WITHDRAWN

ETHICAL CONFLICTS
IN PSYCHOLOGY

ETHICAL CONFLICTS
IN PSYCHOLOGY

DONALD N. BERSOFF

AMERICAN PSYCHOLOGICAL ASSOCIATION
WASHINGTON, DC

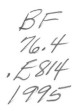

First printing July 1995
Second printing January 1996
Third printing August 1996

Published by
American Psychological Association
750 First Street, NE
Washington, DC 20002

Copies may be ordered from
APA Order Department
P.O. Box 2710
Hyattsville, MD 20784

In the UK and Europe, copies may be ordered from
American Psychological Association
3 Henrietta Street
Covent Garden, London
WC2E 8LU England

Typeset in Berkeley by University Graphics, Inc., York, PA

Printer: Braun-Brumfield, Inc., Ann Arbor, MI
Jacket Designer: Minker Design, Bethesda, MD
Jacket Illustrator: Elena Dvorkina
Technical/Production Editor: Molly R. Flickinger

Library of Congress Cataloging-in-Publication Data
Bersoff, Donald N.
Ethical conflicts in psychology / Donald N. Bersoff.
        p.   cm.
    Includes bibliographical references and index.
    ISBN 1–55798–283–X (acid-free paper). — ISBN 1–55798–302–X (pbk.: acid-free paper)
    1. Psychology—Moral and ethical aspects.   2. Psychologists—Professional ethics.   I. Title.
BF76.4.E814   1995
174′ .915—dc20   95-3252
                                                                                        CIP

British Cataloguing-in-Publication Data
A CIP record is available from the British Library.

Printed in the United States of America

Be not too hasty to trust . . . the teachers of morality
. . . they discourse like angels, but they live like men.

—Samuel Johnson, *Rasselas*

◆   ◆   ◆

To my parents, Mina and Irving, who laid the foundation,
and
to my wife, Deborah Leavy, and my children—Benjamin, David, and Judith—who built an
unassailable edifice on that foundation and truly taught me what love and ethics
were all about.

Contents

Preface

This book represents the final common pathway of over 3 decades of professional work. My experiences as a psychologist working with inpatients and outpatients, collecting data from human subjects in research, or scrutinizing the research proposals of others while serving on institutional review boards; my work as an attorney defending psychologists against claims of malpractice and unethical conduct, or acting as a consultant to state psychology licensing boards seeking to discipline errant professionals; and my service to the American Psychological Association (APA) as its legal counsel for 10 years and, currently, as a member of its Board of Directors—all of this has taught me that there is a need to better inculcate ethical values and virtues in all those who practice, teach, and do research in psychology. In particular, however, it was my role as an academician—directing programs in law and psychology, discussing and debating ethical issues with colleagues and graduate students, and, specifically, teaching ethics to graduate students—that led me to develop this book.

As a teacher, I found that books providing narrative overviews of ethics, although educational, did not always stimulate lively discussion, sometimes failed to adequately represent several sides to the ethical conflicts and dilemmas that contemporary psychologists face, and did not easily facilitate a career-long commitment to treating clients, employees, academic institutions, or research participants with fidelity and integrity. In actuality, students who read published materials, such as journal articles or book chapters, seemed more inspired to invest in particular topics. However, many of these excellent selections often were either burdensomely long or contained information irrelevant to psychology graduate students who were taking their first course in ethics. Moreover, readings alone could not provide the structure, context, and balance that students needed to comprehend the breadth of issues in the field, to understand the conflicts inherent in ethical decision making, and to integrate this material in a meaningful way.

As a result, for a number of years I experimented in the classroom with a hybrid approach—attempting to combine the best of both worlds. First, I gleaned materials from a wide variety of sources, including psychology journals and books, law reviews, legal decisions, statutes, and official policy documents of the APA. When appropriate, I presented only excerpts of the publications to focus attention on their most relevant and salient points, which allowed for comprehensive coverage over the course of a semester of the major ethical conflicts in psychology.

To the articles previously published, I added original explanatory writings before or after some readings as well as provided introductions to each of the topics. In this book, my comments within excerpted articles are called *Editor's Notes,* or *Ed. notes,* whereas my notes before and after articles are offered as *Commentary.* I added these comments to illuminate the issues raised by readings, to provide thought-provoking questions, and, at times, to direct the reader to other important sources. I found that the topical organization helped to structure learning and the brief introductions to the topics provided readers with an overview and context for both the readings and the notes.

I have used successive editions of these materials since 1990, when I began teaching a course in ethics and professional issues through Hahnemann University's Department of Clinical and Health Psychology. Each year I have revised and improved the materials on the basis of informative and candid critiques by students themselves. Once I felt satisfied that they were indeed inculcating sensitivity and awareness of ethical issues and fostering the kind of ethical decision-making strategies that are respectful of the complexity of such issues, I decided to offer them to a broader audience. This book is the result.

Being fully aware of the professional need for guidance in this area, I also designed this book to be of interest and value to psychologists who have finished their formal training and are engaged in teaching, practice, and research. It is in the conduct of day-to-day professional life in psychology that ethical principles become truly compelling. It is then that perception of and sensitivity to ethical issues become paramount and that ethical decision-making skills are put to the test. Most important, it is in these practical situations that ethical problems fully reveal their ambiguity and in which psychologists may feel at sea. At such times, a book such as this can serve as an anchor—allowing psychologists a brief respite on stormy waters to study the scholarly constellations and landmarks before navigating further on their particular ethical voyage. It is my hope that this book will serve this purpose well.

For psychologists as well as students of psychology, the book is particularly timely, as it reflects the major changes that were made by the APA in 1992 to its ethics code, when it was renamed the *Ethical Principles of Psychologists and Code of Conduct.* I take complete responsibility for my interpretation of the past and current ethics codes and for the views expressed throughout the book, while applauding the APA for courageously publishing a volume that is at times critical of official APA policy. I do wish to emphasize, however, that my past and current affiliations with the APA do not imply APA endorsement of or agreement with the views expressed herein.

I now offer some words of appreciation for those who helped in the development of this book. First and foremost, I owe the greatest debt of gratitude to my students for their thoughtful and honest critiques of the material over the years. I also wish to acknowledge the support of the APA Publications and Communications Program. Executive Director Gary VandenBos encouraged me early on to do this project, despite its unusual format. Julia Frank-McNeil, Director of Acquisitions and Development for APA Books, helped shape the contours of the text during its formative stages and secured helpful, early reviews from colleagues whom I can only thank anonymously. Development Editor Peggy Schlegel not only applied just the right amount and mixture of positive reinforcement and necessary prodding but also provided essential suggestions for improving the book's organization and structure. Production Editor Molly Flickinger significantly improved its language and readability, with the assistance of Sarah Trembath, Production Assistant. Both Stan Jones, Director of the APA Office of Ethics, and Ken Pope, one of the most prolific and thoughtful ethics scholars in psychology, prepared detailed critiques of the content and structure of drafts. Each of these contributions immeasurably enhanced this text. Of course, I am fully accountable for the flaws that remain.

Back home, Steven P. Frankino, Dean of the Villanova Law School, sustained me with research grants for four summers while I wrote, edited, and revised the book. The Medical College of Pennsylvania—Hahnemann University, my other academic setting, provided me with Robin Lewis—one of the most efficient, intelligent, and helpful secretaries that a faculty member could hope for. Finally, I wish to thank Lowell Burket, Adam Rosen, Steve Anderer, Drew Messer, Natacha Blain, and Trudi Kirk, all of whom served as my research assistants during the writing of this text and, as such, did the "scut work"—tracking down the materials, securing readable copies, and obtaining the necessary permissions to reprint—that faculty members assiduously attempt to avoid.

If students, psychologists, or other readers have favorite articles relevant to the issues covered in this text that were not included and serve its goals, I would very much like to hear from them. Please provide me with an appropriate reprint or, at least, a citation to the reference. I will be happy to consider your suggestions for future editions.

Introduction

Ethics is the study of those assumptions held by individuals, institutions, organizations, and professions that they believe will assist them in distinguishing between right and wrong and, ultimately, in making sound moral judgments (Bersoff & Koeppl, 1993; Delgado & McAllen, 1982).[1] Making such judgments requires a number of cognitive, affective, and characterological attributes.

Consider the following situations:

1. A male faculty member is supervising the doctoral research of a female graduate student of similar age. After several months, the student informs the professor that she would like to develop a social relationship with him and asks if they could discuss the matter over dinner.
2. In perusing an academic journal, a young assistant professor discovers that, in an article just published, an older colleague has used the work of another psychologist without proper attribution.
3. A client in serious need of intensive and long-term treatment informs his therapist that although 80% of the therapist's fees are covered by insurance, he is unable, because of severe financial problems, to pay the remaining 20% of the fee and requests that the therapist forgive this copayment for the foreseeable future.
4. An industrial psychologist is told by her employer to use a test of questionable validity to assess applicants for unskilled positions in her factory.
5. A forensic psychologist who has tested a criminal defendant to evaluate whether the defendant may be excused from responsibility for a crime because he meets the test of legal "insanity" is asked by the attorney who has retained the psychologist for a hefty fee to testify that the client is, in fact, insane, although the evidence for that assertion is equivocal.

It is unlikely that all of these hypothetical but realistic situations will arise in the course of any single psychologist's work, but they are assuredly problems that confront the everyday academician and professional psychologist. Each requires the psychologist facing the particu-

---

[1] Scholars who study ethics may be divided into two classes. *Descriptive ethicists* are concerned with uncovering and delineating the moral tenets of particular groups. They are like empirical scientists, gathering data about ethical beliefs in an objective and rigorous manner. Once descriptive ethicists have identified and analyzed the basic principles of morality, *normative ethicists* attempt to transform these principles into concrete, behavioral prescriptions designed to guide correct conduct. Thus, normative ethicists are more like philosophers or legislators than scientists. Formal codes of ethics are the expressions of normative ethics.

lar situation to make a sound and reasoned moral judgment. But to do so requires a myriad of skills and attributes.

The psychologist must first be sensitive to and appreciate the fact that the situation does indeed raise an ethical and moral issue. He or she must then know what published sources are available to help resolve the situations in an ethical and moral manner. These sources include, but are not limited to, (a) the APA's (1992) formal code of ethics; (b) other APA documents that guide teaching, practice, and research; (c) federal and state laws and regulations that affect one's work;[2] and (d) institutional or organizational policies of one's work setting.

For several reasons, however, such didactic knowledge is not enough. First, although there may be codes, guidelines, laws, and policies that will be helpful in making and evaluating an ethical decision, they are often fraught with ambiguity or written in generalized language that may not explicitly help to resolve an ethical conflict. Second, it is the rule, rather than the exception, that at any point in time more than one principle can be applied or argument made for and against adopting a particular course of action. Third, at their base level, codes and laws are grounded in such fundamental moral principles and duties as refraining from doing harm, recognizing the right of others to self-determination, or acting justly. Thus, at some point—although armed with knowledge of the rules and appreciative of his or her moral obligations (and recognizing that there may be conflicting points of view)—the psychologist must determine how he or she wants to be viewed. An ethical decision may ultimately depend on one's character and ability to act maturely, wisely, and prudently.

PURPOSE OF THE BOOK

The essential purpose of any book about ethics in psychology is to introduce readers to the formal and enforceable documents that regulate professional, scientific, and academic conduct. That is an inescapable obligation that this book seeks to fulfill. In this regard, the book will be useful to psychology graduate students in their ethics courses. In fact, because its content is relatively comprehensive and reflects the major contemporary ethical conflicts in psychology, the book can be used as a primary text in these classes. In addition, because it covers the major changes made in 1992 in the APA's Ethical Principles and the procedures by which complaints of ethical violations are adjudicated, it can help those who are already psychologists keep abreast of these changing issues.

The book's primary purpose, however, is to help readers develop sensitivity to the ethical aspects of their work as present or future psychologists. It is intended to actuate readers to a deeper level of thought regarding these aspects and to leave them more considerate, critical, and skeptical about their own behavior and the ethical constraints under which they are asked to treat, teach about, and investigate human and animal behavior.

PLAN OF THE BOOK

To accomplish these ends, I have structured and composed this book in a way that should be useful, yet may be unfamiliar, to those in the social and behavioral sciences. I have sought to combine the benefits of historical, classical, and contemporary readings in psychology, law, and ethics with the benefits of narrative structure, engrossing questions and ethical dilemmas, and suggestions for further reading.

---

[2] These laws would include licensure or certification statutes and administrative regulations existing in the jurisdiction in which the psychologist is practicing. Often, these documents contain ethical codes that may vary from that of the APA.

The articles, chapter excerpts, legal decisions, statutes, policy documents, original chapter introductions, editor's notes, and commentaries are organized in a logical progression to teach, juxtapose points of view, stimulate discussion, and analyze and examine contemporary ethical conflicts and issues in psychology. Because I have found that students enjoy and profit from discussing ethical conflicts derived from factual situations, I have included many articles that contain vignettes presenting such conflicts and have developed some original ones as well. I recommend that teachers who use this book take full advantage of the provocative nature of these vignettes to explore the underlying and sometimes competing ethical and moral values they evoke.

The materials are organized into 10 chapters. The first chapter, "Ethics Codes and How They Are Enforced," provides a bit of history and an introduction to the myriad ethical issues facing contemporary psychologists. As a resource, it also includes an unabridged version of the current APA Ethical Principles and the Rules and Procedures by which ethical complaints are adjudicated by the APA Ethics Committee, as well as a description of the sanctions the committee may levy should an ethics violation be found.

The materials in chapter 2, "How Ethics Are Applied," reveal the disparity between the lofty ideals underlying ethical codes and the extent to which those ideals are translated into the real-life behavior of psychologists. This chapter also raises issues concerning the conflict between codes of ethics and other constraints on psychologists' conduct.

Although chapter 3 has an unassuming title—"Learning Ethics"—it is actually an essential and central part of the book. In fact, some teachers may want to begin their ethics course with this chapter. It presents and defines the fundamental moral principles that should serve as the foundation for any ethical code and offers several different strategies for attempting to resolve ethical dilemmas and conflicts.

Whereas the first three chapters provide a general framework for studying ethical issues, each of the remaining seven chapters examines a central and contemporary topical conflict in ethics. Chapter 4—"Confidentiality, Privilege, and Privacy"—defines these essential terms and then tackles such knotty issues as protecting intimate disclosures by violent clients, by children, or by clients infected with the HIV virus. Chapter 5, "Multiple Relationships," shows how unethical behavior can arise through a variety of interactions between psychologists and clients or research participants, presents opposing views on prohibiting sexual intimacies between clients and clinicians, and offers some strategies for avoiding the almost inevitable problems that dual relationships can create. Chapters 6 and 7—"Psychological Assessment" and "Therapy and Other Forms of Intervention," respectively—cover both traditional issues inherent to these topics and more current ones as well, such as computerized testing, treating culturally diverse populations, and the move to gain prescription privileges so that psychologists may administer psychotropic medications.

Chapter 8—"Academia: Research, Teaching, and Supervision"—includes material related to research with humans and animals generally but concentrates on the ethical dilemmas presented by deception research with humans. It also raises issues that may confront teachers of psychology, who will find that ethics codes follow them behind the ivy-covered facades of their academic institutions. Chapter 9, "Forensic Settings," may appear to focus on a narrow and specialized topic, but it actually raises issues that will increasingly face professionals and academics in psychology. The text concludes with another subject—"The Business of Psychology"—that will affect growing numbers in psychology, as the government and the courts more often perceive the provision of mental health services as a matter of commerce and profit making than as an aspect of a learned profession serving the public interest.

Readers will note that there is more in this text on psychological practice than on psychologists in science or academia. Psychologists who serve clients in schools, hospitals, clinics, counseling centers, or business organizations appear to have greater opportunities to evoke complaints of ethical misconduct because of the nature of the tasks in which they engage. Nevertheless, the book does pay serious attention to the ethics of those who perform research. I have also included excerpts from those rare articles that discuss the ethics of teaching and of the student–professor relationship.

I believe that this book fulfills its intended goals and hope that readers will find it not only timely, educational, and interesting but also challenging and engaging.

References

American Psychological Association. (1992). Ethical principles of psychologists and code of conduct. *American Psychologist, 47,* 1597–1611.

Bersoff, D. N., & Koeppl, P. M. (1993). The relation between ethical codes and moral principles. *Ethics and Behavior, 3,* 345–357.

Delgado, R., & McAllen, P. (1982). The moralist as expert witness. *Boston University Law Review, 62,* 869–926.

CHAPTER 1

ETHICS CODES AND HOW THEY ARE ENFORCED

Each profession shares many, varied attributes. They include selective recruitment, lengthy periods of education and training, the development of a shared language (including technical jargon), and controlled entrance into practice. A common characteristic of professions, and of occupations that would like to be perceived as professions, is the development and dissemination of a code of ethics that both emphasizes devotion to fundamental values, such as service to the public and concern for the welfare of those the profession serves, and informs the public of the positive qualities of those who pledge to adhere to the code.

Learning about ethics and the particular code of conduct promulgated by one's professional organization is, thus, one of the major and essential components of a student's socialization into the profession. Ethics teach "the way a group of associates define their special responsibility to one another and to the rest of the social order in which they work" (Erikson, 1967, p. 367). The code of ethics itself, which embodies the formal expression of these responsibilities, should, therefore, instruct those who study it how to relate to their colleagues and how to fulfill their professional roles and responsibilities toward those they serve—clients, patients, employers, research participants, students, institutions, and the public at large.

Ideally, a code of ethics should serve as a guide to resolving moral problems that confront the members of the profession that promulgate it, with its primary emphasis on protecting the public that the profession serves. It should be a grand statement of overarching principles that earn the respect of that public by reflecting the profession's moral integrity. Rarely can a profession fully attain this ideal. Realistically, what a code of ethics does is consensually validate the most recent views of a majority of professionals empowered by their colleagues to make decisions about ethical issues. Thus, a code of ethics is, inevitably, anachronistic, conservative, ethnocentric, and the product of political compromise. But recognition of that reality should not inhibit the creation of a document that fully realizes and expresses fundamental moral principles.

This chapter contributes to the socialization of psychologists by introducing readers to the profession's code of ethics—its voice of conscience. I begin by providing a brief history of the development of a code of ethics by the American Psychological Association (APA). Few know that APA established the Committee on Scientific and Professional Ethics 14 years before adopting its first ethics code in 1952. In fact, the development of an APA code was hotly debated in the 1940s and 1950s. One antagonist, eminent psychologist Calvin Hall (1952), argued that an ethics code

> plays into the hands of. . . . [T]he crooked operator [who] reads the code to see how much he can get away with, and since any code is bound to be filled with

ambiguities and omissions, he can rationalize his unethical conduct by pointing to the code and say[ing], "See, it doesn't tell me I can't do this," or "I can interpret this to mean what I want it to mean." (p. 430)

Modern writers (Schwitzgebel & Schwitzgebel, 1980) have also argued that ethics codes are "vaguely formulated and rarely enforced. Therefore they provide almost no specific and tangible guidance to either practitioners or clients" (p. 3). In this chapter, I present in its entirety the current version of the APA ethics document, adopted in 1992 and titled the "Ethical Principles of Psychologists and Code of Conduct." After studying this most recent version of the code and the material that follows, the reader may want to ask whether the concerns raised by critics of ethics codes in general pertain to this current revision.

If all the APA ethics code did was tweak the conscience and instruct its adherents about "dos" and "don'ts," it would be no more than a book of etiquette—a style manual for how scientists, academics, and practitioners should behave. But it is more than that. This code is enforced by an ethics committee established by the APA, a major purpose of which is to adjudicate complaints of unethical behavior brought by colleagues and members of the public against APA members. In cases where the committee, as a result of its adjudication, finds that a member complained about has committed an ethical violation, it may levy sanctions itself or, in serious cases, may recommend to the APA Board of Directors that the psychologist be dropped from membership. In some very serious cases, such organizationally imposed discipline may lead to complementary sanctions by state licensing boards or institutional employers. How the committee works, on what factual and documentary bases it relies to review complaints, the range of sanctions it may levy, what protections complainants and those psychologists they complain about have, and the extent to which members may appeal adverse findings are all spelled out in the Rules and Procedures drafted by the ethics committee.

Any set of rules that controls the consideration of complaints, that potentially results in a finding that one has committed an ethical violation, that imposes penalties that consequently may damage one's professional or scientific reputation as well as one's economic security (such as increasing malpractice premiums), or that may result in the loss of one's license to practice or the right to apply for federal research grants must be in accord with fundamental principles of fairness, or due process. As readers scrutinize the APA's Rules and Procedures, they might ask whether they afford more due process than is necessary: That is, does the APA provide too much protection for alleged ethics violators, or not enough?

What kinds of ethical dilemmas do psychologists commonly face? In the remaining nine chapters of this text, I examine the answers to that question in great detail. However, by way of introduction, I have included the last excerpt in this chapter to provide an overview. Interestingly, if the results of the survey described in this excerpt are valid, then of the four most troubling categories of ethical incidents, two pertain to practitioners, one pertains to academicians, and one cuts across both domains. Can you speculate as to what those categories are?

In summary, my purposes in this first chapter are to begin the processes of familiarization and socialization into the ethics of psychology and to introduce the reader to the topics addressed in later chapters of this book.

References

Erikson, K. T. (1967). A comment on disguised observation in sociology. *Social Problems, 14,* 366–373.

Hall, C. S. (1952). Crooks, codes, and cant. *American Psychologist, 7,* 430–431.

Schwitzgebel, R. L., & Schwitzgebel, R. K. (1980). *Law and psychological practice.* New York: Wiley.

Ethical Dilemmas Encountered by Members of the American Psychological Association: A National Survey

Kenneth S. Pope and Valerie A. Vetter

Founded in 1892, the American Psychological Association (APA) faced ethical problems without a formal code of ethics for 60 years. As the chair of the Committee on Scientific and Professional Ethics and Conduct in the early 1950s observed,

> In the early years of the American Psychological Association, the problems of ethics were relatively simple. We were essentially an organization of college teachers. The only ethical problems which seemed to present themselves were those of plagiarism and of academic freedom. (Rich, 1952, p. 440)

The Committee on Scientific and Professional Ethics was created in 1938 and began handling complaints on an informal basis. By 1947, the committee recommended that APA develop a formal code. "The present unwritten code . . . is tenuous, elusive, and unsatisfactory" ("A Little Recent History," 1952, p. 427).

The method used to create the formal code was innovative and unique, an extraordinary break from the traditional methods used previously by more than 500 professional and business associations (Hobbs, 1948). Setting aside what Hobbs termed the "armchair approach" (p. 82) in which a committee of those "who are most mature, in wisdom, experience, and knowledge of their fellow psychologists" (p. 81) would study the various available codes, issues, and literature and then submit a draft to the membership for approval, APA decided to create "an empirically developed code" based on an investigation of the

ethical dilemmas encountered by a "representative sample of members": "The research itself would involve the collection, from psychologists involved in all of the various professional activities, of descriptions of actual situations which required ethical decisions" (p. 83). A survey collecting examples of the ethical dilemmas encountered by APA members led to a draft code (APA Committee on Ethical Standards for Psychology, 1951a, 1951b, 1951c) that was refined and approved in 1952 (APA, 1953) . . .

The 1959 revision, the result of nine drafts over a three-year period, was adopted for use on a trial basis (APA, 1959). The committee anticipated that future revisions would be necessary to address changing conditions of practice[.] . . .

To maintain the unique nature and effectiveness of the code, future revisions were to be based not only on discussion among members but also on "additional critical incidents of controversial behavior" (Holzman, 1960, p. 247). To base revisions on recommendations by ethics committees seemed inadequate because "the energies of ethics committees are so totally devoted to fire fighting that fire proofing or concern with problems that have not yet emerged in the form of complaints must take a lower priority" (Golann, 1969, p. 454). Moreover, if the existing code neglected certain issues or dilemmas, individuals would obviously have no basis on which to file complaints relevant to those issues or dilemmas; thus there could be extreme discrepancies between the issues brought to the attention of an ethics committee and the issues encountered by the diverse membership. Even if a committee of experts were to develop ethical standards for diverse areas, they would, according to the rationale of the original code, likely overlook problems in implementing those standards that would be obvious to someone whose day-to-day work was in one of those areas.

The conviction that revisions should be based on subsequent critical incident studies was also based on beliefs about empowerment, management style, group process, and allegiance. . . . This conviction reflected the assumption that two ways of developing a revision would produce very different results. In the first approach, unique to psychology, the revision process would begin by actively soliciting through a formal mail survey the observations, ideas, and questions from those working "on the front lines" in diverse specialties, settings, and circumstances. A revision committee would then base its work on the primary data of this survey. In the alternate approach, used by virtually all other professional and business associations, a committee would decide how the code should be revised. The draft would then be circulated or published along with an announcement inviting comments. The first approach. . . . was considered to empower individual members by involving them meaningfully at the beginning of the project. The process seemed likely not only to lead to a better revision but also to create and benefit from better group dynamics. . . .

The unique nature of the code was that it was "based upon the day-to-day decisions made by psychologists in the practice of their profession, rather than prescribed by a committee" (Golann, 1969, p. 454). Basing revisions on recent critical incidents provided by the membership was believed necessary to maintain an ethical code "close enough to the contemporary scene to win the genuine acceptance of the majority who are most directly affected by its principles" (Holzman, 1960, p. 250). . . .

References

American Psychological Association. (1953). *Ethical standards of psychologists*. Washington, DC: Author.

American Psychological Association. (1959). Ethical standards of psychologists. *American Psychologist, 14,* 279–282.

APA Committee on Ethical Standards for Psychology. (1951a). Ethical standards for psychology: Section 1, Ethical standards and public responsibility. Section 6, Ethical standards in teaching. *American Psychologist, 6,* 626–661.

APA Committee on Ethical Standards for Psychology. (1951b). Ethical standards for psychology: Section 2, Ethical standards in professional relationships. Section 4, Ethical standards in research. Section 5, Ethical standards in writing and publishing. *American Psychologist, 6,* 427–452.

APA Committee on Ethical Standards for Psychology. (1951c). Ethical standards in clinical and consulting relationships: Part 1. *American Psychologist, 6,* 57–64.

Golann, S. E. (1969). Emerging areas of ethical concern. *American Psychologist, 24,* 454–459.

Hobbs, N. (1948). The development of a code of ethical standards for psychology. *American Psychologist, 3,* 80–84.

Holzman, W. H. (1960). Some problems of defining ethical behavior. *American Psychologist, 15,* 247–250.

A little recent history. (1952). *American Psychologist, 7,* 426–428.

Rich, G. J. (1952). A new code of ethics is needed. *American Psychologist, 7,* 440–441.

◆ ◆ ◆

Commentary: The original APA code of ethics, adopted in 1952 and published in 1953, has had many descendants, including the current code's immediate ancestor, published in 1981 and revised in 1989. See, for example,

American Psychological Association. (1981). Ethical principles of psychologists. American Psychologist, 36, 633–638.

American Psychological Association. (1990). Ethical principles of psychologists (amended June 2, 1989). American Psychologist, 45, 390–395.

The 1989 revision was stimulated by concerns expressed by the Federal Trade Commission. For a discussion of why the U.S. government was interested in the APA's code of ethics, see chapter 10 ("The Business of Psychology").

The APA ethics code is considered an expression of association policy. Barring an emergency, all APA policy is adopted by its legislative body—the Council of Representatives. The council also promulgates Association Rules (ARs)—regulations for administering the APA's governance structure. AR 20–4.1 states:

The Ethics Committee shall have the responsibility from time to time of initiating a re-

view of the latest formally adopted version of the ethics code . . . and proposing necessary changes or additions. In carrying out such a review, the Ethics Committee may set up such ad hoc committees as it finds necessary.

Coincident with the Federal Trade Commission's investigation, but begun independently of it, the APA in 1986, under the authority of AR 20–4.1, formed a task force to completely revise its ethical principles. Unlike the original 1953 code, the revision was not based on critical incidents gleaned from the field, but was drafted using the "alternate approach" described by Pope and Vetter (1992) in the article excerpted above. The task force published a draft revision in the June 1990 issue of the APA Monitor for review and comment. As a result of that process, the ethics committee developed a subsequent

revision, renamed the "American Psychological Association Ethics Code." That revision was published in the June 1991 APA Monitor, along with a call for membership and governance reaction. The reaction was mixed, raising a number of controversial issues. Thus, another revision was prepared and printed in the May 1992 APA Monitor for additional comment. This process produced 120 proposed amendments, about 100 of which were considered by the Council of Representatives at the centennial convention of the APA in August 1992. After an 8-hour debate on these amendments, the council voted to adopt the now-current and enforceable code (see Ethical Principles of Psychologists and Code of Conduct, reprinted on the following pages). For a more complete description of the revision process, see APA Ethics Committee. (1993). Report of the Ethics Committee, 1991 and 1992. American Psychologist, 48, 811–820.

Ethical Principles of Psychologists and Code of Conduct

American Psychological Association

INTRODUCTION

The American Psychological Association's (APA's) Ethical Principles of Psychologists and Code of Conduct (hereinafter referred to as the Ethics Code) consists of an Introduction, a Preamble, six General Principles (A–F), and specific Ethical Standards. The Introduction discusses the intent, organization, procedural considerations, and scope of application of the Ethics Code. The Preamble and General Principles are *aspirational* goals to guide psychologists toward the highest ideals of psychology. Although the Preamble and General Principles are not themselves enforceable rules, they should be considered by psychologists in arriving at an ethical course of action and may be considered by ethics bodies in interpreting the Ethical Standards. The Ethical Standards set forth *enforceable* rules for conduct as psychologists. Most of the Ethical Standards are written broadly, in order to apply to psychologists in varied roles, although the application of an Ethical Standard may vary depending on the context. The Ethical Standards are not exhaustive. The fact that a given conduct is not specifically addressed by the Ethics Code does not mean that it is necessarily either ethical or unethical.

Membership in the APA commits members to adhere to the APA Ethics Code and to the rules and procedures used to implement it. Psychologists and students, whether or not they are APA members, should be aware that the Ethics Code may be applied to them by state psychology boards, courts, or other public bodies.

This Ethics Code applies only to psychologists' work-related activities, that is, activities that are part of the psychologists' scientific and professional functions or that are psychological in nature. It includes the clinical or counseling practice of psychology, research, teaching, supervision of trainees, development of assessment instruments, conduct-

Adapted from the *American Psychologist*, 47, 1597–1611. Copyright 1992 by the American Psychological Association.

This version of the APA Ethics Code was adopted by the American Psychological Association's Council of Representatives during its meeting, August 13 and 16, 1992, and is effective beginning December 1, 1992. Inquiries concerning the substance or interpretation of the APA Ethics Code should be addressed to the Director, Office of Ethics, American Psychological Association, 750 First Street, NE, Washington, DC 20002-4242.

This Code will be used to adjudicate complaints brought concerning alleged conduct occurring on or after the effective date. Complaints regarding conduct occurring prior to the effective date will be adjudicated on the basis of the version of the Code that was in effect at the time the conduct occurred, except that no provisions repealed in June 1989, will be enforced even if an earlier version contains the provision. The Ethics Code will undergo continuing review and study for future revisions; comments on the Code may be sent to the above address.

The APA has previously published its Ethical Standards as follows:

American Psychological Association. (1953). *Ethical standards of psychologists*. Washington, DC: Author.
American Psychological Association. (1958). Standards of ethical behavior for psychologists. *American Psychologist*, 13, 268–271.
American Psychological Association. (1963). Ethical standards of psychologists. *American Psychologist*, 18, 56–60.
American Psychological Association. (1968). Ethical standards of psychologists. *American Psychologist*, 23, 357–361.
American Psychological Association. (1977, March). Ethical standards of psychologists. *APA Monitor*, pp. 22–23.
American Psychological Association. (1979). *Ethical standards of psychologists*. Washington, DC: Author.
American Psychological Association. (1981). Ethical principles of psychologists. *American Psychologist*, 36, 633–638.
American Psychological Association. (1990). Ethical principles of psychologists (Amended June 2, 1989). *American Psychologist*, 4, 390–395.

ing assessments, educational counseling, organizational consulting, social intervention, administration, and other activities as well. These work-related activities can be distinguished from the purely private conduct of a psychologist, which ordinarily is not within the purview of the Ethics Code.

The Ethics Code is intended to provide standards of professional conduct that can be applied by the APA and by other bodies that choose to adopt them. Whether or not a psychologist has violated the Ethics Code does not by itself determine whether he or she is legally liable in a court action, whether a contract is enforceable, or whether other legal consequences occur. These results are based on legal rather than ethical rules. However, compliance with or violation of the Ethics Code may be admissible as evidence in some legal proceedings, depending on the circumstances.

In the process of making decisions regarding their professional behavior, psychologists must consider this Ethics Code, in addition to applicable laws and psychology board regulations. If the Ethics Code establishes a higher standard of conduct than is required by law, psychologists must meet the higher ethical standard. If the Ethics Code standard appears to conflict with the requirements of law, then psychologists make known their commitment to the Ethics Code and take steps to resolve the conflict in a responsible manner. If neither law nor the Ethics Code resolves an issue, psychologists should consider other professional materials[1] and the dictates of their own conscience, as well as seek consultation with others within the field when this is practical.

The procedures for filing, investigating, and resolving complaints of unethical conduct are described in the current Rules and Procedures of the APA Ethics Committee. The actions that APA may take for violations of the Ethics Code include actions such as reprimand, censure, termination of APA membership, and referral of the matter to other bodies. Complainants who seek remedies such as monetary damages in alleging ethical violations by a psychologist must resort to private negotiation, administrative bodies, or the courts. Actions that violate the Ethics Code may lead to the imposition of sanctions on a psychologist by bodies other than APA, including state psychological associations, other professional groups, psychology boards, other state or federal agencies, and payors for health services. In addition to actions for violation of the Ethics Code, the APA Bylaws provide that APA may take action against a member after his or her conviction of a felony, expulsion or suspension from an affiliated state psychological association, or suspension or loss of licensure.

PREAMBLE

Psychologists work to develop a valid and reliable body of scientific knowledge based on research. They may apply that knowledge to human behavior in a variety of contexts. In doing so, they perform many roles, such as researcher, educator, diagnostician, therapist, supervisor, consultant, administrator, social interventionist, and expert witness. Their goal is to broaden knowledge of behavior and, where appropriate, to apply it pragmatically to improve the condition of both the individual and society. Psychologists respect the central importance of freedom of inquiry and expression in research, teaching, and publication. They also strive to help the public in developing informed judgments and choices concerning human behavior. This Ethics Code provides a common set of values upon which psychologists build their professional and scientific work.

This Code is intended to provide both the general principles and the decision rules to cover most

[1] Professional materials that are most helpful in this regard are guidelines and standards that have been adopted or endorsed by professional psychological organizations. Such guidelines and standards, whether adopted by the American Psychological Association (APA) or its Divisions, are not enforceable as such by this Ethics Code, but are of educative value to psychologists, courts, and professional bodies. Such materials include, but are not limited to, the APA's *General Guidelines for Providers of Psychological Services* (1987), *Specialty Guidelines for the Delivery of Services by Clinical Psychologists, Counseling Psychologists, Industrial/Organizational Psychologists, and School of Psychologists* (1981), *Guidelines for Computer Based Tests and Interpretations* (1987), *Standards for Educational and Psychological Testing* (1985), *Ethical Principles in the Conduct of Research With Human Participants* (1982), *Guidelines for Ethical Conduct in the Care and Use of Animals* (1986), *Guidelines for Providers of Psychological Services to Ethnic, Linguistic, and Culturally Diverse Populations* (1990), and *Publication Manual of the American Psychological Association* (3rd ed., 1983). Materials not adopted by APA as a whole include the APA Division 41 (Forensic Psychology)/American Psychology–Law Society's *Specialty Guidelines for Forensic Psychologists* (1991).

situations encountered by psychologists. It has as its primary goal the welfare and protection of the individuals and groups with whom psychologists work. It is the individual responsibility of each psychologist to aspire to the highest possible standards of conduct. Psychologists respect and protect human and civil rights, and do not knowingly participate in or condone unfair discriminatory practices.

The development of a dynamic set of ethical standards for a psychologist's work-related conduct requires a personal commitment to a lifelong effort to act ethically; to encourage ethical behavior by students, supervisees, employees, and colleagues, as appropriate; and to consult with others, as needed, concerning ethical problems. Each psychologist supplements, but does not violate, the Ethics Code's values and rules on the basis of guidance drawn from personal values, culture, and experience.

GENERAL PRINCIPLES

Principle A: Competence

Psychologists strive to maintain high standards of competence in their work. They recognize the boundaries of their particular competencies and the limitations of their expertise. They provide only those services and use only those techniques for which they are qualified by education, training, or experience. Psychologists are cognizant of the fact that the competencies required in serving, teaching, and/or studying groups of people vary with the distinctive characteristics of those groups. In those areas in which recognized professional standards do not yet exist, psychologists exercise careful judgment and take appropriate precautions to protect the welfare of those with whom they work. They maintain knowledge of relevant scientific and professional information related to the services they render, and they recognize the need for ongoing education. Psychologists make appropriate use of scientific, professional, technical, and administrative resources.

Principle B: Integrity

Psychologists seek to promote integrity in the science, teaching, and practice of psychology. In these activities psychologists are honest, fair, and respectful of others. In describing or reporting their qualifications,

services, products, fees, research, or teaching, they do not make statements that are false, misleading, or deceptive. Psychologists strive to be aware of their own belief systems, values, needs, and limitations and the effect of these on their work. To the extent feasible, they attempt to clarify for relevant parties the roles they are performing and to function appropriately in accordance with those roles. Psychologists avoid improper and potentially harmful dual relationships.

Principle C: Professional and Scientific Responsibility

Psychologists uphold professional standards of conduct, clarify their professional roles and obligations, accept appropriate responsibility for their behavior, and adapt their methods to the needs of different populations. Psychologists consult with, refer to, or cooperate with other professionals and institutions to the extent needed to serve the best interests of their patients, clients, or other recipients of their services. Psychologists' moral standards and conduct are personal matters to the same degree as is true for any other person, except as psychologists' conduct may compromise their professional responsibilities or reduce the public's trust in psychology and psychologists. Psychologists are concerned about the ethical compliance of their colleagues' scientific and professional conduct. When appropriate, they consult with colleagues in order to prevent or avoid unethical conduct.

Principle D: Respect for People's Rights and Dignity

Psychologists accord appropriate respect to the fundamental rights, dignity, and worth of all people. They respect the rights of individuals to privacy, confidentiality, self-determination, and autonomy, mindful that legal and other obligations may lead to inconsistency and conflict with the exercise of these rights. Psychologists are aware of cultural, individual, and role differences, including those due to age, gender, race, ethnicity, national origin, religion, sexual orientation, disability, language, and socioeconomic status. Psychologists try to eliminate the effect on their work of biases based on those factors, and they do not knowingly participate in or condone unfair discriminatory practices.

Principle E: Concern for Others' Welfare

Psychologists seek to contribute to the welfare of those with whom they interact professionally. In their professional actions, psychologists weigh the welfare and rights of their patients or clients, students, supervisees, human research participants, and other affected persons, and the welfare of animal subjects of research. When conflicts occur among psychologists' obligations or concerns, they attempt to resolve these conflicts and to perform their roles in a responsible fashion that avoids or minimizes harm. Psychologists are sensitive to real and ascribed differences in power between themselves and others, and they do not exploit or mislead other people during or after professional relationships.

Principle F: Social Responsibility

Psychologists are aware of their professional and scientific responsibilities to the community and the society in which they work and live. They apply and make public their knowledge of psychology in order to contribute to human welfare. Psychologists are concerned about and work to mitigate the causes of human suffering. When undertaking research, they strive to advance human welfare and the science of psychology. Psychologists try to avoid misuse of their work. Psychologists comply with the law and encourage the development of law and social policy that serve the interests of their patients and clients and the public. They are encouraged to contribute a portion of their professional time for little or no personal advantage.

ETHICAL STANDARDS

1. General Standards

These General Standards are potentially applicable to the professional and scientific activities of all psychologists.

1.01 Applicability of the Ethics Code

The activity of a psychologist subject to the Ethics Code may be reviewed under these Ethical Standards only if the activity is part of his or her work-related functions or the activity is psychological in nature. Personal activities having no connection to or effect on psychological roles are not subject to the Ethics Code.

1.02 Relationship of Ethics and Law

If psychologists' ethical responsibilities conflict with law, psychologists make known their commitment to the Ethics Code and take steps to resolve the conflict in a responsible manner.

1.03 Professional and Scientific Relationship

Psychologists provide diagnostic, therapeutic, teaching, research, supervisory, consultative, or other psychological services only in the context of a defined professional or scientific relationship or role. (See also Standards 2.01, Evaluation, Diagnosis, and Interventions in Professional Context, and 7.02, Forensic Assessments.)

1.04 Boundaries of Competence

(a) Psychologists provide services, teach, and conduct research only within the boundaries of their competence, based on their education, training, supervised experience, or appropriate professional experience.

(b) Psychologists provide services, teach, or conduct research in new areas or involving new techniques only after first undertaking appropriate study, training, supervision, and/or consultation from persons who are competent in those areas or techniques.

(c) In those emerging areas in which generally recognized standards for preparatory training do not yet exist, psychologists nevertheless take reasonable steps to ensure the competence of their work and to protect patients, clients, students, research participants, and others from harm.

1.05 Maintaining Expertise

Psychologists who engage in assessment, therapy, teaching, research, organizational consulting, or other professional activities maintain a reasonable level of awareness of current scientific and professional information in their fields of activity, and undertake ongoing efforts to maintain competence in the skills they use.

1.06 Basis for Scientific and Professional Judgments

Psychologists rely on scientifically and professionally derived knowledge when making scientific or professional judgments or when engaging in scholarly or professional endeavors.

1.07 Describing the Nature and Results of Psychological Services

(a) When psychologists provide assessment, evaluation, treatment, counseling, supervision, teaching, consultation, research, or other psychological services to an individual, a group, or an organization, they provide, using language that is reasonably understandable to the recipient of those services, appropriate information beforehand about the nature of such services and appropriate information later about results and consultations. (See also Standard 2.09, Explaining Assessment Results.)

(b) If psychologists will be precluded by law or by organizational roles from providing such information to particular individuals or groups, they so inform those individuals or groups at the outset of the service.

1.08 Human Differences

Where differences of age, gender, race, ethnicity, national origin, religion, sexual orientation, disability, language, or socioeconomic status significantly affect psychologists' work concerning particular individuals or groups, psychologists obtain the training, experience, consultation, or supervision necessary to ensure the competence of their services, or they make appropriate referrals.

1.09 Respecting Others

In their work-related activities, psychologists respect the rights of others to hold values, attitudes, and opinions that differ from their own.

1.10 Nondiscrimination

In their work-related activities, psychologists do not engage in unfair discrimination based on age, gender, race, ethnicity, national origin, religion, sexual orientation, disability, socioeconomic status, or any basis proscribed by law.

1.11 Sexual Harassment

(a) Psychologists do not engage in sexual harassment. Sexual harassment is sexual solicitation, physical advances, or verbal or nonverbal conduct that is sexual in nature, that occurs in connection with the psychologist's activities or roles as a psychologist, and that either: (1) is unwelcome, is offensive, or creates a hostile workplace environment, and the psychologist knows or is told this; or (2) is sufficiently severe or intense to be abusive to a reasonable person in the context. Sexual harassment can consist of a single intense or severe act or of multiple persistent or pervasive acts.

(b) Psychologists accord sexual-harassment complaints and respondents dignity and respect. Psychologists do not participate in denying a person academic admittance or advancement, employment, tenure, or promotion, based solely upon their having made, or their being the subject of, sexual-harassment charges. This does not preclude taking action based upon the outcome of such proceedings or consideration of other appropriate information.

1.12 Other Harassment

Psychologists do not knowingly engage in behavior that is harassing or demeaning to persons with whom they interact in their work based on factors such as those persons' age, gender, race, ethnicity, national origin, religion, sexual orientation, disability, language, or socioeconomic status.

1.13 Personal Problems and Conflicts

(a) Psychologists recognize that their personal problems and conflicts may interfere with their effectiveness. Accordingly, they refrain from undertaking an activity when they know or should know that their personal problems are likely to lead to harm to a patient, client, colleague, student, research participant, or other person to whom they may owe a professional or scientific obligation.

(b) In addition, psychologists have an obligation to be alert to signs of, and to obtain assistance for, their personal problems at an early stage, in order to prevent significantly impaired performance.

(c) When psychologists become aware of personal problems that may interfere with their performing work-related duties adequately, they take appropriate measures, such as obtaining professional consultation or assistance, and determine whether they should limit, suspend, or terminate their work-related duties.

1.14 Avoiding Harm

Psychologists take reasonable steps to avoid harming their patients or clients, research participants, students, and others with whom they work, and to minimize harm where it is foreseeable and unavoidable.

1.15 Misuse of Psychologists' Influence

Because psychologists' scientific and professional judgments and actions may affect the lives of others, they are alert to and guard against personal, financial, social, organizational, or political factors that might lead to misuse of their influence.

1.16 Misuse of Psychologists' Work

(a) Psychologists do not participate in activities in which it appears likely that their skills or data will be misused by others, unless corrective mechanisms are available. (See also Standard 7.04, Truthfulness and Candor.)

(b) If psychologists learn of misuse or misrepresentation of their work, they take reasonable steps to correct or minimize the misuse or misrepresentation.

1.17 Multiple Relationships

(a) In many communities and situations, it may not be feasible or reasonable for psychologists to avoid social or other nonprofessional contacts with persons such as patients, clients, students, supervisees, or research participants. Psychologists must always be sensitive to the potential harmful effects of other contacts on their work and on those persons with whom they deal. A psychologist refrains from entering into or promising another personal, scientific, professional, financial, or other relationship with such persons if it appears likely that such a relationship reasonably might impair the psychologist's objectivity or otherwise interfere with the psychologist's effectively performing his or her function as a psychologist, or might harm or exploit the other party.

(b) Likewise, whenever feasible, a psychologist refrains from taking on professional or scientific obligations when preexisting relationships would create a risk of such harm.

(c) If a psychologist finds that, due to unforeseen factors, a potentially harmful multiple relationship has arisen, the psychologist attempts to resolve it with due regard for the best interests of the affected person and maximal compliance with the Ethics Code.

1.18 Barter (With Patients or Clients)

Psychologists ordinarily refrain from accepting goods, services, or other nonmonetary remuneration from patients or clients in return for psychological services because such arrangements create inherent potential for conflicts, exploitation, and distortion of the professional relationship. A psychologist may participate in bartering *only* if (1) it is not clinically contraindicated, *and* (2) the relationship is not exploitative. (See also Standards 1.17, Multiple Relationships, and 1.25, Fees and Financial Arrangements.)

1.19 Exploitative Relationships

(a) Psychologists do not exploit persons over whom they have supervisory, evaluative, or other authority such as students, supervisees, employees, research participants, and clients or patients. (See also Standards 4.05–4.07 regarding sexual involvement with clients or patients.)

(b) Psychologists do not engage in sexual relationships with students or supervisees in training over whom the psychologist has evaluative or direct authority, because such relationships are so likely to impair judgment or be exploitative.

1.20 Consultations and Referrals

(a) Psychologists arrange for appropriate consultations and referrals based principally on the best interests of their patients or clients, with appropriate consent, and subject to other relevant considerations, including applicable law and contractual obligations. (See also Standards 5.01, Discussing the Limits of Confidentiality, and 5.06, Consultations.)

(b) When indicated and professionally appropriate, psychologists cooperate with other professionals in order to serve their patients or clients effectively and appropriately.

(c) Psychologists' referral practices are consistent with law.

1.21 Third-Party Requests for Services

(a) When a psychologist agrees to provide services to a person or entity at the request of a third party, the psychologist clarifies to the extent feasible, at the outset of the service, the nature of the relationship with each party. This clarification includes the role of the psychologist (such as therapist, organizational consultant, diagnostician, or expert witness), the probable uses of the services provided or the information obtained, and the fact that there may be limits to confidentiality.

(b) If there is a foreseeable risk of the psychologist's being called upon to perform conflicting roles because of the involvement of a third party, the psychologist clarifies the nature and direction of his or her responsibilities, keeps all parties appropriately informed as matters develop, and resolves the situation in accordance with this Ethics Code.

1.22 Delegation to and Supervision of Subordinates

(a) Psychologists delegate to their employees, supervisees, and research assistants only those responsibilities that such persons can reasonably be expected to perform competently, on the basis of their education, training, or experience, either independently or with the level of supervision being provided.

(b) Psychologists provide proper training and supervision to their employees or supervisees and take reasonable steps to see that such persons perform services responsibly, competently, and ethically.

(c) If institutional policies, procedures, or practices prevent fulfillment of this obligation, psychologists attempt to modify their role or to correct the situation to the extent feasible.

1.23 Documentation of Professional and Scientific Work

(a) Psychologists appropriately document their professional and scientific work in order to facilitate provision of services later by them or by other professionals, to ensure accountability, and to meet other requirements of institutions or the law.

(b) When psychologists have reason to believe that records of their professional services will be used in legal proceedings involving recipients of or participants in their work, they have a responsibility to create and maintain documentation in the kind of

detail and quality that would be consistent with reasonable scrutiny in an adjudicative forum. (See also Standard 7.01, Professionalism, under Forensic Activities.)

1.24 Records and Data

Psychologists create, maintain, disseminate, store, retain, and dispose of records and data relating to their research, practice, and other work in accordance with law and in a manner that permits compliance with the requirements of this Ethics Code. (See also Standard 5.04, Maintenance of Records.)

1.25 Fees and Financial Arrangements

(a) As early as is feasible in a professional or scientific relationship, the psychologist and the patient, client, or other appropriate recipient of psychological services reach an agreement specifying the compensation and the billing arrangements.

(b) Psychologists do not exploit recipients of services or payors with respect to fees.

(c) Psychologists' fee practices are consistent with law.

(d) Psychologists do not misrepresent their fees.

(e) If limitations to services can be anticipated because of limitations in financing, this is discussed with the patient, client, or other appropriate recipient of services as early as is feasible. (See also Standard 4.08, Interruption of Services.)

(f) If the patient, client, or other recipient of services does not pay for services as agreed, and if the psychologist wishes to use collection agencies or legal measures to collect the fees, the psychologist first informs the person that such measures will be taken and provides that person an opportunity to make prompt payment. (See also Standard 5.11, Withholding Records for Nonpayment.)

1.26 Accuracy in Reports to Payors and Funding Sources

In their reports to payors for services or sources of research funding, psychologists accurately state the nature of the research or service provided, the fees or charges, and where applicable, the identity of the provider, the findings, and the diagnosis. (See also Standard 5.05, Disclosures.)

1.27 Referrals and Fees

When a psychologist pays, receives payment from, or divides fees with another professional other than in an employer–employee relationship, the payment to each is based on the services (clinical, consultative, administrative, or other) provided and is not based on the referral itself.

2. Evaluation, Assessment, or Intervention
2.01 Evaluation, Diagnosis, and Interventions in Professional Context

(a) Psychologists perform evaluations, diagnosis services, or interventions only within the context of a defined professional relationship. (See also Standard 1.03, Professional and Scientific Relationship.)

(b) Psychologists' assessments, recommendations, reports, and psychological diagnostic or evaluative statements are based on information and techniques (including personal interviews of the individual when appropriate) sufficient to provide appropriate substantiation for their findings. (See also Standard 7.02, Forensic Assessments.)

2.02 Competence and Appropriate Use of Assessments and Interventions

(a) Psychologists who develop, administer, score, interpret, or use psychological assessment techniques, interviews, tests, or instruments do so in a manner and for purposes that are appropriate in light of the research on or evidence of the usefulness and proper application of the techniques.

(b) Psychologists refrain from misuse of assessment techniques, interventions, results, and interpretations and take reasonable steps to prevent others from misusing the information these techniques provide. This includes refraining from releasing raw test results or raw data to persons, other than to patients or clients as appropriate, who are not qualified to use such information. (See also Standards 1.02, Relationship of Ethics and Law, and 1.04, Boundaries of Competence.)

2.03 Test Construction

Psychologists who develop and conduct research with tests and other assessment techniques use specific procedures and current professional knowledge for test design, standardization, validation, reduction or elimination of bias, and recommendations for use.

2.04 Use of Assessment in General and With Special Populations

(a) Psychologists who perform interventions or administer, score, interpret, or use assessment techniques are familiar with the reliability, validation, and related standardization or outcome studies of, and proper applications and uses of, the techniques they use.

(b) Psychologists recognize limits to the certainty with which diagnoses, judgments, or predictions can be made about individuals.

(c) Psychologists attempt to identify situations in which particular interventions or assessment techniques or norms may not be applicable or may require adjustment in administration or interpretation because of factors such as individuals' gender, age, race, ethnicity, national origin, religion, sexual orientation, disability, language, or socioeconomic status.

2.05 Interpreting Assessment Results

When interpreting assessment results, including automated interpretations, psychologists take into account the various test factors and characteristics of the person being assessed that might affect psychologists' judgments or reduce the accuracy of their interpretations. They indicate any significant reservations they have about the accuracy or limitations of their interpretations.

2.06 Unqualified Persons

Psychologists do not promote the use of psychological assessment techniques by unqualified persons. (See also Standard 1.22, Delegation to and Supervision of Subordinates.)

2.07 Obsolete Tests and Outdated Test Results

(a) Psychologists do not base their assessment or intervention decisions or recommendations on data or test results that are outdated for the current purpose.

(b) Similarly, psychologists do not base such decisions or recommendations on tests and measures that are obsolete and not useful for the current purpose.

2.08 Test Scoring and Interpretation Services

(a) Psychologists who offer assessment or scoring procedures to other professionals accurately describe the purpose, norms, validity, reliability, and applications of the procedures and any special qualifications applicable to their use.

(b) Psychologists select scoring and interpretation services (including automated services) on the basis of evidence of the validity of the program and procedures as well as on other appropriate considerations.

(c) Psychologists retain appropriate responsibility for the appropriate application, interpretation, and use of assessment instruments, whether they score and interpret such tests themselves or use automated or other services.

2.09 Explaining Assessment Results

Unless the nature of the relationship is clearly explained to the person being assessed in advance and precludes provision of an explanation of results (such as in some organizational consulting, preemployment or security screenings, and forensic evaluations), psychologists ensure that an explanation of the results is provided using language that is reasonably understandable to the person assessed or to another legally authorized person on behalf of the client. Regardless of whether the scoring and interpretation are done by the psychologist, by assistants, or by automated or other outside services, psychologists take reasonable steps to ensure that appropriate explanations of results are given.

2.10 Maintaining Test Security

Psychologists make reasonable efforts to maintain the integrity and security of tests and other assessment techniques consistent with law, contractual obligations, and in a manner that permits compliance with the requirements of this Ethics Code. (See also Standard 1.02, Relationship of Ethics and Law.)

3. Advertising and Other Public Statements
3.01 Definition of Public Statements

Psychologists comply with this Ethics Code in public statements relating to their professional services, products, or publications or to the field of psychology. Public statements include but are not limited to paid or unpaid advertising, brochures, printed matter, directory listings, personal resumes or curricula vitae, interviews or comments for use in media, statements in legal proceedings, lectures and public oral presentations, and published materials.

3.02 Statements by Others

(a) Psychologists who engage others to create or place public statements that promote their professional practice, products, or activities retain professional responsibility for such statements.

(b) In addition, psychologists make reasonable efforts to prevent others whom they do not control (such as employers, publishers, sponsors, organizational clients, and representatives of the print or broadcast media) from making deceptive statements concerning psychologists' practice or professional or scientific activities.

(c) If psychologists learn of deceptive statements about their work made by others, psychologists make reasonable efforts to correct such statements.

(d) Psychologists do not compensate employees of press, radio, television, or other communication media in return for publicity in a news item.

(e) A paid advertisement relating to the psychologist's activities must be identified as such, unless it is already apparent from the context.

3.03 Avoidance of False or Deceptive Statements

(a) Psychologists do not make public statements that are false, deceptive, misleading, or fraudulent, either because of what they state, convey, or suggest or because of what they omit, concerning their research, practice, or other work activities or those of persons or organizations with which they are affiliated. As examples (and not in limitation) of this standard, psychologists do not make false or deceptive statements concerning (1) their training, experience, or competence; (2) their academic degrees; (3) their credentials; (4) their institutional or association affiliations; (5) their services; (6) the scientific or clinical basis for, or results or degree of success of, their services; (7) their fees; or (8) their publications or research findings. (See also Standards 6.15, Deception in Research, and 6.18, Providing Participants With Information About the Study.)

(b) Psychologists claim as credentials for their psychological work, only degrees that (1) were earned from a regionally accredited educational institution or (2) were the basis for psychology licensure by the state in which they practice.

3.04 Media Presentations

When psychologists provide advice or comment by means of public lectures, demonstrations, radio or television programs, prerecorded tapes, printed articles, mailed material, or other media, they take reasonable precautions to ensure that (1) the statements are based on appropriate psychological literature and practice, (2) the statements are otherwise consistent with this Ethics Code, and (3) the recipients of the information are not encouraged to infer that a relationship has been established with them personally.

3.05 Testimonials

Psychologists do not solicit testimonials from current psychotherapy clients or patients or other persons who because of their particular circumstances are vulnerable to undue influence.

3.06 In-Person Solicitation

Psychologists do not engage, directly or through agents, in uninvited in-person solicitation of business from actual or potential psychotherapy patients or clients or other persons who because of their particular circumstances are vulnerable to undue influence. However, this does not preclude attempting to implement appropriate collateral contacts with significant others for the purpose of benefiting an already engaged therapy patient.

4. Therapy
4.01 Structuring the Relationship

(a) Psychologists discuss with clients or patients as early as is feasible in the therapeutic relationship appropriate issues, such as the nature and anticipated course of therapy, fees, and confidentiality. (See also Standards 1.25, Fees and Financial Arrangements, and 5.01, Discussing the Limits of Confidentiality.)

(b) When the psychologist's work with clients or patients will be supervised, the above discussion includes that fact, and the name of the supervisor, when the supervisor has legal responsibility for the case.

(c) When the therapist is a student intern, the client or patient is informed of that fact.

(d) Psychologists make reasonable efforts to answer patients' questions and to avoid apparent misunderstandings about therapy. Whenever possible, psychologists provide oral and/or written information, using language that is reasonably understandable to the patient or client.

4.02 Informed Consent to Therapy

(a) Psychologists obtain appropriate informed consent to therapy or related procedures, using language that is reasonably understandable to participants. The content of informed consent will vary depending on many circumstances; however, informed consent generally implies that the person (1) has the capacity to consent, (2) has been informed of significant information concerning the procedure, (3) has freely and without undue influence expressed consent, and (4) consent has been appropriately documented.

(b) When persons are legally incapable of giving informed consent, psychologists obtain informed permission from a legally authorized person, if such substitute consent is permitted by law.

(c) In addition, psychologists (1) inform those persons who are legally incapable of giving informed consent about the proposed interventions in a manner commensurate with the persons' psychological capacities, (2) seek their assent to those interventions, and (3) consider such persons' preferences and best interests.

4.03 Couple and Family Relationships

(a) When a psychologist agrees to provide services to several persons who have a relationship (such as husband and wife or parents and children), the psychologist attempts to clarify at the outset (1) which of the individuals are patients or clients and (2) the relationship the psychologist will have with each person. This clarification includes the role of the psychologist and the probable uses of the services provided or the information obtained. (See also Standard 5.01, Discussing the Limits of Confidentiality.)

(b) As soon as it becomes apparent that the psychologist may be called on to perform potentially conflicting roles (such as marital counselor to husband and wife, and then witness for one party in a divorce proceeding), the psychologist attempts to clarify and adjust, or withdraw from, roles appropriately. (See also Standard 7.03, Clarification of Role, under Forensic Activities.)

4.04 Providing Mental Health Services to Those Served by Others
In deciding whether to offer or provide services to those already receiving mental health services elsewhere, psychologists carefully consider the treatment issues and the potential patient's or client's welfare. The psychologist discusses these issues with the patient or client, or another legally authorized person on behalf of the client, in order to minimize the risk of confusion and conflict, consults with the other service providers when appropriate, and proceeds with caution and sensitivity to the therapeutic issues.

4.05 Sexual Intimacies With Current Patients or Clients
Psychologists do not engage in sexual intimacies with current patients or clients.

4.06 Therapy With Former Sexual Partners
Psychologists do not accept as therapy patients or clients persons with whom they have engaged in sexual intimacies.

4.07 Sexual Intimacies With Former Therapy Patients
(a) Psychologists do not engage in sexual intimacies with a former therapy patient or client for at least two years after cessation or termination of professional services.

(b) Because sexual intimacies with a former therapy patient or client are so frequently harmful to the patient or client, and because such intimacies undermine public confidence in the psychology profession and thereby deter the public's use of needed services, psychologists do not engage in sexual intima-

cies with former therapy patients and clients even after a two-year interval except in the most unusual circumstances. The psychologist who engages in such activity after the two years following cessation or termination of treatment bears the burden of demonstrating that there has been no exploitation, in light of all relevant factors, including (1) the amount of time that has passed since therapy terminated, (2) the nature and duration of the therapy, (3) the circumstances of termination, (4) the patient's or client's personal history, (5) the patient's or client's current mental status, (6) the likelihood of adverse impact on the patient or client and others, and (7) any statements or actions made by the therapist during the course of therapy suggesting or inviting the possibility of a posttermination sexual or romantic relationship with the patient or client. (See also Standard 1.17, Multiple Relationships.)

4.08 Interruption of Services
(a) Psychologists make reasonable efforts to plan for facilitating care in the event that psychological services are interrupted by factors such as the psychologist's illness, death, unavailability, or relocation or by the client's relocation or financial limitations. (See also Standard 5.09, Preserving Records and Data.)

(b) When entering into employment or contractual relationships, psychologists provide for orderly and appropriate resolution of responsibility for patient or client care in the event that the employment or contractual relationship ends, with paramount consideration given to the welfare of the patient or client.

4.09 Terminating the Professional Relationship
(a) Psychologists do not abandon patients or clients. (See also Standard 1.25e, under Fees and Financial Arrangements.)

(b) Psychologists terminate a professional relationship when it becomes reasonably clear that the patient or client no longer needs the service, is not benefiting, or is being harmed by continued service.

(c) Prior to termination for whatever reason, except where precluded by the patient's or client's conduct, the psychologist discusses the patient's or client's views and needs, provides appropriate pretermination counseling, suggests alternative service providers as appropriate, and takes other reasonable steps to facilitate transfer of responsibility to another provider if the patient or client needs one immediately.

5. Privacy and Confidentiality

These Standards are potentially applicable to the professional and scientific activities of all psychologists.

5.01 Discussing the Limits of Confidentiality

(a) Psychologists discuss with persons and organizations with whom they establish a scientific, or professional relationship (including, to the extent feasible, minors and their legal representatives) (1) the relevant limitations on confidentiality, including limitations where applicable in group, marital, and family therapy or in organizational consulting, and (2) the foreseeable uses of the information generated through their services.

(b) Unless it is not feasible or is contraindicated, the discussion of confidentiality occurs at the outset of the relationship and thereafter as new circumstances may warrant.

(c) Permission for electronic recording of interviews is secured from clients and patients.

5.02 Maintaining Confidentiality

Psychologists have a primary obligation and take reasonable precautions to respect the confidentiality rights of those with whom they work or consult, recognizing that confidentiality may be established by law, institutional rules, or professional or scientific relationships. (See also Standard 6.26, Professional Reviewers.)

5.03 Minimizing Intrusions on Privacy

(a) In order to minimize intrusions on privacy, psychologists include in written and oral reports, consultations, and the like, only information germane to the purpose for which the communication is made.

(b) Psychologists discuss confidential information obtained in clinical or consulting relationships, or evaluative data concerning patients, individual or organizational clients, students, research participants, supervisees, and employees, only for appropriate scientific or professional purposes and only with persons clearly concerned with such matters.

5.04 Maintenance of Records

Psychologists maintain appropriate confidentiality in creating, storing, accessing, transferring, and disposing of records under their control, whether these are written, automated, or in any other medium. Psychologists maintain and dispose of records in accordance with law and in a manner that permits compliance with the requirements of this Ethics Code.

5.05 Disclosures

(a) Psychologists disclose confidential information without the consent of the individual only as mandated by law, or where permitted by law for a valid purpose, such as (1) to provide needed professional services to the patient or the individual or organizational client, (2) to obtain appropriate professional consultations, (3) to protect the patient or client or others from harm, or (4) to obtain payment for services, in which instance disclosure is limited to the minimum that is necessary to achieve the purpose.

(b) Psychologists also may disclose confidential information with the appropriate consent of the patient or the individual or organizational client (or of another legally authorized person on behalf of the patient or client), unless prohibited by law.

5.06 Consultations

When consulting with colleagues, (1) psychologists do not share confidential information that reasonably could lead to the identification of a patient, client, research participant, or other person or organization with whom they have a confidential relationship unless they have obtained the prior consent of the person or organization or the disclosure cannot be avoided, and (2) they share information only to the extent necessary to achieve the purposes of the consultation. (See also Standard 5.02, Maintaining Confidentiality.)

5.07 Confidential Information in Databases

(a) If confidential information concerning recipients of psychological services is to be entered into databases or systems of records available to persons whose access has not been consented to by the recipient, then psychologists use coding or other techniques to avoid the inclusion of personal identifiers.

(b) If a research protocol approved by an institutional review board or similar body requires the inclusion of personal identifiers, such identifiers are deleted before the information is made accessible to persons other than those of whom the subject was advised.

(c) If such deletion is not feasible, then before psychologists transfer such data to others or review such data collected by others, they take reasonable steps to determine that appropriate consent of personally identifiable individuals has been obtained.

5.08 Use of Confidential Information for Didactic or Other Purposes

(a) Psychologists do not disclose in their writings, lectures, or other public media, confidential, personally identifiable information concerning their patients, individual or organizational clients, students, research participants, or other recipients of their services that they obtained during the course of their work, unless the person or organization has consented in writing or unless there is other ethical or legal authorization for doing so.

(b) Ordinarily, in such scientific and professional presentations, psychologists disguise confidential information concerning such persons or organizations so that they are not individually identifiable to others and so that discussions do not cause harm to subjects who might identify themselves.

5.09 Preserving Records and Data

A psychologist makes plans in advance so that confidentiality of records and data is protected in the event of the psychologist's death, incapacity, or withdrawal from the position or practice.

5.10 Ownership of Records and Data

Recognizing that ownership of records and data is governed by legal principles, psychologists take reasonable and lawful steps so that records and data remain available to the extent needed to serve the best interests of patients, individual or organizational clients, research participants, or appropriate others.

5.11 Withholding Records for Nonpayment

Psychologists may not withhold records under their control that are requested and imminently needed for a patient's or client's treatment solely because payment has not been received, except as otherwise provided by law.

6. Teaching, Training Supervision, Research, and Publishing
6.01 Design of Education and Training Programs

Psychologists who are responsible for education and training programs seek to ensure that the programs are competently designed, provide the proper experiences, and meet the requirements for licensure, certification, or other goals for which claims are made by the program.

6.02 Descriptions of Education and Training Programs

(a) Psychologists responsible for education and training programs seek to ensure that there is a current and accurate description of the program content, training goals and objectives, and requirements that must be met for satisfactory completion of the program. This information must be made readily available to all interested parties.

(b) Psychologists seek to ensure that statements concerning their course outlines are accurate and not misleading, particularly regarding the subject matter to be covered, bases for evaluating progress, and the nature of course experiences. (See also Standard 3.03, Avoidance of False or Deceptive Statements.)

(c) To the degree to which they exercise control, psychologists responsible for announcements, catalogs, brochures, or advertisements describing workshops, seminars, or other non-degree-granting educational programs ensure that they accurately describe the audience for which the program is intended, the educational objectives, the presenters, and the fees involved.

6.03 Accuracy and Objectivity in Teaching

(a) When engaged in teaching or training, psychologists present psychological information accurately and with a reasonable degree of objectivity.

(b) When engaged in teaching or training, psychologists recognize the power they hold over students or supervisees and therefore make reasonable efforts to avoid engaging in conduct that is personally demeaning to students or supervisees. (See also Standards 1.09, Respecting Others, and 1.12, Other Harassment.)

6.04 Limitation on Teaching

Psychologists do not teach the use of techniques or procedures that require specialized training, licensure, or expertise, including but not limited to hypnosis, biofeedback, and projective techniques, to individuals who lack the prerequisite training, legal scope of practice, or expertise.

6.05 Assessing Student and Supervisee Performance

(a) In academic and supervisory relationships, psychologists establish an appropriate process for providing feedback to students and supervisees.

(b) Psychologists evaluate students and supervisees on the basis of their actual performance on relevant and established program requirements.

6.06 Planning Research

(a) Psychologists design, conduct, and report research in accordance with recognized standards of scientific competence and ethical research.

(b) Psychologists plan their research so as to minimize the possibility that results will be misleading.

(c) In planning research, psychologists consider its ethical acceptability under the Ethics Code. If an ethical issue is unclear, psychologists seek to resolve the issue through consultation with institutional review boards, animal care and use committees, peer consultations, or other proper mechanisms.

(d) Psychologists take responsible steps to implement appropriate protections for the rights and welfare of human participants, other persons affected by the research, and the welfare of animal subjects.

6.07 Responsibility

(a) Psychologists conduct research competently and with due concern for the dignity and welfare of the participants.

(b) Psychologists are responsible for the ethical conduct of research conducted by them or by others under their supervision or control.

(c) Researchers and assistants are permitted to perform only those tasks for which they are appropriately trained and prepared.

(d) As part of the process of development and implementation of research projects, psychologists consult those with expertise concerning any special population under investigation or most likely to be affected.

6.08 Compliance With Law and Standards

Psychologists plan and conduct research in a manner consistent with federal and state law and regulations, as well as professional standards governing the conduct of research, and particularly those standards governing research with human participants and animal subjects.

6.09 Institutional Approval

Psychologists obtain from host institutions or organizations appropriate approval prior to conducting research, and they provide accurate information about their research proposals. They conduct the research in accordance with the approved research protocol.

6.10 Research Responsibilities

Prior to conducting research (except research involving only anonymous surveys, naturalistic observations, or similar research), psychologists enter into an agreement with participants that clarifies the nature of the research and the responsibilities of each party.

6.11 Informed Consent to Research

(a) Psychologists use language that is reasonably understandable to research participants in obtaining their appropriate informed consent (except as provided in Standard 6.12, Dispensing With Informed Consent). Such informed consent is appropriately documented.

(b) Using language that is reasonably understandable to participants, psychologists inform participants of the nature of the research; they inform participants that they are free to participate or to decline to participate or to withdraw from the research; they explain the foreseeable consequences of declining or withdrawing; they inform participants of significant factors that may be expected to influence their willingness to participate (such as risks, discomfort, adverse effects, or limitations on confidentiality, except as provided in Standard 6.15, Deception in Research); and they explain other aspects about which the prospective participants inquire.

(c) When psychologists conduct research with individuals such as students or subordinates, psychologists take special care to protect the prospective participants from adverse consequences of declining or withdrawing from participation.

(d) When research participation is a course requirement or opportunity for extra credit, the prospective participant is given the choice of equitable alternative activities.

(e) For persons who are legally incapable of giving informed consent, psychologists nevertheless (1) provide an appropriate explanation, (2) obtain the participant's assent, and (3) obtain appropriate permission from a legally authorized person, if such substitute consent is permitted by law.

6.12 Dispensing With Informed Consent

Before determining that planned research (such as research involving only anonymous questionnaires, naturalistic observations, or certain kinds of archival research) does not require the informed consent of research participants, psychologists consider applicable regulations and institutional review board requirements, and they consult with colleagues as appropriate.

6.13 Informed Consent in Research Filming or Recording

Psychologists obtain informed consent from research participants prior to filming or recording them in any form, unless the research involves simply naturalistic observations in public places and it is not anticipated that the recording will be used in a manner that could cause personal identification or harm.

6.14 Offering Inducement for Research Participants

(a) In offering professional services as an inducement to obtain research participants, psychologists make clear the nature of the services, as well as the risks, obligations, and limitations. (See also Standard 1.18, Barter [With Patients or Clients].)

(b) Psychologists do not offer excessive or inappropriate financial or other inducements to obtain research participants, particularly when it might tend to coerce participation.

6.15 Deception in Research

(a) Psychologists do not conduct a study involving deception unless they have determined that the use of deceptive techniques is justified by the study's prospective scientific, educational, or applied value and that equally effective alternative procedures that do not use deception are not feasible.

(b) Psychologists never deceive research participants about significant aspects that would affect their willingness to participate, such as physical risks, discomfort, or unpleasant emotional experiences.

(c) Any other deception that is an integral feature of the design and conduct of an experiment must be explained to participants as early as is feasible, preferably at the conclusion of their participation, but no later than at the conclusion of the research. (See also Standard 6.18, Providing Participants With Information About the Study.)

6.16 Sharing and Utilizing Data

Psychologists inform research participants of their anticipated sharing or further use of personally identifiable research data and of the possibility of unanticipated future uses.

6.17 Minimizing Invasiveness

In conducting research, psychologists interfere with the participants or milieu from which data are collected only in a manner that is warranted by an appropriate research design and that is consistent with psychologists' roles as scientific investigators.

6.18 Providing Participants With Information About the Study

(a) Psychologists provide a prompt opportunity for participants to obtain appropriate information about the nature, results, and conclusions of the research, and psychologists attempt to correct any misconceptions that participants may have.

(b) If scientific or humane values justify delaying or withholding this information, psychologists take reasonable measures to reduce the risk of harm.

6.19 Honoring Commitments

Psychologists take reasonable measures to honor all commitments they have made to research participants.

6.20 Care and Use of Animals in Research

(a) Psychologists who conduct research involving animals treat them humanely.

(b) Psychologists acquire, care for, use, and dispose of animals in compliance with current federal, state, and local laws and regulations, and with professional standards.

(c) Psychologists trained in research methods and experienced in the care of laboratory animals supervise all procedures involving animals and are responsible for ensuring appropriate consideration of their comfort, health, and humane treatment.

(d) Psychologists ensure that all individuals using animals under their supervision have received instruction in research methods and in the care, maintenance, and handling of the species being used, to the extent appropriate to their role.

(e) Responsibilities and activities of individuals assisting in a research project are consistent with their respective competencies.

(f) Psychologists make reasonable efforts to minimize the discomfort, infection, illness, and pain of animal subjects.

(g) A procedure subjecting animals to pain, stress, or privation is used only when an alternative procedure is unavailable and the goal is justified by its prospective scientific, educational, or applied value.

(h) Surgical procedures are performed under appropriate anesthesia; techniques to avoid infection and minimize pain are followed during and after surgery.

(i) When it is appropriate that the animal's life be terminated, it is done rapidly, with an effort to minimize pain, and in accordance with accepted procedures.

6.21 Reporting of Results

(a) Psychologists do not fabricate data or falsify results in their publications.

(b) If psychologists discover significant errors in their published data, they take reasonable steps to correct such errors in a correction, retraction, erratum, or other appropriate publication means.

6.22 Plagiarism

Psychologists do not present substantial portions or elements of another's work or data as their own, even if the other work or data source is cited occasionally.

6.23 Publication Credit

(a) Psychologists take responsibility and credit, including authorship credit, only for work they have actually performed or to which they have contributed.

(b) Principal authorship and other publication credits accurately reflect the relative scientific or professional contributions of the individuals involved, regardless of their relative status. Mere possession of an institutional position, such as Department Chair, does not justify authorship credit. Minor contributions to the research or to the writing for publications are appropriately acknowledged, such as in footnotes or in an introductory statement.

(c) A student is usually listed as principal author on any multiple-authored article that is substantially based on the student's dissertation or thesis.

6.24 Duplicate Publication of Data

Psychologists do not publish, as original data, data that have been previously published. This does not preclude republishing data when they are accompanied by proper acknowledgment.

6.25 Sharing Data

After research results are published, psychologists do not withhold the data on which their conclusions are based from other competent professionals who seek to verify the substantive claims through reanalysis and who intend to use such data only for that purpose, provided that the confidentiality of the participants can be protected and unless legal rights concerning proprietary data preclude their release.

6.26 Professional Reviewers

Psychologists who review material submitted for publication, grant, or other research proposal review respect the confidentiality of and the proprietary rights in such information of those who submitted it.

7. Forensic Activities
7.01 Professionalism

Psychologists who perform forensic functions, such as assessments, interviews, consultations, reports, or expert testimony, must comply with all other provisions of this Ethics Code to the extent that they apply to such activities. In addition, psychologists base their forensic work on appropriate knowledge of and competence in the areas underlying such work, including specialized knowledge concerning special populations. (See also Standards 1.06, Basis for Scientific and Professional Judgments; 1.08, Human Differences; 1.15, Misuse of Psychologists' Influence; and 1.23, Documentation of Professional and Scientific Work.)

7.02 Forensic Assessments

(a) Psychologists' forensic assessments, recommendations, and reports are based on information and techniques (including personal interviews of the individual, when appropriate) sufficient to provide appropriate substantiation for their findings. (See also Standards 1.03, Professional and Scientific Relationship; 1.23, Documentation of Professional and Scientific Work; 2.01, Evaluation, Diagnosis, and Interventions in Professional Context; and 2.05, Interpreting Assessment Results.)

(b) Except as noted in (c), below, psychologists provide written or oral forensic reports or testimony of the psychological characteristics of an individual only after they have conducted an examination of the individual adequate to support their statements or conclusions.

(c) When, despite reasonable efforts, such an examination is not feasible, psychologists clarify the impact of their limited information on the reliability and validity of their reports and testimony, and they appropriately limit the nature and extent of their conclusions or recommendations.

7.03 Clarification of Role

In most circumstances, psychologists avoid performing multiple and potentially conflicting roles in forensic matters. When psychologists may be called on to serve in more than one role in a legal proceeding—for example, as consultant or expert for one party or for the court and as a fact witness—they clarify role expectations and the extent of confidentiality in advance to the extent feasible, and thereafter as changes occur, in order to avoid compromising their professional judgment and objectivity and in order to avoid misleading others regarding their role.

7.04 Truthfulness and Candor

(a) In forensic testimony and reports, psychologists testify truthfully, honestly, and candidly and, consistent with applicable legal procedures, describe fairly the bases for their testimony and conclusions.

(b) Whenever necessary to avoid misleading, psychologists acknowledge the limits of their data or conclusions.

7.05 Prior Relationships

A prior professional relationship with a party does not preclude psychologists from testifying as fact witnesses or from testifying to their services to the extent permitted by applicable law. Psychologists appropriately take into account ways in which the prior relationship might affect their professional objectivity or opinions and disclose the potential conflict to the relevant parties.

7.06 Compliance With Law and Rules

In performing forensic roles, psychologists are reasonably familiar with the rules governing their roles. Psychologists are aware of the occasionally competing demands placed upon them by these principles and the requirements of the court system, and attempt to resolve these conflicts by making known their commitment to this Ethics Code and taking steps to resolve the conflict in a responsible manner. (See also Standard 1.02, Relationship of Ethics and Law.)

8. Resolving Ethical Issues
8.01 Familiarity With Ethics Code

Psychologists have an obligation to be familiar with this Ethics Code, other applicable ethics codes, and their application to psychologists' work. Lack of awareness or misunderstanding of an ethical standard is not itself a defense to a charge of unethical conduct.

8.02 Confronting Ethical Issues

When a psychologist is uncertain whether a particular situation or course of action would violate this Ethics Code, the psychologist ordinarily consults with other psychologists knowledgeable about ethical issues, with state or national psychology ethics committees, or with other appropriate authorities in order to choose a proper response.

8.03 Conflicts Between Ethics and Organizational Demands

If the demands of an organization with which psychologists are affiliated conflict with this Ethics Code, psychologists clarify the nature of the conflict, make known their commitment to the Ethics Code, and to the extent feasible, seek to resolve the conflict in a way that permits the fullest adherence to the Ethics Code.

8.04 Informal Resolution of Ethical Violations

When psychologists believe that there may have been an ethical violation by another psychologist, they attempt to resolve the issue by bringing it to the attention of that individual if an informal resolution appears appropriate and the intervention does not violate any confidentiality rights that may be involved.

8.05 Reporting Ethical Violations

If an apparent ethical violation is not appropriate for informal resolution under Standard 8.04 or is not resolved properly in that fashion, psychologists take further action appropriate to the situation, unless such action conflicts with confidentiality rights in ways that cannot be resolved. Such action might include referral to state or national committees on professional ethics or to state licensing boards.

8.06 Cooperating With Ethics Committees

Psychologists cooperate in ethics investigations, proceedings, and resulting requirements of the APA or any affiliated state psychological association to which they belong. In doing so, they make reasonable efforts to resolve any issues as to confidentiality. Failure to cooperate is itself an ethics violation.

8.07 Improper Complaints

Psychologists do not file or encourage the filing of ethics complaints that are frivolous and are intended to harm the respondent rather than to protect the public.

◆ ◆ ◆

Commentary: There is little doubt that the 1981 and 1989 APA ethical principles needed changing. Although they were serviceable and clear in some respects, many of their provisions were ambiguous. In fact, application of this code was challenged by a clinician who was disciplined by his state licensure board. In that 1990 case,[1] the board voted to revoke the psychologist's license to practice for violating the 1981 Ethical Principles of Psychologists. Such action is not atypical: Many state laws regulating psychologists incorporate the APA ethics code. Where this is true, if a licensed psychologist violates APA ethical principles, then he or she is subject to disciplinary action by the relevant state board. The most severe form of discipline is revocation of the license to practice, a sanction with serious economic consequences. Because of the magnitude of the board's decision, the psychologist filed a complaint against the board in state court, claiming that the various enforceable preambles and principles under which he was charged were unconstitutionally vague and did not provide him with proper notice of potential misconduct. Essentially, he alleged that, under the state and federal constitutions, it was fundamentally unfair for the state to deprive him of his right to practice on the basis of standards that were not comprehensible to the reasonably intelligent psychologist.

With regard to the preambles to various principles in the 1981 code, the court agreed. Their language, the court held, failed to inform licensees of what conduct was forbidden. Although it rejected the psychologist's claim

---

[1] White v. North Carolina State Board of Examiners of Practicing Psychologists, 97 N.C. App. 144, 388 S.E.2d 148 (1990), *review denied*, 326 N.C. 601, 393 S.E.2d 891 (1990).

that the specific principles under which he was charged were also unconstitutional, the court stated:

> Psychologists . . . have a right and funda-
> mental need to be guided by Ethical Codes
> of Conduct of sufficient clarity and speci-
> ficity to meet applicable constitutional stan-
> dards and to adequately apprise practition-
> ers of the boundaries of conduct. While we
> have concluded that those Principles in
> question meet such standards, suffice it to
> say that for the most part it is by the
> slimmest of margins. (White v. North
> Carolina State Board, 1990)

Such indeterminancy showed the ethics code to be a dis-service to organized psychology and its members. Thus, the planned revision was awaited with great and positive anticipation.

The 1992 code was reviewed by a number of re-spected psychologists with experience in ethics in a spe-cial section of an APA journal. See Keith-Spiegel, P. (Ed.). (1994). The 1992 ethics code: Boon or bane? Professional Psychology: Research and Practice, 25, 315–387. Whether from the perspective of science, prac-tice, or public interest, most of the commentators ap-plauded the broadened and specific attention in the new code to important issues. But they also found that, in many respects, the new code lacked clarity, contained qualifying language that may make many provisions dif-ficult to enforce, and may not completely fulfill its mis-sion of protecting the public. As readers examine the Ethical Principles and address the particular issues rep-resented in this book, they should come to their own conclusions about the usefulness of the new Code of Conduct.

One function that a code of ethics should serve is to translate moral values, or prima facie duties, into en-forceable standards. These duties include nonmaleficence, fidelity, beneficence, justice, and autonomy, and each can be defined in the context of professional conduct.

Perhaps the bedrock ethical duty required of psychol-ogists is nonmaleficence, captured in the Latin phrase primum non nocere—"above all, do no harm." Fidelity most often refers to the obligations of faithfulness and loyalty inherent in the client–clinician relationship, but it may be extended to mean fidelity toward the scientific

roots of one's profession. Beneficence is the most com-monsense principle; indeed, the concept of psychology as a "helping profession" is its embodiment. Specifically, it refers to the practitioners' responsibility to benefit those they assess and treat and the obligation of investigators to conduct research with scientific or applied value. Justice refers to psychologists' obligation to treat equi-tably those who they serve and, perhaps, the superordi-nate responsibility to respect the worth and dignity of each individual. Finally—but by no means least impor-tant—is the principle of autonomy, guaranteeing people the freedom to think, choose, and act so long as their ac-tions do not infringe unduly on the rights of others. These principles are explicated more fully in chapter 3. For an analysis of how these prima facie duties have been repre-sented in the current APA Ethical Principles, see Bersoff, D. N., & Koeppl, P. M. (1993). The relation between ethical codes and moral principles. Ethics and Behavior, 3, 345–357.

To keep the ethics code relevant and up-to-date, the APA ethics committee developed an ongoing process of review. The next major revision of the code begins in 1995 with a critical study of the 1992 code; at that time, a decision will also be made about the revision method to be used. This revision is likely to be pub-lished as the world enters the twenty-first century and the APA its 110th year. When readers conclude this text, they may want to revisit the currently enforceable code and suggest to the next revisions committee, work-ing in the year 2001, ways in which the 1992 code can be improved and strengthened to ensure that psychology continues to earn and maintain the public's trust through an ethics document that reflects the profession's moral integrity and its primary mission of promoting human welfare.

The interpretation and enforcement of the Ethical Principles are the responsibility of the APA ethics com-mittee. The structure and work of the committee are gov-erned primarily by the APA bylaws, the ARs passed by the Council of Representatives, and the Rules and Procedures developed by the ethics committee itself. The two portions of the bylaws relevant to ethics are Article XI, Section 5, and Article II, Sections 17–19. See Bylaws of the American Psychological Association. (Amended July 1994.) Washington, DC: American Psychological Association.

Bylaws of the American Psychological Association

American Psychological Association

. . .

[Article XI, Section 5 provides:]

5. The Ethics Committee shall consist of not fewer than eight persons, at least seven of whom shall be Members of the Association, elected from different geographical areas, for terms of not less than three years. Members of the Ethics Committee shall be selected to represent a range of interests characteristic of psychology. The Ethics Committee shall have the power to receive, initiate, and investigate complaints of unethical conduct of Members (to include Fellows), Associate members, and Affiliates; to report on types of cases investigated with specific description of difficult or recalcitrant cases; to dismiss or recommend action on ethical cases investigated; to resolve cases by agreement where appropriate; to formulate rules or principles of ethics for adoption by the Association; to formulate rules and procedures governing the conduct of the ethics or disciplinary process for approval by the Board of Directors acting on behalf of Council; and to interpret, apply, and otherwise administer those rules and procedures.

The work of the Ethics Committee, including information and recommendation on all cases before it, shall be kept confidential, except as provided by the Ethics Committee in rules and procedures approved by the Board of Directors, consistent with the objectives of the Committee and the interest of the Association.

. . .

[Article II, Sections 17–19 provide:]

17. A Member (to include Fellows), Associate member or Affiliate may be dropped from membership or otherwise disciplined for conduct which violates the Ethical Principles of the Association, which tends to injure the Association or to affect adversely its reputation, or which is contrary to or destructive of its objects. Allegations of such conduct shall be submitted to the Ethics Committee.

The Ethics Committee shall formulate rules and procedures governing the conduct of the ethics and disciplinary process. However, such rules and procedures and any changes therein must be approved by the Board of Directors acting on behalf of Council. The Ethics Committee, acting at its own discretion or on direction of the Board of Directors, shall review such rules and procedures periodically and may amend them from time to time, subject to the approval of the Board of Directors, provided, however, that no such amendment shall adversely affect the substantive rights of a Member, Associate member or Affiliate whose conduct is being investigated or against whom formal charges have been filed at the time of amendment.

18. A person who has been dropped from membership pursuant to the rules and procedures of the Ethics Committee may reapply for membership after five years have elapsed from the date of termination of his/her membership. A person who has been permitted to resign under a stipulated agreement may reapply for membership only after the period of time stipulated in the agreement has elapsed, and all other conditions set forth in such agreement have been discharged. In all cases the Member, Associate member or Affiliate must show that he/she is ethically as well as technically qualified for membership. Such reapplications shall be considered first by the Ethics Committee, which shall make recommendation to the Membership Committee.

19. Resignations of Members, Associate members or Affiliates may be accepted only by the Board of Directors. In the ordinary course, the Board of Directors will, in its discretion, refuse to accept a resignation tendered by a Member, Associate member or Affiliate while such Member, Associate member or Affiliate is under the scrutiny of the Ethics Committee. . . .

Rules and Procedures
October 1, 1992

Ethics Committee of the American Psychological Association

INTRODUCTION

The revised Rules and Procedures of the Ethics Committee of the American Psychological Association, which are set forth below, were approved by the APA Board of Directors on August 15, 1992, with an effective date of October 1, 1992. The rules will be applied prospectively to all complaints and cases pending on the effective date, except, as provided in Part II, Subsection 1.2, "no amendment shall adversely affect the rights of a member of the Association whose conduct is being investigated by the Ethics Committee or against whom the Ethics Committee has filed formal charges" as of the effective date. In the event application of the revised Rules and Procedures would adversely affect such rights, the pertinent provisions of the former Rules and Procedures will be applied. Failure by the Committee or APA to follow these rules and procedures shall be cause to set aside action taken pursuant thereto only in the event such failure has resulted in genuine prejudice to the complainee or member.

The revised Rules and Procedures are divided into five parts, which are further subdivided by sections and subsections.

OVERVIEW

This brief overview is intended only to orient the reader to the overall structure of the Rules. The overview is not binding on the Committee or participants in the ethics process, and is not an independent source of authority.

General Provisions

Part I describes the objectives and authority of the Ethics Committee.

Part II sets forth the Committee's general operating rules. These include, among others, rules governing confidentiality and disclosures of information concerning ethics cases; rules governing the maintenance and disposition of Ethics Committee records; rules governing the Committee's jurisdiction, including the time limits within which ethics complaints must be filed; rules governing applications to reopen a closed case; rules describing the various sanctions and directives that may be imposed; and procedures pursuant to which at the outset of the ethics process a member may admit the alleged violation and resign from the Association.

Provisions Bearing on Membership Applications

Part III sets forth the procedures governing Ethics Committee review of applications or reapplications for membership in APA, and procedures governing Ethics Committee review of allegations that membership was obtained based upon false pretenses.

Provisions Governing "Show Cause" Proceedings in Response to Prior Serious Adverse Actions by Other Tribunals

Part IV establishes procedures available to the Committee in cases in which other tribunals—including criminal courts, licensing boards, and state

Adapted from the *American Psychologist*, 47, 1612–1628. Copyright 1992 by the American Psychological Association.

The Board of Directors adopted, in August 1992, Rules and Procedures to replace its earlier set (which were published in the June 1985 issue of the *American Psychologist*, pp. 685–694, with a minor amendment added in June 1991).

psychological associations—have already taken specified serious adverse actions against a member pursuant to presumptively valid procedures. If a member has been convicted of a felony or commensurate criminal offense; has been expelled or suspended by a state psychological association; or has been decertified or unlicensed or had a certificate or license revoked or suspended by a state or local board, the Committee may notify the member that he or she has 60 days to set forth, in writing, why APA should not expel the member from membership on the basis of that prior action. Based solely on the available record leading to the prior action, the member's written response and any evidence developed by the Committee, the Committee may recommend to the Board whether the member should be expelled, some lesser sanction should be applied, or the charges dismissed. The Committee may also choose to adjudicate the matter pursuant to the plenary procedures of Part V, or to offer the member the option of resigning pursuant to stipulated conditions in lieu of other actions, subject to approval by the Board of Directors. The member may file a written response to the recommendation to the Board, which will act based upon the written record in the case.

Provisions Governing Submission and Resolution of Complaints Against Members

Part V establishes the procedures used in resolving and adjudicating complaints of unethical conduct against members. Complaints may be submitted by members or nonmembers of the Association, or may be initiated by the Ethics Committee acting on its own (*sua sponte* complaints). Complaints must be submitted within the time periods set forth in Part II, Section 5, or fall within the exceptions set forth in that section.

Complaints are evaluated initially by the Chair of the Ethics Committee and Director of the Ethics Office to determine whether the Committee has jurisdiction and whether there is cause for action by the Committee (defined in Part V, Subsection 5.1). If necessary, the Chair and Director will conduct a preliminary investigation to assist in making these threshold determinations. If the Committee has no

jurisdiction, or if cause for action does not exist, the complaint will be dismissed at this stage. If the Committee has jurisdiction and cause for action exists, the Director will open a formal case and conduct an investigation.

A formal case is initiated with a charge letter, sent to the complainee. The complainee is afforded an opportunity to review all materials submitted to the Committee and upon which the Committee may rely in adjudicating the complaint. At the conclusion of the investigation, the formal case is referred to the Committee for review and resolution.

In resolving a case, the Committee may dismiss it, recommend that it be resolved with sanctions less than formal charges (i.e., recommend a censure or reprimand, with or without supplemental directives), or issue formal charges (a recommendation to the Board of Directors that the complainee be dropped from membership). The Committee may also offer the member the option of resigning pursuant to stipulated conditions in lieu of other actions, subject to approval by the Board of Directors.

If the Committee votes to recommend resolution without formal charges or issues formal charges, the complainee has a right to an Independent Adjudication or Formal Hearing, respectively. If the Committee has voted to recommend resolution without formal charges, the adjudicatory mechanism is via written submissions to an Independent Adjudication Panel. The decision of the Independent Adjudication Panel is the final adjudication. If the complainee elects *not* to seek an independent adjudication of the Committee's recommendation, the Director implements the recommendation as the accepted adjudication.

If the Committee has issued formal charges, the adjudicatory mechanism is an in-person hearing before a Formal Hearing Committee, which makes an independent recommendation to the Board of Directors. The Board reviews the recommendation of the Hearing Committee, and must adopt that recommendation unless specified defects require the matter to be remanded for further actions. In the event of formal charges, if the complainee elects not to seek adjudication, the Board of Directors reviews the Ethics Committee's recommendation upon the same terms as it would review the recommendation of a Hearing Committee.

PART I. OBJECTIVES AND AUTHORITY OF THE COMMITTEE

1. Objectives

The fundamental objectives of the Ethics Committee (hereinafter the Committee) shall be to maintain ethical conduct by psychologists at the highest professional level, to educate psychologists concerning ethical standards, to endeavor to protect the public against harmful conduct by psychologists, and to aid the Association in achieving its objectives as reflected in its Bylaws.[1]

2. Authority

The Committee is authorized to:

2.1. Formulate rules or principles of ethics for adoption by the Association;

2.2. Investigate allegations of unethical conduct of Fellows, Members, and Associates (hereinafter members) and, in certain instances, applicants for membership;

2.3. Resolve allegations of unethical conduct and/or recommend such action as is necessary to achieve the objectives of the Association;

2.4. Report on types of complaints investigated with special description of difficult cases;

2.5. Adopt rules and procedures governing the conduct of all the matters within its jurisdiction;

2.6. Take such other actions as are consistent with the Bylaws of the Association, the Rules of Council, the Association's Ethics Code, and these Rules and Procedures, and as are necessary and appropriate to achieving the objectives of the Committee; and

2.7. Delegate appropriate tasks to subcommittees of the Ethics Committee or to agents or employees of the Association, such subcommittees, agents, and employees in such event to be fully bound by these Rules and Procedures.

PART II. GENERAL OPERATING RULES

1. General Provisions

1.1 APA documents. The Committee shall base its actions on applicable governmental laws and regulations, the Bylaws of the Association,[2] the Association Rules,[3] the Association's Ethics Code, and these Rules and Procedures.

1.2 Rules and procedures. The Committee may adopt rules and procedures governing the conduct of all matters within its jurisdiction, and may amend such rules from time to time upon a two-thirds vote of the Committee members, provided that no amendment shall adversely affect the rights of a member of the Association whose conduct is being investigated by the Ethics Committee or against whom the Ethics Committee has filed formal charges at the time of amendment. Changes to the Rules and Procedures must be ratified by the Board of Directors acting for the Council of Representatives.

1.3 Compliance with time requirements. The Committee and complainee shall use their best efforts to adhere strictly to the time requirements specified in these Rules and Procedures. Failure to do so will not prohibit final resolution unless such failure was unduly prejudicial.

1.4 Computation of time. In computing any period of time prescribed or allowed by these rules, the day of the act, event, or default from which the designated period of time begins to run shall not be included. The last day of the period shall be included unless it is a Saturday, a Sunday, or a legal holiday, in which event the period runs until the end of the

---

[1] The Ethics Committee seeks to protect the public by deterring unethical conduct by psychologists; by taking appropriate action when an ethical violation has been proved according to these Rules and Procedures; and by setting standards to aid psychologists in understanding their ethical obligations. Of course, in no circumstances can or does the Committee or the Association guarantee that unethical behavior will not occur or that members of the public will never be harmed by the actions of individual psychologists.

[2] APA Bylaws (1991), Article II, Sections 18 and 19, and Article X, Section 5 [now see APA Bylaws (1994), Article II, Sections 17–19 and Article XI, Section 5], pertain to the Committee specifically.

[3] Association Rules (1991) 10-11, 10-12, 10-13, 20-1, 20-2, 20-3, and 20-4 pertain to the Committee specifically.

next day which is not one of the aforementioned days.

2. Meetings and Officers

2.1 Frequency and quorum. The Committee shall meet at reasonable intervals as needed. A quorum at such meetings shall consist of the majority of the elected members of the Committee.

2.2 Selection of officers. The Chair and Vice Chair shall be elected annually at a duly constituted meeting. The Chief Executive Officer of the Association shall designate a staff member to serve as Director of the Ethics Office. Whenever they appear in these rules, "Chair," "Vice Chair," and "Director" shall mean these individuals or their designees.

2.3 Vice chair. The Vice Chair shall have the authority to perform all the duties of the Chair when the latter is unavailable or unable to perform them, and shall perform such other tasks as are delegated by the Chair or by these rules.

2.4 Majority rule. Except as otherwise noted in the Rules and Procedures, all decisions shall be by majority vote of those members present or, in the case of a vote by mail, a majority of those members qualified to vote.

2.5 Attendance. Attendance at the Ethics Committee's deliberation of cases is restricted to elected members of the Committee, the Director of the Ethics Office, the Ethics Office staff, members of the Board of Directors, Legal Counsel of the Association, and other duly appointed persons authorized by the Committee to assist it in carrying out its functions, except when the Committee, by two-thirds vote, authorizes the presence of other persons.

3. Confidentiality and Disclosures

3.1 Requirement of confidentiality. All information concerning complaints against members shall be confidential, except that the Committee may disclose such information when compelled by a valid subpoena, when otherwise required by law, or as otherwise provided in these Rules and Procedures.

3.2 Access by staff, legal counsel, and other duly appointed persons. Information may be shared with Legal Counsel of the Association, with the Chief Executive Officer of the Association, with staff of the Association's Central Office designated by the Chief Executive Officer to assist the Committee with its work, and with other duly appointed persons authorized by the Committee to assist it in carrying out its functions.

3.3 Notification of final disposition of case by the board of directors.

3.3.1 Complainee. The Board of Directors shall inform the complainee or member of its final action, including which Ethical Standard(s)[4] were judged to have been violated, should there be any, and the rationale for the Association's actions. The Director of the Ethics Office (hereinafter Director) shall be provided a copy of the letter to the complainee.

3.3.2 Complainant. The Director shall inform the complainant of the Board of Directors' final action, including which Ethical Standard(s) were judged to have been violated, should there be any, and, if the Board of Directors deems it appropriate, the rationale therefor.

3.3.3 Membership. The Board shall report annually and in confidence to the membership the names of members who have been expelled or dropped from membership and the Ethical Standard(s) involved.

3.3.4 Council of representatives. The Board shall report annually and in executive session to the Council the names of members who have been allowed to resign under stipulated conditions or who have been dropped or expelled from membership and the Ethical Standard(s) involved.

3.3.5 Other entities. When the Board of Directors deems it necessary for the protection of the Association or the public or to maintain the standards of the Association, the Board shall direct the Committee to notify of its final action (a) affiliated state and regional associations,[5] (b) the American

---

[4] In this document "Ethical Standard(s)" refers to the Ethical Standard(s) in the *Ethical Principles of Psychologists and Code of Conduct* or the Ethical Principle(s) in the *Ethical Principles of Psychologists.*

[5] For purposes of these Rules and Procedures, a state association shall include territorial, local, or county psychological associations, and in cases of Canadian members of the Association, provincial psychological associations.

Board of Professional Psychology (ABPP), (c) state or local licensing and certification boards,[6] (d) the Association of State and Provincial Psychology Boards (ASPPB), (e) the Council for the National Register of Health Service Providers in Psychology (CNRHSPP), and/or (f) other appropriate parties.

3.4 Notification of final disposition of case by the ethics committee and/or independent adjudication panel

3.4.1 Complainee. The Committee shall inform the complainee of the final disposition of the case and the rationale therefor, including the Ethical Standard(s) violated, if any.

3.4.2 Complainant. The Committee shall inform the complainant of the final disposition of the case, including the Ethical Standard(s) violated, if any, and, if the Committee deems it appropriate, the rationale therefor.

3.4.3 Other parties informed of the complaint. The Committee may inform such other parties as have been informed of the complaint of the final disposition of the case, including the Ethical Standard(s) violated, if any, and the rationale therefor.

3.4.4 Further disclosure of cases resulting in probation. In cases that have resulted in a member's probation, the Committee may communicate these actions to: (a) members; (b) governance groups, committees, and divisions of the Association; (c) affiliated state and regional associations; (d) ABPP and state licensing and certification boards; (e) the ASPPB; (f) the CNRHSPP; and/or (g) such other individuals or organizations as the Committee shall deem necessary to protect the public.

3.4.5 Disclosure of fact of investigation. The Committee may disclose to any of the entities enumerated in Subsection 3.4.4(a)–(g) of this part the fact that an individual is under ethical investigation in cases deemed to be serious threats to the public welfare (as determined by a two-thirds vote of the Committee at a regularly scheduled meeting), but only when to do so before final adjudication appears necessary to protect the public.

3.4.6 Notification of additional parties at the request of complainee. The Ethics Office may notify such additional parties of the final disposition as are requested by the complainee.

3.4.7 Initiation of legal action constitutes waiver. Initiation of a legal action against the Association or any of its agents, officers, directors, or employees concerning any matters considered or actions taken by the Ethics Committee or Ethics Office shall constitute a waiver by the person initiating such action of an interest in confidentiality recognized in these Rules or other organic documents of the Association with respect to the subject matter of the legal action.

3.5 Communication for investigation or other functions.
Nothing in this section shall be construed to prevent the Committee from communicating with the complainee, complainant, witnesses, or other sources of information necessary to enable the Committee to carry out its functions.

4. Records

4.1 Confidential permanent files.
Files of the Committee related to investigation and adjudication of cases shall be confidential, within the limitations of Section 3 of this part, and shall be maintained, consistent with these Rules and Procedures.

4.2 Preliminary investigation files.
If a preliminary investigation is closed for no cause for action, records containing personally identifiable information shall be maintained for at least one year after the matter is closed.

4.3 Formal case and show cause records

4.3.1 Closure for nonviolation. In cases closed due to finding of nonviolation, records shall be maintained for at least five years after closure.

4.3.2 Closure for insufficient evidence. In cases closed due to evidence insufficient to support a finding of an ethical violation, records shall be maintained for at least five years after closure.

---

[6] For purposes of these Rules and Procedures, state boards shall include boards in Canadian provinces or state or provincial boards of examiners or education in those cases where the pertinent licensing or certification is secured from such entities, or in states or provinces with no licensing authority, nonstatutory boards established for such purpose.

4.3.3 Censure and reprimand. In cases resulting in censure or reprimand, records shall be maintained for at least five years after closure.

4.3.4 Dropped membership and expulsion. In cases in which members have been dropped from membership or expelled, records shall be maintained indefinitely.

4.3.5 Stipulated resignation. In cases in which members have been permitted a stipulated resignation and the complainee does not reapply for membership, records shall be maintained indefinitely. In cases where the complainee is subsequently readmitted, records shall be maintained for at least five years after readmission.

4.4 Death of a member. Records concerning members whom the Association has determined to be deceased shall be maintained for at least one year after that determination was made.

4.5 Records for educative purposes. Nothing in these Rules and Procedures shall preclude the Committee from maintaining records in a secure place for archival or record keeping purposes, or from using or publishing information concerning ethics matters for educative purposes without identifying individuals involved.

5. Jurisdiction

5.1 Persons. The Committee has jurisdiction over individual members, associate members, fellows, and applicants for membership in the American Psychological Association.[7]

5.2 Subject matter. The Committee has jurisdiction to achieve its objectives and perform those functions for which it is authorized in these Rules and Procedures and other organic documents of the Association.[8]

5.3 Time limits for complaints and show cause notices

5.3.1 Complaints by members. Except as provided in Subsections 5.3.5 and 5.3.6 of this part, the Committee may consider complaints brought by members of the Association against other members only if the complaint is received less than one year after the alleged conduct either occurred or was discovered by the complainant.

5.3.2 Complaints by nonmembers. Except as provided in Subsections 5.3.5 and 5.3.6 of this part, the Committee may consider complaints brought by nonmembers only if the complaint is received less than five years after the alleged conduct either occurred or was discovered by the complainant.

5.3.3 Sua sponte complaints. The Committee may initiate a *sua sponte* complaint under Part V of these Rules and Procedures only if it does so less than one year after it discovered the alleged unethical conduct and less than 10 years after the alleged conduct occurred, except that whether or not such periods have expired, the Committee may initiate a *sua sponte* complaint less than one year after it discovered that any of the following actions had become final: (a) a felony conviction, (b) a finding of malpractice by a duly authorized tribunal, (c) expulsion or suspension from a state association for unethical conduct, or (d) revocation, suspension, or surrender of a license or certificate for ethical violations by a state board or while ethical proceedings before such board were pending.

5.3.4 Show cause notices. The Committee may initiate a show cause notice under Part IV of these Rules and Procedures only if it does so less than one year after the date it discovered that the applicable predicate for use of show cause procedures (i.e., an event described in Part IV, Section 1) has become final.

5.3.5 Exceptions to time limits for complaints by members and nonmembers

5.3.5.1 Threshold criteria. Any complaint not received within the time limits set forth in this section shall not be considered unless, with respect to complaints subject to Subsections 5.3.1 and 5.3.2 of this part, at least two thirds of the Committee members voting determine that each of the following criteria are met:

---

[7] Whether an individual is a member of the Association is determined according to the Bylaws, Association Rules, and other pertinent organic documents of the Association. Under the current rules, nonpayment of dues results in discontinuation of membership only after two consecutive calendar years during which dues to the Association have remained unpaid. See Bylaws, Article XVIII, Section 3; Association Rules 10-12.1. For purposes of these Rules and Procedures, an affiliate is not a member of the Association.

[8] Conduct complained of pursuant to this part is subject to the Ethics Code in effect at the time it occurs.

5.3.5.1.1. Considering the version of the Ethics Code under which the case would be judged, the alleged offense is serious enough that the Committee would be likely to recommend that the complainee be dropped from membership in the Association if it is substantiated;

5.3.5.1.2. There is significant supporting evidence for the allegations;

5.3.5.1.3. There is good cause demonstrated for the complaint not having been filed within the applicable time limit; and

5.3.5.1.4. The complaint was received less than 10 years after the alleged conduct occurred.

5.3.5.2 Determination to supersede applicable time limit. Where, pursuant to Subsection 5.3.5.1 of this part, the Committee has determined that the threshold criteria are met, the applicable limit shall be superseded if two thirds of the Committee (excluding recused or otherwise unavailable members), in their sole discretion, vote to do so.

5.3.6 Absolute time limit for member and nonmember complaints. Subsections 5.3.1, 5.3.2, and 5.3.5 of this part notwithstanding, the Committee may not proceed pursuant to any member or nonmember complaint received more than 10 years after the alleged conduct occurred. This rule shall not be construed as prohibiting the Committee from considering the information contained in such a complaint in determining whether to initiate a *sua sponte* action or issuing a show cause notice, where such action would otherwise be consistent with the time limits set forth in Subsections 5.3.3 or 5.3.4 of this part.

5.4 Resignation barred. Except as provided in Subsection 11.4 of this part or Parts IV and V of these Rules, no one under the scrutiny of the Committee will be allowed to resign either by letter of resignation, by nonpayment of dues, or otherwise.

5.5 Litigation not a bar to action by committee; ethics committee authorized to stay ethics process pending resolution. Civil or criminal litigation involving members shall not bar action by the Committee; the Committee may proceed during the course of litigation or may stay the ethics process pending its completion. Delay in conducting the investigation by the Committee during the pendency of civil or criminal proceedings shall not constitute waiver of jurisdiction.

5.6 Other disciplinary proceedings not a bar to action by committee; ethics committee authorized to stay ethics process pending resolution. Disciplinary proceedings or action by another body or tribunal shall not bar action by the Committee; the Committee may proceed during the course of such proceedings or stay the ethics process pending their completion. Delay in conducting the investigation by the Committee during the pendency of such proceedings shall not constitute a waiver of jurisdiction. Where the Committee learns that disciplinary action by another authorized tribunal has been stayed, such stay shall neither require nor preclude action by the Committee.

5.7 Referral and retention of jurisdiction. The Committee may at any time refer a matter to another recognized tribunal for appropriate action. If a case is referred to another tribunal, the Committee may retain jurisdiction and consider the complaint independently pursuant to these Rules and Procedures.

6. Reopening a Closed Case

If the complainant presents significant new evidence of unethical conduct after a matter has been closed, the case may be reopened and acted upon under regular procedures. To be considered under this rule, evidence must meet each of the following criteria:

6.1. The evidence was discovered after the Committee closed the case;

6.2. The evidence could not with reasonable diligence have been discovered before the case was closed; and

6.3. The evidence would probably produce a different result.

7. Choice and Conversion of Procedures

7.1 Choice of procedures. Where a case might be adjudicated pursuant to the show cause procedures set forth in Part IV of these Rules and Procedures, the Committee shall determine whether to proceed pursuant to Part IV or Part V of these Rules and Procedures. The Committee shall also be the sole judge whether a matter shall be disposed of without formal charges, whether a stipulated resignation shall be sought, or whether formal charges shall be brought.

7.2 Conversion of show cause case. In its sole discretion, the Committee may convert a proceeding begun by show cause procedures under Part IV hereof to a plenary case under Part V hereof. In event of such conversion, the complaint shall be deemed timely filed if the show cause proceeding had been initiated in timely fashion.

7.3 Conversion of plenary case. In its sole discretion, where the predicates for use of show cause procedures set forth in Part IV, Section 1 are present, the Committee may convert a plenary proceeding begun by *sua sponte*, member, or nonmember complaint under Part V hereof to a show cause proceeding under Part IV. In such event, the show cause proceeding shall be deemed timely initiated if at the time of conversion it satisfies the provisions of Subsection 5.3.4 of this part.

8. Correspondence and Documentation

8.1 Use of correspondence. The Committee shall conduct as much of its business as is practical through correspondence.

8.2 Personal response required. Although the complainee has the right to consult with an attorney concerning all phases of the ethics process, the complainee must respond to charges of unethical conduct personally and not through legal counsel or another third party. If the complainee shows good cause as to why he or she cannot respond personally, the Director may waive this requirement.

8.3 Transcription of audiotapes, videotapes, and similar data compilations required. It shall be the responsibility of the individual or entity submitting to the Committee an audiotape, videotape, or similar data compilation, to provide an accurate transcription of the information contained thereon. In the sole discretion of the Director, any audiotape, videotape, or similar data compilation provided unaccompanied by a transcription as required in this subsection may be rejected unless and until such transcription is provided.

8.4 Service. For purposes of notice, service shall be made by delivery to the complainee or the complainee's attorney or by mail or common carrier to the complainee or the complainee's attorney at the complainee's or attorney's last known address. Delivery within this rule means handing it to the complainee or the attorney or leaving it at the complainee's office or place of abode or the attorney's office with a receptionist, secretary, clerk, or other person in charge thereof, or, if there is no one in charge, leaving it in a conspicuous place therein. Service by mail is complete upon mailing. Where, after good faith efforts, the Committee has been unable to locate the complainee, it may give notice by causing to be published in a newspaper of general circulation in the complainee's last known place of domicile a notice to contact the Ethics Office concerning an important matter.

9. Failure to Cooperate With Ethics Process

Members are required to cooperate fully and in a timely fashion with the ethics process. Failure to cooperate shall not prevent continuation of any proceedings and itself constitutes a violation of the Ethics Code that may warrant being dropped from membership.

10. Board of Directors' Standing Hearing Panel

The President of the Association shall appoint members of the Standing Hearing Panel. Standing Hearing Panel members shall serve a three-year term. The Standing Hearing Panel shall consist of at least 30 members at least 5 of whom shall be public members, and the remainder shall be members of the Association in good standing, and shall not include any present members of the Ethics Committee.

11. Available Sanctions

On the basis of circumstances that aggravate or mitigate the culpability of the member, a sanction more or less severe, respectively, than would be warranted on the basis of the factors set forth below, may be appropriate.

11.1 Reprimand. Reprimand is the appropriate sanction if there has been an ethics violation but the violation was not of a kind likely to cause harm to another person or to cause substantial harm to the profession, and was not otherwise of sufficient gravity as to warrant a more severe sanction.

11.2 Censure. Censure is the appropriate sanction if there has been an ethics violation, and the violation was of a kind likely to cause harm to another person, but the violation was not of a kind likely to cause substantial harm to another person or to the profession, and was not otherwise of sufficient gravity as to warrant a more severe sanction.

11.3 Drop from membership or expulsion. Dropping from membership or expulsion from membership is the appropriate sanction if there has been an ethics violation, and the violation was of a kind likely to cause substantial harm to another person or the profession, or was otherwise of sufficient gravity as to warrant such action.

11.4 Stipulated resignation. Stipulated resignation may be offered by the Committee:

11.4.1 Pursuant to member/complainee's initial response to the show cause notice, contingent upon execution of an acceptable affidavit admitting responsibility for the violations charged, under Part IV, Subsection 10.1; or

11.4.2 Pursuant to a committee finding that the member/complainee has committed a violation of the ethics code, contingent on execution of an acceptable affidavit and approval by the Board of Directors, under Part IV, Subsection 10.2, or Part V, Subsection 7.5.

12. Available Directives

12.1 Cease and desist order. Such a directive requires the complainee to cease and desist specified unethical behavior(s).

12.2 Supervision requirement. Such a directive requires that the complainee engage in supervision.

12.3 Education, training, or tutorial requirement. Such a directive requires that the complainee engage in education, training, or a tutorial.

12.4 Evaluation and/or treatment requirement. Such a directive requires that the complainee be evaluated to determine the possible need for treatment and/or, if dysfunction has been established, obtain treatment appropriate to that dysfunction.

12.5 Probation. Such a directive requires monitoring of the complainee by the Committee to ensure compliance with Ethics Committee-mandated directives.

13. Matters Requiring the Concurrence of the Chair of the Committee and Director of the Ethics Office

Whenever matters entrusted by these Rules and Procedures to the Chair and Director require the concurrence of those officers before certain action may be taken, either officer in the event of disagreement may refer to the matter to the Vice Chair, who together with the Chair and Director make a final determination by majority vote.

PART III. MEMBERSHIP

1. Applications

1.1 Specific jurisdiction. The Committee has the power to investigate the preadmission scientific and professional ethics and conduct of all applicants for membership in the Association and to make recommendations whether an individual shall become a member or be readmitted to membership.

1.2 Initial application. The Committee shall review applications for membership upon referral by the Membership Committee where there are questions of unethical conduct or false or fraudulent information.

1.3 Procedures for review. The Director shall transmit to the Committee a copy of the membership application and any other materials pertinent to the case. The Ethics Office shall take such steps, including contacting the applicant or other sources of information, as necessary and appropriate to making a fair determination. Upon review, the Committee may recommend to the Board of Directors that membership be denied.

2. Application for Readmission

The Director shall receive from the Membership Committee all applications for readmission by persons who have been (a) expelled or dropped from membership or (b) permitted to resign under stipulated conditions.

2.1 Elapsed time for review. Applications for readmission by members who have been expelled or dropped from membership shall be considered by the Committee only after five years have elapsed from the date of that action. Applications for readmission by members who have been permitted to resign shall be considered only after the stipulated period or, where no period has been stipulated, three years have elapsed.

2.2 Procedures for review. The Director shall transmit to the Committee a summary of the application for readmission and the record of the previous case against the former member. In all cases, the ex-member must show that he or she is technically and ethically qualified, and has satisfied any conditions upon readmission established by the Board. The Committee shall make one of the following recommendations:

2.2.1 Readmission. Recommend to the Membership Committee that the former member be readmitted; or

2.2.2 Denied readmission. Recommend to the Membership Committee that readmission be denied; or

2.2.3 Deferred readmission. Recommend to the Membership Committee that the application for readmission be deferred for a stated period of time; or

2.2.4 Further investigation. Charge the Director to investigate issues specified by the Committee and to place the matter before the Committee at a future date.

3. Allegations That Membership Was Obtained Under False Pretenses

3.1 Specific jurisdiction. The Committee has the power to investigate allegations that membership was obtained on the basis of false or fraudulent information, and to take appropriate action with respect thereto.

3.2 Procedures for review. The Director shall transmit to the Committee a copy of the membership application and any other materials pertinent to the case. The Ethics Office shall take such steps, including contacting the member or other sources of information, conducting or authorizing a hearing for the purpose of ascertaining pertinent facts, etc., as necessary and appropriate to making a fair determination in the circumstances of the case.

3.3 Sanctions. Upon completion of this review, the Committee may recommend to the Board of Directors that it void the election to membership in the Association of any person who obtained membership on the basis of false or fraudulent information.

PART IV. SHOW CAUSE PROCEDURES BASED UPON ACTIONS BY OTHER RECOGNIZED TRIBUNALS

1. Predicates for Use of Show Cause Procedures

1.1 Felony or commensurate offense. The Committee may elect to utilize the process authorized by this part if (a) the Committee finds that a member has been convicted of a felony (as defined by state or provincial law or otherwise a criminal offense with possible term of incarceration exceeding one year) and such conviction is not under appeal, and (b) after review of the publicly available record leading to such conviction, the Committee determines that use of this process appears necessary for the protection of the public.

1.2 Expulsion, suspension, unlicensure, or decertification. The Committee may elect to utilize the process authorized by this part if (a) the Committee finds that a member has been expelled or suspended from an affiliated state or regional psychological association or decertified or unlicensed or had a certificate or license revoked or suspended by a state or local board, and such action is not under appeal, and (b) after review of the publicly available record leading to such action, the Committee determines that use of this process appears necessary for the protection of the public.

2. Notice by the Committee and Response by Member

The member shall be notified by the Committee that he or she has been barred from resigning membership in the Association (subject only to the terms of Section 10 of this part) and, on the basis of Part IV of these Rules and Procedures, will be afforded 60 days in which to show good cause as to why he or she should not be expelled from membership in the Association.

3. Showing by Member That Prior Proceeding Lacked Due Process

In addition to a response to the substance of the charges pursuant to Section 2 of this part, the member may seek within the 60-day period to show that the procedures followed by the other recognized tribunal did not follow fair procedure. If the Committee finds merit to this contention, it may exercise its discretion pursuant to Part II, Subsection 7.2 of these Rules and convert the matter to a *sua sponte* plenary case under Part V hereof or dismiss the complaint.

4. Investigation

The Committee may conduct a further investigation, including seeking additional information from the member or others or requesting that the member appear in person. Any evidence not obtained directly from the member and relied upon by the Committee in connection with adjudication shall first have been provided to the member, who shall have an opportunity to respond in person or shall have been afforded not less than 15 days to respond thereto in writing.

5. Review and Recommendation by the Committee

Upon receipt of the member's response and upon conclusion of any necessary further investigation, or the expiration of 60 days without response, the

Committee may vote to recommend one of the following courses of action to the Board of Directors:

5.1 Dismissal of charges. The Committee may recommend that the case be dismissed, with or without an educative letter.

5.2 Censure or reprimand, with or without directives. The Committee may recommend that the member be censured or reprimanded, with or without one or more directives.

5.3 Expulsion. The Committee may recommend that the member be expelled from the Association; In the alternative, the Committee may elect to recommend the sanction of stipulated resignation, pursuant to the procedure set forth in subsection 10.2 of this part.

6. Notification of Member

The Committee shall notify the member of its recommendation, and shall inform the member of his or her opportunity to file a written statement with the Board of Directors.

7. Member's Statements in Response to Recommendation

Within 15 days of receipt of notification of the Committee's recommendation, the member may file a written statement with the Board of Directors. The statement should be mailed care of the Ethics Office.

8. Committee Response

The Ethics Committee shall have 15 days from the time it receives the member's written statement to file a written response, if any. A copy will be provided to the member.

9. Review by the Board of Directors

Within 180 days after receiving the record, the Committee's recommendation, any written statement by the complainee and any written response by the Committee, the Board of Directors shall vote whether to expel the member from the Association or to issue a lesser sanction. The Board may select a sanction more or less severe than that recommended by the Committee.

10. Stipulated Resignation

10.1 Stipulated resignation with admission of violation pursuant to member's initial response to the show cause notice

10.1.1 Member officer of stipulated resignation with admission of violation. In his or her initial response to the Committee's notice to show cause under Section 2 of this part, the member may offer to resign membership in the Association with admission of violation. Such an offer must include a statement of intent to execute an affidavit, acceptable to the Committee, (a) admitting the violation underlying the criminal conviction, expulsion, unlicensure or decertification, and (b) resigning membership in the Association.

10.1.2 Committee response and proposed affidavit of stipulated resignation. Where the member makes such an offer, the Committee in due course will forward to the member a proposed affidavit of stipulated resignation.

10.1.3 Acceptance by member. Within 30 days of receipt, the member may resign membership in the Association by executing and having notarized the proposed affidavit and returning it to the Committee. Resignation shall be effective upon the Committee's timely receipt of the executed notarized affidavit.

10.1.4 Rejection by member. If the member fails to execute, have notarized, and return an acceptable affidavit within 30 days, or formally notifies the Committee of rejection of the proposed affidavit, the offer of stipulated resignation shall be deemed rejected. The member shall be afforded an additional 30 days within which to supplement his or her response to the Committee's show cause notice. The matter shall thereafter be resolved according to the applicable procedures set forth in this part. All materials submitted by the member shall be part of the file to be considered by the Committee and/or the Board of Directors, in connection with the case.

10.1.5 Stipulated resignation with admission of violation pursuant to this section is available only at the time and in the manner set forth in this section. Unless stipulated resignation with admission of violation is accomplished at the time and in the manner set forth in this section, members may not resign while under scrutiny of the Ethics Committee except as set forth in Subsection 10.2 of this part.

10.2 Stipulated resignation pursuant to review and recommendation by the committee. In lieu of the recommendations set forth in Section 5 of this part, with the agreement of the member, the Committee in its sole discretion may recommend that the member be permitted to resign from the Association under stipulations set forth by the Committee, pursuant to the following procedure:

10.2.1 Offer of stipulated resignation by committee. When the Committee finds that the member has committed a violation of the Ethics Code, the Committee, in its sole discretion, may offer to enter into an agreement with the member, contingent upon approval by the Board of Directors, that the member shall resign from the Association pursuant to mutually agreed upon stipulations. Such stipulations shall include the extent to which the stipulated resignation and underlying ethics violations shall be disclosed and a minimum period of time, after resignation, during which the resigned member shall be ineligible to reapply for membership. The Committee may, in its discretion, also vote to impose, and inform the member of, an alternative recommended sanction, chosen from among Subsections 11.1–11.3 of Part II of these Rules, it would recommend in the event the member does not accept the offer of stipulated resignation.

10.2.2 Notification of member. In such cases, the member shall be notified, in writing, of the Committee's recommended resolution of stipulated resignation and that he or she may accept the Committee's recommended resolution within 30 days of receipt. The member shall also be notified of any alternative recommended sanction.

10.2.3 Acceptance by member. Within 30 days, the member may accept the recommended resolution of stipulated resignation by executing a notarized affidavit of resignation acceptable to both the member and the Committee and forwarding the executed notarized affidavit to the Committee. Such resignation shall become effective only with the approval of the Board, as set forth in this section.

10.2.4 Transmittal to board of directors. If the member accepts the recommended resolution of stipulated resignation, the Committee shall submit a copy of the affidavit of resignation, together with the record in the matter and the rationale for recommending stipulated resignation on the terms set forth in the affidavit, to the Board of Directors.

10.2.5 Action by board of directors. Within 180 days, the Board of Directors shall accept the member's resignation on the terms stated in the affidavit of resignation, unless it is persuaded that to do so would not be in the best interest of the Association and/or of the public. If the resignation is accepted by the Board, the Ethics Office shall notify the member of the resolution of the case.

10.2.6 Rejection of stipulated resignation by member. If the member fails within 30 days to accept the recommended resolution, or formally notifies the Committee of rejection of the offer of stipulated resignation within the 30 day period, the offer of stipulated resignation shall be deemed rejected. The Committee shall reconsider the matter pursuant to these Rules and Procedures or, in the event an alternative recommended sanction has previously been identified by the Committee, such alternative recommended sanction shall automatically become the recommended sanction pursuant to Section 5 of this part. The Committee shall notify the member of the recommendation and of his or her opportunity to file a written statement with the Board of Directors, as set forth in Section 6 of this part. Sections 7–9 of this part shall also apply.

10.2.7 Rejection of stipulated resignation by board. If the Board rejects the affidavit of resignation pursuant to Subsection 10.2.5 of this part, the Committee shall notify the member and reconsider the matter pursuant to these Rules and Procedures.

PART V. PLENARY PROCEDURES FOR COMPLAINTS AGAINST MEMBERS

1. Initiation of Plenary Procedures

Plenary ethics proceedings against a member are initiated by the filing of a complaint or, in the case of a *sua sponte* action, by the issuance of a charge letter pursuant to Subsection 6.1.1 of this part.

2. Complaints

2.1 Complaints submitted by members or nonmembers. Complaints may be submitted by members or nonmembers of the Association. Upon receipt of an inquiry concerning filing a complaint, the Committee shall provide a copy of the Association's Ethics Code, the ethics complaint form, and these Rules and Procedures.

2.2 *Sua sponte* action. When a member appears to have violated the Association's Ethics Code, the Committee may proceed on its own initiative.

2.3 *Sua sponte* action based upon member's filing of capricious or malicious complaint. To prevent abuse of the ethics process, the Committee is empowered to bring charges itself against a complainant if the initial complaint is judged by two thirds of Committee members present to be (a) frivolous and (b) intended to harm the complainee rather than to protect the public. The filing of such a complaint constitutes a violation of the Ethics Code. Such charges shall be investigated and adjudicated under the terms of this part.

2.4 Countercomplaints. The Committee will not consider a complaint from a complainee member against a complainant member during the course of its investigation and resolution of the initial complaint. Rather, the Committee shall study all sides of the matter leading to the first complaint, and consider countercharges only after the initial complaint is finally resolved.

2.5 Anonymous complaints. The Committee shall not act upon anonymous complaints. If material in the public domain is provided anonymously, the Committee may choose to employ such material in support of a *sua sponte* complaint.

2.6 Complaints against nonmembers. If the complaint does not involve a member, the Ethics Office shall inform the complainant and may suggest that the complainant contact another agency or association that may have jurisdiction.

2.7 Consecutive complaints. When a complaint is lodged against a member with respect to whom a case involving similar alleged behavior was previously closed, materials in the prior case may be considered in determining whether to open a case.

2.8 Simultaneous complaints. When more than one complaint is simultaneously pending against the same member, the Committee may choose to combine the cases or to keep them separate. In the event the cases are combined, the Committee shall take reasonable steps to ensure that the legitimate confidentiality interests of any complainant, witness, or complainee are not compromised by combination.

3. Procedures for Filing Complaints

A complaint by a member or nonmember shall comprise:

3.1. A completed APA Ethics Complaint Form;

3.2. Such releases as are required by the Committee;

3.3. A waiver by the complainant of any right to subpoena from the Committee or its agents for the purposes of private civil litigation any documents or information concerning the case;[9] and

3.4. A request that the applicable time limit be waived, if necessary.

4. Preliminary Evaluation of Complaints by Ethics Office

The Ethics Office shall review each complaint to determine if jurisdictional criteria are met and if it can be determined whether cause for action exists.

4.1 Lack of jurisdiction. If jurisdictional criteria are not satisfied, the matter shall be closed and the complainant so notified.

4.2 Information insufficient to determine jurisdiction

4.2.1 Request for supplementation of complaint. If there is not information sufficient to determine whether jurisdictional criteria are met, or if it appears that the complaint is outside the applicable time limit, the Ethics Office shall so inform the complainant, who will be given 30 days from receipt of the request to supplement the complaint and/or ask for a waiver of the applicable time limit.

4.2.2 Consequences of failure to supplement complaint. If no response is received from the complainant within 30 days from receipt of the request, the matter may be closed. If at a later date the complainant shows good cause for delay and demonstrates that jurisdictional criteria can be met, the supplemented complaint shall be considered.

4.3 Process with respect to superseding applicable time limit

4.3.1 Consideration by chair and director. If a complaint otherwise within the jurisdiction of the Ethics Committee appears to have been filed outside the applicable time limit, and the complainant asks the Committee to supersede the time limit, that request will be considered initially by the Chair and the Director pursuant to the criteria set forth in Part II, Subsection 5.3.5. If they do not agree that those criteria appear to be satisfied, the case will be closed pursuant to Subsection 4.1 of this part.

4.3.2 Response by complainee where standards appear to be met. If the Chair and Director agree that the standards of Part II, Subsection 5.3.5 may be satisfied, the Director shall notify the complainee, provide the complainee with a copy of the complaint, the complainant's submission with respect to the time limit, and any other materials the Director deems appropriate. The complainee shall have 30 days from receipt of these materials to address whether the criteria of Part II, Subsection 5.3.5 are met, or reasons, apart from the criteria, why the applicable limit should not be superseded.

---

[9] This waiver is required to help assure participants in the APA ethics process, including complainants, that the process will not be inappropriately used to gain an advantage in other fora.

4.3.3 Determination by committee. In any case not closed pursuant to Subsection 4.3.1 above, the Committee shall consider the request that the time limit be superseded under the standards of Part II, Subsection 5.3.5, based upon any materials provided by the complainant and complainee, and any other information available to or obtained by the Committee. If the Committee votes to supersede the time limit, the matter shall then be considered pursuant to Section 5 of this part. If the Committee does not vote to supersede the time limit, the matter shall be closed pursuant to Subsection 4.1 of this part.

4.4 Information insufficient to determine cause for action

4.4.1 Request for supplementation of complaint. If there is not information sufficient to determine whether cause for action exists, the Ethics Office shall so inform the complainant, who will be given 30 days from receipt of the request to supplement the complaint.

4.4.2 Consequences of failure to supplement complaint. If no response is received from the complainant within 30 days, the matter may be closed. If at a later date the complainant shows good cause for delay and responds to the request for supplementation, the supplemented complaint shall be considered.

5. Evaluation of Complaints by Chair and Director

All complaints not closed by the Ethics Office pursuant to Section 4 of this part shall be reviewed by the Chair and the Director to determine whether cause for action by the Ethics Committee has been shown to exist.

5.1 Cause for action defined. Cause for action shall exist when the complainee's alleged actions and/or omissions, if proved, would in the judgment of the decision maker constitute a breach of ethics. For purposes of determining whether cause for action exists, incredible, speculative, and/or internally inconsistent allegations may be disregarded.

5.2 Preliminary investigation due to insufficient information. If, after supplementation of the complaint by the complainant pursuant to Subsection

4.4.1 of this part, the Chair and the Director determine that they still lack evidence sufficient to determine whether a case should be opened, a preliminary investigation may be initiated.

5.2.1 Notification to complainee. If a preliminary investigation is opened, the Director shall so inform the complainee in writing. The Director will include a copy of the completed Ethics Complaint Form and all materials submitted by the complainant or on the complainant's behalf; a copy of the APA Ethics Code; the Committee's Rules and Procedures; and a statement that information submitted by the complainee shall become a part of the record, and could be used if further proceedings ensue.

5.2.2 Time for complainee response. The complainee shall have 30 days after receipt of the complaint to file an initial response to the complaint. When requested in writing, within the 30 days to respond and when good cause is shown, the Director may extend the time for responding to the complaint.

5.2.3 Response from complainee. The complainee is required to respond as completely as possible, in writing, personally, and within specified time limits. The complainee is free to consult legal counsel, but correspondence must be from the complainee and not from legal counsel or another third party acting for the complainee. If the complainee shows good cause as to why he or she can not respond personally, the Director may waive this requirement.

5.2.4 Information from other sources. The Director, Chair, or the Committee may request additional information from the complainant and/or any other appropriate source. The Committee will not rely upon information submitted by such sources unless it has been shared with the complainee, and the complainee has been afforded an opportunity to respond thereto.

5.2.5 Action if there continues to be insufficient information. At the conclusion of the preliminary investigation, if the Director and Chair determine that they still lack evidence sufficient to determine whether cause for action exists, the matter shall be closed and the complainant notified.

5.3 Finding of cause for action by committee. If the Director and the Chair agree that cause for action exists, they shall open a formal case, unless they also agree that the allegations even if substantiated are trivial or likely to be corrected.

5.4 Finding of no cause for action by committee. If the Director and Chair do not agree that there is cause for action by the Committee, the matter shall be closed. The matter shall also be closed if the Director and Chair agree that, although cause for action otherwise exists, the allegations even if substantiated would constitute a trivial violation or one likely to be corrected. In the event of closure, the Director shall so inform the complainant in writing. A case closed pursuant to this subsection may be reopened only if the complainant presents significant new evidence, as defined in Part II, Section 6.

5.5 Supplementary or alternative action by committee. The Director and Chair may recommend that the complainant refer the complaint to a relevant state psychological association, state board, appropriate regulatory agency, any subsidiary body of the Association, or other appropriate entity, or they may make such referral on their own initiative. Such referral does not constitute a waiver of jurisdiction over the complaint provided that the Committee opens a formal case within 24 months from the date of referral.

6. Formal Case Investigation
6.1 Issuance of charge letter and response from complainee

6.1.1 Charge letter. If a formal case is opened, the Director shall so inform the complainee in a charge letter. The charge letter shall contain a concise description of the alleged behaviors at issue and identify the specific section(s) of the Ethics Code that the complainee is alleged to have violated. The Director shall enclose a copy of any completed Ethics Complaint Form and any materials submitted to date by the complainant or on the complainant's behalf that will be included in the record before the Committee; a copy of the APA Ethics Code and the Committee's Rules and Procedures; and a statement that information submitted by the complainee shall become a part of the record, and could be used if further proceedings ensue.

6.1.2 Significance of charge letter. A charge letter does not constitute or represent a finding that any

unethical behavior has taken place, or that any allegations of the complaint are or are not likely to be found to be true.

6.1.3 Issuance of charge letter to conform to evidence discovered during investigation. At any time prior to final resolution by the Committee, in order to conform the charges to the evidence developed during the investigation, the Director and Chair may issue a new charge letter setting forth Ethical Standard(s) and/or describing alleged behaviors different from or in addition to those contained in the initial charge letter. In a *sua sponte* case, the date of issuance shall, for purposes of applicable time limits, be deemed to relate back to the date of the initial charge letter. The new charge letter shall in all other respects be treated exactly as an initial charge letter issue pursuant to Subsection 6.1.1 of this part.

6.1.4 Time for complainee response. The complainee shall have 30 days after receipt of the charge letter to file an initial response. Any request to extend the time for responding to the charge letter must be made in writing, within the 30 days to respond, and must show good cause for an extension. Based upon such request, the Director may extend the time for responding to the charge letter.

6.1.5 Response from complainee. The complainee is required to respond as completely as possible, in writing, personally, and within specified time limits. The complainee is free to consult legal counsel, but the response must be from the complainee and not through legal counsel or another third party acting for the complainee. If the complainee shows good cause as to why he or she cannot respond personally, the Director may waive this requirement.

6.1.6 Personal appearance. The Director and Chair may request the complainee to appear personally before the Committee. The complainee has no right to such an appearance.

6.2 Information from other sources. The Director, Chair, or the Committee may request additional information from the complainant, complainee, or any other appropriate source.

6.3 Referral to committee. When in the sole judgment of the Chair and Director the investigation is complete, the case will be referred to the Committee for review and resolution. The Ethics Office shall notify the complainant and complainee that the matter has been referred to the Committee.

6.4 Documentation subsequent to investigation and prior to resolution by the committee. Within 30 days after receipt of notification that the case is being referred to the Ethics Committee for review and resolution, the complainant and complainee may submit any additional information or documentation. Any materials timely submitted by the complainant or on the complainant's behalf will be forwarded to the complainee. Within 15 days from receipt of those materials, the complainee may submit any additional information or documentation. All such materials submitted within these time limitations shall be included in the file to be reviewed by the Ethics Committee. Materials submitted out of time will not be included in the file materials relative to the ethics case and will not be reviewed by the Ethics Committee. In the sole discretion of the Director, where good cause for noncompliance with these time limits is shown by the complainant or the complainee, the resolution of the case may be postponed until the next scheduled meeting of the Ethics Committee and the information or documentation provided out of time may be included in the file materials to be reviewed by the Committee at that later time. In the sole discretion of the Director, in the event the complainee fails to comply with these time limits, the information or documentation provided out of time may be included in the file materials to be reviewed by the Committee and the matter maintained for resolution by the Committee as originally scheduled.

7. Review and Resolution by the Committee

Upon conclusion of the investigation, the Committee shall take one of the actions listed below. The Complainee shall then be notified of the Committee's action, the Ethical Standard(s) involved if any, the rationale for the Committee's decision, any sanction, and any directives.

7.1 Remand. The Committee may remand the matter to the Ethics Office for continued investigation or issuance of a new charge letter pursuant to Subsection 6.1.3 of this part.

7.2 Dismiss the charges

7.2.1 No violation. The Committee may dismiss the complaint if it finds the complainee has not violated the Ethical Standard(s) as charged.

7.2.2 Trivial or corrected violation. The Committee may dismiss the complaint if it concludes that any violation it might find would be trivial or has been or is likely to be corrected.

7.2.3 Insufficient evidence. The Committee may dismiss the complaint if it finds insufficient evidence to support a finding of an ethics violation.

7.2.4 Educative letter. Where the Committee deems it appropriate, it may dismiss the complaint and issue an educative letter, to be shared only with the complainee, concerning the behaviors charged.

7.3 Recommend a sanction less than formal charges. If the Committee finds that the complainee has violated the Ethics Code, but decides that the nature of the complainee's behavior is such that the matter would be most appropriately resolved without bringing formal charges, the Committee will recommend censure or reprimand of the complainee, with or without one or more available directives. See Part II, Subsections 11.1, 11.2, and Section 12.

7.4 Issue formal charges. The Committee may issue formal charges if it concludes that there has been an ethics violation, that it was of a kind likely to cause substantial harm to another person or the profession, or that it was otherwise of such gravity as to warrant this action.[10] Formal charges consist of a statement submitted by the Committee to the Board of Directors recommending that the Board of Directors drop the complainee from membership in the Association.

7.5 Stipulated resignation. In lieu of the other resolutions set forth in this section, with the agreement

---

[10] Noncooperation with the APA ethics process is a violation of sufficient gravity, posting danger of substantial harm to the profession, to warrant formal charges.

of the member, the Committee, in its sole discretion, may recommend to the Board that the member be permitted to resign under stipulations set forth by the Committee, pursuant to the following procedure:

7.5.1 Offer of stipulated resignation by the committee. When the Committee finds that the complainee has committed a violation of the Ethics Code, the Committee, in its sole discretion, may offer to enter into an agreement with the complainee, contingent upon approval by the Board of Directors, that the complainee shall resign from the Association pursuant to mutually agreed upon stipulations. Such stipulations shall include the extent to which the stipulated resignation and underlying ethics violation shall be disclosed, and a minimum period of time, after resignation, during which the complainee shall be ineligible to reapply for membership. The Committee may, in its discretion, also vote to impose, and inform the member of, an alternative recommended sanction, chosen from among Subsections 11.1–11.3 of Part II of these Rules, that it would recommend in the event the member does not accept the offer of stipulated resignation.

7.5.2 Notification of complainee. In such cases, the complainee shall be notified, in writing, of the Committee's recommended resolution of stipulated resignation and that he or she may accept the Committee's recommended resolution within 30 days of receipt. The complainee shall also be notified of any alternative recommended sanction.

7.5.3 Acceptance by complainee. Within 30 days, the complainee may accept the recommended resolution of stipulated resignation by executing a notarized affidavit of resignation acceptable both to the complainee and the Committee and forwarding the executed notarized affidavit to the Committee. Such resignation shall become effective only with the approval of the Board, as set forth in Subsection 7.5 of this part.

7.5.4 Transmittal to board of directors. If the complainee accepts the recommended resolution of stipulated resignation, the Committee shall in due course submit a copy of the affidavit of resignation, together with the record in the matter and the rationale for recommending stipulated resignation on the terms set forth in the affidavit, to the Board of Directors.

7.5.5 Action by board of directors. Within 180 days, the Board of Directors shall accept the complainee's resignation on the terms stated in the affidavit of resignation, unless it is persuaded that to do so would not be in the best interest of the Association and/or of the public. If the resignation is accepted by the Board, the Ethics Office shall notify the complainant and complainee of the resolution of the case. A copy of the affidavit of resignation shall be provided to the complainant.

7.5.6 Rejection of stipulated resignation by complainee. If the complainee fails to accept the determination within 30 days, or formally notifies the Committee of rejection of the offer of stipulated resignation within the 30-day period, the offer of stipulated resignation shall be deemed rejected. The Committee shall reconsider the matter pursuant to these Rules and Procedures or, in the event an alternative recommended sanction has previously been identified by the Committee, such alternative recommended resolution shall automatically become the recommended sanction pursuant to Subsection 7.3 or 7.4 of this part.

7.5.7 Rejection of stipulated resignation by board. If the Board rejects the affidavit of resignation pursuant to Subsection 7.5.5 of this part, the Committee shall notify the complainee and reconsider the matter pursuant to these Rules and Procedures.

8. Procedures Subsequent to Committee Action: Dismissal

The complainant may seek reconsideration when the Committee dismisses a case pursuant to Subsection 7.2 of this part only if the complainant furnishes the Committee significant new evidence, consistent with Part II, Section 6. If, in the judgment of the Director, such information is furnished, at its next meeting the Committee will consider whether to reopen the case. If the complainant seeks reconsideration on these grounds within 30 days of notification of dismissal, a reopened complaint shall be deemed to have been filed on the date the original complaint was received. If the complainant seeks reconsideration on these grounds more than 30 days after notification of dismissal, a reopened complaint shall be deemed to have been filed on the date the request for reconsideration was received.

9. Procedures Subsequent to Committee Recommendation: Sanction Less Than Formal Charges

If the Committee proceeds pursuant to Subsection 7.3 of this part, the following procedures shall govern:

9.1 Acceptance of sanction less than formal charges. If the complainee accepts the Committee's recommended sanction and directives, if any, the right of independent adjudication shall be waived, any stipulations will be implemented by the Director, and the case will remain open until the directives are met. The complainee's failure to respond within 30 days of notification shall be deemed acceptance of the Committee's recommended sanction and directives.

9.2 Independent adjudication pursuant to recommended sanction less than formal charges. The adjudicatory mechanism for a recommended sanction less than formal charges is an independent adjudication before a three-person Independent Adjudication Panel.

9.2.1 Request for independent adjudication and rationale for nonacceptance. The complainee may exercise his or her right to independent adjudication by furnishing the Committee within 30 days after notification of the Committee's recommendation a written request for independent adjudication and rationale for nonacceptance of the recommendation.

9.2.2 Personal and prompt response. During the independent adjudication process, the complainee is required to respond personally and not through an agent or representative, as completely as possible, in writing, and within specified time limits. The complainee is free to consult legal counsel. If the complainee shows good cause as to why he or she cannot respond personally, the Director may permit him or her to respond through counsel.

9.2.3 Response by committee. Within 30 days of receipt of the complainee's rationale for nonacceptance, the Committee may prepare a response and provide a copy to the complainee. No response by the Committee is required.

9.2.4 Selection of independent adjudication panel

9.2.4.1 Provision of standing hearing panel list. Within 60 days after the request for an independent adjudication, the Director shall provide the complainee with the names and curricula vitae of six members of the Board of Directors' Standing Hearing Panel, of whom at least one shall be a public member. The Director shall make inquiry and ensure that proposed panel members do not have a conflict of interest as defined by applicable law and appear otherwise able to apply fairly the APA Ethics Code based solely on the record in the particular case.

9.2.4.2 Designation of panel members. Within 15 days after receipt of the six-member list, the complainee shall select three of the six to constitute the Independent Adjudication Panel. The Panel shall include not fewer than two members of the Association. Whenever feasible, the complainee's selection will be honored. If at any time prior to conclusion of the appeal an individual selected by the complainee cannot serve on the Independent Adjudication Panel for any reason, the complainee shall be notified promptly and afforded the opportunity within 10 days of receipt of notification to replace that individual from among a list of not fewer than four members of the Board of Directors' Standing Hearing Panel. In the event the complainee fails to notify the Director of his or her initial or replacement selections in a timely fashion, the right to do so is waived and the President of the Association or designee (hereinafter President) shall select the member(s), whose name(s) shall then be made known to the complainee.

9.2.4.3 Designation of chair of independent adjudication panel. The President shall designate one of the three Panel members to serve as Chair. The Chair of the Panel shall ensure that the Panel fulfills its obligations pursuant to these Rules and Procedures.

9.2.5 Provision of case file to independent adjudication panel. Within 15 days of selection of the Independent Adjudication Panel, receipt of the Committee's response pursuant to Subsection 9.2.3 of this part, or, if no Committee response is received, the expiration of the time period for such response, whichever occurs latest, the Director will provide the case file to the members of the Independent Adjudication Panel.

9.2.6 Consideration and vote by independent adjudication panel. Within 60 days of the receipt of the case file and the rationale for nonacceptance, the members of the Panel shall confer with each other and, solely on the basis of the documentation provided and deliberations among themselves, shall vote to:

9.2.6.1 Adopt the committee's recommended sanction and directives; or

9.2.6.2 Adopt a lesser sanction and/or less burdensome directives; or

9.2.6.3 Dismiss the case.

9.2.7 Decision of the independent adjudication panel. Decisions of the Independent Adjudication Panel will be made by majority vote, and at least two reviewers must agree to written findings, a sanction, if any, and a directive or directives, if any. The Committee bears the burden to prove the charges by a preponderance of the evidence. The panelists' votes and the majority's written decision must be submitted to the Ethics Office within the 60-day period set forth in Subsection 9.2.6 of this part. If no two panelists can agree as to the appropriate outcome or a written decision, the case will be referred to the Committee for further action. The decision of the Independent Adjudication Panel is unappealable and binding on the Committee and the complainee. A decision either to impose a sanction and/or directive(s) or to dismiss the case will be implemented by the Committee as the final adjudication.

9.2.8 Notification. The Committee shall inform the complainee and complainant of the final adjudication. The complainee shall be provided a copy of the majority's written decision.

10. Procedures Subsequent to Committee Recommendations: Formal Charges

If the Committee proceeds pursuant to Subsection 7.4 of this part, the following procedures shall govern:

10.1 Acceptance of formal charges. If the complainee accepts the Committee's recommendation to the Board of Directors that he or she be dropped from membership (formal charge), the right to a formal hearing shall be waived, and the Committee shall proceed with its recommendation to the Board of Directors pursuant to Subsection 10.3.4 and other

subsections of this part. In such event, the recommendation of the Ethics Committee shall be treated as the equivalent of the recommendation of a Formal Hearing Committee that the complainee be dropped from membership. The complainee's failure to respond within 30 days after notification shall be deemed acceptance of the Committee's recommendation.

10.2 Adjudication procedures: formal charges. The adjudicatory mechanism for formal charges issued pursuant to Subsection 7.4 of this part is a formal hearing before a three-member Hearing Committee.

10.2.1 Request for formal hearing. The complainee may exercise her or his right to a formal hearing by furnishing the Committee within 30 days of notification of the Committee's action a written request.

10.2.2 Personal and prompt response. During the adjudicatory process and prior to the formal hearing, the complainee is required to respond personally and not through an agent or representative, as completely as possible, in writing, and within specified time limits. The complainee is free to consult legal counsel. If the complainee shows good cause as to why he or she cannot respond personally, the Director may permit him or her to respond through counsel.

10.2.3 Selection of the formal hearing date and hearing committee

10.2.3.1 Establishment of hearing date and provision of standing hearing panel list. Within 60 days after the complainee requests a formal hearing, the President shall establish the date of the hearing and provide the complainee with the date and the names and curricula vitae of six members of the Board of Directors' Standing Hearing Panel. The six identified members of the Board of Directors' Standing Hearing Panel shall include at least one public member. The Director shall make inquiry and ensure that proposed panel members do not have a conflict of interest as defined by applicable law and appear otherwise able to apply fairly the Ethics Code based solely on the record in the particular case.

10.2.3.2 Designation of hearing committee members. The formal hearing shall be heard by a Hearing Committee of three individuals, selected from among the six individuals from the Board of Directors' Standing Hearing Panel identified pursuant to Subsection 10.2.3.1 of this part. The Hearing Committee shall include not fewer than two members of the Association. Within 15 days after the receipt of the names and curricula vitae pursuant to Subsection 10.2.3.1 of this part, the complainee shall notify the Director of his or her selections for the Hearing Committee. Whenever feasible, the complainee's selections will be honored. In the event an individual timely selected by the complainee cannot serve on the Hearing Committee for any reason, the complainee shall be notified and afforded the opportunity within 10 days of receipt of notification to replace that individual from among a list of not fewer than four members of the Board of Directors' Standing Hearing Panel. In the event the complainee fails to notify the Director of his or her initial or replacement selections in a timely fashion, the right to do so is waived and the President shall select the Hearing Committee members, whose names shall then be made known to the complainee.

10.2.3.3 Voir dire of designated hearing committee members. Within 15 days after receipt of the names of the three designated Hearing Committee members, the complainee may submit in writing, to the Director, a request to question designated Hearing Committee members with respect to potential conflict of interest. Upon receipt of such written request, the Director shall convene by telephone conference call, or otherwise, a formal opportunity for such questioning by the complainee or the complainee's attorney. Legal Counsel for the Association shall preside at such voir dire, shall be the sole judge of the propriety and pertinency of questions posed, and shall be the sole judge with respect to the fitness of designated Hearing Committee members to serve. Failure by the complainee to timely submit a request shall constitute a waiver of the privilege to conduct voir dire.

10.2.3.4 Designation of chair of hearing committee. The President shall designate one of the three Hearing Committee members to serve as Chair. The Chair of the Hearing Committee and Legal Counsel for the Association shall assure proper observance of these Rules and Procedures at the formal hearing.

10.2.4 Documents and witnesses

10.2.4.1 Committee. At least 30 days prior to the scheduled date of the formal hearing, the Ethics Committee shall provide the complainee and the Hearing Committee with copies of all documents and other evidence, and the names of all witnesses that may be offered by the Committee in its case in chief.

10.2.4.2 Complainee. At least 15 days prior to the scheduled date of the formal hearing, the complainee shall provide the Ethics Committee and the Hearing Committee with copies of all documents and other evidence, and the names of all witnesses that may be offered by the complainee.

10.2.4.3 Rebuttal documents and witnesses. At least five days prior to the scheduled date of the formal hearing, the Committee shall provide the complainee and the Hearing Committee with copies of all documents and other evidence, and the names of all witnesses that may be offered in rebuttal.

10.2.4.4 Audiotapes, videotapes, and similar data compilations. Audiotapes, videotapes, and similar data compilations are admissible at the formal hearing, provided usable copies of such items, together with a transcription thereof, are provided in a timely fashion pursuant to the provisions of this section.

10.2.4.5 Failure to provide documents, other evidence, and names of witnesses in a timely fashion in advance of the formal hearing. Failure to provide copies of a document or other evidence or the name of a witness in a timely fashion and consistent with this section and these Rules and Procedures is grounds for excluding such document, other evidence, or witness from evidence at the formal hearing, unless good cause for the omission and a lack of prejudice to the other side can be shown.

10.2.5 Conduct of the formal hearing

10.2.5.1 Presiding officers

10.2.5.1.1. The chair of the hearing committee, assisted by legal counsel for the association, shall preside at the hearing.

10.2.5.1.2. Legal counsel for the association shall be present to advise on matters of procedure and admission of evidence, and shall represent neither the Committee nor the complainee at the formal hearing.

10.2.5.2 Legal representation of the complainee and committee.

10.2.5.2.1 Complainee. The complainee may choose, at complainee's own expense, to be represented by a licensed attorney.

10.2.5.2.2 Committee. The Chair of the Ethics Committee presents the Committee's case. However, the Committee may choose to have legal counsel present its case.

10.2.5.3 Rules of evidence. Formal rules of evidence shall not apply. All evidence that is relevant and reliable, as determined for the Hearing Committee by Legal Counsel for the Association, shall be admissible.

10.2.5.4 Rights of the complainee and the committee. Consistent with these Rules and Procedures, the complainee and the Committee shall have the right to present witnesses, documents, and other evidence, to cross-examine witnesses, and to object to the introduction of evidence.

10.2.5.5 Burden of proof. The Ethics Committee shall bear the burden to prove the charges by a preponderance of the evidence.

10.2.6 Decision of the hearing committee. The decision shall be by a simple majority vote. Within 30 days of the conclusion of the hearing, the Hearing Committee shall submit in writing to the Board of Directors, through the Ethics Committee, its decision and the rationale for that decision. The Hearing Committee may decide to:

10.2.6.1. adopt the Committee's recommendation to the Board of Directors.

10.2.6.2. recommend to the Board of Directors a lesser sanction, with or without directives; or

10.2.6.3. determine that the charges must be dismissed.

10.2.7 Notice to the complainee and the ethics committee. Within 15 days of receipt of the Hearing Committee's decision, a copy of the decision shall be provided to the complainee and the Ethics Committee. If the Hearing Committee determines that the charges must be dismissed, the Ethics Committee will implement this as the final adjudication.

10.3 Proceedings before the board of directors

10.3.1 Referral to board of directors. If the Hearing Committee recommends that the complainee be dropped from membership or otherwise disciplined, the matter will be referred to the Board of Directors. In due course, the Ethics Office shall provide the appeals materials to the Board, including a copy of the Hearing Committee's decision, the complainee's timely response, if any, pursuant to Subsection 10.3.2 of this part, the Ethics Committee's timely response, if any, pursuant to Subsection 10.3.3 of this part, and the record.

10.3.2 Complainee response. Within 30 days from receipt of the Hearing Committee's decision, the complainee shall file a written response, if any, with the Board of Directors, through the Ethics Committee. A copy of the complainee's written response shall be retained by the Chair of the Ethics Committee.

10.3.3 Ethics committee response. If the complainee files a written response, within 15 days from its receipt, the Ethics Committee shall prepare a written statement, if any, and provide a copy to the complainee.

10.3.4 Action by the board of directors. Within 60 days of receipt of the recommendation of the Hearing Committee (or of the Ethics Committee if no hearing was held), together with any timely responses thereto and the record, the Board of Directors will consider these materials, and will take action as follows:

10.3.4.1 Adopt. The Board of Directors shall adopt the recommendation, unless by majority vote it finds grounds for nonacceptance, as set forth in Subsection 10.3.4.2.

10.3.4.2 Grounds for nonacceptance. Only the following shall constitute grounds for nonacceptance of the recommendation by the Board:

10.3.4.2.1 Incorrect application of ethical standard(s). The Ethics Code of the Association was incorrectly applied; or

10.3.4.2.2 Erroneous findings of fact. The findings of fact were clearly erroneous; or

10.3.4.2.3 Procedural errors. The procedures used were in serious and substantial violation of the Bylaws of the Association and/or these Rules and Procedures; or

10.3.4.2.4 Excessive sanction or stipulations. The disciplinary sanction or directives recommended are grossly excessive in light of all the circumstances.

10.3.4.3 Consequences of nonacceptance. If the Board of Directors finds grounds for nonacceptance, it shall refer the case back to the Ethics Committee. In its discretion, the Ethics Committee may return the matter for rehearing before a newly constituted Hearing Committee or may continue investigation and/or readjudicate the matter at the Committee level.

10.4 Notification. If the Board of Directors does not adopt the recommendation, it shall notify the Ethics Committee in writing why the decision was not accepted, citing the applicable ground(s) for nonacceptance under Subsection 10.3.4.2 of this part.

10.5 Rehearing. If a rehearing is instituted the procedures of this part shall apply. Unless any of the following is offered by the complainee, none shall be part of the record before the second Hearing Committee: the original Hearing Committee's report; the complainee or Ethics Committee's written statements made pursuant to Subsections 10.3.2 and 10.3.3 of this part; and the Board of Directors' rationale for nonacceptance of the original Hearing Committee's recommendation. If the complainee offers any portion of any of the foregoing documents as evidence in the rehearing, the Committee may introduce any portion or all of any or all of them.

◆ ◆ ◆

Commentary: What do you think are the most frequent kinds of cases that the ethics committee is adjudicating currently, in comparison with cases seen a decade ago? For answers and other interesting data, see these articles, in chronological order:

Hall, J. E., & Hare-Mustin, R. T. (1983). Sanctions and the diversity of ethical complaints against psychologists. American Psychologist, 38, 714–729.

APA Ethics Committee. (1986). Report of the Ethics Committee: 1985. American Psychologist, 41, 694–697.

APA Ethics Committee. (1987). Report of the Ethics Committee: 1986. American Psychologist, 42, 730–734.

Ethics Committee of the American Psychological Association. (1988). Trends in ethics cases, common pitfalls, and published resources. American Psychologist, 43, 564–572.

APA Ethics Committee. (1990). Report of the Ethics Committee: 1988. American Psychologist, 45, 873–874.

APA Ethics Committee. (1991). Report of the Ethics Committee, 1989 and 1990. American Psychologist, 46, 750–757.

APA Ethics Committee. (1993). Report of the Ethics Committee, 1991 and 1992. American Psychologist, 48, 811–820.

APA Ethics Committee. (1994). Report of the Ethics Committee, 1993. American Psychologist, 49, 659–666.

The 1994 report indicated that from 1985 to 1993, APA expelled 61 members (terminated membership secondary to action by another tribunal) and dropped 51 others (terminated membership as a result of initial action by the ethics committee). What do these data imply about the vigor with which the Ethical Principles have been enforced by APA? Keep in mind that from 1956 to 1980 APA dropped from membership only 8 psychologists for ethical violations.

I conclude this chapter as it began: with an excerpt from Pope and Vetter's 1992 article. This material provides an introduction to the wide variety of ethical issues that psychologists face as teachers, scholars, and professionals. Many of these issues are addressed later in this book in greater detail.

Ethical Dilemmas Encountered by Members of the American Psychological Association: A National Survey

Kenneth S. Pope and Valerie A. Vetter

. . .

METHOD

A cover letter and survey form were developed to invite APA members to provide examples of the ethical dilemmas they faced in their work. . . .

A table of random numbers was used to select 1,319 individuals listed as members or fellows in the APA (1989) membership directory. . . .

RESULTS

Replies were received from 679 psychologists, for a return rate of 51%. . . .

Respondents provided 703 ethically troubling incidents in 23 general categories, as presented in Table 1. Examples of the ethical dilemmas are presented in the Discussion section. . . .

DISCUSSION

The primary purpose of this discussion is to present examples of the critical incidents, highlighting areas and instances in which psychologists find themselves confronting ethical challenges in their day-to-day work. These incidents may be useful as a basis for discussion in graduate courses, workshops, and other settings in which ethics are a focus of formal or informal learning and exploration. Discussion of the issues was limited in order to present as many incidents as possible; however, in some sections, the issues are discussed in light of not only emerging theory and research but also the current ethical code (APA, 1990) and the most recent draft revision ("Draft," 1991).

In the following sections, percentages are used only when based on the total number (703) of incidents; simple frequencies are used to refer to subsets and trends within each of the 23 general categories.

Confidentiality

The most frequently described dilemmas involved confidentiality. Of these troubling or challenging incidents, 38 involved actual or potential risks to third parties, 23 involved child abuse reporting, 8 involved individuals infected with human immunodeficiency virus (HIV) or suffering from acquired immunodeficiency syndrome (AIDS), 6 involved patients who threatened or had committed violence, and 1 involved elder abuse.

An additional 79 dilemmas reveal that respondents are wrestling with agonizing questions about whether confidential information should be disclosed and, if so, to whom. The following were typical:

> One girl underwent an abortion without the knowledge of her foster parents . . . I fully evaluated her view of the adults' inability to be supportive and agreed but worried about our relationship being damaged if I was discovered to know about the pregnancy and her action.

> A colleague withheld information about a client from the therapist to whom she transferred the case (within the same agency). She did so on the grounds of maintaining client confidentiality. This case raises questions not only about client confidentiality and

Adapted from the *American Psychologist*, 47, 397–411. Copyright 1992 by the American Psychological Association.

TABLE 1

Categories of 703 Ethically Troubling Incidents

Category	n	%
Confidentiality	128	18
Blurred, dual, or conflictual relationships	116	17
Payment sources, plans, settings, and methods	97	14
Academic settings, teaching dilemmas, and concerns about training	57	8
Forensic psychology	35	5
Research	29	4
Conduct of colleagues	29	4
Sexual issues	28	4
Assessment	25	4
Questionable or harmful interventions	20	3
Competence	20	3
Ethics (and related) codes and committees	17	2
School psychology	15	2
Publishing	14	2
Helping the financially stricken	13	2
Supervision	13	2
Advertising and (mis)representation	13	2
Industrial–organizational psychology	9	1
Medical issues	5	1
Termination	5	1
Ethnicity	4	1
Treatment records	4	1
Miscellaneous	7	1

professional relationships, but about the limits of confidentiality within an agency setting.

The executive director of the Mental Health Clinic with which I'm employed used his position to obtain and review clinical patient files of clients who were members of his church. He was [clerical title] in an ——— church and indicated his knowledge of this clinical (confidential) information would be of help to him in his role as [clerical title].

Having a psychologist as a client who tells me she has committed an ethical violation and because of confidentiality I can't report it.

One of my clients claimed she was raped; the police did not believe her and refused to follow up (because of her mental history). Another of my clients

described how he raped a woman (the same woman).

The remaining 11 incidents involved respondents' concerns about the careless or unintentional disclosure of confidential information: for example, "A psychiatrist who leases me space and does some of my billing is careless about discussing patient names in front of other patients. What should I do about this?"

In 1990, confidentiality accounted for only 2% of the primary category of active cases before the APA ethics committee ("Report of the Ethics Committee," 1991), yet participants in this research reported more struggles with confidentiality than any other category. This illustrates what the creators of the initial APA ethics code emphasized—that there may be a significant discrepancy between the ethical dilemmas encountered by the membership and the complaints received by the ethics committee, and therefore revisions to the code should be informed by the former as well as the latter.

Perhaps it is not surprising that confidentiality is the most frequently reported ethical dilemma reported by the membership. Although confidentiality is considered one of the most fundamental principles (Knapp & VandeCreek, 1987), and in some research has been endorsed by psychologists as the most important ethical duty (Crowe, Grogan, Jacobs, Lindsay, & Mark, 1985), national studies of psychologists have found that the most frequent *intentional* violations of formal standards involved confidentiality (Pope & Bajt, 1988) and that more than half of the respondents reported *unintentionally* violating confidentiality (Pope, Tabachnick, & Keith-Spiegel, 1987). . . .

Although the incidents raise a variety of concerns, they highlight two critical areas that the most recent draft revision does not address adequately. First, the boundaries of confidentiality when multiple caregivers (including administrators and supervisors) or clients are involved (e.g., clinics, therapy groups, and participants in couple or family therapy) need to be explicitly discussed.

Second, some of the incidents, especially about mandatory child abuse reporting laws, illustrate situations in which some psychologists believe it is better to break the law and act on that belief (Kalichman, Craig, & Follingstad, 1989; Koocher & Keith-Spiegel, 1990; Pope & Bajt, 1988; Pope et al., 1987). Most psychologists are likely to have encountered dilemmas in which following legal requirements seemed clinically and ethically wrong, perhaps placing the client or third parties at needless risk for harm and injustice (Pope & Bajt, 1988). The current ethics code states that psychologists must adhere to the law "in the ordinary course of events" (APA, 1990, p. 391), implying that in extraordinary circumstances some form of resistance to a particular law might be an ethically acceptable course. The most recent draft revision, however, specifies a solution to conflicts between the law and ethics that "complies with the law and yet most nearly conforms to the ethics code" ("Draft," 1991, p. 35), implying that civil disobedience (Gandhi, 1948; King, 1958, 1964; Plato, 1956a, 1956b; Thoreau, 1849/1960) and related approaches are unethical. This issue is in need of careful exploration and vigorous, informed debate. For a presentation of philosophical approaches, research data, and case law on this topic as they are relevant to psychology, see Pope and Bajt (1988) and Pope and Vasquez (1991).

Blurred, Dual, or Conflictual Relationships

The second most frequently described incidents involved maintaining clear, reasonable, and therapeutic boundaries around the professional relationship with a client. In some cases, respondents were troubled by such instances as serving as both "therapist and supervisor for hours for [patient/supervisee's] MFCC [marriage, family, and child counselor] license" or when "an agency hires one of its own clients." In other cases, respondents found dual relationships to be useful "to provide role modeling, nurturing and a giving quality to therapy"; one respondent, for example, believed that providing therapy to couples with whom he has social relationships and who are members of his small church makes sense because he is "able to see how these people interact in group context." In still other cases, respondents reported that it was sometimes difficult to know what constitutes a dual relationship or conflict of interest; for example, "I have employees/supervisees who were former

clients and wonder if this is a dual relationship." Similarly, another respondent felt a conflict between his own romantic attraction to a patient's mother and responsibilities to the child who had developed a positive relationship with him:

> I was conducting therapy with a child and soon became aware that there was a mutual attraction between myself and the child's mother. The strategies I had used and my rapport with the child had been positive. Nonetheless, I felt it necessary to refer to avoid a dual relationship (at the cost of the gains that had been made).

Taken as a whole, the incidents suggest, first, that the ethical principles need to define dual relationships more carefully and to note with clarity if and when they are ever therapeutically indicated or acceptable. . . . Research and the professional literature focusing on nonsexual dual relationships underscores the importance and implications of decisions to enter into or refrain from such activities (e.g., Borys & Pope, 1989; Ethics Committee, 1988; Keith-Spiegel & Koocher, 1985; Pope & Vasquez, 1991; Stromberg et al., 1988).

Second, the principles must address clearly and realistically the situations of those who practice in small towns, rural communities, and other remote locales. . . . Forty-one of the dual relationship incidents involved such locales. Many respondents implicitly or explicitly complained that the principles seem to ignore the special conditions in small, self-contained communities. For example,

> I live and maintain a . . . private practice in a rural area. I am also a member of a spiritual community based here. There are very few other therapists in the immediate vicinity who work with transformational, holistic, and feminist principles in the context of good clinical training that "conventional" people can also feel confidence in. Clients often come to me *because* they know me already, because they are not satisfied with the other services available, or be-

cause they want to work with someone who understands their spiritual practice and can incorporate its principles and practices into the process of transformation, healing, and change. The stricture against dual relationships helps me to maintain a high degree of sensitivity to the ethics (and potentials for abuse or confusion) of such situations, but doesn't give me any help in working with the actual circumstances of my practice. I hope revised principles will address these concerns!

Third, the principles need to distinguish between dual relationships and accidental or incidental extratherapeutic contacts (e.g., running into a patient at the grocery market or unexpectedly seeing a client at a party) and to address realistically the awkward entanglements into which even the most careful therapist can fall. For example, a therapist sought to file a formal complaint against some very noisy tenants of a neighboring house. When he did so, he was surprised to discover "that his patient was the owner-landlord." As another example, a respondent reported,

> Six months ago a patient I had been working with for 3 years became romantically involved with my best and longest friend. I could write no less than a book on the complications of this fact! I have been getting legal and therapeutic consultations all along, and continue to do so. Currently they are living together and I referred the patient (who was furious that I did this and felt abandoned). I worked with the other psychologist for several months to provide a bridge for the patient. I told my friend soon after I found out that I would have to suspend our contact. I'm currently trying to figure out if we can ever resume our friendship and under what conditions.

The latter example is one of many that demonstrate the extreme lengths to which most psychologists are willing to go to ensure the welfare of their patients. Although it is impossible to anticipate every pattern

of multiple relationship or to account for all the vicissitudes and complexities of life, psychologists need and deserve formal principles that provide lucid, useful, and practical guidance as an aid to professional judgment.

Payment Sources, Plans, Settings, and Methods

The third most frequently described incidents involved payment providers, plans, settings, or methods. Fifty-six focused on insurance coverage. Inadequate coverage for clients with urgent needs created a cruel ethical dilemma in which therapists felt forced either to breach their responsibilities to clients ("Insurance companies force me to provide inadequate care for patients because of policy limitations and patients' limited financial resources") or to be less than honest with what sometimes seems an adversarial provider of reimbursement ("I'm forced to lie about clients' mental condition to obtain insurance coverage that is due them, while insurance company psychologists are struggling to deny their customers their rightfully due coverage"). As one respondent put it: "I feel caught between providing the best service and being truly ethical." A vast range of troubling issues were described, including billing for no-shows, billing family therapy as if it were individual, distorting a patient's condition so that it qualifies for coverage, signing forms for unlicensed staff, and not collecting copayments.

Fifteen focused on what are typically called managed health plans, such as health maintenance organizations (HMOs) and employee assistance plans (EAPs). Most of the dilemmas, such as those focusing on more general insurance, highlighted (a) the discrepancy between the needs of the client and the services covered, and (b) the tensions between the interests of clients and the interests of those providing, administering, or investing in the managed health plan. The following examples were typical:

> A 7 year old boy was severely sexually abused and severely depressed. I evaluated the case and recommended 6 months treatment. My recommendation was evaluated by a managed health care agency and approved for 10 sessions by

a nonprofessional inspite of the fact that there is no known treatment program that can be performed in 10 sessions on a 7 year old that has demonstrated efficacy.

[I am] a part-time psychologist in an HMO. Am I an insurance agent or a clinician? . . . The primary obligation of the HMO is towards stockholders, not clients.

A managed care company discontinued a benefit and told my patient to stop seeing me, then referred her to a therapist they had a lower fee contract with.

Twelve dilemmas focused on payment-related issues in hospital settings; again, the emphasis tended to be on the conflict between the needs of the patient and the financial needs of the hospital.

Need to meet admission quotas . . . for private hospital. Pressure to develop diagnosis for inpatients in private hospital that would support hospitalization.

Much of my practice is in a private hospital which is in general very good clinically. However its profit motivation is so very intense that decisions are often made for $ reasons that actively hurt the patients. When patients complain, this is often interpreted as being part of their psychopathology, thus reenacting the dysfunctional families they came from. I don't do this myself and don't permit others to do so in my presence—I try to mitigate the problem—but I can't speak perfectly frankly to my patients and I'm constantly colluding with something that feels marginally unethical.

I have been concerned about the unnecessary hospitalization of teenagers, extensive and expensive testing (often farmed out to MFCCs or interns on commission), 10 minute visits in hospital at $80 to $100 a visit (also often farmed out on a fee splitting basis) with the teenager leaving hospital when med-

ical insurance runs out and receiving no further treatment.

As a clinical psychologist in a large metropolitan area, I have been frustrated on a few occasions recently by the apparent profit motive of the private psychiatric facilities. It appears that decisions to release patients are almost routinely delayed beyond that which I think is in the best interest of the patient. Psychologists appear to be pressured to "go along" with the system, or risk no referrals.

Similarly, in six dilemmas that focused on mental health clinics or centers and two that focused on individuals who paid for someone else's therapy, there was an actual or potential conflict between the interests of the patient and the (generally but not always financial) interests of the party paying for or providing the therapy. . . .

A woman who is married, but unemployed comes to a psychologist for therapy or counseling. The husband of the woman is paying the bills. After a few sessions, it becomes evident that the patient is planning on leaving or divorcing the husband, who is unaware of this. The psychologist is put in a position of helping the patient to carry through an adverse (to the husband) action, which the husband is unknowingly paying for.

Four dilemmas addressed billing issues with clients who were paying for their own therapy; they tended to involve questions about adjusting fees (e.g., "I worry about the ethics of varying fee scale but feel less concerned than I would if I denied services to those unable to pay the higher rate"). Finally, two focused on gifts or financial advantages offered by clients; for example, a consulting psychologist described how "I have had to deal with a number of offers to get expensive items for me 'wholesale.' (I've resisted because it would compromise the relationship but it *is* tempting)."

. . . [T]he growing influence and prevalence of third-party payment sources, from traditional insurance to HMOs and EAPs, seem to have intensified the need for explicit ethical standards that address more directly, realistically, and helpfully the dilemmas created by these payment sources (see, e.g., Cummings & Duhl, 1987; DeLeon, VandenBos, & Kraut, 1986; Dorken & DeLeon, 1986; Kiesler & Morton, 1988a, 1988b; Pope, 1990a; Zimet, 1989). Psychologists who find themselves working for organizations such as HMOs *and* for patients served by those organizations may be facing conflicts parallel to those faced by industrial–organizational psychologists. An author of the 1959 standards noted the unavoidable question that the revision committee confronted: "Can one really serve the needs of management in developing a more effective company while also doing what is always best from the point of view of the man down the line who may be adversely affected by the outcome?" (Holzman, 1960).

Academic Settings, Teaching Dilemmas, and Concerns About Training

Twenty-five dilemmas focusing on teaching, training, and academia involved concern about lax or unenforced standards. Thirteen mentioned "grade inflation" and the pressures of to give "A"s, whether or not deserved. An additional 8 worried about the selection and graduation of unqualified students. Although some were worried about "diploma mills" (termed "a crisis" by one respondent), a majority were concerned about more mainstream programs, as the following examples illustrate.

> My colleagues and I are concerned about the emotional instability and intellectual deficits of several students who have been accepted by APA-approved educational institutions.
>
> I employ over 600 psychologists. I am disturbed by the fact that those psychologists with marginal ethics and competence were so identified in graduate school and no one did anything about it.
>
> Asked to comment to a search committee about a graduate student whom I feel is "ethically dubious" but has a good publication record and is a top candidate for a job.

> I have had students who were clearly emotionally disturbed, yet were completing programs in counseling psychology to become "therapists."

One barrier to addressing the dilemmas associated with unsuitable students seemed to be the threat of lawsuits, mentioned by an additional four respondents.

Three dilemmas mentioned academic discrimination on the basis of race, sex, or physical disability. Another three mentioned psychology graduate programs' failure to offer adequate coursework in the areas of ethics and values, the treatment of minorities, and psychopharmacology. The remaining dilemmas were extremely diverse, including such topics as exploitation of students, teaching group therapy using experimental participation by students, teachers using questions taken from licensing exams and distributing them to students, and misuse of power by professors or administrators.

Forensic Psychology

Some of the respondents' most bitter language (e.g., "whores") was used to describe psychologists who seem willing to present false testimony in court.

> There are psychologists who are "hired" guns who testify for whoever pays them.
>
> A psychologist in my area is widely known, to clients, psychologists, and the legal community to give whatever testimony is requested in court. He has a very commanding "presence" and it works. He will say anything, adamantly, for pay. Clients/lawyers continue to use him because if the other side uses him, that side will probably win the case (because he's so persuasive, though lying).

Four dilemmas stressed the psychologist's willingness to provide such testimony, and an additional three stressed the attorney's pressures or inducements for this kind of testimony. Yet another four, although making no inferences concerning the psychologist's motivations, expressed concern about testimony that is not founded on the data or established scientific principles (e.g., Huber, 1991).

Another psychologist's report or testimony in a court case goes way beyond what psychology knows or his own data supports. How or whether I should respond.

Overstepping of professional knowledge; e.g., testifying in child abuse cases that the perpetrator is "cured" and that there is *no* chance of reabuse (crystal ball predictions).

An additional eight forensic dilemmas reflected these tendencies to go beyond the data or to respond to lawyers' pressure specifically in child custody disputes (especially to provide custody recommendations based on interviews with only one parent).

Colleagues feel uncomfortable in courtroom settings, making recommendations of one parent over another in a custody dispute when the child clearly has a strong relationship with both. Subjective impressions of patients are used as fact.

An attorney wants me to see one patient and the children in a custody case, but won't refer the case to me if I insist on seeing both parents.

Participating in a system in which false or misleading testimony is rendered confronts psychologists with troubling ethical challenges. However, five dilemmas revealed that, bogus testimony aside, psychologists are concerned that presenting *accurate* data in a forensic setting may have harmful consequences.

I find it difficult to have to testify in court or by way of deposition and to provide sensitive information about a client. Although the client has given permission to provide this information, there are times when there is much discomfort in so doing.

I felt compelled to go against a subpoena from a former client's attorney in her divorce proceedings because I strongly believed my written case notes would be severely detrimental to her case. I explained that to her, and barely avoided contempt charges.

Unlike the current code (APA, 1990) which does not explicitly address forensic settings, procedures, and standards, the draft revision ("Draft," 1991) provides a separate section (with seven subsections) on "Forensic Activities." Readers may wish to compare this section with the "Specialty Guidelines for Forensic Psychologists" (Committee on Ethical Guidelines for Forensic Psychologists, 1991).

Research

Twelve dilemmas focusing on research mentioned pressures or tendencies to misstate research procedures or findings.

I design, analyze and write up research reports that identify the advantages for one medium over the other media. Yet with large expenditures for the research, I feel constrained to report *something*. . . . But there is a limit to how many unpleasant findings I come up with— Finally, I have to find some truthful positives or I start looking for another job.

A particular company . . . has been citing my research conclusions . . . without considering my stated cautions, qualifications, and so forth. That is, my work is cited out of the context of conflicting research and the conclusions are uncritically overgeneralized or overstated. I am concerned that my name or my research may be associated with a kind of deceit.

I am co-investigator on a grant. While walking past the secretary's desk I saw an interim report completed by the PI [principal investigator] to the funding source. The interim report claimed double the number of subjects who had actually entered the protocol.

I have consulted to research projects at a major university medical school where "random selection" of subjects for drug studies was flagrantly disregarded. I resigned after the first phase.

A colleague frequently distorts the results of poorly conducted collaborative research with students in order to gain recognition and material to present at conferences. He typically works in applied areas with considerable public interest.

Eight dilemmas reflected concern about the rights of research participants.

With some field experiments, it is unclear whether informed consent is needed and, if so, from whom it should be sought.

As a consultant at a speech clinic, the director wishes to use clinical data for research without informing or getting informed consent.

Deception that was not disclosed, use of a data videotape in a public presentation without the subject's consent (the subject was in the audience), using a class homework assignment as an experimental manipulation without informing students.

The remainder of the dilemmas involved such diverse topics as mistreatment of animals, established researchers squelching new research, inadequate resources, and the difficulties of conducting research for large organizations in which many employees exert influence over how the research should be conducted.

The current draft revision addresses research issues in much more detail than the current code. Its combined section on "Teaching, Research, and Publishing" contains 15 subsections focusing primarily on research. This expansion probably reflects increasing awareness of the ways in which research can, both intentionally and unintentionally, result in harm, violation of human rights, the dissemination of results in a misleading manner, and an erosion of professional integrity (Ceci, Peters, & Plotkin, 1985; Denmark, Russo, Frieze, & Sechzer, 1988; Helms, 1989; Johnson, 1990; Keith-Spiegel & Koocher, 1985; Koocher & Keith-Spiegel, 1990; Levine, 1988; Mulvey & Phelps, 1988; Scarr, 1988; Sieber, 1992; Stanley & Sieber, 1991).

Conduct of Colleagues

Four percent of the responses described dilemmas created by disruptive (e.g., competitive) relationships with colleagues or difficulties confronting colleagues engaging in unethical or harmful behavior.

As a faculty member, it was difficult dealing with a colleague about whom I received numerous complaints from students.

At what point does "direct knowledge" of purportedly unethical practices become direct knowledge which I must report—is reporting through a client "direct" knowledge? . . .

The toughest situations I and my colleague seem to keep running into (in our small town) are ones involving obvious (to us) ethical infractions by other psychologists or professionals in the area. On 3 or more occasions he and I have personally confronted and taken to local Boards . . . issues which others would rather avoid, deal with lightly, ignore, deny, etc., because of peer pressure in a small community. This has had the combined effect of making me doubt my reality (or experience), making me wonder *why* I have such moral compunctions, making me feel isolated and untrusting of professional peers, etc.

During the last 15–20 years, it has been upsetting to me to see my colleagues' primary focus to be image building, income building, status seeking and "equality" with psychiatric brothers and sisters, rather than public service. Not that those things are not important but the priorities are wrong.

. . . Research evidence suggests that only about 58% of psychologists believe that to file an ethics complaint against a colleague is itself an unquestionably ethical act (Pope et al., 1987), that about 5% believe that it is never ethical to help a student to file an ethics complaint against another teacher (Tabachnick, Keith-Spiegel, & Pope, 1991), and that only 21% report that they have never simply ignored unethical behavior by colleagues (Tabachnick et al., 1991). In some instances, the "whistleblower" may risk punishing consequences for not remaining silent (Simon, 1978), even when his or her critique is offered in the context of formal peer review, a process supposedly created to bring inappropriate, unethical, or harmful practices to light (Kleinfield, 1991).

Sexual Issues

Four percent of the dilemmas reflected concerns about sexual issues, particularly the conditions under which sexual involvements are unethical.

> Not often, but I have had female clients indicate their interest in romantic involvement with me.
>
> Therapists asking patients to masturbate in front of them.
>
> A student after seeing a client for therapy for a semester terminated the therapy as was planned at the end of the semester, then began a sexual relationship with the client. . . . I think APA should take a stronger stance on this issue.
>
> I currently have in treatment a psychiatrist who is still in the midst of a six year affair with a patient. He wishes to end the affair but is afraid to face the consequences.
>
> A colleague and friend engaged in sexual activity with an employee of our organization. He was "caught," caused to resign (and did) and is seeking personal help. That seems "punishment" enough without adding reporting the activity to APA ethics.
>
> My psychological assistant was sexually exploited by her former supervisor and threatened her with not validating her hours for licensure if she didn't service his needs.

Sexual involvement with therapy clients (e.g., Bates & Brodsky, 1989; Committee on Women in Psychology, 1989; Ethics Committee, 1988; Feldman-Summers, 1989; Feldman-Summers & Jones, 1984; Gabbard, 1989; Hare-Mustin, in press; Holroyd & Brodsky, 1977; Pope 1990c; Pope & Vasquez, 1991; Sonne, 1987, 1989; Sonne, Meyer,

Borys, & Marshall, 1985; Sonne & Pope, 1991; Stromberg et al., 1988) and with students (e.g., Glaser & Thorpe, 1986; Robinson & Reid, 1985; Pope, Levenson, & Schover, 1979; Pope, Schover, & Levenson, 1980; Tabachnick et al., 1991) has been a difficult issue for the profession to address effectively, as the cited references emphasize and illustrate. Part of the difficulty may be due to surprising historical and related factors (see Brodsky, 1989; Pope 1990b). Part may be due to challenging methodological issues that have been repeatedly emphasized and examined since the earliest research reports; among these enduring methodological issues are "selective memory in retrospective studies, reporting biases, unrepresentative samples, and distortions in data obtained from secondary sources" (Pope, 1990c, p. 477). Part may be due to the incongruity of therapists placing those who come to them for help at risk for significant harm; the harm can be deep and pervasive, meeting the 10 diagnostic criteria of Therapist–Patient Sex Syndrome. This incongruity highlights the problems of responding effectively to those therapists who sexually abuse their clients. The profession has a significant responsibility to address in good faith the ethical, methodological, legal, and policy questions about rehabilitation approaches that have shown no evidence of validity through independently conducted, carefully controlled research published in peer reviewed scientific journals and may place future clients at increased risk for severe harm without their knowledge or consent (Pope, 1991; Pope & Vetter, 1991; Sonne & Pope, 1991). Yet another part of the difficulty may be due to the accelerating evolution of our research-based understanding. Inferences based on research have been modified, as subsequent research findings provide more detailed understanding. For example, numerous variables such as therapist gender, region of residence, and practice setting have emerged as significant in this type of research (e.g., Borys & Pope, 1989); attempts to compare and contrast research findings from different studies without taking into account (e.g., computing statistical adjustments for) the between-studies differences in such variables may lead to confusion when attempting to understand differing findings. . . .

In the mid-1980s, the scientific and professional literature began to examine in more detail the clinical, ethical, and policy implications of posttermination relationships (Brodsky, 1988; Brown, 1988; Gabbard & Pope, 1989; Keith-Spiegel & Koocher, 1985; Shopland & VandeCreek, 1991; Vasquez, 1991), and to provide research data regarding the harm to the patient (Pope & Vetter, 1991) and consequences for the therapist (Sell, Gotlieb, & Schonfeld, 1986) that occurs in cases in which sexual intimacies are initiated only after the termination of therapy. These works, like those examining pretermination relationships, tended to focus less on transference than on a variety of nontransferential factors. . . .

Assessment

As the following examples illustrate, the most typical dilemmas focusing on assessment tended to involve one of two themes: (a) the availability of tests (or computerized interpretations) to those who may not be adequately trained in testing, and (b) basing conclusions on inadequate data or ignoring important sources of data (e.g., observation, interview, or other contact with the client) or expertise.

> Eleven of us cover a 22,000 student population (K–12). When the Binet IV came out, only one person was sent for training. . . . We are often asked to add new tests without appropriate supervision. Test publishers aren't motivated to slow down sales by requiring training to purchase tests. Someone like me needs APA protection via strict access to tests only upon proof of training. It sounds self-serving according to our employer to request appropriate training.
>
> I am often asked by social workers to "interpret" psychological tests which they administer without allowing me to a see the client. I refuse to render an opinion without client contact.
>
> Colleagues in the medical profession have the right to order psychological tests from computer companies that give computer generated interpretations. . . .

Other practitioners, especially internists, wanting to base important decisions on just an MMPI [Minnesota Multiphasic Personality Inventory] result.

Some psychologists will omit subtests from the Wechsler and report verbal and performance IQ scores without indicating that they have omitted subtests. This practice was so common we had to require a copy of the summary sheet to ensure that all tests were administered. . . .

Psychologists use computer-generated test reports as the only report of an evaluation, without integrating the test results with other data.

Questionable or Harmful Interventions

In a concise article, Singer (1980) illuminated the implications of psychology's scientific tradition for providing effective interventions in a safe manner. The importance of attending to this aspect of our work is highlighted by dilemmas reflecting respondents' concern about the efficacy, legitimacy, and safety of treatment approaches, modalities, and conditions.

> A patient of mine . . . left town to attend college. Very shortly before departure, she revealed an early history of sexual abuse. The recurrent thoughts and memories were extremely disturbing to her. She refused to seek a new therapist at school. . . . She asked me to talk with her by phone. I am not licensed in that state. Would I be practicing in that state? Is "phone therapy" a reasonable choice? . . . If . . . not, is it abandonment? . . .
>
> Seeing clients in an unprofessional atmosphere—e.g., in the home with pets present in the consultation room.
>
> Colleagues . . . making/receiving 4–5 phone calls during a session.
>
> As a state psychologist working with retarded clients . . . we may not use response cost or any negative reinforcers with our clients. . . . To me failure to

enforce real controls is unethical, yet it is a very strong national movement to use only positive reinforcement.

Institutions for the developmentally disabled/M/R, especially care from institution, not be supervised properly as to care they get in group homes; foster type care, etc—I've seen some deplorable living conditions and clients almost starved to death.

Competence
About 3% of the dilemmas involved moving into areas without adequate competence or the erosion of competence through time and stress. . . .

In our small town, political community, colleagues are less well trained and often practice beyond their training and competence level.

Some current staff psychologists, trained many years ago, who have not kept their skills and/or knowledge base current and thus, we have a problem with competence.

I often feel exhausted and burned out, but lack supervisory therapy resources for myself. How do I know my own limits?

Ethics (and Related) Codes and Committees
Eleven dilemmas in this area reflected concern about ethics, licensing, and related committees. Three described how committees were too slow to take action or were inactive because of such factors as the threat of litigation. The other diverse concerns about committees included their "presumption of guilt" and "police method," the problem of an ethical violator sitting on the committee, the redundancy of different level (i.e., local, state, and national) committees, and the potential conflict of interest when members are competitive with those they investigate.

The remaining dilemmas reflected concerns that the current ethics code is trivial, that it does not sufficiently address minority values and concerns, that the guidelines are extremely vague, and that it does not reflect adequate concern for clients. . . .

School Psychology
These dilemmas tended to reflect psychologists' struggles to act in the best interests of students despite pressure from administrators.

A retarded boy in a school district is kept isolated from the rest of his class because of his disruptive behavior. The school district hires me to decrease disruptive behaviors while still keeping him isolated. I feel that he should be integrated. Whose agent am I?

My school district administrator would like me to distort test data to show improvement.

I am employed as a school psychologist in a large school district. . . . I am asked to provide a diagnosis which will qualify the examinee for certain services, even if the test results do not justify that diagnosis. I have not done so, but the frequency with which the request is made is troubling.

As a school psychologist there is often pressure from administrators to place children in programs based on the availability of services rather than the needs of the individual student. . . .

Publishing
Dilemmas in the area of publishing tended to focus on giving publication credit to those who do not deserve it, denying publication credit to those who deserve it, and teachers plagiarizing students' papers for their own articles. As one respondent wrote,

I am asked to give P.I. status to M.D. colleagues on training grants that I write and manage within a Dept. of Family Medicine at a large medical school.

Helping the Financially Stricken
Respondents expressed concerns about addressing the needs of those who are poor, unemployed, or homeless.

My concern: not enough educational programs and financial support for those who could help the homeless. . . .

How to be able to serve people of low income.

How to meet the needs of a broad-based socioeconomic clientele in the same offices without alienating them from the pursuit of psychological services.

My fee for psychotherapy makes me unavailable to needy clients, but I cannot afford to do pro bono work . . . I feel wrong (unethical), even though I refer clients to lower-fee therapists.

Although both the current code and the most recent draft revision address the issue of providing services for little or no financial or other personal gain, no sections explicitly address the ethics of interventions, such as those used by community psychologists or primary preventionists, created specifically to serve the needs of those who are poor, unemployed, or homeless, or who are members of other vulnerable populations (e.g., Pope & Garcia-Peltoniemi, 1991; Pope & Morin, 1991). Extensive examinations of the ethics of community psychology and related endeavors have begun to appear somewhat more frequently in the professional literature (e.g., Levin, Trickett, & Hess, 1991; O'Neill, 1989; O'Neill & Hern, 1991), as have discussions of training in the ethics of such activities (Bond & Albee, 1991).

Supervision
Dilemmas in this area reflected concerns about supervisors who were negligent or disrespectful.

Individuals hired and supervised by prominent licensed psychologist, who actually receive little or no supervision.

Clinical supervisors who work with students and impose their own orientation onto the students without regard or respect for different orientations and personality styles. . . .

A psychology intern has a primary supervisor who is psychoanalytically oriented. The intern's final evaluation by the supervisor states that . . . the intern "needs two years of intensive, personal psychotherapy." While there was no

doubt the intern "passed" the internship satisfactorily, this final evaluation was made part of his record. . . . It became evident to the intern years later that this was being sent out in the way of references to potential employers. . . . The intern is barred from all or most jobs which require a recommendation from the internship site. . . . The supervisor left the internship site . . . so that the internship site is not in a position of being able to negotiate a settlement.

Advertising and (Mis)Representations
Dilemmas in this area reflected concerns about how professionals present themselves and their work to the public in a false, misleading, or questionable manner.

My clinic wishes to advertise my services in ways which I find offensive and unprofessional.

Advertising in Yellow Pages stating "Psychological Referral Service" which was nothing more than a number generating referrals for several private practice psychologists.

The Yellow Pages includes "bogus" listings under "Psychologists."

A psychological assistant allows herself to be misrepresented as a psychologist. The hospital for whom she works supports her misrepresentation. . . .

Industrial–Organizational
Dilemmas in this area tended to describe ways in which management interfered with the psychologist's duties, especially instances in which psychologists were expected or pressured to break pledges of confidentiality to employees or survey respondents or in which a company breaks a pledge (which the psychologist had conveyed in good faith) to remedy problems identified in an employee survey. One respondent, however, noted what he or she felt to be an interesting conflict of interest: As an organizational psychologist in charge, he or she was responsible for setting his or her own pay.

Medical Issues

About 1% of the dilemmas focused on several medical issues, as the following examples illustrate.

> A parent of a 10 year old resists taking the child for appropriate medical evaluation. Should I stop working with the child and family?

> I evaluated a nursing home resident whose medical doctor had missed an obvious neurological disease and had misdiagnosed her. Despite my report and telephone conversation with him about considering revising her diagnosis, he did not do so and continued to prescribe medication which worsened her symptoms.

> One of my jobs is to help parents and children adjust to disabling and disfiguring traumatic injuries. I sometimes know that the medical treatment the child has received has increased the disability/disfigurement unnecessarily or that another approach to treatment exists which gets better results. Yet, unless the child/parent can choose some corrective action, no goal would be accomplished in telling them and it seems better to support their belief that they are receiving the most excellent care. By remaining silent, am I in fact supporting poor treatment?

Termination

About 1% of the dilemmas focused on difficulties terminating and rendering appropriate follow-up. Examples include,

> My greatest "ethical crisis" comes from conceptualizing terminations with clients (who have been victims as children of ritual sexual abuse) in whose lives I have been "involved" for 5–7 years. . . .

> A colleague took a 4 month leave of absence and referred a patient to me (as a "babysitter therapist") for the duration. The patient preferred me and did not wish to return to my colleague, who insisted I should force the patient to do so. I am having ambivalent feelings and wondering what is best for the patient—but also, whether to risk losing the friendship of my colleague.

Ethnicity

Dilemmas that focused on ethnicity included the following:

> Many clients when referred to my office show initial shock that I am ethnically different from the mainstream. As a result, more time is needed to establish rapport.

> In my academic institution, there are verbal statements and policies around affirmative action for courses and academic development of ethnic minority students and faculty. However, efforts directed toward those goals are constantly sabotaged and dismantled by the administration of the campus, who are psychologists.

Although both the current code and the most recent draft revision prohibit discrimination on the basis of ethnicity, race, or culture, and the professional literature addresses relevant training and related issues in this area (e.g., Gibbs & Huang, 1989; Mays & Comas-Diaz, 1988; Pedersen, Draguns, Lonner, & Trimble, 1989; Pope & Vasquez, 1991; Stricker et al., 1990), the profession may benefit from a discussion of whether confronting racism and similar forms of discrimination is an ethical responsibility that should be explicitly addressed by the formal code (Brown, 1991).

Treatment Records

About 1% of the dilemmas expressed concerns about what information should go into the record, agency policies of charging for records, providing copies of records to patients who have not paid their bills, and what to do when records are unintentionally destroyed. . . .

References

American Psychological Association. (1989). *Directory of the American Psychological Association.* Washington, DC: Author.

American Psychological Association. (1990). Ethical principles of psychologists (amended June 2, 1989). *American Psychologist, 45,* 390–395.

Bates, C. M., & Brodsky, A. M. (1989). *Sex in the therapy hour: A case of professional incest.* New York: Guilford.

Bond, L. A., & Albee, G. W. (1991). Training preventionists in the ethical implications of their actions. In G. Levin, E. Trickett, & R. Hess (Eds.), *Ethical implications of primary prevention* (pp. 111–126). Binghamton, NY: Haworth.

Borys, D. S., & Pope, K. S. (1989). Dual relationships between therapist and client: A national study of psychologists, psychiatrists, and social workers. *Professional Psychology: Research and Practice, 20,* 283–293.

Brodsky, A. M. (1988, January). *Is it ever o.k. for a therapist to have a sexual relationship with a former patient?* Paper presented at the meeting of Division 12 (Clinical Psychology), San Diego, CA.

Brodsky, A. M. (1989). Sex between patient and therapist: Psychology's data and response. In G. O. Gabbard (Ed.), *Sexual exploitation in professional relationships* (pp. 15–25). Washington, DC: American Psychiatric Press.

Brown, L. S. (1988). Harmful effects of posttermination sexual and romantic relationships between therapists and their former clients. *Psychotherapy, 25,* 249–255.

Brown, L. S. (1991). Antiracism as an ethical imperative: An example from feminist therapy. *Ethics & Behavior, 1,* 113–128.

Ceci, S. J., Peters, D., & Plotkin, J. (1985). Human subjects review, personal values, and the regulation of social science research. *American Psychologist, 40,* 994–1002.

Committee on Ethical Guidelines for Forensic Psychologists. (1991). Specialty guidelines for forensic psychologists. *Law and Human Behavior, 15,* 655–665.

Committee on Women in Psychology. (1989). If sex enters into the psychotherapy relationship. *Professional Psychology: Research and Practice, 20,* 112–115.

Crowe, M., Grogan, J., Jacobs, R., Lindsey, C., & Mark, M. (1985). Delineation of the roles of clinical psychology. *Professional Psychology: Research and Practice, 16,* 124–137.

Cummings, N. A., & Duhl, L. J. (1987). The new delivery system. In L. J. Cummings & N. A. Cummings (Eds.), *The future of mental health services: Coping with crisis* (pp. 85–98). New York: Springer.

DeLeon, P. H., VandenBos, G. R., & Kraut, A. G. (1986). Federal recognition of psychology as a profession. In H. Dorken (Ed.), *Professional psychology in transition* (pp. 99–117). San Francisco: Jossey-Bass.

Denmark, F., Russo, N. F., Frieze, I. H., & Sechzer, J. A. (1988). Guidelines for avoiding sexism in research: A report of the Ad Hoc Committee on Nonsexist Research. *American Psychologist, 43,* 582–585.

Dorken, H., & DeLeon, P. H. (1986). Cost as the driving force in health care reform. In H. Dorken (Ed.), *Professional psychology in transition* (pp. 313–349). San Francisco: Jossey-Bass.

Draft of the APA ethics code published. (1991, June). *APA Monitor,* pp. 30–35.

Ethics Committee of the American Psychological Association. (1988). Trends in ethics cases, common pitfalls, and published resources. *American Psychologist, 43,* 564–572.

Feldman-Summers, S. (1989). Sexual contact in fiduciary relationships. In G. O. Gabbard (Ed.), *Sexual exploitation in professional relationships* (pp. 193–209). Washington, DC: American Psychiatric Press.

Feldman-Summers, S., & Jones, G. (1984). Psychological impacts of sexual contact between therapists or other health care professionals and their clients. *Journal of Consulting and Clinical Psychology, 52,* 1054–1061.

Gabbard, G. O. (Ed.). (1989). *Sexual exploitation in professional relationships.* Washington, DC: American Psychiatric Press.

Gabbard, G. O., & Pope, K. S. (1989). Sexual intimacies after termination: Clinical, ethical, and legal aspects. In G. O. Gabbard (Ed.), *Sexual exploitation in professional relationships* (pp. 115–127). Washington, DC: American Psychiatric Press.

Gandhi, M. K. (1948). *Non-violence in peace and war.* Ahmedabadi, India: Narajivan.

Gibbs, J. T., & Huang, L. N. (1989). *Children of color: Psychological interventions with minority youth.* San Francisco: Jossey-Bass.

Glaser, R. D., & Thorpe, J. S. (1986). Unethical intimacy: A survey of sexual contact and advances between psychology educators and female graduate students. *American Psychologist, 41,* 43–51.

Hare-Mustin, R. T. (in press). Cries and whispers. *Psychotherapy.*

Helms, J. E. (1989). Considering some methodological issues in racial identity counseling research. *The Counseling Psychologist, 17,* 227–252.

Holroyd, J. C., & Brodsky, A. M. (1977). Psychologists' attitudes and practices regarding erotic and nonerotic physical contact with clients. *American Psychologist, 32,* 843–849.

Holzman, W. H. (1960). Some problems of defining ethical behavior. *American Psychologist, 15,* 247–250.

Huber, P. W. (1991). *Galileo's revenge: Junk science in the courtroom*. New York: Basic Books.

Kalichman, S. C., Craig, M. E., & Follingstad, D. R. (1989). Factors influencing the reporting of father–child sexual abuse: Study of licensed practicing psychologists. *Professional Psychology, 20*, 84–89.

Keith-Spiegel, P., & Koocher, G. P. (1985). *Ethics in psychology*. New York: Random House.

Kiesler, C. A., & Morton, T. L. (1988a). Prospective payment system for psychiatric services: The advantages of controversy. *American Psychologist, 43*, 141–150.

Kiesler, C. A., & Morton, T. L. (1988b). Psychology and public policy in the "Health Care Revolution." *American Psychologist, 43*, 993–1003.

King, M. L., Jr. (1958). *Stride toward freedom*. San Francisco: Harper & Row.

King, M. L., Jr. (1964). *Why we can't wait*. New York: Signet.

Kleinfeld, N. R. (1991, August 5). Doctor's critique of care strains hospital's bond. *New York Times*. p. A-12.

Knapp, S., & VandeCreek, L. (1987). *Privileged communications in the mental health professions*. New York: Van Nostrand Reinhold.

Koocher, G. P., & Keith-Spiegel, G. P. (1990). *Children, ethics, and the law: Professional issues and cases*. Lincoln: University of Nebraska Press.

Levin, G. B., Trickett, E. J., & Hess, R. E. (1991). *Ethical implications of primary prevention*. Binghamton, NY: Haworth.

Levine, R. J. (1988). *Ethics and regulation of clinical research* (2nd ed.). New Haven, CT: Yale University Press.

Mays, V. M., & Comas-Diaz, L. (1988). Feminist therapy with ethnic minority populations: A closer look at Blacks and Hispanics. In M. A. Dutton-Douglas & L. E. A. Walker (Eds.), *Feminist psychotherapies: Integration of therapeutic and feminist systems* (pp. 228–251). Norwood, NJ: Ablex.

Mulvey, E. P., & Phelps, P. (1988). Ethical balances in juvenile justice research and practice. *American Psychologist, 43*, 65–69.

O'Neill, P. (1989). Responsible to whom? Responsible for what? Some ethical issues in community intervention. *American Journal of Community Psychology, 17*, 323–341.

O'Neill, P., & Hern, R. (1991). A systems approach to ethical problems. *Ethics & Behavior, 1*, 129–143.

Pedersen, P. D., Draguns, J. G., Lonner, W. J., & Trimble, E. J. (Eds.). (1989). *Counseling across cultures* (3rd ed.). Honolulu: University of Hawaii Press.

Plato. (1956a). The apology (W. H. D. Rouse, Trans.). In E. H. Warmington & P. G. Rouse (Eds.), *Great dialogues of Plato* (pp. 423–446). New York: New American Library.

Plato. (1956b). Crito (W. H. O. Rouse, Trans.). In E. H. Warmington & P. G. Rouse (Eds.), *Great dialogues of Plato* (pp. 447–459). New York: New American Library.

Pope, K. S. (1989). Therapist–Patient Sex Syndrome: A guide to assessing damage. In G. O. Gabbard (Ed.), *Sexual exploitation in professional relationships* (pp. 39–55). Washington, DC: American Psychiatric Press.

Pope, K. S. (1990a). Ethical and malpractice issues in hospital practice. *American Psychologist, 45*, 1066–1070.

Pope, K. S. (1990c). Therapist–patient sexual involvement: A review of the research. *Clinical Psychology Review, 10*, 477–490.

Pope, K. S. (1991). Rehabilitation plans and expert testimony for therapists who have been sexually involved with a patient. *Independent Practitioner, 11*(3), 31–39.

Pope, K. S., & Bajt, T. R. (1988). When laws and values conflict: A dilemma for psychologists. *American Psychologist, 43*, 828.

Pope, K. S., & Garcia-Peltoniemi, R. E. (1991). Responding to victims of torture: Clinical issues, professional responsibilities, and useful resources. *Professional Psychology: Research and Practice, 22*, 269–276.

Pope, K. S., Levenson, H., & Schover, L. R. (1979). Sexual intimacy in psychology training: Results and implications of a national survey. *American Psychologist, 34*, 682–689.

Pope, K. S., & Morin, S. F. (1991). AIDS and HIV infection update: New research, ethical responsibilities, evolving legal frameworks, and published resources. In P. A. Keller & S. R. Heyman (Eds.), *Innovations in clinical practice: A sourcebook* (Vol. 10, pp. 443–457). Sarasota, FL: Professional Resource Exchange.

Pope, K. S., Schover, L. R., & Levenson, H. (1980). Sexual intimacies between clinical supervisors and supervisees: Implications for professional standards. *Professional Psychology, 11*, 157–162.

Pope, K. S., Tabachnick, B. G., & Keith-Spiegel, P. (1987). Ethics of practice: The beliefs and behaviors of psychologists as therapists. *American Psychologist, 42*, 993–1006.

Pope, K. S., & Vasquez, M. J. T. (1991). *Ethics in psychotherapy and counseling: A practical guide for psychologists*. San Francisco: Jossey-Bass.

Pope, K. S., & Vetter, V. A. (1991). Prior therapist–patient sexual involvement among patients seen by psychologists. *Psychotherapy, 28*, 429–438.

Report of the Ethics Committee, 1989 and 1990. (1991). *American Psychologist, 46*, 750–757.

Robinson, W. L., & Reid, P. T. (1985). Sexual intimacies in psychology revisited. *Professional Psychology, 16*, 512–520.

Scarr, S. (1988). Race and gender as psychological variables: Social and ethical issues. *American Psychologist*, *43*, 56–59.

Sell, J. M., Gottlieb, M. C., & Schoenfeld, L. (1986). Ethical considerations of social/romantic relationships with present and former clients. *Professional Psychology: Research and Practice*, *17*, 504–508.

Shopland, S. N., & VandeCreek, L. (1991). Sex with ex-clients: Theoretical rationales for prohibition. *Ethics & Behavior*, *1*, 45–62.

Sieber, J. E. (1992). *Planning ethically responsible research*. Newbury Park, CA: Sage.

Simon, G. C. (1978). The psychologist as whistle blower: A case study. *Professional Psychology*, *9*, 322–340.

Singer, J. L. (1980). The scientific basis of psychotherapeutic practice: A question of values and ethics. *Psychotherapy: Theory, Research and Practice*, *17*, 372–383.

Sonne, J. L. (1987). Proscribed sex: Counseling the patient subjected to sexual intimacy by a therapist. *Medical Aspects of Human Sexuality*, *16*, 18–23.

Sonne, J. L. (1989). An example of group therapy for victims of therapist–client sexual intimacy. In G. O. Gabbard (Ed.), *Sexual exploitation in professional relationships* (pp. 101–127). Washington, DC: American Psychiatric Press.

Sonne, J., Meyer, C. B., Borys, D., & Marshall, V. (1985). Clients' reaction to sexual intimacy in therapy. *American Journal of Orthopsychiatry*, *55*, 183–189.

Sonne, J. L., & Pope, K. S. (1991). Treating victims of therapist–patient sexual involvement. *Psychotherapy*, *28*, 174–187.

Stanley, B., & Sieber, J. E. (1991). *The ethics of research on children and adolescents*. Newbury Park, CA: Sage.

Stricker, G., Davis-Russell, E., Bourg, E., Duran, E., Hammong, W. R., McHolland, J., Polite, K., & Vaughn, B. E. (Eds.). (1990). *Toward ethnic diversification in psychology education and training*. Washington, DC: American Psychological Association.

Stromberg, C. D., Haggarty, D. J., Leibenluft, R. F., McMillian, M. H., Mishkin, B., Rubin, B. L., & Trilling, H. R. (1988). *The psychologist's legal handbook*. Washington, DC: Council for the National Register of Health Service Providers in Psychology.

Tabachnick, B. G., Keith-Spiegel, P., & Pope, K. S. (1991). Ethics of teaching: Beliefs and behaviors of psychologists as educators. *American Psychologist*, *46*, 506–515.

Thoreau, H. D. (1960). *Walden and civil disobedience*. Boston: Houghton Mifflin. (*Civil disobedience* originally published 1849).

Vasquez, M. J. T. (1991). Sexual intimacies with clients after termination: Should a prohibition be explicit? *Ethics & Behavior*, *1*, 35–44.

Zimet, C. A. (1989). The mental health care revolution: Will psychology survive? *American Psychologist*, *44*, 703–708.

CHAPTER 2

HOW ETHICS ARE APPLIED

Suppose you share offices with a close friend and fellow clinician who, like you, is a member of APA. You discover that this office mate has terminated therapy with a female client after two sessions of behavior therapy and that, soon thereafter, he and she have begun a romantic relationship. What should you do? More, interestingly, what *would* you do? If you are like most colleagues, it is probable that you would be among the nearly one third who would not bring his conduct to the attention of any ethics body.

Assume now that you are a psychotherapist asked to consider whether, in the following situations, the psychologists involved acted ethically:

1. A state requires that an applicant for licensure complete 1,500 hours of postdoctoral experience under supervision before becoming eligible to take the licensure examination. An applicant and a licensed psychologist agree that the psychologist will attest in writing that the applicant has completed the requirement even though the applicant has had only 500 hours of supervised experience.
2. At a social gathering attended by people of many professions, a psychologist is overheard discussing one of her patients by name with two of her friends, a physician and an accountant, neither of whom are involved in the case.
3. A patient who has just begun treatment with you tells you that he terminated his professional relationship with his former therapist because the therapist consistently conducted treatment while under the influence of alcohol.

Is there any question that each of these three incidents describes behavior by psychologists that is clearly unethical? Would it surprise you, then, to discover that APA member psychotherapists do not universally agree that the conduct described in these realistic situations is unethical (Pope, Tabachnik, & Keith-Spiegel, 1987)? What about the finding that over 50% of 60 senior psychologists, all of whom had considerable experience with ethics issues, admitted to intentionally violating a law or a formal ethical principle regulating their professional practice (Pope & Bajt, 1988)?

These vignettes and data (or variants thereof) come from research presented throughout this chapter. They may be properly viewed as examples of deplorable and odious behavior. Then again, one could argue that in some instances, violating an ethical rule or even a state or federal law may evidence the proper exercise of professional discretion.

In any event, it is clear that knowledge of ethical provisions and legal rules do not inevitably lead to perfect conformity with these obligations. Thus, putting aside those few colleagues who meet the definition of sociopathy, what stimulates otherwise moral psychologists to take actions that directly contradict what they know they should do?

In some cases, psychologists may violate ethical principles because those principles are vaguely worded. For example, in some informal research, I asked experienced, licensed clinical psychologists to respond to 75 true–false items concerning ethical behavior. To the items I attached the 1989 APA code of ethics. The directions indicated that respondents could refer to the code at any time to answer the items. Yet, in no instance did any of the test takers answer more than 60% correctly.

One could hypothesize that these surprising results, although from an admittedly unsystematic study, show that the old APA ethics code was simply too ambiguous to guide respondents to the presumptively "correct" answer, and that was my guess. But even if an ethical code were written in perfectly clear language, there are plausible and understandable reasons why, at times, psychologists would deliberately violate ethical rules. One of those may be the psychologist's perception that violating the code will satisfy even higher moral values. Is it appropriate, however, for psychologists to engage in civil disobedience, following in the revered footsteps of Henry David Thoreau and Martin Luther King? Or are psychologists obligated to abide by their association's code of ethics and to seek to change those provisions they find objectionable through an orderly, though slow-moving, democratic process?

In this chapter, I explore such issues, providing a great many vignettes and dilemmas that should provoke discussion and debate and, thus, move the reader beyond merely learning ethical rules and procedural regulations to thinking about the meaning and value of a code of ethics. It is my guess, as well, that readers will leave this chapter with a sense of creative uncertainty. But they should not despair. Ideas for best dealing with this uncertainty follow in chapter 3.

References

Pope, K. S., & Bajt, T. R. (1988). When laws and values conflict: A dilemma for psychologists. *American Psychologist, 43,* 828–829.

Pope, K. S., Tabachnik, B. E., & Keith-Spiegel, P. (1987). Ethics of practice: The beliefs and behaviors of psychologists as therapists. *American Psychologist, 42,* 993–1006.

The Failure of Clinical Psychology Graduate Students to Apply Understood Ethical Principles

J. L. Bernard and Carmen S. Jara

. . . With any ethical violation there are two distinct elements that must be recognized: (a) the extent to which the ethical principle applicable to the situation in question is understandable, and (b) the degree of willingness to do what one understands should be done. Of these, it seems unlikely that a lack of understanding is ordinarily the basis for a violation. . . . Rather, in dealings with educated, highly intelligent professionals, it seems much more likely that the crux of the issue with ethical violations is an unwillingness to conform to the demands of the Ethical Principles. . . .

. . . Occasionally, when a psychologist is acting in an unethical manner, it becomes almost common knowledge within the professional community, but no one is willing to file a complaint. In off-the-record discussions, it is often apparent that those who could file the complaint are reluctant to do so out of a concern with possible repercussions (e.g., that it will damage personal or professional relationships with the violator). Butler and Zelen (1977) reported that those therapists who had become sexually involved with clients typically knew of other therapists who were also sexually involved with clients. . . . Yet, Ethical Principle 7(g)[1] clearly places the responsibility for confronting recognized violations squarely on the members of the profession. To ignore an ethical violation is, then, a violation in itself. In this article we report data on the willingness (or, more appropriately, the lack thereof) of graduate students to honor Principle 7(g) when faced with a hypothetical ethical violation by a fellow student who is also a friend.

METHOD
Questionnaire
Packets were distributed to a nationwide sample of clinical graduate students at APA-approved programs with a request that they be returned to the experimenter anonymously. Each packet consisted of an explanatory cover letter soliciting anonymous cooperation, two scenarios constructed to depict ethical violations, a demographic information sheet that the student could discard if he or she felt that it might compromise confidentiality (none did), a questionnaire on which the student would react to the scenarios, and a stamped envelope for the student to use in returning the packet.

In the first scenario, a clinical graduate student was depicted as being sexually involved with a client from a psychotherapy practicum. In the scenarios in half of the packets, the student therapist was female, and in the other half, male. In the second scenario (again balanced for sex) a clinical graduate student was characterized as a problem drinker/alcoholic who is manifesting poor judgment and erratic behavior in various clinical practica, but thus far concealing it from the clinical faculty. In each case, the reader was asked to assume that he or she had discovered the problem, and that the alleged violator was not only a fellow graduate student, but also a friend. Also, according to the scenarios, not only had the reader discovered the problem, but it had already led to one confrontation with the alleged violator that had not produced results. Two Ethical Principles involved, 2(f) and 6(a) (American Psychological Association, 1981), were then presented verbatim in order to eliminate recall

Adapted from *Professional Psychology: Research and Practice, 17,* 313–315. Copyright 1986 by the American Psychological Association.

[1] *Ed. note*: See Standards 8.04 and 8.05 of the APA's current (1992) Ethical Principles.

of the principles as a factor in students' deciding how to answer the questionnaire. These issues were dealt with in other principles as well (e.g., 7(d) prohibits the sexual exploitation of clients), but we felt that by our presenting 2(f) and 6(a), it was adequately clear that both scenarios described unethical acts. At this point the reader was asked two distinct questions. The first, "According to the Ethical Principles, what *should* you do?", was used to assess the degree of understanding that the described behavior constituted an ethical violation requiring some sort of action, and what that action should be. The second question, "Speaking pragmatically, and recognizing that he [she] is a friend and a fellow graduate student, what do you think you probably *would* do?" was used to assess the reader's willingness to do what he or she had already stated should be done. Each of these questions was followed by five possible responses to the situation. To illustrate, those for the problem-drinking/alcoholism scenario in which the student was male were (a) "Nothing"; (b) "Suggest he get help for this problem"; (c) "Keep trying to get him to stop drinking"; (d) "Tell him that if he doesn't get his drinking under control you will have to mention it to the Director of Clinical Training or his clinical supervisor"; and (e) "Tell the Director of Clinical Training or his clinical supervisor." We anticipated that essentially all students would recognize that each scenario depicted a violation that called for a particular course of action. However, we hypothesized that although most students would state a willingness to implement whatever course of action they felt was indicated, a significant number would admit that they would probably do something less than that. Thus the data to be analyzed was the difference between what the reader said should be done and what he or she would actually do if confronted with the situation described in the scenarios. We hypothesized further that to the extent that this was true, some of the demographic items (e.g., whether the student had had coursework in ethics, or the sex of the student who was violating the principles) might enable us to discriminate between these two groups.

As a manipulation check, these scenarios had earlier been presented to the members of a state ethics committee with a request that they respond only to

the question of what should be done. With the sexual scenario there was complete agreement that "Tell the Director of Clinical Training or the student's supervisor" was the appropriate response. With the problem-drinking/alcoholism scenario with a male student, 3 of 5 committee members gave this same reply, whereas 2 chose a response one step less severe ("Tell the student that if he doesn't get his drinking under control you will have to tell the Director of Clinical Training or his/her supervisor").

In the demographic questionnaire mentioned earlier, the student was asked to provide the usual information about age, sex, and so on, but we went beyond this to inquire whether the program led to a PhD or a PsyD, what year the student was in, the geographic location of the school, whether the reader had ever had a course in ethics or substance abuse or both, and whether the orientation of the program was best described as behavioral or psychodynamic.

Subjects

Materials for 10 graduate students were sent, with an explanatory cover letter, to each of 25 clinic directors in APA-approved graduate clinical training programs. . . . In the cover letter we asked the clinic directors to distribute the packets to clinical graduate students, attempting to balance for sex and year in the program. The potential return was 250 questionnaires, and the first mailing resulted in 162 returns. Although these returns were anonymous, it was usually possible, from postmarks on the return envelopes, for us to guess which schools had (and had not) responded to the first mailing. For those few who seemed not to have sent any replies within a month, a second mailing was sent with a cover letter in which we explained that it was difficult to be certain, but it appeared that there had been no replies from that school, and we again solicited cooperation. This second mailing prompted 8 additional returns, which made a total of 170.

RESULTS

The 170 questionnaires returned represent a response rate of 68%. First, we analyzed the data by obtaining percentages of clinical graduate students who stated that they would do the same thing that they had already said they should do, and those who stated that they would do something less than they had already stated they should do. (There were no instances of subjects who said that they would do more than they should.) With the sexual scenario, the split was even: 50% said that they would do what they had already said they should do, and 50% said that they would do less. Applying the binomial expansion to these two groups provides a significant normal approximation to distribution of proportions, $Z(1) = 17.39$, $p < .0001$. With the problem-drinking/alcoholism scenario, 45% of the students said that they would do what they had already stated they should do, and the remaining 55% said that they would do less (again, no one said that they would do more). A comparison of these two groups with the same statistic was also highly significant, $Z(1) = 19.94$, $p < .0001$.

After these analyses had been completed, several multivariate analyses of variance were performed on the demographic and scenario (e.g., sex of violator) variables; again, those students who stated that they would do what they had already said they should do were compared with those who said that they would do less. No significant differences were obtained for any demographic or scenario variables.

DISCUSSION

In this study we did not assess whether graduate clinical students would conform to some abstract standard for ethical behavior when confronted with an hypothetical violation. Rather, we first asked the student what should be done, and then whether the student would do that or something else. In this way, each student indicated his or her own understanding of how the Ethical Principle pertinent to each scenario should be applied, and then whether that understanding would result in appropriate behavior. For both scenarios, at least half of the students stated that they would not live up to their own interpretation of what the Ethical Principles required of them as professionals. Most simply put, this amounts to saying, "I know what I should do as an ethical psychologist, but I wouldn't do it."

The fact that no significant differences were obtained between these two groups of students on any of the demographic variables suggests that factors such as how far along the student was in training,

whether coursework had been taken in ethics or in substance abuse (most respondents had taken a course on ethics), and so on, had no apparent bearing on willingness to put Ethical Principles into action. This may imply that training in ethics is inadequate, or that a willingness to take action when confronted with an ethical violation that involves a colleague/friend is not something that can be taught. Indeed, one fourth-year student who had had coursework in both ethics and substance abuse stated that for both scenarios he believed that he should "Tell the Director of Clinical Training or the student's supervisor"; yet, to the question "What *would* you do?" he replied "Nothing" both times. It seems that psychologists may be teaching the content of the principles without at the same time adequately communicating the importance of their implementation. Furthermore, it seems reasonable (although it remains an empirical question at this point) that these results might generalize to professional psychologists.

Baldick (1980), using the same type of scenario format as we did, found among a sample of clinical psychology interns that those who had had training in ethics were significantly better at understanding ethical dilemmas than were those who had not. Schwitzgebel and Kirkland (1980) observed that

> Most ethical codes are vaguely formulated and rarely enforced. . . . They provide almost no specific and tangible guidance to either practitioner or scientist. (p. 3)

All of this points to a need for a thorough, formal, and systematic approach to training in ethics so that the student will understand what the principles demand of the profession. Yet, our data indicate that although such training is important, the problem is not simply that the Ethical Principles "are vaguely formulated" or "provide almost no guidance." The subjects in this study seemed to understand the ethics of their chosen profession; they simply chose not to apply them in a hypothetical situation involving a peer/friend.

Clearly, there is a problem among those who are training for the profession (and one that may equally well apply to those already practicing). That problem is not how to communicate the ethical principles to students more effectively, but rather how to motivate them to implement principles that they apparently understand quite well. . . .

References

American Psychological Association. (1981). *Ethical standards of psychologists*. Washington, DC: Author.

Baldick, T. L. (1980). Ethical discrimination ability of intern psychologists: A function of training in ethics. *Professional Psychology, 11,* 276–282.

Butler, S., & Zelen, S. L. (1977). Sexual intimacies between therapists and patients. *Psychotherapy: Theory, Research and Practice, 14,* 139–145.

Schwitzgebel, R. L., & Kirkland, R. (1980). *Law and psychological practice*. New York: Wiley.

◆ ◆ ◆

Commentary: Bernard and his colleagues (1987) replicated the preceding study with a sample of members belonging to Division 12 (Clinical) of APA. See Bernard, J. L., Murphy, M., & Little, M. (1987). The failure of clinical psychologists to apply understood ethical principles. Professional Psychology: Research and Practice, 18, 489–491. The scenarios in this study were the same as in Bernard and Jara's (1986) study except that in the first scenario the therapist was a male doctoral-level clinician, and in the second the therapist was a female doctoral-level clinician. Bernard et al. (1987) reported the following results (pp. 490–491):

> First, we analyzed the data by obtaining percentages of (a) clinicians who stated that they would do the same thing that they had already stated they should do and (b) those who said that they would do something less than that. Interestingly, 3 subjects said they would do more than they felt they should do. These were treated as if they had said they would do what they felt they should do.
>
> With the sexual scenario, 63% of clinicians responding said that they would do what they felt they should do, and 37% said that they would do less than they felt they should do. Applying the binomial expansion to these data provides a significant normal approximation to distribution of propor-

tions: $Z(1) = 9.08$, $p < .001$. With the problem-drinking/alcoholism scenario, 74% of the clinicians responding said that they would do what they had already said they should do, whereas 26% said that they would do less. A comparison of these two groups with the same statistic was also highly significant: $Z(1) = 9.96$, $p < .001$. . . .

> . . . [W]e did not attempt to explore whether clinical psychologists would conform to some abstract standard of ethical behavior when confronted with a hypothetical ethical violation. Rather, as was done earlier with clinical graduate students (Bernard & Jara, 1986), the clinician was simply asked what should be done and then whether he or she would do that or something else. Thus each clinician first indicated his or her own understanding of how the Ethical Principles should be applied and then whether he or she would actually take action appropriate to that understanding.

> When clinical graduate students were surveyed in this manner (Bernard & Jara, 1986), about the same results were obtained with each scenario. Approximately half of the students said that they would do less than they knew they should do whether the violation involved alcoholism or sex. This was not the case with clinical psychologists. With the problem-drinking/alcoholism scenario, 25% of the clinicians said that they would do less than their understanding of Ethical Principles demanded of them. However, with the sexual scenario, one third of the clinicians would not live up to their understanding of what should be done. This is even more puzzling when one considers that although the problem-drinking/alcoholism scenario requires that the reader interpret the Ethical Principles as they apply to impaired psychologists, sexual intimacies with patients are flatly described as unethical. . . . [I]t is apparent from this survey that although professionals

say that they would behave more responsibly than do graduate students, significant numbers of clinical psychologists simply would not do what they know they should do when confronted with an ethical violation by a colleague. Still, it is perhaps encouraging that the proportion of clinicians who would "do the right thing" is substantially higher than obtained with graduate students. This may reflect an increased awareness among professionals that even though reporting the unethical behavior of a colleague is personally repugnant, it is an ethical obligation and should benefit the profession in the long run.

As with the graduate students (Bernard & Jara, 1986), there were no significant differences, on any demographic variable, between those clinicians who would do what they felt they should do and those who would not. This suggests that the decision to report the unethical behavior of a colleague is a matter of personal values to a large extent. Yet, it seems that if psychology is to prosper, the ethics of the profession must be taken more seriously by the large numbers of clinicians who are not willing to report the unethical behavior of a colleague. The problem is, then, how our profession can motivate more clinicians to implement the Ethical Principles that they understand quite well.

It may be that a different thrust is needed in the teaching of ethics in graduate programs. It is vitally important that students learn that the function of an ethics committee is to help violators change their unethical behavior, using rehabilitative rather than punitive means whenever possible. It is also important that they come to recognize that their own professional self-interest is protected by their willingness to behave ethically and to report those psychologists who do not. It seems probable, in retrospect, that if more of us had been willing to report those instances of unethical conduct of which we were aware, our malpractice premiums might be lower today. Undoubtedly it would be naive to expect that every psychologist will behave in a moral and ethical manner. There will always be those members of every group who are unwilling to conform to the mores of the group. However, when one fourth to one third of those clinicians surveyed in this study admit that they would not deal appropriately with a colleague's unethical behavior, there is a lot of room for improvement.

In a more recent study, graduate students were confronted with items that identified ethical improprieties by their peers, such as breaching confidentiality or becoming romantically involved with clients (entering "dual relationships"). Twenty-five percent of the students indicated that they would do nothing. Only 3% said that they would contact an outside agency. On the other hand, 47% said they would consult other students about the problem, 31% would express concerns directly to the faculty, and 28% would directly confront their unethical colleagues. Interestingly, faculty underestimated the extent to which their students would take any action. Nevertheless, although students deserve more credit than their teachers give them and, in many instances, "indicate that their feelings of ethical obligation . . . outweigh sentiments of loyalty to problematic peers" (Mearns & Allen, 1991, p. 198), a great deal of impaired performance and unethical behavior remains unattended to. See Mearns, J., & Allen, G. J. (1991). Graduate students' experiences in dealing with impaired peers, compared with faculty predictions: An exploratory study. Ethics and Behavior, 1, 191–202.

Ethics of Practice: The Beliefs and Behaviors of Psychologists as Therapists

Kenneth S. Pope, Barbara G. Tabachnick, and Patricia Keith-Spiegel

The American Psychological Association (APA) has developed elaborate ethical principles and standards of practice to guide the behavior of its membership. . . . However, we still lack comprehensive, systematically gathered data about the degree to which members believe in or comply with these guidelines. Consequently, such data are not available to inform either the clinical decisions of individual practitioners or the attempts of the APA to revise, refine, and extend formal standards of practice.

No implication is intended that norms are the equivalent of ethical standards. In many situations, the formulation and dissemination of formal standards are intended to increase ethical awareness and to improve the behaviors of a professional association. . . . But those who are charged with developing, disseminating, and enforcing professional codes can function much more effectively if they are aware of the diverse dilemmas confronting the membership and of the membership's varied personal codes and behaviors.

METHOD

Survey Questionnaire

A survey questionnaire, a cover letter, and a return envelope were sent to 1,000 psychologists (500 men and 500 women) randomly selected from the 4,684 members of Division 29 (Psychotherapy) as listed in the 1985 *Directory of the American Psychological Association* (APA, 1985).

The survey questionnaire was divided into three main parts.[1] The first part consisted of a list of 83 behaviors. Participants were asked to rate each of the 83 behaviors in terms of three categories [footnote omitted]. First, to what extent had they engaged in the behavior in their practice? Participants either could indicate that the behavior was *not applicable* to their practice or they could rate the behavior's occurrence in their practice as *never, rarely, sometimes, fairly often,* or *very often*. Second, to what extent did they consider the practice ethical? In rating whether each behavior was ethical, participants could use five categories: *unquestionably not, under rare circumstances, don't know/not sure, under any circumstances,* and *unquestionably yes.*

RESULTS

Demographic Characteristics of the Participants and Ratings of the 83 Behaviors

Questionnaires were returned by 456 respondents (45.6%). . . . Table 3 presents the percentage of respondents' ratings for each of the 83 behaviors in terms of occurrence in their own practice and the degree to which they believe the behavior to be ethical. . . .

Behaviors Systematically Related to Sex of Psychologist

In order to assess the degree to which male and female psychologists might be differentially engaging in the 83 behaviors, chi-square analyses were performed on these data. To help eliminate seemingly significant findings actually due to chance—in light of the large number of analyses—a very strict significance level ($p < .001$) was used. Table 6 presents the items significantly related to sex, using this criterion.

---

[1] Only results from the first part of the study are described in this excerpt.

TABLE 3

Percentage of Psychologists (N = 465) Responding in Each Category

	Rating										
	Occurrence in Your Practice?						Ethical?				
Item	1	2	3	4	5ª	NA	1	2	3	4	5ª
1. Becoming social friends with a former client	42.1	45.2	9.2	1.8	1.1	0.7	6.4	51.1	13.4	21.9	6.8
2. Charging a client no fee for therapy	33.3	47.4	15.8	1.1	1.8	2.9	4.6	25.2	14.5	24.8	29.6
3. Providing therapy to one of your friends	70.4	25.2	2.2	0.2	0.7	2.2	47.6	40.1	2.9	4.4	3.7
4. Advertising in newspapers or similar media	72.4	13.2	10.1	2.4	0.4	5.5	12.9	14.7	17.8	33.3	20.6
5. Limiting treatment notes to name, date, and fee	48.2	18.4	13.8	6.6	12.1	1.5	18.6	22.4	21.7	20.8	14.7
6. Filing an ethics complaint against a colleague	61.6	25.2	7.5	0.7	1.1	10.7	2.4	11.8	3.1	22.8	57.9
7. Telling a client you are angry at him or her	9.6	45.0	36.8	5.7	2.2	0.7	3.1	26.8	8.3	35.5	25.4
8. Using a computerized test interpretation service	39.0	21.7	20.8	7.9	7.5	13.2	2.0	9.0	12.9	39.3	34.9
9. Hugging a client	13.4	44.5	29.8	7.7	4.2	0.2	4.6	41.2	8.3	35.5	9.2
10. Terminating therapy if client cannot pay	36.2	36.2	20.0	3.7	2.0	5.3	12.1	27.4	15.4	32.7	11.0
11. Accepting services from a client in lieu of fee	66.9	27.0	3.5	0.2	0.4	7.9	22.6	39.3	14.5	16.0	6.4
12. Seeing a minor client without parental consent	65.8	22.4	5.5	0.2	0.7	14.0	23.5	45.6	13.4	11.6	3.7
13. Having clients take tests (e.g., MMPI) at home	43.9	27.0	16.0	4.8	3.5	10.7	20.2	25.9	19.5	22.1	10.1
14. Altering a diagnosis to meet insurance criteria	36.4	26.5	27.0	5.5	2.6	2.9	37.3	28.9	16.0	14.0	2.0
15. Telling client: "I'm sexually attracted to you."	78.5	16.2	3.5	0.2	0.2	4.8	51.5	33.1	5.5	6.8	2.4
16. Refusing to let clients read their chart notes	33.1	21.3	13.6	5.7	14.9	23.2	14.5	28.3	14.9	21.5	16.0
17. Using a collection agency to collect late fees	48.0	21.9	19.7	5.9	1.8	8.6	5.0	15.1	15.6	35.5	27.4
18. Breaking confidentiality if client is homicidal	15.6	9.6	6.6	24.6	17.3	35.7	1.1	5.0	3.5	18.9	69.1
19. Performing forensic work for a contingency fee	67.3	7.0	6.8	0.9	0.7	42.1	35.5	11.0	29.8	7.0	10.3
20. Using self-disclosure as a therapy technique	5.9	22.1	38.6	19.7	12.9	0.7	2.2	17.1	7.9	43.0	29.2
21. Inviting clients to an office open house	76.3	9.6	5.0	0.7	2.0	19.3	28.9	25.7	23.2	12.1	8.3
22. Accepting a client's gift worth at least $50	72.1	19.1	2.4	0.4	0.0	16.7	34.2	36.2	15.8	8.6	3.3
23. Working when too distressed to be effective	38.8	48.5	10.5	0.4	0.2	5.3	46.7	38.4	8.6	4.4	1.3
24. Accepting only male or female clients	83.8	3.7	2.4	0.2	1.1	18.2	11.0	16.2	18.6	16.9	34.6
25. Not allowing client access to testing report	45.0	23.5	13.6	5.9	6.6	14.3	21.7	32.9	14.0	20.6	8.8
26. Raising the fee during the course of therapy	27.6	23.9	29.4	11.8	5.7	3.5	8.3	15.8	13.2	32.5	28.9
27. Breaking confidentiality if client is suicidal	16.2	24.6	25.0	9.6	19.3	11.8	2.0	10.1	5.5	23.5	57.5
28. Not allowing clients access to raw test data	32.2	10.5	9.0	7.9	30.0	1.8	12.1	12.9	11.2	22.8	36.8

(table continues)

TABLE 3 (*cont.*)

	Rating										
	Occurrence in Your Practice?						Ethical?				
Item	1	2	3	4	5[a]	NA	1	2	3	4	5[a]
29. Allowing a client to run up a large unpaid bill	12.5	44.1	34.4	5.7	1.5	2.9	7.2	35.3	22.8	16.9	16.4
30. Accepting goods (rather than money) as payment	65.1	24.8	6.4	0.2	0.4	12.7	15.8	33.8	21.3	18.2	9.6
31. Using sexual surrogates with clients	81.8	5.7	1.1	0.7	0.2	33.1	36.2	25.7	23.7	8.6	4.6
32. Breaking confidentiality to report child abuse	25.0	16.2	15.1	8.3	22.6	29.4	1.3	4.4	5.3	20.8	64.9
33. Inviting clients to a party or social event	82.9	13.2	2.2	0.2	0.4	4.6	50.0	34.0	8.1	6.1	1.5
34. Addressing client by his or her first name	2.0	2.6	9.4	20.8	65.1	0	0.7	0.9	2.6	30.7	65.1
35. Crying in the presence of a client	42.5	41.5	12.5	1.8	0.7	4.6	5.9	32.0	14.5	18.4	27.6
36. Earning a salary which is a % of client's fee	46.3	4.4	10.1	3.5	5.3	41.0	12.1	8.1	34.2	16.0	16.4
37. Asking favors (e.g., a ride home) from clients	60.5	35.7	2.4	0	0.2	5.0	27.0	45.2	12.3	10.1	4.4
38. Making custody evaluation without seeing the child	76.8	7.2	1.3	0.2	0.2	36.0	64.0	22.8	5.3	2.4	0.9
39. Accepting a client's decision to commit suicide	73.9	16.4	3.7	0.4	0	15.4	45.2	36.6	8.8	4.8	2.9
40. Refusing to disclose a diagnosis to a client	49.8	30.9	10.1	4.6	2.4	4.2	21.5	43.2	13.2	13.4	6.8
41. Leading nude group therapy or "growth" groups	88.6	2.2	0.9	0.2	0	24.3	59.6	16.4	14.9	3.9	2.9
42. Telling clients of your disappointment in them	46.9	39.0	11.4	1.1	0.4	2.6	19.7	37.1	18.0	15.4	7.9
43. Discussing clients (without names) with friends	22.8	46.3	22.4	5.7	2.0	0.9	32.9	38.6	13.8	9.4	4.6
44. Providing therapy to your student or supervisee	63.8	22.4	6.8	0.9	0.9	12.3	45.8	33.6	6.1	8.8	4.2
45. Giving gifts to those who refer clients to you	78.5	11.4	7.0	1.5	1.1	4.2	47.8	21.7	15.6	10.3	4.2
46. Using a law suit to collect fees from clients	62.7	21.3	10.3	0.2	0.4	15.4	10.1	28.3	19.3	19.7	21.1
47. Becoming sexually involved with a former client	88.2	10.5	0.4	0	0.2	7.5	50.2	34.4	7.2	3.9	3.3
48. Avoiding certain clients for fear of being sued	48.9	30.3	13.4	1.3	0.9	13.8	7.9	23.0	23.7	23.9	19.7
49. Doing custody evaluation without seeing both parents	63.8	16.9	6.6	0.7	0.2	30.5	47.1	31.6	10.7	3.9	2.6
50. Lending money to a client	73.7	23.9	1.5	0	0	4.4	40.6	38.8	10.7	5.9	3.3
51. Providing therapy to one of your employees	79.6	12.9	2.0	0	0.7	15.6	55.0	31.1	6.8	2.9	2.4
52. Having a client address you by your first name	3.5	10.5	21.9	21.9	41.9	0.4	1.3	3.3	7.9	23.5	63.6
53. Sending holiday greeting cards to your clients	61.4	16.2	12.9	3.1	4.8	5.3	10.5	12.9	26.8	20.4	28.5
54. Kissing a client	70.8	23.5	4.4	0.2	0.4	2.2	48.0	36.6	4.6	7.7	2.2
55. Engaging in erotic activity with a client	97.1	2.4	0.2	0	0	3.9	95.0	3.5	0.4	0.4	0.4
56. Giving a gift worth at least $50 to a client	95.0	3.7	0.4	0	0	4.6	69.7	16.0	8.1	2.9	2.6

(table continues)

	Rating										
	Occurrence in Your Practice?						**Ethical?**				
Item	**1**	**2**	**3**	**4**	**5**[a]	**NA**	**1**	**2**	**3**	**4**	**5**[a]
57. Accepting a client's invitation to a party	59.6	34.9	4.4	0.2	0.4	2.9	25.7	46.1	10.1	10.7	6.8
58. Engaging in sex with a clinical supervisee	95.0	2.9	0.4	0	0	8.8	85.1	9.0	3.5	1.5	0.2
59. Going to client's special event (e.g., wedding)	23.5	50.7	20.4	3.3	1.5	0.4	5.3	34.0	13.8	28.7	17.5
60. Getting paid to refer clients to someone	98.0	0.4	0.2	0	0	7.2	88.4	7.2	3.3	0	0.2
61. Going into business with a client	95.6	1.5	0.2	0	0.2	9.9	78.5	12.7	5.5	1.1	1.1
62. Engaging in sexual contact with a client	97.8	1.5	0.4	0	0	4.2	96.1	2.6	0.2	0.7	0.2
63. Utilizing involuntary hospitalization	30.5	42.1	16.7	2.4	1.1	17.1	3.1	28.9	8.8	24.3	31.8
64. Selling goods to clients	90.6	5.9	2.0	0	0.4	7.5	71.1	18.4	4.4	2.9	2.0
65. Giving personal advice on radio, t.v., etc.	66.0	18.6	9.2	1.5	0.2	18.6	18.4	28.3	22.1	23.7	6.4
66. Being sexually attracted to a client	9.2	38.8	43.9	5.5	1.3	1.1	11.2	11.0	19.5	19.1	33.3
67. Unintentionally disclosing confidential data	36.0	58.6	3.3	0	0	2.9	75.2	14.3	4.6	1.8	1.8
68. Allowing a client to disrobe	94.5	2.9	1.5	0	0	5.0	81.4	12.1	3.1	1.5	1.3
69. Borrowing money from a client	97.1	1.8	0	0	0	4.4	86.2	10.7	1.1	0.4	0.9
70. Discussing a client (by name) with friends	91.2	7.5	0.4	0.2	0	3.5	94.5	3.5	0.7	0.4	0.4
71. Providing services outside areas of competence	74.8	22.8	1.8	0	0	2.0	80.7	16.9	0.2	0.9	0.7
72. Signing for hours a supervisee has not earned	89.0	7.2	0.9	0	0	9.9	92.5	5.5	0.4	0.4	0.7
73. Treating homosexuality per se as pathological	75.0	12.7	6.4	2.6	1.8	4.4	55.7	12.9	17.3	6.6	5.3
74. Doing therapy while under influence of alcohol	92.8	5.7	0.2	0	0	3.5	89.5	7.7	1.1	0	0.9
75. Engaging in sexual fantasy about a client	27.0	46.3	22.4	2.4	0.7	3.5	18.9	15.1	26.8	13.2	21.9
76. Accepting a gift worth less than $5 from a client	8.6	31.8	45.0	9.4	3.7	0.7	5.0	20.0	16.2	36.4	20.2
77. Offering or accepting a handshake from a client	1.3	3.3	17.5	28.1	48.2	1.1	0.7	1.1	3.3	21.7	71.9
78. Disrobing in the presence of a client	97.8	0.9	0	0.2	0.2	4.6	94.7	3.3	0	0.2	0.7
79. Charging for missed appointments	11.8	15.4	26.3	22.6	22.6	2.4	1.1	6.8	7.2	38.2	45.8
80. Going into business with a former client	83.1	10.1	2.0	0	0.4	15.6	36.8	28.9	17.5	9.0	5.9
81. Directly soliciting a person to be a client	89.3	8.6	0.9	0	0.2	4.4	67.5	22.6	5.7	1.8	1.5
82. Being sexually attracted to a client	9.2	39.5	41.0	6.1	0.9	1.3	9.2	13.4	21.9	18.0	30.0
83. Helping client file complaint re a colleague	52.9	19.4	9.4	1.1	1.1	20.0	6.4	22.6	14.9	29.2	25.2

Note. Rating codes: Occurrence in your practice? 1 = never, 2 = rarely, 3 = sometimes, 4 = fairly often, 5 = very often, NA = not applicable; Ethical? 1 = unquestionably not, 2 = under rare circumstances, 3 = don't know/not sure, 4 = under many circumstances, 5 = unquestionably yes.
[a]Responses 1 through 5 sum to less than 100% due to missing data.

TABLE 6

Items Significantly Related to Sex ($p < .001$)

Item	Direction	χ^2	df
9. Hugging a client	Female more likely	18.70	4
15. Telling a client: "I'm sexually attracted to you."	Male more likely	16.29	2
52. Having a client address you by your first name	Female more likely	20.00	4
73. Treating homosexuality per se as pathological	Male more likely	19.26	4
75. Engaging in sexual fantasy about a client	Male more likely	40.39	4
81. Directly soliciting a person to be a client	Male more likely	11.24	1

DISCUSSION

Relationship Between Behavior and Beliefs

The data suggest that the psychologists' behavior was generally in accordance with their ethical beliefs. This inference is based on the fact that for all but four items, the frequency with which the respondents reported engaging in a behavior was less than the frequency of instances in which the behavior was ethical in their judgment. Of the four exceptions, three involved confidentiality: "discussing a client (by name) with friends," "discussing clients (without names) with friends," and "unintentionally disclosing confidential data." The fourth exception was "providing services outside areas of competence."

Behaviors That Are Almost Universal

For 7 of the 83 items, at least 90% of the respondents indicated that they engaged in the behavior, at least on rare occasions (see Table 3). Two of these almost universal behaviors involved self-disclosure to the clients: "using self-disclosure as a therapy technique" and "telling a client that you are angry at him or her." Thus, it appears that the more extreme versions of the therapist as "blank screen" are exceedingly rare among psychologists. Similarly, the models of the therapist as a distant, almost stand-offish authority figure—which, like the "blank screen" approach, are derived from the classical psychoanalytic

tradition—are infrequently practiced. Fewer than 10% of the respondents indicated that they never engaged in "having a client address you by your first name" (as Table 6 shows, it is mainly male therapists who insist on being addressed by their last names), "addressing your client by his or her first name," "accepting a gift worth less than $5 from a client," and "offering or accepting a handshake from a client." Finally, only 9.2% of the respondents indicated that they had never been sexually attracted to a client. . . .

Behaviors That Are Rare

One of the most surprising results was that only 1.9% of the respondents reported engaging in sexual contact with a client and that only 2.6% reported engaging in erotic activity (which may or may not involve actual contact) with a client. Previously, there have been three national surveys of sexual intimacies between psychologists and their patients. Holroyd and Brodsky (1977) reported 7.7% respondents "who answered positively any of the questions regarding erotic-contact behaviors or intercourse during treatment." Pope, Levenson, and Schover (1979) found that 7% of the therapists in their survey reported engaging in sexual contact with their clients. Pope et al. (1986) reported that 6.5% of their respondents acknowledged engaging in sexual intimacies with clients.

It is difficult to explain the discrepancy between the current findings and those of the previous three studies. It may be that respondents are now less willing to admit, even on anonymous survey, to a behavior that is a felony in some states, or it may be that these findings are reflective of random sampling error or bias in return rate rather than of a change in behavior.

However, the current findings may indicate an actual decrease in the percentage of psychologists engaging in sexual intimacies with their patients. The increasing publicity given to the Therapist–Patient Sex Syndrome (Pope, 1985, 1986) and other devastating consequences of therapist–patient sexual intimacy (Bouhoutsos, Holroyd, Lerman, Forer, & Greenberg, 1983; Feldman-Summers & Jones, 1984; Pope & Bouhoutsos, 1986), as well as the vivid first-person accounts of patients who have been sexually involved with their therapists (Freeman & Roy, 1976; Plaisil, 1985; Walker & Young, 1986), may be significantly altering the behavior of psychologists who are tempted in this area. Clinical strategies developed to help therapists at risk to refrain from sexual contact with their patients may also be contributing to this decline (Pope, in press).

Some other items concerning sexual behaviors—such as nudity as part of therapy or using sexual surrogates with clients—also had extremely low rates. Engaging in sex with a clinical supervisee was reported by only 3.4% of the respondents. This figure corresponds closely to the 4.0% in a prior survey of APA Division 29 members who reported engaging in sexual intimacies with their clinical supervisees (Pope et al., 1979).

Dishonesty in helping candidates to become degreed or licensed without the requisite supervised experience is relatively rare; it was reported by 8.1%.

A number of the rare practices concerned financial or business practices, such as borrowing money from a client, selling goods to clients, going into business with a client, or giving a gift worth at least $50 to a client. The most infrequently reported behavior was getting paid to refer clients to someone (0.6%). It is heartening to note that psychologists are not putting their judgment and influence up for sale.

Although over a fourth (26.1%) of the respondents advertise in newspapers and similar media, only 9.7% report directly soliciting a person to be a client. As Table 6 indicates, men were more likely than women to engage in this practice.

Few psychologists blatantly breach the confidentiality of their clients. However, 8.1% have discussed a client (by name) with friends.

Doing therapy while under the influence of alcohol is also rare (5.9%).

For the most part, psychologists are careful to interview the child when making a custody evaluation, although 8.9% fail to do so.

A gender-based criterion for admission to treatment is rare. Accepting only male or female clients was reported by 7.4%.

Although rare, some of these practices—such as discussing clients by name with friends or doing therapy while under the influence of alcohol—so clearly undermine the rights and welfare of patients

that they need to be addressed much more forcefully and effectively by the profession.

Difficult Judgments

We defined a difficult judgment as one in which at least 20% of the respondents indicated "don't know/not sure." There were 12 behaviors that posed difficult judgments in terms of whether they were ethical: "performing forensic work for a contingency fee," "accepting goods (rather than money) as payment," "using sexual surrogates with clients," "earning a salary which is a percentage of client fees," "avoiding certain clients for fear of being sued," "sending holiday greeting cards to your clients," "giving personal advice on radio, t.v., etc.," "engaging in sexual fantasy about a client," "being sexually attracted to a client," "limiting treatment notes to name, date, and fee," "inviting clients to an office open house," and "allowing a client to run up a large unpaid bill." It is interesting that one third of these directly concerned financial issues, and one fourth concerned sexual issues. The profession may need to develop practical guidelines in these areas.

Topic Areas

Redlich and Pope (1980) have suggested seven principles for meaningfully coordinating ethical guidelines with other standards of professional practice in a way that can be most useful to psychologists and psychiatrists attempting to carry out their professional tasks responsibly. These are (1) above all, do no harm; (2) practice only with competence; (3) do not exploit; (4) treat people with respect for their dignity as human beings; (5) protect confidentiality; (6) act, except in the most extreme instances, only after obtaining informed consent; and (7) practice, insofar as possible, within the framework of social equity and justice. . . . This seven-part framework organizes the following discussion of the questionnaire items.

1. Do no harm.

Lending money to a client. It is ironic that lending money to a client—an act that might seem to be generous and helpful—would be viewed as so harmful to the therapeutic enterprise as to be clearly unethical by 40.6% of the respondents and unethical under most circumstances by an additional 38.8%. Nevertheless, about one fourth of the respondents acknowledged that they had lent money to a client (23.9% rarely; 1.5% sometimes).

Signing for unearned hours. A clear majority (92.5%) believe that signing for hours that a supervisee has not earned is unethical. Producing graduates and licensees whose credentials were fraudulently obtained may subject numerous future clients to harm.

Filing ethics complaints. The injunction to do no harm can be construed to include the mandate not to remain passively acquiescent when fellow professionals are violating ethical principles and standards of practice. A surprising finding was that one fourth of the respondents reported that they had, on a rare basis, filed an ethics complaint against a colleague. An additional 9.3% reported that they did so more frequently.

The view that it is unethical always (2.4%) or under most circumstances (11.8%) to file an ethical complaint against a colleague may reflect the difficulties experienced by an association (the APA) charged with the task of promoting the profession when it also attempts to monitor and discipline the behavior of its members. Furthermore, the practical steps for effective peer monitoring may need to be more widely disseminated (see Keith-Spiegel & Koocher, 1985).

Helping a client file an ethics complaint was a behavior performed by over one third of the respondents on a rare (19.4%) or more frequent (11.6%) basis. Over one fourth believed that this action was unethical (6.4%) or unethical under most circumstances (22.6%). . . .

2. Practice only with competence.

Providing services outside areas of competence. Both the *Ethical Principles of Psychologists* (APA, 1981a) and the *Specialty Guidelines for the Delivery of Services by Clinical Psychologists* (APA, 1981b) make clear statements that psychologists are to practice only within the limits of demonstrable expertise. Nevertheless, almost one fourth of the respondents indicated that they had practiced outside their area of competence either rarely (22.8%) or sometimes (1.8%).

Impaired performance. Psychology has turned increased attention to the impaired or distressed professional (Kilburg, Nathan, & Thoreson, 1986; Laliotis & Grayson, 1985). The results of this survey suggest that those efforts are needed. Over half (59.6%) of the respondents acknowledged having worked—either rarely or more often—when too distressed to be effective. About 1 out of every 15 or 20 (5.7%) respondents acknowledged, on a rare basis, doing therapy while under the influence of alcohol.

Competence in carrying out assessments. In the area of assessment, what seem like efficient and competent short-cuts or innovative strategies to some may seem questionable to others. Sending tests home with clients is said, by its advocates, to be more convenient and to allow clients to fill out the test in more familiar, less stressful surroundings. Critics of the practice argue that psychologists should monitor the administration of such tests—for example, to prevent clients from relying on the advice of friends and family about how to fill out the test. Furthermore, maintain the critics, should the test results become part of important legal proceedings, the psychologist would be unable to testify that the test responses were those of the client unaided by friends or family. The current study indicates that over half of the respondents send such tests home with clients either on a rare (27.0%) or more frequent (24.3%) basis. This practice is viewed as unethical by 20.2% and unethical in most circumstances by 25.9%.

The use of computerized psychological test interpretations has been harshly criticized (Matarazzo, 1986) but seems to have been accepted by the APA, which has issued guidelines for their use (APA, 1986). The current findings indicate that a majority of the respondents have used such services either rarely (21.7%) or more often (36.2%). Few believe that they are unethical (2.0%) or unethical under most circumstances (9.0%).

The literature in the field of child-custody conflicts indicates that a competent custody evaluation cannot be conducted without interviewing both parents. Shapiro (1984), for example, wrote that "under no circumstances should a report on child custody be rendered to the court, based on the evaluation of only one party to the conflict" (p. 99). About half of the respondents agree that doing a custody evaluation without seeing both parents is unethical. Only 16.9% reported that they had done this rarely, 7.5% more frequently.

3. Do not exploit.

Sexual issues and physical contact. As mentioned earlier, the rates of sexual contact and erotic activities with patients are significantly lower than in the three previously reported national studies of psychologists. Over 95% of the respondents believed that both of these behaviors were unethical.

About half of the respondents believed that becoming sexually involved with a *former* client was unethical. (This figure may be compared to the 6.4% who believe that becoming friends with a former client is unethical.) These beliefs seem consistent with the harm associated with these relationships (Pope & Bouhoutsos, 1986), with the awarding of general and punitive damages in malpractice suits in which the sexual intimacies occurred only after termination (e.g., *Whitesell v. Green*, 1973), and with a multiyear study of the adjudications of state licensing boards and state ethics committees (Sell, Gottlieb, & Schoenfeld, 1986). The study found "that psychologists asserting that a sexual relationship had occurred only after the termination of the therapeutic relationship were more likely to be found in violation than those not making that claim" (p. 504). . . .

The focus on erotic contact in therapy has raised questions about the legitimacy and effects of ostensibly nonerotic physical contact (Geller, 1980; Holroyd & Brodsky, 1977, 1980). Holroyd and Brodsky (1980) pointed out that it "is difficult to determine where 'non-erotic hugging, kissing, and affectionate touching' leave off and 'erotic contact' begins" (p. 810). About one fourth of our respondents reported kissing their clients, either rarely (23.5%) or more often (5.0%). About half viewed this practice as unethical. An additional 36.6% believed it to be unethical in most circumstances.

Hugging clients was practiced by 44.5% of the respondents on a rare basis, and by an additional 41.7% more frequently. Few (4.6%) believed the practice to be clearly unethical, but 41.2% believed it to be ethical only under are circumstances.

The findings in the previous two categories may be compared to the results reported by Holroyd and Brodsky (1977) in which 27% of the therapists reported occasionally engaging in nonerotic hugging, kissing, or affectionate touching with opposite-sex patients, and 7% reported doing so frequently or always.

Almost all respondents offered or accepted a handshake from a client, either rarely (48.9%) or more frequently (48.2%). Very few found the behavior to be ethically questionable.

As mentioned earlier, using sexual surrogates with clients was a difficult ethical judgment for almost one fourth of the respondents. A little over one third believed that the behavior was unethical. An additional one fourth believed it was ethical only under rare circumstances. The use of surrogates has been frequently challenged on ethical bases (Redlich, 1977), but so far no complaint has been filed with the APA Ethics Committee concerning the use of a sexual surrogate.

A large majority (85.1%) believe that sexual intimacies with clinical supervisees are unethical, a finding consistent with published analyses of this practice (Pope & Bouhoutsos, 1986; Pope, Schover, & Levenson, 1980).

Over 1 out of every 10 respondents believed that simply "being sexually attracted to a client" was unethical. Approximately an additional one tenth believed that feeling such attraction was ethical under rare circumstances. These findings seem consistent with the results of a prior survey in which 63% of the respondents reported that experiencing sexual attraction to clients made them feel guilty, anxious, or confused (Pope et al., 1986).

Almost half (46.3%) of the respondents reported engaging in sexual fantasy about a client on a rare basis, an additional one fourth (25.5%) more frequently. These figures may be compared to the 28.7% of psychologists in a previous study who answered affirmatively the question, "While engaging in sexual activity with someone other than a client, have you ever had sexual fantasies about someone who is or was a client?" (Pope et al., 1986). Both the current and previous survey found that male psychologists were significantly more likely to engage in sexual fantasies about clients. This difference is consistent with research regarding sexual fantasizing in general, which shows higher rates for men (Pope, 1982).

Financial issues. The vulnerability, dependency, and sometimes confusion of so many who seek help from psychologists call for a strong ethic against financial exploitation, as well as extensive research to determine which financial arrangements work best for therapist and patient. Yet until the 1970s, the subject was virtually absent from the research literature. . . .

In the last 15 years such factors as the increase in third-party payments have brought financial issues into the open. As the results of this study reveal, psychologists have developed a consensus of opinion about the acceptability of some—but by no means all—of the financial approaches to their work.

Over half of the respondents reported altering an insurance diagnosis to meet insurance criteria, either rarely (26.5%) or more frequently (35.1%). This action—which can be legally construed as insurance fraud—is viewed by slightly more than one third as unethical. An additional one fourth viewed it as ethical under rare circumstances. This widespread practice—in light of its legal implications and the use of dishonesty in the therapeutic endeavor—is in need of open discussion among professionals.

Charging for missed appointments seems an acceptable practice to virtually the entire psychological community. Raising a fee during the course of therapy also seems widely accepted. Principle 6d of the *Ethical Principles* (APA, 1981a) stresses that clients must be aware of such financial aspects of the services in advance and that they thus have a right to informed consent to or informed refusal of the financial arrangements.[2]

About half (49.3%) of the respondents have used a collection agency to collect late fees, at least on a rare basis. Only 5% view this practice as unethical.

About one third (21.3% rarely; 10.9% more often) of the respondents have filed a lawsuit to collect fees. One out of 10 (10.1%) view this as unethical. It may be useful for psychologists to be aware that the current APA professional liability policy specifically excludes "disputes concerning fees charged by any

Insured, including but not limited to third party reimbursements sought or received by any Insured" (American Home Assurance Company, undated, p. 3). In addition, psychologists must be aware of the ways in which fee-collection attempts that involve third parties (e.g., collection agencies, the courts) affect both the psychological welfare of the clients as well as such aspects of therapy as privacy and confidentiality.

Accepting a salary that is a percentage of client fees—a practice sometimes known as "kick-backs" or "fee-splitting" (Keith-Spiegel & Koocher, 1985)—was reported by 23.3% of the respondents. It is viewed as unethical by 12.1%. This was the item with the lowest response rate by far, suggesting that many respondents may have been unsure of the meaning of the question.

In another area, forensic psychology, psychologists may be tempted to accept a contingency fee. Standard texts have made clear statements concerning the unacceptability of such arrangements. "The psychologist should never accept a fee contingent upon the outcome of a case" (Blau, 1984, p. 336). "The expert witness should never, under any circumstances, accept a referral on a contingent fee basis" (Shapiro, 1984, p. 95). Only about 15% of the respondents report engaging in this practice either rarely (7.0%) of more often (8.4%).

Bartering of services for therapy has customarily been viewed by the profession as a dual relationship, hence unethical. . . . However, about one fourth of the respondents reported that they had engaged in such bartering, at least on a rare basis. Over half viewed the practice as either unethical or unethical under most circumstances.

Other dual relationships. Both sexual intimacy with clients and bartering for services are dual relationships. However, Principle 6a of the *Ethical Principles* (APA, 1981a) lists other dual relationships that are to be avoided: "Examples of such dual relationships include, but are not limited to, research with and treatment of employees, students, supervisees, close friends, or relatives" (p. 636).[3] The current study inquired into three of these areas: therapy

---

[2] *Ed. note*: See Standard 1.25 of the APA's current (1992) Ethical Principles.

[3] *Ed. note*: See Standard 1.17 of the APA's current (1992) Ethical Principles.

with employees, students/supervisees, and friends. The most frequent dual relationship involved students and supervisees (22.4% rarely; 8.6% more frequently), followed by friends (25.2% rarely; 3.1% more frequently) and employees (12.9% rarely; 2.7% more frequently).

Dual relationships can also be initiated once therapy begins, as happens when a therapist engages in sexual contact with a patient. According to the respondents, initiating business relationships with clients (1.5% rarely; 0.4% more frequently) and former clients (10.1% rarely; 2.4% more frequently) is not a widespread practice.

Advertising for and soliciting clients. Currently, advertising per se is not considered unethical, although direct solicitation of clients can be viewed as potentially exploitive (Keith-Spiegel & Koocher, 1985). About one fourth of the respondents report advertising in newspapers and similar media, either rarely (13.2%) or more frequently (12.9%).

Fewer than 10% of the respondents (generally male psychologists) directly solicit clients. At least two thirds view this practice as unethical.

4. Treat people with respect for their dignity as human beings.

To some extent, the history of psychotherapy has reflected the struggle to arrive at the most effective way in which to express respect. . . . In this study, we found that many of the walls that prevented therapists from engaging in simple human interactions—for example, therapists revealing their emotions—have come down, although therapists are still in a quandary about some of these issues.

An overwhelming majority of the respondents are on a first-name basis with their clients and do not view this as ethically questionable. Three fourths have attended a client's social event, such as a wedding, although only about one third have accepted an invitation to a party. About one fourth view accepting a party invitation as unethical. About the same percentage have invited clients to an office open house, but slightly more (28.9%) view this as unethical.

A large majority (93.3%) use self-disclosure. More specifically, over half tell clients that they are

angry with them (89.7%), cry in the presence of a client (56.5%), and tell clients that they are disappointed in them (51.9%). The most questioned of these was telling clients of disappointment: 56.8% viewed it as unethical or unethical under most circumstances.

5. Protect confidentiality.

Breaking confidentiality to prevent harm. The results of this study suggest that psychologists have accepted the legitimacy of breaking confidentiality in order to prevent danger. Fewer than 10% view this action as unethical in cases involving homicide, suicide, or child abuse.

The data also indicate that such situations are a customary part of general practice for psychologists: 78.5% report having broken confidentiality in regard to suicidal clients, 62.2% in cases of child abuse, and 58.1% when the client was homicidal.

Informally or unintentionally breaking confidentiality. About three fourths discuss clients—without names—with friends. Only 8.1% discuss clients—with names—with friends. Surprisingly, over half (61.9%) have unintentionally disclosed confidential data.

The widespread disclosure of confidential information—whether or not with names—is a practice that needs attention from the profession. Discussion of client information with friends seems to be a clear violation of Principle 5a.[4] "Information obtained in clinical or consulting relationships, or evaluative data concerning children, students, employees, or others, is discussed only for professional purposes and only with persons clearly concerned with the case" (APA, 1981a, p. 636). It also appears to violate the *General Guidelines for Providers of Psychological Services*:

> Psychologists do not release confidential information, except with the written consent of the user involved, or of his or her legal representative, guardian, or other holder of the privilege on behalf of the user, and only after . . . the user has been assisted in understanding the implications of the release. (APA, 1987, p. 717)

[4] *Ed. note:* See Standards 5.01–5.11 of the APA's current (1992) Ethical Principles.

Public psychology. When psychological services are performed in a public forum, of course, there is no confidentiality. Giving personal advice on radio, TV, and so forth, is a very difficult issue. More than one in five indicated that they did not know or were not sure if it was ethical.[5] . . . Surprisingly, over one fourth of the respondents reported giving such advice in the media either rarely (18.6%) or more frequently (10.9%).

6. Acting only with informed consent.

Seeing a minor without parental consent. A major ethical, as well as legal, dilemma is faced by many psychologists when the client is not empowered to give adequate consent to treatment (Koocher, 1976; Melton, 1981; Morrison, Morrison, & Holdridge-Crane, 1979; Plotkin, 1981). Over one fourth of the respondents have elected to see a minor without parental consent either rarely (22.4%) or more frequently (6.4%). Over half of the respondents believe such treatment to be either unethical (23.5%) or unethical under most circumstances (45.6%).

Withholding access to data. Should the clients have full access to assessment and treatment data that concern them? On the one hand, access to data about the client's condition may be important to the client's reaching a truly informed decision about initiating or continuing treatment. For example, if clients are not honestly told the diagnosis, it may be hard for them to know whether they want to be treated without knowing what they are to be treated for. On the other hand, psychologists may feel that certain technical terms or raw data may actually exacerbate the client's condition.

About one in five believe that it is unethical to refuse to disclose the diagnosis (21.5%) or to refuse access to a test report (21.7%). Fewer believe that refusing to allow clients to read their chart notes (14.5%) or that denying clients access to raw test data (12.1%) is unethical. Around half of the respondents have denied their clients access to the diagnosis (48.0%), to the testing report (49.6%), to their chart notes (55.5%), or to raw test data (57.4%).

Access to chart notes may have differential meaning and usefulness depending on how much information is contained in the chart. Over half (50.9%) of the respondents indicated that they had, at least rarely, limited treatment notes to name, date, and fee. The *General Guidelines for Providers of Psychological Services* (APA, 1987) mandate that "accurate, current and pertinent records of essential psychological services are maintained" (p. 717). Lack of adequate documentation of assessment, interventions, and responses to interventions have contributed to successful malpractice actions by establishing lack of care. . . .

Interventions against the client's wishes. Some of the most difficult and painful judgments psychologists must make concern under what, if any, conditions informed consent can be waived. One area of such judgments involves involuntary hospitalization, an area filled with controversy. Over half of the respondents have utilized involuntary hospitalization, either rarely (42.1%) or more often (20.2%). Fewer than 5% view it as unethical.

Whether to accept a client's decision to commit suicide is likewise a difficult and painful dilemma for many psychologists. Some have argued that the informed consent of the patient to accept or to refuse treatment in such cases must be absolute (Szasz, 1986). Only about one in five of the respondents has accepted, either rarely (16.4%) or more frequently (4.1%), a client's decision to kill himself or herself. Almost half (45.2%) believe it to be unethical. An additional 36.6% believe it to be unethical under most circumstances.

7. Promoting equity and justice.

Homosexuality. The profession's struggle to eliminate the stigma and pathologizing of homosexuality has been long, difficult, and not yet complete (Baer, 1981; Malyon, 1986a, 1986b). Slightly more than one in five of the respondents reported treating homosexuality per se as pathological, either rarely (12.7%) or more often (10.8%). However, over half (55.7%) viewed such a practice as unethical.

Sex of client. Whether to make access to one's practice dependent in any way upon the making of discriminations about a potential client's sex, race, religion, and so forth, is another of the very difficult judgments for many psychologists. On the one hand, discrimination as the term is customarily used is ab-

---

[5] *Ed. note*: See Standard 3.04 of the APA's current (1992) Ethical Principles.

horrent. On the other hand, psychologists may wish to specialize, and such specialty areas may be founded in part upon such characteristics as sex, race, or religion. Fewer than 10% engaged in this practice either rarely (3.7%) or more often (3.7%).

Financial barriers. To what extent are people without sufficient funds denied access to needed psychological services? Ever since Freud's (1913/1958) statement that "the absence of the regulating effect offered by the payment of a fee makes itself very painfully felt" (pp. 131–132), there have been strong advocates for the therapeutic necessity of charging fees (e.g., Davids, 1964; Kubie, 1950; Menninger, 1961). Such claims have been made in the absence of empirical support, because systematic studies have found, in general, no therapeutic effect exerted by the fee and no harm to the therapy caused by an absence or lowering of the fee (Balch, Ireland, & Lewis, 1977; Pope, Geller, & Wilkinson, 1975; Turkington, 1984).

Almost half (47.4%) of the respondents report providing free therapy on a rare basis, an additional 18.7% more frequently.

Over half of the respondents had terminated therapy due to the client's inability to pay, either rarely (36.2%) or more often (25.7%). The potential legal liability of the therapist's terminating therapy for other than "therapeutic" reasons may expose the psychologist to a malpractice suit for "abandonment."

Fear of being sued. Do certain clients whose condition may make therapists wary of being sued find access to therapy shut off? Avoiding certain clients for fear of being sued was acknowledged by 30.3% on a rare basis and by 15.6% more often. Fewer than 10% viewed this practice as unethical. . . .

CONCLUSION

The lack of comprehensive normative data about the behaviors of psychologists and their relationship to ethical standards leaves psychologists without adequate guidelines to inform their choices (Rosenbaum, 1982). Ethical issues in general may be relatively neglected in the professional literature. For example, Baldick (1980) reviewed 250 psychotherapy and counseling texts and found that only 2.8% discussed ethical issues encountered in professional practice. . . .

The integrity of psychology is contingent to a great degree on the extent to which we—both as a discipline or profession and as individuals—can regulate our own behavior. Our ability to engage in effective and ethical regulation, in turn, is contingent on our willingness to study our own behavior and our beliefs about that behavior.

References

American Home Assurance Company (undated). *Psychologists' professional liability policy* [Insurance policy], New York: Author.

American Psychological Association. (1981a). *Ethical principles of psychologists* (rev. ed.). Washington, DC: Author.

American Psychological Association. (1981b). *Specialty guidelines for the delivery of services by clinical psychologists.* Washington, DC: Author.

American Psychological Association. (1985). *Directory of the American Psychological Association.* Washington, DC: Author.

American Psychological Association. (1986a). *Guidelines for computer-based tests and interpretations.* Washington, DC: Author.

American Psychological Association. (1987). General guidelines for providers of psychological services. *American Psychologist, 42,* 712–723.

Baer, R. (1981). *Homosexuality and American psychiatry.* New York: Basic Books.

Balch, P., Ireland, J. F., & Lewis, S. B. (1977). Fees and therapy: Relation of source of payment to course of therapy at a community mental health center. *Journal of Consulting and Clinical Psychology, 45,* 504.

Baldick, T. L. (1980). Ethical discrimination ability of intern psychologists: A function of training in ethics. *Professional Psychology, 11,* 276–282.

Blau, T. H. (1984). *The psychologist as expert witness.* New York: Wiley-Interscience.

Bouhoutsos, J. C., Holroyd, J., Lerman, H., Forer, B. R., & Greenberg, M. (1983). Sexual intimacy between psychotherapists and patients. *Professional Psychology: Research and Practice, 14,* 185–196.

Davids, A. (1964). The relationship of cognitive-dissonance theory to an aspect of psychotherapeutic practice. *American Psychologist, 19,* 329–332.

Feldman-Summers, S., & Jones, G. (1984). Psychological impacts of sexual contact between therapists or other health care practitioners and their clients. *Journal of Consulting and Clinical Psychology, 52,* 1054–1061.

Freeman, L., & Roy, J. (1976). *Betrayal.* New York: Stein & Day.

Freud, S. (1958). Further recommendations in the technique of psychoanalysis: On beginning the treatment. In J. Strachey (Ed. and Trans.), *The standard edition of the complete psychological works of Sigmund Freud* (Vol. 12). London: Hogarth. (Original work published 1913).

Geller, J. D. (1980). The body, expressive movement, and physical contact in psychotherapy. In J. L. Singer & K. S. Pope (Eds.), *The power of human imagination: New methods in psychotherapy.* New York: Plenum.

Holroyd, J. C., & Brodsky, A. M. (1977). Psychologists' attitudes and practices regarding erotic and nonerotic physical contact with patients. *American Psychologist, 32,* 843–849.

Holroyd, J. C., & Brodsky, A. M. (1980). Does touching patients lead to sexual intercourse? *Professional Psychology, 11,* 807–811.

Keith-Spiegel, P. C., & Koocher, G. (1985). *Ethics in psychology: Professional standards and cases.* New York: Random House.

Kilburg, R. R., Nathan, P. E., & Thoreson, R. (1986). *Professionals in distress: Issues, syndromes, and solutions in psychology.* Washington, DC: American Psychological Association.

Koocher, G. P. (Ed.). (1976). *Children's rights and the mental health professions.* New York: Wiley.

Kubie, L. S. (1950). *Practical and theoretical aspects of psychoanalysis.* New York: International Universities Press.

Laliotis, D., & Grayson, J. (1985). Psychologist heal thyself: What is available for the impaired psychologist? *American Psychologist, 40,* 84–96.

Malyon, A. K. (1986a). *Brief follow-up to June 24, 1986 meeting with the American Psychiatric Association work group to revise DSM-III.* Unpublished manuscript.

Malyon, A. K. (1986b). *Presentation to the American Psychiatric Association work group to revise DSM-III.* Unpublished manuscript.

Matarazzo, J. D. (1986). Computerized clinical psychological test interpretations: Unvalidated plus all mean and no sigma. *American Psychologist, 41,* 14–24.

Melton, G. B. (1981). Effects of a state law permitting minors to consent to psychotherapy. *Professional Psychology, 12,* 647–654.

Menninger, K. (1961). *Theory of psychoanalytic technique.* New York: Science Editions.

Morrison, K. L., Morrison, J. K., & Holdridge-Crane, S. (1979). The child's right to give informed consent to psychiatric treatment. *Journal of Clinical Psychology, 8,* 43–47.

Plaisil, E. (1985). *Therapist.* New York: St. Martin's/Marek.

Plotkin, R. (1981). When rights collide: Parents, children, and consent to treatment. *Journal of Pediatric Psychology, 6,* 121–130.

Pope, K. S. (1982). *Implications of fantasy and imagination for mental health: Theory, research, and interventions* (Report commissioned by the National Institute of Mental Health. Order No. 82M024784505D). Bethesda, MD: National Institute of Mental Health.

Pope, K. S. (1985, August). *Diagnosis and treatment of Therapist–Patient Sex Syndrome.* Paper presented at the annual meeting of the American Psychological Association, Los Angeles.

Pope, K. S. (1986, May). *Therapist–Patient Sex Syndrome: Research findings.* Paper presented at the annual meeting of the American Psychiatric Association, Washington, DC.

Pope, K. S. (1987). Preventing therapist-patient sexual intimacy: Therapy for a therapist at risk. *Professional Psychology: Research and Practice, 18,* 624–628.

Pope, K. S., & Bouhoutsos, J. (1986). *Sexual intimacy between therapists and patients.* New York: Praeger.

Pope, K. S., Geller, J. D., & Wilkinson, L. (1975). Fee assessment and outpatient psychotherapy. *Journal of Consulting and Clinical Psychology, 43,* 835–841.

Pope, K. S., Keith-Spiegel, P. C., & Tabachnick, B. (1986). Sexual attraction to clients: The human therapist and the (sometimes) inhuman training system. *American Psychologist, 41,* 147–158.

Pope, K. S., Levenson, H., & Schover, L. R. (1979). Sexual intimacy in psychology training: Results and implications of a national survey. *American Psychologist, 34,* 682–689.

Pope, K. S., Schover, L. S., & Levenson, H. (1980). Sexual behavior between clinical supervisors and trainees: Implications for standards of professional practice. *Professional Psychology, 11,* 157–162.

Redlich, F. C. (1977). The ethics of sex therapy. In W. H. Masters, V. E. Johnson, & R. D. Kolodny (Eds.), *Ethical issues in sex therapy and research* (pp. 143–157). Boston: Little, Brown.

Redlich, F. C., & Pope, K. S. (1980). Ethics of mental health training. *Journal of Nervous and Mental Disease, 168,* 709–714.

Rosenbaum, M. (Ed.). (1982). *Ethics and values in psychotherapy.* New York: Free Press.

Sell, J. M., Gottlieb, M. C., & Schoenfeld, L. (1986). Ethical considerations of social/romantic relationships with present and former clients. *Professional Psychology: Research and Practice, 17,* 504–508.

Shapiro, D. L. (1984). *Psychological evaluation and expert testimony: A practical guide to forensic work.* New York: Van Nostrand.

Szasz, T. (1986). The case against suicide prevention. *American Psychologist, 41,* 806–812.

Turkington, C. (1984, April). Austin study questions tenet that free therapy lacks value. *APA Monitor,* p. 6.

Walker, E., & Young, T. D. (1986). *A killing cure.* New York: Henry Holt.

Whitesell v. Green, No. 38745 (Dist. Ct. Hawaii filed November 19, 1973).

Ethical Decision Making and Psychologists' Attitudes Toward Training in Ethics

Alexander J. Tymchuk, Robin Drapkin, Susan Major-Kingsley, Andrea B. Ackerman, Elizabeth W. Coffman, and Maureen S. Baum

Psychologists often face ethical dilemmas without clear decision-making guidelines provided by the profession or by society. Although the American Psychological Association (APA) has established ethical standards, new and sometimes controversial clinical and research technologies as well as increased community concern with the protection of individual rights continually pose new and complex ethical dilemmas. . . .

Although these standards are available, they are most useful when psychologists are familiar with and know how to apply them. When psychologists cannot refer to a specific standard, they must rely more heavily on their own value systems and on their own interpretations of the "spirit" of the APA standards. Such interpretation may lead to variability in professional decision making. Barber (1976) found variability in ethical decision making in medical research, although investigators had utilized human research review committees, had access to federal guidelines and a medical code of ethics, and in some cases had received formal training in ethics. . . .

PURPOSE

The present study had three objectives:[1] The first objective was to determine the extent to which a nationwide sample of clinical psychologists concurred in their responses to a set of hypothetical clinical situations. Consistency of decision making is desirable to ensure that regardless of circumstances, psychological standards will be fairly and equitably applied, and individual rights will be guaranteed to all people seen by psychologists. . . .

METHOD

A two-part questionnaire was developed. The first part contained 13 inquiries regarding the respondents' training in ethics, attitudes toward training in ethics, information about which ethical issues they felt least informed, and clinical orientation. The second part consisted of 12 vignettes that described a clinical or research situation in which ethical issues were involved (Table 1). These vignettes were typical of ethical problems faced by psychologists. . . .

The questionnaire was mailed to a random sample of 500 members of the Division of Clinical Psychology listed in the Directory of the APA (1976). . . . The respondents were asked to agree or disagree with the decision described in each hypothetical situation and to indicate the criteria they considered relevant in determining the appropriateness of the hypothetical decision. These criteria included concerns with (a) the interests of the clients, (b) therapeutic leverage, (c) confidentiality, (d) personal freedom, (e) freedom of expression, (f) individual rights, (g) the interests of the community, (h) public policy, (i) standards of morality, (j) the therapist's judgment, (k) informed consent or agreement, (l) financial issues, and (m) state or federal law. Respondents also were given the opportunity to list additional bases for their decision and to comment on each vignette.

FINDINGS

Of the 500 questionnaires mailed, 23% (113) were returned. The respondents' clinical orientations were characterized as eclectic, 56%; psychoanalytic, 16%; behavioral, 15%; humanistic, 7%; and other, 6%.

Adapted from *Professional Psychology*, 13, 412–421. Copyright 1982 by the American Psychological Association.

[1] *Ed. note*: Only the first objective is discussed in this excerpt.

TABLE 1

Vignettes of Ethical Issues

Vignette	Decision
1. A psychologist at a cocktail party is having a conversation with a woman whom he has just met. He begins to tell her about a client of his, without mentioning names. He reveals to her a set of situations in which the client has recently found himself involved and which the psychologist finds particularly amusing. The woman appears interested in the psychologist's story, until she has heard enough to cause her to believe he is talking about someone she knows. She says, "Are you talking about . . .?" to which the psychologist replies, "Yes, you know him too?" And they both laugh. The next day she calls her ex-husband and asks him if what she hears about him is true. He files a complaint against the psychologist with the local ethics committee.	The psychologist showed a lack of regard for protecting the identity of his client.
2. A psychologist with considerable skill in behavioral engineering is asked by a state institution for the retarded to plan and assist in executing a behavioral program on its adolescent ward. The purpose of this program will be to increase self-help and ward maintenance skills such as bathing, grooming, dressing, feeding, etc. The program will work only on positive incentives, with special treats such as candy, outings, dances, etc. being provided as rewards for those who improve their skills in these areas. The psychologist meets with each adolescent on the ward to explain the program and finds that about 25% of the youngsters do not understand what he is talking about. Even with a film designed to explain his procedures, the psychologist is unable to get his message across to these youngsters.	These youngsters should not be included in the behavior modification program even though the director of the institution wants all the adolescents on the ward to participate.
3. A male clinical psychologist regularly saw a female patient in his apartment to which he had given her a key. Sometimes the therapeutic sessions lasted past midnight. Eventually the patient and her husband accused the therapist of improper relations. The therapist explained that the highly unusual arrangements for psychotherapy resulted from the fact that he had lost control of the relationship and that his patient dominated it.	It would be ethical for a psychologist to see a client on this basis as long as the client had consented to such sessions and was benefiting from the therapy.
4. A psychologist gives information on a figure drawing test to a writer for an article in a popular magazine. The test is not copyrighted and does not require professional training for appropriate interpretation. The psychologist is under the impression that the article would be a dignified statement about how such tests are an aid to the psychologist in giving services to the public. The article appears under the headline "Figure Out Your Own Personality," with a blank space for drawing and instructions for scoring, showing examples.	The psychologist did not violate ethical standards in giving such materials for a popular article.
5. A researcher in autism provides intensive behavioral treatment for one half of the children under age 3 who come to her treatment/research facility. The other children are placed in a control group. Children in the first group receive up to 2 years intensive behavioral treatment. It is known that beyond the age of 5 or 6, the benefits of the treatment program decrease significantly.	This researcher should be obliged to offer 2 years of intensive treatment to the control group children once they have remained in that group for 2 years.
6. A client signs a contract for six weeks of a popularized therapy for which she pays the ($3,000) amount in full prior to treatment. She agrees that after two weeks of the therapy she can receive portions of her money back over the next four-week period. After one week, the client decides she does not like the therapy, has lost trust in the therapist, and wants all of her money back.	The psychologist should return all of the client's money, even though the contract specified none to be returned within the first two weeks.

(table continues)

TABLE 1 *(cont.)*	
Vignette	**Decision**
7. Current legal developments suggest that rights to treatment for the involuntarily committed include "nutritionally adequate meals," which suggests that contingent availability of meals as reinforcers is unacceptable even if it is deemed therapeutic. A psychologist complies with this requirement by offering his patients nutritious food by taking all the courses and mixing them together in a blender. This blended together meal is freely available to all patients, but patients desiring separate course servings must pay for them with earned tokens.	There is nothing unethical about what the psychologist has done as long as it can be shown that such a program is therapeutically desirable.
8. The parents of a public school child demand that a psychologist in private practice give them a written report since they paid for psychological testing. The psychologist gives them a copy of his report in which actual test scores are included. The parents take the report to the school psychologist who refers it to the APA.	In giving such a report to the parents, the psychologist is unethical and lacking in good judgment.
9. A specialist in child development acts as a consultant to a toy manufacturer. Her major function is to test the toys in free-play situations. The manufacturer wants to use the results of this testing in his advertising, and he requests permission to use the name of the psychologist in this connection. This is not to be an endorsement of any particular toy but a statement of the fact that the psychologist has tested the toys.	An ethical psychologist would not lend her name to advertisements. If there were research findings concerning the value of the toy, the results could speak for themselves.
10. A psychologist advertises by mail a service which offers to introduce marriageable clients to each other on a personality analysis basis, thereby increasing the prospects of a compatible relationship. The psychologist does not influence the clients to make any decision to marry but merely obtains from them by mail, information he deems relevant. The data are sorted by computer and used as a basis for arranging introductions of interested clients.	The psychologist's behavior is ethical.
11. Over a weekend a psychologist conducts a growth group at which twelve persons attend. Prior to the beginning of the weekend, the psychologist informs the participants that they have the freedom to leave the group at any time. The following week, one of the participants files a complaint with the State Ethics Committee, charging that there was nudity during the experience, for which he was unprepared and in which he felt pressured to participate. He states that the experience was emotionally humiliating and damaging and requests that action be taken against the psychologist.	The psychologist in question acted unethically in failing to provide advance notice of techniques to be used during the group, including the possibility of nudity, even though he informed the prospective participants that they could leave at any time.
12. A client, at the close of one of his therapy sessions with you, mentions that he has a secret plan to kill his roommate and that he has a gun. You have reason to believe he has the potential for violent behavior (that there may be clear and imminent danger) and you wish to spend more therapy time dealing with this issue. Your client states that he will not return next week. Should you tell anyone his "secret?"	As his psychotherapist, you should inform either the police or his roommate.

Table 2 summarizes the percentage of responses to each vignette as well as the criteria used. The vignettes are rank ordered according to degree of consensus (from highest to lowest), with the decision described in each situation. Where there is relatively strong consensus regarding the actions of the hypothetical psychologist, there is also strong agreement regarding the criteria on which the respondents base their judgments. Additionally, relatively weak consensus regarding the hypothetical psychologist's actions corresponds with less agreement about the relevant criteria. This finding suggests that there may be important distinctions between types of decision-making situations that render some decisions easier than others.

TABLE 2

Percentage of Responses to the Vignettes and the Criteria Used

Degree of Consensus	Vignette Number	Vignette Description	Response Agree	Response Disagree	Response No Response	Criteria 1	2	3	4	5	6	7	8	9	10	11	12	13
High	1	Failure to protect client identity	98	1	1	87[a]	12	92[a]	14	7	46	14	8	22	55[a]	36	3	14
	3	Ethical with client consent	2	96	2	77[a]	50[a]	7	11	5	13	26	16	65[a]	80[a]	14	3	9
	12	Inform police or roommate	84	9	7	62[a]	8	37	15	10	40	72[a]	30	24	24	19	2	54[a]
	11	Failure to provide advance notice	82	15	3	73[a]	15	4	37	20	43	28	16	32	47	55[a]	3	5
	9	Unethical advertising	73	18	9	3	2	13	13	10	10	33	33	7	14	1	18	3
	10	Ethical to advise dating service	22	70	8	49	6	13	11	5	12	29	16	18	35	18	11	2
Moderate	7	Ethical if therapeutically desirable	26	68	6	66[a]	40	3	36	9	56[a]	18	23	24	36	31	3	31
	2	Exclude patients if fail to understand	33	65	2	64[a]	24	2	26	4	42	37	15	10	22	40	2	15
	4	Ethical to provide information for article	49	43	8	7	3	5	11	18	8	48	20	3	30	3	2	3
	5	Must provide treatment and control group	47	42	10	62[a]	7	1	6	13	31	29	7	24	12	19	7	5
Low	6	Should return therapy prepayment	43	47	10	43	18	2	18	3	34	13	19	19	24	38	34	12
	8	Unethical to provide test scores	47	42	10	62[a]	4	25	16	8	36	13	18	6	45	24	1	16

[a]Indicates % use of criteria greater than 50.

In the vignettes that had relatively strong consensus, the issues were current and timely. These vignettes incorporated confidentiality issues, moral issues involving the male therapist–female client relationship, and standards for growth groups.

The issues in the next strongest consensus group of vignettes were not as much in the forefront of professional attention and focused on two basic areas: client rights to obtain or refuse treatment and professional public statements—promotional activities and misrepresentation.

Finally, the vignettes with the weakest consensus (where decisions tended to be approximately equally split between agreement and disagreement) were focused on three basic areas that differed from those of the other vignettes: test security and interpretation, research activities, and remuneration (fees).

These specific findings support the hypothesis that strong consensus in professional decision making may be related to the availability of standards and the nature of the particular situation. When professional or legal standards exist and when the issues are current and related to the therapist–client relationship, the decision-making process appears to be facilitated. Psychologists seem to have more difficulty agreeing either on treatment issues that may be closely intertwined with clinical orientation or on issues that are not in the forefront of the discipline, including those related to "business" or "contract" decisions. . . .

References

Barber, B. The ethics of experimentation with human subjects. *Scientific American*, 1976, 234(2), 25–31.

Directory of the APA. (1976). Washington, DC: American Psychological Association.

Ethical Dilemmas in Psychological Practice: Results of a National Survey

Leonard J. Haas, John L. Malouf, and Neal H. Mayerson

Recent years have been marked by a rise in professional consciousness about ethical and legal responsibilities and by a concurrent rise in public consciousness about legal rights. The result, in part, is a level of concern (and confusion) about proper professional behavior that is unprecedented in all professions and is particularly evident in psychology (Chalk, Frankel, & Chafer, 1980). Much professional attention has been paid to identifying appropriate actions in the face of conflicting ethical, legal, and professional demands (Haas & Fennimore, 1983). In addition, researchers have recently begun to turn their attention to the moral reasoning underlying moral action (Blasi, 1980).

The widespread concern about ethical and legal aspects of practice notwithstanding, relatively little is known about the nature of the actual situations that practitioners find ethically, legally, or professionally problematic. Of the few studies addressed to the issue of ethical concerns, researchers in some (e.g., Baldick, 1980) assess subjects' ability to recognize or identify an ethical dilemma. In other surveys (e.g., Tymchuk et al., 1982) researchers assess the extent of respondents' agreement with a particular choice already made for them. In still other surveys (e.g., Jagim, Wittman, & Noll, 1978), researchers assess a limited sample of psychologists. There has been no study to date in which the nature of respondents' choices from among a range of options has been assessed.

In this study we attempt to investigate some of these unknown areas. Practitioners were presented a set of problems that had at least two potentially workable alternative resolutions, and a set of possible reasons for making those choices. In addition, we at-

tempt to assess the perceived utility of various sources of ethics education. With increasing pressure for standardized ethics education in professional psychology training programs, it is vital to know more about the mechanisms through which ethical practitioners acquire what they consider to be valuable ethics training. Answers to questions such as these may help in the training of ethically responsible psychologists.

METHOD

Instrument
The questionnaire developed for this study consisted of five sections. . . . The first section concerned demographic and background factors such as age, number of years in practice, and theoretical orientation. In the second section respondents indicated the sources of their training in ethics, number of hours spent in various categories of ethical training (e.g., coursework, discussions with colleagues), and the value of each of these experiences (see Table 2).

The third section contained 10 vignettes, each describing a dilemma of professional ethics. . . . The vignettes were chosen to represent five general categories that are considered to encompass the broad range of professional dilemmas: confidentiality problems, issues of informed consent, loyalty conflicts, exploitation, and whistle-blowing (Haas, 1982). In addition, we selected vignettes that involved a *dilemma*, rather than simply knowledge of the relevant standards: that is, vignettes represented situations in which more than one alternative could be considered acceptable on the basis of recognized ethical principles.

For each vignette, alternative ways to respond were presented: as much as possible, the number of

TABLE 2

Amount and Perceived Utility of Education in Ethics

	Hours		Mean Utility[a]	
Source of Education	**M**	**n**	**Rating**	**n**
Discussions with colleagues	79.1	236	4.4	269
Independent reading	31.3	238	4.0	240
Internship supervision	17.1	231	3.8	124
Graduate coursework	11.5	258	4.4	174
Continuing education courses	2.7	233	3.3	26

[a]Mean ratings on a 5-point scale anchored by 1 (*not at all useful*) and 5 (*extremely useful*).

alternatives was restricted and respondents were urged to choose one of them, rather than to "rearrange" the dilemma (e.g., resolving the dilemma by noting that "I would have gotten informed consent beforehand" or making some other shift in the condi-

tions). In several cases it was possible to reduce the behavioral alternatives to two: act or not act. After the alternatives, eight possible reasons for choosing an alternative were presented: upholding the law, upholding the code of ethics, protecting society's interests, protecting client's rights, upholding personal standards, safeguarding the therapy process, financial considerations, and "other." Analysis of these rationales and the categories of moral reasoning that they reflect are presented elsewhere (Haas, Malouf, & Mayerson, 1985). Respondents were asked to indicate their preferred response to each dilemma and the most important reason for making this choice. The vignettes and alternatives are listed in Table 3.

In the fourth section, respondents were asked to rate the frequency with which they had encountered 17 ethical/legal issues in practice (e.g., concern about colleagues' actions, insurance reporting requirements, sexual misconduct) and their rating of the seriousness of each issue (see Table 4). Last, respondents

TABLE 3

Vignettes and Choices Presented in Questionnaire, and Percentage of Respondents Endorsing Each Choice

Vignette	Choice	%
1. You are a therapist in a community mental health center. You are about to move to another state, and must terminate or refer your caseload. Your clinical director tells you to refer a particular individual to a therapist whose ability you do not respect.	Refer the patient.	7
	Refer the patient and indicate your reservations to him.	14
	Refuse to refer the patient to that particular therapist.	79
	Other	1
2. A client of yours tells you that she is still quite upset at her previous therapist for, among other things, making sexual advances toward her. This is the third time you have heard such allegations about this particular therapist.	Discuss the patient's anger but do not discuss the issue of professional standards.	10
	Call the previous therapist and tell him that the behavior you have heard about violates professional ethics.	18
	Tell the patient that she has the right to bring her charge to the ethics committee or the state licensing board.	57
	Call the ethics committee or state licensing board.	14
3. A psychologist whom you have met on occasional meetings but do not know well appears in a TV spot endorsing a local health spa. He says, "As child psychologist I find relaxation important —I go to the Palm Spa to get my head and body together."	Call the psychologist and indicate that you think the ad violates professional standards.	25
	Call the professional standards committee of your psychological association and report the incident.	42
	Do nothing.	33
	Other	0

(table continues)

TABLE 3 (*cont.*)		
Vignette	**Choice**	**%**
4. You have been treating a married couple conjointly for about 6 months. The wife arrives early for the session and tells you that she is thinking of leaving her husband as she has been involved with another man. She also asks you not to tell her husband. You have not previously discussed your policy regarding secrets.	Do not agree to keep the secret. Agree to keep the secret. Other	30 65 5
5. The mother of a 12-year-old boy comes to pick him up after his initial appointment with you. She asks you if he is taking drugs. He has in fact revealed to you that he has been sniffing glue.	Tell her what you know. Tell her the information is her son's to reveal or not as he sees fit. Other	24 72 5
6. A man with no previous experience in therapy contacts you and asks for sex therapy. While you understand the general principles of sex therapy, you would not consider it your area of expertise. However, he looks like an interesting prospective client.	Accept him as a client. Accept him as a client only after discussing your qualifications. Do not accept him as a client and refer him to another therapist. Other	5 45 49 1
7. You are treating a Vietnam veteran with a history of impulsive antisocial actions. You and he have established a good therapeutic relationship (his first after 3 previous attempts in therapy). At the end of the session, he disclosed that he is planning to kill his current girlfriend, because she has been dating another man.	Contact his girlfriend and/or the police without informing him. Plan to discuss this further at the next session. Inform him that you must warn his girlfriend and/or the police. Other	8 5 87 1
8. During the course of your treatment of a 45-year-old male who has drinking problems, his wife telephones and tells you that he has been sexually molesting his 7-year-old stepdaughter (her daughter of a previous marriage).	Report the case to the child protection bureau. Encourage her to report the matter to the child protection bureau. Reflect her concern but take no further action. Other	25 60 11 4
9. A client of yours who is a CPA suggests that he prepare your tax return in partial payment for therapy. You have been preparing your own taxes and find it increasingly burdensome.	Accept his offer. Decline his offer. Other	7 93 0
10. You work in the emergency room of a community mental health center located within a general hospital. You are about to admit a man best diagnosed as a paranoid schizophrenic; his insurance will cover the cost of hospitalization. This diagnosis may make it difficult for him to obtain other kinds of insurance (e.g., life insurance) later. You suspect that learning of this will make him resist hospitalization since he cannot afford it without insurance.	Inform him of the risks involved. Do not inform him of the risks; diagnose him as indicated. Do not inform him of the risks; give him a much "milder" diagnosis. Other	50 30 18 1

were given the option of describing an ethical problem that they themselves had encountered and how they had dealt with it. . . .

Procedure

The sample consisted of 600 randomly selected members of Division 29 (Psychotherapy) of the American Psychological Association (APA) chosen from the APA Directory. . . . [N]ot counting those questionnaires returned as undeliverable, 500 individuals received questionnaires and 294 individuals returned them, which was a response rate of 59%.

Characteristics of Respondents

The median age of respondents was 45.7 years and the mean number of years since they had received their degrees was 15.17. Thirty percent were female and 70% were male.

Overall, the sample had substantial experience, worked largely in private practice delivering clinical

TABLE 4

Mean Ratings of Frequency With Which Areas of Concern Occur and Their Seriousness

Area of Concern	Frequency[a]	Seriousness[b]
1. Confidentiality or privileged communication	3.09	3.94
2. Providing informed consent to clients	2.54	3.33
3. Rights of minors (e.g., in therapy)	2.43	3.52
4. Conflicting interests (employers vs. clients, clients vs. legal system, etc.	2.41	3.59
5. Personal use of advertising or other means of generating referrals	1.58	2.46
6. Talk shows, interviews, or other personal media appearances	1.67	2.43
7. Colleagues' sexual conduct	2.08	4.12
8. Appropriateness of other actions of colleagues	2.66	3.69
9. Own sexual impulses or conduct	1.69	3.21
10. Legality of own actions	1.82	3.33
11. Own malpractice liability	1.76	3.37
12. Own competence to deal with particular problem or provide requested service	2.43	3.45
13. Insurance company requests (e.g., for information or diagnoses)	2.77	3.15
14. Civil (involuntary) commitment	1.70	3.54
15. Behavior of employees or supervisees	2.11	3.34
16. Testing (e.g., use of test results, appropriateness of test requested)	2.05	3.17
17. Research (e.g., protection of subjects' privacy, minimizing risk)	1.72	3.17

[a]Scale ranges from 1 (*never a concern*) to 5 (*constantly a concern*).
[b]Scale ranges from 1 (*not at all serious*) to 5 (*extremely serious*).

services, and was largely composed of PhD-level practitioners. The sample obtained here is quite similar to the clinician sample described in the APA's national work force survey (Stapp & Fulcher, 1983).

RESULTS

Education in Ethics

Subjects' reports of their education in professional ethics are summarized in Table 2. As the table shows, discussions with colleagues is the most widely reported category of ethics education. Graduate coursework, perhaps not surprisingly, is the fourth-ranked category. Subjects were also asked to rate how useful the various sources of education had been in their understanding, coping with, or preventing ethical dilemmas. The means of these ratings are also reported in Table 2. As shown, all categories were rated above 3, but graduate coursework and collegial discussions were both rated as the most useful. Modal number of hours in formal ethics education (e.g., graduate coursework and continuing education courses) was zero.

Responses to Vignettes of Ethical Dilemmas

In Table 3 we show the percentage of respondents who chose each alternative for each vignette in the order in which they were presented to respondents. As the table shows, highest degrees of consensus regarding the appropriate choice were obtained (in descending order) on issues involving the following: conflict of interest (Vignette 9), mandatory reporting of threatened violence (Vignette 7), a superior's order to refer a client to someone who is considered incompetent (Vignette 1), and confidentiality (Vignettes 5 and 4). The modal responses indicated that subjects favored acting in the client's interest when one's own interests might be better served by another response, reporting threatened violence to the police or the intended victim(s), or both, and the protection of clients' rights to confidentiality.

Lower degrees of consensus were obtained on dilemmas involving the following (in ascending order of consensus): others' use of professional credentials in advertising for a local business (Vignette 3), treatment of problems beyond one's established expertise (Vignette 6), and reporting of potentially countertherapeutic diagnoses to insurance companies

(Vignette 10). Regarding both alleged client–therapist sexual contact (Vignette 2) and alleged client-instigated sexual abuse (Vignette 8), slightly more than a majority of the respondents apparently would *not* report the allegation themselves, but instead would try to encourage the client or a family member of the client to make the report.

Frequency and Seriousness of Ethical Dilemmas Actually Experienced

The 17 areas of potential ethical difficulty presented to subjects are listed, along with the overall ratings for each area of concern, in Table 4. Subjects were asked to rate the frequency with which the issues had presented problems for them during the past year. They were also asked to rate the overall severity of those problems, irrespective of how often they had personally encountered them. Interestingly, in terms of mean frequency ratings, none of the issues were reported as more than *ocasionally a concern*. In contrast, 11 of the 17 issues were rated as *fairly serious* or *extremely serious* by more than 50% of the respondents. The two issues that overall seemed to be considered most serious involved confidentiality, or privileged communication, and sexual conduct of colleagues. The two issues rated least serious (e.g., rated about 2) were media appearances and advertising to obtain referrals.

DISCUSSION

. . . One should certainly exercise caution in concluding that our results demonstrate what psychologists would actually do when confronted with ethical dilemmas. Nonetheless, it is precisely the specificity into which we "forced" our respondents that allows us to determine those issues for which there are widely agreed-upon resolutions and those for which there are not.

If one defines high agreement as 75% concordance, then there was a high agreement on what to do in only 3 of the 10 vignettes presented. Psychologists in our sample agreed that it would not be appropriate to refer a client to a therapist whom they did not respect, even when requested to do so by their clinical director. They also agreed that it would not be appropriate to trade therapeutic services for other profes-

sional services. Last, psychologists are apparently quite aware of their duties to warn in cases of threatened violence of the sexual abuse of children, and they appear willing to act accordingly, in contrast to the sample surveyed by Jagim et al. (1978). However, in the vignette relating to the sexual abuse of a child, there was a clear difference of opinion as to whether the therapist's most appropriate response should be to report or to suggest that someone else report the allegation. Despite the increasing prevalence of mandatory reporting laws (DeKraii & Sales, 1984) this result shows that uncertainty about this complex ethical/legal issue is still widespread.

Results suggest a number of other areas in which high agreement does not exist, as defined by the 75% agreement criterion. One problematic area is the issue of confidentiality within families or couples. Although a majority of respondents would maintain the confidentiality of a spouse or minor child (as shown in the results for Vignettes 4 and 5), a significant minority (30.5% and 23.6%, respectively) would reveal certain types of information to a spouse or parent. Despite the existence of legal constraints (DeKraii & Sales, 1984), confidentiality within families is clearly a topic in which much is left to the discretion of the therapist (Margolin, 1982). Clearly, practitioners should be aware of the legal standards and in addition carefully think through the ethical and therapeutic implications of their choices.

Another area of apparent low agreement involves unethical behavior of other professionals. Two vignettes (2 and 3) dealt with this topic, one describing a situation in which a psychologist was alleged to have had sexual relations with clients, the other describing a psychologist who publicly endorsed a health spa. In the first case, approximately 90% felt that some action should be taken, and a significant number felt that the client, rather than the current therapist, should report the previous therapist. In the second case, approximately one third of the respondents felt that they should do nothing about reporting the psychologist who endorsed the health spa, even though such behavior is a clear violation of Principle 4 of the *Ethical Principles* (APA, 1981).[1]

---

[1] *Ed. note:* See Standard 3.01 of the APA's current (1992) Ethical Principles.

One issue that can limit the duty to deal with colleagues' questionable behavior is that of client preferences. It is quite likely that those of our respondents who preferred to let the client report in Vignette 2 held the principle of client control of confidential information to be paramount. This confounding principle was not present in Vignette 3, which suggests that many psychologists find it easier to dismiss as trivial those actions that are not obviously harmful rather than risk being considered vigilantes.

Vignette 6, which concerned a therapist's providing sex therapy despite a lack of specialty training, related to the topic of competence. This vignette highlights another area in which much latitude is given the practitioner by the *Ethical Principles*. Although Principle 2 (APA, 1981)[2] specifies that a therapist be competent to provide the services offered, it is primarily the therapist who determines his or her own competence. In the situation described in the survey, about half of the respondents apparently felt that a knowledge of general principles of sex therapy was not adequate to establish competence in that area, whereas about 45% of respondents would discuss their qualifications with the client and, apparently, let the client determine the therapist's competence. Clients' ability to make such a determination can be seriously questioned.

The final vignette raises the complicated and multifaceted issue of diagnosis. Should a client be informed of his or her diagnosis if this information would possibly be harmful? Should the therapist change the diagnosis to something more "acceptable"? Should the therapist be more concerned about the consequences of the diagnosis itself or about the consequences of decreased trust in professional diagnoses? Half of our respondents would inform a paranoid schizophrenic patient about the risks involved in reporting an accurate diagnosis on an insurance form, whereas 30% would not discuss this with the client but would submit an accurate diagnosis, regardless of the consequences. Eighteen percent would not inform the client but would give a milder diagnosis. This variability highlights the ambiguity in this area, in that all response alternatives can be justified by existing ethical guidelines.

In relation to subjects' reports of the sources and value of their ethics education, results seem to confirm the appropriateness of the APA decision to require the development of formal coursework in ethics. Even though the major reported source of learning, in terms of reported hours, is discussions with colleagues and the number of hours spent studying ethics in graduate school is relatively low, this latter endeavor was as highly valued as the former. Independent reading was reported as the other main source of ethical training. It is also interesting to note that internship (in which many assume that young clinicians get their ethics education) was not rated particularly highly as a source of ethics education. In addition, it is interesting that reading and discussing issues with colleagues (both seemingly intrinsically motivated activities) are extensively used as a means of self education in ethics by this sample. This may be a result of the increasing intensity of concern with ethical and legal issues, or reflect feelings of inadequate preparation in these areas. It is likely that the majority of our respondents completed their graduate training before ethics courses were common in training programs. Given the apparent interest in ethics training and the relatively low ratings given continuing education courses, it seems that further development and improvement of continuing education courses would be appropriate.

Of the 17 areas of potential ethical difficulty that were presented to respondents, only one—confidentiality or privileged communication—received a mean frequency rating of over 3 (*occasionally a concern*). All the other issues received lower ratings. The concerns least frequently encountered involved personal use of advertising and media appearances.

Although the frequency of these 17 topics was not reported to be extremely high, respondents did consider several of them to be serious. The sexual conduct of colleagues was rated as the most serious of the issues, followed by confidentiality or privileged communication, appropriateness of other actions of colleagues, and conflicting interests (e.g., employers vs. clients). Of the 17 issues, all but two received mean ratings of higher than 3 (*somewhat serious*). The questions regarding personal use of advertising and

[2] *Ed. note*: See Standard 1.04 of the APA's current (1992) Ethical Principles.

personal media appearances were rated between 2 (*slightly serious*) and 3 (*somewhat serious*).

One interpretation of these findings is that psychologists consider many issues important but do not encounter problems with them very often. In one sense, this can be considered a positive finding insofar as it may mean that psychologists, at least relatively experienced ones, feel comfortable with the ethical decisions that they make.

IMPLICATIONS

Three major implications stand out. First, psychology as a profession has few generally agreed-on choices of action in several important and difficult areas of professional decision making. The fact that our respondents, all of whom were experienced clinicians, concurred that certain areas of professional decision making were areas of serious concern and that at the same time they failed to reach consensus as a group on these areas may be a troublesome state of affairs or not, depending on how one construes the task of professional ethics education in psychology. If this task is construed to involve the training of professionals in specific *behaviors* that are considered ethical, then our results are troubling. The implication of these results for professional ethics education is that such efforts must focus on teaching psychologists more effectively which are the right behaviors to choose in a variety of professional decision-making situations. On the other hand, if the task of professional ethics education is to inculcate ethical reasoning *processes*, then our results may be somewhat more heartening. As researchers in moral development have shown (Blasi, 1980), the same reasoning processes may lead to quite divergent behavioral outcomes. This is likely to be the case if professional moral decision making is involved. Psychologists who use the same ethical reasoning processes may arrive at quite different conclusions about the proper action. . . .

A second implication of this study is that work to further develop graduate course work in ethics (as required for APA accreditation) should be pursued, perhaps with particular attention to real-world ethical problems involving confidentiality, competence, and colleagues' behavior. In addition, our findings suggest that continuing education courses could be quite appropriate even for the experienced clinician.

A third implication is that particular areas of professional decision making deserve added scrutiny, debate, and consideration. They are competence (e.g., What is it? How do we measure it?), confidentiality (What are the implications of preserving it? of failing to uphold it?), diagnoses (For whom are they being done? What about the issue of stigma?), and whistle-blowing (What is the most appropriate means of reporting? To whom should complaints be addressed?). Some of these are empirical issues and should be dealt with as such. Others deserve added scrutiny and debate by the profession at large.

References

American Psychological Association. (1981). *Ethical principles of psychologists*. Washington, DC: Author.

Baldick, T. (1980): Ethical discrimination ability of intern psychologists: A function of training in ethics. *Professional Psychology, 11*, 276–282.

Blasi, A. (1980). Bridging moral cognition and moral action: A critical review of the literature. *Psychological Bulletin, 88*, 1–45.

Chalk, R., Frankel, M., & Chafer, S. (1980). *AAAS Professional Ethics Project: Professional ethics activities in the scientific and engineering societies*. Washington, DC: American Association for the Advancement of Science.

DeKraii, M. B., & Sales, B. D. (1984). Confidential communications of psychotherapists. *Psychotherapy, 21*, 293–318.

Haas, L. J. (1982). *The teaching of ethics in clinical psychology*. Paper presented at the annual convention of the American Psychological Convention. Washington, DC.

Haas, L. J., & Fennimore, D. (1983). Ethical and legal issues in professional psychology: Selected works, 1970–1981. *Professional Psychology: Research and Practice, 14*, 540–548.

Haas, L. J., Malouf, J. L., & Mayerson, N. H. (1985). *Ethics training, professional characteristics, and ethical "styles" of practicing psychologists*. Paper presented at the annual convention of the American Psychological Association, Los Angeles.

Jagim, R. D., Wittman, W., & Noll, J. (1978). Mental health professionals' attitudes toward confidentiality, privilege, and third-party disclosure. *Professional Psychology, 9*, 458–466.

Margolin, G. (1982). Ethical and legal considerations in marital and family therapy. *American Psychologist, 37*, 788–801.

Stapp, J., & Fulcher, R. (1983). The employment of APA members: 1982. *American Psychologist, 38,* 1298–1320.

Tymchuk, A., Drapkin, R., Major-Kingsley, S., Ackerman, A., Coffman, E., & Baum, M. (1982). Ethical decision making and psychologists' attitudes toward training in ethics. *Professional Psychology, 13,* 412–421.

◆ ◆ ◆

Commentary: In a companion study, Haas et al. (1988) explored the relationship between the particular choices made by the clinicians sampled and the particular reasons for those choices (e.g., upholding the law, upholding the code of ethics, and protecting clients' rights). For pertinent results, see Haas, L. J., Malouf, J. L., & Mayerson, N. H. (1988). Personal and professional characteristics as factors in psychologists' ethical decision making. Professional Psychology: Research and Practice, 19, 35–42.

As demonstrated by the two excerpts from Tymchuk et al. (1982) and Haas et al. (1986), and by the debate concerning the conflict between law and ethics, there are a number of reasons for the variability that one finds in the application, interpretation, and enforcement of the APA's Ethical Principles. For example, Kimmel (1991) has noted that a "growing body of research suggests that individuals systematically differ in the ways they formulate ethical appraisals of research," traced in part "to the fact that the ethical principles that guide research in the scientific community typically are broadly stated and are all too often ambiguous" (p. 786). In addition, he found that psychologists asked to review the ethical acceptability of hypothetical examples of behavioral research could be differentiated in their judgments largely on the basis of personal characteristics:

> *Variation in the ratings could best be accounted for by a set of four predictors: (a) the number of years since the psychologist received his or her terminal academic degree, (b) the general area of that degree, (c) gender of the psychologist, and (d) number of APA membership affiliations ($R^2 = .10$; $p < .001$). Psychologists who tended to be more approving in their ethical evaluations (thereby suggesting a greater emphasis on research benefits) were those who (a) were men, (b) had held their highest degree for a*

> *longer period of time, (c) had received the degree in a basic psychology area (such as social, experimental, or developmental psychology), and (d) were employed in research-oriented contexts. Psychologists who tended to disapprove or reflect conservatism in their judgments (thereby suggesting a greater emphasis on research costs) were those who (a) were women, (b) had held their highest degree for a shorter period of time, (c) had received the degree in an applied psychology area (such as counseling, school, or community psychology), and (d) were employed in service-oriented contexts. (p. 787)*

See Kimmel, A. J. (1991). Predictable biases in the ethical decision making of American psychologists. American Psychologist, 46, 786–788.

There are other, more systemic reasons why codes of ethics do not always engage the respect and authority sought for them. Using the vignettes developed by Haas and his colleagues, Smith, McGuire, Abbott, and Blau (1991) surveyed a sample of 102 eclectically oriented clinicians practicing either in private or in community mental health agencies in an attempt to assess the clinicians' reasoning in resolving professional ethical conflicts. The sample was predominantly White, female, and nondoctoral (70%). Smith et al.'s results supported the research by Bernard and his colleagues, presented earlier in this chapter, indicating a discrepancy between what clinicians recognize they should do and what they actually are willing to do:

> *These findings suggest that clinicians are most likely to act consistently with how they believe they should act when they believe the ethical violation involves one of the relatively clear rules of existing professional codes. This is particularly true when such professional rules of conduct are further supported by legal statutes or precedents (e.g., clear danger and duty to protect; prohibition against sexual contact with clients). On the other hand, existing professional codes and standards are more often utilitarian guidelines, not rules of conduct. Utilitarian principles suggest*

that what is ethically correct depends on an assessment of the effects of one's behavior on oneself and others. Such situations demand increased judgment by the clinician and result in greater inconsistency between perceived *should* versus *would* choices. In such conflict situations, what clinicians indicate that they would do is affected not only by professional or legal codes of conduct, but also by personal values and practical considerations of the situation. . . .

. . . Our findings suggest that professional–ethical decision making among nondoctoral-level providers involves processes similar to those previously demonstrated among doctoral level clinicians (Haas et al., 1986, 1988; Wilkins et al., 1990).

References

Haas, L. J., Malouf, J. L., & Mayerson, N. H. (1986). Ethical dilemmas in psychological practice: Results of a national survey. Professional Psychology: Research and Practice, 17, 317–321.

Haas, L. J., Malouf, J. L., & Mayerson, N. H. (1988). Personal and professional characteristics as factors in psychologists' ethical decision making. Professional Psychology: Research and Practice, 19, 35–42.

Wilkins, M., McGuire, J., Abbott, D., & Blau, B. (1990). Willingness to apply understood ethical principles. Journal of Clinical Psychology, 46, 539–547. (pp. 238–239)

See *Smith, T. S., McGuire, J. M., Abbott, D. W., & Blau, B. I. (1991). Clinical ethical decision making: An investigation of the rationales used to justify doing less than one believes one should.* Professional Psychology: Research and Practice, 22, 235–239.

When Laws and Values Conflict: A Dilemma for Psychologists

Kenneth S. Pope and Theresa Rose Bajt

Edmund Burke (1790/1961) stated the importance of absolute compliance with the law: "One of the first motives to civil society, and which becomes one of its fundamental rules, is, *that no man should be judge in his own cause*" (p. 71). The U.S. Supreme Court, in *Walker v. Birmingham* (1967), underscored this "belief that in the fair administration of justice no man can be judge in his own case, however exalted his station, however righteous his motives, and irrespective of his race, color, politics, or religion" (pp. 1219–1220).

Henry David Thoreau (1849/1960), however, urged that if a law "requires you to be the agent of injustice to another, then, I say, break the law" (p. 242). Even the California Supreme Court seemed to give tacit approval to breaking the law *as long as it is done within the framework of civil disobedience*: "If we were to deny to every person who has engaged in . . . nonviolent civil disobedience . . . the right to enter a licensed profession, we would deprive the community of the services of many highly qualified persons of the highest moral courage" (*Hallinan v. Committee of Bar Examiners of State Bar*, 1966, p. 239).

Neither stance may seem acceptable to psychologists who believe that compliance with a legal or professional obligation would be harmful, unjust, or otherwise wrong. Absolute compliance connotes a "just following orders" mentality all too ready to sacrifice personal values and client welfare to an imperfect system of rules and regulations. Selective noncompliance connotes an association of people who have annointed themselves as somehow above the law, able to pick and choose which legal obligations and recognized standards they will obey.

Civil disobedience itself may be precluded in significant areas of psychology. Coined as a term by Thoreau, civil disobedience as a concept has been developed, defined, and justified as an act involving open and public violation of the law while volunteering to accept the legal penalties. . . . This absolute openness—the lack of any attempt to avoid detection and prosecution—is essential in reaffirming respect for the process of law and accountability. But how can a psychologist, for example, *publicly* refuse to make a mandated report (e.g., regarding child abuse or potential harm to third parties) about a student, client, or subject without betraying the supposedly secret information?

We used an anonymous survey, with a 60% return rate, to explore this dilemma. The questionnaire was mailed to 100 senior psychologists, presumably acknowledged by their peers as knowledgeable and scrupulous regarding professional accountability: 60 current or former members of state ethics committees (50 of whom had served as chairs), 10 current or former members of the American Psychological Association (APA) Ethics Committee, 10 authors of textbooks focusing on legal or ethical aspects of psychology, and 20 diplomates of the American Board of Professional Psychology.

The first question was: "In the most serious, significant, or agonizing instance, if any, what law or formal ethical principle have you broken intentionally in light of a client's welfare or other deeper value?" A majority (57%) acknowledged such instances. Of these 34 instances, the following were reported by more than one respondent: 7 (21%) involved refusing to report child abuse, 7 (21%) involved illegally divulging confidential information,

3 (9%) involved engaging in sex with a client, 2 (6%) involved "dual relationships" (no details), and 2 (6%) involved refusing to make legally mandated warnings regarding dangerous clients. It is interesting to note that 48% involve the issue of whether certain information should be kept confidential. It is dismaying to note that 9% involve psychologists' using "client welfare or other deeper value" as a rationale for engaging in sex with a client.

Incidents reported by one respondent each were giving a student an inappropriately high grade to "help" the student, helping a colleague to fake a credential, using one's professional status and expertise to help someone obtain an illegal abortion, committing perjury to keep a client from going to jail, engaging in "insurance fraud" (respondent's phrase) to help the client pay for services, treating a minor without parents' consent, refusing to turn over a former client's records in response to a legitimate request, accepting a very expensive gift from a client, withholding significant information from a patient, refusing to collect insurance copayment, blurring a personal and professional relationship, continuing therapy beyond the point at which it should have ended, and "lied about my experience treating a particular disorder, in order to instill confidence in the patient-to-be."

Exactly half of the respondents consulted someone before taking the action; 68% discussed the incident afterwards. Beneficial results were reported by 91%; ill effects by 44%. Only one psychologist was, as a result of the incident, the object of a formal complaint. Seventy-three percent would, in hindsight, take the same action if the circumstances were the same.

Seventy-seven percent of the respondents believed "that formal legal and ethical standards should ever be violated on the basis of patient welfare or other deeper values." In light of the fact that three fourths of this select sample believed that psychologists should sometimes violate formal legal and ethical standards, and that a majority have actually done so, it is regrettable that only 18% report that the topic of conflicts between deeply held values and formal legal or ethical obligations was adequately addressed in their education, training, and supervision, and that only 22% believe that the topic is adequately addressed in the professional literature.

Are the aims toward which our laws and formal ethical standards strive ultimately supported or subverted when psychologists intentionally violate explicit legal and ethical standards that conflict with the psychologists' deeply held values? How can psychologists who believe that the authority of the legal and ethical codes are not absolute ensure that their actions are based on sound professional judgment rather than on self-interest, prejudice, rationalization, and the sense that one is "above the law"? Are the integrity, effectiveness, and fairness of our mechanisms of accountability—such as university grievance committees, human subjects review committees, and ethics committees—enriched or eroded when those who sit in judgment on the behavior of others have themselves intentionally broken the rules that they are seeking to enforce? Such dilemmas are in need of open acknowledgment and serious study.

References

Burke, E. (1961). *Reflections on the revolution in France*. Garden City, NY: Doubleday. (Original work published 1790)

Hallinan v. Committee of Bar Examiners of State Bar, 55 Cal. Rptr. 228 (1966).

Thoreau, H. D. (1960). *Walden and civil disobedience*. Boston: Houghton Mifflin. (*Civil disobedience* originally published 1849)

Walker v. City of Birmingham. 388 U.S. 307, 18 L ed 2d 1210 (1967).

Reply To Pope and Bajt

Charles Ansell and Harvey L. Ross

We are dismayed at Pope and Bajt's (October 1988) shocked reaction to their survey. In a survey sample of "100 senior psychologists, presumably acknowledged by their peers as knowledgeable and scrupulous" a majority revealed that they willingly violated laws or certain ethical principles, and would so do again on the basis of "client welfare or other deeper values" (Pope & Bajt, 1988, p. 828). Our reply here is concerned specifically with the reported failures to obey reporting laws.

We are puzzled that Pope and Bajt failed to understand the reasons for these responses. It was clear to us that the "100 senior psychologists" chose their client's welfare over mindless obedience to reporting laws. We are aware of the grim statistics on child abuse, and it is precisely our concern over such tragic behavior that prompted us to frame this reply.

The fact is that psychologists did not design reporting laws. Had psychologists been initially involved in designing and submitting such legislation they would have given serious thought to the effect of such laws on clinical practice, their probable effects on clients, and certainly their effects on the best interests of the child and his or her family. Instead of these thoughtful considerations, a handful of psychologists rushed to spread alarm among psychologists by equating the demand for obedience to reporting laws with ethical practice. Clearly, that kind of thinking subordinates the clinical function to a policing function.

We are distressed that organized psychology failed to address the deeper implications inherent in the new reporting laws. The impact of reporting laws has forced psychologists to accept a redefinition of professional responsibility. Given the practitioner's inability to predict violence, can reporting potential violence really prevent such acts? Have we instituted any studies to help us learn something of the eventual consequences of mandating the immediate reporting of potential child abuse, or suicide threats, or past sexual intimacies between clients and therapists (whether clients wanted to make such reports or not)? Methodologies of evaluation research are (or should be) well known and fully available to the new breed of psychological ethicists, but none has attempted to use research methods before they rushed into legislation. The ethicist might have assumed that a psychotherapist who suspected a client of child abuse might consider a range of options before rushing to report. Those options lie within the clinical function to make a judgment call. To deny therapists that judgment is a clear usurpation of professional function. Worse, it compels psychologists to turn away from their professional responsibilities to become agents of the police. . . .

Reference

Pope, K. S., & Bajt, T. (1988). When laws and values conflict: A dilemma for psychologists. *American Psychologist, 43,* 828–829.

When Laws and Values Conflict: Comment on Pope and Bajt

John R. Van Eenwyk

A small group of us who offer our services as pro bono psychologists for the Marjorie Kovler Center for the Treatment of Survivors of Torture have discovered an interesting dilemma wherein failure to report child abuse can actually undermine the therapeutic alliance with the abuser.

During a staffing of cases at the Kovler Center, one of our clinical staff reviewed his work with a family that had been referred to us by a local hospital. The parents had taken their daughter to a hospital for treatment of injuries sustained in a fall. The examining physician felt that the injuries could not have come from a fall and accused the parents of child abuse. As they vehemently denied that any abuse had taken place and as the father had been a victim of torture before immigrating to the United States, they were referred to the Kovler Center. During the staffing of the case, it was noted that if the parents admitted that the child had been abused, the child would most likely be removed from the home. Furthermore, if the parents felt that the Kovler Center was in any way involved with that removal, they would certainly terminate the therapy.

Up to this point, the picture is relatively familiar. Although our views do not necessarily reflect official policy of the Kovler Center, we all felt the conflict between observing the law and maintaining the therapeutic alliance. Nevertheless, as we discussed our concerns, a very interesting paradox emerged. That is, victims of torture are routinely subjected to abuse from those who locate themselves beyond the formal constraints of government. For example, torturers commonly say to their victims, "I am the law. I am the courts. I am the state." Although we felt ourselves torn between the extremes of those who are "just following orders" and those who "have anointed themselves as somehow above the law, able to pick and choose which legal obligations and recognized standards they will obey" (Pope & Bajt, p. 828), it was clear on which side we had to be. That is, to assure the parents that any admission of abuse would be held in strictest confidence and not reported as required by law would be to recreate the very premises on which the torture had been carried out in the first place.

The paradox was ruthlessly simple: To spare the parents was to be guilty by association of the same justifications used by those responsible for the problem—being beyond the law. Although cases like this are probably quite rare in the general practice, those of us involved in psychotherapy with survivors of torture might do well to keep this paradox in mind. It is essential that victims of torture understand that residents of the United States are protected by laws that apply to all and that no individual has the right to suspend them, for it is only within such a context that they can begin to rebuild their world, which has been so cruelly and arbitrarily shattered.

Reference

Pope, K. S., & Bajt, T. (1988). When laws and values conflict: A dilemma for psychologists. *American Psychologist, 43,* 828–829.

Reporting Laws, Confidentiality, and Clinical Judgment: Reply to Ansell and Ross

Seth C. Kalichman

... I share Pope and Bajt's (1988) surprise in the number of psychologists who, despite their knowledge of reporting laws, do not report suspected abuse. Not unlike the ethical experts in Pope and Bajt's survey, as many as 60% of psychologists have elected not to report suspected child abuse (Kalichman, Craig, & Follingstad, 1989). In a recently completed study of 328 licensed practicing psychologists from Minnesota and Oklahoma, Kalichman et al. found that 37% had suspected abuse and decided not to report it. Psychologists indicated a variety of reasons for failure to report. Contrary to Ansell and Ross's [1990] opinion, their data showed that the most influential factor in reporting decisions was not the clinician's concern over potential disruption to therapy (indicated by 22% of the sample), but rather the level of evidence available to substantiate abuse (indicated by 39%). Degree of confidence in the occurrence of abuse accounted for 18% of the variance in psychologists' decisions to report. ...

Failure to report suspected abuse (a) is at present illegal, (b) may result in reduced public trust in psychologists, and (c) may diminish a child's right to an investigation and potential prosecution of the perpetrator. Failure to report, therefore, violates Principle 3: Moral and Legal Standards of the "Ethical Principles of Psychologists" (APA, 1990).[1] Thus, in contrast to Ansell and Ross's (1990) statement suggesting that obedience of the law is not equal to ethical practice, it appears to be so in the case of reporting abuse.

Although I share Ansell and Ross's [1990] concern over limitations placed on clinical judgment, justification of disregarding reporting laws is potentially dangerous for practitioners as well as their clients. As receivers of sensitive information, psychologists have the obligation to "respect the confidentiality of information obtained from persons in the course of their work as psychologists" (APA, 1990, p. 392).[2] Likewise, psychologists have an obligation to handle information legally. Decisions to report suspected child abuse often entail dilemmas and always involve either adherence to or violation of the law. Indeed, it is paradoxical that ethical psychologists so frequently choose to break the law.

References

American Psychological Association. (1990). Ethical principles of psychologists (Amended June 2, 1989). *American Psychologist, 15,* 390–395.

Ansell, C., & Ross, H. (1990). Reply to Pope and Bajt. *American Psychologist, 45,* 399.

Kalichman, S. C., Craig, M., & Follingstad, D. (1989). Factors influencing the reporting of father–child sexual abuse: Study of licensed practicing psychologists. *Professional Psychology: Research and Practice, 20,* 84–89.

Pope, K., & Bajt, T. (1988). When laws and values conflict: A dilemma for psychologists. *American Psychologist, 43,* 828–829.

[1] *Ed. note*: See Standards 1.02 and 5.05 of the APA's current (1992) Ethical Principles.

[2] *Ed. note*: See Standard 5.02 of the APA's current (1992) Ethical Principles.

Professional Ethics and Legal Responsibilities: On the Horns of a Dilemma

Donald N. Bersoff

It should be evident . . . that codes of ethics and the law may present competing demands. . . . It is not so clear, however, why this phenomenon should exist. One would expect that the law would provide only minimal standards and require less exacting behavior than idealistic codes of ethics designed to guide the conduct of highly trained, carefully selected, service-oriented professionals. Several factors may be responsible for this anomaly.

A basic reason for the failure of ethical codes to provide adequate bases for behavior is their ethnocentrism. Ethics "refer to the way a group of associates define their special responsibility to one another and to the rest of the social order in which they work" (K. Erikson, 1967, p. 367). Thus, codes represent the professional group's point of view and are rarely developed with help from the consumers who receive the professional's services. Psychologists may be living under the false presumption that their ethic is shared by the people they serve. As Nettler (1959) has pointed out, "When the student of behavior works in a . . . community, he cannot assume that his scientifically honorable intentions will be considered morally justifiable by those whom he seeks to help" [p. 683].

Another fundamental problem is that ethical principles are formulated on such an abstract level that they merely provide general guides to actual behavior (Fox, 1959); practitioners rarely understand how these principles are to be applied in specific situations. Enforcement procedures do not provide for the dissemination of decisions arrived at by ethics committees whose judgments and recommendations are made known only to the profession and is limited to those instances when a member has been ex-

pelled for a violation. As a consequence, codes may be seen as meaningless rules extraneous to the everyday functioning of the practitioner.

A corollary outcome is that the value of codes may be perceived soley as a means of providing practitioners with a symbol that they are truly professionals, not merely employees, who thereby have a legitimate claim to autonomy. One of the traditional hallmarks of a profession (along with selective recruitment, extended training, and controlled entrance to practice) is a code of ethics which emphasizes devotion to service, concern for the client, and the positive attributes of its adherents (Becker, 1962). With a code in hand and elaborate procedures for its enforcement, the profession may feel that it is now entitled to the trust and confidence of the public it serves. But, as Friedson (1970) has indicated, a code of ethics "has no necessary relationship to the actual behavior of members of the occupation. . . . In this sense, a code of ethics may be seen as one of many methods an occupation may use to induce general belief in the ethicality of its members, without necessarily bearing directly on individual ethicality" [p. 187].

A most painful possibility is that our ethical codes are but hollow symbols of a myth of professionalism. . . . As long as it appears to courts and to the public that psychology is a cacophony of competing claims to workable procedures, the judgment of its members, regardless of the profession's high-minded ethical standards, will be open to challenge. Psychology is fragmented into many different schools each espousing its own theoretical orientation, a state of affairs which may motivate research and enliven the professional journals but which may inspire little confidence in society. With the field so divided it is not difficult to explain why codes of ethics remain vague and abstract and why a wide variety of specific behavior is tolerated. But, while psychology may permit different interpretations of its ethical guidelines, the courts may not be so benevolent. They do not find it all difficult to disregard a profession's claim to autonomy when the behavior of its practitioners is perceived to interfere with the rights of individuals or the public at large. . . .

A number of fundamental changes may be in order if . . . psychologists . . . are to become less vulnerable to litigation and more reliant on workable codes of ethics. To reduce ethnocentrism, it may be helpful for future committees, whose charge it is to rework existing codes, to make parents, children, school officials, and others who will be directly affected by the actions of professionals, integral parts of their membership. To make codes more pertinent and applicable, it may be helpful to consider publishing cases heard by ethics committees. The cases could be collected and printed in much the same way judicial decisions are currently collected. The reports could include the facts involved (with anonymity assured where appropriate), the precise issues in question, the decision of the committee, and the rationale for its judgment. In this way students and practitioners alike would gain heightened awareness of the myriad ethical problems faced by their colleagues and would learn consensually-arrived-at techniques for preventing or remediating such problems.

Psychologists may need to expose themselves more freely to the professional scrutiny and criticism of their colleagues. Acting in a vacuum tends to develop an exaggerated sense of self-correctness. Such conduct makes practitioners assailable when their work is subjected to close examination by courts and attorneys who are not likely to defer to opinion, reputation or professional aura of "expert" on the witness stand (see Ziskin, 1975). This is a time when many professionals are experiencing searching inquiry into their behavior. Courts, particularly, have become less tolerant of claims to autonomy and are less willing to accept self-regulation by professionals as those society [has] trusted are shown to be untrustworthy. . . .

References

Becker, H. C. (1962). The nature of a profession. In N. B. Nelson (Ed.), *The sixty-first yearbook of the National Society for the Study of Education*. Chicago: NSSE, 1962.

Erikson, K. T. A comment on disguised observation in sociology. *Social Problems*. 1967. 14, 366–373.

Fox, R. *Experiment perilous*. Glencoe, Ill.: The Free Press, 1959.

Friedson, E. *The profession of medicine*. New York: Dodd, Mead, 1970.

Nettler, G. Test burning in Texas. *American Psychologist*, 1959, 14, 682–683.

Ziskin, J. *Coping with psychiatric and psychological testimony*. Beverly Hills: Law and Psychology Press, 1975.

◆ ◆ ◆

Commentary: Other authors also have addressed the value of a code of ethics and criticized the method of its development. Pope and Vetter (1992), who provided a brief and informative history of the development of the first APA ethical code (see chapter 1), complained that the revision process that led to the 1992 Code of Conduct was flawed because that code was not drafted in the same was as the original code, that is, "guided by contemporary empirical data about the incidents faced by the full range of APA's current membership" (p. 409). They argued that unless a critical incident or empirical approach is used, "the code risks losing relevance and applicability" (p. 409). See Pope, K. S., & Vetter, V. A. (1992). Ethical dilemmas encountered by members of the American Psychological Association: A national survey. American Psychologist, 47, 397–411.

Barlow (1989) has asserted that although "respected, quoted, and esteemed by all," ethics codes "have influence, but little, if any actual authority" (p. 9). He believes that, in addition to often containing contradictory principles, such codes have limited moral authority because they undergo regular revision:

> *Sponsoring agencies tend to proceed with regard to special interests and a democratic process of voting to affirm the declarations they compose. By nature the statements can be emended, amended, or revised as the voting body decides. This policy allows for important updating and adjustments called*

for by technological innovation. But it also allows for amended restatement in response to changes in social policy and moral sentiment.

Moreover, contemporary promulgations are often little more than consensus statements affirming no more than what everyone in the group at that moment agrees upon. The larger, more heterogeneous is the sponsoring body, the more general, simplified, and minimalist is the position taken. A mark is chiseled into the ethical bench, but its reach is usually only as high as the least common denominator. (p. 13)

See Barlow, J. (1989). The practical limits of codes and declarations. In L. P. Bird & J. Barlow (Eds.), Codes of medical ethics, oaths, and prayers: An anthology (pp. 9–14). Richardson, TX: Christian Medical and Dental Society.

Welfel and Lipsitz (1984) were in accord with Barlow's (1989) view:

In recent years, the profession has shown an increased awareness that even thorough familiarity with the code and powerful sanctions against nonconforming psychologists are insufficient in themselves to guarantee ethical practice. For example, a number of authors . . . have pointed out that the ethical codes serve only as general guidelines for practice. They suggest that changes in professional practice happen so quickly that not even regular revision of the standards can address every aspect of current practice. They also contend that many ethically sensitive situations arising in the course of practice are difficult to categorize according to the tenets of the code. In some extreme cases, adherence to one portion of the code even seems to result in violation of another portion. Most importantly, they argue that the purpose of the code was never to provide blueprints that would remove all need for the use of judgment by individual psychologists, but rather, to act as a foundation to assist the psychologist in determining the applicability of the code to his or her unique and often complex situation. (p. 31)

See Welfel, E. R., & Lipsitz, N. E. (1984). The ethical behavior of professional psychologists: A critical analysis of the research. The Counseling Psychologist, 12(3), 31–41.

CHAPTER 3

LEARNING ETHICS

Since the late 1970s, every graduate program training professional psychologists that seeks to be accredited by the APA has been required to offer instruction in ethics and to familiarize students with whatever version of the APA ethics code is current at the time. APA does not accredit programs that train graduate students solely for research positions, but a great many such programs offer similar instruction in ethics, at the very least concentrating on the ethics of experimentation and scholarship. Does this training ensure that those who complete these programs act ethically as professionals? As the data and material presented in chapters 1 and 2 illustrate, this is often not the case.

As we have begun to explore, there are a variety of reasons for psychologists to act in ways that violate the code of ethics. A few miscreants deliberately flout their professional and scientific responsibilities for personal gain—monetary, reputational, and sexual, among others. For example, the psychologist who, without consulting his or her client, rushes to the media with the news that he or she is the therapist of a famous personage just charged with a heinous crime is acting in a purely self serving and inexcusable manner. Other psychologists violate ethical principles because of imprudence, ignorance, or insensitivity about the ethical consequences of their behavior. For instance, consider the psychologist who calls child protection services after she learns that the parents she is counseling are punishing their 10-year-old child with a rattan cane. When the parents file an ethics complaint, the psychologist responds that she thought she was mandated by law to report child abuse but never realized that the APA ethics code also required her to inform clients of the limits of confidentiality or that failing to do that would damage the development of the therapeutic relationship.

These are relatively simple cases to adjudicate. But there are at least two others kinds of cases that are more complex. In the first case are psychologists who attempt to comply with the rules but, perceiving that they lack the guidance of clearly written, explicit, and precise ethical provisions, rely on their own interpretation of those rules. To illustrate, under the 1992 ethics code, psychologists are supposed to discuss the limits of confidentiality with clients very close to the beginning of a therapeutic relationship, "unless it is not feasible or is contraindicated" (APA, 1992, p. 1606). Suppose now that a patient in the third year of intensive psychoanalysis begins to fall behind in paying for his therapy. For several months the analyst and the patient discuss the patient's failure to pay as part of his resistance to therapy. Finally, however, with the unpaid bills mounting, the analyst and the patient agree to terminate therapy. The analyst then turns over the outstanding account to a collection agency. The client complains that his right to confidentiality was violated when the analyst submitted his name to the collection agency without telling him at any time during treatment that she would do so. In response, the analyst explains that her conduct violated no ethical rule because she believed that any discussion of the limits of confidentiality at the outset of treatment would have interfered with transference issues so crucial to successful psychoanalysis. Thus, in her mind, disclosure was "contraindicated." Lacking specific guidance in this situation by those who drafted the code, the psychologist made a not implausible interpretation of her own.

The most complex situations are those that present ethically sensitive and knowledgeable psychologists with fundamental and profound ethical dilemmas. Psychologists in these cases understand the rules (or the law) but break them because they consider violation to be in the service of higher moral principles. Consider the following case example. A 10th-grade boy is enrolled in research studying violence in adolescents and how it might be prevented through short-term intervention. During an interview portion of the study, the student reveals to the female investigator that he has had many fantasies about harming his next-door neighbor, a slightly older female teenager who refuses to pay him any attention. On further inquiry, the investigator also learns that the student is contemplating the purchase of a gun. The investigator suggests to the student that it would be a good idea to inform his parents of the situation, even though she is aware that he has no history of violent behavior. The student adamantly refuses to inform his parents or to let the investigator do so, warning that he will drop out of the study and treatment if she does not honor his refusal. Believing that preserving confidentiality would, in the long run, be in the student's best interest by not driving him out of needed treatment and would most closely express the psychologists' moral principle of fidelity, the investigator agrees not to tell his parents.

One week later, the psychologist reads in the newspaper that, with a gun bought the day before, her research subject has shot and wounded his teenage neighbor after she ignored him one evening. The parents of the 10th-grade student file a complaint with APA, stating that the psychologist should have informed them of their son's potentially violent and harmful behavior, regardless of his wishes. The psychologist concedes that the code permits disclosure without consent to protect third parties from harm, but she argues that supporting the boy's right to privacy and autonomy and the need to establish trust in therapy outweighed any putative entitlement in the code of ethics to inform his parents.

Although the psychologist's decision in this case may have contributed to a negative outcome, the situation did present her with a genuine ethical dilemma. It would have been perfectly ethical for her to disclose the student's confidences and even to refuse to abide by his demand for secrecy. Nevertheless, she decided that this course of action conflicted with more universal moral principles—the promotion of autonomy and the development of faithfulness to her subject's expressed interests—that were an inherent part of her value system as a psychologist.

All psychologists will be faced with such dilemmas sometime in their careers. They may find that, by necessity or design, the APA code of ethics contains few absolute and explicit prohibitions regarding a particular dilemma. The psychologist who wishes to act ethically in an ethically uncertain world needs to have both a philosophical base from which to make decisions and a method for using that base to build workable options.

In this chapter, I offer some frameworks for recognizing a genuine ethical dilemma, for generating possible solutions to it, and, perhaps for arriving at a reasonable resolution in line with the ethical principles of one's professional association and one's personal value system.

However, as the authors of material in this chapter argue, acting ethically is not a compartmentalized function. Instead, ethical behavior results from integrating didactic knowledge, including a thorough familiarity with the APA ethics code; an understanding of problem-solving and decision-making approaches; a clear conception of the philosophical principles (each of which may compete with one another) that underlie the formal code of ethics; and a basically sound character that leads one to respond with maturity, judgment, discretion, wisdom, and prudence.

In the remainder of this book I concentrate on seven central topics that inevitably confront and test the psychology practitioner, researcher, and professor with ethical dilemmas surrounding confidentiality, multiple relationships, assessment, therapeutic interventions, teaching and doing research in an academic institution, serving as an expert witness, and dealing with the commercial and business aspects of psychology. Because this chapter provides the foundation for ethical decision making under each of these topics, I consider it absolutely crucial to understanding and integrating the material in the remaining chapters of the book.

References

American Psychological Association. (1992). Ethical principles of psychologists and code of conduct. *American Psychologist, 47,* 1597–1611.

Problems With Ethics Training by "Osmosis"

Mitchell M. Handelsman

Ethical training by osmosis refers to the practice of allowing ethics to be taught in the context of supervision, in which a sensitivity to issues will seep through during discussions of cases. In this article I argue that relying on such informal methods to teach ethics is a dangerous practice.

There is an old and widespread belief that ethics can best be taught in the context of supervised clinical work rather than as a separate, formal course. Veatch and Sollitto (1976) cited one respondent from their survey of medical schools: "Probably the most important teaching of ethics takes place between preceptors and students when students are actually involved with patient care and ethical issues arise" (p. 1031). In a recent survey of ethics training among master's degree programs in psychology, I (Handelsman, 1986) found that although a relatively high percentage of programs had a formal course or part of a course devoted to ethics, a majority of the programs with no formal ethics courses felt that ethics can best be taught in the context of supervision. One respondent to that survey said, "I do not see any reason why this should be a whole course. I see ethics as a topic that "naturally" comes up in *all* (or almost all) graduate seminars, i.e., rather than a course on its own."

The first argument against training in the context of practica concerns the nature and extent of supervision. "It is usually assumed that adequate supervision will always be provided in the clinic or hospital, but this is far from universally true" (Arnhoff & Jenkins, 1969, p. 441). Often, needs and time constraints of the agency take precedence over careful exploration of ethical issues. Competence of supervisors in ethics is also an issue. Dalton (1984) noted that "students' learning is limited by the supervisor's awareness of ethical dilemmas and assumptions; is-

sues not recognized by the supervisor are not recognized or mentioned by students" (p. 186). The "extended supervision" argument, then, may be an instance of transferring responsibility. . . .

Even if one knows that supervisors do an adequate job of exploring ethical issues (this remains, of course, an empirical question) when such issues arise in the course of clinical work, this method does not guarantee that a broad range of ethical issues will arise. In their survey, Tymchuk et al. (1982) found that 58% of doctoral-level psychologists felt "that they were not well informed enough about ethical issues in psychology" (p. 419). One may overcome such a gap in knowledge by exposure to such issues in a formal way, rather than leaving it up to chance.

Informal methods of ethics training do not prepare practitioners to handle future ethical dilemmas through the application of relevant principles. Memorizing lists of case examples is no longer adequate, given the rapidly changing nature of the field (Tymchuk, 1981). The ability to generalize from one situation to others may not be adequately developed if a general conceptualization of ethical issues is not taught. Pressure to deal with individual cases and to cover treatment issues in a limited supervision session make the development of such general skills unlikely.

There is no doubt that important learning takes place in relation to meaningful events, and ethical issues encountered during clinical practice will remain salient. However, to rely on such learning to take place seems to be a dangerous practice. Reconceptualizing ethics and its training is needed in training programs. It is necessary to treat ethical thinking as a skill that must be developed and that is not intimately bound to the process of therapy, testing, and so on. . . .

Adapted from *Professional Psychology: Research and Practice*, 17, 371–372. Copyright 1986 by the American Psychological Association.

One can make room for an ethics course by dropping a core course, such as perception or learning, from the curriculum. Although this certainly weakens the scientist–practitioner model, it may be unethical to preserve this model at the expense of ethics training. When one joins the American Psychological Association, one is sent a copy of the Ethical Principles, not of reinforcement schedules. A compromise solution would be to make the ethics course, the core courses, or both less than full credit. A danger in this arrangement may be that students would perceive these courses as less important, but this could be offset by the rigor of the courses themselves and by the enthusiasm of the instructors.

Another reason for lack of ethics courses may be that faculty, given their own areas of expertise, are not qualified to teach general ethics courses. A psychotherapist, for example, may not be well qualified to teach about the ethics of deception and informed consent to research. One approach to this problem would be to team-teach the course. In this way, each faculty member would be responsible for covering issues that he or she is (or should be) familiar with. Also, guest lecturers could be recruited from various sources, such as state psychological association ethics committees. This would tap a valuable and underused resource, but might also, because of the contact, facilitate trainees' consultation of such committees in the future. The danger in such an approach is that the course could amount to an appendage to a program for which nobody takes full responsibility. One must take care not to model such an attitude towards ethics.

Ethics courses can be made more stimulating and relevant by being taught with a variety of methods that blend theory and application. Learning can include general ethical concepts (Solomon, 1984), ethical thinking processes (Tymchuk, 1981), values clarification (Abeles, 1980), use of comprehensive textbooks (e.g., Keith-Spiegel & Koocher, 1985; Steininger, Newell, & Garcia, 1984), and exploration of ethical dilemmas (e.g., Mills, 1983). Bloch (1980) described one such multifaceted approach to a psychiatric ethics course. Bloch enlisted the services of moral philosophers, who acted as "respondents" to class discussions and facilitated the integration of general ethical theories and principles with specific rules and dilemmas.

Just as psychologists have abandoned the apprenticeship model of psychotherapy training and have recognized that courses in therapeutic theory and techniques are desirable and effective, so they need to think of ethical reasoning as a skill that can be taught and studied in much the same way.

References

Abeles, N. (1980). Teaching ethical principles by means of values confrontations. *Psychotherapy: Theory, Research and Practice, 17*, 384–391.

Arnhoff, F. N., & Jenkins, J. W. (1969). Subdoctoral education in psychology: A study of issues and attitudes. *American Psychologist, 24*, 430–443.

Bloch, S. (1980). Teaching of psychiatric ethics. *British Journal of Psychiatry, 136*, 300–301.

Dalton, J. H. (1984). Discussing ethical issues in practicum courses. *Teaching of Psychology, 11*, 186–188.

Handelsman, M. M. (1986). Ethics training at the master's level: A national survey. *Professional Psychology: Research and Practice, 17*, 24–26.

Keith-Spiegel, P., & Koocher, G. P. (1985). *Ethics in psychology: Professional standards and cases.* Hillsdale, NJ: Erlbaum.

Mills, D. H. (1983, April). *Professional ethics.* Invited workshop presented at the meeting of the Rocky Mountain Psychological Association, Snowbird, UT.

Solomon, R. C. (1984). *Ethics: A brief introduction.* New York: McGraw-Hill.

Steininger, M., Newell, J. D., & Garcia, L. T. (1984). *Ethical issues in psychology.* Homewood, IL: Dorsey.

Tymchuk, A. J. (1981). Ethical decision-making and psychological treatment. *Journal of Psychiatric Treatment and Evaluation, 3*, 507–513.

Tymchuk, A. J., Drapkin, R. S., Major-Kingsley, S., Ackerman, A. B., Coffman, E. W., & Baum, M. S. (1982). Ethical decision making and psychologists' attitudes toward training in ethics. *Professional Psychology, 13*, 412–421.

Veatch, R. M., & Sollitto, S. (1976). Medical ethics teaching: Report of a national medical school survey. *Journal of the American Medical Association, 235*, 1030–1033.

◆ ◆ ◆

Commentary: Compare the argument above by Handelsman (1986) to the following, written by Welfel and Lipsitz 2 years earlier:

> *In spite of the dramatic increase in availability of ethics courses in graduate pro-*

grams there has been little systematic investigation of the impact of such experiences on students. In fact, there is little information regarding exactly what is being taught in those courses. . . .

[The] literature only very weakly supports the interpretation that ethics courses have a positive impact on students. No study has been reported that examines the influence of such training on actual behavior with clients or assesses whether the effects of ethics courses are temporary or permanent. In addition, there are no data to compare whether ethics is best taught in a separate

course or integrated into existing courses in the curriculum. Thus, the push to initiate separate ethics courses in graduate programs is based more on the "good hearted assumption" that such courses will have a positive impact than on any scientific data. Given the cost in faculty time and in tuition for such training systematic research into such courses seems imperative. (p. 37).

See Welfel, E. R., & Lipsitz, N. E. (1984). The ethical behavior of professional psychologists: A critical analysis of the research. Counseling Psychologist, 12(3), 31–41.

Psychologist as Ethics Educator: Successes, Failures, and Unanswered Questions

Elizabeth Reynolds Welfel

The American Psychological Association began mandating ethics training in its accreditation standards in 1979, thirty-one years after it accredited its first clinical psychology program in 1948. This modification of the standards to include ethics training reflected the profession's growing recognition of the importance of ethical behavior and of the need for more explicit instruction in ethics during graduate school. This recognition grew out of a burgeoning literature on ethics in therapy and clearer evidence of flagrant violations of ethical standards by some therapists. . . .

HISTORY AND CURRENT STATUS OF ETHICS EDUCATION

In the first published survey of ethics education in psychology programs, DePalma and Drake (1956) queried faculty from both practice and nonpractice specialties in psychology. They found that only 6% of the graduate programs included a separate required course in ethics. Another 34% offered ethics either as an elective or as a discussion topic in other courses. In other words, they reported that 60% of the programs provided little or no training in professional ethics. In addition, they noted little dissatisfaction with this state of affairs among respondents and cited examples of department chairs who were "frankly skeptical about the need for such a course" (p. 555) or expressed the view that ethics need not be taught if the admissions committee does its work properly. The sentiment among many psychology educators at the time was that ethical behavior was almost fully determined by moral character, which was established and essentially unchangeable by adulthood. Needless to say, subsequent research in

moral development has effectively challenged the accuracy of that belief. (See Rest et al., 1986, for a detailed description of that literature.)

By the time the next survey of ethics education was published in 1973, modifications in curricula and faculty attitudes were apparent. Jorgensen and Weigel (1973) reported required ethics courses in 14% of the clinical programs and exposure to professional ethics, either informally or through structured units in other courses, in some other part of the curriculum in 80% of the sample. While Jorgensen and Weigel did not inquire directly about the beliefs of faculty about ethics education, their findings implied a growing acceptance of the position that professional ethical behavior requires more than good moral character. Nevertheless, they still encountered individual faculty who believed that ethics could not be taught in a classroom.

In 1979 Tymchuk et al. reported that 55% of the programs in clinical psychology they surveyed required an ethics course of all students. Some other formal instruction in ethics (such as a planned unit in another course) was provided in another 12% of the programs. Still another 29% indicated that ethics was taught in an informal format as the topic emerged from class discussion or at the judgment of the individual instructor. In other words, by 1979, a full 96% of the clinical programs reported some attention to ethics, but only 67% of these used a formal structure such as a separate course or planned units within other courses. In addition, when Tymchuk et al. asked training directors whether ethics should be taught in graduate school, 98% agreed and 71% supported a separate, required course on professional ethics. In short, by 1979 endorsement of ethics training as a necessary part of professional education was almost universal among clinical programs. Moreover, the implementation of formal ethics instruction had increased but still lagged behind stated beliefs of faculty.

By 1990, the transformation in approaches to ethics education was even more dramatic. Vanek (1990) reported that all of her 209 respondents from APA-approved clinical and counseling psychology programs stated that ethics was included in the graduate curriculum. The majority (69%) had a separate required course, and almost all of these had also included additional attention to ethics in other parts of the curriculum. The remainder of her sample had some other planned format for attention to ethics, usually lectures on ethics in other established courses. Only 4% of the programs offered ethics as an elective. Vanek also reported that 74% of the respondents allocated more than 20 class hours to ethics and more than 50% allocated in excess of 30 hours. Thus, between 1979 and 1990 informal discussion of ethics as a primary mode of teaching appears to have largely vanished from the curriculum. Whether such universality in ethics education characterizes all clinical and counseling psychology programs or just those programs willing to complete a survey is an open question. . . .

. . . [T]he pattern of responses by faculty over a period of years and across different surveys lends credibility to the interpretation that ethics classes now occur more frequently and are supported by more faculty. Moreover, other studies of ethical decision-making skills of psychologists report the same pattern. For example, Lipsitz (1985), Tymchuk, Drapkin, Major-Kingsley, Ackerman, Major, and Baum (1982), Tymchuk (1985), Wilkins, McGuire, Abbott, and Blau (1990) and Wood, Klein, Cross, Lammers, and Elliott (1985) reported substantial percentages of psychologists who indicated that they had been exposed to some planned ethics instruction during graduate school.

At first glance, then, it appears that psychology educators have made important strides in ethics education in recent times. The majority of psychology educators now appear to view ethics education as their responsibility, not the responsibility of admissions committees or clinical supervisors (Handlesman,

1986a; Tymchuk et al., 1979; Vanek, 1990). Faculty also appear to provide planned attention to ethics in the curriculum rather than relying on the informal methods of teaching common in earlier decades. In addition, Vanek (1990) reported that faculty identified the primary motivation for teaching ethics as its intrinsic importance to the profession rather than the pressures of accreditation or licensing bodies. . . .

References

DePalma, N., & Drake, R. (1956). Professional ethics for graduate students in psychology. *American Psychologist, 11*, 554–557.

Handelsman, M. M. (1986a). Ethics training at the master's level: A national survey. *Professional Psychology: Research and Practice, 17*, 24–26.

Jorgensen, G. T., & Weigel, R. G. (1973). Training psychotherapists: Practices regarding ethics, personal growth, and locus of responsibility. *Professional Psychology: Research and Practice, 4*, 23–27.

Lipsitz, N. E. (1985, August). *The relationship between ethics training and ethical discrimination ability.* Paper presented at the Annual Meeting of the American Psychological Association, Los Angeles.

Rest, J. R., Barnett, R., Bebeau, M., Deemer, D., Getz, I., Moon, Y., Spickelmeir, J., Thoma, S., & Volker, J. (1986). *Moral development: Advances in research and theory.* New York: Praeger.

Tymchuk, A. J. (1985). Ethical decision-making and psychology students' attitudes toward training in ethics. *Professional Practice of Psychology, 6*, 219–232.

Tymchuk, A. J., Drapkin, R. S., Ackerman, A. B., Major, S. M., Coffman, E. W., & Baum, M. S. (1979). Survey of training in ethics in APA-approved clinical psychology programs. *American Psychologist, 34*, 1168–1170.

Tymchuk, A. J., Drapkin, R. S., Major-Kingsley, S., Ackerman, A. B., Major, S. M., & Baum, M. S. (1982). Ethical decision making and psychologists' attitudes toward training in ethics. *Professional Psychology: Research and Practice, 13*, 412–421.

Vanek, C. A. (1990). Survey of ethics education in clinical and counseling psychology. *Dissertation Abstracts International, 52*, 5797B. (University Microfilms No. 91-14, 449)

Wilkins, M., McGuire, J., Abbott, D., & Blau, B. (1990). Willingness to apply understood ethical principles. *Journal of Clinical Psychology, 46*, 539–547.

Wood, B. J., Klein, S., Cross, H. J., Lammers, C. J., & Elliott, J. K. (1985). Impaired practitioners: Psychologists' opinions about prevalence and proposals for intervention. *Professional Psychology: Research and Practice, 16*, 843–850.

◆ ◆ ◆

Commentary: *Tymchuk et al. (1982) have argued that*

the profession . . . needs to attend more
closely to decision-making processes and develop decision-making standards that can be
applied to situations as they arise. What
may be most useful for the professional are
broader and more basic decision-making
standards rather than specific rules that attempt to define behavior as "right" or

"wrong." Models are needed that incorporate
a comprehensive range of ethical considerations in order to assist psychologists in the
process of making critical decisions. (p. 420)

See *Tymchuk, A. J., Drapkin, R. S., Major-Kingsley, S.,
Ackerman, A. B., Major, S. M., & Baum, M. S. (1982).
Ethical decision making and psychologists' attitudes to-
ward training in ethics.* Professional Psychology:
Research and Practice, 13, 412–421.

*Consider whether the next two excerpts provide those
models.*

Integrating Psychology and Philosophy in Teaching a Graduate Course in Ethics

Mark A. Fine and Lawrence P. Ulrich

. . . To explicitly state our position from the outset, we regard the teaching of graduate-level courses in ethics to be a critical and necessary component of graduate training in psychology. It is not sufficient merely to add a short footnote about ethics to the subject matter of various courses. Although this common practice may be helpful in showing how ethical concerns are an integral part of psychological practice, these issues are often addressed in terms of conclusions without sufficient conceptual justification for the positions taken. A separate course is necessary, we believe, because an adequate ethical analysis can occur only when there is a formulation and critical appraisal of the justifications that underlie ethical decisions.

. . . [I]t is important to justify why we feel that it is critically important to include a philosophical component in ethics courses for psychology graduate students. First, philosophers have studied ethics much more thoroughly than have psychologists. Ethics is generally considered the appropriate subject matter of philosophy, insofar as psychologists typically treat ethics as a tool to assist them in conducting their clinical activities, but not as a primary subject matter in itself. Second, as a result of philosophy's greater acquaintance with ethical subject matter, it is better suited to assist when there arise ethical dilemmas that cannot easily be resolved with reference to ethical codes. . . . As Kitchener (1984) and Eberlein (1987) noted, when such situations arise, one must resort to underlying principles and theories, which are within the expertise of philosophy. Third, a greater understanding of ethical theory may assist psychology as a profession in the continual process of articulating ethical guidelines or codes.

Our model of the ethical decision-making process derives from work by Beauchamp and Walters (1982) and has similarities to a discussion by Kitchener (1984). It consists of four distinct levels. The most general level of ethical reasoning consists of ethical frameworks or theories. We address two of the most commonly articulated frameworks, utilitarianism and deontology. *Utilitarianism*, often associated with John Stuart Mill and Jeremy Bentham, is based on the major principle that an action as ethically appropriate when it leads to the greatest possible balance of good consequences or to the least possible balance of bad consequences in the world as a whole (Beauchamp & Walters, 1982). Thus from a utilitarian perspective, one must carefully evaluate and weigh the relative value of the consequences that are expected to arise from an ethical decision and choose that action that maximizes the ratio of benefits to costs. *Deontology*, initially associated with Immanuel Kant, is based on the major principle (categorical imperative) that one must act to treat every person as an end and never as a means only (Beauchamp & Walters, 1982). This reflects inherent respect for the dignity of all persons. The morality of actions is based on their intrinsic rightness, is independent of the consequences of the behaviors, and thus permits no exceptions to the major principle. . . .[1]

The case of *Tarasoff v. Board of Regents of the University of California* (1976) may help to clarify the meaning of the two ethical frameworks. A utilitarian

[1]*Ed. note*: Another term often contrasted with *deontology* is *teleology*. Teleological ethical theory holds that actions are judged by the goodness of their consequences. Thus, it is closely akin to utilitarianism.

judgment would involve a careful assessment of the benefits and costs of violating confidentiality and warning potential victims. Because of individual variation in the assessment of benefits and costs, differing conclusions may be reached. In fact, a majority of the justices of the California Supreme Court argued on utilitarian grounds that the potential victim should have been warned, but a minority of the justices, also using utilitarian guidelines, maintained that the greater good arose from not breaking confidentiality in such instances because the integrity of the therapeutic relationship would be enhanced and potentially violent individuals would be more likely to seek and benefit from psychotherapy. A deontological argument would suggest that one should maintain confidentiality in *all* cases because an individual's right to privacy is a moral absolute and should never be violated.

The next level of ethical reasoning represents specific principles derived from the frameworks. Examples of principles (Beauchamp & Walters, 1982) include autonomy (i.e., a person should be free to perform whatever action he or she wishes, regardless of risks or foolishness, provided that it does not impinge on the autonomy of others), beneficence (i.e., one should render positive assistance to others, and abstain from harm, by helping them to further their important and legitimate interests), justice (i.e., one should give to persons what they are owed, what they deserve, or what they can legitimately claim), and paternalism (i.e., one should restrict an individual's action against his or her consent in order to prevent that individual from self-harm or to secure for that individual a good that he or she might not otherwise achieve). These flow logically from the frameworks; that is, a utilitarian perspective would suggest that one should respect an individual's autonomy, provided that it does not impinge on the autonomy of others, because this maximizes the ratio of benefits to harm. Although deontological perspectives have similar principles, they may take a somewhat different form from those derived from utilitarian perspectives. One such difference is that the

purest form of deontological principles permits no exceptions.

The third level in the ethical decision-making process consists of rules. Rules are derived from principles and are general guidelines asserting what ought to be done in a range of particular cases. Ethical codes may be considered rules, insofar as they provide guidelines to assist psychologists in a range of situations.

The final and most particular level in the process consists of judgments, which represent decisions about specific actions of decisions. Kitchener (1984) noted that people make most ethical decisions at this level ("intuitive level") without probing more deeply at the rule, principle, or framework level. We believe that ethical decisions typically are made at the level with which the decision maker feels most comfortable; that is, if individuals feel comfortable with an ethical rule as stated in a code, they are unlikely to probe more deeply to the level of principle or theory. At times, this may lead to questionable decisions, particularly when intuition alone is used as the basis for making ethical decisions. However, some ethical decisions are made routine in such a way that there is no need to probe more deeply because the analysis has been done for similar dilemmas in the past. Maintaining confidentiality, for example, by not revealing that an individual is receiving psychotherapy unless that person grants permission to do so should become a habit and should not require careful analysis for each client. . . .

References

Beauchamp, T., & Walters, L. (Eds.) (1982). *Contemporary issues in bioethics* (2nd ed.). Belmont, CA: Wadsworth.

Eberlein, L. (1987). Introducing ethics to beginning psychologists: A problem-solving approach. *Professional Psychology: Research and Practice, 18,* 353–359.

Kitchener, K. S. (1984). Intuition, critical evaluation and ethics principles: The foundation for ethical decisions in counseling psychology. *The Counseling Psychologist, 12*(3), 43–55.

Tarasoff v. Board of Regents of the University of California, 551 P.2d 334 (Cal. S. Ct. 1976).

Introducing Ethics to Beginning Psychologists: A Problem-Solving Approach

Larry Eberlein

Dr. Phillis Sawyer, a clinical psychologist in private practice, also hosts a popular radio call-in show twice a week. During one program dealing with depression, a male caller wanted to talk about his feelings of inadequacy. Dr. Sawyer indicated that she couldn't discuss his individual case on the radio but suggested that he might want to talk with a psychologist about his concern. She provided a free help number to call and indicated her willingness to provide the names of several qualified psychologists when she went off the air. A few days later, without indicating he had been the caller, Gregory Greenwood made an appointment to see Dr. Sawyer. During the first interview Mr. Greenwood revealed that he had been the caller and had been so impressed with Dr. Sawyer on the radio that he was sure she could help him. Dr. Sawyer decided that she could be of help to him and arranged for a series of sessions. During the second interview Mr. Greenwood revealed that he was taking medication prescribed by Dr. Gendrau, his family physician. Mr. Greenwood asked Dr. Sawyer not to talk with Dr. Gendrau, who had been seeing him every other week for 4 months. Mr. Greenwood explained that Dr. Gendrau had been helpful to

Mrs. Greenwood and their two children, but that he does not like psychologists. He might stop seeing the family if any member were also seeing a psychologist, no matter how well qualified the psychologist was. Dr. Sawyer felt an obligation to talk with Dr. Gendrau, especially to find out about the medication, but did not want to do so without Mr. Greenwood's consent. She was also concerned about seeing Mr. Greenwood without Dr. Gendrau's knowledge, even though it appeared that Dr. Gendrau had been unable to deal with Mr. Greenwood's feelings of inadequacy.

This is the kind of ethical dilemma that was used in a case study approach to the study of ethics by clinical and counseling master's students at the University of Alberta. The course focus was on the process of thinking through the many dimensions of a dilemma with the use of a problem-solving model. . . .

There exist good reasons for Dr. Sawyer to choose any of several different courses of action. Immediate responses, such as "Dr. Sawyer shouldn't have taken this case in the first place," or "She must terminate therapy," or "She must ignore Dr. Gendrau and do what's best for her client," were discouraged in favor of a more careful and balanced consideration of the moral, legal, and ethical elements present in the dilemma. The discussion focused on the short- and long-term consequences of any action taken and on how each action would affect the dignity of and the responsible caring for all the people involved. Students were encouraged to consult with colleagues to develop and consider many alternative actions by the psychologist with the understanding that in many ethical dilemmas there is no single correct (or perhaps even best) response. This kind of process-oriented, problem-solving approach was very much appreciated by the first-year students; for many, this was the first sustained contact with legal and ethical issues faced by professional psychologists. . . .

THE CURRENT NATURE OF ETHICS EDUCATION

Although there is evidence of an increasing emphasis on education in ethics, there is little information in the literature about the content of such courses. Welfel and Lipsitz (1983) suggested that more information and research are necessary. They asked, for example, what activities occur in these courses, whether they have an impact on behavior, whether they sensitize practitioners, and which approaches are most effective. "How do practitioners, when recognizing an ethical dilemma, sort through the complex considerations involved in making ethical decisions?" (p. 321). . . .

If we accept the importance of morals and values in ethical decision making, the current nature of ethics education is severely lacking. In the formal courses reviewed by Tymchuk et al. (1979), APA standards were used as the basic text, with additional coverage on research standards, confidentiality, right to treatment, and professional and legal issues. Personal values was the item least frequently discussed: "clarification of values plays no integral part in graduate education" (Tymchuk et al., 1979, p. 1170). Welfel and Lipsitz (1983) said that in addition to simply reviewing a code, many writers feel that "ethics education must broaden its base and include instruction in moral philosophy" (p. 322). Consideration of personal values and the ability to reason on moral issues are considered essential. . . .

Four goals for ethics education, integrated with the psychological process underlying moral behavior, form the basis of Kitchener's (1986) approach to

teaching applied ethics in counselor education. The goals, based on those of Rest (1984), include sensitizing students to ethical issues and improving their ability to reason about ethical issues and to develop moral responsibility and the ego strength to take action. Kitchener also suggested that educators can encourage young professionals to develop a sense of responsibility for ethical action by modeling, through discussions, and by their own personal valuing of ethical behavior.

Pelsma and Borgers (1986) combined a learning process with Van Hoose's (1980) developmental ethics in an "experience-based ethics model." Using Kolb's (1984) reasoning, they postulated that improvements in ethical reasoning will occur as counselors successfully adapt to their environment: "The learner needs four different kinds of abilities: concrete experience (feeling), reflective observation (watching), abstract conceptualization (thinking), and active experimentation (doing)" (p. 311). Although the importance of process is considered in the model, their example seems to indicate that learning occurs by means of getting one's fingers burned, an impulsivity dimension, and seems to downplay the importance of preplanning with the use of a problem-solving model.

THE CORRECT ANSWER APPROACH

Many of the models examined, even those involving a moral emphasis, focus on the "right" or "best" answer. Bailey (1980), for example, provided a quiz for school counselors. He offered 26 questions, keyed to the official ethical standards of the American Personnel and Guidance Association; one of five responses to each question was the "correct" answer. Casebooks often present real dilemmas and then a judgment as to whether the action was proper (Callis, 1976; Keith-Spiegel & Koocher, 1985). By contrast, the workbook for beginning professionals by Corey, Corey and Callanan (1979) is more issue oriented, more thought provoking, and less judgmental.

This correct-answer approach is also common in many professional examinations. For example, the Examination of Professional Practice in Psychology is used by many licensing boards. A substantial part of the exam covers "professional conduct, affairs, and ethics; interdisciplinary relations, and knowledge of professional affairs" (Hess, 1977, p. 367). This exam of 150 or more items is graded as being right or wrong. Although forced-choice responses provide data that can be subjected to statistical manipulation, such a format does not always provide the framework and freedom to think about a question in ways that could lead to a more productive resolution of the issue. . . .

Sometimes in the area of professional ethics no response is very satisfying, although more than one may meet the bare requirements of ethical behavior. Members of professional ethics committees usually do not articulate their thought processes or the principles that they apply to a case; the "facts" are reported together with a decision as to whether the situation was seen as unethical behavior (Sanders, 1979). In addition, there are conflicts between code provisions, between the codes of different professional associations, and between codes and the legal requirements of a particular jurisdiction (Bersoff, 1975; Huey, 1986; Mappes, Robb, & Engles, 1985). . . .

This lack of uniformity as to what constitutes legal or ethical action extends to psychologists, as was well illustrated by Tymchuk et al. (1982). They presented members of the APA Division of Clinical Psychology with vignettes of clinical and research situations, together with a proposed response. Among the 113 respondents there was strong consensus about the decision taken in 5 of the 12 vignettes, but almost equal disagreement about the decision in 4 others. Aside from issues of sexual behavior, client identity, and client dangerousness to others (all issues addressed in recent code revisions), there was not wide agreement about what constitutes ethical behavior in the situations presented. In a similar, more recent survey of the Division of Psychotherapy, Haas, Malouf, and Mayerson (1986) presented a choice of at least two potentially workable alternatives. They found high (75%) agreement on only 3 of 10 vignettes presented.

On many issues for which there is not a strong consensus and when individual psychologists cannot refer to a specific standard, they fall back on their own value systems and their interpretation of the spirit of the code. There has to be a better approach than trying to apply a limited set of rules to problems of human relationships, a major issue underlying all ethical dilemmas; such an approach must include a value component.

A PROBLEM-SOLVING APPROACH

Problems of human relationship almost always involve some conflict among the values, rights, and responsibilities of the psychologist, the client, related persons, one or more agencies, other professionals, and the community at large. In much of the literature referred to earlier, the researchers considered that ethics involve values. Van Hoose and Kottler (1977) considered values to be part of a person's identity (whether psychologist or client) and that behavioral decisions involve conflicting demands, a weighing, a balancing, and finally an action that reflects a multitude of forces. We now realize that values are present in any relationship, and psychologists must confront and deal with attitudes and values within the professional relationship as well as with the respective rights and responsibilities involved.

Frequently, the presence of such conflicting claims presents difficulties for a conscientious psychologist. If we consider Dr. Sawyer's dilemma, the most obvious conflicts involve Gregory Greenwood's autonomy, right to privacy, confidentiality, and self-determination, on the one hand, and the obligation to protect and promote the welfare of the Greenwood family (including Gregory) while maintaining good interprofessional relationships, on the other. Kitchener (1984) discussed two levels of moral thinking: an immediate (intuitive) level and a critical–evaluative level. The "shoulds" and "musts" tend to reflect the intuitive level, the ordinary or perhaps impulsive moral judgments. Upon further reflection and consideration of the conflicting values, rights, and responsibilities, an open-minded psychologist usually will modify or qualify a first response, even though the first response may be ethically acceptable. This is especially true when different ethical guidelines are in conflict. This reflects the critical–evaluative level, which Kitchener described as having three components: rules and codes, ethical principles, and ethical theory. The goal for the University of Alberta course was to challenge students to go beyond a code to the underlying principles, to consider ethical theory when possible, to consult widely, and to maintain flexibility when considering alternatives during the problem-solving process.

Several authors have developed problem-solving models; a common pattern involves the development of alternatives, analysis, choice of action, and evaluation. Several deal directly with ethical concerns. Keith-Spiegel and Koocher (1985, pp. 19–20) offered an eight-step model:

1. Describe the parameters of the situation.
2. Define the potential issues involved.
3. Consult the guidelines, if any, already available that might apply to the resolution of each issue.
4. Evaluate the rights, responsibilities, and welfare of all affected parties.
5. Generate the alternative decisions possible for each issue.
6. Enumerate the consequences of making each decision.
7. Present any evidence that the various consequences or benefits resulting from each decision will actually occur.
8. Make the decision.

Tymchuk (1986) had a useful approach that included seven steps. In the most important step, one determines which alternative to implement by looking at the short-term, ongoing, and long-term consequences and at the psychological, social, and economic costs with a risk–benefit analysis of each alternative.

The problem-solving model recommended by the CPA [Canadian Psychological Association] Committee on Ethics (1986), is reflective of the Tymchuk approach and the following six questions used in the development of the new code (Sinclair et al. 1987):

1. Indicate the individuals and/or groups that need to be considered in arriving at a solution to the dilemma posed by the situation.
2. Take each of the individuals or groups that you feel should be considered, and explain in detail what consideration each is owed and why, particularly in terms of the rights and responsibilities involved.
3. What would be your choice of action, and why would you choose it?
4. What alternative choices of action would you consider, and why did you not choose them?
5. What is the minimal circumstance in the situation that you can conceive of that could lead you to a different choice of action? What would that action be, and why would you choose it?
6. Do you have any further thoughts or comments about this or similar situations? If so, explain.

. . .

Students in professional graduate programs often are socialized "not to look for moral problems or recognize moral issues in their work" (Rest, 1984, p. 21). The goal of the University of Alberta course was to counter this attitude and to alert clinical, counseling, and school psychology students at the beginning of their studies to the disparate professional problems involved in the field of psychology. The expectation was that a sensitivity to the myriad legal and ethical issues involved in any type of professional relationship could be coupled with a problem-solving approach. This combination should bring into focus the importance of developing a personal structure of moral thought and action that would provide a basis for future ethical decision making. This type of problem-solving approach also meets the need found by Tymchuk et al. (1982) for decision-making guidelines rather than just case-related materials.

Most problem-solving models finish with an evaluation of the action taken. Perhaps the most important omission of such models is the following step that the CPA, Committee on Ethics (1986), included as the seventh and final step:

Assumption of responsibility for the consequences of the action taken, including correction of negative consequences, if any, or re-engaging in the decision-making process if the ethical issue is not resolved. (p. 6E)

Following a code of conduct does not render a psychologist immune from an ethical complaint or lawsuit. Even more difficult is the choice of action when one is facing an ethical dilemma that is not easy to resolve. There may be conflicts among code provisions or with legal requirements. One example is the lack of competence in some area of practice when there is no other more competent referral source reasonably available. Another is the potential breach of an ethical confidence when one is facing a court subpoena. Such decisions should be well thought out and not taken lightly. The CPA recognizes that final resolution of such dilemmas is a matter of personal conscience, but "psychologists are expected to engage in an ethical decision-making process that is explicit enough to bear public scrutiny" (CPA, Committee on Ethics, 1986, p. 6E).

Psychologists need educational experiences involving a value component that can help them to reach responsible decisions after all consequences have been fully explored. These experiences should help psychologists to develop a structure of ethical or moral decision making that will be useful when they face future dilemmas. The problem-solving approach described here can be of use to practitioners and to professional associations requiring continuing education experiences that are relevant to practicing psychologists. . . .

If all psychologists had the same moral value system, a code of conduct would not be necessary, complaints would not be filed, and most lawsuits would be avoided. As it is, there are dramatic value differences, and a code is usually a consensual validation of what *has been* the most recent view of a majority of psychologists ensconced in decision-making roles, often in response to public pressures or specific problematic behavior. Codes are at best incomplete guidelines; ultimately the individual psychologist must decide upon a personal course of action and live with the consequences of that decision.

CONCLUSION

. . .

The reality of the training experience is that students are usually given a copy of a code of ethics, along with the clinic or placement rules, and provided an awareness that consent forms have to be signed and client interviews kept confidential. Few supervisors spend time discussing ethical implications of action taken unless a problem arises. Occasionally an ethical concern might surface, but most of the real issues in the areas of informed consent, confidentiality, and competence are never addressed in the students' classes, seminars, or practicum experiences. Students also are not made aware of the professional issues that they will meet after graduation. Perhaps as psychology continues its professional development outside of university settings, students will need a different exposure to heighten their awareness that there exist more professional dilemmas than are usually recognized and that mere knowledge of a set of guidelines does not a professional make.

Beginning and practicing psychologists all need a comprehensive, more inclusive approach when making decisions that involve ethical issues. Many decisions are easily made and cause no difficulty. In others, the ethical implications are implicit in the action taken but receive no conscious consideration. I recommend that all supervisors in a practicum or institutional setting regularly ask, "What are the ethical issues involved in what we have done or are doing?" I also recommend that regular case conferences be held, not only to discuss the handling of a case, but to discuss the ethical nuances that are involved. I favor a continuing exposure to ethical, problem-solving experiences, but I recognize that the real test comes when principles discussed in the reflective atmosphere of a workshop setting have to be applied in a real-life situation.

References

Bailey, J. A. (1980). School counselors: Test your ethics. *The School Counselor, 27,* 285–293.

Bersoff, D. N. (1975). Professional ethics and legal responsibilities: On the horns of a dilemma. *The Journal of School Psychology, 13,* 359–376.

Callis, R. (1976). *Ethical standards casebook* (2nd ed.). Washington, DC: American Personnel & Guidance Association.

Canadian Psychological Association. Committee on Ethics (1986). Code of ethics. *Highlights, 8*(1), 6E–12E.

Corey, G., Corey, M. S., & Callanan, P. (1979). *Professional and ethical issues in counseling and psychotherapy.* Monterey, CA: Brooks/Cole.

Haas, L. J., Malouf, J. L., & Mayerson, N. H. (1986). Ethical dilemmas in psychological practice: Results of a national survey. *Professional Psychology: Research and Practice, 17,* 316–321.

Hess, F. F. (1977). Entry requirements for professional practice of psychology. *American Psychologist, 32,* 365–368.

Huey, W. C. (1986). Ethical concerns in school counseling. *Journal of Counseling and Development, 64,* 321–322.

Keith-Spiegel, P., & Koocher, G. P. (1985). *Ethics in psychology: Professional standards and cases.* New York: Random House.

Kitchener, K. S. (1984). Intuition, critical evaluation and ethical principles: The foundation for ethical decision in counseling psychology. *The Counseling Psychologist, 12*(3), 43–55.

Kitchener, K. S. (1986). Teaching applied ethics in counselor education: An integration of psychological processes and philosophical analysis. *Journal of Counseling and Development, 64,* 306–310.

Kolb, B. (1984). *Experience as the source of learning and development.* Englewood Cliffs, NJ: Prentice-Hall.

Mappes, D. C., Robb, G. P., & Engels, D. W. (1985). Conflicts between ethics and law in counseling and psychotherapy. *Journal of Counseling and Development, 64,* 246–252.

Pelsma, D. M., & Borgers, S. B. (1986). Experience-based ethics: A development model of learning ethical reasoning. *Journal of Counseling and Development, 64,* 311–314.

Rest, J. R. (1984). Research on moral development: Implications for training counseling psychologists. *The Counseling Psychologist, 12*(3), 19–29.

Sanders, J. R. (1979). Complaints against psychologists adjudicated informally by APA's committee on scientific and professional ethics and conduct. *American Psychologist, 34,* 1139–1144.

Sinclair, C., Poizner, S., Gilmour-Barrett, K., & Randall, D. (1987). The development of a code of ethics for Canadian psychologists. *Canadian Psychology, 28,* 1–8.

Tymchuk, A. J. (1986). Guidelines for ethical decision making. *Canadian Psychology, 27,* 36–43.

Tymchuk, A. J., Drapkin, R. S., Ackerman, A. B., Major, S. M., Coffman, E. W., & Baum, M. S. (1979). Survey of training in ethics in APA-approved clinical psychology programs. *American Psychologist, 34,* 1168–1170.

Tymchuk, A. J., Drapkin, R., Major-Kingsley, S., Ackerman, A. B., Coffman, E. W., & Baum, M. S. (1982). Ethical decision making and psychologists' attitudes toward training in ethics. *Professional Psychology, 13,* 412–421.

Van Hoose, W. H. (1980). Ethics and counseling. *Counseling and Human Development, 13*(1), 1–12.

Van Hoose, W. H., & Kottler, J. A. (1977). *Ethical and legal issues in counseling and psychotherapy.* San Francisco: Jossey-Bass.

Welfel, E. R., & Lipsitz, N. E. (1983). Wanted: A comprehensive approach to ethics research and education. *Counselor Education and Supervision, 22,* 320–332.

◆ ◆ ◆

Commentary: *Gawthrop and Uhlemann (1992) have provided empirical support for the approaches espoused by Eberlein (1987) and by Tymchuk et al. (1982). They presented a vignette containing an ethical dilemma to undergraduate students who were preparing for careers in mental health professions. The treatment group received a 3-hour workshop on ethical decision making using a problem-solving approach. In comparison with two control groups, the treatment group performed significantly better on a rating scale designed to measure quality of the decision-making process. See Gawthrop, J. C., & Uhlemann, M. R. (1992). Effects of the problem-solving approach in ethics training. Professional Psychology: Research and Practice, 23, 38–42. The authors offered the following insights on their study and its implications for teaching students about ethics:*

> *The results of this study are consistent with those found in earlier work (Baldick, 1980; Granum & Erickson, 1976; Morrison & Teta, 1979; Paradise, 1976) in that formal exposure to ethics education had a significant positive effect on the dependent variable. In addition, the refinements of the present study made possible several specific conclusions in light of the results.*
>
> *. . . When the brevity of the workshop experience is considered, the strength of the observed treatment effect is notable. Moreover, the lack of effect in the informed control group suggests that increased quality in decision making could not be elicited by written instructions alone and that such a level of decision making was not already present in participants' behavioral repertoire. The results suggest that the problem-solving approach in teaching ethics . . . is effective in fostering quality in ethical decision making and that simply presenting*

written instructions is not sufficient for eliciting that quality of decision making.

It is important to point out that the problem-solving approach . . . was augmented in this study with elements of other ethics teaching models. The workshop goals were to sensitize participants to ethical issues and to maximize the quality of ethical decision making by using reading and discussion of ethical codes and case vignettes, self-generation of ethical dilemmas from experience, and generating and justifying ethical decisions about specific vignettes (Kitchener, 1986). Discussions of ethical dilemmas during the workshops often included an exploration of how values form the basis of codes and decision rationales (Abeles, 1980). The case vignette also served to recognize the contribution made by several teaching models (Eberlein, 1987; Fine & Ulrich, 1988; Kitchener, 1984, 1986; McGovern, 1988) with regard to making participant evaluation and accountability an integral part of ethics education.

The present results, in conjunction with findings from earlier studies, permit several suggestions regarding the training of counselors and psychologists in ethical issues. First, it is becoming increasingly clear that the limitations of the informal teaching of ethics need to be accepted (Handelsman, 1986b). The mere provision of ethics information is not sufficient. Rather, the present results support the notion that ethics education be made a formal endeavor in which specific attention is given to the content and process of teaching ethical decision making. Second, the results make it reasonable to suggest that those trainees who do not receive formal exposure to ethics education cannot be assumed to possess the same ethical decision-making skills as trainees who have gone through formal ethics education in which such skills are taught. Third, it seems reasonable to suggest that separate sections of courses or full courses devoted to professional ethics be included in all training programs in the helping professions and that all such courses include the teaching of ethical decision making. Fourth, the results of the present study support the suggestion that educators consider using the problem-solving approach . . . in teaching ethical decision making. . . .

. . . [A]lthough research is developing that indicates how to teach ethics in the classroom, it cannot be assumed that ethics education will generalize to ethical behavior in clinical practice (Bernard & Jara, 1986; Pope, Tabachnick, & Keith-Spiegel, 1987, 1988). Once the problem of how to teach effective ethical decision making is addressed, continuing challenges lie in (a) motivating practitioners to implement their ethical decisions and (b) determining the personal and professional risk factors that can come between such decisions and their implementation. . . .

References

Abeles, N. (1980). Teaching ethical principles by means of value confrontations. Psychotherapy: Research and Practice, 17, 384–391.

Baldick, T. (1980). Ethical discrimination ability of intern psychologists: A function of training in ethics. Professional Psychology, 11, 276–282.

Bernard, J., & Jara, C. (1986). The failure of clinical psychology graduate students to apply understood ethical principles. Professional Psychology: Research and Practice, 17, 313–315.

Eberlein, L. (1987). Introducing ethics to beginning psychologists: A problem-solving approach. Professional Psychology: Research and Practice, 18, 353–359.

Fine, M., & Ulrich, L. (1988). Integrating psychology and philosophy in teaching a graduate course in ethics. Professional Psychology: Research and Practice, 19, 542–546.

Granum, R., & Erickson, R. (1976). How a learning module can affect confidential decision making. Counselor Education and Supervision, 15(4), 276–284.

Handelsman, M. (1986b). Problems with ethics training by "osmosis." Professional

Psychology: Research and Practice, 17, 371–372.

Kitchener, K. (1984). *Intuition, critical evaluation and ethical principles: The foundation for ethical decisions in counseling psychology.* Counseling Psychologist, 12(3), 43–55.

Kitchener, K. (1986). *Teaching applied ethics in counselor education: An integration of psychological processes and philosophical analysis.* Journal of Counseling and Development, 64(5), 306–310.

McGovern, T. (1988). *Teaching the ethical principles of psychology.* Teaching of Psychology, 15(1), 22–26.

Morrison, J., & Teta, D. (1979). *Impact of a humanistic approach on students' attitudes, attributions, and ethical conflicts.* Psychological Reports, 45, 863–866.

Paradise, L. (1976). *Towards a theory on the ethical behavior of counselors* (Doctoral dissertation, University of Virginia). Dissertation Abstracts International, 1977, 37, 4140A-4141A. (University Microfilms No. 77–204)

Pope, K., Tabachnick, B., & Keith-Spiegel, P. (1987). *Ethics of practice: Beliefs and behaviors of psychologists as therapists.* American Psychologist, 42, 993–1006.

Pope, K., Tabachnick, B., & Keith-Spiegel, P. (1988). *Good and poor practices in psychotherapy: National survey of beliefs of psychologists.* Professional Psychology: Research and Practice, 19, 547–552.

Introduction to the Special Section: Ethics Education—An Agenda for the '90s

Elizabeth Reynolds Welfel and Karen Strohm Kitchener

[T]he . . . ethical dimensions of the education and supervision of psychologists in training have received only minimal attention in the professional literature. . . .

. . . Rest has postulated a model for understanding the components of moral behavior that is useful in organizing the empirical literature on ethics. By contrast, Kitchener's work is helpful in tying the ethical issues in training to the work of ethics scholars and in providing an ethical rationale for the statements in the Ethical Principles of Psychologists (APA, 1990). . . .

THE COMPONENTS OF MORAL BEHAVIOR

Rest has defined morality as "standards or guidelines that govern human cooperation—in particular, how rights, duties and benefits are allocated." (1983, p. 558). Morality from this perspective provides guidance for how the individual's welfare and intrinsic value is balanced with the welfare of others in the social system. The question he asks is, "What psychological processes are involved in the production of such behavior? He concludes that the psychological processes can be divided into four components, each of which involves both cognition and affect. In any given circumstance, the failure to act ethically can be traced to a deficiency in one of these four component processes.

The first component of moral behavior, *interpreting the situation as a moral one*, involves the recognition that one's actions affect the welfare of another. This component is sometimes called *moral sensitivity*. For the psychologist, moral sensitivity means the ability to recognize the ethical dimensions of a situation along with its clinical, scholarly, or pragmatic aspects. For example, when a client without insurance asks whether the psychologist will allow her to provide carpentry services in exchange for psychotherapy, the psychologist recognizes that this request is not just pragmatically difficult or possibly symptomatic of the client's difficulties but is also an ethical problem that can affect the welfare of both the client and others.

The second component involves deciding which course of action is just, right, or fair. It includes deciding what ought to be done in light of sometimes conflicting moral obligations. It is also called *moral reasoning*. In other words, once the ethical issue is recognized, the psychologist must have the capacity to differentiate ethical from unethical choices. This capacity is informed, of course, by one's knowledge of the current code of ethics, the published literature, the philosophical principles underlying the code, and by the individual's level of moral reasoning. Sometimes the code of ethics provides adequate guidance; other times, the dilemma is "at the cutting edge of practice" or one ethical principle seems to conflict with another. In cases of the latter, the capacity of the professional to analyze the moral theory underlying the code and use mature moral reasoning greatly affects the definition of what constitutes an ethical choice.

Deciding what one intends to do is the third component of Rest's model, and it involves choosing whether or not to carry out the ethical action in the face of competing values. Here, the psychologist has recognized that a moral issue exists and has identified a morally defensible action. The psychologist

Adapted from *Professional Psychology: Research and Practice*, 23, 179–181. Copyright 1992 by the American Psychological Association.

must now decide whether to go forward with the ethical action in spite of possible costs and in light of competing nonmoral values. For example, a faculty member decides that she will confront a colleague about that person's unethical actions with a student despite the awkwardness inherent in that confrontation and the subsequent unpleasantness that may come from it. The psychologist has weighed the ethical values against values such as smooth relations with colleagues and possible professional gain and has selected the ethical value as the value of greatest importance.

The fourth component of the model is the *implementation of the moral action*, or the ability to execute the ethical action despite the costs to self or external pressures to act differently. In essence, this is the ability to be steadfast in doing what is right through a process that may be tedious and isolating. It involves what we often think of as ego strength. In the above example, the psychologist may be threatened by legal action from the colleague she confronts and viewed by other colleagues as causing trouble and jeopardizing the future of the training program. Only if she is able to weather these harsh penalties and not withdraw from the decision to act ethically will the ethical behavior be maintained.

Rest's theory not only provides a framework that allows the empirical literature on ethics training to be organized, it also provides a model for training itself. In other words, it suggests that if psychologists are to train new professionals to act ethically, the profession must be concerned with students' moral sensitivity, their moral reasoning, their ability to sort the moral from the nonmoral issues, and their ego strength. . . .

KITCHENER: PRINCIPLES UNDERLYING ETHICAL STANDARDS

The second model . . . was based on the work of Beauchamp and Childress (1983, 1989) in biomedical ethics and applied to psychology by Kitchener (1984) and Steere (1984). Kitchener has observed that in real life the ethical issues people face often present extremely difficult choices. Initially, individuals rely on their ordinary moral sense (i.e., a person's moral "intuition") in responding to these issues. In some cases, however, one's ordinary moral

sense may be misleading or inadequate. When this happens, professionals turn to codes of ethics as the first level of justification when their moral intuitions leave them without clear choices. In this circumstance, psychologists are obligated to evaluate their ethical choices in light of the Ethical Principles of Psychologists (APA, 1990). Ethics codes have their limits, however. For example, they are often conservative, balancing the protection of the consumer against the protection of the professional from outside regulation. Further, they are time limited. Issues that are on the cutting edge of the profession or that arise after the publication of the code are not discussed. In addition, they cannot address every possible ethical issue a professional may encounter.

On the basis of Beauchamp and Childress (1983, 1989), Kitchener (1984) has suggested that the problem stemming from the limitations of professional codes can be addressed by considering more fundamental ethical principles. These principles provide the ethical foundation for professional codes along with a conceptual vocabulary that allows psychologists to analyze ethical issues when codes are silent or do not give clear advice. In psychology, five ethical principles appear most fundamental: benefit others, do no harm, respect others' autonomy, be just or fair, and be faithful. The following defines each principle.

The principle of benefiting others, of accepting a responsibility to do good, underlies the profession. Psychologists are dedicated to promoting the welfare of others, whether in research, teaching, or practice. In fact, benefiting others is one of the primary reasons psychology exists as a profession. When clients contract for services or students enter graduate programs, they are doing so with the expectation that they will profit from our services or tutelage.

The principle of doing no harm, also called non-maleficence, includes not perpetrating physical or psychological harm on another or engaging in activities that have a high risk of harming others. This principle is fundamental to any helping profession dedicated to promoting the welfare of others, because by engaging in harmful activities the professional would contradict a core concept of the profession.

Similarly, the principle of respecting autonomy underlies the concept of ethical choice. It encompasses the concept of freedom of thought and freedom of action. In the latter case, individuals are at liberty to act in ways that they freely choose as long as their actions do not interfere with similar actions of others. Both concepts imply a reciprocal relationship with others. In other words, if a person wishes his or her choices to be respected by others, then that person must similarly respect the rights and choices others make, even if they appear mistaken. This principle means that the professional position of psychologists does not give psychologists the right to interfere in others' lives just because those persons' decisions seem wrong. The critical factor is the ability of the individual to think and act rationally and with understanding of the consequences of the action. Acting paternalistically (i.e., in violation of the choice of the individual) is ethically justifiable only under special circumstances. (See Beauchamp & Childress, 1989, or Kitchener, 1984, for a more complete discussion.)

The fourth ethical principle is acting fairly or justly. It refers to the fair treatment of an individual when his or her interests must be balanced against the rights and interests of others. For psychology, justice is fundamental because the profession is concerned with the welfare of others. How could others trust psychologists to act in their best interests if they did not believe we would treat them fairly?

Being faithful to commitments, also called fidelity, is the last ethical principle to be considered here. Fidelity includes promise keeping, trustworthiness, and loyalty. Although Beauchamp and Childress suggest that it is derived from the respect due to autonomous persons, Kitchener (1984) has argued that in the helping professions fidelity is at the core of relationships between the professional and client. By virtue of their role, psychologists carry a special ethical obligation to be faithful to promises and commitments and not to deceive or exploit those with whom they work.

References

American Psychological Association. (1990). Ethical principles of psychologists. *American Psychologist, 45,* 390–395.

Beauchamp, T. L., & Childress, J. F. (1983). (2nd ed.). *Principles of biomedical ethics.* Oxford, England: Oxford University Press.

Beauchamp, T. L., & Childress, J. F. (1989). *Principles of biomedical ethics* (3rd ed.). Oxford, England: Oxford University Press.

Kitchener, K. S. (1984). Intuition, critical evaluation and ethical principles: The foundation for ethical decisions in counseling psychology. *The Counseling Psychologist, 12,* 43–56.

Rest, J. R. (1983). Morality. In J. Flavell & E. Markham (Eds.), *Cognitive development* (Vol. IV). P. Mussen (General Ed.). Manual of child psychology (pp. 520–629). New York: Wiley.

Steere, J. (1984). *Ethics in clinical practice.* Cape Town: Oxford University.

◆ ◆ ◆

Commentary: Consider the following cases:

1. *Under immense pressure to be a success, a first-year graduate student with considerable academic potential cheats on a final paper in a required course. Such conduct could justify expulsion. What should the professor do?*

2. *A psychologist tests a 52-year-old resident of an institution for people with mental retardation and finds that the resident's intellectual deficits are not as severe as was previously thought. The psychologist recommends that the resident be moved to a group home in the community, not only making the woman more independent but relieving crowded conditions on the ward where she is institutionalized. The shift will save the state about $10,000. When the psychologist reveals the plan to the resident, she becomes depressed and argues that the institution is her home and she does not want to leave it.*

3. *A psychologist proposes to compare behavioral and pharmacological approaches to the treatment of bulimia. He wants to use a wait-list control group and a placebo group in addition to the two treatment groups.*

Identify the ethical dilemmas facing the professor, the clinical psychologist, and the researcher in each of these vignettes adapted from Kitchener's (1984) article: See Kitchener, K. S. (1984). Intuition, critical evaluation and ethical principles: The foundation for ethical decisions in counseling psychologists. Counseling Psychologist, 12(3), 43–55. What provisions in the APA Code of Conduct would apply in each vignette? For each situa-

tion, specify the relevant philosophical ethical principles from those articulated by Welfel and Kitchener in the previous article and those found in the general principles of the code. Using any of the decision-making models you have read about in this chapter, what action would you ultimately take in each of these cases? In completing this exercise, consider the following, also from Kitchener (1984):

> The point has been made that neither the identification of ethical principles nor accepting them as prima facie valid relieves the psychologist from the burden of decision making in ethical dilemmas. A dilemma, after all, is a situation in which there are good reasons to take different courses of action. However, we must still ask: Are there better ways to decide what to do when ethical principles conflict? This question is a very complex one and one which is open for debate among twentieth century ethicists (Abelson & Nielsen, 1967). Because the issue is complex, it is beyond the scope of this article to address in detail. However, a brief account of several answers follows. Readers are referred to the authors referenced in this section for more thorough discussions.
>
> Beauchamp and Childress (1979) and Drane (1982) direct us to ethical theories such as utilitarianism or formalism, which provide reasons for giving priority to one ethical principle over another. However, classical utilitarian and deontological theories are subject to serious criticisms (see Abelson & Nielson, 1967, for a summary), which suggests their helpfulness is limited.
>
> A second approach is to establish by convention a particular ordering of principles for a set of similar issues. (This ordering may rely on an implicit, but unarticulated theory.) Thus, for example, the APA code of ethics has established that not doing harm should take precedence over fidelity in regard to the issue of confidentiality, and over beneficence in the area of research.
>
> This approach is problematic because pre-established conventions cannot always anticipate issues that arise. In addition, just as with trying to establish a single principle as absolute, establishing a single ordering of principles as absolute may sometimes lead to bad ethical decisions. For example, if autonomy was always weighed more heavily than beneficence, it would always be unethical to interfere in someone's life against their will. . . .
>
> In addressing the issue of ethical decision making when ethical principles conflict, many twentieth century ethicists (e.g., Toulmin (1950), Nielsen (1959), Baier (1958)), have taken what has been dubbed the "good reasons" approach to moral judgment (Abelson & Nielsen, 1967). Their concern has been to identify what counts as a good reason to make an ethical judgment and the logic of moral justification. Drawing from Kant they suggest that ethical decisions first, must be universalizable. Kant argued that an act is ethical only if it can be unambiguously generalized to all similar cases (e.g., if we would want ourselves or our children to be treated the same way as we are proposing to treat someone else, under the same circumstances). Translated into more familiar terms it can be stated as the golden rule, "do unto others as you would have them do unto you," which is a fundamental principle of all the great religions. What it suggests is that when we must decide between moral principles, we should decide in a way that is consistent with what we would want for ourselves, our loved ones, and all people under the same conditions.
>
> Second, these ethicists suggest that in making a judgment there should be an attempt to balance the possible harms against the possible benefits or to create the greatest balance of value over disvalue. Toulmin (1950), for example, has suggested that

moral principles may be justified by considering which principles, if consistently acted upon, would lead to the least amount of avoidable suffering all around. Such a position, as Abelson & Nielsen point out, relies on the belief that while it is hard to agree on what will make people happy, it is easier to determine what causes pain and suffering.

While the problems of applying ethical principles in decision making need to be acknowledged, this does not keep them from being useful or important. By accepting them as prima facie valid, we imply that their relevance always needs to be considered in ethical situations. Because they are at a more general level than ethical rules, they can be applied across many situations when ethical codes remain silent or conflict. (See Brown and Krager . . .)

In addition, they provide a framework and a set of helpful guidelines to use in critical evaluation of our ethical intuitions. What this implies is that our moral insight may be sharpened and our moral intuitions refined and reformulated after careful consideration of our ethical actions in light of ethical principles. Via this kind of feedback process, we may improve as ethical decision makers.

Often, books written on ethics and values in psychology treat each ethical issue as if it were independent of all others. One author uses the vocabulary of "rights," another of "obligations," a third of "issues." As a consequence, it is difficult for the reader to generalize across situations. We often end up with a conflicting set of specific rules and/or very personal advice. The principles proposed by Beauchamp and Childress (and elaborated here), however, have three advantages. First, they offer us a common vocabulary and a set of prima facie *valid principles that ought to be relevant whether we are thinking about ethical problems in vocational counseling*

or behavioral research. Beauchamp and Childress have observed: "Only by examining moral principles and determining how they apply to cases and how they conflict can we bring some order and coherence to the discussion of these problems" (1979, p. vii).

Secondly, the principles provide a more general justification for ethical codes and identify areas which ethical codes may need to address. For example, as has been noted, respect for individual autonomy, not harming clients, truthfulness, and justice are minimally addressed by the current APA code. Furthermore, they may illuminate inconsistencies within the code itself.

Third, when we move to the level of ethical principles we move beyond believing that we have fulfilled our ethical responsibility if we have not broken a specific rule in our professional code. If, as Drane (1982) and others have argued, the helping professions are involved in ethical issues at their very core, we need to pay attention to more general ethical principles as we evaluate our own ordinary moral judgments as well as those of our colleagues and our profession. The five ethical principles discussed in this article constitute an initial foundation for the critical evaluation of ethical reasoning in the context of counseling and psychology.

References

Abelson, R., Nielsen, K. (1967). History of ethics. In P. Edwards (Ed.). The encyclopedia of philosophy (Vol. 3). New York: Macmillan.

Baier, K. (1958). The moral point of view. Ithaca, NY: Cornell University.

Beauchamp, T. L., & Childress, J. F. (1979). Principles of biomedical ethics. *Oxford: Oxford University Press.*

Brown, R., & Krager, L. A. (1983). Ethical issues in graduate education: Faculty and student responsibilities. *Paper presented* at the meeting of the American College Personnel Association, Houston, TX.

Drane, J. F. (1982). *Ethics and psychotherapy: A philosophical perspective. In M. Rosenbaum (Ed.).* Ethics and values in psychotherapy. *New York: Free Press.*

Nielsen, K. (1959). *The 'good reasons approach' and 'ontological justifications of morality.'* Philosophical Quarterly, 9, *116–130.*

Toulmin, S. (1950). An examination of the place of reason in ethics. *Cambridge: Cambridge University.*

The Relation Between Ethical Codes and Moral Principles

Donald N. Bersoff and Peter M. Koeppl

Each of the prima facie duties . . . has been translated in some form in the code (APA, 1992). The duty of nonmaleficence is exemplified throughout the aspirational General Principles and in the enforceable Ethical Standards. In General Principle E (Concern for Others' Welfare), psychologists are importuned to resolve "conflicts and to perform their roles in a responsible fashion that avoids or minimizes harm" (p. 1600) and, more specifically in Principle B (Integrity), to "avoid improper and potentially harmful dual relationships" (p. 1599). Similarly, psychologists are required in enforceable Provision 1.14 to "take reasonable steps to avoid harming [those] with whom they work, and to minimize harm where it is foreseeable and unavoidable" (p. 1601). The concern that psychologists' personal problems may harm clients and research participants (Provision 1.13), the highly cautionary statements about engaging in multiple relationships of any sort (Provision 1.17), and the absolute ban on sexual relations with current and recently terminated therapy clients (Provisions 4.05 and 4.07) because they "are so frequently harmful" (p. 1605) also exemplify the principle. The significant emphasis on nonmaleficence in the code may be explained by the fact that plaintiffs in malpractice actions must prove that injury has occurred as a foreseeable result of the practitioners' actions before they are awarded damages. Thus, a code that attempts to ensure that, at the very least, psychologists do not harm those they serve helps insulate them from litigation.

Fidelity, requiring that psychologists ally themselves with their clients, respect their needs and fundamental rights, and promote a relationship based on veracity and trust, is perhaps (along with non-maleficence) the most legally salient moral principle. A duty to act in a fiduciary capacity toward those psychologists assess, treat, and study is one that should find robust expression in a code of ethical conduct. The current code (APA, 1992) does not always live up to this hope. Fidelity is best exemplified by the Preamble, which states that the "primary goal" of the code is "the welfare and protection of the individuals and groups with whom psychologists work" (p. 1599). It is represented, among others, in enforceable Provision 1.19, prohibiting the exploitation of research participants, clients, and supervisees, and in Provision 4.09, absolutely forbidding the abandonment of patients. The most obvious application of the fidelity principle, however, is in the obligation to protect the intimate disclosures we obtain in the course of evaluation, treatment, and research. As was true in the debates concerning the adoption of prior APA ethical principles (Bersoff, 1995; Siegel, 1979), how assiduously psychologists are required to protect confidential communications was a source of controversy in the adoption of the current code.

In the original version of the code presented to the Council of Representatives, the central provision read: "Psychologists take reasonable precautions to respect the confidentiality rights of those with whom they work or consult, recognizing that confidentiality may be established by law, institutional rules, or professional or scientific relationships" ("APA's Ethics Code Draft," 1992). Confidentiality is a bedrock value that undergirds a sense of trust and allegiance that must necessarily exist between psychologists and their patients, clients, and research subjects. When we expect and exhort clients to disclose intimate in-

From *Ethics and Behavior, 3,* 345–357. Copyright 1993 by Erlbaum. Adapted with permission of the publisher.

formation, they and the public at large should expect that we will protect those communications by taking more than reasonable precautions. Perhaps the greatest contribution of the late Max Siegel, president of the APA in 1983 and a warmly regarded practitioner and trainer, was his constant and compelling arguments in favor of absolute confidentiality in clinical relationships (Siegel, 1979). It would be naive to argue for absolute prohibition of unconsented disclosures given such real-world intrusions as the opinion in *Tarasoff v. Regents of the University of California* (1976), child abuse reporting statutes, and exceptions to privileged communications laws. However, such intrusions do not call for unnecessary dilution of the ethical value of confidentiality.

In an attempt to strengthen the provision, during the debate in Council on the new code I moved to amend the proposed principle to state: "Psychologists take the utmost care to respect and protect the confidentiality rights of those with whom they work or consult, and disclose confidential information only when compelled by law." The APA attorney hired to consult on this project asserted that the amendment would create undue burdens on practitioners. But the purpose of a code of ethics is to protect the public, not to protect the professionals that are bound by it. Nevertheless, the amendment failed, although some additional wording was added to the original version. Principle 5.02 now states that "Psychologists have a primary obligation and take reasonable precautions to respect . . . confidentiality rights . . ." (p. 1606). This ambivalent protection of clients' private communications does not seem to be an adequate translation of such a central prima facie duty as fidelity.

In contrast, the new code (APA, 1992) appears to endorse the principle of beneficence openly. Just as the predecessor to the current code required that psychologists use their specialized knowledge for the "promotion of human welfare" (APA, 1990, p. 390), the 1992 version encourages psychologists in the Preamble to "improve the condition of both the individual and society" (APA, 1992, p. 1599) and in Principle E to "contribute to the welfare of those with whom they interact professionally" (p. 1600). The duty to act beneficently is also carried forward in a number of the more specific, enforceable princi-

ples in the code. For example, psychologists are responsible for providing "proper training and supervision" to those they teach and oversee so they will learn to apply their services responsibly and competently (Provision 1.22, p. 1602). They are required to "consider" the "best interests" of those legally incapable of giving informed consent (Provision 4.02, p. 1605) and to terminate any professional relationship when the recipient of psychological services "is not benefiting" (Provision 4.09, p. 1606). Scientists are responsible for conducting "research competently and with due concern for the dignity and welfare of the participants" (Provision 6.07, p. 1608).

The principle of justice has also influenced the development of the new code (APA, 1992). For instance, Principle A (Competence) suggests that the competent psychologist be cognizant of the unique needs of distinct groups of people. More explicitly, Principle D (Respect for People's Rights and Dignity) encourages psychologists to "accord appropriate respect to the fundamental rights, dignity, and worth of all people" (p. 1599). Similarly, in enforceable Provision 1.10, psychologists are forbidden in their work from engaging in "unfair discrimination based on age, gender, race, ethnicity, national origin, religion, sexual orientation, disability, socioeconomic status, or any basis proscribed by law" (p. 1601). If they are not competent to work with these diverse groups, psychologists are required to "obtain the training, experience, consultation, or supervision necessary" (Provision 1.08, p. 1601) to do so. The code also prohibits harassing or demeaning behavior toward minority or underrepresented groups, students, and women (see, e.g., Provisions 1.11, 1.12, and 6.03).

Finally, the moral principle of autonomy is also directly addressed in the aspirational components of the code (APA, 1992). Several references endorse the right of users of psychological services to self-determination and free choice. Principle D reminds psychologists to "respect the rights of individuals to privacy, confidentiality, self-determination, and autonomy . . ." (p. 1599). In Principle E, psychologists are advised to be aware of the "real and ascribed differences in power between themselves and others" (p. 1600) and to avoid abusing this potential imbalance.

Whether this essential respect for the integrity and sovereignty of clients so powerfully and elegantly translated in the aspirational sections of the code (APA, 1992) is reflected in its Ethical Standards is questionable. Certainly, there are many enforceable provisions in which choice, consent, and self-determination are valued. Provision 1.07, for example, requires psychologists to provide "appropriate information before" (p. 1600) psychologists may assess, treat, teach, or gather research data. This general principle is more explicitly reiterated in provisions ensuring that the public is accorded the rights to be sufficiently informed and to consent before one participates in therapy (Provision 4.02) or as a research subject (Provision 6.11). Although, curiously, the code has no specific provision requiring informed consent before one undergoes a psychological evaluation, the code does ensure that clients have the right to an explanation of the results of such an assessment (see Provision 2.09).

Yet, when it comes to autonomy, the code (APA, 1992) is clearly teleological and utilitarian in its approach, consistently balancing autonomy against other interests. This is particularly true when psychologists view autonomy as antagonistic to their perception of their clients' best interests; when they believe there are higher values, such as the safety of the public, that must be satisfied; or when organizational demands conflict with autonomy. For example, we have already noted that confidentiality is not fully protected in the code. But respect for private disclosures is further compromised by Provision 5.05 permitting psychologists to "disclose confidential information without the consent of the individual" (p. 1606) when psychologists consult with their colleagues, seek to protect the patient or third parties from harm, or wish to secure payment for services. Confidentiality may be limited not only by law but by "institutional rules" (Provision 5.02, p. 1606) as well. Similarly, disclosure of assessment results to test takers may be precluded by organizational concerns, by the needs of employers, and in certain forensic

evaluations (Provision 2.09). When children and those adults who are not legally capable of giving informed consent receive therapy, psychologists are only required to "consider such persons' preferences" (Provision 4.02, p. 1605), not to be bound or even guided by those preferences. Despite the beneficent intent of Provision 4.07, absolutely barring sexual intimacies with former therapy patients for 2 years and after that only if several significant factors are considered, the provision can be perceived as relegating clients to the role of passive victims rather than as autonomous, self-determining consenting adults.

One can see from this exposition of a sample of relevant provisions there are very few moral absolutes in the current code (APA, 1992). Beyond unequivocally forbidding sexual intimacies with current therapy patients or those whose treatment ceased within 2 years of termination and absolutely precluding the abandonment of patients, there are few, if any other, deontological provisions in the code. It is very much a document full of moral compromise, larded with the lawyerly language of "reasonableness" and constantly balanced by the interests of professional and academic psychologists, organizations, institutions, and what are perceived to be the best interests of clients and research participants.

References

American Psychological Association. (1990). Ethical principles of psychologists. *American Psychologist, 45,* 390–395.

American Psychological Association. (1992). Ethical principles of psychologists and code of conduct. *American Psychologist, 47,* 1597–1611.

American Psychological Association's ethics code draft. (1992, May). *APA Monitor,* pp. 38–42.

Bersoff, D. N. (1995). *Ethical conflicts in psychology.* Washington, DC: American Psychological Association.

Siegel, M. (1979). Privacy, ethics, and confidentiality. *Professional Psychology: Research and Practice, 10,* 249–258.

Tarasoff v. Regents of the University of California, 17 Cal.3d 425, 551 P.2d 334 (Cal. 1976).

Ethics and the Professional Practice of Psychologists: The Role of Virtues and Principles

Augustus E. Jordan and Naomi M. Meara

Currently, the teaching and practice of ethics in professional psychology tend to focus on the application of ethical principles to situations involving dilemmas. These dilemmas take a variety of forms, but they typically emphasize the competing rights and claims of clients or institutions and the related responsibilities faced by service providers. An emphasis on the application of relevant principles in such settings has provided researchers and clinicians with tools to conceptualize and sort through the competing demands of a complex and pluralistic society. However, philosophical and practical limitations to this approach have been identified. We review some of these limitations and identify an additional approach to ethical analysis called virtue ethics. Our analysis of virtue ethics suggests that this approach offers a supplement to the application of ethical principles in dilemmas. . . .

We believe that the difference between this focus on what we call *principle ethics* (i.e., approaches that emphasize the use of rational, objective, universal, and impartial principles in the ethical analysis of dilemmas) and *virtue ethics* (i.e., characterized by an emphasis on historical virtues) is significant and could have implications for the professional development and practice of psychologists. For example, ethical systems that emphasize universally or prima facie valid principles tend to become salient in the presence of dilemmatic situations and tend to claim objective independence from the people involved. In contrast, virtue ethics focus on the historically formed character of identifiable persons; such character development provides the basis for professional judgment. In addition, principle ethics typically fo-

cus on acts and choices. Through the application of what are taken to be objective, rational standards, rules, or codes, they attempt to answer the question "What shall I do?" Virtues, on the other hand, emphasize agents or actors. Through the formation of internal qualities, traits, or mature habits, virtue ethics attempt to answer the question "Who shall I be?"

Our analysis focused on the salient differences between principle and virtue approaches. This is not, however, meant to suggest that these approaches are necessarily mutually exclusive. For example, the distinctions that we make do not imply that all systems that emphasize principle ethics are unconcerned with virtue, character, or agents (see, e.g., Drane, 1982, for a possible synthesis of these approaches). Nor are virtue ethics a unified philosophical perspective that avoids the difficulties inherent in dilemmas or in the application of competing principles. Indeed, we are not analyzing two competing philosophical systems (one called *virtue ethics* and another *principle ethics*), although philosophical differences may well exist. Rather, the distinctions that we identify represent a matter of focus, emphasis, and orientation in the current debate. . . .

THE LIMITATIONS OF ETHICAL PRINCIPLES AND DILEMMAS

The form of ethics currently reigning as the "paradigmatic center of moral reflection" (Hauerwas, 1981, p. 114) in medical, psychological, and religious contexts is that of principle ethics. Given focused articulation in the modern psychological context by Kohlberg (1971) and brought to maturity by

Adapted from *Professional Psychology: Research and Practice, 21*, 107–114. Copyright 1990 by the American Psychological Association. Table 1 has been omitted.

the unique dilemmas of biomedicine, principle ethics have gained a solid foothold in the training and practice of professional psychologists (Kitchener, 1984). The prevalent pedagogy of this approach is the evaluation of competing prima facie valid principles in the context of significant quandaries or dilemmas (Beauchamp & Childress, 1983). These principles typically include justice, autonomy, nonmaleficence, and beneficence, although particular approaches may emphasize the pervasive role of one or another principle over others. For example, Kohlberg (1970) focused on justice, Mill (1861/1957) emphasized the principle of utility, and Gilligan (1982) more recently called for consideration of an ethic of care.

All in all, however, the primary content or subject matter of these approaches involves dilemmas cast in the form of brief case histories that typically highlight a significant conflict between the perceived rights, demands, duties, or obligations of several individuals or groups, agencies, or institutions. Such an approach has led some to call this type of ethical discourse *quandary ethics* or *decisionism* (McClendon, 1974; Pincoffs, 1971). The methodology is to sort through the principles involved and then evaluate the actions taken by participants in the case or articulate what actions are appropriate on the basis of relevant but competing principles, or both (Beauchamp & Childress, 1983; Callahan, 1988). The identities of the people involved in the dilemma are typically irrelevant. Rather, the goal is to provide objective and universally valid interpretations that can be reconciled with and applied to any perspective in the dilemma (Kohlberg, 1971). . . .

However, others have suggested that principle ethics may be too narrow a characterization of what it means to be engaged in ethical discourse (Dykstra, 1981; Kilpatrick, 1986; Pincoffs, 1971) and thus may be professionally limiting (May, 1984). A narrowing of focus on problem solving in an atmosphere of reasoned deliberation could limit the relevant contextual and methodological resources of the professional psychologist. For instance, Kilpatrick (1986) suggested that "even handed, dispassionate discussion of values . . . may habituate students to the notion that moral questions are merely intellectual problems rather than human problems that nat-

urally call up strong emotion" (p. 189). Principle ethics attempt to tie together cognitive analysis and behavioral responses (Kohlberg 1976) while formally distancing the affective and habitual dimensions of human decisions and interactions (Meilaender, 1984; Steininger et al., 1984). When this happens, case studies risk becoming primarily abstract thought puzzles to be analyzed according to specified rules. Other critical psychological dimensions, such as human pain, pathos, and historical particularity, tend to be underestimated or forgotten.

In addition, the heavy reliance on the reasoned application of principles and rules may unintentionally accentuate the impact of individual differences in the use of ethical criteria apart from a theoretically coherent framework. By definition, ethical principles seek grounding in a universal context freed from individual bias, and yet the definitive nature of quandaries places principles in direct conflict with each other. The question then becomes "Which principle(s) will prevail?" For example, researchers often face a conflict between doing the most good for the most people (beneficence) and doing no harm to specific subjects (nonmaleficence). The principles of beneficence, nonmaleficence, and autonomy all stand in potential conflict. To solve this dilemma, appeal must be made to a fundamental moral principle supported by one's moral theory (Steininger et al., 1984). However, different solutions may be achieved, depending on whether one is a utilitarian who emphasizes the public good or a deontologist who advocates a duty to "above all, do no harm" (Jonsen, 1977). Even within a given theoretical orientation, there may exist disagreement regarding the relative weight of competing principles. As Drane (1982) reported, "There is no evident way to determine which principles should take precedence over which others. In such painful dilemmas the psychotherapist simply does the best he (or she) can" (p. 37). The empirical result is that universal principles, as well as their overarching theories, come to be applied idiosyncratically.

. . . Different professionals who are considered to be conscientious and ethical can review the same facts and use the same reasoned methodology and yet come to different conclusions. This calls into question the exclusive use of principle ethics to provide a solid foundation for critical dimensions of ethical behavior. . . .

Kitchener (1984) pointed out that even careful analysis does not lift the burden of a decision. But how does one make the decision? On what basis does one choose among the justifiable, but often contradictory, solutions? Given a situation in which principles stand in opposition, what variables will one allow to influence one's preference, or to whom will one entrust the decision? As professional psychologists migrate with increasing frequency into large industrial and health maintenance organizations, the likelihood of conflicting principles increases. Professionals, the clients whom they serve, and the service organizations that they create risk becoming hostage to the reasoned, principle based, but potentially controversial choices of these organizations (Eyde & Quaintance, 1988; May, 1984).

VIRTUES AND THE HISTORY OF MORAL DISCOURSE

Only in relatively modern times have quandaries received central focus in ethical reflection. An ethics system consisting primarily of problem solving might seem choiceworthy to the modern professional faced with innumerable social and technological dilemmas. However, the focus of philosophers from Plato to Hegel has been not so much on what one ought to do as on who one ought to be (Pincoffs, 1971). From this perspective, professionals would do well to focus on the kinds of persons whom they recruit for their training programs and the kinds of experiences that they seek throughout their careers to enhance their personal and professional integrity. . . .

In contrast to principles, virtues historically have been viewed neither as situation specific nor as universal maxims but rather as character and community specific. Thus they are nurtured habits grown mature in the context of a formative community and a shared set of purpose and assumptions. This process begins in the community of one's childhood and continues throughout life. Professional training and practice introduce new contexts and communities wherein professional virtues can be articulated and nurtured by students and professionals. People socialize one another into a professional culture that they continually construct and shape and from

which they seek inspiration and support. As time passes, certain shared assumptions and values are "taken for granted" and form the character of the profession and are part of the individual characters of the professionals.

Some writers have suggested that principle ethics are not without virtue but rather emphasize a single virtue, that of conscientious rule following (see MacIntyre, 1984, and Pincoffs, 1971, for relevant discussions). Conscientiousness is the orientation with which principle ethicists approach dilemmas. With the advent of litigiousness in the United States, conscientiousness is a common orientation in much of psychologists' professional training and life. Other virtues may be recognized but typically are seen as derivative of and subordinate to the principles (Beauchamp & Childress, 1983); that is, Beauchamp and Childress contended that for every virtue, there is a corresponding rule or principle that can be used. However, May (1984) disagreed and suggested that historical virtues can come into play precisely when principles are in irreconcilable dispute. These virtues, he suggested, are essential for professional development and the maintenance of professional character. For May (1984) they included fidelity, prudence, discretion, perseverance, courage, integrity, public spiritedness, benevolence, humility, and hope.

May (1984) contended that these virtues are not simply correlates of related principles . . . rather, they represent ideals for the professional that go beyond the boundaries of rules or principles. Unlike Beauchamp and Childress (1983), however, May held that the pursuit of such ideals is not ethically optional for the professional. Indeed, the professional "lives under the *imperative* to *approximate* the ideal" with respect to these virtues (May, 1984, p. 252). According to May, this is in part what it means to be a professional.

EMPLOYING VIRTUE ETHICS IN PSYCHOLOGY

. . . Two examples of how specific virtues influence professional practice are offered in this section. The first concerns the use of informed consent in a counseling relationship; the second involves the role of professional virtues in conceptualizing therapeutically relevant constructs such as "genuineness." Although explicitly psychotherapeutic in content, these examples are intended to offer a starting point for more general discussions of potentially relevant virtues for professional psychologists.

Informed Consent

A client's right to informed consent has received increasing attention (Berger, 1982; Burstein, 1987). Respect for the principles of autonomy and beneficence have encouraged therapists to design explicit contracts in response to the rights of clients (Everstine et al., 1980). Debate on this issue has centered on what information rightly belongs to the client and whether one can ever determine what truly constitutes informed consent. Clearly, information is due the client, but do therapists tell the client all of their plans, thoughts, and opinions, or are they selective? For instance, how can one provide complete information with respect to the technique of paradoxical intention and then use this technique in therapy? This issue focuses careful attention to prima facie valid principles that must be weighed and balanced in light of legal concerns and therapeutic effectiveness.

There is, however, another layer of ethical concern that is typically overlooked in the midst of such quandaries: Whereas most attention has focused on what information a therapist ought to tell a client, or what information rightly belongs to a client, there is yet a more subtle but equally important ethical issue that concerns *how* the client will be told (May, 1984). As therapists know, how the truth is spoken in therapy is as morally relevant as what truth is spoken.

For example, Everstine et al. (1980) fully illustrated what information ought to be included in an informed consent procedure, but they did not adequately consider the ethical dimension associated with *how* such information is presented. In an effort to address legal and ethical concerns over informed consent, they developed a therapist–client contract that identified clients' legal rights. Issues were explored in depth and clearly delineated. Client autonomy was respected. However, Everstine et al. did not call into question how to present these matters to clients. As they put it, "The form taken by these con-

sent procedures is irrelevant by contrast with the procedure itself. What is important is that specific ground rules be decided upon in advance and endorsed with a signature before the hard work of therapy begins" (p. 832). Such a legalistic procedure, however, may not be in the client's best interests, nor does it adequately reflect the mutual trust and respect or therapist's integrity that are essential for productive therapy. Specifically, at face value, the rights, the contract, and the consent forms provided by Everstine et al. subtly suggest that therapy is first and perhaps foremost a legal transaction of commodities or services. Modern therapy often includes such a transaction, but it is not clear that therapy is best understood, first and foremost, within the limits of such categories. What is more, the forms imply that the client is a passive recipient of these services, for which the client will be billed. Indeed, the client's rights and the therapist's responsibilities are listed in great detail, but little is said of the client's responsibilities, the mutuality of the therapy process, or what "set" such a document provides for the client.

Clearly, Everstine et al. (1980) developed these forms in an environment that presses escalating legal responsibilities on therapists. The prevailing question was, and continues to be, What are therapists legally required to do in order to protect client rights and their own legal culpability? Everstine et al. addressed these issues, and virtue ethics does not deny the importance of the question. But in virtue ethics, such concerns would be seen as an outgrowth of a professional's concern for the integrity of the process and practice of psychotherapy itself and an abiding respect for clients who engage in it. Such concern adds another, equally valid question: Who are therapists required to be in order to competently and credibly inform clients about their rights and responsibilities, as well as concerning the nature and tradition of the practice of psychotherapy? The virtues of prudence and discretion and of fidelity to a particular client with whom the therapist is in a particular relationship are ethically relevant to informed consent. It may be that standardized, legal contracts are necessary and can be presented articulately and sensitively (i.e., professionally) to a depressed client without the need of a lawyer to interpret the contract's legal implications. But this is precisely the point: How professionals present such information is morally relevant without being necessarily rule dependent. The character of the professional is as ethically decisive as the content of the contract.

Genuineness

A second example extends this concern for how therapists present themselves and how well they tell clients the truth into the dynamics of therapy. Rogers (1959; Meador & Rogers, 1984) considered genuineness to be essential to the development of a therapeutic relationship. But apart from a person, how does one define genuineness? For example, to what extent does the therapist reveal personal values, perspectives, and problems to a client or clients (Brammer & Shostrom, 1977)? Such questions have both therapeutic and ethical dimensions that are difficult to differentiate. The therapeutic dimensions usually involve a clinical and empirical evaluation of the effectiveness or curative value of genuineness and related constructs proposed by Rogerians, such as transparency, congruence, realness, and authenticity (Truax & Carkhuff, 1964). Similarly, ethical considerations are typically utilitarian. Genuineness is appropriate insofar as it advances the therapeutic interest of the client and does not violate other relevant ethical principles. The exact parameters and nuances of genuineness that are most effective, however, are difficult to isolate and require continued study.

From the perspective of virtue ethics, genuineness might be approached and defined in a different way. In addition to, and perhaps before, questions concerning the curative value of genuineness in the therapeutic encounter is this question: Is genuineness an essential attribute of being a professional in a therapeutic relationship? Many would argue that genuineness, as articulated by Rogers (1959), is not essential, that it is a technique or approach and not a quality. Some might further argue that as such it can be therapeutically counterproductive. But beyond such theoretical arguments is a fundamental question: Is there a sense in which one expects professionals *to be*, for example, genuine, trustworthy, or competent in a way that is not completely dependent on therapeutic consequences? These questions place our deliberations regarding effectiveness in a wider

context that includes astute considerations of what is meant by *professionalism*.

From this second perspective, the virtue-oriented dimensions of genuineness become salient. Genuineness is a complex concept based on a quality of truthfulness. Genuineness includes both a principle-oriented guide to proper action (e.g., tell the truth) and a virtue-oriented characteristic of professionals (e.g., integrity or trustworthiness). But these two admonitions (i.e., "tell the truth" and "be trustworthy") are not necessarily or logically interdependent. . . . [T]he maintenance of trust sometimes demands of trustworthy therapists a certain measured deliberateness with respect to the truth that they speak. "Measured deliberateness" is not a code for subtle and deceptive manipulations but rather is a reference to three additional virtues: discretion, prudence, and humility. Not speaking or speaking with care and discretion can be just as critical to maintaining integrity and trustworthiness of the therapist as speaking out. . . .

Thus the "genuine" therapist is involved in an intricate interaction that balances honesty and subtle therapeutic manipulation. How the therapist manages this interaction is an ethical, as well as a therapeutic, issue. The ethical nuances of this encounter go far beyond the categories of principled analysis, empirical effectiveness, or technical skills. Such an analysis does not imply support for ineffective therapists so long as they are virtuous. In fact, the concept of an incompetent virtuous therapist is an oxymoron. Rather, ethics from a virtue perspective serves to remind us that professional psychology is a discipline with pervasive moral, as well as scientific, dimensions. These moral dimensions are intimately tied to the character of the professional.

BEYOND PRINCIPLE TO CHARACTER

Last, a focus on virtues, in addition to principles, may offer a tentative response to the problem of individual inconsistencies in the use of ethical principles. Specifically, on what criteria do therapists rely when choosing among rationally justifiable alternatives in a dilemma? Eyde and Quaintance (1988) appealed in such situations to Kant's universal imperative to act according to maxims that can and ought to be obeyed by all people. Thus they suggested that psychologists ask themselves, in the midst of a dilemma, "Would I wish my action to become a universal law?" (p. 149). Such a "universal principle" has, however, received severe critical analysis in recent discourses in moral philosophy (MacIntyre, 1984). For example, such a principle does not provide logical access to a normative rule's exceptions. Controversies surrounding confidentiality is a case in point. Initially, the universal rule was "Therapists do not break confidentiality." Careful reexamination of this rule, along with painful and expensive court battles, now indicates that confidentiality *must* be abridged in certain cases. But which cases? And does the particular case in which a particular therapist happens to be involved meet the relevant criteria? Who decides? It is clear that in some instances—child abuse, for example—the community, through legislation, has decided. But in other cases the decision is less clear, and the history of these questions undermines any consistent application of Kant's universal imperative.

In such situations, the client and the community rely not simply on a therapist's rational, cognitive processing of universal or prima facie valid principles, nor simply on his or her specific technical skills or legal expertise. Principles, technical skills, and legal knowledge are necessary in evaluating a course of action but are not logically sufficient or necessarily primary. What is demanded of professionals is a dimension of character appropriately understood by way of the virtues. Professionals use words such as *maturity, professional judgment, discretion, wisdom*, or *prudence*, which depend for their exercise not so much on rational, objective principles as on a quality of character identified by the virtues. A serious consideration in psychological training and practice of what constitutes virtuous character will not eliminate professional disagreement about what is proper or ethical, but it could result in the development of professionals who are better prepared to make such judgments. Such professionals might more easily identify their bias, more carefully guard against imposing their values on clients, and be more vigilant in separating personal and cultural preferences from the psychological and therapeutic phenomena. . . .

References

Beauchamp, T. L., & Childress, J. F. (1983). *Principles of biomedical ethics*. New York: Oxford University Press.

Berger, M. (1982). Ethics and the therapeutic relationship: Patient rights and therapist responsibilities. In M. Rosenbaum (Ed.), *Ethics and values in psychotherapy* (pp. 67–95). London: Free Press.

Brammer, L., & Shostrom, E. (1977). *Therapeutic psychology: Fundamentals of counseling and psychotherapy*. Englewood Cliffs, NJ: Prentice-Hall.

Burstein, A. G. (1987). The virtue machine. *American Psychologist, 42*, 199–202.

Callahan, J. C. (1988). *Ethical issues in professional life*. New York: Oxford University Press.

Drane, J. (1982). Ethics and psychotherapy: A philosophical perspective. In M. Rosenbaum (Ed.), *Ethics and values in psychotherapy: A guidebook* (pp. 15–50). New York: Free Press.

Dykstra, C. (1981). *Vision and character: A Christian educator's alternative to Kohlberg*. New York: Paulist Press.

Everstine, L., Everstine, D. S., Heymann, G. M., True, R. M., Johnson, H. G., & Seiden, R. H. (1980). Privacy and confidentiality in psychotherapy. *American Psychologist, 35*, 828–840.

Eyde, L. D., & Quaintance, M. K. (1988). Ethical issues and cases in the practice of personnel psychology. *Professional Psychology: Research and Practice, 19*, 148–154.

Gilligan, C. (1982). *In a different voice: Psychological theory and women's development*. Cambridge, MA: Harvard University Press.

Hauerwas, S. (1981). *A community of character*. Notre Dame, IN: University of Notre Dame Press.

Jonsen, A. (1977). Do no harm: Axiom of medical ethics. In S. Spicker & T. Engelhardt, Jr. (Eds.), *Philosophical medical ethics: Its nature and significance* (pp. 27–41). Dordrecht, The Netherlands: Reidel.

Kilpatrick, W. K. (1986). Moral character, story-telling and virtue. In R. Knowles & G. McLean (Eds.), *Psychological foundations of moral education and character development* (pp. 183–199). New York: University Press of America.

Kitchener, K. S. (1984). Intuition, critical evaluation and ethical principles: The foundation for ethical decisions in counseling psychology. *The Counseling Psychologist, 12*(3), 43–55.

Kohlberg, L. (1970). Education for justice: A modern statement of the Platonic view. In T. R. Sizer & N. F. Sizer (Eds.), *Moral education: Five lectures* (pp. 57–83). Cambridge, MA: Harvard University Press.

Kohlberg, L. (1971). Stages of development as a basis for moral education. In C. M. Beck, B. S. Crittenden, &

E. V. Sullivan (Eds.), *Moral education: Interdisciplinary approaches* (pp. 23–92). Toronto, Ontario, Canada: University of Toronto Press.

Kohlberg, L. (1976). Moral stages and moralization: The cognitive–developmental approach. In T. Lickona (Ed.), *Moral development and behavior* (pp. 31–53). New York: Holt, Reinhart & Winston.

MacIntyre, A. (1984). *After virtue.* Notre Dame, IN: University of Notre Dame Press.

May, W. F. (1984). The virtues in a professional setting. *Soundings, 67,* 245–266.

McClendon, J. W. (1974). *Biography as theology: How life stories can remake today's theology.* Nashville, TN: Abingdon.

Meador, B., & Rogers, C. (1984). Person-centered therapy. In R. Corsini (Ed.), *Current psychotherapies* (pp. 142–195). Itasca, IL: Peacock Publishers.

Meilaender, G. C. (1984). *The theory and practice of virtue.* Notre Dame, IN: University of Notre Dame Press.

Mill, J. S. (1957). *Utilitarianism* (O. Piest, Ed.). Indianapolis: Bobbs-Merrill. (Original work published 1861)

Pincoffs, E. (1971). Quandary ethics. *Mind, 80,* 552–571.

Rogers, C. (1959). Client-centered therapy. In S. Arieti (Ed.), *American handbook of psychiatry* (Vol. 3, pp. 183–200). New York: Basic Books.

Steininger, M., Newell, J., & Garcia, L. (1984). *Ethical issues in psychology.* Homewood, IL: Dorsey.

Truax, C., & Carkhuff, R. (1964). The old and the new: Theory and research in counseling and psychotherapy. *Personnel and Guidance Journal, 42,* 860–866.

◆   ◆   ◆

Commentary: Do "virtue ethics" give too much discretion to the professional, for example, when, to maximize the potential for a successful outcome in therapy, a clinician engages in the "virtue" of sexual intercourse with the client? To guard against such rationalizations requires "ethical principles and guidelines . . . to protect psychologists against themselves" (Miller, 1991, p. 107). For a short but lively debate between Miller and the proponents of virtue ethics, see these analyses, in order of their appearance:

Miller, D. J. (1991). The necessity of principles in virtue ethics. Professional Psychology: Research and Practice, 22, 107.

Jordan, A. E., & Meara, N. M. (1991). The role of virtues and principles in moral collapse: A response to Miller. Professional Psychology: Research and Practice, 22, 107–109.

CHAPTER 4

CONFIDENTIALITY, PRIVILEGE, AND PRIVACY

Except for the ultimate precept—above all, do no harm—there is probably no ethical value in psychology that is more inculcated than confidentiality. Whether psychologists engaging in research, assessing children, families, employees, criminal defendants, or others, or providing any of the several forms of psychological intervention—regardless of whether they are employed in private or public settings—they know that they bear responsibility for protecting information disclosed to them in the context of a professional relationship. Yet, there is probably no ethical duty more misunderstood or honored by its breach rather than by its fulfillment.

There is ample evidence that protecting intimate disclosures by patients, clients, and even research subjects is valued in society. Even though the word *privacy* does not appear in the U.S. Constitution, the Supreme Court has recognized it as a fundamental right. In part, the right of privacy means that federal and state governmental agencies are barred from unreasonable gathering, storage, and dissemination of their citizens' private information. Many states have passed even more particularized statutes that regulate the disclosure of psychological information. Some of these laws call for civil or even criminal penalties if psychologists or other professionals breach confidentiality without the informed consent of those they assess, treat, or study. Other states—but not all—have enacted statutes, called privileged communications laws, that permit a client to bar his or her psychologist from testifying about certain matters in legal proceedings. And, of course, medicine and every mental health profession embed in their codes of ethics provisions for protecting confidential communications.

But, to the same degree that this litany of protections evidences the heightened importance of confidentiality and privacy in society, like the ozone layer of the atmosphere, there has been a gradual but constant erosion of these fundamental values. When clients seek reimbursement for psychotherapy from their insurers, they are almost always compelled to waive their right to bar dissemination to the reimbursing agency of vital and personal information, such as their diagnosis, prognosis, and aspects of their history. Although privileged communications laws sound protective, they most often contain exceptions permitting psychologists to report child abuse, to testify in civil commitment hearings, and to sue for collection of debts. Thus, when read in their entirety, many privilege laws contain more holes than fabric.

To those who view confidentiality as a preeminent value, the most noteworthy and troubling example of its dilution was the decision made by the California Supreme Court in *Tarasoff v. Regents of the University of California* (1976). This was perhaps the most well-known and notorious case in mental health law, and so, in this chapter, I provide extensive material written about the *Tarasoff* case and its ramifications.

Briefly, California's highest court held that psychotherapists have certain obligations to nonpatient third parties whom they may not know and have never seen when their patients disclose believable and serious threats to harm those third parties. In possibly the most quoted line from *Tarasoff*, the court stated: "The protective privilege ends where the public peril begins" (*Tarasoff v. Regents*, 1976, p. 347). Although poetically alliterative, this mandate had stark and even frightening implications. It clearly put mental health professionals on notice that society did not hold confidentiality in as high esteem as do most psychologists. Speaking through its legal system, society told psychologists—including, as you will see, researchers—as well as mental health professionals in general that fidelity to one's client must recede when it is necessary to protect third parties from harm.

There should be many questions rustling around in the reader's mind about the long- and short-term effects of *Tarasoff*. What are the consequences, for example, of establishing a role for psychologists as protectors of private third parties external to therapy? How does this affect the client–clinician relationship? What additional obligations to the client does *Tarasoff* suggest? If clients are told that not everything they say in therapy is confidential, will they be less honest and trusting? What if the client is not threatening to harm another person by force but by infecting a lover with AIDS? If confidentiality is such a core value to the psychological profession and to those it serves, then why does the rest of society seem to hold that value in lesser esteem than psychologists? Is the protection of intimate disclosures to a therapist more important to the therapist than it is to the client? Is, in fact, the profession making too much of confidentiality as an ethical value? And at this point in my litany, the risk-averse reader should be asking how a conscientious therapist (and researcher) can handle the complex treatment, ethical, and legal problems that arise when faced with a dangerous client.

The material in this chapter raises these questions, debates the issues, and, perhaps, even provides some answers. It also has some didactic goals that should not be ignored, such as understanding the distinctions among privacy, privilege, and confidentiality and gaining an appreciation of the confidentiality provisions in the APA code of ethics. But clearly there are more important lessons to be learned. Perhaps more than any other topic, confidentiality provides a springboard for contemplating the consequences for psychologists torn between their duty and ethical obligations to clients and their responsibilities to the larger society in which they live. A consideration of these dual roles is the overarching purpose of this chapter.

Reference

Tarasoff v. Regents of the University of California, 551 P.2d 334 (Cal. 1976).

Privacy, Confidentiality, and Privilege in Psychotherapeutic Relationships

Michele Smith-Bell and William J. Winslade

. . .

PRIVACY

Concept of Privacy

The concept of privacy embraces the idea of limiting the access of others in certain respects (Gavison, 1980), such as limiting the access of others to one's body or mind, including information about the self contained in dreams, fantasies, thoughts, and beliefs. Privacy in the law is sometimes linked to freedom from intrusion by the state or third persons; it also designates a domain of personal associations, abortion, and bodily integrity. Privacy is important because it preserves and protects individuals as they exercise their freedom to develop their personal identity, choose their values, and shape the course of their lives.

Some legal commentators argue for a constitutional right to privacy, seeing personal information as an integral part of an individual's identity and as crucial to most theories of personhood. This personal interest can be protected from unwarranted governmental intrusions by recognizing a constitutional right to informational privacy based on personhood (Note, 1991). It has been argued that personal interest in mental and emotional health is as basic and fundamental to ordered liberty as are constitutional rights related to family life and childbearing; significant interference with such fundamental interests, in the absence of a compelling state interest, violates the right to privacy (Smith, 1980). Although there is a recognized constitutional right to privacy, the scope of that right is quite narrow. Moreover, the Supreme Court has specifically held that there is no federal constitutional right to informational privacy for medical records, casting further doubt on the idea that there might be a constitutional right to privacy applicable to psychotherapeutic communications (*Whalen v. Roe*, 1976).

Constitutional Right to Privacy

The Supreme Court first recognized a constitutional right to privacy in the case of *Griswold v. Connecticut* (1965), which struck down a Connecticut statute prohibiting use of contraceptives by married couples. The right to privacy was expanded in the case of *Eisenstadt v. Baird* (1972), in which the Supreme Court reversed the defendant's conviction for distributing contraceptives to unmarried persons. In *Roe v. Wade* (1973), the Court held that criminal abortion laws, which proscribed abortion except for the purpose of saving the life of the mother, are unconstitutional. However, the *Roe* Court limited the right to privacy by stating that "only personal rights that can be deemed 'fundamental' or 'implicit in the concept of ordered liberty' . . . are included in this guarantee of personal privacy."

The constitutional right to privacy was restricted in the subsequent case of *Whalen v. Roe* (1976), in which the Court ruled that a patient does not have a constitutional right to informational privacy of communications or records generated in the course of medical treatment when the records are adequately protected from unauthorized disclosure. A more recent Supreme Court case further limits the constitutional right to privacy. In *Bowers v. Hardwick* (1985), the Court upheld a Georgia state antisodomy statute, and rejected the assertion that the right to privacy includes the

From the *American Journal of Orthopsychiatry*, 64, 180–193. Copyright 1994 by the American Orthopsychiatry Association. Adapted with permission of the publisher.

fundamental right of homosexuals to engage in sodomy. Few federal appellate courts or state courts have recognized a constitutional right to privacy for the psychotherapeutic relationship; only California, Pennsylvania, and the United States Court of Appeals for the Ninth Circuit (covering Alaska, Arizona, California, Guam, Hawaii, Idaho, Montana, Nevada, the North Mariana Islands, Oregon, and Washington) have recognized a constitutionally based psychotherapist–patient privilege for psychotherapeutic communications (Smith, 1980, citing *Bremer v. State*, 1973), and those decisions are 15 to 20 years old.

In the California case (In re Lifschutz, 1970), a psychotherapist claimed that he had a privacy interest in psychotherapeutic communications with his patients; the court held that only the patient has a constitutionally protected privacy interest in preventing the release of psychotherapeutic communications. In another case (*Caesar v. Mountanos*, 1976), a psychotherapist refused to answer questions about one of his patients even after the patient specifically waived the psychotherapeutic privilege. The court held that the nature of communications between a patient and his therapist brings the relationship within the constitutional right of privacy through the psychotherapist–patient privilege. But on appeal, the court held that the right to privacy may be limited when necessary to advance a compelling state interest, such as ascertaining truth in court proceedings; moreover, it was held to be the patient's right to waive or assert the privilege.

The case of *Hawaii Psychiatric Society v. Ariyoshi* (1979) supported a constitutional right to privacy. A federal district court enjoined the State of Hawaii from enforcing a statute that permitted the issuance of administrative inspection warrants to review the mental health records of Medicaid patients. The court held that an individual's decision to seek the aid of a psychiatrist, or to communicate certain personal information to that psychiatrist, fell squarely within the constitutional right to privacy. The court balanced the patient's privacy interest against the state's interest in protecting the Medicaid program from fraud; it found that the state failed to show that the issuance of warrants to inspect the confidential medical records of a psychiatrist was necessary to advance a compelling state interest (Smith, 1980).

The constitutional law of privacy is currently a dormant issue and does not seem likely to awaken much interest in the near future, especially with regard to psychotherapy. Thus, whether other federal and state courts will agree that there is a constitutional right to privacy, and what the boundaries of that right are, are unresolved issues.

CONFIDENTIALITY

Distinction From Privacy

Privacy and confidentiality are essential features of the psychotherapeutic relationship, despite the limited recognition of the right to privacy in constitutional law. Both are linked to the general notion of limited access and the exclusion of others; sometimes these concepts are used loosely and interchangeably. For example, privacy and confidentiality both stand as polar opposites to what is public and open to everyone. Nevertheless, it is useful to distinguish these concepts in the context of the psychotherapeutic relationship.

When a person enters into a therapeutic relationship, the client relinquishes his or her personal privacy of thoughts, feelings, beliefs, etc., in exchange for the prospect of therapeutic understanding and assistance. In this respect privacy is an aspect of *individuals*. Once private information has been disclosed to a therapist with an expectation that such information will not ordinarily be disclosed to third parties, it becomes confidential, and one refers to the confidentiality of information in the relationship. Thus, giving a therapist access to private information is necessary by definition for establishing a confidential relationship; and confidentiality is essential. . . .

In some instances, no third parties have access to private information disclosed in confidence to the therapist or even know that the relationship exists at all. Some clients, for example, choose to pay cash for therapy rather than to file an insurance claim (Domb, 1990–1991, citing Sosfin, 1985). Some therapists organize their offices to protect client privacy by the use of separate entrances and exits and of answering machines rather than answering services. The classic image of the exclusive dyadic relationship of the therapist–client, though increasingly rare, is not extinct.

Obstacles to Preservation

Individual and, increasingly, group therapeutic practice often occurs in a larger context of therapist, client, and an array of third parties including family members, employers, insurers, courts, and government agencies. Therapists' general obligation to protect clients' confidential information is overridden by specific obligations to disclose information at the client's request, when the law requires it, or when ethics demands it. For example, a client in a commitment, competency, sanity, or custody proceeding might desire that a therapist testify about disclosures made in therapy. The law might also require disclosures in such contexts even if the client does not consent to them. Legally mandated reporting requirements, such as those concerning child or elder abuse, override confidentiality. Ethics may dictate disclosures in the absence of specific legal authority. Conflicts arise, for example, concerning therapists' obligation to protect third parties threatened by dangerous patients.

The therapeutic consequences of external pressures on the preservation of confidentiality are that therapists may become wary of seeking sensitive information and clients of disclosing it. Even if therapists do not explicitly notify clients of the limits of confidentiality, the style of conducting therapeutic inquiry is influenced by the encroaching shadow of third-party access to information. If therapists inform clients of the limits of confidentiality, clients may then be inhibited in their communication and thereby hamper therapeutic effectiveness. The challenge to policymakers is to balance the need for confidentiality essential to the therapeutic process with the need for access to otherwise confidential information when necessary to protect legitimate public interests.

Patient expectations. Most therapists should be familiar, even if not happy, with the numerous restrictions placed on the right to confidentiality, but studies indicate that patients have greater expectations of privacy and confidentiality (Weiss, 1982). In a 1986 study, a majority of student psychotherapy patients and nonpatients believed that all communications to psychotherapists are confidential; almost all patients wanted to be informed of exceptions to confidential-

ity; and most reported that they would react negatively to unauthorized breaches of confidentiality that would undermine their right to privacy (VandeCreek, Miars, & Herzog, 1987). Another study (Weiss, 1982) questioning patients, house staff, and medical students about their expectations concerning patient privacy demonstrated that only a small number of patients expected that their cases would be shared with physicians' spouses (17%) or at parties (18%). House staff and medical students indicated that such discussions occur commonly (57% and 70%, respectively).

Therapists should, of course, protect confidentiality to the extent permitted by law and required by ethical standards. But in view of clients' sometimes unrealistic expectations about the scope of confidentiality, it is important to clarify its limits at the outset of therapy or at least early on. Therapeutic relationships are often tentative and fragile until a client trusts a therapist. Trust is threatened, if not undermined, if a client feels misled by the therapist, and such a client may withhold information or not cooperate in the therapy in overt or subtle ways—by cancelling sessions, coming late, failing to pay, etc. Misunderstandings about confidentiality may even irrevocably rupture a therapeutic relationship. Thus, it is important for therapists to know and disclose what clients can reasonably expect concerning confidentiality. Its precise boundaries may be difficult to mark out in advance, but at least the general issues should be addressed.

When therapists are confronted with a specific conflict between a client's interest in confidentiality and a third party's claim to access, it is almost always appropriate to explore the conflict with the client first. This advances the therapeutic process because it demonstrates respect for both the client and the integrity of the therapeutic relationship. Clients may choose to authorize disclosure even if not legally required to do so. When a client does not want to permit disclosure, therapists have a duty to seek protection of confidentiality to the extent that the law and ethics allow. In specific situations, therapists may find it helpful to consult ethics committees of their professional organizations, ethics consultants or attorneys, or experienced colleagues who are familiar with confidentiality rules and practices.

Demands to disclose confidential information are sometimes excessive; it may be possible for the client or the therapist to negotiate a limited disclosure that satisfies both the client and the third party. In other situations a client may have waived or forfeited the right to confidentiality by, for instance, signing a waiver or revealing private information to a third party; the therapist may then have no choice but to disclose otherwise confidential information. The damage to the therapeutic relationship can be minimized, however, if the client has been adequately informed and educated by the therapist early in the relationship.

PRIVILEGE

Concept of Privilege

The concept of privilege should be distinguished from that of confidentiality. Privilege is an exception to the general rule that the public has a right to relevant evidence in a court proceeding; confidentiality refers more broadly to legal rules and ethical standards that protect an individual from the unauthorized disclosure of information. Confidentiality alone is not enough to support a privilege; without a privilege statute or a common-law rule, a therapist may be charged with contempt of court for refusing a court order to testify about a patient's psychotherapeutic communications. Thus, confidentiality is a professional duty to refrain from speaking about certain matters, while privilege is a relief from the duty to speak in a court proceeding about certain matters (Domb, 1990–1991, citing In re Lifschutz, 1970). While the impact of privilege laws, or of their lack, on the utilization of psychotherapeutic services in general is beyond the scope of this article, the impact on the use of such services by child abusers is discussed below.

Patient Rights

The patient's right to privacy and confidentiality is partially protected by the doctrine of privileged communications. Confidential information that would otherwise be admissible in a judicial proceeding may be withheld if it is classified as a privileged communication. Privilege thus protects patients' privacy and confidentiality and, in doing so, renders them more disposed to seek mental health services. Privilege

generally belongs to the patient, who decides whether it will be exercised or waived. Although the holder of the privilege is the patient, in appropriate circumstances the therapist may invoke the privilege on behalf of the patient, unless that privilege has been waived or the communication in question falls within a statutory exception to the privilege (Brakel, Parry, & Weiner, 1985, citing In re Lifschutz, 1970).

To be considered privileged, communications from a patient to a therapist must meet a number of requirements. First, the communications must be to a licensed or certified therapist as described in the state's privilege statute, or to an assistant of the therapist, depending upon state law. Second, a professional relationship must exist between the patient and the therapist. Third, the communications must be related to the provision of professional services. Fourth, the communications must be confidential; they may not be released by the client to a third party (Smith, 1986–1987).

Privilege Statutes

While patients tend to expect confidentiality for their communications within the context of psychotherapy, they rarely consider the matter of privilege. Therapists, however, view privilege laws as an important restraint on litigant and governmental intrusion on the therapeutic process. Support for privilege laws also comes from the deontological school of thought, which views privilege as a way to protect significant human interests of the holders of the privileges. It focuses on the societal values preserved by a privilege and considers the disclosure of confidences revealed in certain relationships in and of itself wrong (Shuman, 1985). The fact that privilege laws sometimes result in the exclusion of relevant and probative evidence from a trial is then secondary and incidental.

Accordingly, privilege statutes are enacted to encourage full disclosure by patients to their therapist; these statutes usually provide that such communications cannot be revealed without the patient's consent. The term "privileged communication" refers solely to information that is at issue in litigation. There are generally three forms of privilege statutes applicable to MHPs: a general physician–patient and psychiatrist–patient privilege, a psychologist–patient privilege, and a psychotherapist–patient privilege (Brakel, Parry, & Weiner, 1985). Most states and the District of Columbia have adopted statutes that guarantee the physician-patient and psychologist-patient privilege in judicial settings. A smaller number of states have adopted the psychotherapist-patient testimonial privilege.

Criticism of Privilege

There is no consensus about the importance of a privilege to effective psychotherapy. It has been argued that most people are unaware of the existence of privilege, and it therefore does not affect their seeking therapy or their conduct within therapy (Brakel, Parry, & Weiner, 1985, citing Shuman & Weiner, 1982). Others have concluded that the concept of privilege should be abandoned as a means of determining whether psychotherapeutic communications should be disclosed, noting that standard guidelines in evidentiary matters, materiality and relevancy, adequately protect against unwarranted intervention in the therapeutic relationship (Brakel, Parry, & Weiner, 1985, citing Slovenko, 1974). Still others see privilege laws as insulating therapists from public scrutiny, rather than protecting patients' interests.

Privilege laws and the general obligation of confidentiality have become increasingly subject to exceptions and limitations, effectively reduced by inconsistent federal and state rules, and threatened by changes in health-care financing. . . . In addition, privilege statutes afford only limited protection to confidentiality because of the narrowness of their application; in the litigation setting, they are often only applicable to psychiatrists and psychologists, thereby decreasing their scope and effectiveness (Brakel, Parry, & Weiner, 1985). The scope of psychotherapeutic privilege is also reduced when it is waived, sometimes unwisely, by patients.

Waiver

Patients waive the privilege for psychotherapeutic communications when they file a tort or Workers' Compensation claim for a psychiatric injury, or when litigants otherwise put their mental states at issue. Unlike exception, in which normally privileged information is not privileged in certain situations

prescribed by law (as when a defendant to a criminal charge raises his mental state as a defense), waiver requires action or acquiescence from the patient.

At least one court has held that the physician–patient, and hence the psychiatrist–patient, privilege is waived if the patient does not raise it when information concerning psychotherapeutic communications is first sought. There are situations in which a patient's psychotherapeutic communications are at issue, but the patient is not a party to the immediate matter before the court. In those situations, some courts have asserted the privilege on behalf of the patient, to protect the patient's right to confidentiality (Brakel, Parry, & Weiner, 1985). . . .

References

Bowers v. Hardwick, 478 U.S. 186. (1985).

Brakel, S. J., Parry, J., & Weiner, B. A. (1985). *The mentally disabled and the law* (3rd ed.). Chicago: American Bar Foundation.

Bremer v. State, 18 Md. App. 291, 307A.2d 503. (1973).

Caesar v. Mountanos, 542 F.2d 1064 (9th Cir. 1976), *cert. denied*, 430 U.S. 954. (1977).

Domb, B. (1990–1991). I shot the sheriff, but only my analyst knows: Shrinking the psychotherapist-patient privilege. *Journal of Law and Health, 5,* 209–236.

Eisenstadt v. Baird, 405 U.S. 438. (1972).

Gavison, R. (1980). Privacy and the limits of the law. *Yale Law Journal, 89,* 421–472.

Griswold v. Connecticut, 381 U.S. 479. (1965).

Hawaii Psychiatric Society v. Ariyoshi, 481 F. Supp. 1028. (D. Hawaii, 1979).

In re Lifschutz, 2 Cal. 3d 415, 467 P.2d 557, 85 Cal. Rptr. 829. (1970).

Note. (1991). The constitutional protection of informational privacy. *Boston University Law Review, 71,* 133–160.

Roe v. Wade, 410 U.S. 113. (1973).

Shuman, D. W. (1985). The origins of the physician–patient privilege and professional secret. *Southwestern Law Journal, 39,* 661–687.

Shuman, D. W., & Weiner, B. A. (1982). The privilege study: An empirical examination of the psychotherapist-patient privilege. *North Carolina Law Review, 60,* 893–942.

Slovenko, R. (1974). Psychotherapist-patient testimonial privilege: A picture of misguided hope. *Catholic University Law Review, 23,* 649–673.

Smith, S. R. (1980). Constitutional privacy in psychotherapy. *George Washington Law Review, 49,* 1–60.

Sosfin, E. S. (1985). The case for a federal psychotherapist-patient privilege that protects patient identity. *Duke Law Journal,* 1217–1244.

VandeCreek, L., Miars, R. D., & Herzog, C. E. (1987). Client anticipations and preferences for confidentiality of records. *Journal of Counseling Psychology, 34,* 62–67.

Weiss, B. D. (1982). Confidentiality expectations of patients, physicians, and medical students. *Journal of the American Medical Association, 247,* 2695–2697.

Whalen v. Roe, 429 U.S. 589. (1976).

◆ ◆ ◆

Commentary: Max Siegel, President of the APA in 1983, subscribed to the "absolute position that psychologists may not break confidentiality of a patient or client under any circumstances" (p. 269). See Siegel, M. (1979). Privacy, ethics, and confidentiality. Professional Psychology, 10, *249–258. The APA has never adopted that view in its ethical codes. For example, the language of General Principle 5, the primary confidentiality provision of the 1981 version, read as follows:*

> *Psychologists have a primary obligation to respect the confidentiality of information obtained from persons in the course of their work as psychologists. They reveal such information to others only with the consent of the person or the person's legal representa-tive, except in those unusual circumstances in which not to do so would result in clear danger to the person or to others. Where appropriate, psychologists inform their clients of the legal limits of confidentiality.*

Confidentiality is now covered in 11 separate provisions of Section 5 of the 1992 Ethical Principles of Psychologists and Code of Conduct. *Standards 5.02 and 5.05 are the major provisions. As in the adoption of the 1981 code, considerable debate took place about the language of the 1992 confidentiality provisions. For example, one member of the Council of Representatives moved that Standard 5.02 should read: "Psychologists take the utmost care to respect and protect the confidentiality rights of those with whom they work or consult, and disclose confidential information only when compelled by law." The motion was defeated by a large margin in favor of this statement: "Psychologists have a primary obligation and take reasonable precautions to respect the confidentiality rights of those with whom they work or consult, recognizing that confidentiality may be established by law, institutional rules, or professional and scientific relationships."*

As you read the material that follows, it may be useful to compare Siegel's (1979) view with prevailing sentiments and to ask this: In what ways does the current provision disserve the ethical ideals of self-determination, the independence to decide matters about one's own private interests, and the right to privacy generally, reflected in aspirational Principle D of the 1992 Ethical Principles?

Privacy and Confidentiality in Psychotherapy

*Louis Everstine, Diana Sullivan Everstine, Gary M. Heymann, Reiko Homma True,
David H. Frey, Harold G. Johnson, and Richard H. Seiden*

. . .

OVERVIEW

. . .[T]he issue is not whether guilt properly falls
upon a particular therapist who breaches or declines
to breach confidentiality; instead, the issue is one of
defining the line between proper and improper conduct. Here in truth is a "doctor's dilemma," created
by the tension between two powerful forces that ra-
diate from opposite poles: (a) the client, a private
citizen who wishes that the right to privacy be respected and (b) society, which wants to be informed
about certain acts or intentions on the part of individual citizens. In choosing a path between these adversaries, a therapist can be excused for seeking the
intercession of a guiding star. . . .

INFORMED CONSENT
FOR PSYCHOTHERAPY

The need to protect client privacy invokes the issue
of consent for treatment. Even when a client seeks
out a therapist, he or she may face some risk owing
to lack of knowledge concerning some inherent consequence of that decision. In effect, the client may
inadvisedly waive his or her right to privacy by entering into a therapeutic relationship. . . .

This discussion primarily concerns the rights of
clients who seek help in noninstitutional settings.
Naturally, in crisis intervention situations, or when
a client needs to be hospitalized, alternative rules
concerning when and how informed consent is to
be obtained will apply. Nevertheless, clients should
be made aware of their rights, and some agreement
on a course of treatment should be obtained at the
earliest appropriate time. Thus, some general princi-

ples apply to both institutional and noninstitutional
settings.

What Is Consent?

Consent as a legal concept has three basic
elements: . . . capacity of competence, information,
and voluntariness.

Competence. The basic question is, Can the person
engage in rational thought to a sufficient degree to
make competent decisions about his or her life?
Competence is assumed unless a person has been
legally declared to be "mentally incompetent." *Direct*
consent should be obtained from all competent persons. For persons legally declared incompetent (such
as minors under the age of 18), *substitute* consent
from parents, guardians, or court-appointed conser-
vators should be obtained. In fact, both the required
substitute's consent and the incompetent person's
consent should be obtained when possible.

Information. For consent to be "informed," clients
must possess relevant information about the procedures that are to be performed. Two major considerations are what information is provided and how the
information is communicated. The kind of information that should be provided generally includes (a) an
explanation of the procedures and their purpose, (b)
the role of the person who is providing therapy and
his or her professional qualifications, (c) discomforts
or risks reasonably to be expected, (d) benefits reasonably to be expected, (e) alternatives to treatment
that might be of similar benefit, (f) a statement that
any questions about the procedures will be answered
at any time, and (g) a statement that the person can

Adapted from the *American Psychologist, 35,* 828–840. Copyright 1980 by the American Psychological Association.

withdraw his or her consent and discontinue participation in therapy or testing at any time. This information should be presented in language that the
client can understand (e.g., by means of simple, de-
clarative sentences and the avoidance of jargon).

Voluntariness. At times of extreme crisis, when serious bodily harm or the death of a client or another
person is involved, consent is not an issue. In such
cases, the law generally operates on the principle of
compelling or justifiable interest; that is, society's
best interests outweigh the client's right to give or
withhold consent. In such cases, it is a good idea to
obtain consent as soon as possible after the crisis has
subsided. Similarly, when someone is forced to participate in assessment or therapy by order of a court,
the concept of consent takes on a different meaning.
Our recommendation is that consent be obtained
even in these nonvoluntary situations. And while the
consent itself may be legally empty, in many cases it
will very likely have a clinical usefulness. . . .

SAMPLE DOCUMENTS FOR
OBTAINING INFORMED CONSENT

If a clinician accepts in principle the need for informed consent as a means to protect client privacy,
he or she will probably see the value of employing a
written document to record the implied contract that
consent for treatment represents. . . . The following
documents incorporate the basic elements of informed
consent: (a) a client's rights statement, (b) an initial
contract form, and (c) an informed consent form. [*Ed.
note*: The contract and consent forms have been omit-
ted].

Client's Rights Statement

This statement begins with the therapist's professional qualifications, including (at a minimum)
name, office address, and telephone number, highest
relevant degree, and certification or license number.
The sentences that follow suggest what a client's basic rights in psychotherapy ought to include: . . .

> You have the right to prevent electronic
> recording of any part of the therapy ses-
> sions: permission to record must be
> granted by you in writing on a form that

explains exactly what is to be done and
for what period of time. I shall explain
my intended use of the recordings and
provide a written statement to the effect
that they will not be used for any other
purpose; you have the right to withdraw
your permission to record at any time.

You have the right to review your
records in the files at any time.

One of your most important rights
involves confidentiality: Within certain
limits, information revealed by you during therapy will be kept strictly confidential and *will not be revealed* to any
other person or agency *without your
written permission.*

If you request it, any part of your
record in the files can be released to any
person or agencies you designate. I shall
tell you, at the time, whether or not I
think making the record public will be
harmful to you.

You should also know that there are
certain situations in which, as a psychotherapist, I am required *by law* to reveal information obtained during therapy
to other persons or agencies—*without
your permission.* Also, I am not required
to inform you of my actions in this regard. These situations are as follows: (a)
If you threaten grave bodily harm or
death to another person, I am required
by law to inform the intended victim
and appropriate law enforcement agencies; (b) if a court of law issues a legitimate subpoena, I am required by law to
provide the information specifically described in the subpoena; (c) if you are in
therapy or being tested by order of a
court of law, the results of the treatment
or tests ordered must be revealed to the
court. . . .

CONFIDENTIALITY AND
QUALITY ASSURANCE

In recent years, more and more elements of the nation's health care system have been required to im-

plement programs of *quality assurance* (or some variant of treatment evaluation by another name). The motivating forces behind this trend are, very likely, increasing public criticism concerning the astronomical costs of health care services and the need to prepare a feasible design for national health insurance.

Current developments in the quality assurance movement will have major impact on mental health practitioners. Whatever form these evaluation programs may take, they will involve the opening of clients' records for scrutiny by others and will thus carve a path for the potential breaching of client-therapist confidentiality. To safeguard the clients' and our welfare, we should be acquainted with the nature of these systems and their pitfalls. . . .

The main difficulty is engendered by the "blanket" release-of-information clauses of insurance claims forms. These clauses serve to provide more or less unlimited access to clinical records on the part of a wide range of insurance company and/or government agency employees, most of whom are not mental health professionals but are clerical workers. The net effect is a dilemma for both parties to a therapeutic relationship: Clients are placed under pressure to sign because they need (and are entitled to receive) covered services, and clinicians encourage them to sign because insurance reimbursement is important to earning a living. . . .

DUTY TO WARN

Confusion remains about the case of *Tarasoff v. Board of Regents of the University of California*, confusion that was not dispelled by a final decision handed down by the California Supreme Court in July 1976. Many do not know full details of the events that occurred in 1969 in Berkeley which led to the case being brought. . . .

On August 20, 1969, . . . Prosenjit Poddar, who was a voluntary outpatient at Cowell Memorial Hospital [footnote omitted] on the Berkeley campus, informed his therapist, a psychologist, that he was planning to kill a young woman. Poddar did not name the woman, but as established later, the psychologist could easily have inferred who she was [footnote omitted]. The murder was to be carried out when the woman returned to Berkeley from her summer vacation.

Following this session, the psychologist telephoned the campus police to ask them to observe Poddar for possible hospitalization as a person who was "dangerous to himself or others"; he then wrote a letter, containing a formal request for assistance, to the chief of the campus police. The campus officers took Poddar into custody for the purpose of questioning, but later released him when he gave evidence of being "rational." Soon afterward the psychologist's supervisor, Director of the Department of Psychiatry at Cowell Hospital, asked the campus police to return the psychologist's letter, ordered that the letter and therapy notes that had been made in Poddar's case be destroyed, and directed that no further action be taken to hospitalize Poddar. No warning was given either to the intended victim or to her parents. The client, naturally enough, did not resume his therapy.

On October 27, 1969, Prosenjit Poddar killed Tatiana Tarasoff. The victim's parents filed suit against the Board of Regents of the university, several employees of Cowell Hospital, and the chief of the campus police plus four of his officers. A lower court dismissed the suit, the parents appealed, and the California Supreme Court upheld the appeal in 1974 and reaffirmed its decision in 1976. In July 1977, the suit was settled out of court and the Tarasoff family received a substantial award. Without public scrutiny, a bizarre tragedy had been adjudicated in camera, and a far-reaching and intensely value-laden controversy had been stifled by the fiat of legal precedent.

A crucial point of the Supreme Court decision was this: It was not the failure of the psychologist or his supervisor to predict violence that made the case a viable one (the psychologist had clearly decided that his client was dangerous), but the failure of the psychologist and his supervisor to provide an adequate warning of violence either to the intended victim or to her parents.

In a brief amicus curiae filed by CSPA and other professional organizations acting in concert (see Gurevitz, 1977), it was argued that (a) a therapist cannot predict violence with certainty and (b) warning the intended victim would have breached the confidentiality of the therapist–client relationship, thus jeopardizing both the climate of trust that is necessary for therapy to occur and the effectiveness of therapy itself. The Court ignored the first argument because the therapist *had* accurately predicted that a violent act would be committed. The second argument was flatly rejected by the majority[.] . . . And to the contention that the essential nature of psychotherapy is altered by the stated exception to privilege, the Court responded with the view that a therapy relationship, whether effective or not, is of secondary importance to the preservation of life and safety. In its conclusion, the Court affirmed a guiding principle that had weighed heavily in its decision: "The public policy favoring protection of the confidential character of patient–psychotherapist communications must yield to the extent to which disclosure is essential to avert danger to others. The protective privilege ends where the public peril begins" (p. 24) [footnote omitted]. That was the cornerstone of the decision. No psychologist can be immune to the force of this conclusion, and each must ponder its implications.

What is the major impact of *Tarasoff?* In essence, the Court has chosen to make a narrow interpretation of therapist–client privilege, believing that the privilege should be sharply restricted. In deliberating the concept of privilege, the Court took a dim view of the notion that psychotherapy must occur in an atmosphere of secrecy (the canon of sanctum sanctorum). In reaction, Siegel (1976) and others have concluded that by making these value judgments, the Court has struck yet another blow against individual freedom of conscience and has come down hard on the side of conformity. Still others are willing to accept that the "duty to warn" is, at least for the present time and indefinite future, a legal requirement.

Although a therapist, a person is still a citizen, and he or she must protect and contribute to the common good. As a private citizen, the person of good conscience will not hesitate to warn an intended victim. That, as far as can be determined, is the meaning of *Tarasoff*.

EROSION OF THE PROFESSIONAL TRUST RELATIONSHIP

A hallmark of psychotherapy is the establishment of a relationship of trust between client and therapist,

and this relationship must be carefully protected through the course of the therapeutic experience. Yet a gradual and continuous weakening has occurred in the confidentiality privilege, one legal mechanism by which this professional trust relationship is implemented in our social system. . . . [I]t is urgent that we make every effort to reestablish and strengthen the sociolegal nature of the trust relationship that is so central to our professional work. . . .

There is a psychotherapist–client privilege. In California law, *psychotherapist* is defined as a clinical psychologist, a school psychologist, a clinical social worker, or a psychiatrist. This privilege is controlled by the client, is not independently held by the psychotherapist, and *must* be breached by the psychotherapist under six legal conditions: (a) when criminal action is involved; (b) when the information is made an issue in a court action; (c) when the information is obtained for the purpose of rendering an expert's report to a lawyer; (d) when the psychotherapist is acting in a court-appointed capacity; (e) when the psychotherapist believes that the client is a danger to himself, herself, or others and feels that it is necessary to prevent an actual threat of danger from being carried out; and (f) when a client is under the age of 16 and the therapist believes that the client has been the victim of a crime (e.g., incest, rape) and judges such disclosure to be in the client's best interest. . . .

Ironically, it is the psychotherapy client whose privilege of confidentiality is most vulnerable to breach under the law.[1] . . .

CONCLUSIONS AND RECOMMENDATIONS

The Committee on Privacy and Confidentiality has . . . encountered three compelling mysteries. First, . . . Does he who pays the piper call the tune? . . . Who is the client of psychotherapy? Is it a governmental agency and/or its fiscal intermediary or another type of third-party payer such as an insurance company? Is it the ostensible client's personal agent or representative, such as an attorney, guardian, or conservator? Is it a "significant other" or some per-

---

[1] *Ed. note*: The psychotherapy client's privilege of confidentiality is most vulnerable in comparison with physician–patient, lawyer–client, and clergy–penitent privileges.

son who would in some way be the beneficiary of successful treatment as applied to the ostensible client? Is it the public at large? Or is it the client self-declared? . . .

A second mystery we have encountered pertains to the current legal status of confidentiality per se. We found that the concept of confidentiality (defined as the security of personal information) is a relatively new arrival on the legal scene. As referred to earlier, the Fourth Amendment is our principal guarantor of the civil right to privacy. . . . It may be that what is needed is a kind of "freedom of anonymity," and it may ultimately be necessary to draft a constitutional amendment that will legitimize this right. Such an amendment would specify that protection of personal information be added to the safeguards afforded by the Fourth Amendment.

Finally, we have observed a mysterious trend toward legislation that would seriously impair our efforts to strengthen confidentiality. This trend is embodied by the ever more stringent regulations that are being imposed to require the swift and aggressive reporting of an ever widening array of suspected crimes against the person. A current list of these kinds of crimes would include (in California) child abuse, child molestation, and incest. And while no one in our profession questions the imperative of putting a stop to these aberrations, many of us are appalled that it has been necessary to pass laws threatening penalties if we fail to report our suspicions. Even so, these laws exist and their intent is clear; psychotherapists are being called upon to serve as gatekeepers of the criminal justice system, at least with respect to the kinds of crimes just referred to. The basic question raised by this development is, When does the healer become the informer? . . .

Our committee offers certain *proverbs* to therapists, as follows:

1. When in doubt, provide your client with information[.] . . .
2. When in deeper doubt, obtain consent; the client who is fully informed of his or her rights in psychotherapy is only partially protected unless he or she has been asked to make a decision concerning the kind and extent of protective measures to be taken.

3. The "duty to warn" implies an obligation to warn a client that such a duty exists; it is only fair to let your client know, in advance, that certain statements are inadmissible to therapy. . . .

We can with confidence put forward the following *prophesies:* (a) More laws will be passed and more court decisions handed down that will mandate respect for privacy and preservation of confidentiality; (b) more laws will be passed and more court decisions handed down which will require that confidentiality be breached and privacy invaded. . . .

References

Gurevitz, H. *Tarasoff*: Protective privilege versus public peril. *American Journal of Psychiatry*, 1977, *134*, 289–292.

Siegel, M. Confidentiality. *Clinical Psychologist* (Newsletter of Division 12 of the American Psychological Association), Fall 1976, pp. 1; 23.

Tarasoff v. Board of Regents of the University of California, Cal. Rptr. 14, No. S.F. 23042 (Cal. Sup. Ct., July 1, 1976) 131.

Commentary: No judicial decision has had more of an impact on professional psychologists (and, in some respects, on researchers as well) than Tarasoff v. Regents of the University of California *(1976). The basic facts of the case are described in the excerpt above by Everstine et al. There were actually two decisions rendered by California's Supreme Court: one in 1974 (Tarasoff I) and another in 1976 (Tarasoff II). The defendants, including Dr. Moore (the psychologist who treated Poddar), Dr. Powelson (the psychiatrist who ran the university hospital clinic where Poddar was in outpatient treatment), and the Regents of the University of California (their employer), asserted that Tatiana Tarasoff's parents had no legal claim against them for the death of their daughter because she was not their patient, but a private third party to whom they owed no professional duty. Nevertheless, a majority of the state supreme court held that the parents could sue the defendants for failure to warn Ms. Tarasoff or others of Poddar's threat. The following statement by the court sent psychological shock waves across the psychotherapy landscape—far beyond the borders of California:*

Tarasoff v. Regents of the University of California (*Tarasoff I*)

We shall explain that defendant therapists, merely because Tatiana herself was not their patient, cannot escape liability for failing to exercise due care to warn the endangered Tatiana or those who reasonably could have been expected to notify her of her peril. When a doctor or a psychotherapist, in the exercise of his professional skill and knowledge, determines, or should determine, that a warning is essential to avert danger arising from the medical or psychological condition of his patient, he incurs a legal obligation to give that warning. Primarily, the relationship between defendant therapists and

Poddar as their patient imposes the described duty to warn.

◆ ◆ ◆

Commentary: Tarasoff I *stimulated a plethora of critical analysis. See, for example, Slovenko, R. (1975). Psychotherapy and confidentiality. Cleveland State Law Review, 24, 375–396; Stone, A. (1976). Suing psychotherapists to safeguard society. Harvard Law Review, 90, 358–378. The following article addressed the ethical implications of the decision.*

Adapted from *Tarasoff v. Regents of the University of California,* 529 P.2d 553 (Cal. 1974).

Therapists as Protectors and Policemen: New Roles as a Result of *Tarasoff*?

Donald N. Bersoff

The emphasis on the clinician's duty to disclose threats to potential victims has obscured the concomitant duty of clinicians to disclose to clients the limits of confidentiality. Thus, *Tarasoff* has relevance in terms of the informed consent doctrine, an emerging rule of law developed in the context of physician–patient malpractice suits. . . . The philosophical underpinning to the informed consent doctrine is that everyone has the right to self-determination and, more specifically, the right to determine what happens to his or her body. As a result, the patient is entitled to all the facts necessary to make an informed, intelligent choice prior to consenting to medical intervention.

Typically, however, the duty to disclose is not absolute. It is tempered by what may be called the materiality rule. Physicians need not disclose risks that are likely to be known to the average patient or are in fact known to the particular patient as a result of past experience. Rather, the extent of disclosure is determined by the materiality of the risk. As defined in a leading case,

> Materiality may be said to be the significance a reasonable person, in what the physician knows or should know is his patient's position, would attach to the disclosed risk or risks in deciding whether to submit or not to submit to surgery or treatment. (*Wilkinson v. Vesey*, 1972, p. 689)

Some of the information falling within the materiality rule and thus necessitating disclosure are inherent and potential hazards of the proposed treatment, alternatives to that treatment, and the results likely if the patient remains untreated.

With this background, the implications of *Tarasoff* with regard to informed consent become self-evident. The possibility that therapists may be under a duty to make known to both the intended victim and police authorities threats to third persons made by their clients would clearly seem to be a material piece of information requiring disclosure to prospective clients. That such information is material to an individual client is manifest in the consequences of disclosure. Certainly, liberty and privacy interests are at stake (Fleming & Maximov, 1974). Communication of violent threats outside the therapeutic relationship may lead to involuntary incarceration because the standard for emergency commitment in most states is "danger to self or others." Knowledge by the putatively potential victim may lead to abrupt disruption of the relationship between client and third party in instances where such disruption would not, in fact, be warranted. The disclosure clearly violates the confidential association between client and clinician. . . .

It is thus evident that clinicians must now reveal to potential clients the limits of confidentiality. To blithely ensure the secrecy of all communications is to engage in blatant misrepresentation of facts that should now be known to all therapists. To fail to disclose these limits is to hold oneself open to liability under the materiality test. In fact, the failure to disclose the limits of confidentiality in the face of a concomitant duty to disclose threats to third parties may be to entrap the client. Clients, believing that the therapeutic relationship is inviolate, may lay bare heretofore unrevealed secrets, including their most violent urges. Therapists, fearful that their clients' verbal expression of aggression may become manifest in overt behavior, aware of the *Tarasoff* decision, and

Adapted from *Professional Psychology*, 7, 267–273. Copyright 1976 by the American Psychological Association.

frightened of the threat to their economic security and professional reputation, may too quickly and frequently inform police officials about the possibility of danger to society. The result will be an increase in involuntary civil commitment of therapy clients who would otherwise have not been incarcerated. . . .

THE DUTY OF DISCLOSURE TO THIRD PERSONS

Tarasoff, important in itself for the implications it has with regard to informed consent, is also important in a larger context. Decisions such as *Tarasoff* make it increasingly clear that therapists not only serve their clients but are also agents of the society in which they work. Psychotherapists have long struggled with the problem of conflicting loyalties to their clients and to society. The traditional cant is that the relationship between client and clinician is an especially private one in which confidentiality is entitled to the utmost respect. The primary allegiance the budding practitioner is told, is to the client. Recently, writers such as Bersoff (in press), Halleck (1971), Kittrie (1971), Szasz (1963), and Torrey (1974) have surfaced the many ways in which mental health professionals serve the state and the public, often to the detriment of the individual client. . . .

[W]hile the psychologist in *Tarasoff* was employed by a state agency, the effect of the decision is not limited to those practitioners who work in the government-funded institutions. The therapist in *Tarasoff* was held liable, in part, for breach of a state statute concerning privileged communication that governs the behavior of private, as well as institutional, practitioners. Private therapists who might seek refuge in professional codes of ethics as counterweights in a struggle to protect their clients' confidences will fail to find them safe havens. In fact, the *Tarasoff* court quoted Section 9 of the Principles of Medical Ethics of the American Medical Association to further justify its decision. Section 9 reminds physicians that they may not reveal confidences "unless . . . required to do so by law or unless it becomes necessary in order to protect the welfare of the individual or of the community."[1]

. . . As psychiatrists and psychologists become more identified with the law and its enforcement, there is the danger of discouraging people from seeking psychotherapy and of trusting those whom society has taught are the most trustworthy of professionals (excluding clergypersons, perhaps). Therapists may find themselves in insolvable conflicts as they attempt to reconcile their own personal morality and training regarding confidentiality, the vague reminders of their professional codes of ethics that warn of the consequences of violating the moral and legal standards of the community, and the developing legal requirements that demand complex decision making and a balancing between client and public interests. In any event, it is evident that there are ever decreasing guarantees to client–clinician privacy and that the therapeutic relationship is not immune from the scrutiny of society. Such limits must clearly be conveyed to the prospective client because failure to do so can result in both loss of liberty and privacy to the client as well as loss to the clinician of reputation and money damages to unwarned victims.

References

Bersoff, D. N. Coercion and reciprocity in psychotherapy. In C. T. Fischer & S. Brodsky (Eds.), *The Prometheus principle: Informed participation by clients in human services*. New Brunswick: Transaction, in press.

Fleming, J. G., & Maximov, B. The patient or his victim: The therapist's dilemma. *California Law Review*, 1974, *62*, 1025–1068.

Kittrie, N. N. *The right to be different*. Baltimore, Md.: Johns Hopkins University Press, 1971.

Halleck, S. L. *The politics of therapy*. New York: Science House, 1971.

Szasz, T. S. *Law, liberty, and psychiatry*. New York: Macmillan, 1963.

Tarasoff v. Regents of University of California, 13 C.3d 177, 529 P.2d 553, 118 Cal. Rptr. 129 (1974).

Torrey, E. F. *The death of psychiatry*. Radnor, Pa.: Chilton, 1974.

Wilkinson v. Vesey, 110 R.I. 606, 295 A.2d 676 (1972).

◆ ◆ ◆

Commentary: In a rare move, the California Supreme Court agreed to hear new arguments and reconsidered its opinion in Tarasoff II.

---

[1] *Ed. note:* See also Standards 5.01 and 5.05 of the APA current (1992) Ethical Principles.

Tarasoff v. Regents of the University of California (*Tarasoff II*)

... We shall explain that defendant therapists cannot escape liability merely because Tatiana herself was not their patient. When a therapist determines, or pursuant to the standards of his profession should determine, that his patient presents a serious danger of violence to another, he incurs an obligation to use reasonable care to protect the intended victim against such danger. The discharge of this duty may require the therapist to take one or more of various steps, depending upon the nature of the case. Thus it may call for him to warn the intended victim or others likely to apprise the victim of the danger, to notify the police, or to take whatever other steps are reasonably necessary under the circumstances. . . .

. . . As a general principle, a "defendant owes a duty of care to all persons who are foreseeably endangered by his conduct, with respect to all risks which make the conduct unreasonably dangerous."

. . . As we shall explain, however, when the avoidance of foreseeable harm requires a defendant to control the conduct of another person, or to warn of such conduct, the common law has traditionally imposed liability only if the defendant bears some special relationship to the dangerous person or to the potential victim. Since the relationship between a therapist and his patient satisfies this requirement, we need not here decide whether foreseeability alone is sufficient to create a duty to exercise reasonable care to protect a potential victim of another's conduct.

Although . . . under the common law, as a general rule, one person owed no duty to control the conduct of another . . . nor to warn those endangered by such conduct . . . the courts have carved out an exception to this rule in cases in which the defendant stands in some special relationship to either the person whose conduct needs to be controlled or in a relationship to the foreseeable victim of that conduct. . . . Applying this exception to the present case, we note that a relationship of defendant therapists to either Tatiana or Poddar will suffice to establish a duty of care: as explained in section 315 of the Restatement Second of Torts, a duty of care may arise from either "(a) a special relation . . . between the actor and the third person which imposes a duty upon the actor to control the third person's conduct, or (b) a special relation . . . between the actor and the other which gives to the other a right of protection."

Although plaintiffs' pleadings assert no special relation between Tatiana and defendant therapists, they establish as between Poddar and defendant therapists the special relation that arises between a patient and his doctor or psychotherapist [footnote omitted]. Such a relationship may support affirmative duties for the benefit of third persons. Thus, for example, a hospital must exercise reasonable care to control the behavior of a patient which may endanger other persons [footnote omitted]. A doctor must also warn a patient if the patient's condition or medication renders certain conduct, such as driving a car, dangerous to others [footnote omitted].

Although the California decisions that recognize this duty have involved cases in which the defendant stood in a special relationship *both* to the victim and to the person whose conduct created the danger, we do not think that the duty should logically be constricted to such situations. . . .

In their summary of the relevant rulings Fleming and Maximov conclude that the "case law should dispel any notion that to impose on the therapists a duty to take precautions for the safety of persons threatened by a patient, where due care so requires, is in any way opposed to contemporary ground rules

Adapted from *Tarasoff v. Regents of the University of California (Tarasoff II)*, 551 P.2d 334 (Cal. 1976).

on the duty relationship. On the contrary, there now seems to be sufficient authority to support the conclusion that by entering into a doctor-patient relationship the therapist becomes sufficiently involved to assume some responsibility for the safety, not only of the patient himself, but also of any third person whom the doctor knows to be threatened by the patient." (Fleming & Maximov, *The Patient or His Victim: The Therapist's Dilemma* (1974) 62 Cal.L.Rev. 1025, 1030.)

Defendants contend, however, that imposition of a duty to exercise reasonable care to protect third persons is unworkable because therapists cannot accurately predict whether or not a patient will resort to violence. In support of this argument amicus representing the American Psychiatric Association and other professional societies cites numerous articles which indicate that therapists, in the present state of the art, are unable reliably to predict violent acts; their forecasts, amicus claims, tend consistently to overpredict violence, and indeed are more often wrong than right. Since predictions of violence are often erroneous, amicus concludes, the courts should not render rulings that predicate the liability of therapists upon the validity of such predictions.

The role of the psychiatrist, who is indeed a practitioner of medicine, and that of the psychologist who performs an allied function, are like that of the physician who must conform to the standards of the profession and who must often make diagnoses and predictions based upon such evaluations. Thus the judgment of the therapist in diagnosing emotional disorders and in predicting whether a patient presents a serious danger of violence is comparable to the judgment which doctors and professionals must regularly render under accepted rules of responsibility.

We recognize the difficulty that a therapist encounters in attempting to forecast whether a patient presents a serious danger of violence. Obviously we do not require that the therapist, in making that determination, render a perfect performance: the therapist need only exercise "that reasonable degree of skill, knowledge, and care ordinarily possessed and exercised by members of (that professional specialty) under similar circumstances." . . . Within the broad range of reasonable practice and treatment in which professional opinion and judgment may differ, the therapist is free to exercise his or her own best judgment without liability; proof, aided by hindsight, that he or she judged wrongly is insufficient to establish negligence.

In the instant case, however, the pleadings do not raise any question as to failure of defendant therapists to predict that Poddar presented a serious danger of violence. On the contrary, the present complaints allege that defendant therapists did in fact predict that Poddar would kill, but were negligent in failing to warn.

Amicus contends, however, that even when a therapist does in fact predict that a patient poses a serious danger of violence to others, the therapist should be absolved of any responsibility for failing to act to protect the potential victim. In our view, however, once a therapist does in fact determine, or under applicable professional standards reasonably should have determined, that a patient poses a serious danger of violence to others, he bears a duty to exercise reasonable care to protect the foreseeable victim of that danger. While the discharge of this duty of due care will necessarily vary with the facts of each case, in each instance the adequacy of the therapist's conduct must be measured against the traditional negligence standard of the rendition of reasonable care under the circumstances. As explained in Fleming and Maximov, *The Patient or His Victim: The Therapist's Dilemma* (1974) 62 Cal.L.Rev. 1025, 1067: ". . . the ultimate question of resolving the tension between the conflicting interests of patient and potential victim is one of social policy, not professional expertise. . . . In sum, the therapist owes a legal duty not only to his patient, but also to his patient's would-be victim and is subject in both respects to scrutiny by judge and jury." . . .

Defendants . . . argue that free and open communication is essential to psychotherapy. . . . The giving of a warning, defendants contend, constitutes a breach of trust which entails the revelation of confidential communications.

We recognize the public interest in supporting effective treatment of mental illness and in protecting the rights of patients to privacy. . . .

We realize that the open and confidential character of psychotherapeutic dialogue encourages patients to express threats of violence, few of which are ever executed. Certainly a therapist should not be encouraged routinely to reveal such threats: such disclosures could seriously disrupt the patient's relationship with his therapist and with the persons threatened. To the contrary, the therapist's obligations to his patient require that he not disclose a confidence unless such disclosure is necessary to avert danger in others, and even then that he do so discreetly, and in a fashion that would preserve the privacy of his patient to the fullest extent compatible with the prevention of the threatened danger. . . .

The revelation of a communication under the above circumstances is not a breach of trust or a violation of professional ethics: as stated in the Principles of Medical Ethics of the American Medical Association (1957), section 9: "A physician may not reveal the confidence entrusted to him in the course of medical attendance . . . *unless he is required to do so by the law or unless it becomes necessary in order to protect the welfare of the individual or of the community.* (Emphasis added.) We conclude that the public policy favoring protection of the confidential character of patient-psychotherapist communications must yield to the extent to which disclosure is essential to avert danger to others. The protective privilege ends where the public peril begins.

Our current crowded and computerized society compels the interdependence of its members. In this risk-infected society we can hardly tolerate the further exposure to danger that would result from a concealed knowledge of the therapist that his patient was lethal. If the exercise of reasonable care to protect the threatened victim requires the therapist to warn the endangered party or those who can reasonably be expected to notify him, we see no sufficient societal interest that would protect and justify concealment. The containment of such risks lies in the public interest. For the foregoing reasons, we find that plaintiffs' complaints can be amended to state a cause of action against defendants Moore, Powelson, Gold, and Yandell and against the Regents as their employer, for breach of a duty to exercise reasonable care to protect Tatiana. . . .

MOSK, Justice (concurring and dissenting).

I concur in the result in this instance only because the complaints allege that defendant therapists did in fact predict that Poddar would kill and were

therefore negligent in failing to warn of that danger. . . .

I cannot concur, however, in the majority's rule that a therapist may be held liable for failing to predict his patient's tendency to violence if other practitioners, pursuant to the "standards of the profession," would have done so. The question is, what standards? . . .

I would restructure the rule designed by the majority to eliminate all reference to conformity to standards of the profession in predicting violence. If a psychiatrist does in fact predict violence, then a duty to warn arises. The majority's expansion of that rule will take us from the world of reality into the wonderland of clairvoyance.

CLARK, Justice (dissenting).

Until today's majority opinion, both legal and medical authorities have agreed that confidentiality is essential to effectively treat the mentally ill, and that imposing a duty on doctors to disclose patient threats to potential victims would greatly impair treatment. Further, recognizing that effective treatment and society's safety are necessarily intertwined, the Legislature has already decided effective and confidential treatment is preferred over imposition of a duty to warn.

The issue whether effective treatment for the mentally ill should be sacrificed to a system of warnings is, in my opinion, properly one for the Legislature, and we are bound by its judgment. Moreover, even in the absence of clear legislative direction, we must reach the same conclusion because imposing the majority's new duty is certain to result in a net increase in violence. . . .

Overwhelming policy considerations weigh against imposing a duty on psychotherapists to warn a potential victim against harm. While offering virtually no benefit to society, such a duty will frustrate psychiatric treatment, invade fundamental patient rights and increase violence. . . .

Assurance of confidentiality is important for three reasons. . . .

First, without substantial assurance of confidentiality, those requiring treatment will be deterred from seeking assistance. . . .

Second, the guarantee of confidentiality is essential in eliciting the full disclosure necessary for effective treatment.

Third, even if the patient fully discloses his thoughts, assurance that the confidential relationship will not be breached is necessary to maintain his trust in his psychiatrist—the very means by which treatment is effected. . . .

Given the importance of confidentiality to the practice of psychiatry, it becomes clear the duty to warn imposed by the majority will cripple the use and effectiveness of psychiatry. Many people, potentially violent—yet susceptible to treatment—will be deterred from seeking it; those seeking it will be inhibited from making revelations necessary to effective treatment; and, forcing the psychiatrist to violate the patient's trust will destroy the interpersonal relationship by which treatment is effected. . . .

By imposing a duty to warn, the majority contributes to the danger to society of violence by the mentally ill and greatly increases the risk of civil commitment—the total deprivation of liberty—of those who should not be confined. The impairment of treatment and risk of improper commitment resulting from the new duty to warn will not be limited to a few patients but will extend to a large number of the mentally ill. Although under existing psychiatric procedures only a relatively few receiving treatment will ever present a risk of violence, the number making threats is huge, and it is the latter group—not just the former—whose treatment will be impaired and whose risk of commitment will be increased.

Both the legal and psychiatric communities recognize that the process of determining potential violence in a patient is far from exact, being fraught with complexity and uncertainty. . . .

This predictive uncertainty means that the number of disclosures will necessarily be large. As noted above, psychiatric patients are encouraged to discuss all thoughts of violence, and they often express such thoughts. However, unlike this court, the psychiatrist does not enjoy the benefit of overwhelming hindsight in seeing which few, if any, of his patients will ultimately become violent. Now, confronted by the majority's new duty, the psychiatrist must instantaneously calculate potential violence from each patient on each visit. The difficulties researchers have encountered in accurately predicting violence will be heightened for the practicing psychiatrist

dealing for brief periods in his office with heretofore nonviolent patients. And, given the decision not to warn or commit must always be made at the psychiatrist's civil peril, one can expect most doubts will be resolved in favor of the psychiatrist protecting himself.

Neither alternative open to the psychiatrist seeking to protect himself is in the public interest. The warning itself is an impairment of the psychiatrist's ability to treat, depriving many patients of adequate treatment. It is to be expected that after disclosing their threats, a significant number of patients, who would not become violent if treated according to existing practices, will engage in violent conduct as a result of unsuccessful treatment. In short, the majority's duty to warn will not only impair treatment of many who would never become violent but worse, will result in a net increase in violence.

The second alternative open to the psychiatrist is to commit his patient rather than to warn. Even in the absence of threat of civil liability, the doubts of psychiatrists as to the seriousness of patient threats have led psychiatrists to overcommit to mental institutions. . . . This practice is so prevalent that it has been estimated that "as many as twenty harmless persons are incarcerated for every one who will commit a violent act." (Steadman & Cocozza, *Stimulus/Response: We Can't Predict Who is Dangerous* (Jan. 1975) 8 Psych. Today 32,35.). . .

◆ ◆ ◆

Commentary: Max Siegel (1979) made the following comments after Tarasoff II *was decided:*

> This was a day in court for the law and not for the mental health professions. If the psychologist had accepted the view of absolute, inviolate confidentiality, he might have been able to keep Poddar in treatment, saved the life of Tatiana Tarasoff, and avoided what was to become the Tarasoff decision. (p. 253)

Siegel, M. (1979). Privacy, ethics, and confidentiality. Professional Psychology, 10, 249–258.

Other commentators have suggested that a good client–clinician relationship is based on trust rather than on confidentiality. Thus, they argue, if trust is maintained, then the therapeutic relationship may endure even after a mandated breach in confidentiality. See Brosig, C. L., & Kalichman, S. C. (1992). Child abuse reporting decisions: Effects of statutory wording of reporting requirements. Professional Psychology: Research and Practice, 23, 486–492; Watson, H., &

Levine, M. (1989). Psychotherapy and mandated reporting of child abuse. American Journal of Orthopsychiatry, 59, 246–256. Some of the materials that follow may help you judge the respective merits of these positions. In any event, Tarasoff II was the first of a long string of similar cases that soon spread across the United States.

Protecting Third Parties: A Decade After *Tarasoff*

Mark J. Mills, Greer Sullivan, and Spencer Eth

. . . The ethical roots of the *Tarasoff* decision are found in the principles of medical confidentiality and beneficence, recognized for two millennia. The Hippocratic oath affirms that "What I may see or hear in the course of the treatment or even outside of the treatment in regard to the life of men . . . I will keep to myself" (24). In the present era, physicians continue to prize the sanctity of the doctor–patient relationship, even as it is encroached upon by the demands of insurance companies, peer review organizations, and other interested third parties (25,26).

Two arguments have been proposed to justify the enduring importance of confidentiality. Moral deontologists assert that privacy and absolute control over personal information are among the natural rights of man. They argue that since a breach of confidentiality constitutes an assault on human dignity, it is always wrong. The alternative and more widely held justification for the importance ascribed to confidentiality is based on a utilitarian calculation of effects (an assessment of likely outcomes). This position holds that the consequences of violating confidentiality outweigh the possible benefits. Some psychiatrists claim that confidentiality is essential to psychiatric treatment (27). They believe that without the assurance of complete secrecy, patients would be less inclined to enter treatment and those already in therapy would be unwilling to disclose charged material. Therefore, violating confidentiality would seriously affect the care of the mentally ill, to the detriment of patients and society alike.

Another historic tradition in medicine emphasizes the physician's ethical obligation to act beneficently. This responsibility for altruistic service applies not only to patients but to the community as well.

Specific public health interventions, such as quarantining contagious patients, have been common in medical practice for hundreds of years. In direct response to the publication of a series of professional articles on the battered child syndrome, every state in the union has adopted laws requiring physicians to report cases of child abuse (28). . . .

We believe that the responsibility to protect patient confidentiality and to protect community welfare forms the foundation of medical ethics. We do not question the fundamental importance of either duty, despite the inherent potential for conflict. Rather, we recognize that, in accord with the current *Principles of Medical Ethics*, neither duty is absolute: "Psychiatrists at times may find it necessary, in order to protect the patient or the community from imminent danger, to reveal confidential information disclosed by the patient" (31). When examining issues raised by *Tarasoff*, one in effect considers the limits of the duty to protect, not the legitimacy of that duty. . . .

In 1976 Dr. Alan Stone warned that the imposition of a duty to protect would "destroy the patient's expectation of confidentiality, thereby thwarting effective treatment and ultimately reducing public safety" (3). The available data suggest otherwise. . . . In a more recent report Stone reconsidered his position and concluded that "the duty to warn is not as unmitigated a disaster for the enterprise of psychotherapy as it once seemed to critics like myself" (35). The utilitarian balance seems, then, to shift in favor of confidentiality generally but to permit selected violations when they are justified by the conflicting duty to prevent harm. "It is, indeed, difficult to formulate a moral argument against the position that therapists should act to protect those whom they believe to be endangered, as should all human beings" (36).

We maintain that both medical ethics and legal jurisprudence prefer that confidentiality be preserved whenever possible. Furthermore, there is abundant evidence that in instances where the welfare of society or third parties is seriously threatened, confidentiality should, and indeed must, be breached. . . .

Within a relatively short time a series of cases followed *Tarasoff* both within and outside of California. Perhaps the cases that most concerned psychotherapists were the 1980 *Lipari* decision (7) and the 1983 *Petersen* decision (15). In the first instance an outpatient, evidently disgruntled with his care, threatened to harm others but did not specify whom he would attack or when. The therapist apparently made no intervention, and the patient then purchased a shotgun and fired it in a nightclub, injuring and killing several people. The subsequent court decision extended the duty to protect to apply even in cases where a victim had not been and could not be specifically identified. However, it is important to note that the court, as with *Tarasoff* itself, was dealing with the issue in demur. In such cases, the court assumes the facts as presented by the plaintiff's brief. The court thus addresses a theoretical issue: Was there a duty if the facts were as the plaintiff alleges? Virtually always the defendant's version of the facts is quite different. The *Lipari* case, like *Tarasoff*, did not impose liability; in fact, both cases were settled out of court.

The *Petersen* case extends the *Tarasoff* decision the furthest to date. In this case the female plaintiff was awarded monetary damages for injuries incurred as a result of an automobile accident with a patient who had been released from a state mental hospital 5 days previously. The plaintiff claimed that the patient should not have been released and that the psychiatrist should have reported the patient's parole violation. (It was alleged that the psychiatrist knew that the patient had been convicted of murder and rape.) At the time of discharge, the treating psychiatrist had perceived the patient as fully recovered from a drug-induced (phencyclidine) psychosis. Liability was imposed although at the time of discharge the victim was unknown, the violence was unforeseeable, and the patient had not directly

threatened anyone. Perhaps the court could find no other legal mechanism to compensate the plaintiff. However, in a situation in which the patient was threatening to no one in particular, the decision appears to demand predictive powers that are completely beyond present-day psychiatry.

In a previous paper, Mills reviewed many of the post-*Tarasoff* court decisions concerning the protection of third parties from potentially violent psychiatric patients (37). Using a normative analysis, Mills concluded that these cases largely turn on the issue of foreseeability. When the courts have imposed liability, the identity of the subsequently injured party was known to the psychotherapist (*Macintosh*) (5) or the victim would reasonably have been expected to be in close proximity to the target of violence, as in the case of a young child (*Hedlund*) (14) or a home in the vicinity of a building burned by arson (*Peck*) (18,38). In addition, threats were specific, the patient's history was overwhelming, and there were breaches of conventional practice, such as failure to obtain the patient's prior medical record (*Jablonski*) (12), (*Peck*) (18,38), or to examine carefully the patient and his or her medical record (*Clark*) (16). When liability has not been imposed, the patient has, at the time of evaluation, been perceived as not being a threat to any individual or group (*Thompson*) (6), (*Leedy*) (8), (*Doyle*) (9), (*Brady*) (13), (*Furr*) (11), even when the patient had a history of violent behavior or alcoholism (*Hasenei*) (10).

Although the use of a normative approach may seem to suggest that courts are concerned primarily with the overall policy, this is not a fully accurate portrayal of judicial decision making. Public policy evolves only as the courts, attempting to achieve justice in each case, make individual decisions. In the majority of states, no cases involving the issue of third-party protection have been brought to the bar. A few states—for example, Pennsylvania and Maryland—have even considered the issue and have decided against following the policy established in *Tarasoff* (39,40). Nevertheless, the evident trend continues toward a policy of a duty to warn for psychotherapists. In states where the issue has not been litigated, the conservative assumption is that the court will find a *Tarasoff*-like duty when the issue arises.

In August 1985, the California legislature adopted the first state statute concerning the psychotherapist's duty to warn and protect third parties. The law states more clearly the circumstances in which the duty is applicable. A psychotherapist is liable only "where the patient has communicated to the psychotherapist a serious threat of physical violence against a reasonably identifiable victim or victims." The statute further directs that the duty to warn and protect shall be discharged by "reasonable efforts to communicate the threat to the victim or victims and to a law enforcement agency" (2). . . .

Although the new law limits psychotherapists' liability in some cases, it encourages clinicians to respond to a circumstance in a rote way. No mention is made of protecting a third party through clinical interventions. Further, the statute encourages "defensive medicine." Breaching confidences by warning routinely is analogous to ordering laboratory tests that are not indicated clinically, for fear of liability. Rather than being placed in a defensive position, therapists should be encouraged to approach a situation of potential violence thoughtfully, to use clinical interventions whenever possible to contain the potential violence, and to warn when public policy so counsels (52). . . .

References

2. California Assembly Bill 1133, McAllister, 1984

3. Stone AA: The Tarasoff decisions: suing psychotherapists to safeguard society. Harvard Law Review 1976; 90:358–378

5. Macintosh v Milano, 168 NJ 966, 403 A 2d 500 (1979)

6. Thompson v County of Alameda, 27 Cal 3d 741, 614 P 2d 728 (1980). Mental Disability Law Reporter 1980; 4:313–314

7. Lipari v Sears, Roebuck & Co, 497 F Supp 185 (D Neb 1980)

8. Leedy v Hartnett, 510 F Supp 1125 (MD, Pa 1981). Mental Disability Law Reporter 1981; 5:161–162

9. Doyle v United States, 530 F Supp 1278 (CD Cal 1982). Mental Disability Law Reporter 1982; 6:336–337

10. Hasenei v United States, 541 F Supp 999 (D Md 1982)

11. Furr v Spring Grove State Hospital, 53 Md App 474, 454 A 2d 414 (1983)

12. Jablonski v United States, 712 F 2d 391 (9th Cir 1983)

13. Brady v Hooper, 570 F Supp 1333 (D Colo 1982). Mental Disability Law Reporter 1983; 7:453–454

14. Hedlund v Orange County, 34 Cal 3d 695, 669 P 2d 41 (1983)

15. Petersen v State, 100 Wn2d 421, 671 P 2d 230 (Wash 1983)

16. Clark v State of New York, 99 AD 2d 616, 472 NYS 2d, 170 (1984)

18. Peck v Counseling Service of Addison County, Inc, No 83-062 (Vt Sup Ct June, 1985). Mental and Physical Disability Law Reporter 1985; 9:364–365

24. Beauchamp TL, Childress JF: Principles of Biomedical Ethics. New York, Oxford University Press, 1979

25. Rosner BL: Psychiatrists, confidentiality, and insurance claims. Hastings Cent Rep 1980; 10(6):5–7

26. Siegler M: Confidentiality in medicine—a decrepit concept. N Engl J Med 1982; 307:1518–1521

27. Group for the Advancement of Psychiatry: Confidentiality and Privileged Communication in the Practice of Psychiatry: Report 45. New York, GAP, 1960

28. Heins M: The "battered child" revisited. JAMA 1984; 251:3295–3300.

31. American Psychiatric Association: The Principles of Medical Ethics With Annotations Especially Applicable to Psychiatry. Washington, DC, APA 1985.

35. Stone AA: Law, Psychiatry and Morality. Washington, DC, American Psychiatric Press, 1984

36. Appelbaum PS: *Tarasoff* and the clinician: problems in fulfilling the duty to protect. Am J Psychiatry 1985; 142:425–429

37. Mills MJ: The so-called duty to warn: the psychotherapeutic duty to protect third parties from patients' violent acts. Behavioral Sciences and the Law 1984; 2:237–257

38. Stone AA: Vermont adopts *Tarasoff*: A real barnburner. Am J Psychiatry 1986; 143:352–355

39. Hopewell v Adibempe, Number GD78-28756, Civil Division, Court of Common Pleas of Allegheny County, Pennsylvania, June 1, 1981

40. Shaw v Glickman, 415 A 2d 625 (Md Ct Spec App 1980)

52. Klein JI, Macbeth JE, Onek JN: Legal Issues in the Private Practice of Psychiatry. Washington, DC, American Psychiatric Press, 1984

◆ ◆ ◆

Commentary: There are other useful collections of post-Tarasoff cases. See, for example, Knapp, S., & Vandecreek, L. (1982). Tarasoff: *Five years later.* Professional Psychology, 13, 511–516; Fulero, S. M. (1988). Tarasoff: *10 years later.* Professional Psychology, 19, 184–190. In an Appendix, Fulero provided a useful and relatively complete compendium of 70 judicial opinions decided between 1974 and 1987 in which the courts applied the Tarasoff "duty to protect" principle. For an even more extensive discussion, see Vandecreek, L., & Knapp, S. A. (1989). Tarasoff and beyond: Legal considerations in the treatment of life-endangering patients. *Sarasota, FL: Professional Resource Exchange. Among the more noteworthy cases these sources discuss are (a)* Bellah v. Greenson, *141 Cal. Rptr. 92 (Cal. App. 1977)—in which a California appellate court (but not its Supreme Court) held that the duty to protect does not extend to a patient's suicidal threats; (b)* Peck v. Counseling Service of Addison County, *499 A.2d 422 (Vt. 1985)—in which the Vermont Supreme Court extended the duty to protect to a master's-level counselor whose adolescent patient threatened to burn down his father's barn, creating the possibility that the Tarasoff duty may extend to protecting property (or at least damage to property that may also create risk to people); and (c)* Hedlund v. Superior Court, *34 Cal.3d 995, 194 Cal. Rptr. 805 (1983)—in which the California Supreme Court held that a foreseeable, innocent bystander who witnesses the violence inflicted by a patient may sue the patient's therapist for negligent infliction of emotional distress in addition to the victim's suit for failure to protect.*

Tarasoff and the Researcher: Does the Duty to Protect Apply in the Research Setting?

Paul S. Appelbaum and Alan Rosenbaum

A field-worker in an epidemiologic survey of psychiatric disorders among a cohort of young men is startled to hear one of her subjects confess a desire to "get even" with his former boss, whom he blames for his current problems. A research psychologist in a longitudinal study of spouse abusers learns from a subject's wife that he is again beating her regularly. A clinician in a controlled trial of psychotherapy explores the roots of a patient-subject's depression, only to uncover homicidal fantasies about his ex-wife.

The above situations are hypothetical, but each example was posed to us by an investigator of an actual research project. These examples represent real concerns among investigators in the behavioral sciences. All of the scenarios present the same dilemma: To what extent are researchers responsible for preventing the occurrence of violent behavior by one of their research subjects? . . .

DOES THE DUTY APPLY IN THE RESEARCH SETTING?

Despite researchers' concerns, we know of no case in which an attempt has been made to apply the duty to protect in the context of a research project. Nonetheless, without analyzing the reasons for its possible applicability, it would be premature to conclude that a court might not apply the duty in the future, given the proper set of circumstances. . . .

Although it might be argued that the duty to protect was formulated in, and applies only to, the clinical setting, and therefore no further consideration need be given to its application to investigators, such a position seems too simplistic. Research and clinical functions are often integrally related, and they are difficult to tease apart (Fried, 1974). Furthermore, they are often conducted by the same persons. Consider, for example, a controlled trial of psychotherapy. The functions of the therapist–researchers, apart from filling out evaluation forms, differ little from those of their nonresearch colleagues and from the researchers' own functions in nonresearch contexts. One cannot simply maintain that duties that are applied to one group are irrelevant to the other. On the other hand, much behavioral science research—for example, social psychological studies of interactions among small groups of undergraduates—takes place in settings so different from the treatment context and is performed by people who may be so different in their training and functions from clinicians that it would be equally misleading to assume that the duty to protect will invariably be applied to investigators. Some basis is needed for distinguishing between research situations in which a duty to protect may be invoked and those in which it is unlikely to be found.

The courts will be attempting here to determine whether there is something intrinsic to clinical relationships themselves that warrants their being deemed "special" for the purpose of invoking a duty to protect, or whether some characteristic of the actors that transcends the clinical setting is determinative. Given the analysis in *Tarasoff* [1974], it would appear that the abilities of psychotherapists with regard to prediction and prevention of violence—not the context in which contact with a potentially violent person occurs—will determine whether the relationship is "special enough" for a duty to protect to be invoked. Thus, the courts will need to inquire into the resemblance between the researchers in

Adapted from the *American Psychologist, 44*, 885–894. Copyright 1989 by the American Psychological Association.

question and clinicians with regard to these abilities [footnote omitted].

Ability to Predict Violence: Clinical Training

Courts will have to look at more than just the researchers' general disciplines (e.g., psychology vs. sociology) to make this determination. Social and experimental psychologists without clinical training should fall outside the requirements of the duty to protect, as should relatively untrained research assistants who collect data. Thus, one can envision a variety of research situations to which the duty to protect should not apply. Industrial psychologists conducting research on personnel issues in a corporate setting; developmental psychologists examining child behavior in connection with a public health early intervention program; social psychologists, sociologists, or anthropologists examining the behavior of police officers in the field—all should be free of legal obligations (although some ethical duties may apply in given circumstances, as we will discuss later) to protect potential victims of their subjects. Even investigators who have spent many years studying violence—such as social psychologists evaluating the effectiveness of an intervention program to assist police officers in preventing family violence—lack the putative ability to predict dangerousness, based on clinical training, to which the courts have looked as a basis for the special relationship needed to impose a duty.

What if a nonclinician investigator heads a project, but data collection is performed by clinicians, who have direct contact with subjects? According to our analysis, the data collectors themselves may have an obligation to protect endangered persons. Does their nonclinician supervisor bear any responsibilities? The closest parallel here would seem to be to a nonclinical administrator of a hospital or clinic. The administrator is held responsible for the formulation of policies that inform clinicians of their obligations and enable them to fulfill their duties. Similarly, nonclinician researchers might be expected to be aware that their data gatherers may have a duty to protect, to make this duty known to them, and to oversee the formulation of policies for fulfilling the duty.

Ability to Predict Violence: Data Available

. . .

The reliability and validity of data concerning potential violence are dependent, in part, on an interviewer's ability to determine the accuracy of available information, to probe the seriousness of the subject's resolve and to seek confirmation of alternative explanations of the subject's apparent violent intent. This requires at a minimum that the data be gathered in direct, face-to-face contact between the clinician–investigator and the subject, a *sine qua non* of ordinary clinical settings (Appelbaum, 1984). Such contact will militate in favor of applying a duty to protect. On the other hand, even assuming a general ability to predict violence, the expectation that the data relevant to capacity for violence can be gathered validly without substantial face-to-face contact, such as from a questionnaire completed by the subject or a telephone interview, is untenable. . . .

The scope of the data available is another important factor that may differentiate between clinical and research settings. Clinicians conduct wide-ranging assessments, with the freedom to inquire about all relevant aspects of thought and behavior; such a broad-ranging inquiry is essential for a predictive process that comports with professional, clinical norms (Monahan, 1981). Some research projects may adopt similar methodologies, using multiple clinical indexes or unstructured interviews. They would seem to be susceptible, on the basis of their comparability to the clinical setting, to the imposition of a duty to protect. Many studies, however, focus their data collection exclusively on particular areas of functioning (e.g., depressive symptoms). Researchers in the latter type of project ought not to be held to have a duty to detect a predisposition for violence and to take appropriate protective measures when the data that clinicians would find relevant to that determination ordinarily would not be uncovered in the course of the study.

The cross-sectional versus longitudinal nature of the data available to researchers, a third major factor in the analysis of whether a duty to protect should apply, affects the mental health professional's ability to determine whether there is a reproducible link between a particular constellation of circumstances (e.g., patients' threats) and their violent behavior. These relationships can be measured only over time. In the clinical setting, repeated contact between therapist and patient allows assessment of the seriousness of a patient's threat by comparison with the patient's previous history. Threats repetitively evoked by given circumstances, particularly when they have resulted previously in violence, should be taken more seriously. Conversely, frequent and diffuse threats that are never actualized over time will appropriately be discounted (Appelbaum, 1986). Repeated contact with subjects, therefore, may encourage application of the duty to protect. This process of assessing the stability of causal relationships in subjects' behavior, however, cannot occur in research projects that involve only single encounters between researchers and subjects. Although one cannot rule out the possibility that even in this situation information might be obtained that would be sufficiently alarming that a reasonable person might act on it after a single contact, the courts might well choose not to impose a duty in such cases. . . .

Facilitating the Prediction of Violence

A more difficult set of questions concerns the degree to which researchers might be held to have a duty to alter their methodologies to facilitate assessment of potential violence, and consequent application of a duty to protect. Data gatherers, as noted earlier, will often collect insufficient information to allow reasonable evaluation, by clinical standards, of subjects' potential for violence. . . .

. . . In most research projects, the risk of subject violence is small and, given difficulties in prediction, even with optimal data, the likelihood that researchers will accurately detect such propensities is even smaller. In contrast, the burdens placed on researchers to alter methods or conduct additional evaluations may be so substantial as materially to impede or even prevent the conduct of their research. One would hope that courts would not lightly impose affirmative obligations on the vast proportion of research investigations.

Studies of populations at high risk for violent behavior, however, may present a different balance of interests. A follow-up study of violent criminals may be an example of such a project. Not only is the

likelihood increased that someone may be harmed, but the higher base rate of violence makes accurate prediction more probable. Even in research projects addressing groups at low risk for violence, a given subject might present so blatant a threat to third parties that most reasonable mental health professionals would feel impelled at least to extend their evaluations and perhaps to take other actions. It is an open question whether courts would require affirmative steps to be taken to facilitate evaluation of violence potential in these cases.

On ethical grounds alone, though, it may be reasonable for investigators to consider building provisions for the protection of potential victims into their protocols. Professional associations' codes of ethics contain language permitting disclosures to be made to protect third parties in therapeutic and research contexts. . . .

Our contact with researchers around the country who are studying high-risk groups suggests to us that investigators, funding agencies, and institutional review boards (IRBs) are just beginning to think through when additional precautions may be indicated. For example, two nonclinician researchers studying ascriptions of dangerousness to mental patients reported to us that only after approval and funding of their study by a federal agency (and approval by their university's IRB) were they approached by the funding agency and asked to consider how they might deal with these issues, a question they had not considered before. . . .

A somewhat different situation may exist in cases in which a researcher, though a nonclinician, actually alters subjects' propensity for engaging in violent behavior, for example, by manipulating their level of anger. Here the researcher, by inducing the potentially dangerous situation, may have both legal . . . and ethical . . . obligations to ensure that no untoward effects ensue.

STATUTORY AND REGULATORY SOURCES OF A DUTY TO PROTECT

In some states, as noted earlier, the duty to protect has been established or modified by statute. This adds another level of complexity to the analysis. The statutes adopted to date invariably frame the duty in terms of a "patient's" or "client's" potential violence.

It is unclear, therefore, what effect they might have in nontherapeutic research settings, although they would seem to apply, at a minimum, to research in which treatment is also being received (e.g., a trial of psychotherapy). Courts, which will ultimately interpret the laws, might determine that the statutes were meant to be exclusive and therefore only apply to situations in which treatment is rendered. Alternatively, they may read the statutes as evidence of the legislatures' intent to place responsibility on mental health professionals in general for the protection of endangered persons without attempting to specify all circumstances in which the duty might arise. It seems safe to conclude that at this point the statutes' effects on researchers are unclear. Legal consultation in states with such laws (currently California, Colorado, Indiana, Kentucky, Louisiana, Massachusetts, Minnesota, Montana, New Hampshire, Utah, and Washington) is advisable. . . .

There are some circumstances in which uncertainty about the existence of a duty disappears. When disclosure is statutorily required, as is true in all states for situations involving child abuse (Green, 1980), researchers who fall into one of the categories of professionals designated by the law must report their information to the authorities. Statutes differ from state to state—for example, sometimes limiting the duty only to professionals who have actually seen the child (e.g., Pa. Stat. Ann. Tit. 11, Sec. 2204)—and should be consulted for particular questions. A growing number of states have adopted similar requirements for reporting of elder abuse (Salend, Kane, Satz, & Pynoos, 1984), abuse of the mentally impaired, and harm to similar groups (e.g., Mass. Gen. Laws Ann. Chap. 19B). They too are binding on researchers who meet statutory designation as mandated reporters. It should be noted that this class of statutes requires more in some respects and less in others than the *Tarasoff*-like duty to protect. The statutes exceed the scope of *Tarasoff*, in most cases, by mandating reporting when an act of abuse has occurred, regardless of whether it is likely to recur. On the other hand, they generally do not require action in the absence of past abuse, and the obligation they impose is limited to reporting the situation to state authorities, who take whatever further measures are necessary.

Circumstances exist, however, in which these requirements may be abrogated. In order to facilitate research on certain sensitive topics, particularly substance abuse, Congress has permitted the Secretary of Health and Human Services to issue confidentiality certificates (Public Health Service Act, 1975). These documents authorize researchers to protect subjects' privacy by withholding "the names or other identifying characteristics" of subjects from "any Federal, State, or local civil, criminal, administrative, legislative, or other proceedings" (42 U.S.C. 242[a]). Although court tests are again lacking, the Department of Health and Human Services (DHHS) has interpreted the statute to mean that researchers holding such certificates are exempt from state and local reporting requirements (Lanman, 1980). The certificates are available to "persons engaged in research on mental health, including research on the use and effect of alcohol and other psychoactive drugs," who make proper application to DHHS ("Protection of Identity-Research Subjects," 1979).

The existence of confidentiality certificates raises the question of what impact they may have on a *Tarasoff*-like duty to protect. Again, in the absence of a court test, the answer is uncertain. There are several reasons why issuance of a certificate might not affect researchers' obligations. First, the certificate does not prevent voluntary disclosure by investigators; it only allows researchers to resist compulsion. Thus, researchers retain the capacity to breach subjects' confidentiality if necessary to protect third parties. Arguably, therefore, if a court found that the duty to protect would otherwise apply, the certificate might not change that conclusion. Similarly, because measures to protect potential victims (such as hospitalizing the threatening subject) can often be taken without breaching confidence (Roth & Meisel, 1977), the certificate may be irrelevant for that reason too. . . .

THE DUTY TO PROTECT AND INFORMED CONSENT

Federal regulations, applicable to most research with human subjects, require that subjects be informed of any limitations that may apply to the confidentiality of information they provide ("Protection of Human Subjects," 1981). Should an investigator who anticipates that a duty to protect may apply, potentially requiring the release of information or other measures, inform potential subjects of that fact? Should IRBs require this information to be included on consent forms?

Although federal requirements for disclosure to subjects of limits on confidentiality are framed in absolute terms, suggesting that these two questions should always be answered affirmatively, the matter is not that simple. There is, in any study, the risk that information might be disclosed or other steps taken in emergent or extraordinary situations. For example, should a medical emergency occur, information about a subject will be communicated to allow treatment to take place. If research data are subject to release on court order, investigators will have no choice but to reveal them. Some IRBs may require these eventualities to be included in consent disclosures, but most recognize the impossibility of covering all conceivable situations in a form of reasonable length. Some discretion is required. . . .

. . . Even in most studies in which provisions are made to protect potential victims, the probability that any given subject's communications will have to be revealed is quite small. Evidence suggests that warnings that confidentiality may be imperiled will restrict full participation by research subjects (Singer, 1978). Because little will be gained from such warnings, the balance of advantages and disadvantages will tip against including them routinely. On the other hand, there will be studies (e.g., research on populations with a high incidence of violence) in which the need to take measures protective of potential victims can be foreseen with reasonable probability. In such cases, we would advocate notifying subjects at the time of recruitment. Subjects' right to be informed of the high likelihood that some action will need to be taken seems to us to have precedence in these cases over the interests of researchers in recruiting subjects. It is probable, however, that these disclosures will have negative impact on recruitment, and thus on the conduct of certain research projects, especially those directly examining phenomena related to violence.

The American Psychological Association has articulated a statement regarding the ethical responsibilities of researchers that addresses some of these issues (American Psychological Association, 1982). Of particular relevance to the present discussion is Principle J, which concerns the anonymity of subjects and the confidentiality of data. It states,

> Information obtained about the research participant during the course of an investigation is confidential unless otherwise agreed in advance. When the possibility exists that others may obtain access to such information, this possibility, together with the plans for protecting confidentiality, is explained to the participant as part of the procedure for obtaining informed consent. (p. 70)

In the explication of this principle, Item 6 discusses deliberate disclosure to protect the participant or other from harm, specifically stating that "the protection afforded research participants by the maintenance of confidentiality may be compromised when the investigator discovers information that serious harm threatens the research participant or others" (p. 72). Finally, Principle J imposes on investigators a "special obligation . . . to inform the individual that the information may have to be disclosed" (p. 72). This ethical principle, although emphasizing the desirability of disclosing to potential subjects the risks of breaching confidentiality, is not necessarily in conflict with the analysis presented earlier, which suggested that such disclosures be limited to high-risk situations. . . .

CONCLUSION

. . . [T]his discussion should not be interpreted as encouraging the imposition by courts or legislatures of broad *Tarasoff*-like duties on researchers. Research on sensitive topics, such as violence, child maltreatment, substance abuse, AIDS, and sexuality, might seriously be compromised by such obligations. If we value research, the validity of data must be protected to the extent possible by assuring subjects' confidentiality. Countervailing obligations, such as the duty to protect potential victims, should be imposed only after careful consideration of their probable impact and in as circumscribed a manner as possible.

References

American Psychological Association. (1982). *Ethical principles in the conduct of research with human participants.* Washington, DC: Author.

Appelbaum, P. S. (1984). Hypotheticals, psychiatric testimony, and the death sentence. *Bulletin of the American Academy of Psychiatry and the Law, 12,* 169–177.

Appelbaum, P. S. (1986). Tarasoff and the clinician: Problems in fulfilling the duty to protect. *American Journal of Psychiatry, 142,* 425–429.

Fried, C. (1974). *Medical experimentation: Personal integrity and social policy.* New York: American Elsevier.

Green, A. H. (1980). Child abuse. In D. H. Schetky & E. P. Benedek (Eds.), Child psychiatry and the law (pp. 71–88). New York: Brunner–Mazel.

Lanman, R. B. (1980, April 10). Memorandum opinion. Washington, DC: U.S. Department of Health and Human Services.

Melton, G. B., & Gray, J. N. (1988). Ethical dilemmas in AIDS research: Individual privacy and public health. *American Psychologist, 43,* 60–64.

Monahan, J. (1981). *The clinical prediction of violent behavior.* Rockville, MD: National Institute of Mental Health.

Protection of Identity–Research Subjects, 42 C.F.R. Part 2a (1979).

Protection of Human Subjects, 45 C.F.R. Part 46 (1981).

Public Health Service Act (as amended 1975), 42 U.S.C. 242a(a).

Roth, L. H., & Meisel, A. (1977). Dangerousness, confidentiality, and the duty to warn. *American Journal of Psychiatry, 134,* 508–511.

Salend, E., Kane, R. A., Satz, M., & Pynoos, J. (1984). Elder abuse reporting: Limitations of statutes. *The Gerontologist, 24,* 61–69.

Singer, E. (1978). Informed consent: Consequences for response rate and response quality in social surveys. *American Sociological Review, 43,* 144–162.

Tarasoff v. Regents of University of California, 13 C.3d 177, 529 P.2d 553, 118 Cal. Rptr. 129 (1974).

◆ ◆ ◆

Commentary: *Because* Tarasoff *was a duty-to-protect case, its rulings left therapists with more options than merely informing the potential victim. One of those options is to civilly commit the client. Although in many cases that may satisfy one's legal obligations under* Tarasoff, *involuntary hospitalization has its own drawbacks. First, depriving one's clients of liberty over their objections will likely impair the therapeutic relationship. Second, civil commitment necessarily involves breaching confidentiality. Third, commitment usually requires not only a finding of potential danger to self and others, but also the presence of serious mental illness. Many outpatient therapy clients may not fit that criterion. Voluntary admission to a hospital, on the other hand, circumvents these pitfalls.*

Other options include (a) involving the potential victim in therapy (although that would most likely require the potential victim to be closely related in some way to the client); (b) manipulating the social environment, for example, seeing that the client rids himself or herself of deadly weapons; (c) referring the client for psychotropic medication or for an increased dosage if he or she is already being medicated; and (d) obtaining permission from the client to contact the potential victim, a suggestion that eliminates the involuntary disclosure of confidential communications. What follows is the most recently published set of recommendations for therapists.

Limiting Therapist Exposure to *Tarasoff* Liability: Guidelines for Risk Containment

John Monahan

. . .

RISK ASSESSMENT

Four tasks form the basis of any professionally adequate risk assessment: The clinician must be educated about what information to gather regarding risk, must gather it, must use this information to estimate risk, and, if the clinician is not the ultimate decision maker, must communicate the information and estimate to those who are responsible for making clinical decisions.

Education

The essence of being a "professional" is having "specialized knowledge" not available to the general public. In this context, specialized knowledge consists of both knowledge of mental disorder in general (e.g., assessment, diagnosis, and treatment) and knowledge of risk assessment in particular. In addition, one should be thoroughly conversant with the laws of the jurisdiction in which one practices regarding the steps to follow when a positive risk assessment is made.

Clinical education. Familiarity with basic concepts in risk assessment (e.g., predictor and criterion variables, true and false positives and negatives, decision rules and base rates) and with key findings of risk assessment research (e.g., past violence as the single best predictor of future violence) is becoming an important aspect of graduate education in psychology, psychiatry, and social work. For clinicians whose graduate education predated this emphasis or neglected it, many books and articles are readily available (e.g., Appelbaum & Gutheil, 1991; Bednar, Bednar, Lambert, & Waite, 1991; Simon, 1987; Tardiff, 1989). One does not have to commit these works to memory. But I have seen the blood drain from clinicians' faces when a plaintiff's attorney begins a cross-examination by reading a list of well-known titles in the area and asks whether the witness has read them, and the clinician is forced to mumble "no" (see Brodsky, 1991).

It is not enough to learn the basic concepts and classic findings in the field of risk assessment once and consider one's education complete. Research findings evolve and become modified over time, and the conventions of professional practice become more sophisticated. Continuing education in risk assessment through formal programs sponsored by professional or private organizations is one way to keep apprised of developments in the field. Periodically perusing original research journals (e.g., *Law and Human Behavior, Behavioral Sciences and the Law,* the *International Journal of Law and Psychiatry* is another. . .).

Legal education. The standards to which clinicians will be held in making judgments on risk are set largely by state law. In the past, these standards were usually articulated by judges who applied common law tort principles to the context of clinical risk assessment. This is what happened in *Tarasoff* and similar cases in other states. Increasingly, and after intense lobbying by professional mental health organizations, state legislatures are passing statutes to make standards for liability and immunity in this area explicit (Appelbaum, Zonana, Bonnie, & Roth,

1989). These statutes, however, will still require much adjudication to interpret inevitably ambiguous terminology (e.g., what counts as a "serious threat" or a "reasonably identifiable victim" in California's, 1990, statute?). The point here is that there is no national legal standard for what clinicians should do when they assess risk and that it behooves clinicians to know precisely what the legal standards in their own jurisdiction are regarding violence prevention. State mental health professional associations ought to have this information readily available.

Information

Once a clinician knows what information, in general, may be relevant to assessing risk, he or she must take efforts to gather that information in a given case. Most of the *Tarasoff*-like cases on which I have worked have faulted clinicians not for making an inaccurate prediction but for failing to gather information that would have made a reasonable effort at prediction possible. There are generally four sources in which relevant information can be found: in the records of past treatment, in the records of current treatment, from interviewing the patient, and from interviewing significant others. In some criminal contexts (e.g., assessments for suitability for release on parole or from insanity commitment) additional records in the form of police and probation reports, arrest records, and trial transcripts may also be available and should be consulted. But in the civil context, these records are generally not available to clinicians.

Past records. The only cases in which I have been involved that were, in the words of the defense attorneys, "born dead" were those in which the patient had an extensive history of prior violence that was amply documented in reasonably available treatment records, but those records were never requested. In these cases, the clinician has been forced to acknowledge on the witness stand that if he or she had seen the records, preventive action would have been taken.

. . . [A] line has to be drawn as to what constitutes a reasonable effort to obtain records of past treatment. I know of no standard operating procedure on this question. "Records" does not have to mean the entire hospital file; a discharge summary

may often suffice. More of a priority might be accorded to requesting the records of patients whose hospitalization was precipitated by a violent incident, or who exhibited violence in the hospital, than to requesting the records of other patients. In the context of long-term hospitalization, of course, there will be more opportunity to obtain records from distant facilities than would be the case for short-term treatment (this opportunity to obtain records is also present for patients with repeated short-term hospitalizations).

Current records. Reading the chart of the current hospitalization when making risk judgments about hospitalized patients is essential. I am continually amazed, however, at how often clinicians peruse the chart as if it were a magazine in a dentist's waiting room. In particular, nursing notes, in which violent acts and threats are often to be found, are frequently glossed over. Yet, I have seen plaintiff's attorneys introduce exhibits consisting of eight-foot-by-four-foot photographic enlargements of pages from nursing notes containing statements such as, "assaulted several other patients without provocation tonight," and "patient threatening to kill spouse as soon as released." These exhibits certainly concentrated the jury's attention.

Inquiries of the patient. Clinicians appear to question patients more often about a history of violence to self or current suicidal ideation, than about a history of violence to others or current violent fantasies. There seems little justification for this inconsistency. Directly asking patients about violent behavior and possible indices of violent behavior (e.g., arrest or hospitalization as "dangerous to others") is surely the easiest and quickest way to obtain this essential information. Open-ended questions such as "What is the most violent thing you have ever done?" or "What is the closest you have ever come to being violent?" may be useful probes, as might "Do you ever worry that you might physically hurt somebody?" The obvious problem, of course, is that patients may lie or distort their history or their current thoughts. This is always a possibility, but often corroborating information will be available from the records (above) or from significant others (below). Quite often, however, patients are remarkably forthcoming about violence. And although there may be reasons to suspect a negative answer in a given case, a positive answer should always be pursued. Unless a question to the patient is ventured, potentially valuable information on risk will not be gained.

Inquiries of significant others. Records are often unavailable, and patients are sometimes not reliable informants. A significant other, usually a family member, is frequently available in the case of inpatient hospitalization, however, either in person (accompanying the patient to treatment or seen later in conjunction with the patient's therapy) or at least by telephone. Asking the significant other about any violent behavior or threats in the event that precipitated hospitalization, or in the past, as well as open-ended questions such as "Are you concerned that X might hurt someone?" with appropriate follow-up questions as to the basis for any expressed concern, may yield useful information.

Estimation

I have elsewhere suggested a clinical model for estimating a patient's risk of violent behavior (Monahan, 1981). Although the mental health professions have yet to demonstrate that the accuracy of their estimations of risk is high in absolute terms, it is clearly high relative to chance. For example, Kozol, Boucher, and Garofalo (1972), in one of the most cited prediction studies, identified a group of patients, 35% of whom were found to have committed a violent act within five years of release. The base (i.e., chance) rate of violence was 11%. Thirty-five percent is both much lower than 100% and much higher than 11%. Whether these clinical predictions were any more accurate than those that could have been made by nonclinicians for actuarial tables) using simple demographic variables, however, is unknown. More recent research (e.g., Klassen & O'Connor, 1988) has demonstrated considerably more accurate predictions with narrowly defined groups of high-risk patients. . . .

Communication

In the individual practice of psychotherapy, the clinician who gathers information on risk is also the

clinician who makes decisions based on this information. But in outpatient treatment agencies and in mental hospitals, a division of labor often exists: One person may do the intake, another may be responsible for patient care, a team of several professionals may provide a variety of assessment and treatment modalities, and one person will have formal responsibility for making or approving discharge decisions. Although this division of labor may be an efficient use of resources, it does raise an issue not present in the solo practitioner context: the communication of relevant information from one mental health professional to another. Here, information must be transferred between or among clinicians, and significant information must be made salient to the person responsible for making the ultimate decisions regarding the patient. . . .

Placing all relevant information in the chart, of course, is the primary way of transferring information among treatment professionals. As long as the person ultimately responsible for making the institutionalization or discharge decision reads the entire file, the information is thereby communicated to the person who needs to know it.

In the real world of professional practice, however, information is not always effectively communicated by simply passing on a chart. The ultimate decision maker may be a harried senior staff member whose signature is often a pro forma endorsement of the recommendations of line staff, based only on a brief discharge summary. Or the amount of information in the chart, including information from numerous past hospitalizations, may be literally so voluminous that no final decision maker would be expected to read it verbatim. . . .

It is not sufficient to dump undigested information on the desk of the ultimate decision maker and to claim that he or she assumed the risk of liability by taking possession of the file. Rather, information pertinent to risk should explicitly . . . be brought to the attention of the decision maker. Only by making the information salient can one be assured that the decision maker has had the option to make use of it.

From the decision maker's vantage point, the implications of information overload are equally clear. When the transfer or discharge summary prepared by others makes no explicit positive or negative reference to risk, one should directly ask what information relevant to risk is in the chart and should record the answer.

RISK MANAGEMENT

. . .

Planning

Choice of a plan. For a patient flagged as *high risk*, it is important to explicitly consider preventive action. Such actions usually fall into three categories (see Appelbaum, 1985, p. 426). Following the literature on crime prevention, the first category might be called *incapacitation*, or negating the opportunity for violence in the community by hospitalizing the patient (voluntarily or involuntarily), or if it is hospital violence that is anticipated, negating that opportunity by transferring the patient to a more secure ward until the level of risk is reduced. The second category could be termed *target hardening*, or warning the potential victim when one can be identified, so that the victim can take precautionary measures. The final category might be called *intensified treatment*, in which outpatient status is maintained but sessions are scheduled more frequently, medication is initiated or increased, or joint sessions are held with the patient and others significant to the occurrence of violence, possibly including the potential victim (Wexler, 1981). More creative options may also be possible (Dietz, 1990).

The issue here is not that the clinician must necessarily adopt one of these violence-prevention strategies as part of a risk management plan but that the clinician consciously *consider* such options and make a reasoned and reasonable decision to adopt or not to adopt one of them. If the steps taken to prevent violence are seen as reasonable, the clinician should not be held liable, even if harm occurs.

Second opinions. The problem with choosing a risk management plan, in terms of tort liability, is that because the plan didn't work (or else there would be no law suit), the plaintiff can often retain another mental health professional as an expert witness to say, with the wisdom of hindsight, that any competent clinician would have known that the plan was defective. The more well thought out the preventive measures taken in a case, the more difficulty

the plaintiff will have in finding a credible witness who can with integrity make such a claim.

One way for a clinician to immunize himself or herself from this kind of Monday morning quarterbacking is for the clinician to initiate it on Friday afternoon, by consulting with a respected colleague about a difficult case before risk management decisions are made (Rachlin & Schwartz, 1986). Getting a second opinion has two advantages. First, the clinician may learn something. He or she may learn that the consulting colleague does not think that the contemplated actions are reasonable. The clinician may have missed a significant risk or protective risk factor, or may be overreacting to some aspect of the case—we all have blind spots. Or, the planned course of action may be reasonable, but the consultant may have a more creative suggestion.

The second advantage of obtaining a consultation is that it is a concrete way of demonstrating that the clinician took the case seriously and considered a variety of options for violence prevention. If the consultant is an experienced clinician . . . it becomes much more difficult to claim after the fact that "anyone" would have known that the risk management plan was negligent.

There are two clear disadvantages to obtaining consultation, however. The first is that it takes time to familiarize a colleague with a difficult case and to talk through strategy. In many busy practice settings, there is barely enough time to make a reasoned initial decision, much less to review that decision with someone else. The second disadvantage is that in obtaining consultation the clinician may be exposing the chosen consultant to potential liability should the patient commit a violent act (although I emphasize that I know of no cases in which consultants who have not seen the patient have been found to share liability). Perhaps the most equitable ways to obtain consultation are case conferences or grand rounds in which each clinician gets to discuss a difficult case, thereby broadly sharing potential liability with other colleagues, while incurring potential liability from their cases.

Adherence

Without doubt, the single largest category of cases on which I have served as an expert witness have involved patient noncompliance with aftercare recommendations. The typical case is one in which a patient is seriously violent when acutely disordered, is treated in a mental hospital until the disorder is under control, and is discharged with the recommendation to continue treatment as an outpatient. The patient comes to few, if any, appointments and then stops showing up altogether. No one on the hospital staff calls to find out what the problem is or to assess the patient's condition. The patient decompensates over the course of a few weeks or months and, while acutely disordered, kills someone. This situation is even more egregious when the patient is known to have a long history of noncompliance with treatment (typically, with psychotropic medication) and is also known from the record to become disordered when off medication and to become violent when disordered. It does not take the jury long to complete the syllogism and to conclude that the clinician or hospital could and should have avoided the tragedy by pursuing the missed appointments and nonadherence to treatment recommendations.

I know how understaffed many mental health facilities are. It is hard enough to see those people who do show up for aftercare treatment, much less to track down those who do not. Furthermore, unless the former patient satisfies the criteria for civil commitment (or outpatient commitment), there may be little the clinician can legally do to force the patient to comply with treatment recommendations (but see Meichenbaum & Turk, 1987, for an excellent account of *adherence enhancement*). Yet, it is very hard to convince a jury, with the children of the deceased in the front row of the courtroom, that a good faith effort to assure the patient's compliance with treatment was not worth the clinician's time (Klein, 1986).

DOCUMENTATION

It would be an exaggeration to state that in a tort case what is not in the written record does not exist—but not much of an exaggeration. The violent event that gives rise to the suit may occur weeks or months after the patient was last seen. The resolution of the case through settlement or trial will be a minimum of several years from the time of the vio-

lent event. Memories fade or become compromised when numerous, or innumerable, other patients are seen in the interval. The record requested by telephone, the questioning of the patient or family member about violence, the hallway conversation with a colleague to communicate information, or the careful consideration of options is unlikely to be retrieved intact from memory; nor would it make much difference if it were. Juries are rightly skeptical of self-interested statements by people who have a lot to lose. "If you did it, why didn't you write it down?" they will reason. "I was busy," is not a credible retort. Unrecorded warnings to a patient's family member that he or she has been threatened with harm are useless when that family member is dead as a result of the threatened violence or is the plaintiff in a suit for damages against the therapist. From the perspective of violence prevention, the suggestions made regarding obtaining and communicating information and developing and monitoring a risk management plan are equally applicable whether or not a record is made. From the perspective of reducing exposure to liability, there is little point in doing any of them unless they are memorialized in ink or on a dated disk (or by a videotaped exit interview; see Poythress, 1990, 1991).

Documenting information received and actions taken, or "building the record," is an essential exposure-limitation technique. When recording information relevant to risk—for example, a statement from a family member that a patient made a violent threat—one should note three things: the *source* of the information (e.g., the name of the family member), the *content* of the information (e.g., the nature and circumstances of the threat), and the *date* on which the information was obtained or communicated. In addition, when noting an action taken in furtherance of a risk reduction plan (e.g., committing or not committing a patient, warning or not warning a potential victim), it is essential to include a statement, however brief, of the *rationale* for the action. A comment in the chart or discharge summary reading—for example, "Called mother on 6/21. She said that she did not take patient's threats seriously, and that he had always complied with medication in the past"—is worth its weight in gold (perhaps literally) in demonstrating a good faith effort to attend to risk.

POLICY

The time for a clinician to think through difficult issues regarding risk assessment and management is not when a patient makes a threat or misses a follow-up appointment. Rather, general policy choices should be made and reflected upon before the need for them arises in a given case. These policies or guidelines should be committed to writing and should be reviewed by experienced clinicians and lawyers. Staff should be educated in the use of the guidelines, and their compliance should be audited. Finally, forms should be revised to prompt and record the actions contemplated by the policy statement.

Written Guidelines

Memorializing "risk policy" in writing has several virtues (Bennett, Bryant, VandenBos, & Greenwood, 1990). It promotes clarity of thought and thus is conducive to formulating effective procedures, from both the viewpoints of violence prevention and the reduction of exposure to liability. In an organizational context, it allows for consistency of application, so that staff members are not acting at cross purposes ("I thought that it was *your* responsibility to warn the family!"). And it is efficient in the sense that novice clinicians, or clinicians new to the organization, can more quickly be brought up to the level of practitioners experienced in handling potentially violent patients. The guidelines should periodically (e.g., annually) be reviewed, with an eye to revision in light of developments in research, practice, or state law.

The absolutely essential point here is that the guidelines should reflect *the minimal standards necessary for competent professional practice* and not the ideals to which an organization would aspire if it had unlimited resources. . . .

External Review

Experienced clinicians should be the ones to draft risk policy. But the draft should be reviewed by other clinicians from comparable facilities elsewhere (Poythress, 1987). As with securing consultation on difficult cases . . . policy consultation serves two purposes. It allows the drafting clinicians to learn from the experience of others and, thus, to substantively improve the quality of their procedures. If the question of the reasonableness of the policies is later impugned in a tort suit, it is very helpful to announce that they received the blessing of the most relevant slice of the professional community before the events that gave rise to the suit. A leadership role can productively be played by state and local professional organizations in drafting model guidelines in this area. . . . In addition to review by external clinicians, review by house or retained counsel is also essential to make certain that the policies comport with the statutory and case law of the jurisdiction.

Staff Education and Compliance

It is not enough—indeed, it is counterproductive—to draft exemplary guidelines and subject them to clinical and legal review if the guidelines are merely to be filed in some cabinet or entombed in a staff handbook, never to be read. Again, *it is much better to have no policies at all than to have policies that are not followed in actual practice.* . . .

Once the staff have been educated in the use of the guidelines, their compliance should be the subject of periodic "audits." A senior colleague . . . should review files to see whether the guidelines are being followed in practice, whether, for example, records are requested, information is communicated, and all actions are properly documented. Corrective action—including the revision of unworkable policies—should then be taken.

Useful Forms

The creation of user friendly forms for documenting actions called for by policy guidelines can both prompt and memorialize appropriate inquiries and responses. I have seen many a case saved for defendants by clinicians having simply checked off "no" to a list of intake questions, including the items "violent history" and "violent ideation." Expanding that list to incorporate more items contemplated in the risk-policy statement—for example, fill-in-the-blanks for "records requested from _____" "concerns communicated to _____" and "attempted to follow-up by _____"—would be very useful both in terms of violence prevention and exposure limitations. Forms should facilitate, rather than impede, gathering necessary information, taking appropriate action, and documenting both information and actions. . . .

DAMAGE CONTROL

Risk assessment and risk management involve probabilistic judgments. By definition, these judgments will sometimes be wrong—not wrong in the sense of mistake, but wrong in the sense that low probability events do happen. . . . In the context of being a mental health professional, having a patient kill or severely injure another qualifies as a major life event. I am amazed at how often clinicians panic and take actions that are unwise, unethical, and sometimes illegal. The two most prevalent forms of maladaptive clinician reaction to the stress of patient violence and the fear of liability are tampering with the record and making inculpatory public statements.

Tampering With the Record

In several of the cases on which I have served as an expert witness, a treating clinician has learned of his or her patient's violence from the media and shortly thereafter has gone to the patient's chart and inserted new material tending to support the reasonableness of the decisions that the clinician had made. In each of these cases, to my knowledge, the new material was factually correct. The clinician was not lying about the events that took place, for example, the questioning of family members about the patient's violent history or the attempt to follow up on missed aftercare appointments. But the clinician was lying about the date that these events were recorded: The entries were back-dated to appear as if they had been written before the violent act took place. . . .

. . . [I]t should be clear why tampering with the record is *always* wrong, even when the intent is to make the record more accurately reflect what actually transpired in a case. It may be legally actionable, and it is strategically catastrophic.

If a suit has not been filed, one can argue that the record does not yet constitute evidence and so changing it is not illegal. But once a suit is filed, changing the record can constitute obstruction of justice. If the clinician is asked under oath whether the records—and the dates of entry are part of the records—are accurate and testifies affirmatively and

if the late entries come to light, the clinician is guilty of perjury, a criminal offense.

The most likely outcome of tampering with the record . . . is to completely destroy whatever chances one had of winning the case. . . . It is much better to admit that you didn't keep good records and hope that the jury believes you when you tell them what happened than to manufacture good records after the fact at the cost of your own integrity and credibility.

Public Confessions

Therapists often feel responsible when a patient commits suicide. It is at least as traumatic for the therapist when a patient kills an innocent third party. Clinicians are not immune from the hindsight effect: Everything seems clear and determined in retrospect (Wexler & Schopp, 1989). Given the nature of their occupation, clinicians will often want to talk through their feelings of guilt; however, they are strongly advised to resist such public confessional urges (and might if necessary be advised to go to their own therapist to express their affect in the context of a confidential relationship). Whatever the clinician says can only hurt his or her case if a suit is filed, and, indeed, it may make the filing of a suit more likely. . . .

Clinicians must learn that when their worst fantasies come true, they should take the time-honored course of defendants in criminal cases: Imitate a potted plant. Say nothing. . . .

References

Appelbaum, P. (1985). *Tarasoff* and the clinician: Problems in fulfilling the duty to protect. *American Journal of Psychiatry, 142,* 425–429.

Appelbaum, P., & Gutheil, T. (1991). *Clinical handbook of psychiatry and the law* (2nd ed.). Baltimore: Williams & Wilkins.

Appelbaum, P., Zonana, H., Bonnie, R., & Roth, L. (1989). Statutory approaches to limiting psychiatrist's liability for their patients' violent acts. *American Journal of Psychiatry, 146,* 821–828.

Bednar, R., Bednar, S., Lambert, M., & Waite, D. (1991). *Psychotherapy with high-risk clients: Legal and professional standards.* Pacific Grove, CA: Brooks/Cole.

Bennett, B., Bryant, B., VandenBos, G., & Greenwood, A. (1990). *Professional liability and risk management.* Washington, DC: American Psychological Association.

Brodsky, S. (1991). *Testifying in court: Guidelines and maxims for the expert witness.* Washington, DC: American Psychological Association.

Dietz, P. (1990). Defenses against dangerous people when arrest and commitment fail. In R. Simon (Ed.). *Review of clinical psychiatry and the law* (Vol. 1, pp. 205–219). Washington, DC: American Psychiatric Press.

Klassen, D., & O'Connor, W. (1988). A prospective study of predictors of violence in adult male mental patients. *Law and Human Behavior, 12,* 143–158.

Klein, J. (1986). The professional liability crisis: An interview with Joel Klein. *Hospital and Community Psychiatry, 37,* 1012–1016.

Kozol, H., Boucher, R., & Garofalo, R. (1972). The diagnosis and treatment of dangerousness. *Crime and Delinquency, 18,* 371–392.

Meichenbaum, D., & Turk, D. (1987). *Facilitating treatment adherence: A practitioner's guidebook.* New York: Plenum Press.

Monahan, J. (1981). *The clinical prediction of violent behavior.* Washington, DC: U.S. Government Printing Office.

Poythress, N. (1987). Avoiding negligent release: A risk-management strategy. *Hospital and Community Psychiatry, 38,* 1051–1052.

Poythress, N. (1990). Avoiding negligent release: Contemporary clinical and risk management strategies. *American Journal of Psychiatry, 147,* 994–997.

Poythress, N. (1991). [Letter]. *American Journal of Psychiatry, 148,* 691–692.

Rachlin, S., & Schwartz, H. (1986). Unforseeable liability for patients' violent acts. *Hospital and Community Psychiatry, 37,* 725–731.

Simon, R. (1987). *Clinical psychiatry and the law.* Washington, DC: American Psychiatric Press.

Tarasoff v. Regents of the University of California, 131 Cal. Rptr. 14, 551 P.2d 334 (1976).

Tardiff, K. (1989). *Concise guide to assessment and management of violent patients.* Washington, DC: American Psychiatric Press.

Wexler, D. (1981). *Mental health law: Major issues.* New York: Plenum Press.

Wexler, D., & Schopp, R. (1989). How and when to correct for juror hindsight bias in mental health malpractice litigation: Some preliminary observations. *Behavioral Sciences and the Law, 7,* 485–504.

◆ ◆ ◆

Commentary: *For another helpful article on managing violent patients, see Appelbaum, P. S. (1985). Tarasoff and the clinician: Problems in fulfilling the duty to protect.* American Journal of Psychiatry, 142, 425–429.

The Impact of *Tarasoff* on Clinical Practice

Kathleen M. Quinn

. . .

There is only one systematic study of therapists post-*Tarasoff* (Wise, 1978). A mailed questionnaire surveyed the attitudes of a total of 1,272 California psychiatrists and psychologists. The sample, which was overwhelmingly male and middle-aged, replied that over 80% treated at least one patient each year whom they considered potentially dangerous. Almost all of the respondents reported some familiarity with the case approximately one year after the second *Tarasoff* decision. Nearly one-half had been informed as to how it specifically affected their practices (pp. 177–178).

In the Wise survey (1978) there was only tenuous evidence to suggest that there was any increase in frequency of actual warnings occurring (p. 179). However, there was one obvious change in the therapist's warning behavior—a greater percentage were now including the potential victim among those they warned since the *Tarasoff* ruling (p. 180).

Other changes in clinical practice noted by the survey included a change in the method of dealing with dangerousness during therapy. Approximately one-fourth of the therapists reported directing more attention to the subject of dangerousness in general. One-fifth of the therapists concentrated their attentions on less serious threats than before *Tarasoff*. Consultations with colleagues were increased on cases involving potentially dangerous patients (p. 182).

The Wise survey (1978) also noted direct effects on the therapists with the majority of therapists reporting increased anxiety when the subject of dangerousness arose during therapy. More than one-fourth indicated that *Tarasoff* had led them to change their methods of keeping records. Most of the changes were done with the goal of avoiding future legal liability which the majority feared more since *Tarasoff* (p. 190).

In the Wise survey (1978) almost 70% of the therapists believed confidentiality could be justifiably breached in some circumstances during treatment (p. 176). The survey, as noted earlier, showed that therapists had traditionally acted on this belief by taking action, including warning potential victims pre-*Tarasoff*.

An alarming incidental finding showed that a significant minority (16%) of therapists were now *more* reluctant to probe the topic of potential dangerousness (Wise, 1978, p. 182). Several therapists also spontaneously volunteered that the *Tarasoff* finding had caused them to discontinue treating potentially dangerous patients.

Finally, the Wise survey (1978) reported that therapists were changing their criteria for warning. These changes, although not fully described, generally suggested that the therapists had lowered the threshold at which they considered a patient dangerous and subsequently either warned a third party or committed the patient (p. 181). The Wise study concluded that although the *Tarasoff* ruling did not mandate a radical change in therapeutic practice, its overall impact was potentially detrimental to the practice of psychotherapy because of heightened therapist anxiety, increased emphasis on violence as a topic in therapy, altered practice habits, and changes in confidentiality (p. 190).

A more recent study (Beck, 1982) looked at the role of the patient's informed consent and of the clinical validity of the assessment of the dangerousness on a warning's impact on the therapy. A small sample of 38 psychiatrists, all having both private practices and clinical or administrative responsibility in an institution that served violent patients, were given a semi-structured interview. Forty-two percent of the sample ($N = 38$) had been involved in giving an actual warning. The warnings seldom had an adverse effect on the therapeutic relationship as judged by the therapists. Only warnings either not discussed with the patient or those given without good clinical evidence of dangerousness were judged to be harmful to the therapeutic relationship. "The results support the conclusion that warnings per se have little or no apparent effect; how they are integrated into the therapy is the important variable" (p. 199).

Beck (1982) noted that the psychiatrists in his sample did not find the *Tarasoff* duty burdensome. He hypothesized that the greater availability of colleagues for consultation and the existence of a wide network of services might contribute to this finding of relative ease as compared with clinicians working in greater isolation. Unexpectedly, Beck found that all the warnings but one had occurred in institutional settings, not in the therapists' private practices.

In comparing the Wise and Beck surveys it is important to note that only 10% of the much larger Wise sample were associated with public institutions (Wise, 1978, p. 175). The Wise sample being primarily private-practice-oriented may have been more likely to experience greater anxiety and unfamiliarity in the clinical management of dangerousness. The Beck study, however, which used face-to-face interviewing and practitioners frequently known to the author is unlikely to have fully sampled the negative reactions or fears of the sample in handling *Tarasoff* situations. No study to date has surveyed the patient's or potential victim's reaction to a *Tarasoff*-type warning. . . .

Beck's survey indicated that the clinicians in his sample chose commitment when there was a threat of imminent danger to a specific victim. Warnings were given when the threatened violence was not imminent, when the threat was vague as to time, or when the therapist judged the likelihood of violence to be remote due to the absence of a history of violence and the presence of a good therapeutic alliance. Frequently those cases with a presence of a good therapeutic alliance and the absence of a past history of violence influenced the therapists to address the threats solely within the therapy rather than by warning third parties (p. 200). The Wise

survey (1978), however, suggests an apparent lack of flexibility in discharging the duty to protect in actual clinical practice. The survey showed that, after *Tarasoff*, potential victims are much more likely to be among the persons warned by those therapists who gave warnings. This is despite the evidence that in some cases a threatened victim can take virtually no realistic prevention action. Potential victims are frequently relatives or close acquaintances of the people who threaten them (Skodol & Karusu, 1978). The police may lack the resources to protect all threatened people fully. . . .

References

Beck, J. C. (1982). When the patient threatens violence: An empirical study of clinical practice after *Tarasoff*. *American Academy of Psychiatry and the Law Bulletin*, 10, 189–202.

Skodol, A. E. & Karosu, T. B. (1978). Emergency psychiatry and the assaultive patient. *American Journal of Psychiatry*, 135, 202–205.

Wise, T. P. (1978). Where the public peril begins: A survey of psychotherapists to determine the effects of *Tarasoff*. *Stanford Law Review*, 31, 165–190.

◆ ◆ ◆

Commentary: In 1984, the Wisconsin Law Review *(Givelber, Bowers, & Blitch, 1984), criticizing Wise's (1978, see above) methodology, reported the results of its own survey of 2,875 psychiatrists, psychologists, and social workers located in the eight largest metropolitan population centers in the United States. The most relevant major findings from Givelber et al. were as follows:*

1. *Almost all mental health professionals had heard of Tarasoff or a case like it: "These data demonstrate that the court and its critics were justified in believing that the . . . decision would be well known and therefore might have a substantial influence on therapeutic practice" (pp. 458–459).*

2. *About one in four respondents mistakenly believed that the decision applied whenever a client made a threat. The majority recognized that the Tarasoff obligation arises "when a therapist actually believes someone is dangerous and also when a reasonable therapist would believe this" (p. 461).*

3. *Contrary to the positions taken in the American Psychiatric Association's amicus curiae brief in the*

California Supreme Court, about 75% of the respondents "felt that they could make a prediction [about future violence] ranging from 'probable' to 'certain'" (p. 463). Only 5% felt that there was no way to predict violent behavior. In addition, a majority of therapists believed that "there are objective professional standards for evaluating dangerousness" (p. 464).

4. A majority of therapists wrongly believed that Tarasoff *requires warning the intended victim. Only a small minority understood that the case requires mental health professionals to use reasonable care to protect the intended victim.*

5. *In the 12 months prior to the survey, an "overwhelming majority" of therapists surveyed had communicated confidential information disclosed in therapy to third parties (although of psychiatrists, social workers, and psychologists, the latter were least likely to do so). Thus, "while confidentiality may well represent an important ethical and therapeutic value, it is*

apparently a value which therapists . . . will frequently be forced to compromise" (p. 468).

6. *About 50% of the therapists who had communicated with potential victims believed that they "had to violate their own clinical judgment" (p. 470) in doing so.*

7. *However, a significant majority of therapists considered "responsibility to potential victims to be a professional [or personal] ethical obligation" (p. 475).*

8. *In addition to producing an increased willingness to notify third parties of their dangerous patients, Tarasoff had "influenced willingness to take notes and to initiate involuntary hospitalization" (p. 478), but it had not lessened willingness to treat dangerous patients.*

See Givelber, D. J., Bowers, W. J., & Blitch, C. L. (1984). Tarasoff, *myth and reality: An empirical study of private law in action.* Wisconsin Law Review, 1984, 443–497.

If It's Not Absolutely Confidential, Will Information Be Disclosed?

David Nowell and Jean Spruill

Recent literature on ethical issues in psychology has focused on informing the psychotherapy client regarding the nature of, and the exceptions to, confidentiality in client–therapist communications. Historically, clinical wisdom has been that effective psychotherapy can take place only in an absolutely confidential relationship and that, unless clients are offered complete confidentiality, they will avoid self-disclosure (Reynolds, 1976; Siegel, 1979). However, legally and ethically, clients cannot be promised absolute confidentiality because most states have laws providing some exceptions to confidentiality. Some therapists, fearing that detail in the explanation of the limits of confidentiality would be "disruptive to the patient and the therapeutic experience" (Langs, 1982, p. 476), discourage informing clients of those limits. Others are concerned that information regarding the limits of confidentiality may discourage some people from seeking therapy (e.g., Roth & Meisel, 1977) or instill client distrust of the therapist (e.g., Kimmons, cited in Muehleman, Pickens, & Robinson, 1985). However, there is little empirical research to support such views.

What do therapists tell clients about confidentiality in the therapy relationship? The 1981 and 1990 versions of the *Ethical Principles of Psychologists* state that "where appropriate, psychologists inform their clients of the legal limits of confidentiality" (American Psychological Association [APA], 1990, p. 392). The latest revision of the ethical principles (APA, 1992) is much more detailed than previous versions in discussing issues of confidentiality, indicating that psychologists should discuss the relevant limitations on confidentiality at the onset of the rela-

tionship unless it is not feasible or is contraindicated. In Baird and Rupert's (1987) survey of psychotherapists, only 61% of the respondents reported discussing confidentiality with their clients, and 19% of those reported telling clients that "everything they say in therapy is confidential." Such a statement has been referred to as a "blatant misrepresentation of facts that should be known to all therapists" (Bersoff, 1975, p. 270).

Does telling the client about limits to confidentiality affect the therapeutic relationship or client self-disclosure? Clients have been shown to value the confidentiality of client–therapist communications (Hillerbrand & Claiborn, 1988; McGuire, Toal, & Blau, 1985; Miller & Thelen, 1986). Appelbaum, Kapen, Walters, Lidz, and Roth (1984) found that psychiatric patients believed that, if information about them was revealed without their consent, such disclosure would negatively affect the therapeutic relationship, unless they believed that the information was revealed "in their best interests."

In an interview situation with nondistressed undergraduate subjects, Woods and McNamara (1980) found that subjects who were offered absolute confidentiality were more self-disclosing than those who were informed that their responses might be available to others. Muehleman et al. (1985) conducted single-session "diagnostic" interviews with 24 undergraduate students identified as depressed by a screening instrument. Subjects were given either general or detailed information about the limits of confidentiality. The two groups were not significantly different in their willingness to self-disclose about their depressive symptoms. In their investigation of 32 single

Adapted from *Professional Psychology: Research and Practice*, 24, 367–369. Copyright 1993 by the American Psychological Association.

mothers' willingness to disclose regarding disciplinary practices, Haut and Muehleman (1986) concluded that most clients are not "overwhelmed by limits to confidentiality," especially when the limits are presented with clarity and specificity.

The purpose of the present study was to investigate, in a survey situation, the effect of varying information regarding limits of confidentiality on subjects' anticipated disclosure about a variety of topics. Additionally, the effects of specific inhibition and severity level of the material to be disclosed were investigated. Perhaps psychotherapy clients refrain from divulging sensitive or personal information only in those areas specifically addressed by the therapist in his or her discussion of limits of confidentiality. The typical focus of such discussions concerns the potential to harm oneself or others; therefore, it was predicted that subjects would be less willing to disclose information in the areas specifically addressed in the discussion of the limits of confidentiality than in the areas not specifically discussed. Additionally, it was expected that the subjects would report greater willingness to disclose information considered to be of "low-severity than high-severity" (e.g., symptoms of depression vs. symptoms of psychosis).

METHOD

Subjects

Subjects were 75 undergraduate students enrolled in an introductory psychology course at a large southern university. The majority of students in the course were college freshmen or sophomores. Fifty percent of students at this university are women, and 85% are White and non-Hispanic. Approximately 13% of the subjects in this study indicated some prior experience in therapy.

Measure

A questionnaire developed by David Nowell in a preliminary study (Nowell, 1991) was used to assess subjects' anticipated willingness to self-disclose information about several common clinical concerns: depression/anxiety; substance use/abuse; physical/psychological aggression; suicidal thought/behavior; and psychotic thought/behavior. The questionnaire consisted of 2 items of high severity and 2 items of low severity for each of the five areas, along with 25 filler items. Examples of high- and low-severity items in the psychotic thought/behavior category were, respectively, statements such as "hearing voices (that others cannot hear) that command you to perform some act" and "having friends recently tell you that they like you because you are a bit 'odd' or 'eccentric.' "

Procedure

Subjects were randomly assigned to one of three experimental groups. All subjects received a Psychology Clinic Client Awareness Form that gave information about psychological services offered, limits of confidentiality, fees, and appointment cancellation policy. The forms were identical for all subjects except for the information about confidentiality. The absolute confidentiality group was told that all information they disclosed would be held confidential. Subjects in the short-form group were given general information about limits to confidentiality and were told that, in general, information was confidential unless the therapist had reason to believe the client might harm him or herself or others. Subjects in the long-form group were given information about these exceptions plus detailed information about other specific exceptions to confidentiality, such as the reporting of actual or suspected child abuse, court subpoenas, and so on [footnote omitted].

After reading and signing the Psychology Clinic Client Awareness Form, subjects were given the questionnaire and the following instructions: "Imagine you are seeking psychotherapy and that you have engaged in or experienced each of the behaviors or experiences described in this questionnaire." Subjects then responded to each item of the questionnaire, indicating their degree of willingness to disclose to a therapist information about each of the behaviors or experiences. A 7-point Likert-type scale was used, ranging from *unwillingness to disclose information* (1) to *willingness to disclose information* (7). Subjects were informed that they could discontinue the study at any time without penalty. Subjects were encouraged to contact the experimenters with any questions or concerns they had regarding the study. [*Ed. note:* The Results section had been omitted. In summary, subjects in the absolute confidentiality condition (M = 5.52) were more willing to disclose information than were subjects in the limited confidentiality group (M = 4.88). The difference between the means of the short- and long-form (M = 5.11) groups was not significant.

Subjects were more willing to disclose information concerning low-severity items than about high-severity items, regardless of content area or group membership; but subjects in the absolute confidentiality group were significantly more willing to disclose information about high-severity items than were subjects in the limited confidentiality group.

With regard to content, subjects were more willing to disclose information about aggressive thoughts than suicidal thoughts and were less willing to disclose information about substance abuse than about depression and thought disorder; but they were more willing to disclose information about depression than about thought disorder.]

. . .

DISCUSSION

. . .

One implication of this study is that clients' understanding of the limits of confidentiality may influence their willingness to self-disclose regarding behaviors or experiences considered serious or extreme. Once informed that there are limits to the confidentiality of the therapeutic relationship, clients may engage in less self-disclosure. However, as indicated by this study and an earlier study comparing levels of information regarding limits of confidentiality (Muehleman et al., 1985), a complete explanation of the limits of confidentiality may not produce more inhibition than would a brief, cursory explanation. Whether they are offered absolute confidentiality or limited confidentiality, subjects in this study anticipated less disclosure about intent to harm others than about other experiences, such as depression. There appears to be an understood taboo against disclosing aggressive behaviors and experiences, independent of the explanation of the limits of the therapist's ability to keep such material confidential.

Caution should be taken in generalizing from the population of this study to the population of interest: psychotherapy clients. What subjects in this study—undergraduate students in an introductory psychol-

ogy course—did and said may not be predictive of what psychotherapy clients would say or do. Additionally, this was a survey in which subjects were asked to indicate "what they would disclose if in therapy" rather than what they "did disclose in therapy." Studies comparing the experience of clients who have received differential information regarding the limits of confidentiality are needed to address this issue. Concerns held by some clinicians that a discussion with a client about the limits of therapeutic confidentiality will lead to decreased self-disclosure appear to be supported by this and other research (e.g., Woods & McNamara, 1980). However, it should be noted that therapists have an ethical and, in some states, a legal obligation to inform clients of the limits of confidentiality as defined in their state. Indeed, in contrast to previous versions, the latest version of the ethical principles for psychologists (APA, 1992) specifically requires psychologists to discuss the limits of confidentiality at the outset of therapy. This research suggests that, contrary to some clinical beliefs, complete, detailed information regarding limits of confidentiality may not lead to greater inhibition of self-disclosure than would a brief, cursory discussion of these limits. As a matter of self-protection for the therapist, and of consumers' rights for the client, offering a detailed description of the circumstances under which confidentiality can be broken may be the therapist's best course of action when establishing a therapy relationship.

References

American Psychological Association. (1990). Ethical principles of psychologists. *American Psychologist, 45,* 390–395.

American Psychological Association. (1992). Ethical principles of psychologists and code of conduct. *American Psychologist, 47,* 1597–1611.

Appelbaum, P. S., Kapen, G., Walters, B., Lidz, C., & Roth, L. H. (1984). Confidentiality: An empirical test of the utilitarian perspective. *Bulletin of the American Academy of Psychiatry and the Law, 12,* 109–116.

Baird, K. A., & Rupert, P. A. (1987). Clinical management of confidentiality: A survey of psychologists in seven states. *Professional Psychology: Research and Practice, 18,* 347–352.

Bersoff, D. N. (1975). Professional ethics and legal responsibilities: On the horns of a dilemma. *Journal of School Psychology, 13,* 359–376.

Ethical Conflicts in Psychology

Haut, M. W., & Muehleman, T. (1986). Informed consent: The effects of clarity and specificity on disclosure in a clinical interview. *Psychotherapy, 23*(1), 93–101.

Hillerbrand, E. T., & Claiborn, C. D. (1988). Ethical knowledge exhibited by clients and nonclients. *Professional Psychology: Research and Practice, 19,* 527–531.

Langs, R. (1982). *Psychotherapy: A basic text.* New York: Jason Aronson.

McGuire, J. M., Toal, P., & Blau, B. (1985). The adult client's conception of confidentiality in the therapeutic relationship. *Professional Psychology: Research and Practice, 16,* 375–384.

Miller, D. J., & Thelen, M. H. (1986). Confidentiality in psychotherapy: Knowledge and beliefs about confidentiality. *Professional Psychology: Research and Practice, 17,* 15–19.

Muehleman, T., Pickens, B. K., & Robinson, F. (1985). Informing clients about the limits to confidentiality, risks, and their rights: Is self-disclosure inhibited? *Professional Psychology: Research and Practice, 16,* 385–397.

Nowell, D. D. (1991). *The effects of varying information regarding limits of confidentiality on willingness to self-disclose.* Unpublished master's thesis, University of Alabama, Tuscaloosa.

Reynolds, M. M. (1976). Threats of confidentiality. *Social Work, 21,* 108–113.

Roth, L. H., & Meisel, A. (1977). Dangerousness, confidentiality, and the duty to warn. *American Journal of Psychiatry, 134,* 508–511.

Siegel, M. (1979). Privacy, ethics, and confidentiality. *Professional Psychology, 10,* 249–258.

Woods, K. M., & McNamara, J. R. (1980). Confidentiality: Its effect on interviewee behavior. *Professional Psychology, 11,* 714–721.

◆ ◆ ◆

Commentary: As Nowell and Spruill (1993) stated, Standard 5.01 of the APA's 1992 Code of Conduct mandates that all research and professional psychologists dis-

cuss confidentiality "at the outset of the relationship" unless "it is not feasible or is contraindicated." Standard 4.01 specifically requires therapists to discuss confidentiality with their patients "as early as is feasible." Yet, in surveying 204 midwestern psychologists about what procedures they would follow concerning the mandatory reporting of child abuse, Nicolai and Scott (1994) noted these findings with alarm:

> Almost 20% of respondents indicated that they sometimes, rarely, or never provide this information to clients and that more than 5% misleadingly tell clients that everything disclosed in therapy is confidential. We are disturbed by these and other findings and their implications.
>
> Without explicit presentation of information regarding confidentiality limits, the novice client may well assume that all disclosures, regardless of content, will be kept confidential. Moreover, clinicians who tell clients that everything they say will be held in confidence are clearly putting clients, as well as themselves, at risk. Legal and ethical guidelines for mental health professionals clearly state that clinicians must breach confidentiality when certain information is disclosed by clients in therapy. (p. 158)

Nicolai, K. M., & Scott, N. A. (1994). Provision of confidentiality information and its relation to child abuse reporting. Professional Psychology: Research and Practice, 25, 154–160.

The next article is one of the few to investigate how the public at large views client–clinician confidentiality. After reviewing the results, one might ask how well the 1992 APA ethics code addresses the public's expectations of confidentiality, particularly in Standards 5.01, 5.05, 5.06, and 5.08.

188

Public Attitudes Toward Psychotherapist–Client Confidentiality

Daniel E. Rubanowitz

. . .

According to Winslade (1978, p. 196), policy makers in our society are often faced with a basic conflict in this area. On the one hand, there is a need to promote the confidentiality of sensitive communications within certain professional relationships; on the other hand, there is pressure for open communication of information that serves to protect the safety and welfare of the general public. Bersoff and Jain (1980) suggested that these conflicting legal and social policy pressures are particularly problematic for the institution of psychotherapy. Although the protection of confidentiality may be a commendable aim and may in fact be quite important for effective treatment, it may nonetheless come into direct conflict with other fundamental interests of society, such as the administration of justice and the protection of the innocent from violence. . . .

In this study, data on public attitudes regarding specific situations in which a psychotherapist might break confidentiality or reveal information to specific third parties are presented. These kinds of data can help mental health professionals begin to examine the extent to which the expectations of potential consumers of psychotherapy are congruent with professional practice. Because this area has not been extensively researched, several individual difference variables were examined for exploratory purposes: city, gender, age, and family role (e.g., parent vs. nonparent).

METHOD

Subjects

Two hundred subjects 18 years of age and older were used; 100 were from the rural area of greater Grand Forks, North Dakota, and 100 were from the urban area of greater Los Angeles, California.

. . .

Procedure

A 15-statement questionnaire was written for the telephone survey. Eight of the statements described situations in which a psychotherapist might break confidentiality in order to save a life, prevent violence, or otherwise represent the best interests of society. Six of the statements described the unauthorized release of therapy information to some specific third party. One item on the questionnaire stated that a psychotherapist should never reveal information without a client's permission (i.e., a statement of absolute confidentiality). Subjects responded to each statement on a 5-point Likert-type scale ranging from *strongly agree* (1) to *strongly disagree* (5). Seven of the statements were randomly selected to be worded in a "should" manner, and the remaining eight statements were worded in a "should not" form (thus numerical anchors were reversed). The final order of the statements was randomized. . . .

RESULTS

. . .

Responses to questionnaire items were scored so that 1 indicated strong agreement that a psychotherapist *should* disclose therapy information and 5 represented strong agreement that confidentiality *should not* be breached. The questionnaire statements, means, standard deviations, and percentages of responses at each level are presented in Table 2. . . .

Table 2

Individual Questionnaire Items

Item	M	SD	Strongly Agree		Agree		Neutral		Disagree		Strongly Disagree	
			n	%	n	%	n	%	n	%	n	%
1. If a client admits to taking illegal drugs, the therapist *should not* notify the police.	3.22	1.13	29	14.5	101	50.5	16	8.0	45	22.5	9	4.5
2. If a child or teenager is in therapy, the parents *should not* have access to information or records without the child's permission.	2.81	1.23	20	10.0	75	37.5	12	6.0	74	37.5	18	9.0
3. A therapist *should not* notify the police if a client reveals that he/she has committed a major theft.	2.55	1.08	8	4.0	50	25.0	28	14.0	94	47.0	20	10.0
4. A therapist should *never* reveal information about a client without first getting written permission from the client.	3.27	1.13	34	17.0	80	40.0	26	13.0	56	28.0	4	2.0
5. The family doctor *should* be given therapy information *without* the client's permission.	3.10	1.03	4	2.0	60	30.0	27	13.5	95	47.5	14	7.0
6. If a client is going to commit suicide, the therapist *should* contact the family or the police.	1.86	0.70	59	29.5	125	62.5	10	5.0	4	2.0	2	1.0
7. A therapist *should* notify the police if a client is planning to kill someone.	1.50	0.61	95	47.5	99	49.5	4	2.0	1	0.5	1	0.5
8. If a therapist is summoned to court to testify about one of his/her clients, the therapist *should not* testify unless the client authorizes this.	3.10	1.07	12	6.0	71	35.5	40	20.0	66	33.0	11	5.5
9. If the spouse of someone in therapy requests information, the therapist *should not* provide it without the client's permission.	3.71	0.85	26	13.0	125	62.5	28	14.0	18	9.0	3	1.5
10. A therapist *should* be able to discuss his/her clients with other mental health professionals.	2.50	0.97	7	3.5	121	60.5	24	12.0	40	20.0	8	4.0
11. If a client confesses during therapy to an unsolved murder, the therapist *should not* notify the police.	2.10	0.85	0	0.0	22	11.0	15	7.5	122	61.0	40	20.5
12. If a client admits to treason or sabotage against the United States, the therapist *should* inform the authorities.	2.17	0.90	36	18.0	116	58.0	19	9.5	29	14.5	0	0.0
13. If a client is planning to kill someone, the therapist *should* warn the intended victim.	2.44	0.99	29	14.5	109	54.5	21	10.5	39	19.5	2	1.0
14. A therapist *should* notify the police if a client admits to child abuse.	2.11	0.84	37	18.5	124	62.0	16	8.0	16	8.0	0	0.0
15. Insurance companies *should not* have access to therapy records without clients' permission.	3.71	0.82	41	20.5	120	60.0	21	10.5	18	9.0	0	0.0

Note. Means greater than 3.00 indicate the confidentiality *should not* be broken; means less than 3.00 indicate that confidentiality *should* be broken.

DISCUSSION

. . . Overall, the results of this study indicate that the public may expect therapists to maintain confidentiality as a general rule. However, it appears that the public may also expect therapists to break confidentiality when doing so represents the best interests of society. They expect therapists to notify appropriate parties when a client in therapy reports murder (planned or confessed), suicide plans, child abuse, major theft, and treason or sabotage against the United States. Older subjects may also expect therapists to notify the police when a client admits illegal drug use. Younger subjects, however, may expect a therapist to maintain confidentiality in this latter situation.

Overall, the public seemed to expect therapists to protect a client's confidences from the courts, the client's spouse, insurance companies, and even the family doctor. Younger subjects felt more strongly than older subjects about protecting confidential information from insurance company access. The two age groups disagreed in regard to parents' access to a child's therapy information and to information access by the family doctor. Older subjects endorsed routine access to information by parents and the family doctor, whereas younger subjects believed that confidentiality should be maintained with these third parties. In regard to the age group differences found in this study, it is conceivable that younger members of society have grown up in an environment that is less trusting or accepting of recognized authority figures, leaders, government agencies, and corporations. . . .

Overall, the results suggest that the expectations of the public are in some respects compatible, and in some respects incompatible, with the laws and ethical guidelines regulating confidentiality in psychotherapy. It appears that the general public may readily endorse the ideal that a therapist should never reveal information about a client without written authorization. At the same time, the public may allow for consultation between mental health professionals and may clearly expect confidentiality to be broken when a serious danger to physical well-being exists (e.g., murder, suicide, child abuse). To the extent that reported treason or sabotage against the United States may involve danger to innocent people (e.g., terrorism) or may involve threats toward elected officials, then public expectations for breaking confidentiality would be congruent with the legal and ethical requirements for psychotherapists. Discrepancies between public expectations and regulations for clinical practice may be evident in situations of reported illegal drug use and major theft. In the absence of clear dangerousness, it does not appear that there are laws or ethical codes that specifically mandate breaking confidentiality under these circumstances. Public expectations may also conflict with the rules and regulations in terms of access to therapy information by the courts, insurance companies, and the parents of a minor client. Clients may be unaware of the various circumstances under which a therapist cannot protect the confidentiality of communications from the courts (e.g., sanity or competency hearings, court ordered evaluations, malpractice suits). Parents may be surprised to find out that they do not always have routine access to disclosures made by their child in therapy or to their child's case records. Finally, the results clearly indicate that insurance company access to treatment information is liable to be a particularly sensitive issue among potential consumers of psychotherapy.

In view of these results, it seems reasonable to suggest that psychotherapists and their professional organizations should take into consideration public expectations regarding confidentiality in psychotherapy. Insofar as professional guidelines and laws protecting confidentiality conflict with the expectations of the potential consumer of psychotherapy, it would be helpful for therapists to practice dispensing to their clients information regarding the actual limits of confidentiality and the obligations of the therapist. It would also be helpful for professional organizations to facilitate public education on this subject.

References

Bersoff, D. N., & Jain, M. (1980). A practical guide to privileged communication for psychologists. In G. Cooke (Ed.), *The role of the forensic psychologist* (chap. 5). Springfield, IL: Charles C Thomas.

Winslade, W. J. (1978). Confidentiality. In W. T. Reich (Ed.), *Encyclopedia of bioethics* (Vol. 1, pp. 194–199). New York: Free Press.

◆ ◆ ◆

Commentary: I conclude this chapter with articles addressing two issues that are perhaps more complex than those difficult issues to which the reader has already been exposed. First, I review the extent to which a minor's confidential communications are protected from disclosure. And second, I present views of the potentially conflicting duties and obligations of psychologists who provide services to people infected with HIV or AIDS.

McGuire (1974) asserted that the 1963 APA code of ethics was difficult to understand and apply to the relationship between a clinician and child clients, particularly with regard to confidentiality. It may be interesting to review Standards 1.21, 4.02, and 5.01 of the 1992 Ethical Principles and judge whether they offer any greater clarity or guidance to those who work with children than the 1963 code did. McGuire also conducted a survey of 45 clinicians employed by mental health agencies and found a growing trend among professionals to act as if minors' confidential disclosures could be accorded the same protection as adults. See McGuire, J. M. (1974). Confidentiality and the child in psychotherapy. Professional Psychology, 5, 374–379. Was that trend justified from either a legal or an ethical perspective? The following excerpts may help illuminate the issue.

Confidentiality With Minor Clients: Issues and Guidelines for Therapists

Kathryn E. Gustafson and J. Regis McNamara

. . .

LEGAL CONSIDERATIONS IN CONSENT TO TREATMENT

Increasingly, minors are legally allowed to pursue treatment without parental consent. Most jurisdictions allow minors to consent to treatment without parental knowledge in specific situations in which obtaining parental consent may jeopardize the likelihood that the minor will receive that treatment (Wilson, 1978). These specific situations include counseling or medical care for sexual abuse, substance abuse, pregnancy, sexually transmitted diseases, and contraception.

In addition, the law has recognized four general exceptions to the requirement of parent consent for treatment of minors (Plotkin, 1981). The first, the "mature minor" exception, pertains to minors with sufficient maturity to understand the nature and consequences of treatment. The second, "emancipated minor," refers to minors who are legally entitled to the rights and duties of adulthood for reasons that vary from state to state (e.g., a married minor). "Emergency treatment" is the third circumstance in which parental consent is not necessary. It is assumed that parental consent is implied because of the urgency of the situation. The final exception to obtaining parental consent is when treatment is court ordered.

These exceptions, although originally designed to clarify the rights of minors, have actually confused practitioners because the exceptions are vague, vary from state to state, and are open to a great amount of interpretation. Thus Plotkin (1981) recommended that the age at which individuals may give consent to treatment be lowered according to data in the child development literature.

DEVELOPMENTAL CONSIDERATIONS IN CONSENT TO TREATMENT

There is accumulating evidence that minors of certain ages may have obtained sufficient developmental maturity to make well-informed decisions about psychotherapeutic treatment. Grisso and Vierling (1978) reviewed the cognitive developmental literature and concluded that "there is little evidence that minors of age 15 and above as a group are any less competent to provide consent than are adults" (p. 423). Below age 11, however, minors are not capable of voluntary consent because they do not have the necessary intellectual capabilities, and they have a tendency toward deference to authority. Weithorn (1982) concurred that when children acquire formal operational thinking, between ages 11 and 14, they are able to conceptualize abstract possibilities and hypothetical outcomes of multiple courses of action and therefore are competent to provide consent. . . .

Moreover, by age 15, adolescents are capable of comprehending and exercising their rights. In a therapy analogue, information provided about clients' rights improved 15-year-old, but not 9-year-old, boys' recognition of rights violations and their capacity to protect those rights (Belter & Grisso, 1984). The 15-year-olds in this study performed as well on these variables as did the 21-year-old subjects.

Another important component in informed consent is the ability to identify potential risks and benefits of therapy. Kaser-Boyd, Adelman, and Taylor

Adapted from *Professional Psychology: Research and Practice, 18*, 503–508. Copyright 1987 by the American Psychological Association.

(1985) found that minors with learning and behavior problems were capable of identifying relevant therapy risks and benefits. There was a tendency for minors who were older who had had previous therapeutic experience to identify more risks and benefits and to describe these risks and benefits more abstractly. Younger minors and those without previous therapy experience, however, were able to identify risks and benefits that were relevant and practical to their situation.

There is a growing body of evidence that minors can effectively participate in at least some types of treatment decisions. Minors with learning and related behavior problems reported an interest in, and felt competent to participate in, the psychoeducational decisions that affect them, took the steps necessary to get involved, and then felt satisfied with the results of their involvement (Adelman, Lusk, Alvarez, & Acosta, 1985; Taylor, Adelman, & Kaser-Boyd, 1983, 1985). Older students had a greater desire to participate, had a greater tendency to follow through with their plans, and were rated as more effective in doing so by their parents and teachers (Taylor et al., 1985). In addition, adolescents appear to respond more positively to treatment when involved in treatment planning and evaluation (Janzen & Love, 1977) and when they perceive themselves as having a choice about participation (Bastien & Adelman, 1984).

Messenger and McGuire (1981), investigating the child's conception of confidentiality in the therapeutic relationship, also found that older children (ages 12–15) have a significantly better understanding of confidentiality than do younger children (ages 6–8). Thus it appears that children gradually evolve a concept of confidentiality. . . .

DETERMINING THE BEST INTEREST OF THE CHILD

. . . Several authors believe that minors are entitled to the same rights of confidentiality as are adults (Myers, 1982; Patterson, 1971; Wrenn, 1952). As stated by Myers (1982), "the fact of minority in no fashion lessens the importance of the sanctity of confidential communications" (p. 310). Myers maintained that the therapist's duty of confidentiality is not to the parents but to the child because the child

is the client. The American Psychiatric Association's Task Force on Confidentiality of Children's and Adolescents' Clinical Records has recommended in their "Model Law of Confidentiality" that the age at which minors may give consent to release confidential information is 12 years or over (American Psychiatric Association, 1979). . . .

Some authors endorse limited confidentiality with minors. Pardue, Whichard, and Johnson (1970) recommended forewarning minors that their parents or guardians might need to become involved, and minors thus informed of this limitation are then free to choose whether to participate in therapy.

Glenn (1980) and Ross (1966) proposed that the determination of whether confidentiality is necessary with minor clients should be decided on an individual, case-by-case basis. Thompson (1983) maintained that "the therapist should decide how the client's guardian is apt to use the disclosed information before deciding whether or not to release it" (p. 99).

There is a paucity of research on what minors perceive as being in their own best interests in regard to confidentiality in the therapeutic relationship. Kobocow et al. (1983) investigated the effects of varying degrees of assurance of confidentiality on self-disclosure in early adolescents. Subjects were reluctant to admit to behaviors that were not socially sanctioned and appeared not to trust the interviewer, even when confidentiality was ensured. Establishing a trusting relationship may be more important than promises of confidentiality when one is dealing with minors (Koocher, 1976, 1983; Ross, 1966). Messenger and McGuire (1981) also suggested that verbal explanations of confidentiality, although necessary, may not be as important as real-life experiences with a therapist who maintains confidentiality. Thus it does appear that confidentiality is important to the older minor.

PROFESSIONAL ATTITUDES AND BEHAVIORS

There is some variability in professionals' consent and confidentiality practices with minor clients. Many therapists apparently provide psychotherapeutic services to minors without parental consent regardless of whether state statutes allow such action (Apsler, cited in Wilson, 1978; Melton, 1981). When providing services to a minor without parental consent, many clinics and practitioners charge either a nominal fee or no fee at all or base the fee on the adolescent's income. Clinics that do not offer such special payment arrangements for minors may discourage minors from seeking treatment because costs would be too exorbitant or because payment by parental insurance would result in parental notification of treatment.

In regard to confidentiality with minor clients, some clinics limit parental access to the minor's treatment records, whereas others allow unlimited parental access to such information (Melton, 1981). McGuire (1974) assessed community mental health professionals' behaviors regarding confidentiality with minors in therapy. He found that the majority of the mental health professionals supported the position that minors should be extended the same rights of confidentiality as adults. Whether this belief was consistent with agency policy or state law was not assessed. . . .

GUIDELINES FOR THERAPISTS

. . .

Whether confidentiality will be ensured may influence the adolescent's decision to enter psychotherapy. An adolescent not guaranteed confidentiality may decide not to enter therapy or may reluctantly participate without disclosing his or her concerns. Thus as with adult clients, ensuring confidentiality serves the interests of society in that it induces individuals in need of treatment to seek that treatment.

Involving adolescents in treatment planning and assuring confidentiality in the relationship may have therapeutic benefits as well. Minors who construe themselves as active participants in a confidential relationship are more likely to be allied with the therapist and hence less likely to resist therapeutic progress.

Moreover, adolescent involvement in treatment decision making, including what information can be revealed to whom, also provides an important social learning experience. It provides them with experience for future decision making and gives them a sense of being active, responsible participants in their own welfare (Weithorn, 1983).

The degree of confidentiality afforded a minor client should be based on consideration of several factors. First, the therapist should consider the age of the client. . . . The therapist should consider the needs and desires of the child, the concerns of the parents, the particular presenting problem, and relevant state statutes in deciding what degree of confidentiality is appropriate with preadolescent children. Second, because age is only a rough indicator of cognitive functioning, the therapist should make an informal assessment of the minor's cognitive capacity, including factors such as intelligence, Piagetian stage, and Kohlbergian reasoning level. . . .

There are a number of strategies that the clinicians can use to optimize the therapeutic experience while simultaneously upholding the rights of both the minor and the parents:

1. Once the therapist has made a decision regarding the degree of confidentiality believed to be necessary and appropriate, the therapist should schedule a pretreatment family meeting with the parents and the adolescent and explain his or her rationale for this decision. The therapist should develop rapport with all family members, and all family members should demonstrate sufficient understanding of the conditions of treatment, including confidentiality. He or she should then prepare a written professional services agreement . . . fully detailing the conditions and the limits of the confidential relationship. All participating parties—parents, the adolescent, and the therapist—should sign the professional services agreement, and it should become part of the minor's permanent file.

The professional services agreement, as well as open communication and rapport, is likely to discourage parents from demanding information obtained in therapy. In some cases, however, the parents may subsequently demand access to the files. It is unclear whether courts would decide in favor of the parents or uphold the professional service contract. . . .

2. Depending on the nature of the presenting concern and the preferences of the therapist, the parents may be involved in the treatment in different capacities. Indeed, family involvement can be therapeutically beneficial, and it is often the treatment of choice in work with minors. Yet, the adolescent's communications may still remain confidential. Parents are sometimes involved directly in treatment,

such as when an improved parent–adolescent relationship is the ultimate therapeutic goal. Maintaining confidentiality does not necessarily interfere with this goal. In some cases, family relationships have deteriorated to a point to preclude immediate, productive family work. Relationship and communication skills enhancement may first be necessary with the therapist and adolescent before it is extended to the parent and adolescent. At other times, parents may be involved indirectly, such as through monitoring the adolescent's behavior at home for change outside of therapy. In cases in which the adolescent has personal concerns, parent involvement may be even more limited. In those cases, the parents should be cautioned that adolescents often develop a strong trusting relationship with the therapist; the adolescent may reveal more intimate information to the therapist than to the parents. The therapist should explore with the parents whether such a relationship between the therapist and their child is likely to be threatening or to provoke jealousy in the parents. A frank, honest discussion of these feelings can be beneficial. . . .

3. Parents should be encouraged to initiate future family meetings if at any time during treatment they have concerns about the therapeutic process. It should be clear to both the parents and the adolescent (as stated in the professional service agreement) that family sessions will not compromise the confidential relationship between the therapist and the minor. It is important to maintain a relationship with the parents while still maintaining confidentiality of the adolescent's private disclosures. This allows the parents to more adequately assess the competence of the therapist and the effectiveness of therapy.

4. Throughout the duration of treatment, the clinician should make an attempt to provide treatment rationales and explanations that are developmentally appropriate for the adolescent. . . .

5. It is imperative that the clinician be familiar with any relevant statutes in his or her state of residence and adopt policies consistent with these statutes. Confidentiality with minors is a subject on which the law is unclear (Herr, Arons, & Wallace, 1983). Some states have adopted inconsistent policies in which minors are allowed to consent to treatment and yet parents have access to minors' treatment records or financial responsibility for any fees incurred. Other states' statutes make no mention of the situation in which parents want access but the minor wants confidentiality.

6. If at any time the therapist is confronted with a situation in which he or she is unclear regarding appropriate professional conduct, he or she should first consult a book on ethics. . . . as well as a mental health law text. . . . If there is any uncertainty or concern remaining after such a review, appropriate professional and/or legal consultation should be considered. . . .

References

Adelman, H. S., Lusk, R., Alvarez, V., & Acosta, K. (1985). Competence of minors to understand, evaluate, and communicate about their psychoeducational problems. *Professional Psychology: Research and Practice, 16*, 426–434.

American Psychiatric Association (1979). Task force on confidentiality of children's and adolescents' clinical records. *American Journal of Psychiatry, 136*, 138–144.

American Psychological Association (1981). *Ethical principles of psychologists*. Washington, DC: Author.

Bastien, R. T., & Adelman, H. S. (1984). Noncompulsory versus legally mandated placement, perceived choice, and response to treatment among adolescents. *Journal of Consulting and Clinical Psychology, 52*, 171–179.

Belter, R. W., & Grisso, T. (1984). Children's recognition of rights violations in counseling. *Professional Psychology: Research and Practice, 15*, 899–910.

Everstine, L., Everstine, D. S., Heymann, G. M., True, R. H., Frey, D. H., Johnson, H. G., & Seiden, R. H. (1980). Privacy and confidentiality in psychotherapy. *American Psychologist, 35*, 828–840.

Glenn, C. M. (1980). Ethical issues in the practice of child psychotherapy. *Professional Psychology, 11*, 613–619.

Grisso, T. (1981). *Juvenile's waiver of rights: Legal and psychological competencies*. New York: Plenum.

Grisso, T., & Vierling, L. (1978). Minors consent to treatment: A developmental perspective. *Professional Psychology, 9*, 412–427.

Herr, S. S., Arons, S., & Wallace, R. E. (1983). *Legal rights and mental health care*. Lexington, MA: Lexington.

Janzen, W. B., & Love, W. (1977). Involving adolescents as active participants in their own treatment plans. *Psychological Reports, 41*, 931–934.

Kaser-Boyd, N., Adelman, H., & Taylor, L. (1985). Minors' ability to identify risks and benefits of therapy. *Professional Psychology: Research and Practice, 16*, 411–417.

Kobocow, B., McGuire, J. M., & Blau, B. (1983). The influence of confidentiality conditions on self-disclosure of early adolescents. *Professional Psychology: Research and Practice, 14*, 435–443.

Koocher, G. P. (1976). A bill of rights for children in psychotherapy. In G. P. Koocher (Ed.), *Children's rights and the mental health professions* (pp. 23–32). New York: Wiley.

Koocher, G. P. (1983). Competence to consent: Psychotherapy. In G. B. Melton, G. P. Koocher, & M. J. Saks (Eds.), *Children's competence to consent* (pp. 111–128). New York: Plenum.

McGuire, J. M. (1974). Confidentiality and the child in psychotherapy. *Professional Psychology, 5*, 374–379.

Melton, G. B. (1981). Effects of a state law permitting minors to consent to psychotherapy. *Professional Psychology, 12*, 647–654.

Messenger, C., & McGuire, J. (1981). The child's conception of confidentiality in the therapeutic relationship. *Psychotherapy: Theory, Research & Practice, 18*, 123–130.

Myers, J. E. B. (1982). Legal issues surrounding psychotherapy with minor clients. *Clinical Social Work Journal, 10*, 303–314.

Pardue, J., Whichard, W., & Johnson, E. (1970). Limited confidential information in counseling. *Personnel and Guidance Journal, 49*, 14–20.

Patterson, C. H. (1971). Are ethics different in different settings? *Personnel and Guidance Journal, 50*, 254–259.

Plotkin, R. (1981). When rights collide: Parents, children, and consent to treatment. *Journal of Pediatric Psychology, 6*, 121–130.

Reisner, R. (1985). *Law and the mental health system: Civil and criminal aspects.* St. Paul, MN: West.

Reynolds, M. M. (1976). Threats to confidentiality. *Social Work, 21*, 108–113.

Ross, A. O. (1966). Confidentiality in child therapy: A reevaluation. *Mental Hygiene, 50*, 360–366.

Taylor, L., Adelman, H. S., & Kaser-Boyd, N. (1983). Perspective of children regarding their participation in psychoeducational treatment decision making. *Professional Psychology: Research and Practice, 14*, 882–884.

Taylor, L., Adelman, H. S., & Kaser-Boyd, N. (1985). Minors; attitudes and competence toward participation in psychoeducational decisions. *Professional Psychology: Research and Practice, 16*, 226–235.

Thompson, A. (1983). *Ethical concerns in psychotherapy and their legal ramifications.* New York: University Press of America.

Wagner, C. A. (1978). Elementary school counselors' perceptions of confidentiality with children. *The School Counselor, 25*, 240–248.

Wagner, C. A. (1981). Confidentiality and the school counselor. *Personnel and Guidance Journal, 59*, 305–310.

Weithorn, L. A. (1982). Developmental factors and competence to make informed treatment decisions. *Child and Youth Services, 5*, 85–100.

Weithorn, L. A. (1983). Involving children in decisions affecting their own welfare: Guidelines for professionals. In G. B. Melton, G. P. Koocher, & M. J. Saks (Eds.), *Children's competence to consent* (pp. 235–260). New York: Plenum.

Wilson, J. (1978). *The rights of adolescents in the mental health system.* Lexington, MA: Heath.

Wrenn, C. G. (1952). The ethics of counseling. *Educational and Psychological Measurement, 12*, 161–177.

Reframing the Confidentiality Dilemma to Work in Children's Best Interests

Linda Taylor and Howard S. Adelman

LIMITS ON CONFIDENTIALITY

. . .

There are times when professionals would prefer to maintain confidences but cannot do so legally or ethically. Examples include instances when clients indicate an intention to harm themselves or someone else and when they have been abused. . . .

In order to adequately inform minors of exceptions to the promise of privacy, therapists must add a statement about exceptions, such as this:

> Although most of what we talk about is private, there are three kinds or problems you might tell me about that we would have to talk about with other people. If I find out that someone has been seriously hurting or abusing you, I would have to tell the police about it. If you tell me you have made a plan to seriously hurt yourself, I would have to let your parents know. If you tell me you have made a plan to seriously hurt someone else, I would have to warn that person. I would not be able to keep these problems just between you and me because the law says I can't. Do you understand that it's OK to talk about most things here but that these are three things we must talk about with other people?

Because youngsters may feel a bit overwhelmed about the exceptions to privacy and the serious problems described, they may simply nod their acquiescence or indicate that they are unsure about how to respond. To soften the impact, therapists may add statements, such as this:

> Fortunately, most of what we talk over is private. If you want to talk about any of the three problems that must be shared with others, we'll also talk about the best way for us to talk about the problem with others. I want to be sure I'm doing the best I can to help you.

. . .

CONFIDENTIALITY AS A LIMITATION ON HELPING

. . .

In its ethical guidelines on confidentiality, the American Psychological Association recognizes that there are instances when information obtained in clinical or counseling relationships should be shared with others. In doing so, the guidelines stress that such sharing should occur "only with persons clearly concerned with the case" (APA, 1981, p. 636).[1] Given that teachers and parents are clearly connected and see themselves as also working in a minor's best interests, some interveners feel it appropriate—even essential—to discuss information with them. In other words, there are times when an intervener sees keeping a specific confidence shared by a minor client as working against the youngster's best interests and will evaluate the costs of not communicating the information to others as outweighing the potential benefits of maintaining the minor's privacy.

On a practical level, this concern arises whenever

Adapted from *Professional Psychology: Research and Practice, 20,* 79–83. Copyright 1989 by the American Psychological Association.

[1] *Ed. note:* See Standard 5.05 of the APA's current (1992) Ethical Principles.

parents threaten to withdraw their child because of dissatisfaction about too little access to the information passing between their child and the intervener. It seems clear that the best interests of the child cannot be served if an intervener's unrelenting stance regarding confidentiality results in the child's no longer having access to counseling or to other important resources. In other instances, interveners find that some minors misuse the confidential nature of the counseling relationship by making it secretive and yet another weapon in their conflict with parents and other authority figures, thereby further alienating support systems that the intervener may find are essential links in the helping process.

GUIDELINES FOR RESOLVING THE DILEMMA

Thinking in terms of what would be most beneficial and least damaging to an intervener's efforts to help the client, we have found it best to approach problems related to confidentiality by reframing them. In particular, we have come to focus less on how to avoid breaching confidences and more on how to establish the type of working relationship in which clients take the lead in sharing information when this is indicated. To accomplish this, we stress processes for enhancing youngsters' motivational readiness and empowering them with the ongoing motivation and skills to share information that can help them to solve problems that they are experiencing. In addition, we emphasize steps to minimize the negative consequences of divulging confidences.

Enhancing Motivational Readiness for Sharing

Informing youngsters about reporting requirements can compound negative attitudes toward participating in the intervention (e.g., see Adelman & Taylor, 1986). Thus there may be a need for systematic efforts to enhance motivation to participate. The problem, of course, is a bit paradoxical: that is, how to elicit sufficient participation to allow the therapist to demonstrate that participation is worthwhile.

One strategy involves demonstrating to the youngster that there is an intrinsic payoff for taking the risk of disclosing very personal thoughts and feelings to the therapist. We start with the assump-

tion, born of experience, that the first sessions with most youngsters allow sufficient access to encourage attendance for a couple of sessions. In other words, we know that skilled therapists use a range of nonthreatening activities to help establish enough rapport that most youngsters are willing to return at least for a second session. . . .

Several problems may have to be worked through before a youngster will disclose something perceived as risky. It is hoped that when the risk is taken, the matter is one that can be kept private. Whenever a matter that must be shared is raised, we suggest use of strategies that enable clients to take the lead in sharing the information with others.

Enabling Clients to Share Information

. . . [A] fundamental concern of an intervener in offering a helping relationship is to act in the best interests of the client, as defined by the client, through an informed agreement about ongoing client participation in decision making about means and ends. The ultimate intent is to enable clients to independently pursue their best interests (Swift & Levin, 1987). To accomplish this, intervention focuses on ways to enhance a client's ongoing motivation and skills for autonomous functioning.

In contrast, intervention designed as a socialization process gives primary consideration to the society's best interests. The individual's consent and decision making are not necessarily sought, and empowerment of the individual is pursued only if it is consonant with the socialization agenda (Adelman & Taylor, 1985).

Fortunately, the interests of the individual and the society often are in harmony. However, instances in which confidentiality has been limited by law are indicative of circumstances in which individual and societal interests conflict and society's interests have predominated.

For the most part, clinicians and counselors try to act in the best interests of their clients and look for honest confirmation from clients that they are doing so. Of course, some clients, especially young ones, initially lack the ability to understand and communicate in ways that allow for informed agreements and shared decision making. In such cases, the commitment to empower clients calls for efforts to increase their level of understanding, communication skills, and ability to participate in decision making (Taylor & Adelman, 1986).

All of this has direct implications for the problem of divulging information when the intervener views this as in the client's best interests. In a helping process, the first responsibility of the intervener is to determine whether the client agrees that information should be shared. If the client does not agree, the intervener must be prepared to help the client to explore (in a developmentally appropriate way) the costs and benefits involved (Kaser-Boyd, Adelman, & Taylor, 1985). This may take some time to accomplish, especially insofar as the point is not to convince or seduce but to facilitate comprehension (e.g., understanding of the positive impact that sharing would have on relationships with significant others). In the end, the individual still may not agree, and the ethics of the situation may dictate that the intervener break confidentiality without consent.

If the client sees it in his or her interest to have others informed of certain matters, then discussion shifts to how this will be accomplished. Again, in keeping with a commitment to enabling the client to pursue his or her interests, the client should be in control of what information is shared and, if feasible, should be the one who does the sharing. . . .

Minimizing Negative Consequences of Disclosure

In general, when legal or ethical considerations compel an intervener to divulge confidences, three steps must be taken to minimize the repercussions: (a) an explanation to the client of the reason for disclosure, (b) an exploration of the likely repercussions in and outside of the counseling situation, and (c) a discussion of how to proceed so that negative consequences are minimized and any potential benefits are maximized.

For example, in explaining reasons, one might begin by saying,

> What you have shared today is very important. I know you're not ready to talk about this with your parents, but it is the kind of thing that I told you at the beginning that I am required to tell them.

One might begin an exploration of repercussions for the helping relationship by stating,

> I know that if I do so, you will be upset with me and it will be hard for you to trust me anymore. I feel caught in this situation. I'd like us to be able to work something out to make this all come out as good as we can make it.

With respect to how to proceed, often it is feasible simply to encourage the client to take actions in keeping with his or her best interests or to give consent to allow the counselor to do so:

> This may work best for you if you tell them rather than me. Or, if you don't feel ready to handle this, we both could sit down with your parents while I tell them.

. . .

References

Adelman, H. S., & Taylor, L. (1985). Toward integrating intervention concepts, research, and practice. In S. L. Pfeiffer (Ed.), *Clinical child psychology: An introduction to theory, research, and practice* (pp. 57–92). Orlando, FL: Grune & Stratton.

Adelman, H. S., & Taylor, L. (1986). Children's reluctance regarding treatment: Incompetence, resistance, or an appropriate response? *School Psychology Review, 15,* 91–99.

American Psychological Association (1981). *Ethical principles of psychologists.* Washington, DC: Author.

Kaser-Boyd, N., Adelman, H. S., & Taylor, L. (1985). Minors' ability to identify risks and benefits of therapy. *Professional Psychology: Research and Practice, 16,* 411–417.

Swift, C., & Levin, G. (1987). Empowerment: An emerging mental health technology. *Journal of Primary Prevention, 8,* 71–94.

Taylor, L., & Adelman, H. S. (1986). Facilitating children's participation in decisions that affect them: From concept to practice. *Journal of Clinical Child Psychology, 15,* 346–351.

◆ ◆ ◆

Commentary: See also Sobocinski, M. R. (1990). Ethical principles in the counseling of gay and lesbian adolescents: Issues and autonomy, competence, and confidentiality. Professional Psychology: Research and Practice, 21, 240–247. *This important and controver-*

sial article presents a number of vignettes containing ethical dilemmas facing psychologists who work with gay and lesbian youth. Which provisions in the 1992 APA Ethical Principles might be helpful in resolving such dilemmas?

Balancing the interests of minors and their parents is a difficult task for practitioners and researchers. Because the law considers children to be generally incompetent in making decisions for themselves, whether children are granted the power to make those decisions is determined by constitutional analyses and state law. For psychologists who work in governmental institutions, such as schools or state hospitals, it is very risky to serve minors without parental involvement unless there is an explicit statute permitting it. Psychologists in private institutions—whether in independent practice, nonpublic universities, or mental health clinics—should clearly delineate expectations among themselves, their minor clients, and the minors' parents. For a more complete discussion of legal issues related to assessment, intervention, and research with minors, see Bersoff, D. N., & Hofer, P. (1990). The legal regulation of school psychology. In C. Reynolds & T. Gutkin (Eds.), Handbook of school psychology (2nd ed., pp. 937–961). New York: Wiley.

AIDS: Ethical Implications for Psychological Intervention

Constance F. Morrison

AIDS (acquired immune deficiency syndrome) is perhaps the most frightening disease to be faced in modern times. It is transmissible, severely debilitating, and inevitably fatal, and it has an incubation period of between 6 months and more than 5 years. Current estimates in the United States place the number of people with AIDS (PWAs) at 40,051, and the number of AIDS cases are increasing each year ("Epidemiological notes," 1987). In addition to PWAs, there are an estimated 2 million people now believed to be infected with the human immunodeficiency virus (HIV), although they may display no symptoms of the disease. Of these 2 million people, 10%–50% are expected to develop AIDS or AIDS-related complex within 10 years of their exposure (Faulstich, 1987; Ostrow & Gayle, 1986). . . .

CONFIDENTIALITY

Record Keeping

. . . Membership in a high-risk group may be considered grounds for cancellation of insurance; testing positive for HIV may result in the loss of one's home or job; and one's friendship with a PWA may result in one's being shunned socially. Therefore, one should exercise caution in including potentially damaging information with regard to AIDS in records that might end up with insurance companies, with peer-review groups, or in court.

Cohen (1979) recommended that client records include a summary of all contacts with the client and with others concerning the client, regular summaries of progress, documentation of informed consent to treatment, and all psychological test data. On the other hand, Soisson, VandeCreek, and Knapp (1987)

suggested that information about illegal behavior, sexual practices, or other sensitive information that may harm the client is rarely appropriate for records. One option available to psychotherapists is the use of dual record keeping, whereby working notes are separate from the client's formal record in order to ensure the confidentiality of potentially damaging information.

Right to Privacy Versus Duty to Warn

Practitioners may find themselves facing an ethical dilemma when their responsibility to maintain the confidentiality of a client's personal information is at odds with their duty to warn. . . . Consider the following scenario based on a case study appearing in the *Hastings Center Report* (Winston, 1987):

> Mr. A requested to see a therapist at a Sexually Transmitted Diseases Clinic after receiving a positive result on the HIV test. He has no symptoms.
>
> The therapist informed Mr. A of the probability of his developing the disease within the next 5 years, the typical course of the disease, and its probable outcome. He then explained to Mr. A that he could infect others through sexual contact, sharing needles, or donating blood. The therapist told Mr. A about "safe sex" and what he could do to protect sexual partners from infection.
>
> At that point Mr. A confided to the therapist that he was bisexual and that he believed he had contracted the virus

during one of his homosexual encounters. He went on to say that he had made a decision to discontinue his homosexual activities and had, in fact, recently become engaged. The therapist advised Mr. A to share his diagnosis with his fiancee and again warned him of the risk of transmitting the virus. Mr. A refused to do so, saying that it would wreck his marriage plans.

This therapist is faced with a conflict between maintaining his client's confidentiality and warning his client's fiancee of a potential threat of harm. Perhaps the first step in dealing with this dilemma is to weight the risks involved to each party. Informing Mr. A's fiancee about a possible risk to her may, as Mr. A fears, result in a loss of this relationship and thus Mr. A could feel emotionally devastated. It would also place the therapist/client relationship in a serious jeopardy. Once this information was given to Mr. A's fiancee, she could disclose it to whomever she chose, which could possibly cause Mr. A further harm. But what of the risks to Mr. A's fiancee if she is not warned of the possible threat to her? There is some question as to the medical risks that she might face. Not all persons who test positive for the HIV are viremic and therefore infectious (Winston, 1987) Although there is substantial evidence that the HIV can be transmitted through heterosexual contact (Chamberland & Dondero, 1987; Redfield et al., 1985), the efficiency of transmission is still in question. Also, the outcome of infection with the HIV is not predictable. At present, 10%–50% of persons with the HIV are expected to develop AIDS. Although there is also the possibility that his fiancee has already been exposed to the virus by Mr. A, Chamberland and Dondero (1987) suggested that repeated unprotected sexual contact with an infected partner over time may increase the likelihood of transmission, and epidemiological evidence suggests that an average of 100 incidents of unprotected vaginal intercourse may be required for male-to-female transmission (Landers, 1988). Therefore, in weighing the risks to each party, the practitioner must also take into consideration the possibility that further

unprotected sexual contact will increase the risks of harm to the fiancee.

The therapist in this situation is also bound by legal considerations. If she breaches Mr. A's confidentiality, she may be sued or sanctioned for wrongful disclosure and could be held liable for any personal suffering that he experiences. If the therapist does not inform Mr. A's fiancee and his fiancee does develop AIDS, the therapist may be liable for failing to warn the fiancee of potential harm. State and case laws concerning confidentiality and duty to warn vary from state to state. For example, in California, the *Tarasoff* decision and the California Civil Code (cited in Weinstock, 1988) make clear the therapist's duty to warn. However, California also recently passed legislation imposing fines or imprisonment or both for willful disclosure of HIV test results without prior written consent (Binder, 1987). . . .

In arguing the importance of maintaining client confidentiality, Landesman (1987) suggested that breaching the client's confidentiality in such a case as the one just described might cause the client immediate harm and may also result in the client's failure to seek help at a later date. It can also discourage others from seeking testing and treatment. Kain (1988) suggested that the role of the psychotherapist in AIDS prevention lies not so much in reporting the behavior but rather in the working through the issues of rejection, abandonment, loneliness, homophobia, and infidelity, which may be restraining a client from informing sexual partners. Winston (1987), on the other hand, argued that failing to warn the fiancee may put her, as well as any children she might bear, at risk. She may also unknowingly transmit the HIV to future sexual partners. In a discussion of the limits of confidentiality with clients who have AIDS or are HIV seropositive, Gray and Harding (1988) recommended more direct methods. They suggested that the therapist directly inform identified sexual partners of the imminent danger when the client is unwilling to do so. In the case of anonymous sexual partners, they suggested that the therapist inform appropriate state health officials and professional or civil authorities. Last, the Council on Ethical and Judicial Affairs of the American Medical Association (1988) suggested that should persuasion fail, the physician should inform appropriate health authorities or the endangered third party.

Obviously, there are no clear or easy answers. In the ideal situation, the therapist would be able, in a relatively short time, to persuade Mr. A to tell his fiancee about the test results. Failing that, the therapist might convince her client to practice safe sex while he continued to consider revealing his HIV status to his fiancee. Last, the therapist should consult with knowledgeable medical and legal advisers and with colleagues before taking any action. If a decision is made to breach the client's confidentiality in order to protect a third party, the client should be informed beforehand (Kerr, 1987). Informing the client first and explaining the legal and ethical bases for the decision may help to minimize the harm to both the client and the therapeutic relationship. Until greater clarity results from either case law or statutes, cases such as these will probably have to be resolved on a case-by-case basis. . . .

Suicide

Another ethical dilemma faced by physicians that psychotherapists may also confront when working with PWAs and HIV-seropositive people is determining an appropriate response to an intention to commit suicide. In a recent study in New York City, Marzuk et al. (1988) demonstrated a substantially increased risk for suicide among men with AIDS. Male PWAs who are between the ages of 20 and 59 are approximately 36 times more likely to commit suicide than are men in the general population. Issues that must be addressed by the practitioner include consideration of the PWA or the HIV-seropositive individual's right to commit suicide, the impact of HIV infection on the capacity of the individual to make a rational choice, and the practitioner's legal liability.

Mental health professionals have traditionally accepted an ethical and sometimes legal responsibility to prevent a client's suicide. Preventive measures have ranged all the way from persuasion to involuntary commitment in a psychiatric facility. It has been in the area of what Szasz (1986) termed *coercive interventions*, wherein the client's consent is not obtained and confidentiality is breached, that controversy has developed. Individual psychotherapists and groups such as the Hemlock Society have argued that people

have a right to make a rational, competent choice to die, especially in cases of terminal illness or severe, untreatable, debilitating pain (Fujimura, Weis, & Cochran, 1985). On the other hand, some have contended that even in such cases, suicide may be motivated by emotions that are temporary, whereas suicide is permanent (Bursztajn, Gutheil, Warren, & Brodsky, 1986). Central to the issue is the question of the individual's capacity to rationally and competently choose suicide. In the case of the client with HIV infection, the question of capacity is complicated by the infection itself. Many individuals infected with the HIV show signs of progressive dementia similar to that of Alzheimer's disease (Faulstich, 1987; Volberding & Abrams, 1985). This AIDS-related dementia has been reported to sometimes develop before a definitive diagnosis of AIDS (Ostrow & Gayle, 1986). Central nervous system dysfunction or neuropsychiatric impairment obviously raises questions concerning the client's competency to make a rational choice for suicide, as well as to consent to treatment. Even such staunch advocates of clients' rights as Szasz (1986) justify coercive intervention when there is demonstrable malfunctioning of the brain.

The psychologist must also consider the issue of legal liability. Not only do the Ethical Principles of Psychologists allow a practitioner to breach a client's confidentiality in order to prevent suicide, but in recent reviews, researchers have also found no successful lawsuit against a therapist who breached confidentiality to protect the life of a suicidal client. However, should a practitioner fail to take reasonable action to prevent a suicide, a wrongful death action could be brought against him or her, although the courts are more likely to impose liability in inpatient settings (Kjervik, 1984). Last, although a psychotherapist may view suicide as a rational choice for a client, actually assisting the client to die is clearly defined as a crime, and there would be little question regarding legal liability. . . .

References

American Psychological Association (1981). Ethical principles of psychologists. *American Psychologist, 36,* 633–638.

Baird, K. A., & Rupert, P. A. (1987). Clinical management of confidentiality: A survey of psychologists in seven states. *Professional Psychology: Research and Practice, 18*, 347–352.

Binder, R. L. (1987). AIDS antibody tests on inpatient psychiatric units. *American Journal of Psychiatry, 144*, 176–181.

Bursztajn, H., Gutheil, T. C., Warren, M. J., & Brodsky, A. (1986). Depression, self-love, time, and the "right" to suicide. *General Hospital Psychiatry, 8*, 91–95.

Chamberland, M. E., & Dondero, T. J. (1987). Heterosexually acquired infection with human immunodeficiency virus (HIV). *Annals of Internal Medicine, 107*, 763–766.

Cohen, R. J. (1979). *Malpractice: A guide for mental health professionals.* New York: Free Press.

Council on Ethical and Judicial Affairs of the American Medical Association (1988). Ethical issues involved in the growing AIDS crisis. *Journal of the American Medical Association, 259*, 1360–1361.

Epidemiological notes and reports: Update: Acquired immunodeficiency syndrome—United States (1987, August 14). *Morbidity and Mortality Weekly Report,* pp. 522–526.

Faulstich, M. E. (1987). Psychiatric aspects of AIDS. *American Journal of Psychiatry, 144*, 551–556.

Fujimura, L. E., Weis, D. M., & Cochran, J. R. (1985). Suicide: Dynamics and implications for counseling. *Journal of Counseling and Development, 63*, 612–615.

Gray, L. A., & Harding, A. K. (1988). Confidentiality limits with clients who have the AIDS virus. *Journal of Counseling and Development, 66*, 219–223.

Kain, C. D. (1988). To breach or not to breach: Is that the question? *Journal of Counseling and Development, 66*, 224–225.

Kerr, C. P. (1987). AIDS and the issue of confidentiality. *Postgraduate Medicine, 81*(8), 95, 98, 101.

Kjervik, D. K. (1984). The psychotherapist's duty to act reasonably to prevent suicide: A proposal to allow reasonable suicide. *Behavioral Sciences and the Law, 2*, 207–219.

Landers, S. (1988). Practitioners and AIDS: Face-to-face with pain. *APA Monitor, 19*(1), 1, 14–15.

Landesman, S. H. (1987). AIDS and a duty to protect: Commentary. *Hastings Center Report, 17*(1), 23.

Marzuk, P. M., Tierney, H., Tardiff, K., Gross, E. M., Morgan, E. B., Hsu, M., & Mann, J. J. (1988). Increased risk of suicide in persons with AIDS. *Journal of the American Medical Association, 259*, 1333–1337.

Ostrow, D. G., & Gayle, T. C. (1986). Psychosocial and ethical issues of AIDS health care programs. *Quality Review Bulletin, 12*, 284–294.

Redfield, R. R., Markham, P. D., Salahuddin, S. Z., Wright, D. C., Sarngadharan, M. G., & Gallo, R. C. (1985). Heterosexually acquired HTLV-III/LAV disease (AIDS-related complex and AIDS): Epidemiological evidence for female-to-male transmission. *Journal of the American Medical Association, 254*, 2094–2096.

Soisson, E. L., VandeCreek, L., & Knapp, S. (1987). Thorough record keeping: A good defense in a litigious era. *Professional Psychology: Research and Practice, 18*, 498–502.

Szasz, T. (1986). The case against suicide prevention. *American Psychologist, 41*, 806–812.

Tarasoff v. Regents of the University of California, 17 Cal.3d 425, 551 P.2d 334 (1976). (Tarasoff II)

Volberding, P., & Abrams, D. (1985). Clinical care and research in AIDS. *Hasting Center Report, 15*(4), 16–17.

Weinstock, R. (1988). Confidentiality and the new duty to protect: The therapist's dilemma. *Hospital and Community Psychiatry, 39*, 607–609.

Winston, M. (1987). AIDS and a duty to protect: Commentary. *Hastings Center Report, 17*(1), 22–23.

◆ ◆ ◆

Commentary: For another helpful article that discusses applying the duty to protect to clients who present issues concerning sexually transmitted diseases, see Lamb, D. H., Clark, C., Drumheller, P., Frizzell, K., & Surrey, L. (1989). Applying Tarasoff to AIDS-related psychotherapy issues. Professional Psychology: Research and Practice, 20, *37–43.*

In a follow-up study to Lamb et al's (1989) conceptual piece, Lamb and other colleagues (1990) empirically investigated the degree to which (a) the dangerousness of a client and (b) the identifiability of their potential victims influenced clinicians to break confidentiality. On the basis of surveys from 241 clinical members of APA, they concluded that both variables were important but that clients' dangerousness appeared to be more relevant than victims' identifiability. Lamb et al. also found that clinicians who had prior contact with AIDS patients in therapy were less likely to disclose confidential information. See Totten, G., Lamb, D. H., & Reeder, G. D. (1990). Tarasoff and confidentiality in AIDS-related psychotherapy. Professional Psychology: Research and Practice, 21, *155–160.*

Finally, nowhere is the conflict between psychologists' ethical duty to protect client disclosures and the demands of society more salient than in settings where it has been deemed that national security or public safety interests override client interests, such as in correctional facilities, police departments, and the military. For an introduction to the ethical problems that psychologists face in these settings, see, for example,

Archibald, E. M. (1986). Confidentiality when the police psychologist is evaluator and caregiving practitioner. In J. T. Reese & H. A. Goldstein (Eds.), Psychological services for law enforcement (pp. 215–217). Washington, DC: Federal Bureau of Investigation, U.S. Department of Justice.

D'Agostino, C. (1986). Police psychological services: Ethical issues. In J. T. Reese & H. A. Goldstein (Eds.), Psychological services for law enforcement (pp. 241–247). Washington, DC: Federal Bureau of Investigation, U.S. Department of Justice.

Dietz, P. E. (1986). The perils of police psychology: 10 strategies for minimizing role conflicts when providing mental health services and consultation to law enforcement agencies. Behavioral Sciences and the Law, 4, 385–400.

Howe, E. G. (1989). Confidentiality in the military. Behavioral Sciences and the Law, 7, 317–337.

Jeffrey, T. B. (1989). Issues regarding confidentiality for military psychologists. Military Psychology, 1, 49–56.

Jeffrey, T. B., Rankin, R. J., & Jeffrey, L. K. (1992). In service of two masters: The ethical–legal dilemma faced by military psychologists. Professional Psychology: Research and Practice, 23, 91–95.

Saxton, G. H. (1986). Confidentiality dilemmas for psychologists and psychiatrists in the criminal justice system. American Journal of Forensic Psychology, 4, 25–31.

Weinberger, L. E., & Sreenivasan, S. (1994). Ethical and professional conflicts in correctional psychology. Professional Psychology: Research and Practice, 25, 161–167.

Weiner, B. A. (1986). Confidentiality and the legal issues raised by the psychological evaluations of law enforcement officers. In J. T. Reese & H. A. Goldstein (Eds.), Psychological services for law enforcement (pp. 97–102). Washington, DC: Federal Bureau of Investigation, U.S. Department of Justice.

Zelig, M. (1988). Ethical dilemmas in police psychology. Professional Psychology: Research and Practice, 19, 336–338.

Also, see, generally, Monahan, J. (Ed.). (1980). Who is the client? Washington, DC: American Psychological Association.

CHAPTER 5

MULTIPLE RELATIONSHIPS

When Borys and Pope (1989) surveyed 2,352 psychologists, social workers, and psychiatrists, only about 16 of them considered "engaging in sexual activity with a current client" to be ethical. One of the few absolute prohibitions in the current APA code, as well as in its predecessor, is that barring sexual intimacies with current psychotherapy clients (see Principle 6a, APA, 1990; Standard 4.05, APA, 1992). Yet, the APA ethics committee (1994) reported that, in 1993, "the largest single category of unethical behavior in cases that end[ed] in the loss of membership is sexual misconduct" (p. 663).

Accusations that professionals in positions of power have engaged in inappropriate sexual intimacies have evoked publicity and absorbed the public's attention, particularly during the past decade. This notoriety has not been limited to mental health practitioners but has touched senators, governors, presidents, and Supreme Court justices.

Although sexual impropriety between clients and clinicians is the most written about and troubling form of multiple relationship, it is a relatively low probability event. Many other potential forms of multiple relationships are more likely to confront not only the therapist but the researcher, tester, supervisor, and professor as well. For example, what if a carpenter cannot afford to pay for a psychological assessment of his or her child and offers to build some bookshelves in lieu of the psychologist's fee? What if a research subject asks the experimenter for a date? Can faculty members invite their graduate students to their houses for social gatherings? What should the chair of an admissions committee do if a close friend applies to the chair's doctoral program and it is the only one in the area that the friend can afford to attend? What if patients want to give their therapists inexpensive gifts? Can a psychologist supervising a graduate student in a practicum also become the supervisee's therapist? These are potentially knotty problems that are not always easily resolved by explicit prohibitory language in the ethics code.[1]

In this chapter, then, one of the goals is to delineate the wide variety of multiple relationships that can confront psychologists, regardless of the settings in which they work or the roles they perform. With these readings, I also seek to educate readers about the consequences of engaging in multiple relationships and to provide some guidance in avoiding the harm that such relationships can cause.

But this chapter has more implicit and far-ranging aims. For example, one of the topics

---

[1] As an example of really low probability events, consider a case brought before the Arizona Board of Psychologist Examiners. It involved a psychologist, also ordained as a minister, who performed an exorcism on a 10-year-old boy and then billed child protective services for his treatment.

the reader considers is the barring of sexual intimacies with former clients. Under Standard 4.07 of the 1992 ethics code, sexual relationships are absolutely forbidden for 2 years after therapy is terminated and, then, after that, only if the therapist can demonstrate that the relationship is not exploitative. The 1992 Ethical Principles was the first of all the ethics codes that APA has promulgated to contain such a provision, and its inclusion was seen as a major advance. Ironically, however, the rule as adopted pleases practically no one (perhaps not even the reluctant majority of the APA Council of Representatives who voted for it as a compromise).

Although the provision barring posttermination sexual relationships for 2 years promotes such moral principles as nonmaleficence, the fact that such relationships are not banned in perpetuity angers those who believe that any possibility of a future nonprofessional relationship will harm therapy and the patient. On the other hand, one could argue that any ban constitutes a form of "ethical imperialism" (Gergen, 1973, p. 910). Because the typical sexual dual relationship involves a male therapist and a female patient, does the ban, in fact, produce a perverse kind of antifeminism, forbidding women to exercise their autonomous right to choose to enter into such a relationship—placing them, therefore, in the role of powerless, passive victims?

Even more broadly, one can ask to what extent a code of ethics should interfere in private relationships. Although one can acknowledge that the profession universally condemns sexual relationships with current and former patients—for all the reasons that the following material advances and the vast majority of psychologists adopt—that does not mean that the issue cannot be debated rationally and in good faith. This chapter, because of its intellectually controversial and emotion-arousing content, lends itself well to a debate, for the larger purposes that such a debate can serve.

References

American Psychological Association. (1990). Ethical principles of psychologists (amended June 2, 1989). *American Psychologist, 45,* 390–395.

American Psychological Association. (1992). Ethical principles of psychologists and code of conduct. *American Psychologist, 47,* 1597–1611.

APA Ethics Committee. (1994). Report of the ethics committee, 1993. *American Psychologist, 49,* 659–666.

Borys, D. S., & Pope, K. S. (1989). Dual relationships between therapist and client: A national study of psychologists, psychiatrists, and social workers. *Professional Psychology: Research and Practice, 20,* 283–293.

Gergen, K. J. (1973). The codification of research ethics: Views of a doubting Thomas. *American Psychologist, 28,* 907–912.

Dual Relationships in Psychotherapy

Kenneth S. Pope

. . .

Dual relationships are relatively easy to define; they are much more difficult for many of us to recognize in our practice. A dual relationship in psychotherapy occurs when the therapist is in another, significantly different relationship with one of his or her patients. Most commonly, the second role is social, financial, or professional.

In some cases, one relationship follows the other. The mere fact that the two roles are apparently sequential rather than clearly concurrent does not, in and of itself, mean that the two relationships do not constitute a dual relationship. . . .

In part it may be the relative simplicity and abstraction of the definition that lulls many of us into a lack of alertness to the diverse ways, many of them exceptionally subtle, that dual relationships occur in psychotherapy, often with potentially devastating results. Specific examples, more than abstract definitions, may provide us with a useful awareness of how these entanglements occur. The following five fictional scenarios, dismayingly typical of actual practice, were among those created by Keith-Spiegel and Koocher (1985) to illustrate their discussion of dual relationships.

> Jan Job worked as a records clerk for a large community mental-health agency. She was supervised by Helmut Honcho, Ph.D. Jan was experiencing personal problems and asked Dr. Honcho if she could be a client. He agreed. Jan would later bring an ethics complaint against Honcho, charging him with blocking her promotion based on assessments of her as a client rather than as an employee. (p. 270)

> Soon after Patty Pal began counseling with Richard Chum, Ed.D., Patty asked Dr. Chum and his wife to spend the weekend at their family beach house. The outing was enjoyable for all parties. During therapy, however, Patty became increasingly reluctant to talk about her problems and insisted that things were going quite well. Other social interactions among the foursome continued to occur on weekends. Chum finally confronted Patty during the therapy with his impression that "nothing was moving." It was at that point that Patty admitted that she was experiencing numerous pressures and problems. But she felt that if she were honest about them in therapy, Chum might choose not to socialize with her and her husband. (p. 271)

> Feline Breed, Ph.D., spent much of her time outside her professional role raising pedigree cats. Most of her weekends were devoted to traveling the cat-show circuit. Many of her therapy clients were "cat people" whom she had met through her hobby contacts. The small-talk before and after the therapy sessions was usually devoted to discussion about cats. Interest in purchasing kittens that she raised was often expressed, and she did sell them to clients. In more than one instance, the sale of kittens to clients caused difficulties. Once, for example, the therapy process was not proceeding as the client wished, and the client accused Dr.

Breed of "using" him as a way of selling high-priced cats and not really caring about his problems. In another instance, a woman client was upset because Dr. Breed sold her an animal that had never won a single prize. The client assumed that if the therapist raised such defective cats, then the trustworthiness of her therapy skills should be questioned as well. (p. 276)

Kurt Court, Esq., and Leonard Dump, Ph.D., met at a cocktail party. Mr. Court's law practice was suffering because of his debilitating personal problems. Dr. Dump was about to embark on a bitter divorce proceeding. They hit upon the idea of swapping professional services. Dr. Dump would see Mr. Court as a psychotherapy client, and Mr. Court would represent Dr. Dump in the divorce proceeding. Mr. Court proved to be a difficult and more disturbed client than Dr. Dump had anticipated. Furthermore, Court's representation of Dump was erratic and the likelihood of a favorable outcome looked bleak. Yet Mr. Court brought ethics charges against Dr. Dump. Court charged that the therapy he received was inferior and that Dump spent most of the time expressing anger and berating him for not getting better. (p. 278)

Elmo Brush agreed to paint the house of Peel Schuff, Ph.D., in exchange for psychotherapy for Brush's teenage daughter. Dr. Schuff saw the girl for six sessions and terminated her therapy. Brush complained that his end of the bargain would have brought him $900 in a conventional deal. Thus it was as though he had paid $150 a session for the services of a person who normally charged $50 a session. Dr. Schuff argued that he had satisfactorily resolved the daughter's problems, and the deal was valid because task was traded for task, not dollar for dollar value. (p. 279)

PROBLEMS WITH DUAL RELATIONSHIPS

. . .

First, the dual relationship erodes and distorts the professional nature of the therapeutic relationship. The professional therapeutic relationship is secured within a reliable set of boundaries on which both therapist and patient can depend. When the therapist is also the patient's lover, landlord, best friend, or employer, the crucial professional nature of the therapeutic relationship is compromised. . . .

Second, dual relationships create conflicts of interest and, thus, compromise the disinterest (not lack of interest) necessary for sound professional judgment. The therapist as professional professes to place the interests of the patient foremost (except in those rare instances in which to do so would place third parties at unacceptable risk for harm). If the therapist allows another relationship to occur, however, the therapist creates a second set of interests to which he or she will be subject. . . . In dual relationships, the therapist is engaged in meeting his or her own needs (e.g., sexual or social). Further, in dual relationship therapies, recognition, analysis, and management of transference and countertransference become all but impossible.

Third, both during the course of therapy and at any time thereafter, the therapist may be invited or compelled (through subpoena or court order) to offer testimony regarding the patient's diagnosis, treatment, prognosis, and so forth. Such testimony can be crucially important to the patient in personal injury suits, custody hearings, criminal trials, and other judicial proceedings. If the therapist were also the business partner, live-in lover, or "we frequently share vacations together" type of friend, the objectivity, reliability, and integrity of the testimony as well as the information and documents reflecting the therapy (e.g., chart notes and insurance form diagnoses) would be suspect.

Fourth, because of the therapist–patient relationship, the patient cannot enter into a business or other secondary relationship with the therapist on equal footing (see Pope, 1988). . . . [T]he patient who feels seriously wronged in a business, financial, or social transaction with his or her therapist faces troubling obstacles in seeking legal redress. The "secrets" and intensely private material about the patient that the therapist became aware of during the psychotherapy can be used by the therapist in planning the most effective defense. Further, therapists may use a variety of false diagnostic labels by which to discredit the patient, a practice that is unfortunately not infrequent (Pope, 1988).

Fifth, if it became acceptable practice for therapists to engage in dual financial, social, and professional relationships with their patients, whether prior or subsequent to termination, then the nature of psychotherapy would be drastically changed. Psychotherapists could begin using their practices to screen their patients for each patient's likelihood of meeting—either during therapy or some time after termination—the therapist's social, sexual, financial, or professional needs or desires. . . .

Sixth, dual relationships would affect the cognitive processes that research has shown to play a role in the beneficial effects of therapy that help the patient to maintain the benefits of therapy after termination (see Gabbard & Pope, 1989). . . .

STRATEGIES OF TOLERATION AND JUSTIFICATION

If both sexual (Gabbard, 1989) and nonsexual (Borys & Pope, 1989) dual relationships have historically been viewed by the mental health professions as harmful, what strategies enable us to tolerate or justify them? . . .

Selective Inattention

One of the most prevalent ways in which dual relationships—and many other forms of unethical behavior—are made tolerable is through selective inattention. The therapist blocks out sustained, useful awareness of the duality of relationships by splitting the two relationships and refusing to acknowledge that both relationships involve the same patient and have implications for the patient and the patient's treatment.

One indication that selective inattention may have played a role in the development of a dual relationship is the lack of any mention of a second relationship in the treatment notes. . . . The chart contains no mention of the duality of the relationship, no consideration of how the two relationships may be interacting, and no discussion of how the dual re-

lationship may affect the patient's clinical status, prognosis, treatment plan, or response to the treatment plan. . . .

Selective inattention may foster dual relationships in another manner. Often, the colleagues of a therapist who is entering a dual relationship may choose to screen out and remain selectively inattentive to evidence that the therapist is engaging in activities that put the patient at risk for harm. Again, such selective inattention regarding some of our closest colleagues is common to virtually all of us who practice as clinicians. At times, we may not want to risk losing the friendship or the collegial amiability; we fear that the warmth of our relationship with a colleague who is engaging in a harmful dual relationship with a patient might disappear, perhaps permanently. At times, we may fear the anger or the power of our colleague. Perhaps he or she is our employer or supervisor or, perhaps, a valuable source of referrals. At times, we may not want to rock the boat and upset the tranquility of a formal organization, such as a clinic, or an informal network of colleagues. And at times, we may experience the "glass house" phenomenon: We may avoid raising ethical issues with others because we are afraid that they will begin raising them with us. Thus, we may enter into a tacit pact with our colleagues: Everyone will ignore everyone else's ethical violations. In such situations, selective inattention becomes an important aspect of the interpersonal or social ecology. . . .

Benefits

A second way in which dual relationships are sometimes justified is that they are beneficial for the patient. . . . The addition of the sexual relationship was said to provide the patient with a more nurturantly human, warmer professional relationship; to provide the patient with a more complete sense of acceptance; to help the patient develop—under the watchful eye of the therapist—a more healthy view of his or her own sexuality and a more varied and completed array of sexual responses; to provide the patient with sexually corrective experiences that would help the patient recover from dysfunction caused by prior sexual trauma; to help the patient overcome a disabling "mind–body" split in which the patient's reactions were overly intellectualized; to provide a way in which the patient could experience and work through "overt transference"; and to provide a safe "bridge" between the therapeutic and nontherapeutic environment (i.e., the patient could "try out" on the therapist what the patient had discovered about sex and intimacy during the early stages of therapy so that the patient could be sure of making it work "in real life").

One difficulty the proponents of this view experienced was that mention of the dual relationship—supposedly a key component of the treatment plan—was often absent from any part of the chart notes or informed consent procedures. Therapists had difficulty explaining why, if they had carefully considered why a dual relationship was the treatment of choice and had implemented it carefully, they had neglected to obtain the patient's informed consent for the procedure and why they failed to note the consideration or use of the treatment strategy in the chart notes.

A second difficulty faced by those who sought to justify their behavior . . . was their difficulty finding substantial research evidence that implementing dual relationship treatment was a safe and effective way to produce positive therapeutic change. . . .

Some therapists acknowledged that there was virtually no research evidence or other systematic data supporting the hypothesis that dual relationships are a safe and effective method to produce therapeutic change. They maintained that their implementation of the dual relationship was on a trial basis, as part of a research or quasi-research effort to obtain just such evidence. However, it was often difficult for these therapists to establish that they had provided adequate procedural safeguards (such as informed consent) to the patients on whom this experimental method was being tested (see Levine, 1988; Pope, 1990a, 1990b).

Prevalence

Therapists may attempt to justify engaging in dual relationships with their patients by asserting that many other therapists engage in the practice. . . . This approach was used in some of the early malpractice trials in which therapists who acknowledged engaging in sexual dual relationships with their patients emphasized that the early surveys of therapist–patient sexual intimacies (e.g., Holroyd &

Brodsky, 1977) indicated that around 10% of male therapists reported engaging in sexual relationships with their patients. This 10% figure, according to the defense, represented a sizable minority of the professional community who accepted and endorsed, via their own behavior with patients, the legitimacy of therapist–patient sexual relations.

The reflexive acceptance of the "prevalence" argument may have encouraged or facilitated both sexual and nonsexual dual relationships. The argument itself, however, does not seem to address the issue of whether dual relationships are indeed a safe and effective way to produce beneficial change in the patient. Various behaviors that may be unethical, illegal, or clinically contraindicated may unfortunately be practiced, from time to time, by a sizable minority and sometimes even by a majority of the professional community. . . . The fact that a substantial number of professionals engage in a practice, does not, in and of itself, indicate whether the practice is ethical, legal, safe, or effective. . . .

Necessity

Dual relationships may be accepted with virtually no ethical or clinical scrutiny when they are asserted to be necessary. The therapist claims that there was no alternative but to engage in a dual relationship. The therapist using this justification refuses to accept any responsibility for entering a dual relationship; the therapist must simply accept what is determined by forces beyond his or her control. Thus, dual relationships may be termed *inevitable* or *unavoidable*.

Yet the "my hands were tied" and the "what else could I have done?" approach may represent a combination of a failure to explore and create alternative approaches that meet the highest clinical, legal, and ethical standards and a not-too-subtle attempt to evade responsibility. Careful, determined, imaginative attempts to meet the needs of patients without resorting to sexual or nonsexual dual relationships can overcome the rationalization of necessity. . . .

References

Borys, D. S., & Pope, K. S. (1989). Dual relationships between therapist and client: A national study of psychologists, psychiatrists, and social workers.

Professional Psychology: Research and Practice, 20, 283–293.

Gabbard, G. O. (Ed.). (1989). *Sexual exploitation in professional relationships.* Washington, DC: American Psychiatric Press.

Gabbard, G. O., & Pope, K. S. (1989). Sexual intimacies after termination: Clinical, ethical, and legal aspects. In G. O. Gabbard (Ed.), *Sexual exploitation in professional relationships* (pp. 115–127). Washington, DC: American Psychiatric Press.

Holroyd, J. C., & Brodsky, A. M. (1977). Psychologists' attitudes and practices regarding erotic and nonerotic physical contact with clients. *American Psychologist, 32,* 843–849.

Keith-Spiegel, P., & Koocher, G. P. (1985). *Ethics in psychology.* New York: Random House.

Levine, R. J. (1988). *Ethics and regulation of clinical research* (2nd ed.). New Haven: Yale University Press.

Pope, K. S. (1988). Dual relationships: A source of ethical, legal, and clinical problems. *Independent Practitioner, 8*(1), 17–25.

Pope, K. S. (1990a). Therapist–patient sex as sex abuse: Six scientific, professional, and practical dilemmas in addressing victimization and rehabilitation. *Professional Psychology: Research and Practice, 21,* 227–239.

Pope, K. S. (1990b). Therapist–patient sexual involvement: A review of the research. *Clinical Psychology Review, 10,* 477–490.

Dual Relationships Between Therapist and Client: A National Study of Psychologists, Psychiatrists, and Social Workers

Debra S. Borys and Kenneth S. Pope

[*Ed. note:* The results reported below were gleaned from a survey of an equal number of 4,800 psychiatrists, psychologists, and social workers who were asked about their beliefs and behaviors regarding a range of dual relationships.]

. . .

RESPONSES REGARDING BELIEFS

In Table 1 we present the degree to which the 1,108 participants in this part of the study considered each behavior to be ethical. . . .

. . . In Table 2 we present the items constituting each factor and their factor loadings. Factor 1 (Incidental Involvements), accounting for 69.8% of the common variance, described three behaviors involving incidental, typically one-time events or special occasions in which therapeutic boundaries were altered at the initiation of the client. Factor 2 (Social/Financial Involvements), accounting for 17% of the common variance, described the involvement of the therapist and the client in extratherapeutic social, financial, or business activities. Factor 3 (Dual Professional Roles), accounting for 13.2% of the common variance, contained three items concerning the therapist's engaging in a dual role of the sort that is explicitly prohibited by the Ethical Principles (APA, 1981) and a fourth item concerning the therapist's entering a professional relationship with a significant other of an ongoing client. The ranges of possible values were 0 to 9.69 for the Incidental Involvements factor, 0 to 32.83 for the Social/

Financial Involvements factor, and 0 to 13.10 for the Dual Professional Roles factor.

. . .

RESPONSES REGARDING BEHAVIORS

In Table 3 we present the frequencies with which the 1,021 clinicians in this part of the study reported engaging in each of the listed activities. . . .

DISCUSSION ·

. . .

In regard to one item alone could social desirability response bias be reasonably inferred from comparison with prior studies. In our study, only 0.2% of the women ($n = 1$) and 0.9% of the men ($n = 4$) reported engaging in sexual intimacies with an ongoing client. These figures are lower than those reported for women (2.5%–3.1%) and for men (7.1%–12.1%) in any of the previously published national studies (Gartrell et al., 1987; Holroyd & Brodsky, 1977; Pope et al., 1986, . . . 1987). There are three major possibilities, which are not mutually exclusive, for interpreting this discrepancy:

First, it may, of course, represent an actual decline in the rate of sexual intimacies with clients. In the most recent previous study, Pope et al. (1987) found a significantly lower rate than in prior studies and discussed possible factors contributing to an actual decline. Our study may be charting a continuation of this trend.

Adapted from *Professional Psychology: Research and Practice, 20,* 283–293. Copyright 1989 by the American Psychological Association.

TABLE 1

Percentage of Clinicians (*N* = 1,108) Responding in Each Ethicality Category

Item	Rating						
	1	2	3	4	5	NS	NR
Accepting a gift worth under $10	3.0	13.0	38.4	40.1	5.0	0.4	0.2
Accepting a client's invitation to a special occasion	6.3	26.3	41.0	20.8	4.6	0.8	0.1
Accepting a service or product as payment for therapy	21.4	30.0	28.2	12.7	2.7	4.2	0.7
Becoming friends with a client after termination	14.8	38.4	32.0	10.2	2.1	1.9	0.6
Selling a product to a client	70.8	18.0	7.5	0.9	0.3	2.1	0.5
Accepting a gift worth over $50	44.9	37.0	13.1	1.4	0.8	2.3	0.5
Providing therapy to an employee	57.9	26.2	10.9	2.1	0.2	2.4	0.4
Engaging in sexual activity with a client after termination	68.4	23.2	4.2	0.6	0.3	2.6	0.7
Disclosing details of current personal stresses to a client	26.0	39.3	29.5	2.9	1.3	0.5	0.5
Inviting clients to an office/clinic open house	26.6	24.7	21.5	15.4	5.8	5.0	0.9
Employing a client	49.9	29.5	14.5	2.8	1.2	1.5	0.5
Going out to eat with a client after a session	43.2	37.9	13.6	2.4	0.8	1.4	0.5
Buying goods or services from a client	36.7	35.4	20.6	4.7	0.7	1.5	0.3
Engaging in sexual activity with a current client	98.3	0.5	0.0	0.1	0.6	0.4	0.0
Inviting clients to a personal party or social event	63.5	29.2	4.6	0.7	0.5	1.2	0.2
Providing individual therapy to a relative, friend, or lover of an ongoing client	12.6	21.4	38.8	21.4	4.2	1.0	0.5
Providing therapy to a current student or supervisee	44.4	31.0	16.0	5.4	1.0	2.0	0.4
Allowing a client to enroll in one's class for a grade	39.0	28.0	18.0	7.6	1.9	5.2	0.4

Note. Rating codes: 1 = *never ethical*, 2 = *ethical under rare conditions*, 3 = *ethical under some conditions*, 4 = *ethical under most conditions*, 5 = *always ethical*. NS = *not sure*. NR = *no response* (i.e., missing data). Rows may not sum to 100% because of rounding.

Second, the discrepancy may be due to a decline in reporting—even on an anonymous survey—a behavior that is becoming recognized as a felony in an increasing number of states. No other item on the form concerns a behavior that constitutes a felony.

Third, the wording on this survey may have led to a misunderstanding among some participants. It is possible that participants may have interpreted "engaged in sexual activity with an ongoing client" as referring to sexual intimacies with someone who was still a client at the time of this survey rather than sexual intimacies with any client—past or present—before termination of therapy.

Ratings of the Beliefs About the Behaviors

The percentage of respondents viewing a behavior as ethical under most or all conditions was invariably less than the percentage viewing it as never ethical or ethical under only some or rare conditions. A majority of the 1,108 respondents rated five behaviors as *never ethical*: sexual activity with a client before

TABLE 2

Factor Indices for Ethicality Ratings

Item	Loading
Factor 1: Incidental Involvements	
Accepting a gift worth under $10	.83
Accepting a client's invitation to a special occasion	.43
Accepting a gift worth over $50	.68
Factor 2: Social/Financial Involvements	
Accepting a service or product as payment for therapy	.61
Becoming friends with a client after termination	.68
Selling a product to a client	.66
Engaging in sexual activity with a client after termination	.68
Disclosing details of one's current personal stresses to a client	.42
Inviting clients to an office/clinic open house	.76
Employing a client	.70
Going out to eat with a client after a session	.74
Buying goods or services from a client	.63
Inviting clients for a personal party or social event	.68
Factor 3: Dual Professional Roles	
Providing therapy to a then-current employee	.57
Providing individual therapy to a relative, friend, or lover of an ongoing client	.51
Allowing a client to enroll in one's class for a grade	.70
Providing therapy to a current student or supervisee	.83

termination of therapy (98.3%; $n = 1,089$), selling a product to a client (70.8%; $n = 784$), sexual activity with a client after termination of therapy (68.4%; $n = 758$), inviting clients to a personal party or social event (63.5%; $n = 704$), and providing therapy to an employee (57.9%; $n = 641$). In only two cases did fewer than 10% of the respondents rate a behavior as never ethical: accepting an invitation to a client's special occasion (6.3%; $n = 70$) and accepting a gift worth less than $10 (3.0%; $n = 33$). Fewer than 10% of the respondents were uncertain about the degree to which any particular item was ethical.

. . . Thus behaviors that are directly prohibited by the Ethical Principles (APA, 1981) or other formal policy statements appear to be endorsed as presenting more serious ethical problems than the other behaviors.

Ratings of the Frequency of the Behaviors

For all behaviors, the percentage of respondents who had reportedly engaged in the behavior with few or no clients was greater than the percentage who had done so with some, most, or all clients. There were only two behaviors in which a majority of the 1,021 participants had engaged with at least one client: accepting a gift worth less than $10 (85.2%; $n = 870$) and providing concurrent individual therapy to a client's significant other (61.2%; $n = 625$). The behavior with the lowest reported frequency was sexual relations with a client before termination of therapy (0.5%; $n = 5$). Overall, these results suggest that the average respondent had engaged in most of the behaviors with few or no clients.

Behaviors and Beliefs as a Function of Profession

This study permits the first direct comparison of the behaviors of the three major mental health professions in terms of sexual and nonsexual dual relationships. Although psychologists tended to engage with greater frequency in incidental involvements, there was *no significant difference* among the professions in terms of (a) sexual intimacies with clients before or after termination of therapy, (b) nonsexual dual professional roles, (c) social involvements, or (d) financial involvements with patients. . . .

Behaviors and Beliefs as a Function of Theoretical Orientation

One of the most consistent findings was that to a significantly greater degree than their colleagues, psychodynamically oriented clinicians affirmed the unethical nature of dual professional, financial, and social involvements of the type that have been prohibited explicitly through, for example, the formal ethical policy of the APA, and they refused to engage in these activities. It is possible that training in psychodynamic therapy promotes greater awareness of the importance of clear, nonexploitive, and therapeutically oriented roles, boundaries, and tasks, as well as of the sometimes subtle but potentially far-reaching consequences of violating these norms. . . . Furthermore, psychodynamic training, with its attention to the needs, motives, and desires of the therapist, may better enable its practitioners to recognize and avoid exploitive relationships that advance the welfare or pleasure of the therapist at the expense of the client. . . .

TABLE 3

Percentage of Clinicians (*N* = 1,021) Responding in Each Practice Category

Item	Rating					
	1	2	3	4	5	NR
Accepted a gift worth under $10	14.0	56.5	11.3	5.9	11.5	0.8
Accepted a client's invitation to a special occasion	64.0	28.0	3.3	2.4	1.4	0.8
Accepted a service or product as payment for therapy	82.6	13.9	2.8	0.2	0.1	0.8
Became friends with a client after termination	69.0	26.5	3.2	0.2	0.3	0.7
Sold a product to a client	97.1	1.4	0.7	0.0	0.1	0.7
Accepted a gift worth over $50	92.4	5.8	0.3	0.2	0.2	1.1
Provided therapy to an employee	87.5	9.3	1.7	0.3	0.2	1.1
Engaged in sexual activity with a client after termination	95.3	3.9	0.0	0.0	0.0	0.8
Borrowed less than $5 from a client	97.0	1.7	0.0	0.2	0.1	1.1
Disclosed details of current personal stresses to a client	60.1	30.7	7.4	0.6	0.2	1.0
Borrowed over $20 from a client	98.7	0.1	0.1	0.0	0.0	1.1
Invited clients to an office/clinic open house	88.7	3.7	3.5	1.1	2.0	0.9
Employed a client	91.2	7.5	0.4	0.1	0.0	0.8
Went out to eat with a client after a session	87.4	10.5	0.9	0.2	0.0	1.1
Bought goods or services from a client	77.6	20.5	1.1	0.1	0.0	0.8
Engaged in sexual activity with a current client	98.7	0.4	0.1	0.0	0.0	0.8
Invited clients to a personal party or social event	92.1	6.7	0.3	0.2	0.0	0.8
Provided individual therapy to a relative, friend, or lover of an ongoing client	38.0	36.0	21.6	2.1	1.4	0.8
Provided therapy to a then-current student or supervisee	88.9	8.4	1.5	0.2	0.1	0.9
Allowed a client to enroll in one's class for a grade	95.2	2.3	1.1	0.1	0.3	1.3

Note. Rating codes for proportion of clients with whom clinician has engaged in the behavior: 1 = *no clients or no opportunity* (combines both categories), 2 = *few clients*, 3 = *some clients*, 4 = *most clients*, 5 = *all clients*, NR = *no response* (i.e., missing data). Rows may not sum to 100% because of rounding.

References

American Psychological Association (1981). Ethical principles of psychologists. *American Psychologist, 36,* 633–638.

Gartrell, N., Herman, J., Olarte, S., Feldstein, M., & Localio, R. (1987). Psychiatrist–patient sexual contact: Results of a national survey, I: Prevalence. *American Journal of Psychiatry, 143,* 1126–1131.

Holroyd, J. C., & Brodsky, A. M. (1977). Psychologists' attitudes and practices regarding erotic and nonerotic physical contact with clients. *American Psychologist, 32,* 843–849.

Pope, K. S., Keith-Spiegel, P., & Tabachnick, B. (1986). Sexual attraction to clients: The human psychologist and the (sometimes) inhuman training system. *American Psychologist, 41,* 147–158.

Pope, K. S., Tabachnick, B. G., & Keith-Spiegel, P. (1987). Ethics of practice: The beliefs and behaviors of psychologists as therapists. *American Psychologist, 42,* 993–1006.

The Concept of Boundaries in Clinical Practice: Theoretical and Risk-Management Dimensions

Thomas G. Gutheil and Glen O. Gabbard

. . .

ROLE

Role boundaries constitute the essential boundary issue. To conceptualize this entity, one might ask, "Is this what a therapist does?" Although subject to ideological variations, this touchstone question not only identifies the question of clinical role but serves as a useful orienting device for avoiding the pitfalls of role violations.

> A middle-aged borderline patient, attempting to convey how deeply distressed she felt about her situation, leaped from her chair in the therapist's office and threw herself to her knees at the therapist's feet, clasping his hand in both of her own and crying, "Do you understand how awful it's been for me?" The therapist said gently, "You know, this is really interesting, what's happening here—but it isn't therapy; please go back to your chair." The patient did so, and the incident was explored verbally.

Although such limit setting may appear brusque to some clinicians, it may be the only appropriate response to halt boundary-violating "acting in" (especially of the impulsive or precipitous kind) and to make the behavior available for analysis as part of the therapy.

Almost all patients who enter into a psychotherapeutic process struggle with the unconscious wish to view the therapist as the ideal parent who, unlike the real parents, will gratify all their childhood wishes (19). As a result of the longings stirred up by the basic transference situation of psychotherapy or psychoanalysis, it is imperative that some degree of abstinence be maintained (20). However, strict abstinence is neither desirable nor possible, and total frustration of all the patient's wishes creates a powerful influence on the patient in its own right (8, 19).

In attempting to delineate the appropriate role for the therapist via-à-vis the patient's wishes and longings to be loved and held, it is useful to differentiate between "libidinal demands," which cannot be gratified without entering into ethical transgressions and damaging enactments, and "growth needs," which prevent growth if not gratified to some extent (21). Greenson (22) made a similar distinction when he noted that the rule of abstinence was constructed to avoid the gratification of a patient's neurotic and infantile wishes, not to lead to a sterile form of treatment in which all the patient's wishes are frustrated. . . .

TIME

Time is, of course, a boundary, defining the limits of the session itself while providing structure and even containment for many patients, who derive reassurance because they will have to experience the various stresses of reminiscing, reliving, and so forth for a set time only. The beginnings and endings of sessions—starting or stopping late or early—are both susceptible to crossings of this boundary. Such crossings may be subtle or stark.

> A male psychiatrist came in to the hospital to see his female inpatient for marathon sessions at odd times, such as

from 2:00 to 6:00 in the morning, rationalizing that this procedure was dictated by scheduling problems. This relationship eventually became overtly sexual.

An interesting prejudice about violating the boundary of time has evolved in sexual misconduct cases, a prejudice deriving from the fact that a clinician interested in having a sexual relationship with a patient might well schedule that patient for the last hour of the day (although, of course, after-work time slots have always been popular). In the fog of uncertainty surrounding sexual misconduct (usually a conflict of credibilities without witnesses), this factor has gleamed with so illusory a brightness that some attorneys seem to presume that because the patient had the last appointment of the day, sexual misconduct occurred! Short of seeing patients straight through the night, this problem does not seem to have a clear solution. Admittedly, however, from a risk-management standpoint, a patient in the midst of an intense erotic transference to the therapist might best be seen, when possible, during high-traffic times when other people (e.g., secretaries, receptionists, and even other patients) are around. . . .

PLACE AND SPACE

The therapist's office or a room on a hospital unit is obviously the locale for almost all therapy; some exceptions are noted in the next section. Exceptions usually constitute boundary crossing but are not always harmful. Some examples include accompanying a patient to court for a hearing, visiting a patient at home, and seeing a patient in the intensive care unit after an overdose or in jail after an arrest.

Some boundary crossings of place can have a constructive effect. As with medication, the timing and dosage are critical.

> After initially agreeing to attend his analysand's wedding, the analyst later declined, reasoning that his presence would be inappropriately distracting. Later, after the death of the analysand's first child, he attended the funeral service. Both his absence at the first occasion and his presence at the second were felt as helpful and supportive by

the analysand. They both agreed later that the initial plan to attend the wedding was an error.

A relevant lesson from this example is that boundary violations can be reversed or undone with further consideration and discussion. At times, an apology by the therapist is appropriate and even necessary. . . .

Sorties out of the office usually merit special scrutiny. While home visits were a central component of the community psychiatry movement, the shift in the professional climate is such that the modern clinician is best advised to perform this valuable service with an opposite-sex chaperon and to document the event in some detail.

Sessions during lunch are an extremely common form of boundary violation. This event appears to be a common way station along the path of increasing boundary crossings culminating in sexual misconduct. Although clinicians often advance the claim that therapy is going on, so, inevitably, is much purely social behavior; it does not *look* like therapy, at least to a jury. Lunch sessions are not uncommonly followed by sessions during dinner, then just dinners, then other dating behavior, eventually including intercourse.

Sessions in cars represent another violation of place. Typically, the clinician gives the patient a ride home under various circumstances. Clinician and patient then park (e.g., in front of the patient's house) and finish up the presumably therapeutic conversation. From a fact finder's viewpoint, many exciting things happen in cars, but therapy is usually not one of them.

The complexity of the matter increases, however, when we consider other therapeutic ideologies. For example, it would not be a boundary violation for a behaviorist, under certain circumstances, to accompany a patient in a car, to an elevator, to an airplane, or even to a public restroom (in the treatment of paruresis, the fear of urinating in a public restroom) as part of the treatment plan for a particular phobia. The existence of a body of professional literature, a clinical rationale, and risk–benefit documentation will be useful in protecting the clinician in such a situation from misconstruction of the therapeutic efforts.

MONEY

Money is a boundary in the sense of defining the business nature of the therapeutic relationship. This is not love, it's work. Indeed, some would argue that the fee received by the therapist is the only appropriate and allowable material gratification to be derived from clinical work (28). Patient and clinician may each have conflicts about this distinction (29), but consultative experience makes clear that trouble begins precisely when the therapist stops thinking of therapy as work.

On the other hand, most clinicians learned their trade by working with indigent patients and feel that some attempt should be made to pay back the debt by seeing some patients for free—a form of "tithing," if you will. Note that this *decision*—to see a patient for free and to discuss that with the patient—is quite different from simply letting the billing lapse or allowing the debt to mount. The latter examples are boundary crossings, perhaps violations.

Consultative experience also suggests that the usual problem underlying a patient's mounting debt is the clinician's conflict about money and its dynamic meanings. Initially reluctant to bring up the unpaid bill, the clinician may soon become too angry to discuss it. Explorations of the dynamic meaning of the bill are more convincing when they do not take place through clenched teeth. A clinician stuck at this countertransference point may simply let it slide. In the minds of fact finders, this raises a question: "The clinician seems curiously indifferent to making a living; could the patient be paying in some other currency?"—a line of speculation one does not wish to foster.

In rural areas even today, payments to physicians may take the form of barter: when the doctor delivers your child, you pay with two chickens and the new calf. For the dynamic therapist this practice poses some problems, because it blurs the boundary between payment and gift (covered in the next section). The clinician should take a case at a reasonable fee or make a *decision* to see the patient for a low fee (e.g., one dollar) or none. Barter is confusing and probably ill-advised today. Of course, all such decisions require documentation.

GIFTS, SERVICES, AND RELATED MATTERS

A client became very upset during an interview with her therapist and began to cry. The therapist, proffering a tissue, held out a hand-tooled Florentine leather case in which a pocket pack of tissues had been placed. After the patient had withdrawn a tissue, the therapist impulsively said, "Why don't you keep the case?" In subsequent supervision the therapist came to understand that this "gift" to the patient was an unconscious bribe designed to avert the anger that the therapist sensed just below the surface of the patient's sorrow.

This gift was also a boundary violation, placing unidentified obligations on the patient and constituting a form of impulsive acting in. A related boundary violation is the use of favors or services from the patient for the benefit of the therapist, as Simon's startling vignette illustrates:

Within a few months of starting . . . psychotherapy, the patient was returning the therapist's library books for him "as a favor." . . . The patient began having trouble paying her treatment bill, so she agreed—at the therapist's suggestion—to clean the therapist's office once a week in partial payment. . . . The patient also agreed to get the therapist's lunch at a nearby delicatessen before each session. (6, p. 106)

The obvious exploitive nature of these boundary violations destroys even the semblance of therapy for the patient's benefit. . . .

In contrast to the potentially harmful or at least confusing effects of the preceding examples, compare the practice (not uncommon among psychopharmacologists) of giving patients, as part of treatment, educational texts designed for laypersons (e.g., giving *Moodswing* [31] to a patient with bipolar disorder). Such a boundary crossing may foster mastery of the illness through information—a positive result. A similar point might be made for judicious "gifts" of medication samples for indigent patients. These two instances represent clear boundary crossings that have some justification. Ideally, even these should be discussed with an ear to any possible negative effects.

> A patient in long-term therapy had struggled for years with apparent infertility and eventually, with great difficulty, arranged for adoption of a child. Two years later she unexpectedly conceived and finally gave birth. Her therapist, appreciating the power and meaning of this event, sent congratulatory flowers to the hospital.

In this case, the therapist followed social convention in a way that—though technically a boundary crossing—represented a response appropriate to the real relationship. Offering a tissue to a crying patient and expressing condolences to a bereaved one are similar examples of appropriate responses outside the classic boundaries of the therapeutic relationship.

CLOTHING

Clothing represents a social boundary the transgression of which is usually inappropriate to the therapeutic situation, yet a patient may appropriately be asked to roll up a sleeve to permit measurement of blood pressure. Excessively revealing or frankly seductive clothing worn by the therapist may represent a boundary violation with potentially harmful effects to patients[.] . . .

Berne (32) noted the technical error of the male clinician who, confronting a patient whose skirt was pulled up high, began to explain to the patient his sexual fantasies in response to this event. Berne suggested instead saying to the patient, "Pull your skirt down." Similar directness of limit setting appears to be suited to the patient who—either from psychosis or the wish to provoke—begins to take off her clothes in the office. As before, the comment, "This behavior is inappropriate, and it isn't therapy; please put your clothes back on," said in a calm voice, is a reasonable response.

LANGUAGE

As part of the otherwise laudable efforts to humanize and demystify psychiatry a few decades back, the use of a patient's first name was very much in vogue. While this may indeed convey greater warmth and closeness, such usage is a two-edged sword. There is always the possibility that patients may experience the use of first names as misrepresenting the professional relationship as a social friendship (28). There may well be instances when using first names is appropriate, but therapists must carefully consider whether they are creating a false sense of intimacy that may subsequently backfire. . . .

There are distinct advantages to addressing the adult in the patient, in terms of fostering the adult observing ego for the alliance. Trainees often do not see the paradox of expecting adult behavior on the ward from someone they themselves call "Jimmy," which is what people called the patient when he was much younger. Last names also emphasize that this process is work or business, an atmosphere which may promote a valuable mature perspective and minimize acting out. In addition, calling someone by the name used by primary objects may foster transference perceptions of the therapist when they are not desirable, as with a borderline patient prone to forming severe psychotic transferences. For balance, however, recall that use of last names may also sound excessively distant, formal, and aloof. . . .

SELF-DISCLOSURE AND RELATED MATTERS

Few clinicians would argue that the therapist's self-disclosure is always a boundary crossing. Psychoanalysis and intensive psychotherapy involve intense personal relationships. A useful therapeutic alliance may be forged by the therapist's willingness to acknowledge that a painful experience of the patient is familiar to himself (19). However, when a therapist begins to indulge in even mild forms of self-disclosure, it is an indication for careful self-scrutiny regarding the motivations for departure from the usual therapeutic stance. Gorkin (33) observed that many therapists harbor a wish to be known by their patients as a "real person," especially as the termination of the therapy approaches. While it may be technically correct for a therapist to become more spontaneous at the end of the therapeutic process, therapists who become more self-disclosing as the therapy ends must be sure that their reasons for doing so are not related to their own unfulfilled needs in their private lives but, rather, are based on an objective assessment that increased focus on the real relationship is useful for the patient in the termination process.

Self-disclosure, however, represents a complex issue. Clearly, therapists may occasionally use a neutral example from their own lives to illustrate a point. Sharing the impact of a borderline patient's behavior on the therapist may also be useful. The therapist's self-revelation, however, of personal fantasies or dreams; of social, sexual, or financial details; of specific vacation plans; or of expected births or deaths in the family is usually burdening the patient with information, whereas it is the patient's fantasies that might best be explored. The issue is somewhat controversial: a number of patients (and, surprisingly, some therapists) believe that the patient is somehow entitled to this kind of information. In any case, it is a boundary violation and as such may be used by the legal system to advance or support a claim of sexual misconduct. The reasoning is that the patient knows so much about the therapist's personal life that they must have been intimate[.] . . .

Finally, the boundary can be violated from the other side. An example would be the therapist's using data from the therapy session for personal gain, such as insider information on stock trading, huge profits to be made in real estate, and the like.

PHYSICAL CONTACT

. . . [Professionals] working with a patient with AIDS or HIV seropositivity often describe wishing to touch the patient in some benign manner (pat the back, squeeze an arm, pat a hand) in every session. They reason that such patients feel like lepers, and therapeutic touch is called for in these cases. But even such humane interventions must be scrutinized and, indeed, be documented to prevent their misconstruction in today's climate.

From the viewpoint of current risk-management principles, a handshake is about the limit of social physical contact at this time. Of course, a patient

who attempts a hug in the last session after 7 years of intense, intensive, and successful therapy should probably not be hurled across the room. However, most hugs from patients should be discouraged in tactful, gentle ways by words, body language, positioning, and so forth. Patients who deliberately or provocatively throw their arms around the therapist despite repeated efforts at discouragement should be stopped. An appropriate response is to step back, catch both wrists in your hands, cross the patient's wrists in front of you, so that the crossed arms form a barrier between bodies, and say firmly, "Therapy is a talking relationship; please sit down so we can discuss your not doing this any more." If the work degenerates into grabbing, consider seriously termination and referral, perhaps to a therapist of a different gender.

What is one to make of the brands of therapy that include physical contact, such as Rolfing? Presumably, the boundary extends to that limited physical contact, and the patient expects it and grants consent; thus, no actual violation occurs. Massage therapists may struggle with similar issues, however. In other ideologies the issue may again be the impact of the appearance of a violation:

> A therapist—who claimed that her school of practice involved hugging her female patient at the beginning and end of every session, without apparent harm—eventually had to terminate therapy with the patient for noncompliance with the therapeutic plan. The enraged patient filed a sexual misconduct claim against the therapist. Despite the evidence showing that this claim was probably false (a specious suit triggered by rage at the therapist), the insurer settled because of the likelihood that a jury would not accept the principle of "hug at the start and hug at the end but no hugs in between." If the claim was indeed false, this is a settlement based on boundary violations alone.

At another level this vignette nicely suggests how nonsexual boundary violations may be harmful to a patient in much the same way that actual sexual misconduct is. Instead of engaging the patient in a mourning process to deal with the resentment and grief about the deprivations of her childhood, the therapist who hugs a patient is often attempting to provide the physical contact normally offered by a parent. The patient then feels entitled to more demonstrations of caring and assumes that if gratification in the form of hugs is available, other wishes will be granted as well (compare Smith's concept of the "golden fantasy" that all needs will be met by therapy [34]). When actual physical contact occurs, the crucial psychotherapeutic distinction between the symbolic and the concrete is lost (21), and the patient may feel that powerful infantile longings within will finally be satisfied. . . .

References

6. Simon RI: Sexual exploitation of patients. how it begins before it happens. Psychiatr Annals 1989; 19:104–122

8. Lipton SD: The advantages of Freud's technique as shown in his analysis of the Rat Man. Int J Psychoanal 1977; 58:255–273

19. Viederman M: The real person of the analyst and his role in the process of psychoanalytic cure. J Am Psychoanal Assoc 1991; 39:451–489

20. Novey R: The abstinence of the psychoanalyst. Bull Menninger Clin 1991; 55:344–362

21. Casement PJ: The meeting of needs in psychoanalysis. Psychoanal Inquiry 1990; 10:325–346

22. Greenson RR: The Technique of Psychoanalysis, vol 1. New York, International Universities Press, 1967

28. Epstein RS, Simon RI: The exploitation index: an early warning indicator of boundary violations in psychotherapy. Bull Menninger Clin 1990; 54:450–465

29. Krueger DW (ed): The Last Taboo: Money As Symbol and Reality in Psychotherapy and Psychoanalysis. New York, Brunner/Mazel, 1986

31. Fieve R: Moodswing: The Third Revolution in Psychiatry. New York, Bantam Books, 1976

32. Berne E: What Do You Say After You Say Hello? The Psychology of Human Destiny. New York, Grove Press, 1972

33. Gorkin M: The Uses of Countertransference. Northvale, NJ, Jason Aronson, 1987

34. Smith S: The golden fantasy: a regressive reaction to separation anxiety. Int J Psychoanal 1977; 58:311–324

◆ ◆ ◆

Commentary: "*The true base rate of sexual misconduct among psychologists is not known*" *(p. 455). See Gottlieb, M. (1990). Accusation of sexual misconduct: Assisting in the complaint process.* Professional Psychology: Research and Practice, 21, 455–461. *In part, that is because of the methodological problems involved in gathering data about sexual intimacies with clients. See, for example, Williams, M. H. (1992). Exploitation and inference: Mapping the damage from therapist–patient sexual involvement.* American Psychologist, 47, 412–421. *Nevertheless,*

> *the American Psychological Association's Ethics Committee [in 1991] reported that exploitation of clients, including sexual acting out, is the most frequently investigated complaint. Additionally, the APA [Insurance] Trust reported that 53 cents out of each malpractice dollar goes to sexual misconduct. (p. 168)*

See Rodolfa, E., Hall, T., Holms, V., Davena, A., Komatz, D., Antunez, M., & Hall, A. (1994). The management of sexual feelings in therapy. Professional Psychology: Research and Practice, 25, 168–172.

Keeping in mind these methodological issues, Pope (1993) compiled the following helpful and intriguing data that has been gathered over the past 2 decades.

Licensing Disciplinary Actions for Psychologists Who Have Been Sexually Involved With a Client: Some Information About Offenders

Kenneth S. Pope

. . .

TABLE 1

Self-Report Studies of Sex With Clients, Using National Samples of Psychologists

Study	Publication Date	N	Return Rate (%)	Subjects Male (%)	Subjects Female (%)
1. Holroyd & Brodsky	1977	1,000	70	12.1	2.6
2. Pope, Levenson, & Schover	1979	1,000	48	12.0	3.0
3. Pope, Keith-Spiegel, & Tabachnick	1986	1,000	58.5	9.4	2.5
4. Pope, Tabachnick, & Keith-Spiegel[a]	1987	1,000	46	3.6	0.4
5. Akamatsu[b]	1988	1,000	39.5	3.5	2.3
6. Borys & Pope[c]	1989	1,600	56.5	1.0	0.4

Note. Exceptional caution is warranted in comparing the data from these various surveys. For example, the frequently cited percentages of 12.1 and 2.6, reported by Holroyd and Brodsky (1977), exclude same-sex intimacies. Moreover, when surveys included separate items to assess posttermination sexual involvement, these data are reported in footnotes in this table. Finally, some published articles did not provide sufficiently detailed data for this table (e.g., return rate and frequencies for psychologists in an article reporting aggregate data for psychologists, social workers, and psychiatrists; percentages of male and female psychologists' responses to an item); the investigators supplied the data needed for the table. Although the gender percentages presented in the table for Studies 2–6 represent responses to one basic survey item in each survey, the percentages presented for Study 1 span several items. The study's senior author confirmed through personal communication to me that the study's findings were that 12.1% of the male and 2.6% of the female participants reported having engaged in erotic contact (whether or not it included intercourse) with at least one opposite-sex patient; that about 4% of the male and 1% of the female participants reported engaging in erotic contact with at least one same-sex patient; and that, in response to a separate survey item, 7.2% of the male and 0.6% of the female psychologists reported that they had "had intercourse with a patient within three months after terminating therapy" (p. 846).

[a]The survey also included a question about "becoming sexually involved with a former client" (p. 996). Gender percentages about sex with current or former clients did not appear in the article but were provided by an author. Fourteen percent of the male and 8% of the female respondents reported sex with a former client.

[b]The original article also noted that 14.2% of male and 4.7% of female psychologists reported that they had "been involved in an intimate relationship with a former client" (p. 454).

[c]The original article also asked if respondents had "engaged in sexual activity with a client after termination" (p. 288). Gender percentages for psychologists, which did not appear in the article but were supplied by an author, were 10.5% for male and 2.0% for female psychologists. . . .

Adapted from *Professional Psychology: Research and Practice, 24,* 374–377. Copyright 1993 by the American Psychological Association. Table 2 has been omitted.

References

Akamatsu, T. J. (1988). Intimate relationships with former clients: National survey of attitudes and behavior among practitioners. *Professional Psychology: Research and Practice, 19,* 454–458.

Borys, D. S., & Pope, K. S. (1989). Dual relationships between therapist and client: A national study of psychologists, psychiatrists, and social workers. *Professional Psychology: Research and Practice, 20,* 283–293.

Holroyd, J. C., & Brodsky, A. M. (1977). Psychologists' attitudes and practices regarding erotic and nonerotic physical contact with patients. *American Psychologist, 32,* 843–849.

Pope, K. S., Keith-Spiegel, P., & Tabachnick, B. G. (1986). Sexual attraction to clients: The human therapist and the (sometimes) inhuman training system. *American Psychologist, 41,* 147–158.

Pope, K. S., Levenson, H., & Schover, L. R. (1979). Sexual intimacy in psychology training: Results and implications of a national survey. *American Psychologist, 34,* 682–689.

Pope, K. S., Tabachnick, B. G., & Keith-Spiegel, P. (1987). Ethics of practice: The beliefs and behaviors of psychologists as therapists. *American Psychologist, 42,* 993–1006.

◆ ◆ ◆

Commentary: What explains the trend toward an increasingly lower incidence of self-reported sexual intimacies with clients by psychologists?

In light of the issues and arguments contained so far in this chapter, readers may profit from discussing the sexually oriented dual-relationship vignettes presented in chapters 2 and 3, as well as the following hypothetical but realistic vignette from Hall, J. E. (1987). Gender-related ethical dilemmas and ethics education. Professional Psychology: Research and Practice, 18, 573–579:

> *A psychologist in a full-time, solo private practice advertises that he limits his practice to marital problems. In 20 years in private practice, he has been successful in solving his clients' marital problems but not in saving his own marriage. Because he works 60–70 hr per week, he is able to avoid focusing on his own problems.*

> *His secretary schedules his 5:00 opening with a new client, a 35-year-old married woman, and leaves to catch the 5:00 bus. The client impresses him as someone in need of confirmation of her own worth; after several sessions she admits that she was molested as a child by her father and that her sexual relationship with her husband is both unsatisfactory and coerced. After 3 months pass, the psychologist realizes that he is looking forward to seeing his client each week and is beginning to feel sexually attracted to her. (p. 575)*

Hall (1987) suggested several choices that the male psychologist might make:

1. *Deny attraction to the client as well as "their vulnerability to each other" and continue to see the client in therapy;*

2. *Consult with a colleague and ask for peer supervision on the case;*

3. *Tell the client that it is unethical to have a sexual relationship with her and, therefore, that he must terminate the therapeutic relationship immediately;*

4. *Tell the client that it is unethical to have a sexual relationship with her, and suggest that if they terminate therapy and she initiates treatment with another therapist they could see each other socially after a reasonable period of time; or*

5. *Provide a referral to another therapist, and explain to the client that he cannot help her and that the other therapist is better qualified. He then seeks therapy for himself.*

What boundary violations occurred in this situation? What standards of the 1992 APA Ethical Principles are implicated? Which of these options are in accord with those provisions? Which options are unethical? Which simply reflect poor judgment? See the original article for Hall's own perspectives on each option.

It is noteworthy that Hall did not list an option in which the therapist, after careful evaluation, concludes that the client is not psychotic and is capable of making competent judgments, discusses the issue thoroughly with the client, and decides (with the client's consent) to continue therapy while beginning a social and romantic relationship with her. Are there any conditions under which such an option would be ethical? This response by Pope, Sonne, and Holroyd (1993) represents the professional consensus:

> Under no circumstances should a therapist ever engage in sexual intimacies with a patient. No matter what the situation. No matter who the patient. No matter what the patient has said and done. No matter how the therapist or the patient feels. Therapist–patient sexual intimacies are in all instances wrong and must be avoided. (p. 180)

See Pope, K. S., Sonne, J. L., & Holroyd, J. (1993). Sexual feelings in psychotherapy. Washington, DC: American Psychological Association.

Are there any reasonable counterarguments to this consensus that one can put forth, under the conditions I have described above?

Although there is near unanimity regarding sexual intimacies with current clients, professional opinions do diverge over the propriety of absolutely prohibiting sexual intimacies with former clients. In one survey, Sell, Gottlieb, and Schoenfeld (1986) found that, of 54 cases before ethics committees and 48 cases before state licensing boards involving sexual intimacies, not one psychologist was exonerated solely because the adjudicating body agreed that a sufficient amount of time had elapsed between termination of treatment and initiation of a sexual relationship. However, they also found that very few of these bodies had developed guidelines to determine whether sexual relationships between psychologists and former clients would be permissible. Sell et al. urged APA to amend the Ethical Principles to create an absolute ban on sexual intimacies between psychologists and either current or former clients. See Sell, J. M., Gottlieb, M. C., & Schoenfeld, L. (1986). Ethical considerations and social/romantic relationships with present and former clients. Professional Psychology: Research and Practice, 17, 504–508.

In a later survey (Akamatsu, 1988) of 395 members of APA Division 29 (Psychotherapy), 44.7% said that intimate relationships with former clients were highly unethical. However, 31.3% felt that such relationships were neither ethical nor unethical, or even felt them to be ethical to some degree; 23.9% felt that such relationships were only somewhat unethical. The primary factor that respondents stated should be taken into account in determining whether posttherapy intimacy was ethical was time since termination. Other factors included the length and nature of therapy, the mental health of the client, whether therapy would resume, and promotion of the patient's freedom of choice. Interestingly, 14.2% of men and 4.7% of women admitted to intimate relationships with former patients. The average interval between termination and the commencement of the relationship was 15.6 months. See Akamatsu, T. J. (1988). Intimate relationships with former clients: National survey of attitudes and behavior among practitioners. Professional Psychology: Research and Practice, 19, 454–458. Akamatsu then concluded as follows:

> My results strongly suggest that ethical guidelines be established by the APA. However, because of the divergent interpretations possible for current results, it may be that the recommendations . . . for a blanket prohibition of sexual intimacies with clients and former clients is more conservative than the views of many practitioners. Guidelines clearly are necessary, but they should delineate contingencies or circumstances that might be considered in determining the ethics of a particular case. This compromise would probably necessitate the individual handling of each case, but the task would be made considerably easier if guidelines were clear to therapists and their state boards or ethics committees. (p. 457)

As events transpired, Akamatsu's (1988) conjecture that an absolute ban on sex with former clients would not gain consensus turned out to be correct. The 1992 Ethical Principles retains an unconditional prohibition on sexual intimacies with current clients (Standard 4.05), but limits the prohibition to 2 years after termination for intimacy with former therapy patients. After that, however, the burden is on the psychologist to show that the development of a sexual relationship is a "most unusual circumstance" and that there has been no exploitation of the former client as a result of the relationship, considering all the factors set out in Standard 4.07.

Is Standard 4.07 sufficiently specific, and does it take into account all of the factors that should be balanced in developing a reasonable rule? Does it go far enough to protect psychotherapy clients, or does even a 2-year ban interfere with autonomous decision making, as long as both parties are adults and there is appropriate disclosure of the risks to the client? Consider the following.

Explicit Ambiguity: The 1992 Ethics Code as an Oxymoron

Donald N. Bersoff

. . .

Gabbard (1994) raised and rebutted "nine arguments frequently set forth as favoring a policy permitting posttermination sexual involvements" (p. 331). He called this permissive policy "premature" (p. 334), however, and urged the APA to permanently bar any sexual intimacies with former therapy clients. In support of his argument, he, as well as many others (Brown, 1988; Gabbard & Pope, 1989; Sell, Gottlieb, & Schoenfeld, 1986; Shopland & VandeCreek, 1991; Vasquez, 1991), provided powerful reasons for such a ban.

There may be excellent reasons for reconsidering the APA's position, and it is worthy of further debate. Certainly, Standard 4.07, as currently written or as it might be revised to bar sexual relations in perpetuity, does reflect such central moral principles as non-maleficence and beneficence (Beauchamp & Childress, 1989; Bersoff & Koeppl, 1993; Kitchener, 1984). In considering the validity of the current provision or its alternative, however, I suggest that other competing moral or ethical principles be kept in mind. Foremost among those competing principles is autonomy—"forebearing from interfering in the expression of self-determination by those who wish to make decisions for themselves" (Bersoff, 1992, pp. 1569–1570). Society in general and our professional association in particular should be committed to, among other values, respecting each individual's right to choose his or her own fate, even if the choices the individual makes do not serve, in some objective sense, what the majority would consider to be the individual's best interests. To use a more felicitous translation of this idea, "autonomy in a democratic society might be defined as an adult's capacity to choose what his parents might not have chosen for him or for themselves" (Burt, 1975, p. 126).

Concern about posttermination sexual intimacies, at least in part, is predicated on the belief that there will always be an unequal relationship between the powerful therapist—usually a man—and the subservient patient—usually a woman (Gabbard, 1994; Vasquez, 1991). Coleman (1988), however, suggested that any permanent bar

> raises fundamental questions about . . . unconscious sexist motivations.
>
> The first such question is the appearance of paternalism. An absolute prohibition means [therapists] are deciding for patients that they will always be incapable of giving informed consent to a sexual relationship with their former therapists. Although such a rule ostensibly applies to both male and female patients, in reality those involved are almost exclusively women. Consequently, an absolute prohibition effectively renders female patients incapable of giving informed consent because they always remain under the influence of their male [therapists]. (p. 48)

Or to use Slovenko's (1992) crisp query, "Does transference turn women but not men into helpless waifs?" (p. 654).

That women who were once in therapy will not be able to make an informed, voluntary, and intelligent decision about their sexual partners is precisely the claim proponents make in favor of an absolute ban. There should be more data to support such a

Adapted from *Professional Psychology: Research and Practice*, 25, 382–387. Copyright 1994 by the American Psychological Association.

hypothesis, however, before it is converted into an ethical rule relegating female clients to the role of passive victims rather than reinforcing their status as autonomous, self-determining, consenting adults. . . .

References

Beauchamp, T. L., & Childress, J. F. (1989). *Principles of biomedical ethics*. New York: Oxford University Press.

Bersoff, D. N. (1992). Autonomy for vulnerable populations: The Supreme Court's reckless disregard for self-determination and social science. *Villanova Law Review, 37*, 1569–1605.

Bersoff, D. N., & Koeppl, P. M. (1993). The relation between ethical codes and moral principles. *Ethics and Behavior, 3*, 345–357.

Brown, L. S. (1988). Harmful effects of posttermination sexual and romantic relationships between therapists and their former clients. *Psychotherapy, 25*, 249–257.

Burt, R. A. (1975). Developing constitutional rights of, in, and for children. *Law and Contemporary Problems, 39*(3), 118–143.

Coleman, P. (1988). Sex between psychiatrist and former patient: A proposal for a "no harm, no foul" rule. *Oklahoma Law Review, 41*, 1–52.

Gabbard, G. O. (1994). Reconsidering the American Psychological Association's policy on sex with former patients: Is it justifiable? *Professional Psychology: Research and Practice, 25*, 329–335.

Gabbard, G. O., & Pope, K. (1989). Sexual intimacies after termination: Clinical, ethical, and legal aspects. In G. O. Gabbard (Ed.), *Sexual exploitation in professional relationships* (pp. 115–127). Washington, DC: American Psychiatric Press.

Kitchener, K. S. (1984). Intuition, critical evaluation and ethical principles: The foundation for ethical decisions in counseling psychology. *The Counseling Psychologist, 12*, 43–55.

Sell, J. M., Gottlieb, M. C., & Schoenfeld, L. S. (1986). Ethical consideration of social/romantic relationships with present and former clients. *Professional Psychology: Research and Practice, 17*, 504–508.

Shopland, S. N., & VandeCreek, L. (1991). Sex with ex-clients: Theoretical rationales for prohibition. *Ethics and Behavior, 1*, 35–44.

Slovenko, R. (1992). Undue familiarity or undue damages? *Whittier Law Review, 13*, 643–667.

Vasquez, M. (1991). Sexual intimacies with clients after termination: Should a prohibition be explicit? *Ethics and Behavior, 1*, 45–61.

◆ ◆ ◆

Commentary: Gabbard (1994; cited above) had a different role for statistics:

> *In the absence of data that would persuasively demonstrate such relationships to be harmless, the prudent course of action would be to proscribe posttermination relationships under the same rationale used to prohibit sex with* current *[emphasis added] patients. When one considers that there are 5 billion people on the planet, the choice of a former patient as a sexual partner must raise serious questions about the judgment and ethics of the psychotherapist. (p. 334)*

There are a variety of ways to discipline psychologists and other mental health professionals who violate prohibitions on sexual intimacies with their clients. These include actions by APA and state ethics committees, licensing boards, and plaintiffs bringing malpractice suits. Some insurance companies refuse to cover such conduct under professional liability policies or severely limit what they will pay to damaged plaintiff–clients, leaving the bulk of any payments to the therapist. For the most comprehensive and recent review of the issue of client–clinician sexual intimacies, including an extensive discussion of legal remedies available to clients (e.g., civil actions, administrative complaints to licensing boards, and criminal prohibitions), see Jorgenson, L., Randles, R., & Strasburger, L. (1991). The furor over psychotherapist–patient sexual contact: New solutions to an old problem. William and Mary Law Review, 32, 647–732. The passage of laws in an increasing number of states making client–therapist sex a criminal activity has continued to fuel the debate.

Criminalization of Psychotherapist–Patient Sex

Larry H. Strasburger, Linda Jorgenson, and Rebecca Randles

OVERVIEW OF CRIMINALIZATION

. . . In 1983 Wisconsin became the first state to enact a statute making psychotherapist–patient sexual exploitation a criminal offense (8). Minnesota (9), North Dakota (10), and Colorado (11) soon followed. Such statutes were adopted by California (12) and Maine (13) in 1989 and by Florida in 1990 (14). Currently, the legislatures of Iowa, Maryland, Massachusetts, New Mexico, and Pennsylvania are considering similar bills. Although seven states have criminalized the conduct, the issue is far from settled. Criminalization is a complex and controversial matter. There are a number of clinical, ethical, and legal considerations to be weighed in deciding its appropriateness as social policy.

ARGUMENTS FOR CRIMINALIZATION

Deterrence

Deterrence is the primary argument in favor of criminalization of psychotherapist–patient sexual activity. A criminal law articulates to everyone the wrongfulness of such behavior. Proponents believe that sexual contact would be restrained by an unmistakable legal message that such behavior is severely damaging and totally unconscionable backed by the threat of a felony conviction and a prison sentence. Controversy exists over the probable effectiveness of this deterrence, but among the categories of exploitative therapists (1, p. 402; 15), those who are naive, uninformed, or undergoing the effects of midlife crisis may well respond to the prospect of punishment.

Retribution

In addition to the utilitarian function of deterrence, retribution is also a primary goal of criminal statutes. . . . This morally justified retaliation constitutes a vindictive justice that metes out suffering to pay back the wrongdoers. One of the strongest arguments for criminalization may now be that sexual exploitation, in the light of the evidence documenting its ill effects on patients, is so outrageous a transgression of societal rules that retribution is called for. Although therapist behavior rooted in the character pathology of impulsive, narcissistic, or sociopathic personalities may not be deterred by criminalization, retribution for such individuals may nonetheless be socially appropriate.

Additional Redress

A criminal statute would augment existing procedures that, for one reason or another, have not functioned effectively. In the past, an exploited victim could obtain redress for sexual exploitation only through complaints to professional societies' ethics committees, complaints to licensing authorities, or lawsuits for civil damages. Each of these routes has presented problems. Ethical procedures are ponderous, often involving long delays and ineffective action from the professional societies, themselves fearful of being sued by therapists. Licensing authorities have often been unresponsive or impotent. A civil lawsuit can be very expensive and may drag on for years. Criminalization, then, provides an additional option for a victim when other avenues fail. Implementing this option, however, may itself be lengthy and be delayed by the motions of a defendant exercising due process rights.

Dealing With Unlicensed Therapists

Although no panacea, criminalization may also provide a practical way to deal with unlicensed thera-

From the *American Journal of Psychiatry*, 148, 859–863. Copyright 1991 by the American Psychiatric Association. Adapted with permission of the publisher.

pists and to incapacitate practitioners who continue to practice unregulated after their licenses have been revoked (17). Licensure boards cannot sanction them, and many of them have so few financial resources that a civil suit would be fruitless. A weakness of the criminal process, however, has been demonstrated in Minnesota, where the relatively short sentences imposed on convicted therapists have allowed them to return to practice after brief incarcerations. . . .

Money to Treat Victims

Proponents of criminalization point out that such laws can provide access to money for both prevention and treatment of victims. Minnesota, for example, has used money from federal criminal justice programs to fund educational efforts dealing with the problem (18). Money may be available to help fund ongoing victim treatment in states where public funds are dedicated to assistance of crime victims. Such financial restitution, however, may represent an unkept promise. Although funds for assistance to crime victims do exist in theory, the current austerity of state budgets has led to large cuts in the funding of such programs.

ARGUMENTS AGAINST CRIMINALIZATION

Obscuring the Issue

Paradoxically, criminalization may cause psychotherapist–patient sex to be reported even less. Colleagues may be less willing than they currently are to report an offending psychotherapist if an ethics complaint would lead to criminal charges. This might be the case despite an ethical duty to report (2) and the statutes on mandatory reporting that some states have passed (19). A patient may also be reluctant to complain, appalled at the idea that the psychotherapist would be subject to criminal sanctions. While some complainants want retribution or restitution, others may want help for their impaired therapists. Although some patients may not be aware of it, criminal prosecutions cannot proceed without their testimony, which they can choose to withhold.

Voiding Malpractice Coverage

One of the gravest concerns of victims of therapist exploitation is that criminalization may void mal-

practice insurance coverage. Although insurers continue to recognize an obligation to defend accused therapists, the trend has been to exclude paying judgments for sexual exploitation. Criminalization provides additional justification for such exclusion, as most policies specifically exclude criminal acts from coverage. Criminalization, then, may eliminate a resource that victims sorely need to finance continuing treatment. There is no victim compensation fund comparable to the therapist's malpractice policy. Although the victim may be able to reach the personal assets of the psychotherapist, these resources are frequently inadequate or nonexistent.

This concern about loss of malpractice coverage may be exaggerated. There are indications that insurers may be required to indemnify such claims even in states which have criminalizing statutes (20). Successful suits are frequently based on assertions of mishandled transference. One appellate opinion has held that in such circumstances, "It is the mishandling of transference, and not the resulting sexual conduct, which gives rise to the alleged malpractice. . . . The sexual acts are an incidental outgrowth of the primary malpractice, not the proximate cause" (21). Some plaintiffs have won lawsuits despite these exclusionary policies by alleging concurrent proximate causes for their injuries—where the injuries have been caused by both the excluded risk (sexual misconduct) and an insured risk (such as wrongful or improper termination of therapy).

Impairment of Civil Actions

Criminalization may make it more difficult for patients to win civil suits for damages. The risk of criminal prosecution certainly will make offending therapists less likely to admit their behavior. The therapist may exercise Fifth Amendment rights. This in effect will prevent the process of discovery by civil and administrative boards until the criminal trial is completed. This could delay not only an award of (money) damages but also restriction or revocation of the therapist's license by the licensing board. Even the simple matter of apology, which some victims find healing, becomes difficult in the face of a possible criminal prosecution. . . .

Inappropriate Catharsis

Victims' advocates observe that pursuit of criminal prosecution provides an anodyne to the shame and feeling of powerlessness experienced by victims of sexual exploitation. Whether this emotional relief is greater than that obtained through a civil lawsuit or action before a licensing board is unclear. Nevertheless, it may be inappropriate to use the blunt instrument of criminal law to palliate and enable victims. . . .

Loss of Control of Process

Many victims of sexual exploitation by psychotherapists feel that they have lost control of their lives, and involvement in criminal prosecution may heighten this feeling. Although some writers believe that a decision to file a criminal complaint helps recover a sense of control, the victim does not control a criminal process and civil process in the same way. Although the victim is free to choose whether or not to come forward with a complaint and a prosecutor cannot proceed if the only witness against the therapist refuses to testify, victims have been concerned that after a complaint is entered the prosecutor's decisions will determine how the case is run.

Unproven Deterrence

Although anecdotal information and common sense suggest that criminalization may act as a deterrent, there is as yet no empirical evidence to demonstrate this premise. In fact, few people even file criminal charges in states where statutes exist. Over 1,600 victims of therapist sexual contact have been seen in the Walk-In Counseling Center in Minneapolis, but Minnesota has prosecuted only nine criminal charges to date.

Absence of Rehabilitation

The absence of a provision for the rehabilitation of offenders is a major omission in the current criminal statutes. Although some sexual exploiters victimize multiple patients, appear to be without conscience, and are probably not treatable, others commit a single offense that may be a response to a situational or life cycle crisis, and these psychotherapists might benefit from treatment and be restored to social productivity. Casting these latter individuals in the role of unredeemable criminals may not be wise social policy.

SPECIAL CONSIDERATIONS
Consent

Some criminal laws, such as those against rape and indecent assault, already apply to therapist sexual misconduct. As a practical matter these laws cover only the most egregious cases, and consent of the victim is an absolute defense (17). Eliminating consent as an issue by defining psychotherapist–patient sexual contact as a specific crime provides a more effective statute. Most statutes criminalizing patient–therapist sex exclude consent as a defense, defining such contact as a crime regardless of the victim's behavior. This strict liability standard means that the only matter to be adjudicated is whether the sexual contact occurred.

Some commentators believe that removing the defense of consent in effect portrays psychotherapy patients as incompetent "presumptive sillies" (23). If this were to occur, the status of patients would clearly be stigmatized. As a practical matter, in our experience victims are not concerned that they will be demeaned through the removal of the issue of consent. Obviously, competent adults are presumed capable of consent and the law is reluctant to remove this presumption. Drawing an analogy between psychotherapy patients and rape victims, as in Masters and Johnson's original proposal, appears to infantilize them by saying that patients are ipso facto unable to consent. This, however, is not the best way to conceptualize the issue.

It is not that the victim cannot consent or that consent is improperly obtained—as through undue influence of transference or lack of information about risks. Consent is irrelevant. The issue is fiduciary breach and abuse of power in the therapeutic relationship. A fiduciary is in a position of special trust, analogous to that of a trustee, involving "a duty to act primarily for another's benefit" and requiring "scrupulous good faith and candor" (24). Trust and confidence are reposed in the therapist on the basis of a perception of social role. Even a sophisticated patient must place himself or herself in a vulnerable, less powerful position vis-à-vis a therapist who has more knowledge, training, and experience of the therapeutic process. It is the duty of the therapist as fiduciary to attend only to the needs of the patient and to do no harm. Sexual contact is countertherapeutic behavior that will harm patients. The consequences of such acts are so socially deleterious that they call for proscription regardless of consent. Attention should focus entirely on the therapist's behavior, not on that of the victim. . . .

False Accusations

For psychotherapists the possibility of having to defend themselves against false accusations of sexual misconduct is terrifying, and false accusations do occur (26). The criminal law, although it exposes the accused therapist to greater jeopardy, provides better protection against false accusations of sexual exploitation than the civil law. The standard of proof in a criminal trial is "beyond reasonable doubt," whereas in a civil trial a jury can find for the plaintiff on "the preponderance of the evidence." In an ambiguous situation a properly instructed criminal court jury should be less likely to enter a judgment against a therapist than a jury in a civil trial. In actuality the difficulty of proving a criminal case beyond reasonable doubt may make prosecutors hesitant to proceed. The vast majority of these cases involve alleged actions in an office in which only two people were present, and the evidence is limited to one person's word against another's. The narrow and specific definition of behavior in a criminal statute, which is necessary to avoid constitutional challenge of the statute on the basis of vagueness, means that a therapist may avoid criminal conviction for acts that could incur civil liability. The criminal law also offers more due process protection to the accused therapist than proceedings before licensure boards, which may allow testimony that would be excluded under strict rules of evidence and which may not be governed by a statute of limitations. . . .

References

1. Schoener G, Milgrom J, Gonsiorek J, et al: Psychotherapists' Sexual Involvement With Clients: Intervention and Prevention. Minneapolis, Walk-In Counseling Center, 1989

2. The Principles of Medical Ethics With Annotations Especially Applicable to Psychiatry. Washington, DC, American Psychiatric Association, 1989

8. Wisconsin Statutes Annotated, Section 940.22(2), 1983

9. Minnesota Statutes, Section 609.341 et seq

10. North Dakota Revised Statutes Annotated, Section 12.1-20-06.1(1) (Michie Supp 1989)

11. Colorado Revised Statutes, Section 18-3-405.5(4)(c) (Supp 1988)

12. California Business and Professional Code, Section 729 (Supp 1989)

13. Maine Revised Statutes, Title 17-A, Section 253(2)(I) (Supp 1989)

14. Florida Statutes Annotated, Section X (West 1990)

15. Pope K, Bouhoutsos J: Sexual Intimacy Between Therapists and Patients. New York, Praeger, 1986, pp 33–45

17. Jorgenson L, Randles R, Strasburger LH: The furor over psychotherapist-patient sexual contact: new solutions to an old problem. William and Mary Law Review 1991; 32:643–729

18. Sanderson B (ed): It's Never OK: A Handbook for Professionals on Sexual Exploitation by Counsellors and Therapists. St Paul, Minnesota Department of Corrections, 1989

19. Strasburger L, Jorgenson L, Randles R: Mandatory reporting of sexually exploitative psychotherapists. Bull Am Acad Psychiatry Law 1990; 18:379–384

20. Vigilant Insurance Co v Kambly, 114 Mich App 683, 319 NW 2d 382 (1982)

21. St Paul Fire and Marine Insurance Co v Love, 447 NW 2d 5 (Minn Ct App 1989)

23. Leff AA: Unconscionability and the code—the emperor's new clause. University of Pennsylvania Law Review 1967; 115:485–559

24. Black HC: Black's Law Dictionary, 4th ed. St Paul, West Publishing, 1968, p 753

26. Gutheil TG: Borderline personality disorder, boundary violations, and patient-therapist sex: medicolegal pitfalls. Am J Psychiatry 1989; 146:597–602

◆ ◆ ◆

Commentary: The issue of sexual intimacy also confronts those who train psychologists. Pope, Levensen, and Schover (1979), in a survey of 481 APA members, found that almost 10% of respondents reported sexual contact as a student with at least one of their educators. By a significant margin, more women (17%) reported such contact in comparison with men (3%). For women, the bulk of their sexual contact was with teachers, whereas for men it was with their clinical supervisors. See Pope, K. S., Levenson, H., & Schover, L. R. (1979). Sexual intimacy in psychology training. American Psychologist, 34, 682–689.

From another perspective, Pope et al. (1979) reported that 12% of psychology teachers, 4% of supervisors, and 3% of administrators disclosed sexual contact with their students (in comparison with about 7% of therapists in the survey who reported such contact with their clients). Only 2% unequivocally endorsed the benefit of educator–trainee sexual relations, 21% thought it might be beneficial, and the remainder indicated that they thought it could not be of benefit.

Based on responses to a questionnaire from 464 female members of the APA's Division 12 (Clinical Psychology), Glaser and Thorpe (1986) found much greater disapproval of sexual intimacy between students and faculty. Seventeen percent of the women reported having had sexual contact with an educator, which was essentially identical to that reported by Pope et al. However, in comparison with 77% of respondents in the Pope et al. study who believed sexual contact was damaging, Glaser and Thorpe (1986) found that "over 95% of all respondents judged such contact as unethical, coercive, and harmful to the working relationship to a considerable degree" (p. 49), even though at the time of contact most saw no ethical problems or felt coerced or exploited. See Glaser, R. D., & Thorpe, J. S. (1986). Unethical intimacy: A survey of sexual contact and advances between psychology educators and female graduate students. American Psychologist, 41, 43–51.

Although sexual intimacy is a troubling issue, other kinds of multiple relationships also occur in training and teaching settings.

The Ethics of Dual Relationships in Higher Education

Belinda Blevins-Knabe

The ethics of dual relationships between professors and students are unclear and largely unexplored. When dual relationships are discussed, it is often in the context of the therapist–client relationship (e.g., Pope, 1991). As both Matthews (1991) and Keith-Spiegel and Koocher (1985) indicated, however, there are multiple opportunities for dual relationships in the educational context.

Dual relationships in an educational setting have received relatively little attention perhaps because those in higher education are often not given explicit training on how to teach. The training that is provided does not include the ethical issues of professor–student relationships. One indicator of this is that there is very little literature on the ethics of teaching (Keith-Spiegel & Koocher, 1985). A specific example of the lack of coverage comes from the work of Glaser and Thorpe (1986), who reported that only 22% of those responding to a survey of all the female members from the 1983 Division 12 (Clinical Psychology) membership roles of the American Psychological Association (APA) had received instruction in graduate school on the issue of sexual relationships between professors and students. . . .

Several situations involve dual relationships. For example, professors may have a professional colleague, a family member, or a friend who wants to take their class; professors may have a desire to become friends with a member of a class they are currently teaching; professors may want to engage in a business relationship with a member of a current class; professors and their students may be members of the same social organization or church; professors may desire to date their current students; professors may desire to become sexually involved with current students; or professors who are also therapists may have clients who wish to take their courses. All of these situations have a possible conflict of interest, but how do we decide which ones pose a significant threat to the educational process? . . .

The teaching role is rather complex. The professor's role includes teaching, not only in the narrow sense of the specific course material involved, but also in the wider sense of modeling for students how to use authority and knowledge appropriately. Trustworthiness is part of this role. Students often reveal sensitive information to professors, as they might to a therapist or a medical doctor, and they trust professors not to use this information to exploit them. Another component of this role is objective and equitable evaluation of students. In addition, professors should provide equal learning opportunities for all students. If one student has access to a professor's notes or extended tutoring sessions, then all students should have the opportunity for such access. The final component of the professor's role is power. Inherent in the professor–student relationship is the power of the professor over the student. The power comes from two sources; the professor both evaluates the student and is the authority in the subject matter (Paludi, 1990; Zalk et al., 1990). . . . [A] step in determining the ethical risk of a relationship is to use a set of four decision criteria. . . . First, is the professorial role negatively compromised? Here it is necessary to refer back to the components of the professor's role and to remember that more is taught by a professor than course material. Students are also learning about the ethics of dealing with others. Second, is the professor exploiting the student? Two important issues are (a) the extent to which the power of the pro-

From *Ethics and Behavior*, 2, 151–163. Copyright 1992 by Erlbaum. Adapted with permission of the publisher.

fessor is responsible for establishing the relationship and (b) the extent to which a student can choose not to participate in the relationship. Third, is the professor increasing the likelihood of being exploited? This can happen in situations in which keeping the relationship secret becomes important or in situations in which the student has privileged access to the professor. Fourth, is the professor's behavior interfering with the professional roles of other faculty? At issue here is whether a professor's behavior has gone far enough beyond the appropriate professional boundaries that others must intervene.

Two themes that underlie these criteria need to be made explicit. One is that professors are professionals and as such their behavior should be governed by principles such as those specified by APA. The specific principle applying to dual relationships is that psychologists (and here professors can be substituted) should avoid dual relationships that interfere with their role as a professional. Professors must decide whether the relationship interferes with their teaching behavior. The second theme is based on virtue ethics as discussed by Jordan and Meara (1990). Virtue ethics stresses the importance of the question, "Who shall I be?" In making decisions about dual relationships, professors must ask themselves not only whether their behavior will be influenced, but also whether their professional self-concept will be influenced. The issue for the professor making a decision about a dual relationship is, "Will the integrity of my professorial self be damaged?" . . .

How does [a] sexual dual relationship between a professor and a current student fit with the decision criteria mentioned earlier? Is the professor's role negatively compromised? Yes, every aspect of the professor's role is influenced negatively by such a relationship. Assuming that the professor does not have such a relationship with all class members, the professor has taught other students that favoritism exists and that there are not equal opportunities for all. This means that the professor is discriminating based on gender and sexual preference. Female students receive the message that their sexuality is important in attracting a professor's attention, and male students have learned that in this case they do not have equal status with female students. Their resentment can lead them to trivialize the accomplishments of female students. In addition, male students may receive the message that if you are a man in a position of power it entitles you to sexual privilege (Franklin, Moglen, Zatlin-Boring, & Angress, 1981).

Is the professor exploiting the student or increasing the risk of being exploited? The professor has violated the trust of the student that he as a professional can be counted on not to exploit her. Even if the professor makes every effort to grade the student fairly, there is a perception on the part of others that the student has received unequal treatment. The student herself may question whether she has been treated fairly. The professor has also increased the risk of exploiting the student due to ill feelings once the relationship is over, and he has also increased the risk of being exploited by the student. For many students, these ill feelings can have long-term consequences. Many undergraduate students will be continuing their education and may have to take required classes either from the professor or in the professor's department, and many need letters of recommendation.

Graduate students also run risks, perhaps even greater than those of undergraduates (Schneider, 1987). Graduate students often will remain in the same department as the professor; in fact, that professor may be the only one in their speciality area. Faculty make frequent decisions about the future of graduate students in terms of who will be retained in the program and who will be given funding. Letters of recommendation are critical to getting a professional job. It is important to note that the assumption that older students or graduate students are adults and should be considered as mutually consenting in these relationships ignores the very real power of the professor. Older, more mature students are not immune to the power of the professor, and they risk damaging their careers and self-images both during and after the relationship.

Is the behavior of the professor interfering with the professional roles of other faculty? The answer to this question is likely to be yes. To the extent that the relationship between the professor and the student has become recognized, other faculty members have to spend time deciding how to ensure that all students are being treated fairly. In addition, other faculty members may find that students generalize from the behavior of one faculty member to the rest of the department and expect similar behaviors. Female faculty members may find that the message that women should be treated as sexual objects interferes with their own performance.

The discussion up to this point has focused on evaluating the decision criteria in terms of the principle of avoiding relationships that interfere with the professional role. The other issue in the decision criteria is whether the integrity of the self-concept, as it relates to the professional role, is damaged. If a professor is engaging in a relationship that involves exploitation, treating students unfairly, and burdening other faculty members, then the integrity of the professorial self-concept is likely to be damaged. It will be difficult to uphold professional standards in other situations if the answer to the question "Who am I?" is "I am a person who is willing to use my power to enter an exploitative relationship."

So far the discussion has focused on a consensual relationship between a male professor and a female student. Certainly other combinations are possible (e.g., homosexual relationships). Does the application of the decision criteria change when the genders of participants in the relationship change? To a large extent, the answer is no. . . .

What about nonsexual dual relationships? For example, what if a friend of long standing wishes to take a professor's course? In many ways this relationship poses the same problems as a sexual relationship. This type of relationship can negatively compromise the professional role of the professor. If the professor has a more intimate relationship with the friend than other students, this can interfere with evaluating the student objectively and with treating other students fairly. Other students may feel that it is "not what you know, but who you know" that is important for success. By engaging in this dual relationship, the professor may be increasing the risk of exploiting the student and the risk of being exploited. The friend, who is now a student, may not feel free to say no to social invitations or requests for favors. Alternatively, the friend might try to take advantage of the relationship to gain access to information about tests or special consideration on papers. The professor's behavior may interfere with the roles of other faculty. Other students may generalize that all faculty members show favoritism. Faculty members may find that any evaluation decisions they make about the student are influenced by the fact that the student is a friend of a colleague.

Obviously the cleanest solution to handling the potential problems raised by a dual relationship is to avoid it. In many cases this is possible and desirable given the serious problems raised by dual relationships. There will be occasions, however, when this option presents as many problems as the dual relationship. For example, if the professor is the only one teaching a required course, a close friend may have to take it in order to graduate. Does this mean that the professor is forced to choose between committing a breech of ethics or denying a student entry into a required course?

There are no easy solutions to the question of how to handle a dual relationship that seems unavoidable. The decision criteria and the themes underlying them, however, can provide ideas about workable solutions. . . .

References

Franklin, P., Moglen, H., Zatlin-Boring, P., & Angress, R. (1981). *Sexual and gender harassment in the academy*. New York: The Modern Language Association of America.

Glaser, R., & Thorpe, J. (1986). Unethical intimacy: A survey of sexual contact and advances between psychology educators and female graduate students. *American Psychologist, 41*, 43–51.

Jordan, A., & Meara, N. (1990). Ethics and the professional practice of psychologists: The role of virtues and principles. *Professional Psychology: Research and Practice, 21*, 107–114.

Keith-Spiegel, P., & Koocher, G. (1985). *Ethics in psychology: Professional standards and cases*. New York: Random House.

Matthews, J. (1991). The teaching of ethics and the ethics of teaching. *Teaching of Psychology, 18*, 80–85.

Paludi, M. (1990). Creating new taboos in the academy: Faculty responsibility in preventing sexual harassment. *Initiatives, 52*, 29–34.

Pope, K. (1991). Dual relationships in psychotherapy. *Ethics & Behavior, 1*, 21–34.

Schneider, B. (1987). Graduate women, sexual harassment, and university policy. *Journal of Higher Education, 58*, 46–65.

Zalk, S., Paludi, M., & Dederich, J. (1990). Women students' assessment of consensual relationships with their professors: Ivory power reconsidered. In E. Cole (Ed.), *Sexual harassment on campus: A legal compendium* (pp. 103–133). Washington, DC: National Association of College and University Attorneys.

Multiple Role Relationships During Internship: Consequences and Recommendations

P. Ann O'Connor Slimp and Barbara K. Burian

Multiple or dual role relationships in . . . training (Bartell & Rubin, 1990; Glaser & Thorpe, 1986; Pope, Levenson, & Schover, 1979; Stadler, 1986) have received increased attention during the last decade. Although multiple relationships between trainees and trainers have been addressed by some authors, such relationships that occur specifically during the internship year have largely been left unexplored. Such relationships may confuse interns, influence their professional identities, and prove problematic to the internship site itself. . . .

Dual role or multiple relationships occur when psychologists have "social or other nonprofessional contacts with persons such as patients, clients, students, supervisees or research participants" (American Psychological Association [APA], 1992, p. 1601). In fact, the recently adopted *Ethical Principles of Psychologists and Code of Conduct* of the American Psychological Association clearly directs psychologists to avoid multiple relationships with clients, students, and supervisees because of the recognized risk of harm and exploitation intrinsic in these relationships. Furthermore, psychologists are encouraged to maintain a sensitivity to the "real and ascribed differences in power" and to not "exploit or mislead other people during or after professional relationships" (APA, 1992, p. 1606). Although some dual roles are considered allowable (e.g., bartering for psychological services), engaging in such relationships is generally discouraged.

Although the current *Ethical Principles of Psychologists and Code of Conduct* (APA, 1992) acknowledges that it may not be feasible to avoid all multiple roles, Kitchener (1988) believed that "all

dual role relationships can be ethically problematic and have the potential for harm" (p. 217). Nonetheless, it has been noted by Pope and Vasquez (1991) that some professionals point to potential benefits of such relationships and often refer to these benefits as justification for such interactions. Indeed, Pope and Bajt (1988) found that 9% of survey respondents, who were considered authorities in psychological professional accountability, reported engaging in sex with a client "in light of the client's welfare or other deeper value" (p. 828). Because the prevalence of multiple role relationships involving trainees has been noted by several authors (Glaser & Thorpe, 1986; Pope & Bajt, 1988; Pope, Keith-Spiegel, & Tabachnick, 1986; Pope et al., 1979), it is important to consider why such relationships may develop during the internship year and the subsequent consequences of these interactions. . . .

During the internship year, staff may at times find it almost impossible to keep from engaging in dual role relationships with interns (Bernard & Goodyear, 1992; Keith-Spiegel & Koocher, 1985). This is particularly so for professionals who also hold faculty status in graduate programs or at internship training sites that emphasize self-exploration (Herlihy & Corey, 1992; Keith-Spiegel & Koocher, 1985). . . .

These guidelines are applied in the following discussion of four specific types of multiple roles that may occur during the internship: sexual, social, therapy, and business relationships. In addition, this discussion is limited to the possible negative impact of dual roles. Although there may be benefits gained from engaging in such relationships, we contend that

Adapted from *Professional Psychology: Research and Practice*, 25, 39–45. Copyright 1994 by the American Psychological Association.

most often, negative consequences outweigh the advantages, especially for the individuals who possess the least power in these relationships, the interns. In addition, we explore possible motivations for engaging in various dual roles and the subsequent impact on training.

SEXUAL RELATIONSHIPS

Many have recognized that the expectations and obligations of the role of sexual partner diverge greatly from those of supervisor or evaluator (Bartell & Rubin, 1990; Harrar, VandeCreek, & Knapp, 1990; Kitchener, 1988; Kitchener & Harding, 1990). However, staff members and interns may be motivated to engage in "mutually consensual" sexual relationships with each other for a variety of reasons, including natural attraction, gratification of physical, sexual, or emotional needs, the need to please a favored individual or to feel "special," and the need to feel powerful or in control of another person. The degree to which an intern can actually give true and full consent to any dual role relationships is explored later in this article.

The consequences of engaging in such relationships can be numerous and quite serious. First, a staff member engaged in such a relationship may have difficulty in keeping the intern's training interests and needs primary (Pope, Schover, & Levenson, 1980); self-interest and the preservation of the sexual relationship will generally take precedence. As a result, the interns involved may not be expected to complete the same requirements and may not be sufficiently challenged. Second, when engaged in these kinds of dual role relationships, interns may refrain from challenging or disagreeing with staff members or may avoid appropriately exploring various issues in seminars or supervision. For example, an intern who is in a sexual relationship with a member of the training staff may abstain from discussing issues of a sexual or intimate nature (e.g., his or her attraction to clients) for fear of eliciting an undesired reaction by the staff member (Pope et al., 1986). In addition, the staff member's ability to objectively evaluate the intern's skills is compromised. A supervisor in such a relationship is vulnerable to direct and vicarious liability because of inadequate supervision. Should such a sexual relationship end, the trainee might

consequently become, or at least feel like, a target for abuse or unfair negative evaluations.

Furthermore, sexual relationships that are coerced and not "mutually consensual" (e.g., sexual harassment) can have effects on interns ranging from mild discomfort to extreme anxiety and depression that impair the intern's professional or personal functioning (Salisbury, Ginorio, Remick, & Stringer, 1986). An intern may consider or actually leave the internship or the profession or both (Glaser & Thorpe, 1986). Moreover, the current *Ethical Principles of Psychologists and Code of Conduct* (APA, 1992) prohibits psychologists from engaging in sexual harassment, which leaves those that engage in such behavior vulnerable to subsequent ethical and possibly legal consequences.

It is also well documented that the transference phenomenon exists in supervisory relationships (Doehrman, 1976; McNeill & Worthen, 1989). At times, transference may well be the motivating force behind an intern's decision to engage in a sexual relationship with a staff member. According to the recently revised *Ethical Principles of Psychologists and Code of Conduct* (APA, 1992), psychologists are expected to be sensitive to the real or ascribed power in professional relationships, including situations involving transference. Thus, it is the responsibility of the psychologist to prevent the exploitation of this phenomenon. . . .

The transference phenomenon, in addition to the power differential between interns and staff members (Bernard & Goodyear, 1992; Cormier & Bernard, 1982; Harrar et al., 1990; Kitchener, 1988), compromises an intern's ability to provide true consent for entering into a dual role relationship. Cormier and Bernard (1982) suggested that "it could be argued that because of this, a supervisee is not able to give voluntary consent to participate in *any* form of dual relationships (p. 487, emphasis ours). In addition, Glaser and Thorpe (1986) found that the perception of the degree of coercion involved in such relationships increased with the passage of time and distance from the relationship. This supports Kitchener's (1988) belief that, because trainees are in positions of diminished power, interns' abilities to make knowledgeable and informed decisions that are in their own best interests are compromised.

SOCIAL RELATIONSHIPS

Upon first reflection it may not appear that the role expectations of a professional trainer differ that much from those of a social acquaintance, particularly when one considers friendly collegial interactions that occur during the work day. Those social relationships or interactions can take many forms and can be an important factor in maintaining a congenial work environment and good working relationships with colleagues. Hence, one might conclude that the potential for harm and exploitation in social relationships is much less than in sexual relationships. However, the role expectations and obligations of a friend or social acquaintance do differ from and can conflict with those of a staff member or supervisor. Supervisors are expected not only to evaluate interns but also to recommend interns for future employment. Should a supervisor share a social relationship with an intern, his or her objective evaluation of the intern's readiness for employment may be influenced. Therefore, even seemingly benign social relationships with positive intentions can still have an adverse effect on the training process (Keith-Spiegel & Koocher, 1985; Kitchener & Harding, 1990). . . .

The consequences or potential problems that may develop when engaging in a social dual role relationship are much the same as those involved in a sexual relationship. A staff member's objectivity may be compromised and interns may avoid issues or topics that threaten the social relationship. In either case the quality of the intern's training is likely to suffer. In addition, Gutheil and Gabbard (1993) observed that sexual relationships with clients usually begin with the crossing of other boundaries such as those involving time, place, and self-disclosure. If this premise is applied to training or supervisory relationships, the boundary crossings involved in social relationships would make it more likely that sexual relationships and other dual role relationships could occur.

THERAPY RELATIONSHIPS

Possible incentives for interns and staff members to engage in therapy relationships with each other are diverse, and such relationships may occur unintentionally. As previously noted, the internship can be a difficult period as trainees, often isolated from their support networks, make the transition to becoming full professionals. When the intense focus on interpersonal relationships and clinical skills is also considered, it is understandable that many interns might benefit from and even need therapy.

Some staff members may feel that they are the most qualified people to provide therapy to interns given their relationships with them (Roberts, Murrell, Thomas, & Claxton, 1982; Stadler, 1986), and an ethical mandate may exist for staff or supervisors to provide such therapy to interns in the event of a crisis (Cormier & Bernard, 1982; Stadler, 1986). In addition, some internship sites (and postdoctoral training institutes), particularly those with psychoanalytic orientations, may require interns to receive therapy as a part of their training. In some graduate programs, it is common for faculty members to serve not only as instructors but also as clinical supervisors. In fact, Borys and Pope (1989) found that approximately 10% of survey respondents reported providing therapy to clients who were also students or supervisees at the time. However, Stoltenberg and Delworth (1987) suggested that in such situations students should be given a choice about such arrangements and the implications of these relationships should be openly discussed. If we apply this recommendation to internship sites and postdoctoral training programs regardless of theoretical orientation, then trainees should be allowed choices regarding multiple relationships at their training sites. Opportunities for obtaining therapy from someone with whom they have no other type of relationship should be available to all trainees.

Many have noted the therapy-like aspects of supervision (Newman, 1981; Upchurch, 1985), including the development of transference (Corey, Corey, & Callahan, 1984; Doehrman, 1976; Ethics Committee of the American Psychological Association, 1987). Others maintain that therapy is a proper activity within supervision (Hess, 1980). We agree with Cormier and Bernard (1982) that "this type of dual role relationship probably does occur to some degree in supervision because of the perceived importance of focusing on the supervisee's inter- and intrapersonal dynamics" (p. 487). This may be particularly relevant when one considers the parallel process between the therapy relationship and the supervisory relationship (Doehrman, 1976; McNeill & Worthen, 1989). However, Doehrman (1976) pointed out that the purpose of exploring a trainee's interpersonal and intrapersonal concerns should be confined to assisting the trainee in his or her relationship with the supervisor or client and that it is the supervisor who should take responsibility for providing any needed clarification regarding this relationship dynamic (Bernard & Goodyear, 1992).

Supervisors or staff members who provide therapy to interns place themselves in situations involving a conflict of interest (Stadler, 1986). The role of a staff member is often evaluative. In addition, those responsible for training can significantly influence an intern's future career goals and employment. Supervisors, who have a clear evaluative role with the intern, have the added duty to protect the welfare of the intern's clients (Cormier & Bernard, 1982; Harrar et al., 1990; Wise, Lowery, & Silverglade, 1989). Evaluation, however, is antithetical to the nature and process of therapy and the role of a therapist (Kitchener, 1988). As clients, interns need the same protection of confidentiality that is afforded other clients; they should feel free to explore their thoughts and feelings without fearing that such information might be used in an evaluative context. Hence, interns who engage in therapy dual role relationships with staff might withhold or censor the information they choose to disclose, and thus both endeavors would suffer. Ethical guidelines (American Association for Counseling and Development, 1988; American College Personnel Association, 1990; APA, 1992) and several authors (Ethics Committee of the APA, 1987; Stadler, 1986; Wise et al., 1989) have suggested that interns who are in need of therapy should be referred to someone with whom they have no other relationship.

BUSINESS RELATIONSHIPS

Although business dual role relationships have typically received rather limited exploration in the literature (see Harrar et al., 1990; Keith-Spiegel & Koocher, 1985; Kitchener & Harding, 1990), we believe that it is not uncommon for interns to be hired as staff members' employees. Examples of this employment might range from house-sitting or baby-sitting to assisting staff members in research, consultation, or other private practice activities. Reasons for such relationships may include easing one's work load while providing professional and economic opportunities for trainees. However, although the intentions may be partially charitable or educational, the risk of exploitation and the potential for harm do exist.

Because of the power differential, transference, and the intern's developmental needs, discussed earlier, it may be quite difficult for an intern to resist staff requests for paid services. Keith-Spiegel and Koocher (1985) noted that, once an intern is in such a relationship, "the elements of power, control, and influence are even more marked . . . since a 'double power base' accrues to the psychologist" (p. 270). This places the intern in double jeopardy and clearly has implications for the intern's training.

As with other types of multiple role relationships, the staff member's ability to objectively evaluate the intern's performance, as a supervisor or employer, is compromised (Kitchener & Harding, 1990). In addition, consider how the intern–staffmember relationships could be affected should a child get hurt, a house burn, or a lucrative consulting contract fall through during the intern's employment. . . .

References

American Association for Counseling and Development (1988). *Ethical standards*. Alexandria, VA: Author.

American College Personnel Association (1990). A statement of ethical principles and standards of the American College Personnel Association. *Journal of College Student Development, 31,* 11–16.

American Psychological Association (1992). Ethical principles of psychologists and code of conduct. *American Psychologist, 47,* 1597–1611.

Bartell, P. A., & Rubin, L. J. (1990). Dangerous liaisons: Sexual intimacies in supervision. *Professional Psychology: Research and Practice, 21,* 442–450.

Bernard, J. M., & Goodyear, R. K. (1992). *Fundamentals of clinical supervision*, Boston: Allyn & Bacon.

Borys, D. S., & Pope, K. S. (1989). Dual relationships between therapist and client: A national study of psychologists, psychiatrists, and social workers. *Professional Psychology: Research and Practice, 20,* 283–293.

Corey, G., Corey, M. S., & Callahan, P. (1984). *Issues and ethics in the helping professions* (2nd ed.). Monterey, CA: Brooks/Cole.

Cormier, L. S., & Bernard, J. M. (1982). Ethical and legal responsibilities of clinical supervisors. *Personnel and Guidance Journal, 60,* 486–491.

Doehrman, M. J. G. (1976). Parallel processes in supervision and psychotherapy. *Bulletin of the Menninger Clinic, 40,* 3–104.

Ethics Committee of the American Psychological Association. (1987). Report of the Ethics Committee: 1986. *American Psychologist, 42,* 730–734.

Glaser, R. D., & Thorpe, J. S. (1986). Unethical intimacy: A survey of sexual contact and advances between psychology educators and female graduate students. *American Psychologist, 41,* 43–51.

Gutheil, T. G., & Gabbard, G. O. (1993). The concept of boundaries in clinical practice: Theoretical and risk-management dimensions. *American Journal of Psychiatry, 150,* 188–196.

Harrar, W. R., VandeCreek, L., & Knapp, S. (1990). Ethical and legal aspects of clinical supervision. *Professional Psychology. Research and Practice, 21,* 37–41.

Herlihy, B., & Corey, G. (1992). *Dual relationships in counseling.* Alexandria, VA: American Association for Counseling and Development.

Hess, A. K. (Ed.). (1980). *Psychotherapy supervision: Theory, research, and practice.* New York: Wiley.

Keith-Spiegel, P., & Koocher, G. P. (1985). *Ethics in psychology.* Hillsdale, NJ: Random House.

Kitchener, K. S. (1988). Dual role relationships: What makes them so problematic? *Journal of Counseling and Development, 67,* 217–221.

Kitchener, K. S., & Harding, S. S. (1990). Dual role relationships. In B. Herlihy & L. B. Golden (Eds.), *Ethical standards casebook* (4th ed.). Alexandria, VA: American Association for Counseling and Development.

McNeill, B. W., & Worthen, V. (1989). The parallel process in psychotherapy supervision. *Professional Psychology: Research and Practice, 20,* 329–333.

Newman, A. S. (1981). Ethical issues in the supervision of psychotherapy. *Professional Psychology, 12,* 690–695.

Pope, K. S., & Bajt, T. R. (1988). When laws and values conflict: A dilemma for psychologists. *American Psychologist, 43,* 828–829.

Pope, K. S., Keith-Spiegel, P., & Tabachnick, B. G. (1986). Sexual attraction to clients: The human therapist and the (sometimes) inhuman training system. *American Psychologist, 41,* 147–158.

Pope, K. S., Levenson, H., & Schover, L. R. (1979). Sexual intimacy in psychology training: Results and implications of a national survey. *American Psychologist, 34,* 682–689.

Pope, K. S., Schover, L. R., & Levenson, H. (1980). Sexual behavior between clinical supervisors and trainees: Implications for professional standards. *Professional Psychology, 11,* 157–162.

Pope, K. S., & Vasquez, M. J. T. (1991). *Ethics in psychotherapy and counseling: A practical guide for psychologists.* San Francisco: Jossey-Bass.

Roberts, G. T., Murrell, P. H., Thomas, R. E., & Claxton, C. S. (1982). Ethical concerns for counselor educators. *Counselor Education and Supervision, 22,* 8–14.

Salisbury, J., Ginorio, A. B., Remick, H., & Stringer, D. M. (1986). Counseling victims of sexual harassment. *Psychotherapy, 23,* 316–324.

Stadler, H. A. (1986). To counsel or not to counsel: The ethical dilemma of dual relationships. *Journal of Counseling and Human Service Professions,* 134–140.

Stoltenberg, C. D., & Delworth, U. (1987). *Supervising counselors and therapists: A developmental approach.* San Francisco: Jossey-Bass.

Upchurch, D. W. (1985). Ethical standards and the supervisory process. *Counselor Education and Supervision, 25,* 90–98.

Wise, P. S., Lowery, S., & Silverglade, L. (1989). Personal counseling for counselors in training: Guidelines for supervisors. *Counselor Education and Supervision, 28,* 326–336.

◆ ◆ ◆

Commentary: For another recent discussion of these issues, see Russell, R. K., & Petrie, T. (1994). Issues in training effective supervisors. Applied and Preventive Psychology, 3, *27–42.*

Standard 1.19 of the 1992 APA Ethical Principles now explicitly prohibits psychologists from engaging in sexual relationships and other potentially exploitative conduct with students and supervisees in training that they evaluate or over whom they have direct authority.

Perhaps more important than punishing those who violate the code's basic standards for multiple relationships (i.e., Standards 1.13–1.15 and 1.17–1.19) is preventing their occurrence and helping those who may be injured by psychologists' inappropriate conduct. The final set of materials in this chapter confronts those issues.

Avoiding Exploitive Dual Relationships: A Decision-Making Model

Michael C. Gottlieb

. . . Seven assumptions are required to use the model. First, the model is applicable to all professional relationships in which psychologists engage. . . .

Second, the aspirational goal of striving to avoid all dual relationships (APA, 1990) is unrealistic in many circumstances. . . . The purpose of the model is to assist colleagues in managing these relationships more sensitively and effectively, when they cannot be avoided.

Third, due to the inherent high risk, all additional relationships with consumers should be evaluated to assess potential harm.

Fourth, the model assumes that not all dual relationships are exploitive per se. It presumes that in some circumstances, dual relationships may be pursued with low risk and may be beneficial; dual relationships must, however, be avoided whenever there is a reason to believe that they may prove harmful.

Fifth, the model is intended to sensitize the psychologist to the relevant issues, and make recommendations for action.

Sixth, the model assumes that the professional's dilemma is the result of contemplating the addition of a second relationship to an existing one. It is not intended for situations where multiple relationships are already in existence.

Seventh, the dimensions below must be assessed from the perspective of the consumer, not from that of the professional. Since the psychologist generally does not have access to the consumer's feelings in these situations, decisions must be made on the most conservative basis to insure consumer welfare.

THE MODEL

The model is based upon the use of three dimensions . . . that are believed to be basic and critical to the ethical decision-making process.

The first dimension is *Power*. It refers to the amount or degree of power which a psychologist may have in relation to a consumer. Power can vary widely. The psychologist who gives a speech at the local PTA on childrearing practices has relatively little power over members of the audience when compared with a therapist's influence over someone in long-term, insight-oriented psychotherapy.

Second, *Duration of the Relationship*, an aspect of power, is important because it is assumed that power increases over time. Power is lower when relationships are brief, such as in a single assessment session for referral, and increases as relationships continue, such as that of a student and teacher.

Third, *Clarity of Termination* refers to the likelihood that the consumer and the psychologist will have further professional contact. Performing a psychological assessment of a job applicant involves an unambiguous termination, with little chance of further contact. On the other hand, some family psychologists assume that their obligation to a family never ends. How does one decide when the professional relationship has been terminated? In this model one must assume that the professional relationship continues, as long as the consumer assumes that it does, regardless of the amount of time elapsed or contact in the interim. When the psychologist does not know the consumer's feelings, the ethical choice is to assume that the consumer always has the right to renew the professional relationship in the future.

Adapted from *Psychotherapy*, 30, 41–47. Copyright 1993 by Division 29 of the American Psychological Association. Figures 1 and 2 and Cases 1 and 2 have been omitted.

Using the Decision-Making Model

When a psychologist is contemplating an additional relationship, the model is to be used as follows.

Step 1. Assess the current relationship according to the three dimensions. From the consumer's perspective, where does the relationship fall on each? How great is the power differential, how long has the relationship lasted, and has it clearly ended? If the relationship falls to the right side on two or three of the dimensions (i.e., higher power, longer duration and no termination), the potential for harm is high, and no other relationship should be contemplated.

For traditional individual psychotherapy, group, marital, and family therapy the case is clear. The power differential is great, the duration of treatment can be long, and termination is not always clear cut. Furthermore, the consumer may presume it their right to return for service at any time in the future. . . .

If the relationship falls to the left side on the three dimensions (i.e., low power, short duration, and clearly terminated), one may move down to the next level. When the relationship falls at mid-range on the three dimensions, some types of additional relationships may be permissible, and the psychologist may move down to the next level.

Step 2. Examine the contemplated relationship along the three dimensions, as was done for the current relationship. If the contemplated relationship falls to the right side of the dimensions (i.e., it would involve great power over a long time with an uncertain termination), then it should be rejected if the existing relationship also falls to the right. If the proposed relationship falls either in the mid-range or to the left side of the dimensions, it may be permissible, and the psychologist should move down to step three. . . .

Another possibility is that the first relationship may fall to the left side on the dimensions, but the contemplated relationship might fall to the right. In this case, the new relationship may be acceptable. For example, a psychologist could consider treating a child in psychotherapy after he gave a speech on children's reactions to divorce which the mother had attended.

Step 3. Examine both relationships for role incompatibility if they fall within the mid-range or to the

left side of the dimensions. According to Kitchener (1988) role incompatibility increases as a function of greater differences in expectations of the two roles, greater divergence of the obligations of the two roles, and an increase in the power differential. If the two different roles are highly incompatible, then the contemplated relationship should be refused. For example, a psychologist should not accept an employee as a brief psychotherapy patient. Faculty members should not initiate business relationships with students.

If both relationships fall within the mid-range, or to the left side of the dimensions, and the incompatibility is low, the psychologist might proceed. For example, a faculty member may consider having a student in one of his or her classes work as a research assistant under his or her direction. A psychologist who has treated a man for smoking cessation may consider treating him and his wife for marital problems.

Step 4. Obtain consultation from a colleague. . . . A colleague familiar with the circumstances, the consumer, and the decision-maker is the ideal choice. . . .

Step 5. Discuss the decision with the consumer if the psychologist chooses to proceed with the additional relationship. He or she must review the essence of the decision-making model, its rationale, the pertinent ethical issues, available alternatives, and potential adverse consequences as a matter of informed consent. If the consumer is competent, and chooses to engage in the second relationship, the psychologist may proceed, once the consumer has had adequate time to consider the alternatives. If the consumer is unable to recognize the dilemma or is unwilling to consider the issues before deciding, he or she should be considered at risk, and the contemplated relationship rejected. . . .

References

American Psychological Association. (1990). Ethical principles of psychologists. *American Psychologist, 45,* 390–395.

Kitchener, K. S. (1988). Dual role relationships: What makes them so problematic? *Journal of Counseling and Development, 67,* 217–221.

Dual Relationships Between Therapist and Client: A National Study of Psychologists, Psychiatrists, and Social Workers

Debra S. Borys and Kenneth S. Pope

4,800 psychologists, psychiatrists, and social workers were surveyed (return rate = 49%) to examine attitudes and practices regarding dual professional roles, social involvements, financial involvements, and incidental involvements. Half of the Ss rated the degree to which each behavior was ethical; the other half reported how often they engaged in each behavior. A majority believed dual role behaviors to be unethical under most conditions; most reported that they had rarely or never engaged in the behaviors. 10 factors (therapist gender, profession, age, experience, marital status, region of residence, client gender, practice setting, theoretical orientation, and practice locale) were examined for their relation to beliefs and behaviors. A higher proportion of male than of female therapists were perpetrators of sexual and nonsexual dual relationships. The professions did not differ among themselves in terms of (a) sexual intimacies with clients before or after termination, (b) nonsexual dual professional roles, (c) social involvements, or (d) financial involvements with patients. 10 specific training implications are discussed in light of the exploitive and clinically harmful nature of dual relationships.

IMPLICATIONS FOR EDUCATION AND TRAINING

Graduate training programs, internships, teaching hospitals and clinics, organizations providing continuing education, and other providers of formal and informal learning opportunities can, through careful attention to program planning and evaluation, help to increase sensitivity to dual relationships that are unethical and harmful and to ethical issues more generally. The following 10 steps may be useful to help to ensure that clinicians do not collude in a process of denial regarding particular ethical issues and of tolerating and enabling the perpetuation of exploitive and clinically harmful behavior.

1. Programs need to present the research-based literature in which the nature, causes, and consequences of dual relationships are explored. . . .

2. The ethical and clinical implications of both sexual and nonsexual dual relationships, as well as of incidental involvements, need to be reflected in virtually all clinical coursework, supervision, and other forms of education. . . .

3. Departmental chairs, training directors, and others with administrative responsibilities must avoid shortcuts and negligence in following formal policies and procedures to select faculty and staff who are sensitive to ethical issues. . . .

4. There is a need for clear and explicit institutional standards regarding potential dual relationships between students and educators. . . .

5. There is a need for written, operationally defined procedures for avoiding conflicts of interest in monitoring and enforcing the institutional standards regarding dual relationships. . . . Because the efforts to rehabilitate and to prevent recidivism among therapists who have engaged in sexual intimacy with a patient unfortunately have *not* demonstrated greater effectiveness than those involving other sex abusers

Adapted from *Professional Psychology: Research and Practice*, 20, 283–293. Copyright 1989 by the American Psychological Association. Tables 1, 2, and 3 have been omitted.

such as child molesters and rapists (Pope, 1989c), the ability of organizations to respond promptly, knowledgeably, and satisfactorily to instances of abuse and to abusers seems particularly important. A negligent, cursory, or trivializing approach to violations involving sexual or nonsexual dual relationships can place numerous future patients of the abuser at risk for serious harm and can send a clear message to actual and potential victims/survivors, as well as to other actual or potential perpetrators, that such abuse is not taken seriously.

6. The practical consequences for those (professionals, students, clients, and others) who report violations of the standards need to be candidly acknowledged and adequately addressed. . . .

7. Beyond the formal standards, programs need to provide an authentically safe and supportive environment in which students and educators alike can acknowledge and examine the seemingly unacceptable impulses that might tempt them to enter into unethical dual relationships. Beginning and seasoned clinicians may feel sexually aroused by or attracted to a client or a clinical supervisee . . . , may experience a desire to make a financial killing and therefore to enter into business partnerships or other lucrative arrangements with clients, or may be uncomfortable setting appropriate boundaries or limits and thus find it difficult to refuse to provide psychotherapy to an employee, and so on. Students are unlikely to disclose their genuine impulses if they infer that discussing one's sexual impulses may be labeled "seductive" and may serve as the basis for a teacher's advances or departmental gossip, that disclosing an enthusiastic love of money will result in a less-than-glowing letter of recommendation, and that revealing an embarrassing reluctance to disappoint people may be diagnosed as a pathognomonic sign that one needs to make a different career choice.

8. Students and clinicians alike need to be able to recognize and appreciate the human dimensions of an abstract-sounding issue such as "dual relationships." . . . First-person accounts by clients who have experienced sexualized dual relationships are provided in published works by Freeman and Roy (1976), Plaisil (1985), Walker and Young (1986), and Bates and Brodsky (1988). . . .

9. Training institutions must encourage, conduct, learn from, and disseminate the findings of systematic research and serious investigations into the gender implications of dual relationships. A disproportionately large percentage of male professionals approve of and engage in a range of nonsexual and sexual dual relationships of the sort prohibited by the APA. . . .

10. Training institutions need to identify, through careful research, those factors that encourage ethical sensitivity and behavior in contrast with those that increase the likelihood that clinicians will act in ways that put their clients or others at risk for harm. . . .

References

Bates, C. M., & Brodsky, A. M. (1988). *Sex in the therapy hour*. New York: Guilford.

Freeman, L., & Roy, J. (1976). *Betrayal*. New York: Stein & Day.

Plaisil, E. (1985). *Therapist*. New York: St. Martin's/Marek.

Pope, K. S. (1989c). Therapists who become sexually intimate with a patient: Classifications, dynamics, recidivism and rehabilitation. *Independent Practitioner, 9*(3), 28–34.

Walker, E., & Young, T. D. (1986). *A killing cure*. New York: Holt.

◆ ◆ ◆

Commentary: For other articles on prevention and remediation, see:

Pope, K. S., Keith-Spiegel, P., & Tabachnik, B. G. (1986). Sexual attraction to clients: The human therapist and the (sometimes) inhuman training system. American Psychologist, 41, 147–158.

Slimp, P. A. O'Connor, & Burian, B. K. (1994). Multiple role relationships during internship: Consequences and recommendations. Professional Psychology: Research and Practice, 25, 39–45.

See also *Rodolfa, E., Hall, T., Holms, V., Davena, A., Komatz, D., Antunez, M., & Hall, A. (1994). The management of sexual feelings in therapy.* Professional Psychology: Research and Practice, 25, 168–172:

> *In 1986, Pope et al. called for the integration of this topic into the resources for teaching counseling and therapy skills. Lerman (1990) provides an annotated bibliography*

of the 3,000 publications on this topic. There is currently an abundance of material, and models exist for training (Brodsky, 1989; Rodolfa et al., 1990; Vasquez, 1988). It is now up to the training program faculty to decide to integrate this material, for the good of their students, for the good of those who seek our psychological services, and for the good of our profession. It is time to train psychologists to accept and understand their sexual feelings and do no harm.

References

Brodsky, A. (1989). Sex between patient and therapist: Psychologist's data and response. In G. G. Gabbard (Ed.), Sexual exploitation in professional relationships (pp. 15–25). Washington, DC: American Psychiatric Press.

Lerman, H. (1990). Sexual intimacies between psychotherapists and patients: An annotated bibliography of mental health, legal and public media literature and relevant legal cases. (2nd ed.). Washington, DC: American Psychological Association.

Pope, K., Keith-Spiegel, P., & Tabachnik, B. (1986). Sexual attraction to clients: The human therapist and the (sometimes) inhuman training system. American Psychologist, 41, 147–158.

Vasquez, M. (1988). Counselor–client sexual contact implications for ethics training. Journal of Counseling and Development, 67, 238–241. (pp. 171–172)

Accusation of Sexual Misconduct: Assisting in the Complaint Process

Michael C. Gottlieb

. . .

ASSISTANCE TO VICTIMS

The profession has made initial attempts to assist victims in four ways. First, the APA took a major step forward in public education by publishing a work of the Committee on Women in Psychology entitled *If Sex Enters into the Psychotherapy Relationship* (1989). This document explicitly defines the problem, takes the unequivocal position that sex in the therapy relationship is improper, supports and normalizes the feelings of victims, and explains the various options one may take in pursuing a complaint.

Second, there have been recent attempts to urge ethics committees to accept broader responsibilities. For example, Schoenfeld, Gottlieb, and Sell (1989) emphasized that ethics committees are "underutilized resources", able to educate both the profession and the public regarding such problems. They noted that the ethics committee [members] . . . could, if they were to reach out, serve a wider role in consulting to victims as well. Unfortunately, this role is institutionally limited because the ethics committee must avoid dual relationships itself. Because it must serve an objective, investigative, and adjudicative function, it cannot be an advocate for a complainant and is limited in the direct assistance it can offer.

Third, some colleagues have advanced the alternative of assisting victims through mediation. This model, pioneered in 1983 by Schoener, Milgrom, and Gonsiorek offers a rapid and less formal means of dealing with the problem and has been successfully used by others (Bouhoutsos & Brodsky, 1985). With successful mediation, however, the victim may not file a formal complaint, thereby allowing the offending psychologist to escape formal disciplinary procedures (Pope & Bouhoutsos, 1986).

A fourth method is consultation. Anderson and Hays (1988) reminded us that when psychologists find themselves in ethical dilemmas, they should seek consultation from a colleague. Stone (1983) has taken this notion one step further. He properly notes the conflict in which therapists find themselves when clients reveal sexual abuse by a previous therapist. The present therapist must help the client in any way possible, but cannot directly pursue the complaint, for to do so would violate confidentiality. Only the client may file such a complaint. Because clients are often reluctant to have such information revealed (Pope & Bouhoutsos, 1986), they frequently ask the therapist to say and do nothing. The therapist now has knowledge of misconduct but is prevented from using it on behalf of the client. Stone's excellent suggestion is that both client and therapist discuss the situation with a consultant. If after such a meeting the client chooses to file a complaint, the consultant can play an advocacy role and press for appropriate remedies while the therapist and client resume their therapeutic work. Although Stone notes potential disadvantages, his proposal can remove significant barriers to the complaint process.

An effort to help victims has also come from self-help groups of consumers who consider themselves abused by therapists (Pope & Bouhoutsos, 1986). Although sometimes antagonistic toward mental health professionals, these groups do offer support to their members and will make direct offers of assistance to victims in the complaint process. . . .

Adapted from *Professional Psychology: Research and Practice*, 21, 455–461. Copyright 1990 by the American Psychological Association.

References

Anderson, J., & Hays, J. R. (1988). Dual relationships. *Texas Psychologist, 40*, 5–6.

Bouhoutsos, J. D., & Brodsky, A. M. (1985). Mediation in therapist–client sex: A model. *Psychotherapy: Research and Practice, 22*, 189–193.

Committee on Women in Psychology, American Psychological Association. (1989). If sex enters into the psychotherapy relationship. *Professional Psychology: Research and Practice, 20*, 112–115.

Pope, K. S., & Bouhoutsos, J. C. (1986). *Sexual intimacy between therapists and patients*. New York: Praeger.

Schoener, G., Milgrom, J., & Gonsiorek, J. (1983). *Responding therapeutically to clients who have been sexually involved with their psychotherapists*. Minneapolis, MN: Walk-In Counseling Center.

Schoenfeld, J. S., Gottlieb, M. C., & Sell, J. M. (1989). Managing sexual misconduct complaints: The role of a state association ethics committee. *Professional Practice of Psychology: Legal, Regulatory, and Licensing Issues, 8*, 109–119.

Stone, A. A. (1983). Sexual misconduct by psychiatrists: The ethical and clinical dilemma of confidentiality. *American Journal of Psychiatry, 140*, 195–197.

CHAPTER 6

PSYCHOLOGICAL ASSESSMENT

Assessment, particularly testing, permeates every facet of people's lives. Almost every subset of psychologists uses tests. Researchers use tests to acquire data from those who participate in their studies. Clinical psychologists administer tests for diagnostic purposes and to monitor the course of psychotherapy. School psychologists assess children to determine their eligibility for possible placement in special education programs. Counseling psychologists use vocational, occupational, and interest tests to guide career development and measure problem-solving skills throughout the life span. Forensic psychologists use tests to help courts determine the best placement for children whose parents are divorcing or to assess whether a criminal defendant is competent to stand trial or should be held responsible for an otherwise criminal act. Industrial and organizational psychologists measure skills and job knowledge of those seeking employment or promotion. And, of course, academics often devise their own instruments to assess what their undergraduate and graduate students have learned.

As the nonexhaustive list above illustrates, assessment can take many forms. Each form may have its own ethical implications. For example, when clinicians use intelligence scales, paper-and-pencil personality tests, or projective techniques, issues of privacy and informed consent arise. When psychologists in employment settings use tests, issues of dual loyalties arise: For whom is the psychologist working and to whom does the psychologist owe the primary obligation of fidelity—the test taker or the employer? When school psychologists assess children for special education placement, who is the client—the child, the parent, or the school system that is paying the evaluator? When a researcher gathers data through tests, questions of informed consent and deception become important (see chap. 8, this volume). When forensic clinicians evaluate a criminal defendant, are they working on behalf of the prosecution, the defense, or the court (see chap. 9)? And regardless of the assessor's role, the issue of competence becomes pervasive. Are the tests that are used psychometrically sound, and are the interpretations and judgments that psychologists make from the data valid? Finally, the advent of computerized testing in general and the increased use of so-called honesty or integrity tests in employment in particular open such discussions to a whole new set of issues.

This chapter can only provide an introduction to the complex ethical issues inherent to gathering, storing, interpreting, and disseminating information about test takers that is gleaned from assessment. Such technical issues as validity, reliability, norming, and standardization are addressed here only if they are relevant to ethical and social issues. To gain a broader perspective on both technical and social policy questions, see the two special issues of the *American Psychologist* devoted to testing and edited by Amrine (1965) and by Glaser and Bond (1981). In addition, the National Academy of Sciences has produced two major works evaluating standardized tests in general (Heller, Holtzman, & Messick, 1982; Wigdor & Garner, 1982).

The ethical problems raised in this chapter cannot be fully understood if they are examined outside of their historical, social, and legal contexts. Thus, I urge readers to also examine such classical articles as Cronbach's (1975) and Haney's (1981). For recent reviews of some of the more controversial issues, see Elliot's (1987) book and Helms's (1992) article. I too have contributed significantly to the legal literature on this topic (Bersoff, 1979, 1981, 1982, 1984).

References

Amrine, M. (Ed.). (1965). Testing and public policy [Special issue]. *American Psychologist, 20*(11).

Bersoff, D. N. (1979). Regarding psychologists testily: Legal constraints on psychological testing in the public schools. *Maryland Law Review, 39,* 27–120.

Bersoff, D. N. (1981). Testing and the law. *American Psychologist, 36,* 1047–1056.

Bersoff, D. N. (1982). *Larry P. and PASE:* Judicial report cards on the validity of individual intelligence scales. In T. Kratochwill (Ed.), *Advances in school psychology* (Vol. 2, pp. 61–95). Hillsdale, NJ: Erlbaum.

Bersoff, D. N. (1984). Social and legal influences on test development and usage. In B. Plake (Ed.), *Social and technical issues in testing* (pp. 87–109). Hillsdale, NJ: Erlbaum.

Cronbach, L. J. (1975). Five decades of public controversy over mental testing. *American Psychologist, 30,* 1–14.

Elliot, R. (1987). *Litigating intelligence: IQ tests, special education, and social science in the courtroom.* Dover, MA: Auburn House.

Glaser, R., & Bond, L. (Eds.). (1981). Testing: Concepts, policy, practice, and research [Special issue]. *American Psychologist, 36*(10).

Haney, W. (1981). Validity, vaudeville, and values: A short history of social concerns over standardized testing. *American Psychologist, 36,* 1021–1034.

Heller, K., Holtzman, W., & Messick, S. (Eds.). (1982). *Placing children in special education: A strategy for equity.* Washington, DC: National Academy Press.

Helms, J. (1992). Why is there no study of cultural equivalence in standardized *cognitive* ability testing? *American Psychologist, 47,* 1083–1101.

Wigdor, A. K., & Garner, W. R. (Eds.). (1982). *Ability testing: Uses, consequences, and controversies* (Vols. 1 & 2). Washington, DC: National Academy Press.

Test Validity and the Ethics of Assessment

Samuel Messick

Fifteen years ago or so, in papers dealing with personality measurement and the ethics of assessment, I drew a straightforward but deceptively simple distinction between the psychometric adequacy of a test and the appropriateness of its use (Messick, 1964, 1965). I argued that not only should tests be evaluated in terms of their measurement properties but that testing applications should be evaluated in terms of their potential social consequences. I urged that two questions be explicitly addressed whenever a test is proposed for a specific purpose: First, is the test any good as a measure of the characteristics it is interpreted to assess? Second, should the test be used for the proposed purpose in the proposed way? The first question is a scientific and technical one and may be answered by appraising evidence for the test's psychometric properties, especially construct validity. The second question is an ethical one, and its answer requires a justification of the proposed use in terms of social values. Good answers to the first question are not satisfactory answers to the second. Justification of test use by an appeal to empirical validity is not enough; the potential social consequences of the testing should also be appraised, not only in terms of what it might entail directly as costs and benefits but also in terms of what it makes more likely as possible side effects.

These two questions were phrased to parallel two recurrent criticisms of testing—that some tests are of poor quality and that tests are often misused—in an attempt to separate the frequently blurred issues in the typical critical interchange into (a) questions of test bias or the adequacy of measurement, and (b) questions of test fairness or the appropriateness of use (Messick, 1965).

. . . Also at issue is whether the measures *should* serve as means to the given end, in light of other ends they might inadvertently serve and in consideration of the place of the given end in the social fabric of pluralistic alternatives. For example, should a psychometrically sound measure of "flexibility versus rigidity" be used for selection in a particular college if it significantly improves the multiple prediction of grade point average there? What if the direction of prediction favored rigid students? What if entrance to a military academy were at issue, or a medical school? What if the scores had been interpreted instead as measures of "confusion versus control"? What if there were large sex differences in the score distributions? . . .

It seemed clear at this point that value issues in measurement were not limited to personality assessment, nor to selection applications, but should be extended to all psychological and educational measurement (Messick, 1975). This is primarily because psychological and educational variables all bear, either directly or indirectly, on human characteristics, processes, and products and hence are inherently, though variably, value-laden. . . . Values thus appear to be as pervasive and critical for psychological and educational measurement as is testing's acknowledged touchstone, validity. Indeed, "The root remaining of the word 'validity' is the same as that of the word 'value': both derive from a term meaning strength" (Kaplan, 1964, p. 198). . . .

VALIDITY AS EVALUATION OF IMPLICATIONS

Since validity is an evaluation of evidence, a judgment rather than an entity, and since some evidential basis should be provided for the interpretation and use of any test, validity has always been an ethical imperative in testing. As Burton (1978) put it, "Validity (as the word implies) has been primarily an

Adapted from the *American Psychologist, 35,* 1012–1027. Copyright 1980 by the American Psychological Association. Figures 1 and 2 have been omitted.

ethical requirement of tests, a prerequisite guarantee, rather than an active component of the use and interpretation of tests" (p. 264). . . .

If test validity is the overall degree of justification for test interpretation and use, and if human and social values encroach on both interpretation and use, as they do, then test validity should take account of those value implications in the overall judgment. The concern here, as in most ethical issues, is with evaluating the present and future consequences of interpretation and use (Churchman, 1961). If, as an intrinsic part of the overall validation process, we weigh the actual and potential consequences of our testing practices in light of considerations of what future society might need or desire, then test validity comes to be based on ethical as well as evidential grounds. . . .

References

Burton, N. W. Societal standards. *Journal of Educational Measurement*, 1978, *15*, 263–271.

Churchman, C. W. *Prediction and optimal decision: Philosophical issues of a science of values.* Englewood Cliffs, N.J.: Prentice-Hall, 1961.

Kaplan, A. *The conduct of inquiry: Methodology for behavioral science.* San Francisco: Chandler, 1964.

Messick, S. Personality measurement and college performance. *Proceedings of the 1963 Invitational Conference on Testing Problems.* Princeton, N.J.: Educational Testing Service, 1964.

Messick, S. Personality measurement and the ethics of assessment. *American Psychologist*, 1965, *20*, 136–142.

Messick, S. The standard problem: Meaning and values in measurement and evaluation. *American Psychologist*, 1975, *30*, 955–966.

On Competence and Ethicality in Psychodiagnostic Assessment

Irving B. Weiner

Psychologists who engage in psychodiagnostic assessment are frequently asked to comment on the validity of their instruments. Influenced by needs to affirm their opinions and assert their worth as professionals, they may at times be tempted to claim more certainty for their conclusions than can be documented and to stretch test findings beyond the known boundaries of their relevance. At other times, seeking to avoid any appearance of having gone beyond the facts or deviated from reasonable certainty, they may be tempted to sell their assessment techniques short and understate the valid and useful information that can be extracted from them.

Neither braggadocio nor diffidence serves professional purposes well, however, and psychologists should resist being tempted in either of these directions. Instead, they should draw on a careful analysis of what their tests can and cannot do, guided by a distinction among three types of referral questions that differ in how definitively they can be answered.

One type of question concerns aspects of current psychological functioning, such as intellectual ability or level of anxiety. These questions can usually be answered somewhat directly and objectively with instruments tailored for the purpose; on the Wechsler Adult Intelligence Scale (WAIS) and the State–Trait Anxiety Inventory (STAI), for example, intelligence and anxiety level, respectively, are ordinarily indicated with considerable certainty by the subject's performance. However, such narrowly focused assessments, although they may be valid, rarely satisfy either those who request or those who provide them. Psychological consultation typically addresses the way in which such specific aspects of psychological functioning combine to elucidate broader features of a person's capacities and coping style.

Accordingly, a second type of referral question concerns the presence of some state or condition, such as whether a person is schizophrenic or learning disabled, has a posttraumatic stress disorder, or is in need of therapy. The degree of certainty with which questions of this type can be answered depends on: (a) the clarity and reliability with which a condition in question has been delineated in terms of psychological functioning and (b) the adequacy with which the psychological functions that identify the condition can be measured by the tests that the psychologist is using.

The more fully a condition is understood and the more precisely its psychological manifestations can be assessed, the more certainly its presence or absence can be inferred from psychodiagnostic test data. However, the inescapable role of inference in answering this second type of question means that psychologists can rarely be as sure of themselves as when they are merely describing functioning in response to questions of the first type. Examiners commenting on the presence of a state or condition need to keep in mind how inferential they are being and to express their opinions accordingly, with a degree of certainty consonant with how closely their test data correspond to known corollaries of condition-specific psychological characteristics.

A third type of referral question concerns predictions of behavior, such as whether a person is potentially dangerous or suicidal or is likely to benefit from therapy or be a good parent. How accurately such questions can be answered through psychodiagnostic assessment depends on the extent to which individual psychological factors, as opposed to environmental and/or nonpsychological factors, determine the behavior in question. The more that intellectual or personality variables account for a behavior to be predicted, the more effectively psychodiagnostic assessment can be put to use. Earning passing grades in school, participating actively in psychotherapy, and acting in self-destructive ways are examples of behaviors that have substantial individual psychological determinants and that, in many cases, test data can help to predict. Even so, numerous circumstances unrelated to or unmeasurable by psychological tests will influence outcome in these behaviors. Presenting predictions about them with any suggestion of certainty is, therefore, usually unwarranted and ill-advised.

There are also instances in which even tentative predictions based solely on psychodiagnostic assessment are difficult to justify. Among seriously disturbed patients being discharged from hospitals and felons being released from prisons, for example, there is good reason to believe that their being able to remain in the community will be determined mainly by the nature of the environment to which they return. Psychodiagnostic test data contribute weakly at best to prediction in these cases and, in light of present knowledge, should not be portrayed otherwise in clinical practice.

Reference to present knowledge invokes the main theme of this article. Expressing certainty in considered relationship to the type of referral question being asked contributes to effective consultation only when psychodiagnosticians: (a) know what their tests can do and (b) act accordingly. Knowing what one's tests can do—that is, what psychological functions they describe accurately, what diagnostic conclusions can be inferred from them with what degree of certainty, and what kinds of behavior they can be expected to predict—is the measure of a psychodiagnostician's competence. Acting accordingly—that is, expressing only opinions that are consonant with the current status of validity data—is the measure of his or her ethicality.

Circumstances arise in which competent psychodiagnosticians confront ethical dilemmas that tax their sense of how best to use their knowledge of what tests can do. Perhaps most common in this regard is choosing between a less and a more serious diagnosis when reporting to a third party. The more serious diagnosis may help the person get needed treatment and insurance coverage. The less serious diagnosis may spare the person from an official mental health record that may be used prejudicially against him or her at some later time. Presumably, one could merely weigh the test data, select the diagnosis that fits them best, and let the chips fall where they may. In practice, however, survey data indicate that psychologists often struggle with this kind of situation, especially when the data would justify more than one option, and they differ in the alternatives toward which they lean.

Rarely can competent psychodiagnosticians avoid entirely having to grapple with gray areas of ethicality, especially in matters that have not yet been codified. Two equally ethical practitioners can end up behaving differently in such circumstances. Regrettably, there are also times when competent practitioners exercise poor judgment in the absence of any ethical dilemma. The harried examiner who saves time by signing his or her name to a computer printout and sending it off as a report and the expert psychologist witness who inflates up his or her credentials to lend weight to testimony are being unethical, even though they may be highly competent.

Although it is, therefore, possible in psychodiagnostic work to be competent without being ethical, it is not possible to be ethical without being competent. Competence is prerequisite for ethicality, and psychologists who practice or teach psychodiagnosis without being fully informed concerning what tests can and cannot do are behaving unethically. . . .

◆ ◆ ◆

Commentary: Because assessment may infringe on the test taker's sense of privacy and because it has such serious consequences for both society and the individual, there have been constant calls for either its abolition or its strict regulation. But as Messick warned 30 years ago,

> *absolute rules forbidding the use of . . . tests . . . would be an intolerable limitation both to scientific freedom and to professional freedom. . . . [I]n our consideration of pos-*

sible ethical bases for self-regulation in assessment, it seems imperative that we go beyond ethical absolutism . . . and espouse an "ethics of responsibility," in which pragmatic evaluations of the consequences of alternative actions form the basis for particular ethical decisions. . . . In this sense, then, we need continual assessments of ethics as the basis for an ethics of assessment. (p. 140)

See Messick, S. (1965). Personality measurement and the ethics of assessment. American Psychologist, 20, 136–142.

As you read the next group of materials, consider whether there has been too much self-regulation by the profession and too intrusive involvement in assessment by the federal government and the courts. On the other hand, given the enormous social consequences of testing, has the plethora of professional and legal regulation in the past 25 years been insufficient to deal with the problems?

The Legal Regulation of School Psychology

Donald N. Bersoff and Paul T. Hofer

TESTING AND EVALUATION

Nondiscriminatory Assessment

While every person in the United States probably has been affected in some way by tests, schoolchildren are its most frequent targets. It has been estimated that more than 250 million standardized tests of academic ability, perceptual and motor skills, emotional and social characteristics, and vocational interests and talent are used each year in education (Holman & Docter, 1972). Undoubtedly, test results have been used to admit, advance, and employ, but for the majority of persons scores derived from psychometric instruments serve as exclusionary devices—to segregate, institutionalize, track, and deny access to desired goals. . . .

While criticism of testing by social, political, and psychological commentators arose within the test industry itself, the legal system seriously began to examine the issue of nondiscriminatory assessment only since the mid-1960s. In part, judicial interest in testing may be explained by the Supreme Court's mandate in *Brown v. Board of Education* (1954) that the public schools must be desegregated. Civil rights advocates view educational and psychological tests as tools to hinder integration and, more broadly, as discriminatory instruments, denying the full realization of the constitutional rights of racial and ethnic minorities. As a result, from the mid-1960s to the 1980s there was an explosion of litigation and legislation affecting the administration, interpretation, and use of psychological tests. . . .

. . . In 1975 Congress passed P.L. 94-142 (20 U.S.C. §§ 1401–1461), the Education for All Handicapped Children Act (EAHCA). Two years earlier it had enacted § 504 of the Rehabilitation Act of 1973 (29 U.S.C. § 794). Implementing regulations

for the EAHCA were drafted by the Department of Health, Education, and Welfare (now the Department of Education) and for § 504 by what is now the Department of Health and Human Services, both of which took effect in 1977.

P.L. 94-142 is essentially a grant-giving statute providing financial support to sate and local education agencies for special education and related services if they meet certain detailed eligibility requirements. P.L. 94-142 and its implementing regulations reaffirmed earlier mandates concerning nondiscriminatory evaluation and fleshed out the meaning of this requirement. Section 300.532 of the regulations states:

> (a) Tests and other evaluation materials:
>
> (1) Are provided and administered in the child's native language or other mode of communication . . .
>
> (2) Have been validated for the specific purpose for which they are used; and
>
> (3) Are administered by trained personnel in conformance with the instructions provided by their producer. . . .

Other provisions also affect psychological and educational assessment. Children with sensory, manual, or speaking impairments are to be given tests that reflect genuine deficits in aptitude or achievement, not those impairments. Further, all assessment is to be comprehensive, multifaceted, and multidisciplinary. Evaluations for placement must be conducted by persons from education, medicine, and psychology who assess children "in all areas related to the suspected disability, including where appropriate, health, vision, hearing, social and emotional status, general intelligence, academic performance, communicative status, and motor abilities." Tests cannot be used which are "merely . . . designed to provide a single general intelligence quotient" nor can one single procedure be "used as the sole criterion for determining an appropriate educational program for a child." In making placement decisions the school is required to "draw upon information from a variety of sources, including aptitude and achievement tests, teacher recommendations, physical condition, social and cultural background and adaptive behavior." Thus, P.L. 94-142 makes it quite clear that assessment and placement decisions are the responsibility not of a school psychologist acting alone, but of a multidisciplinary team. The apparent reasons behind this diffusion of duty are to reduce individual bias and broaden accountability.

To ensure that all these provisions are effectuated, both the statute and the regulations provide mechanisms enabling parents "to present complaints with respect to any matter relating to the identification, evaluation, or educational placement" of their children. The complaints are presented in an impartial administrative hearing in which parents have the right to compel the attendance of, and to cross-examine, witnesses involved in the assessment and programming decisions. The consequence is that psychologists are vulnerable to intense scrutiny of their credentials and performance, including the reliability and validity of the evaluation measures they employ, the interpretations they make from the information gathered, or the recommendations they offer as a result of their evaluation. . . .

With regard to the Rehabilitation Act, a multipurpose law to promote the education, employment, and training of handicapped persons, Congress declared in § 504 that "no otherwise qualified handicapped individual in the United States . . . shall, solely by reason of his handicap, be excluded from participation in, be denied the benefits, of, or be subjected to discrimination under any program or activity receiving federal financial assistance." This section thus represents the first federal civil rights law protecting the rights of handicapped persons and reflects a national commitment to end discrimination on the basis of handicap. Unlike P.L. 94-142, the requirements of § 504 are not triggered by receipt of funds under a specific statute but protect handicapped persons in all

institutions receiving federal financial assistance. Thus, any school system, public or private, receiving federal monies for any program or activity whatsoever is bound by its mandates.

The regulations implementing the broad right-granting language of § 504 were published in 1977. In addition to general principles already established under P.L. 94-142, it sets forth regulations pertaining to the evaluation of children suspected of being handicapped. The language of those provisions, requiring preplacement evaluations, validated tests, multidisciplinary comprehensive assessment, and periodic reevaluations, are almost identical to that which now appears in the implementing regulations to P.L. 94-142. . . .

Reference

Holman, M., & Docter, R. (1972). *Educational and Psychological Testing*. New York: Russell Sage.

◆ ◆ ◆

Commentary: The Rehabilitation Act of 1973 is applicable to employment settings as well as to schools. Section 84.13 of the act's implementing regulations prohibits the use of employment tests that screen out applicants who are disabled, unless the test is job related and there are no alternative selection devices available that do not screen out such applicants. Even more broadly applicable to employers is the Americans for Disabilities Act (ADA). The ADA covers all employers engaged in interstate commerce that have 15 or more employees, even if these employers receive no federal financial assistance. Like the Rehabilitation Act, it prohibits the use of employment tests with an adverse impact on people who are disabled unless the tests are job related and are consistent with business necessity. On July 26, 1991, the Equal Employment Opportunity Commission published detailed regulations implementing the ADA. See the Federal Register, 56, 35726–35753, 1991.

Novick provided a useful history and summary of existing laws, regulations, and guidelines promulgated by the federal government concerning testing. See Novick, M. R. (1981). Federal guidelines and professional standards. American Psychologist, 36, 1035–1046. The most detailed and relevant of these documents is the Uniform Guidelines on Employee Selection Procedures, published in the 1978 Federal Register (Vol. 43, pp. 38290–38315), and a series of questions and answers designed to clarify and interpret the Uniform Guidelines, published in the 1979 Federal Register (Vol. 44, pp. 11996–12009).

Novick also discussed the work of such organizations as APA, the American Educational Research Association (AERA), and the National Council on Measurement in Education (NCME) in developing professional standards, including the then-current version of the APA, AERA, and NCME *Standards for Educational and Psychological Tests* (1974), which, for the first time, addressed issues of social importance, such as invasion of privacy and discrimination against women and minorities. But he and others were critical of the 1974 *Standards* and called for their revision. Not coincidentally, Novick was asked to chair a committee of AERA, APA, and NCME representatives who were to draft new testing standards. The revisions committee completed its work and published the *Standards for Educational and Psychological Testing* in 1985. The tripartite committee specifically noted that the "standards were formulated with the intent of being consistent with" (p. vii) the then-current (1987) APA code of ethics. Are the *Standards* enforceable under the provisions of Standard 2 of the 1992 Ethical Principles?

Any psychologist involved in the development, administration, scoring, interpretation, or publication of tests should read the *Standards for Educational and Psychological Testing* thoroughly. However, be aware that they are undergoing major revision under the auspices of the same three organizations that produced the 1985 version. This revision is due to be published in 1998.

References

AERA, APA, & NCME. (1974). *Standards for educational and psychological tests.* Washington, DC: American Psychological Association.

AERA, APA, & NCME. (1985). *Standards for educational and psychological tests.* Washington, DC: American Psychological Association.

Ethical Issues and Cases in the Practice of Personnel Psychology

Lorraine D. Eyde and Marilyn K. Quaintance

. . .

We examine factors contributing to the mounting concern with ethical issues and examine the professional practices of psychologists working in employment settings in light of increasing competition in the business community. Within this context, we explore the way in which a unifying principle of ethics facilitates consideration and discussion of five disparate ethical principles (American Psychological Association [APA], 1981a). We examine ethical obligations of personnel and counseling psychologists to serve their clients and the public as scientists/practitioners. Although the ethical principles are related to examples of test misuse, they apply to a broad spectrum of ethical behaviors, including the misrepresentation of and failure to consider professional competence, submission to managerial, financial, personal, and political pressures, and the issuance of misleading public statements.

BACKGROUND CONSIDERATIONS

. . .

For the use of psychologists, the American Psychological Association has issued the *Standards for Educational and Psychological Tests* (American Educational Research Association et al., 1985), the *General Guidelines for Providers of Psychological Services* (APA, 1987), and the *Specialty Guidelines for the Delivery of Services by Industrial/Organizational Psychologists* (APA, 1981b) to provide general guidance for ensuring quality in the delivery of psychological services. The Society for Industrial and Organizational Psychology's (1987) *Principles for the Validation and Use of Personnel Selection Procedures* also provide relevant guidance.

To assist industrial/organizational psychologists, of whom 47% identify themselves as personnel psychologists (Howard, 1982), in applying APA's *Ethical Principles*, the Society for Industrial and Organizational Psychology produced an ethics casebook, based on cases solicited from its membership (Lowman, 1985). . . .

The ethical concerns of psychologists working in business and industry relate to the roles that they play in organizations and

> from the fact that the ethics of psychology and the ethics of business are not usually congruent. . . . Most ethical complaints from business settings concern responsibility-to-client, assessment, and advertising issues. Often one senses that the psychologist in the business world about whom a complaint is received may have become a servant of power or may have lost some focus on human values to those of productivity and the company. (Keith-Speigel & Koocher, 1985, p. 333)

CASE APPROACH TO ETHICS

. . .

The applicability of the unifying principle may be illustrated by five cases that involve disparate ethical principles. . . .

Adapted from *Professional Psychology: Research and Practice*, 19, 148–154. Published by the American Psychological Association, 1988. In the public domain.

Case 1: Inappropriate Use and Interpretation of an Assessment Procedure

A psychologist administered the California Psychological Inventory (CPI) to assess candidates for promotion to senior management positions within an organization. The CPI results were the only information used by the psychologist in making the promotional decision, and these results were accepted as the "truth" regardless of the situational factors involving the inventory administration process. The psychologist was not familiar with the research evidence suggesting that test and retest CPI profiles differ considerably, depending on specific family or work stresses at the time of administration. No other inventories were administered, and no other evidence (e.g., appropriate performance ratings) was considered. The psychologist used only the CPI because the organizational management wanted to announce the promotions immediately. The psychologist recommended that a job analysis be performed to link the CPI's constructs to the requirements of the managerial job, but the recommendation was rejected by management because the linkage appeared obvious. The psychologist handled the matter rapidly because the contract to conduct the assessment had tight time requirements.

Several ethical principles apply to this case. According to Ethical Principle 8, Assessment Techniques, psychologists "guard against the misuse of assessment results. . . . They strive to ensure the appropriate use of the assessment techniques by others" (p. 637). In this case, the psychologist misused the CPI by relying on it as the sole measure for the determination of managerial promotional decisions. In addition, the CPI was misused in that its results were not interpreted correctly (i.e., in light of situational factors that may have affected CPI performance). By being unfamiliar with the CPI research literature regarding the influence of situational factors and by not taking the necessary time to prepare, the psychologist violated Ethical Principle 2, Competence, which requires that "psychologists responsible for decisions involving individuals or policies based on test results have an understanding of psychological or educational measurement, validation problems, and test research" (p. 634).

Last, the fact that the psychologist succumbed to management pressure for quick promotional decisions by using the CPI and no other assessment techniques or evidence (e.g., relevant performance evaluations) indicates that Ethical Principle 1, Responsibility, was violated: "As practitioners, psychologists know that they bear a heavy social responsibility because their recommendations and professional actions may alter the lives of others. They are alert to personal, social, organizational, financial, or political situations and pressures that might lead to misuse of their influence" (p. 633).

Case 2: Lack of Competence in Test Interpretation and Misrepresentation

A personnel psychologist who lacked training in the interpretation of the Minnesota Multiphasic Personality Inventory (MMPI) hired a clinical psychologist to purchase MMPI materials from the test publisher. The clinical psychologist was trained to read and interpret the test records of job applicants for nuclear power plant positions and to determine their emotional fitness for work in one of two power companies. Because of financial pressures, the personnel psychologist discontinued the use of the services of the clinical psychologist. The personnel psychologist continued to purchase the MMPI from the test publisher and did not inform the test publisher that the services on the clinical psychologist had been discontinued. The test publisher's agreement to provide the needed test materials was based on the understanding that consultation by the clinical psychologist, trained in the interpretation of the MMPI, was ongoing. The personnel psychologist also continued to provide the psychological screening service to the two power companies without informing these two organizations of the lack of his knowledge of MMPI procedures.

Clearly, the personnel psychologist violated Ethical Principle 2, Competence, which requires psychologists to "accurately represent their competence, education, training, and experience" (p. 634) by not informing the two power companies of the need for the assistance of the clinical psychologist in the administration and interpretation of the MMPI. The personnel psychologist did not "recognize the boundaries of [his] competence and the limitations of [his] techniques" (p. 634); nor did he "only provide services and only use techniques for which [he was] qualified by training and experience" (p. 634). It is possible that the personnel psychologist could have corrected this situation by attending appropriate workshops or through postgraduate training.

In addition, the personnel psychologist violated Ethical Principle 1, Responsibility, by succumbing to financial pressures that led him to continue providing to the power companies services that he was unqualified to provide while simultaneously discontinuing the services of the clinical psychologist who was qualified to interpret the MMPI. According to Ethical Principle 1, "As practitioners, psychologists know they bear a heavy social responsibility because their recommendations and professional actions may alter the lives of others. They are alert to personal, social, organizational, financial, or political situations and pressures that might lead to misuse of their influence" (p. 633). According to the Preamble, psychologists show concern for serving the best interests of society. Certainly an incorrect hiring decision for the position of nuclear power plant worker would not only affect the life of the job applicant, but it might also have disastrous effects on the lives of others if that applicant were hired and failed on the job.

Case 3: Violation of Legal Standards and Submission to Personal Pressures

A psychologist responsible for administering a test procedure to candidates for hire knows one of the candidates personally as a friend. The psychologist assists the candidate in attaining a good score on the selection instrument by coaching.

This psychologist has succumbed to the personal pressures of friendship and violated Ethical Principle 1, Responsibility: "As practitioners, psychologists know that they bear a heavy social responsibility because their recommendations and professional actions may alter the lives of others. They are alert to personal, social, organizational, financial, or political situations and pressures that might lead to misuse of their influence" (p. 633).

By giving the personal friend an advantage on this particular hiring measure, the psychologist has violated the civil rights of the other applicants (i.e., the right to equal employment opportunity). Thus

the psychologist violated Ethical Principle 3, Moral and Legal Standards: "In their professional roles, psychologists avoid any action that will violate or diminish the legal and civil rights of clients or of others who may be affected by their actions" (p. 634).

Case 4: Misleading Public Statements

Promotional material prepared by a psychologist for a personnel test that she published was misleading in that it suggested that it was the only test of its kind favorably reviewed in a given edition of *Mental Measurements Yearbook*. The promotional literature made no mention of the fact that subsequent editions of the *Yearbook* contained favorable reviews of other instruments that were similar in nature. In addition, the promotional material stated that the *Mental Measurements Yearbook* contains all published psychological tests; in fact, the *Yearbook* contains only new tests and tests revised since the last edition of the *Yearbook* or tests that have generated 20 or more references since the last *Yearbook* edition.

The psychologist violated Ethical Principle 4, Public Statements, in that her promotional materials did not "serve the purpose of helping the public make informed judgments and choices" (p. 634). The promotional material contained "a misinterpretation of fact . . . [that may] deceive because in context it makes only a partial disclosure of relevant facts" (p. 634). In addition, the literature contained a statement implying unusual or unique abilities by suggesting that the test was the only one reviewed favorably by the *Yearbook*, although in later editions other similar tests had been reviewed favorably as well.

Case 5: Lack of Competence in Test Selection and Interpretation

A counseling psychologist, who lacked formal training and experience in the use of written examinations for personnel selection and classification, was asked to recommend a test to evaluate competency of teachers in a northeastern state. The psychologist suggested that the Wesman Personnel Classification Test be administered to all practicing teachers to evaluate teacher competency level. The test manual for the Wesman indicated that the examination was a measure of skills in verbal and numerical areas, but gave no reference to applications of the Wesman to evaluate teacher competency. Although such an application of the Wesman might constitute a legitimate use, there was no research evidence to support it.

In the absence of normative data for teachers, the psychologist recommended a pass–fail score of 70%. This score was established partly for political reasons because that level was "what was expected of school children."

The test manual showed that scores of 70% (28) on the Verbal Wesman are at the 76th percentile for salaried workers and the 73rd percentile for the Air Force Captains. Similarly, scores of 70% (14) on the Numerical Wesman are at the 76th percentile for salaried workers and the 78th percentile for Air Force Captains. However, these same scores of 28 and 14 were considered failing for the examinees.

About half of the teachers, as well as an even larger proportion of school administrators who also took the examination, "failed." The pass rate for minorities was significantly lower than the pass rate for nonminorities. When a summary of the test results appeared in the press, along with a description of the scoring procedures, the state school system experienced a public relations disaster.

Clearly, the counseling psychologist violated Ethical Principle 2, Competence: "Psychologists [who are] responsible for decisions involving individuals or policies based on test results have an understanding of psychological or educational measurement, validation problems, and test research" (p. 634). Had the counseling psychologist had an understanding of psychological or educational measurement, then she would have known how to interpret the normative data that had been gathered previously for the Wesman and to assess the practical implications of setting a passing score of 70% for teachers. Ideally, the psychologist would have suggested to the state school system that a large group of satisfactory teachers be tested initially to establish norms. Another situation, less ideal, would have been to set the standard on the basis of the scores of the examinees taking the test or "grading on the curve."

The counseling psychologist should have informed the state school system of her lack of formal training and experience in personnel selection and classification. By proceeding with the assignment without in-forming her employer of the limitations of her competence, she violated Principle 2, which requires that "psychologists accurately represent their competence, education, training, and experience" (p. 634).

In this case, the psychologist suggested a cutoff score, recognizing that the Wesman Test Manual contained neither evidence to support that score nor validity evidence to support the use of the Wesman to evaluate teacher competency. In addition, the 70% cutoff was selected for political rather than professional reasons because that is "what was expected of the children." Thus the counseling psychologist also violated Ethical Principle 1, Responsibility: "[Psychologists] are alert to . . . political situations and pressures that might lead to misuse of their influence" (p. 633).

DISCUSSION

. . .

What commonalities do the five cases present? If the psychologists had invoked the universal principle, they might have foreseen the destructive aspects of their behavior and avoided unethical conduct. In the test for universal applicability, deontics and teleology converge. The universality principle calls for actions for the common good, and the teleological aspects focus on the psychologists' purposive behavior and its potential effects. . . .

. . . By discussing ethical principles in terms of moral philosophy, we are likely to raise our ethical consciousness relating to our scientific and professional obligations, to our organizational clients, and to consumers whose lives are affected by our practices. Ethical violations might then be avoided. . . .

References

American Educational Research Association, American Psychological Association, and the National Council on Measurement in Education (1985). *Standards for educational and psychological tests.* Washington, DC: American Psychological Association.

American Psychological Association (1981a). Ethical principles of psychologists. *American Psychologist, 36,* 633–638.

American Psychological Association (1981b). *Specialty guidelines for the delivery of services by industrial/organizational psychologists.* Washington, DC: Author.

American Psychological Association (1987). General guidelines for providers of psychological services. *American Psychologist, 42,* 712–723.

Howard, A. (Chair). (1982, March). *Who are the industrial/organizational psychologists? An analysis of data from the 1981 APA Directory Survey.* Report prepared for the Executive Committee of Division 14, American Psychological Association, Washington, DC.

Keith-Spiegel, P., & Koocher, G. P. (1985). *Ethics in psychology: Professional standards and cases.* New York: Random House.

Lowman, R. L. (Ed.) (1985). *Casebook on ethics and standards for the practice of psychology in organizations.* College Park, MD: Society for Industrial and Organizational Psychology, Inc., Division 14 of the American Psychological Association.

Society for Industrial and Organizational Psychology (1987). *Principles for the validation and use of personnel selection procedures* (3rd ed.). College Park, MD: Author.

◆ ◆ ◆

Commentary: The citations in this article are for the 1981 ethics code. Can you identify the relevant provisions in the 1992 Ethical Principles?

An outgrowth of the 1981 Conference on Testing, Assessment, and Public Policy was the creation of the Test User Qualifications Working Group (TUQWoG)—a subcommittee of the AERA, APA, and NCME Joint Committee on Testing Practices, which devised the 1985 Standards for Testing. TUQWoG's ultimate mission was to develop a model test-user-qualification system, consistent with professional standards and ethical principles. TUQWoG identified seven major factors related to the misuse of tests: (a) failure to conduct a comprehensive assessment, (b) improper test use (such as lack of proper training and use of quality control), (c) ignorance of standard error of measurement, (d) failure to maintain integrity of test results, (e) inaccurate scoring, (f) inappropriate use of norms, and (g) the failure to give proper interpretive information to test takers. See Edye, L. E., Moreland, K. L., & Robertson, G. J. (1988). Test user qualifications: A data-based approach to promoting good test use. *Washington, DC: American Psychological Association, Test User Qualifications Working Group. More recently, a successor group to TUQWoG—the Test User Training Work Group—has developed a helpful book of cases that were based on real-life testing situations and were designed to raise questions about proper test use and interpretation. See Eyde, L. D., Robertson, G. J., Krug, S. E., Moreland, K. L., Robertson, A. G., Shewan, C. M., Harrison, P. L., Porch, B. E., Hammer, A. L., & Primoff, E. S. (1993).* Responsible test use: Case studies for assessing human behavior. *Washington, DC: American Psychological Association.*

Ethical Issues in Testing and Evaluation for Personnel Decisions

Manuel London and Douglas W. Bray

[Professional standards and ethics] have had an impact on personnel research and practice in at least three ways. First, the professional standards and federal guidelines clearly delineate appropriate procedures for developing and validating evaluation devices. The values implied by these standards are that high-quality information should be used to make decisions about people and that psychologists are responsible for developing procedures that result in the most accurate decisions. Second, equal employment legislation has placed emphasis on the meaning and extent of unfair discrimination and how it can be avoided by affirmative action programs. Third, growing concerns for individual privacy and freedom of information are beginning to raise new research questions and challenges. For example, what is the impact on employees of suddenly having access to their supervisors' view of their potential for advancement? Does such access affect supervisors' ratings? To what extent does informing individuals about the purpose of an evaluation affect the results? How can confidentiality of information be guaranteed and invasion of privacy avoided while providing information to those who make personnel decisions? . . .

. . . Theories that serve as a basis for ethical principles should be formed by observing interrelationships rather than vice versa. If the available evidence is not sufficient to establish guidelines for specific ethical problems, research questions must be formulated and answered before resolutions are suggested.

Another caveat is that a law or standard does not exist for all situations. Laws and standards are frequently ambiguous and are subject to change. Many ethical questions require personal judgment at least until cases accumulate that provide a body of collec-

tive experience to guide ethical practice in similar situations. According to Mirvis and Seashore (1979), "The challenge of being ethical lies not simply in the application of moral prescriptions but in the process of creating and maintaining research relationships in which to address and moderate ethical dilemmas that are not and cannot be covered by prescription" (p. 768). . . .

ETHICAL OBLIGATIONS OF PSYCHOLOGISTS

Organizational staff members who are responsible for formulating and applying evaluation procedures have ethical obligations to their profession, to the people they evaluate, and to their employers. . . .

Psychologists' Obligations to the Profession

Organizations often employ individuals with advanced degrees in personnel-related fields. Psychologists who are members of APA or who are licensed by a state to practice psychology are expected to abide by the standards and principles for ethical practice set forth by APA, regional professional organizations, and/or state statutes. However, nonpsychologists involved in evaluation are not formally responsible for adhering to these standards. Nevertheless, the federal *Uniform Guidelines on Employee Selection Procedures* sets standards for all personnel experts in organizations subject to federal regulations regarding equal employment opportunity. . . . Desirable behaviors for ethical conduct generally include keeping informed of advances in the field, reporting unethical practices, and increasing colleagues' sensitivity to ethical issues.

Adapted from the *American Psychologist*, 35, 890–901. Copyright 1980 by the American Psychological Association.

Maintaining professional competence is necessary for effective application of evaluation techniques. The *Standards for Educational and Psychological Tests* devotes a section to qualifications of test users. Test users must have a general knowledge of measurement and validation principles and the limitations of test interpretation as well as an understanding of the literature relevant to the evaluation devices they use. The *Ethical Standards of Psychologists* emphasizes the need for continuing education, being open to new procedures, and remaining abreast of relevant federal, state, and local regulations concerning practice and research. . . .

Psychologists' Obligations to Those Who Are Evaluated

Social and legal influences mandate that career decisions be made with a concern for accuracy and equality in employment opportunity (Division of Industrial and Organizational Psychology, 1975). A concern for the person who is affected by career decisions, however, leads to a number of ethical principles that go beyond improving and maintaining accuracy and ensuring equal employment opportunity. These principles include guarding against invasion of privacy, guaranteeing confidentiality, obtaining employees' and applicants' informed consent before evaluation, respecting employees' right to know, imposing time limitations on data, minimizing false positive and false negative decisions, and treating employees with respect and consideration. . . .

Questions of invasion of privacy arise in the use of certain types of tests. Gross (1962) has argued that personality tests in particular violate personal privacy and encourage conformity and lying. He wonders why someone should be required to share private thoughts as a condition of employment and why people are penalized for responding truthfully. Guion (1965) responds to these arguments by stating, "It is a clear invasion of privacy to ask an applicant to reveal details of thought or emotion that are not relevant to performance on the job for which he is considered" (p. 576). Ewing (1977) recommends that employees or applicants not be required or pressured to take a personality test or any other examination, for that matter, which constitutes, in their opinion, an invasion of privacy, regardless of the

test's validity. This is an extreme view that must be balanced against the value of accurate employment and placement decisions to the organization, society, and individuals themselves. . . .

Some organizations routinely provide evaluation results to employees in the hope that knowledge of results will improve performance. Other organizations maintain a policy of secrecy or leave it up to individual supervisors to decide whether to provide feedback. Legislation now guarantees public employees access to this information, and pending legislation, if enacted, will do the same in the private sector. Research on the effects of access on the quality of information and the behavior and attitudes of the employee is necessary. . . .

Another issue pertaining to the confidentiality of evaluations such as recommendations deals with protecting the identity of individuals providing the information. Specifically, should employees have access to recommendations written about them? A similar question was answered by Congress in 1974 when it enacted a law giving students the right to inspect their records (Ewing, 1977). Now students choose whether or not to waive this right before asking someone to complete a recommendation form. Allowing employees to decide whether or not to waive their right to access to recommendations and other information in their personnel files may be a viable solution to employee complaints about confidential information they believe may be used against them. Here, as in other areas, there is a conflict between the rights of the individual and the validity of information obtained. An important research question is whether those named as references will supply negative information if they know the applicant will have access to it.

An especially difficult ethical problem involves maintaining the confidentiality of test results within an organization. Typically, many individuals outside the personnel staff have legitimate access to the information. For instance, a manager who is responsible for filling a position vacancy by promotion from within the company may use information about an employee's job experience and performance. Such information is often used without the knowledge of the employee. This raises the issue of informed consent—that is, of informing candidates about the intended use of test results prior to their taking the test. Tests given by an organization for one purpose are often used later for additional purposes. Thus, a score on an employment test may be used later for selection to a training program, assignment to a specific type of work, or promotion to a higher level. A person has the right to be told every potential use of the test results. This does not mean that the individual has to be informed every time a decision is made. Rather, it simply means that he or she should be aware of the types of decisions that may depend in part on the test results.

If information collected early in an employee's career is to be used later to make decisions about that employee, the salience of the information should be checked when the decisions are made. Both the *Standards for Educational and Psychological Tests* and the *Ethical Standards of Psychologists* state that test score information that has become obsolete because of lapse of time should be removed from data files. The idea is to prevent such information from being misused or misconstrued to the disadvantage of the person being evaluated. But how old must data be before they are of little use? One study demonstrated that assessment center ratings predict advancement 8 years later (Bray, Campbell, & Grant, 1974). Further research indicated that the same ratings retained predictive validity 16 years after they were collected. . . . In some cases, destroying data in personnel files may be illegal, as when such information is discoverable in a lawsuit. It is reasonable to remove old evaluative information that has not been used for personnel decisions, particularly if it has been updated. Before destroying data used to make personnel decisions, however, it is desirable to determine their likely utility for making future predictions and for serving as evidence of the rationale for prior decisions. Data with such utility should not be indiscriminantly destroyed. . . .

Ethical treatment of employees during and after evaluation is another obligation of psychologists. How employees or applicants are treated when they are evaluated can influence the results of the evaluation and their acceptance of the ensuing decision. In general, evaluation procedures should be standardized to guarantee equal treatment and to enable examinees to do their best. . . . Standard procedures

should include personal and considerate treatment, a clear explanation of the evaluation process, and direct and honest answers to examinees' questions.

Psychologists' Obligations to the Employer

Ethical obligations to the employer go beyond the basic design and administration of decision-making procedures. These obligations include conveying accurate expectations for evaluation procedures, ensuring high-quality test data, implementing and periodically reviewing the adequacy of decision-making procedures, respecting the employer's proprietary rights, and balancing vested interests of the employer with government regulations, with commitment to the psychology profession, and with the rights of those evaluated for personnel decisions. . . .

Psychologists must attempt to provide high-quality information for personnel decisions, namely, reliable, valid, and fair data. However, psychologists are often unable to use the most rigorous scientific methods to ascertain a test's reliability and validity because of limited resources, time pressure, or other constraints imposed by the employer. . . .

Fairness relates to the absence of discrimination on the basis of race, sex, national origin, or other characteristics not related to the job. The law has responded to this issue in the form of legislation and judicial rulings. In general, a reasonably reliable and valid test that does not exhibit differential validity may still be unfair if it results in a substantially smaller proportion of favorable personnel decisions for one or more protected classes than for the majority group. (A substantially smaller proportion is defined in the *Uniform Guidelines* as less than 80% of the majority group selection rate, but this criterion does not necessarily define unfairness.) Therefore, in addition to determining that an evaluation device is reliable and valid, a psychologist must ascertain that it is free from bias. . . .

The advent of new knowledge, changes in job requirements, and recent legislation and judicial rulings may require adjustments in the use of evaluation techniques. For example, procedures will have to be established for providing feedback to candidates. Psychologists have an obligation to their employers as well as to their profession to keep abreast of such requirements and to inform the employers when changes are relevant. In addition, psychologists should oppose guidelines, rulings, and policies that are not in keeping with professional practice.

Psychologists must respect the proprietary rights of the employer as long as it is possible to maintain standards of ethical practice. Many organizations insist that their selection methods remain confidential, and in some cases they maintain this policy even when under review by government agencies. Companies in a competitive environment that invest heavily in personnel methods may be reluctant to publicize the details of their procedures. Moreover, organizations may fear that information given out about their procedures will lead to difficult questions even if the procedures are perfectly proper. The APA expects in-house psychologists and independent psychologists serving as consultants to support the proprietary rights of their employer as long as the employer does not demand or use unethical practices. . . . Therefore, psychologists working in industry may be constrained from publishing data regarding test development and validation or other research results sponsored by the employer.

Another ethical issue arises when psychologists are constrained from conducting research because the results may in some way be detrimental to their employer. . . . In such a case, the psychologist must abide by the wishes of the employer, try to persuade the employer otherwise, or change jobs. The ethical issue must be resolved by the psychologist. The issue becomes salient when the psychologist believes that proper practice has been hindered. Indeed, this is the crux of many ethical issues in psychology. Ethical responsibility is a personal and individual issue. Although the situation may be constructed by the employer, the psychologist perceives and interprets the situation and must deal with restrictions that he or she believes contribute to unethical practice. . . .

Balancing obligations to the employer, the profession, and those evaluated for personnel decisions is difficult. . . .

The potential for conflict among the professional's obligations to the employer, the profession, and employees is perhaps most likely in the area of confidentiality. Management's need to know must be sat-

isfied while keeping promises to employees and applicants that evaluation results will remain confidential and while ensuring that the contents of evaluation devices are not disclosed to the extent that they are invalidated. . . .

SUMMARY AND CONCLUSION

. . .

This review clearly indicates that the times are changing. What was considered ethical several years ago is not necessarily considered ethical today. A growing concern for human rights has placed career decision-making procedures and associated psychological research and practices in the public domain. At one time organizations felt they had a right to hire, transfer, and fire whomever they wished for the good of the business, but recent union agreements and civil suits have markedly altered the situation. Just as more and more organizations are beginning to abide by and respect the need for equal employment opportunity (whether they are forced by regulatory agencies or not), so the emphasis on freedom on information and individual privacy is awakening employees and employers to new concerns.

These changes have led to what may seem to be an ever growing morass of edicts, laws, and implicit values constituting ethical standards. Moreover, these standards are often ambiguous, contradictory, and far from intuitively obvious. Many researchers, practitioners, and administrators are wondering how to cope with this turbulent environment. If psychologists maintain a reactive stance and allow legislation and judicial rulings to define ethical practice, then the outlook is depressing. If psychologists creatively resolve ethical issues and deal with conflicting rights, however, then the outlook is challenging. We suggest the need for research on conditions leading to unethical conduct. Research is also needed on ways to enforce ethical principles, particularly when these principles are promulgated in the profession but not supported by legislation. . . .

Finally, we must recognize that today's ethical standards are frequently tomorrow's laws. Professional standards are often incorporated into laws and used as the basis for judicial rulings. When published professional standards are insufficient, Congress and the courts do not hesitate to impose their own. Consequently, psychologists must play active roles in lobbying and writing legislation. Recognizing that ethical prescriptions and legal requirements are intertwined and are likely to become more so should be impetus enough for adopting ethical personnel practices and conducting research that will influence legislation.

References

Bray, D. W., Campbell, R. J., & Grant, D. L. *Formative years in business*. New York: Wiley, 1974.

Division of Industrial and Organizational Psychology, American Psychological Association. *Principles for the validation and use of personnel selection procedures*. Dayton, Ohio: Author, 1975.

Ewing, D. W. *Freedom inside the organization: Bringing civil liberties to the workplace*. New York: Dutton, 1977.

Gross, M. L. *The brain watchers*. New York: Random House, 1962.

Guion, R. M. *Personnel testing*. New York: McGraw-Hill, 1965.

Mirvis, P. H., & Seashore, S. E. Being ethical in organizational research. *American Psychologist*, 1979, *34*, 766–780.

Commentary: Although London and Bray (1979 and excerpt above) did not cite it, in 1979 the U.S. Supreme Court decided a case that raised many of the issues discussed in their article. More important, although the case involved an interpretation of the National Labor Relations Act and the use of tests in employment settings, it had broader ramifications for all psychologists. The case was not only relevant to issues of confidentiality of test results but, in the larger context, it pitted all of APA's ethics code against competing legal obligations (see chap. 2). The following excerpt from Eberlein's 1980 article summarizes the facts and issues in the case— Detroit Edison Co. v. National Labor Relations Board, 440 U.S. 301 (1979).

Confidentiality of Industrial Psychological Tests

Larry Eberlein

. . .

THE CASE

In late 1971, Detroit Edison posted notice of six vacancies in its classification "Instrument Man B" at a new power plant. All 10 employees who applied for the posted positions failed to achieve the "acceptable" cutoff score set by the Company on a battery of psychological aptitude tests. The vacancies were then filled by promoting employees with less seniority from other units of Detroit Edison who had scored at or above the recommended level on the test. Under the terms of the collective bargaining agreement, the Union filed a grievance against the Company and claimed the testing procedure was unfair. The Union requested that the Company deliver the administered tests as well as the employees' answer sheets, scores, and other data referring to the tests. The Union claimed that this would be essential for processing the grievance through the normal arbitration channels.

There was no dispute that the Company had established the right to use standardized tests as a measure of an employee's qualifications. The Union contended, however, that it could only monitor the collective agreement by examining copies of tests and actual protocols whenever an issue of fairness relating to the testing procedure was raised. The Company, on the other hand, argued that since the tests were designed only to predict future success in a particular job, the sample questions and descriptive literature together with validation studies were all that would be required to judge the fairness of the test. The Company also claimed that disclosure of the actual test battery would make it useless in the future because dissemination of the questions and answers would be sure to follow. In addition, Detroit Edison refused to deliver data on any specific person on the basis of the confidential relationship between the psychologist and the testee. If each Union member would agree in writing to the release of information, then it would be made available. The Union refused to obtain this permission and claimed the test data as a matter of right.

THE LAW JUDGE

An administrative law judge for the NLRB [National Labor Relations Board] decided on January 29, 1975 that the test results of individual employees should be turned over to a qualified industrial psychologist "selected by the Union to act in its behalf in this matter." The argument that seemed to influence the law judge was that the Company and its psychologists were using the issue of confidentiality under an ethical code for their own purposes. The Company used psychological tests to determine the right of an employee to be promoted and then tried to hide behind the shield of confidentiality to prevent revelation of critical elements in the promotion process. The judge concluded that this was an attempt to return to individual bargaining and that it negated the collective process provided by law. The "asserted code of conduct of a psychological association" does not insulate the Company "from the obligations imposed by the Act as a result of (Detroit Edison's) own voluntary course of conduct [footnote omitted]."

The Union was granted the right, utilizing a psychologist's services, to view and study all the data and to use the tests in its arbitration process. The decision recommended the imposition of certain safeguards, however, to protect the security of the

Adapted from *Professional Psychology*, 11, 749–754. Copyright 1980 by the American Psychological Association.

test data. It prohibited the Union from copying and disclosing questions to employees who had taken or might take the tests or to anyone who might advise employees about test contents.

THE NLRB AND THE COURT OF APPEALS

By a 2–1 vote, the NLRB subsequently ordered that the test results and raw data be turned *directly* over to the Union. If the Union felt the need of a psychologist to interpret the test results or the test profiles, it would be free to hire one [footnote omitted].

On appeal to the Court of Appeals for the Sixth Circuit, that Court agreed in 1977, also by a 2–1 vote, that the NLRB order should be enforced. The Court held:

> It is possible that the union will not be able to make any determinations about the fairness of the tests by itself and that it will need the advice of a psychologist. Nevertheless, that is a decision that the union should be allowed to make rather than a condition to its right to examine the tests [footnote omitted].

Over the objections of the American Psychological Association (APA), as well as Detroit Edison, the Court of Appeals held that protection of confidentiality was adequately maintained by the NLRB's order to the Union not to copy the tests or otherwise disclose the test contents. In response to a Company claim that any disclosure of the actual test battery or individual test scores would involve their industrial psychologists in a breach of their professional ethical code, the court concluded that:

> Detroit Edison cannot rely upon an asserted privilege which is personal to the employees who took the examination, and we are not informed of any rule of law under which the professional code of the American Psychological Association can stand as a barrier to the right of a duly chosen and certified collective bargaining representative to receive information of use to it in carrying out its duties and responsibilities [footnote omitted].

. . .

◆ ◆ ◆

Commentary: *The U.S. Supreme Court, in reviewing the Sixth Circuit Court's decision, began its opinion by acknowledging that "psychological aptitude testing is a widely used employee selection and promotion device in both industry and government. Test secrecy is concededly critical to the validity of any such program, and confidentiality of scores is undeniably important to the examinees" (p. 304). The Court held that the National Labor Relations Board's order, enforced by the Court of Appeals, failed to adequately accommodate those concerns. The Board, it said, abused its discretion in ordering the company to turn over the test battery and answer sheets directly to the union. It then addressed the ethical issues.*

Detroit Edison Co. v. National Labor Relations Board

   The dispute over Union access to the actual scores received by named employees is in a somewhat different procedural posture[.] . . . The Company argues that even if the scores were relevant to the Union's grievance (which it vigorously disputes), the Union's need for the information was not sufficiently weighty to require breach of the promise of confidentiality to the examinees, breach of its industrial psychologists' code of professional ethics, and potential embarrassment and harassment of at least some of the examinees. The Board responds that this information does satisfy the appropriate standard of "relevance," . . . and that the Company, having "unilaterally" chosen to make a promise of confidentiality to the examinees, cannot rely on that promise to defend against a request for relevant information. The professional obligations of the Company's psychologists, it argues, must give way to paramount federal law. Finally, it dismisses as speculative the contention that employees with low scores might be embarrassed or harassed.

   We may accept for the sake of this discussion the finding that the employee scores were of potential relevance to the Union's grievance, as well as the position of the Board that the federal statutory duty to disclose relevant information cannot be defeated by the ethical standards of a private group. . . . Nevertheless we agree with the Company that its willingness to disclose these scores only upon receipt of consents from the examinees satisfied its statutory obligations under § 8 (a)(5).

   The Board's position appears to rest on the proposition that union interests in arguably relevant information must always predominate over all other interests, however legitimate. But such an absolute rule has never been established [footnote omitted], and we decline to adopt such a rule here [footnote omitted]. There are situations in which an employer's conditional offer to disclose may be warranted. This we believe is one.

   The sensitivity of any human being to disclosure of information that may be taken to bear on his or her basic competence is sufficiently well known to be an appropriate subject of judicial notice [footnote omitted]. There is nothing in this record to suggest that the Company promised the examinees that their scores would remain confidential in order to further parochial concerns or to frustrate subsequent Union attempts to process employee grievances. And it has not been suggested at any point in this proceeding that the Company's unilateral promise of confidentiality was in itself violative of the terms of the collective-bargaining agreement. Indeed, the Company presented evidence that disclosure of individual scores had in the past resulted in the harassment of some lower scoring examinees who had, as a result, left the Company.

   Under these circumstances, any possible impairment of the function of the Union in processing the grievances of employees is more than justified by the interests served in conditioning the disclosure of the test scores upon the consent of the very employees whose grievance is being processed. The burden on the Union in this instance is minimal. The Company's interest in preserving employee confidence in the testing program is well founded.

   In light of the sensitive nature of testing information, the minimal burden that compliance with the Company's offer would have placed on the Union, and the total absence of evidence that the Company had fabricated concern for employee confidentiality only to frustrate the Union in the discharge of its responsibilities, we are unable to sustain the Board in its conclusion that the Company, in resisting an unconsented-to disclosure of individual test results, violated the statutory obligation to bargain in good faith. . . . Accordingly, we hold that the order requiring the Company unconditionally to disclose the employee scores to the Union was erroneous. . . .

Adapted from *Detroit Edison Co. v. National Labor Relations Board*, 440 U.S. 301 (1979).

Confidentiality of Industrial Psychological Tests

Larry Eberlein

. . .

In the Detroit Edison case the psychologists were APA members, certified by the state of Michigan. Their practice was to administer tests to job applicants on the express understanding that neither Company management nor Union officials would see actual results, although the psychologists were prepared to go through test results with individual employees. Circuit Judge Weick, the lone dissenting judge in the Court of Appeals, was of the opinion that any other disclosure could subject the psychologists to the sanctions of disciplinary action and suspension or even revocation of licenses by the state of Michigan [footnote omitted]. Indeed, Michigan subjects psychologists to APA ethical standards [footnote omitted] and provides for revocation of certification for violation of those standards or for "dishonorable or unprofessional conduct [footnote omitted]."

The majority of the Supreme Court recognized both the APA Standards for Educational and Psychological Tests and the Ethical Standards of Psychologists. Justice White, speaking for the minority, however, argued that these standards were unimportant, since this was *not* an employee rights issue. It was up to the NLRB to achieve the "difficult and delicate task" of balancing the competing concerns of unions and management without court interference. In fact, the dissent took the view that a company psychologist in going over test results with an employee outside the presence of a union representative violates the spirit of the grievance procedure.

Justice White, speaking for four of nine justices, was of the strong opinion that giving test questions solely to a third-party psychologist is fundamentally at odds with the collective bargaining process. Thus, services of a psychologist "may be totally unnecessary" and there is no need to "justify compulsory retention" of a professional with its attendant cost [footnote omitted]. Nothing in Justice White's argument addresses the APA's professional obligation to provide materials only to another professional but, rather, suggests that the union leadership may be as qualified as a psychologist to understand and interpret test data. . . .

IMPLICATIONS FOR PROFESSIONAL PRACTICE

. . . The Detroit Edison case involved "in-house" psychologists who were seen to be part of management. Even with the best history of good labor relations, unions approach management with a certain degree of skepticism. Psychologists in such a practice must realize that their job responsibilities will be dictated in part by the collective agreement and can be changed by the collective bargaining process.

In any employment setting, psychologists are involved in deciding where their allegiance lies when inherent conflicts surface. The union's responsibility is to protect the collective rights of its members more than one individual's right. Psychologists must, therefore, clearly indicate the limitations of their role when dealing with union members. Since confidentiality is a privilege reserved to the client, the psychologist would not have breached an ethical duty in providing data to a duly authorized representative of the client. In such an event, however, the employee must consent and understand that he or she is delegating to the union the right to inspect psychological test results.

Consultants face a less severe problem as long as their role is clearly defined at the time a consulting contract is arranged (and is permissible under the labor–management agreements in force). Psychologists

Adapted from *Professional Psychology, 11,* 749–754. Copyright 1980 by the American Psychological Association.

may be called on to deviate from their standard practice in some consulting requests and must be prepared to reject a contract as potentially involving conflict of interest or calling for unprofessional conduct. Ethical standards are only guidelines; psychologists should be prepared to deviate from them when substantial reason exists. A legal requirement or court order provides such a reason, and it becomes a matter of conscience whether a psychologist is willing to suffer the consequences of contempt of court or provide the information required by the appropriate legal process. . . .

It is basically clear from the history of this case that psychologists are having difficulty in convincing courts that the nature of psychological test results necessitates protection in all but the most serious cases. . . .

Commentary: By far, the overarching point in Detroit Edison *is the Supreme Court's apparent agreement with the National Labor Relations Board that a federal law requiring the disclosure of relevant information cannot be defeated by the ethical standards of a private group like the APA. Thus, the decision in* Detroit Edison *implies that psychologists cannot rely solely on professional ethics and standards to protect them when they are faced with overriding obligations imposed by the law. In what other*

areas than testing may this conflict create problems for scientists and professionals?

In any event, Standard 15.7 of the Standards for Testing states as a primary obligation that "test users should protect the security of test materials." Similarly, standard 2.10 of the current Ethical Principles requires that psychologists "make reasonable efforts to maintain the integrity and security of tests and other assessment techniques consistent with law, contractual obligations, and in a manner that permits compliance with the requirements of this Ethics Code." Detroit Edison *shows that there are obvious limits to protecting test security. For example, with the advent of televised trials, consider the position of the psychologist who is compelled by the court to exhibit and discuss the questions, results, and interpretation of such tests as intelligence scales, the Minnesota Multiphasic Personality Inventory, and projective instruments. And, of course, psychologists have no control over the conduct of judges. For example, in a case challenging the validity of the Wechsler and Stanford–Binet scales—*PASE v. Hannon, 506 F. Supp. 831 (N.D. Ill. 1980)—*the judge, in evaluating the tests, disclosed all the questions and correct answers to both tests. So even though he held that the tests were not culturally biased, their security had been seriously compromised, if not destroyed. For a more complete discussion of these issues, see Bersoff, D. N. (1982). Larry P. and PASE: Judicial report cards on the validity of individual intelligence tests. In T. Kratochwill (Ed.), Advances in school psychology (Vol. 2, pp. 61–95). Hillsdale, NJ: Erlbaum.*

The Release of Psychological Data to Nonexperts: Ethical and Legal Considerations

Daniel Tranel

. . .

The purpose here is to discuss ethical and legal considerations pertaining to the release of raw psychological data, in the context of the new Ethical Principles of Psychologists and Code of Conduct (hereinafter, the Ethical Principles) recently approved by the American Psychological Association (APA, 1992). The guidelines provided in the new Ethical Principles are more clear and specific than those available previously, enabling psychologists to take a more definitive position on the issue of whether or not to share raw psychological data with others. . . .

A DEFINITION OF RAW PSYCHOLOGICAL DATA

What are raw psychological data? In keeping with the Ethical Principles, and following distinctions proposed by Matarazzo (1990) regarding the nature of psychological assessment and psychological testing, several different types of psychological information can be distinguished:

1. Written reports, in which the psychologist typically summarizes the history, test findings, and other pertinent data, and then presents conclusions, diagnoses, and perhaps recommendations and predictions.
2. Notes, which generally include the handwritten information recorded by a psychologist in the course of interviewing, observing, and testing a client or patient.
3. Scores, typically numerical, which can be raw (e.g., the number of items answered correctly on a test) or standardized (e.g., IQ scores, percentile scores).

4. Test stimuli, which are the actual items used by the psychologist to elicit responses from the client or patient that form the basis for determining levels of cognitive and behavioral function.
5. Responses (i.e., the actual verbal, written, or other responses generated by the client/patient to test stimuli).
6. Test manuals, which typically comprise, in addition to the test stimuli, information regarding how the test was constructed, its reliability and validity, normative data, appropriate applications, and detailed instructions for administration.

SHARING RAW PSYCHOLOGICAL DATA WITH OTHERS

When a client or patient places his or her mental or emotional condition into litigation, this produces a waiver of privilege, and all pertinent information is "discoverable" by both sides of the case. Given that the privilege has been waived, there is usually no great concern regarding the sharing of written reports and summaries among different parties involved in a case. It is also generally accepted that notes, which are usually not considered to constitute raw data or results, may be shared among different parties in a case. . . .

A much different situation obtains, however, when it comes to the types of information defined in 3 to 6 above (viz., test scores, stimuli, responses, and manuals). The test scores, stimuli, and responses compose what is commonly known as raw psychological data, raw test results, or simply raw data [footnote omitted]. At the center of the problem is the fact that there is a direct conflict between law and ethics when it comes to the release of raw psychological data. The law says one thing ("Provide the data"); the ethics code says the opposite ("Do not provide the data"). Detailed below is a discussion of pertinent issues regarding this problem and a recommended course of action for resolving such a conflict.

Preventing Misuse of Psychological Data

The new Ethical Principles, which went into effect officially on December 1, 1992, state the following in Ethical Standard 2.02(b):

> Psychologists refrain from misuse of assessment techniques, interventions, results, and interpretations and take reasonable steps to prevent others from misusing the information these techniques provide. This includes refraining from releasing raw test results or raw data to persons, other than to patients or clients as appropriate, who are not qualified to use such information.

It is clear that the APA has taken a position against the release of raw data to unqualified persons. There are two main reasons behind this, both of which pertain directly to several standards explicated in the new Ethical Principles (e.g., Sections 2.02, 2.06, 2.10).

Potential misuse. Release of raw data creates numerous potentialities for misuse. For example, laypersons lack an appreciation of the context in which psychological test stimuli are administered and may reach erroneous conclusions about the meaning of individual answers. When this occurs, for example, in a courtroom, by lawyers, judges, and jurors, the ramifications of the errors may be great.

By way of example, consider the following scenario. An attorney for the defense has obtained all the raw data from a neuropsychologist in a case in which a plaintiff is claiming permanent cognitive disability from a brain injury. In the courtroom, the attorney attempts to convince the jury that the plaintiff cannot possibly be suffering the extent of memory impairment claimed, because the plaintiff was able to complete several difficult items on a test of nonverbal memory. The attorney also points out that the items the plaintiff failed are so difficult that it would be unreasonable to expect any normal person to pass them. This line of arguing, perhaps accompanied by exhibits depicting the "difficult" memory items that the patient passed, may be quite compelling to laypersons. In all likelihood, however, the attorney and other nonexperts in this situation do not appreciate several fundamental and critical components of the assessment process. Most tests, for example, include both easy and difficult items, and most tests include very difficult items in order to avoid ceiling effects. Also, the testing process is usually arranged so that even a very impaired person can pass some items in order to form the right "set" and to have "success" experiences. Thus, analysis of individual items taken out of context can be quite misleading. Add the likelihood that laypersons have limited understanding of how factors such as age, gender, and educational background may play a role in performance on the test, and one is left with a potentially extremely misleading depiction of the plaintiff's abilities.

Raw data may become part of the public domain. Release of raw data may allow psychological test stimuli to become part of the public domain, the domain of information that is in principle accessible by virtually anyone. This opens up the possibility that test stimuli could be disseminated among the public, perhaps even widely. A potential consequence of this is that future test takers (i.e., persons receiving psychological tests) would not be naive. As one example, a particular individual may have studied all the questions on the Information subtest of the Wechsler Adult Intelligence Scale—Revised (WAIS–R; Wechsler, 1981). This would invalidate the test. Most psychological tests, particularly those used in measurement of intellect, memory, and other aspects of cognition, assume complete or near-complete naivete on the part of the client or patient. (Even in the case of practice effects, which refer to improvements in test performance attributable to prior exposure to the test and not to a change in ability level, it is assumed that all test exposures have occurred under standard, controlled conditions prescribed by the test instructions.) Psychologists cannot risk invalidating tests due to widespread dissemination among the public. It is unreasonable and impractical that psychologists would have to recreate tests on a frequent basis. Thus onus would not be in the best interests of anyone, including psychologists, attorneys, and clients or patients. . . .

The new APA Ethical Principles imply that raw data should only be released to another qualified individual (i.e., someone who is competent to interpret the data). A qualified individual is someone who, by virtue of his or her training and experience, is in a position to appreciate fully the meaning of raw data, including considerations of reliability and validity. In most cases, this will be a licensed psychologist who meets recognized standards of training and experience. In most states, licensure can be taken as evidence that the psychologist has acquired a minimum level of knowledge regarding pertinent issues of reliability and validity, test construction, and psychological appraisal. Licensure also indicates (again, in most states) that the psychologist is responsible for operating in accordance with the Ethical Principles. For the types of raw data typically under consideration in personal injury litigation cases, such as raw test results from neuropsychological and psychological tests, the clearest example of a qualified recipient would be a licensed clinical psychologist or clinical neuropsychologist. . . .

Shapiro (1991) has written about the problems surrounding the release of raw psychological data and how one should go about resolving the conflict between law and ethics. . . . Shapiro reasons very cogently that the only acceptable strategy is to release raw data only to another qualified individual. He points out that the "courts have essentially recognized the legitimacy of this demand, though none has commented on the specific practice" (p. 236). Shapiro goes on to cite legal precedent for this, including one case in which the court denied the claim that a psychiatrist could serve as a "qualified person" to receive raw psychological data. The court ruled that psychiatrists are not, without special training, qualified to interpret psychological tests [footnote omitted].

A comment should also be made here regarding the statement in the Ethical Principles that raw test results or raw data may be released to "patients or clients as appropriate." This wording does not imply that raw data should be released directly to clients or patients but rather that it is appropriate for a psychologist to explain and interpret the findings to the client or patient and provide other pertinent feedback. In many circumstances, it would be appropriate for the client or patient to have access to the written report authored by the psychologist. (The client or patient has a legal right to this report in virtually all situations.) But with regard to raw data, including raw test results, it is not advisable in most cases to provide clients or patients with meaningless or misleading test scores, stimuli, and responses. This topic is dealt with directly in Section 2.09 of the Ethical Principles. . . .

A Recommended Course of Action for the Release of Raw Psychological Data

The APA Ethical Principles prohibit the release of raw data to unqualified individuals, and with rare exception, attorneys are not qualified individuals. A viable course of action if an attorney should request raw data from a psychologist (A), would be to advise the attorney to engage the consultation of another psychologist (B), who is qualified, by virtue of licensure, training, and experience, to receive the data. Psychologist A then could send the raw data to Psychologist B (provided the client or patient has given appropriate consent). Psychologist B could then interpret the data to the attorney. Needless to say, Psychologist B must operate under the same rules and standards of ethics and confidentiality as Psychologist A.

By and large, attorneys and judges are reasonably understanding of the dilemma faced by psychologists regarding the sharing of raw data. When given an explanation about why psychologists are restricted from releasing raw data to unqualified persons, attorneys and judges tend to be amenable to the course of action recommended above. This explanation is likely to be more effective, however, if the particular reasons are explained (e.g., that psychologists cannot afford to have test stimuli disseminated in the public domain; that raw data are difficult or impossible for a nonexpert to interpret), rather than simply citing the Ethical Principles that prohibit such release.

There may be instances in which attorneys will be quite insistent on receiving raw data and will go to considerable lengths to secure it. In the well-known series of books by Ziskin and Faust (1988; Faust et al., 1991), the authors recommend strongly that lawyers secure raw data from psychologists in all cases. Lawyers familiar with this series of books can be expected to make adamant requests for raw data. The principal aim of this strategy, though, is to have an opportunity to scrutinize the psychologist's work product for incorrect scoring, miscalculations, misuse of test manuals, and other errors that might be used by the opposing attorney to impugn the psychologist's competence. Obviously another psychologist would be in a much better position than the attorney to conduct such an analysis; thus, there would appear to be little justification for not following the course of action recommended above (i.e., insisting that the attorney secure the consultation of a qualified expert). In short, there is considerable precedent, legal and professional, for holding to the position that the raw data can only be sent to another qualified individual, and this course of action should be pursued unless there are unusually compelling reasons not to do so.

If a psychologist is served with a subpoena ordering the release of raw data, the psychologist should explain why she or he cannot comply with the request and recommended an alternative course of action (as detailed above). The explanation might be provided to the judge in the case, as well as to the attorneys. In some cases, psychologists may want to consult legal counsel of their own, which will help clarify the particular legal considerations of the matter. Psychologists may be intimidated by being served a subpoena; legal counsel and full understanding of the operative contingencies are usually quite reassuring. Psychologists need not automatically translate the serving of a subpoena into prompt acquiescence to legal demands without regard for the ethics of the situation. One additional point that psychologists should understand is that a subpoena can be resisted (e.g., through a "motion to quash"). A court order, by contrast, cannot be legally resisted (only appealed). If a psychologist is given a court order to produce raw data, manuals, and so on, the psychologist should take immediate steps to clarify for the court the ethical dilemma this creates. In

such situations, psychologists are strongly encouraged to seek their own legal counsel.

Recording Psychological Information

Another topic relevant to the current discussion pertains to the manner in which information is recorded in the course of psychological assessment and test administration. The new Ethical Principles (Section 1.23(b)) state the following:

> When psychologists have reason to believe that records of their professional services will be used in legal proceedings involving recipients of or participants in their work, they have a responsibility to create and maintain documentation in the kind of detail and quality that would be consistent with reasonable scrutiny in an adjudicative forum.

This standard has important implications for the types of notes that are recorded for a particular client or patient. Obviously one intent is to ensure that psychologists will record information in a manner that allows subsequent accurate reconstruction; that is, the recording should be complete, accurate, and legible.

There is another aspect of this standard, however, that also merits careful consideration. It is common for attorneys to request the handwritten notes from a patient's file, even if the raw data (test scores, stimuli, and responses) are allowed to remain confidential. With this in mind, and given the position that notes are probably not subsumed under the rubric of raw data, a psychologist should be cautious about writing things down on paper that might later be used in a legal proceeding. For example, the jotting down of initial impressions or judgmental observations must be done in a circumspect fashion, with thoughtful consideration of how such statements might later be used, perhaps out of context, to the detriment of the patient or psychologist. Notes should never comprise unsupportable judgments or pejorative descriptors.

TEST MANUALS

An attorney or the court will occasionally request the test manuals on which the psychologist relied to score and interpret psychological tests. The considerations here are much the same as those that pertain to the release of other raw psychological data—test manuals should not be released to unqualified persons. Several portions of the Ethical Principles speak to this issue:

> Psychologists do not promote the use of psychological assessment techniques by unqualified persons. (2.06)
>
> Psychologists make reasonable efforts to maintain the integrity and security of tests and other assessment techniques consistent with law, contractual obligations, and in a manner that permits compliance with the requirements of this Ethics Code. (2.10)

Standard 2.02(b), quoted above, also speaks to this issue. Test manuals contain data and information that are part of a specialized discipline (e.g., psychological appraisal, neuropsychological assessment). It is simply not permissible for a layperson (unqualified individual) to attempt to use such information. Use and dissemination of such information by an unqualified person could reduce or vitiate entirely the value of the tests. Many manuals are distributed by reputable test publishers, who require evidence of purchaser qualification (e.g., a license to practice psychology) before selling such manuals. If publishers fail to respect such guidelines and engage in practices that would be considered a violation of law and APA Ethics, this matter should be brought to the attention of the APA. Ziskin and Faust (1988) recommend that lawyers hire an expert consultant to deal with the types of information that are part of test manuals.

If a psychologist receives a court order or subpoena for test manuals, the psychologist might consider one of the following courses of action: (a) The psychologist could request to provide the test manuals in person, in a situation in which the psychologist could explain appropriately various qualifications, limitations, and other important contextual information; or (b) the psychologist could ask the requestor to retain an expert (e.g., licensed psychologist) who would be qualified to interpret the test manuals. The manuals could then be provided to that expert.

TEST SCORES

. . . [T]est scores, both raw and standardized, constitute yet another domain of psychological information that may be requested for release. When the requestor is a qualified person (i.e., a licensed psychologist), there is no problem in releasing the scores. In fact, in many cases it is actually the scores (rather than the test forms, responses, etc.) in which the requesting psychologist is most interested (e.g., for purposes of comparing performances across time). There are a few other special situations, such as in the determination of disability by social security officials or in a worker's compensation claim, in which it may be permissible to release test scores. These agencies often have employees with special expertise in the interpretation of psychological data (especially IQ scores). Provided the psychologist is confident the test scores will be used appropriately, it is reasonable in these situations to provide requested test scores (assuming the client or patient has given appropriate consent).

For unqualified persons, the matter of releasing test scores should be treated in the same way as the release of other raw psychological data. That is, psychologists should refrain from releasing scores to unqualified individuals, and if asked for such information by attorneys or other nonexperts, psychologists should follow a course of action along the lines elaborated here earlier under the heading *A Recommended Course of Action for the Release of Raw Psychological Data.*

A few other considerations pertaining to test scores warrant mention. As noted earlier, two types of test scores can be specified—raw and standardized. Raw scores (e.g., the fact that a patient earned a score of "6" items correct on a test) are often uninterpretable to nonexperts, which may more or less preclude opportunities for misuse. However, this should not justify the release of such scores to unqualified persons, because the psychologist has no way of assuring that even apparently uninterpretable raw scores would not eventually be used inappropriately. Standardized scores, including IQs and percentiles, clearly fall under the domain of raw psychological information that should not be released to unqualified persons. These scores, unlike raw test scores, are often open to possible "interpretation" by nonexperts. For instance, an attorney may conclude that an IQ score of 100 indicates intact intelligence, when in fact it could indicate a major impairment if the patient's premorbid intelligence had been in the superior range. The nonexpert cannot be expected to appreciate critical considerations such as standard error of measurement, the nature of the underlying distribution of scores, the importance of background information for determining whether the observed score differs or not from the expected score, and numerous other factors.

Another consideration regarding test scores is the question of whether such scores should be included in the text of a psychological report. As discussed earlier, reports are generally shared rather freely among various parties in a case, including nonexperts. Obviously, if test scores are included in reports, the scores will be shared along with the reports. This has the potential of creating opportunities for misuse. Some scores are especially vulnerable in this regard, and considerable care should be taken by a psychologist in deciding whether or not to include them in narrative reports. For example, IQ scores have a great deal of connotative value for most persons, experts and laypersons alike; however, the meaning can vary widely from one individual to the next, and may in many cases fail to reflect accurately the intended meaning. Hence, the inclusion of IQ scores in reports should be done only with careful consideration of the consequences. As a general policy, test scores should be included in narrative reports only when the psychologist is confident that such inclusion is in the best interests of the client or patient and that those scores will not be subject to misuse.

OTHER CONSIDERATIONS

Determination of the qualifications of a requesting party (or the party named as the intended recipient of raw data) is the responsibility of the psychologist from whom the data are being requested. It is recommended that if a psychologist is unsure of the credentials of an intended recipient, the psychologist should request evidence on which a judgment regarding competency can be made. In most cases, the curriculum vitae (CV) of the intended recipient would provide such evidence. . . .

. . . [T]he attitude or demeanor of the psychologist can influence substantially the degree of cooperation from members of the legal profession (lawyers, judges, etc.). When an attorney senses that the psychologist is trying to conceal something, or to resist cooperation, the attorney is likely to mount an all-out effort to get everything possible out of the psychologist. By contrast, if the attorney senses that the psychologist is attempting to cooperate fully with the spirit of the proceedings, within the bounds of his or her ethical principles, the attorney is far more likely to go along with the psychologist's recommended course of action. The Ethical Principles do not, in fact, have force of law; thus, it is very much in the best interest of psychologists to solicit cooperation and collegiality from attorneys. . . .

References

American Psychological Association. (1992). Ethical principles of psychologists and code of conduct. *American Psychologist, 47*, 1597–1611.

Faust, D., Ziskin, J., & Hiers, J. B. (1991). *Brain damage claims: Coping with neuropsychological evidence* (Vol. 1–2). Los Angeles: Law and Psychology Press.

Matarazzo, J. D. (1990). Psychological assessment versus psychological testing: Validation from Binet to the school, clinic, and courtroom. *American Psychologist, 45*, 999–1017.

Shapiro, D. L. (1991). *Forensic psychological assessment.* Boston: Allyn and Bacon.

Wechsler, D. (1981). *Manual for the Wechsler Adult Intelligence Scale—Revised.* San Antonio, TX: Psychological Corporation.

Ziskin, J., & Faust, D. (1988). *Coping with psychiatric and psychological testimony* (4th ed., Vols. 1–3). Marina del Rey, CA: Law and Psychology Press.

◆ ◆ ◆

Commentary: Tranel raises many significant issues. It would certainly compromise many single-form instruments, such as individually administered intelligence scales, if the questions and the manuals for scoring answers were widely disseminated (although, as I have noted, an Illinois federal judge did already do this). But, is not Tranel's assertion that attorneys and their clients are not qualified to use the information that raw data imparts paternalistic? More fundamentally, is it not just plain wrong when he states that Standard

2.02(b) does not really mean that patients or clients may receive raw data? The least twisted reading of that provision—that psychologists refrain "from releasing raw test results or raw data to persons, other than to patients or clients as appropriate"—states the opposite. The only qualification is the "as appropriate" language, a condition that, unfortunately, is vague and unexplained. But if, in the main, clients can obtain their own raw data, does it not follow that their legal repre- sentatives, at the client's request, should also have access to those data? Whatever one's interpretation of the disclosure principles in the Ethical Principles, it is better to anticipate problems rather than to confront them after the fact. What steps can psychologists take at the initiation of an assessment to avoid or minimize the real problems that Tranel has brought to our attention? (There is more discussion of this issue in chap. 9 [Forensic Settings]).

Ethical and Professional Considerations in Psychological Assessment

David J. Berndt

. . .

. . . Two different kinds of justifications have been put forth for sharing much, if not all, of the material with the person who is tested. One justification is that assessment instruments may be usefully employed as an adjunctive mode of treatment (e.g., Harrison, 1965; Harrower, 1960). Others (e.g., Ladkin & Levine, 1976) have argued that it is the patient's right to know and that witholding information from the client reinforces the sick role by adding the authority of the psychological battery to the diagnosis.

The current investigation was designed to provide descriptive data about professional and ethical practices of psychologists who administer, interpret, and store the results of psychological assessment. . . .

Respondents were asked a series of questions on how they describe their role to the patient and on how they obtain informed consent. Two open-ended questions concerning a hypothetical consultation from a psychiatrist or colleague asked: "How would you usually introduce your role to the patient?" and "Would you give an example of informed consent?" Typical responses to the question about the role of the tester included some variant of the following: "Dr. _____ has asked me to see you (give you some psychological tests) today, to help you (try and understand yourself)." Nearly all respondents either left it at that or indicated that they considered rapport, willingness to proceed, or the patient's compliance as sufficient. Most also stressed that they attempted to ensure that the patient understood what the testing procedure was, and many stressed that they explored with the patient full understanding of the consultation. A few respondents indicated that they offered to discuss the testing after it was over. In response to more structured questions, 18% of the respondents indicated that they did not attempt to get informed consent for testing, and oral consent was obtained in a 3:1 ratio over written.

The respondents were also asked to respond to a question regarding the feedback process, but they rarely gave written feedback when it was not requested (see Table 1). On the other hand, it was also infrequent for the respondents to refuse to discuss the results. Overall, the respondents tended to agree most with an approach that utilized clinical judgment and took the patient's needs into account. Testing appeared to be frequently used as a supplement to therapy.

The percentage of respondents who indicated how likely they were to go over test results with the subject for each test is listed in Table 2. Comparing the 2 "least likely" points on the 5-point scale for each test, note that results from the Rorschach (41%), Projective Drawings (38%), and the Thematic Apperception Test (34%) are least likely to be shared; there appears to be less concern over sharing results of the IQ instruments (8%) or the Minnesota Multiphasic Personality Inventory (20%). Despite the apparent trend to share results of more objective measures and not go over the more projective measures, more respondents were likely (46%) to share their results of the Rorschach than not share them.

Subjects were also asked in an open-ended question to list the kind of feedback they would give their patients. By far the most frequently men-

TABLE 1

Average Likert Scale Ratings Indicating Feedback Techniques Preferred by Respondents

Response	M	SD
If a patient or research subject asks you what the testing results are, how often do you typically		
Refuse to discuss the results with the person?	1.84	1.23
Ask the patient to have the referral source (e.g., psychiatrist) go over the results?	3.53	1.41
Discuss as little as possible, only talking in vague generalities?	2.10	1.15
Discuss only what the patient can readily understand and use?	3.86	.99
Give full disclosure, avoiding material that would be detrimental in your clinical judgment?	3.23	1.33
Actively share as much of the results as time permits with the patient, believing testing can be used as a supplement to therapy?	3.47	1.15
Always tell the patient everything because I believe they have a right to know?	2.89	1.35
Make a practice of giving the patient a written report when they ask for such information?	2.67	1.54
Give all the patients you test written feedback even if they don't ask?	1.29	.59

Note. Anchor points on the 5-point Likert Scale were 1 (never) and 5 (always).

tioned feedback was the IQ range, with most respondents emphasizing the range rather than the score and several stating they would not share below normal IQ information. Others said they would use the interest scatter or patients' intellectual strengths and weaknesses and the consequent implications. All the above were spontaneously mentioned by at least one fourth of the respondents.

Other areas mentioned 10 or more times included emotional and situational conflicts; potential for improvement and ability to use therapy; object relations and attitudes toward significant others, including social roles and postures; recommendations; and strengths and weaknesses. Areas mentioned four

or more times included relating the results to the referral or presenting complaint; profile interpretation; defensive styles; and self-concept or self-image.

Finally, another set of questions inquired about record-keeping practices. A high percentage (91%) of all respondents had kept a record of old test batteries in which they had the ability to find a particular patient's file. For those who kept old batteries on file, the oldest record ranged from 2 years to 35 years ($M = 12.8$ years). Only 24% maintained they would not release their personal testing files to an outside agency if the agency had the patient's consent, whereas 59% would refuse to supply it to the patient. As far as safety was concerned, 16% admitted to not locking their files, and only 12% used a

TABLE 2

Likelihood That Respondents Would Share Specific Assessment Instruments With Their Clients

Instrument	Likert scale				
	1	2	3	4	5
Rorschach	11[a]	30	13	19	27
MMPI	10	10	11	23	46
Projective Drawings	15	23	23	8	31
IQ instruments	4	4	12	35	45
Bender-Gestalt	7	20	18	27	28
Sentence Completion	5	22	24	24	25
Personality Measures	9	16	18	25	32
Thematic Apperception Test	8	26	24	20	22

Note. Likert Scale ranged from 1 (not at all) to 5 (likely). Number of subjects varied among instruments.
MMPI = Minnesota Multiphasic Personality Inventory.
[a]All figures represent percentage of respondents agreeing to points on a 5-point scale (rows sum to 100%).

master code that kept the patient's name coded and in a separate place from the data.

DISCUSSION

... Many of the respondents fall into one of two groups. One group enthusiastically advocated sharing most if not all of the information with the patient; as one respondent put it, "using tests as a self-discovery procedure typically results in much growth. . . . I personally feel that using tests in this manner is worth 1–3 months of therapy." A second group of respondents favored sharing some information with the client but had diverse views on how much should be shared. Most felt that as much as could be used by the patient should be shared, but considerable disagreement existed about the fragility of patients. Some advocated sharing only positive results; others opted for consciously experienced phenomena; and others insisted that if it was too troublesome for the patient, they probably would not hear it.

... A few indicated that sharing the information was desirable but that institutional constraints, especially lack of time, prevented using tests in this preferred manner. Others commented on the importance of using tests as a supplement to therapy only when one is treating the patient oneself. . . . When the patient is seen in a consultation, coordination with the consultant is important, and patient feedback is sometimes resented. . . .

As for specifics of feedback, respondents rarely gave written feedback, especially if it was not requested; but they usually did not refuse a patient's request to discuss the information. They tended to avoid talking in vague generalities. Rather, they most frequently discussed what the patient could readily understand and use. They also asked the patient to go over the results with the referral source, although as many commented, it depended on the clinical skills of the person who referred the patient. Blind consumerism ("I always tell my patient everything because I believe they have a right to know"), although sometimes advocated, was less frequent than a broader emphasis on clinical judgment used to temper complete disclosure. . . .

The data on how the tester presents the assessor's role indicate a general lack of agreement. Although a majority, but by no means all, of the respondents indicated that they explained to the patient what the testing would be like, several commented that rapport or the willingness to proceed was adequate. In some states, such as Illinois, assessment is considered by the law to be a form of treatment and, hence may be subject to informed consent. Additionally, the ethical standards compel psychologists to see to it that clients understand both the nature and purposes of not only the test results but the tests themselves.

The results on the record-keeping practices also raise some questions. Nearly all of the respondents kept old records on file, and most of them had files dating quite far back. These files were typically stored in locked places; however, only 12% kept the names in a separate code book, apart from the data. Additionally, 76% said they would release such information to an outside agency, with the patient's consent. This implies that the data are stored with the name either attached or linked in some way to the data. Both the *Ethical Principles of Psychologists* (APA, 1981, Principle 8d)[1] and the *Standards for Educational and Psychological Tests* (APA, 1974) stress that obsolete test material should be carefully handled. The "test user should develop procedures for systematically eliminating from data files test score information that has become obsolete" (APA, 1974, p. 73), and data that are being kept for research purposes, according to the *Standards for Educational and Psychological Tests* (APA, 1974), should have the names detached from the data. Safely locking the data is important, but clearly not sufficient. . . .

References

American Psychological Association. *Standards for educational and psychological tests.* Washington, D.C.: Author, 1974.

American Psychological Association. Ethical principles of psychologists. *American Psychologist*, 1981, *36*, 633–638.

Harrison, R. Thematic apperceptive methods. In B. Wolman (Ed.), *Handbook of clinical psychology.* New York: McGraw-Hill, 1965.

Harrower, M. Projective counseling—a psychotherapeutic technique. In M. Harrower, P. Vorhaus, M. Roman, & G. Bauman (Eds.), *Creative variations in the projective technique.* Springfield, Ill.: Charles C Thomas, 1960.

Ladkin, J. F., & Levine, L. Interpreting psychological test results to the hospitalized consumer. *Professional Psychology*, 1976, *7*, 161–166.

[1] *Ed. note:* See Standard 2.07 of the APA's current (1992) Ethical Principles.

School Psychology as "Institutional Psychiatry"

Donald N. Bersoff

Commentary: *I have likened certain testing practices of school psychologists to institutional psychiatry, a term coined by Thomas Szasz in* The Manufacture of Madness *(1970). Institutional psychiatrists are bureaucratic employees who impose themselves on patients who are compelled to use the services of the psychiatrists' organizational employer. I have argued that, in many ways, school psychologists at one time were (and, to some extent, still are) agents of the school system— which, creates problems of dual loyalty. Children are often referred for evaluations without a clear understanding of the purposes of the assessment and without their assent. I described the ethical implications of this problem in my 1971 article on school psychology (see excerpt that follows).*

. . .

Although the psychologist and those who have referred the child to him see this referral in terms of a "This is being done to help you" attitude, it is often forgotten that the child is an involuntary participant of any evaluation or modification procedure. The psychologist may explain to the child why he is being tested, but his permission is rarely asked before an intelligence or other test is administered. Even this explanation to the child is hardly ever honest. One can only imagine a school psychologist saying to a child, "You are being evaluated today because your teacher finds you a highly disturbing individual and seeks to have you removed from her class. My job is to see if that is possible. If you do not behave on the tests I am about to give you within certain acceptable limits of intelligence and/or emotional indicators, you will be transferred to an adjustment class or be excluded from school, the choice of which depends

on how deviant you are from these norms." While that is essentially the real reason for testing, it is more likely that the child hears some brief speech about how this testing session will be very beneficial to him because it will aid in securing more information that will eventually lead to helping him. Thus, . . . for almost all children evaluated by a school psychologist, the testing situation is characterized by a high degree of "response uncertainty" wherein the child does not know the nature of the testing instruments, the purpose of testing, or the use to which the information he provides may be put. Thus, we have an involuntary client almost completely in the dark about why he is there, being tested by someone whose primary responsibility is not to him. Any resistance to this procedure by the child (or his parents) is not viewed, however, as being evoked by this situation but is more likely to be seen as either (or a combination of) lack of motivation, passive-aggressivity, internally stimulated anxiety, evasion, or paranoid suspiciousness.

Not only does the child run the danger of being placed in a situation where he is asked to reveal information about himself, though he does not know how the information will be used, but only infrequently is he likely to come out of this situation without some damaging label. Szasz likens psychological testing to the water ordeal used in witch finding. If an alleged witch, completed restrained by ropes and dumped into deep water, floated, she was guilty; if she sank, she was innocent. In either case, she was dead. And, like the witch, the child referred for testing by a teacher or principal usually ends up in the same position; though not dead he is tagged and labeled, if not for life then for the academic portion of it. The fact of referral leads to a bias to uncover pathology or exceptionality, especially when additional special education units and subsequent financial support from the state for these units depend on children to fill the classes. . . .

◆ ◆ ◆

Commentary: *The article above evoked considerable debate in subsequent issues of* Professional Psychology. *In responding to the points made in the context of that debate, I proposed what I considered a more ethical model for interacting with children who are referred for psychological testing and their parents. (See the next article.)*

The Ethical Practice of School Psychology: A Rebuttal and Suggested Model

Donald N. Bersoff

. . .

The following is not meant to be an all-encompassing model, but is limited to the process of assessment. It rests on three assumptions:

1. Test responses are a function not only of the characteristics of the organism to whom the test is administered but also of the stimulus properties of the test and the background or environments (e.g., instructions, setting, nature of the experimenter) in which the test is administered (Fiske, 1967; Hamilton, 1970; Murstein, 1965; Sattler & Theye, 1967).

2. Each person perceives the testing situation differently and thus develops an idiosyncratic style or strategy in responding to test material. Without discerning these strategies, the validity of test interpretation is highly attenuated (Fulkerson, 1965).

3. Parents are at least equally capable as the school staff in deciding what is best for their children (Goldman, 1971).

Accepting these assumptions allows the psychologist to include the client in all aspects of the evaluation. In fact, it makes it imperative that he do so if he wants to obtain data that are not obfuscated by mistrust, misunderstanding, and the inhibition of self-disclosure. Because we have not included the client (both the child and his parents) in the assessment transaction it is possible that most of our test data and their subsequent interpretation may be of doubtful veracity. As Jourard (1971) conjectured,

> the millions of psychometric tests
> mildewing in agency files might be lies
> told by untrusting clients and patients
> to untrustworthy functionaries. If psy-
> chologists were serving the interests of

bureaucracies, wittingly or unwittingly, in their . . . activities, then it would be quite proper for . . . patients not to trust us; functionaries masquerading as professionals are not to be trusted too far [p. 2].

If we are to achieve intimate, ethical relationships consonant with the empirical data concerning the interactive nature of test productions, it may be necessary to reconceive of the assessment process as one in which there is mutual disclosure. In a series of papers, Fischer (1970, 1971a, 1971b, 1972, in press-a, in press-b) detailed both the theoretical foundations and the practical expression of just such a relationship in which tester and client become "co-evaluators" (Fischer, 1970). Specifically, the following steps are recommended.

1. *Coadvisement.* This is an expansion of the principle of informed consent. The psychologist tells the child and his parents how he functions; informs them of the identity of the referral agent and the purpose for referral; and describes the nature of the assessment devices he will use, the merits and limitations of those devices, what kinds of information will be put in a report, and who might eventually read the report. The psychologist then asks the child to tell how he perceives the purposes of testing and what he feels the consequences of such an evaluation might be. The psychologist secures agreement from the child and his parents to proceed with the assessment subsequent to full and mutual disclosure concerning the purposes of the evaluation.

2. *Sharing impressions.* Immediately after the administration of the psychometric instruments the

Adapted from *Professional Psychology, 4,* 305–312. Copyright 1973 by the American Psychological Association.

psychologist, the child, and his parents engage in a dialogue in which the psychologist gives his interpretation of the child's test behavior as he has just experienced it. By conferring with the child he further attempts to extrapolate from the testing situation to other situations similar to the one represented by the test stimuli. Such a dialogue provides immediate feedback to the child about how others perceive his behavior and enables the assessor to check out hypotheses about how equivalent the test behavior observed is to actual classroom behavior and to develop possible strategies he may use to intervene in the instructional environment (see Fischer, 1970, for an example of how such an interaction might proceed). It also gives the child a chance to disagree with the psychologist's initial interpretations and to offer his perceptions about his own behavior. Rather than assuming that the behavior observed in the testing situation can be extrapolated to all other situations, the psychologist has an opportunity to discover the situations or contexts in which the behavior does occur. Such an approach has been variously called psychosituational (Bersoff, 1971a; Bersoff & Grieger, 1971) or contextual (Fischer, in press) assessment, but whatever its title, such a method prevents the child from being mislabeled and interpretations of his behavior from being overgeneralized.

3. *Critique of the written evaluation.* This concludes the sequence of mutually disclosing events. After the evaluation is complete and the psychologist has prepared his report, he shows the child and his parents a copy of the written evaluation. This insures that the report will be recorded so that it is understandable to all concerned. In addition, as Fischer (1970) described,

> This procedure also produces a beneficial side effect: Knowing that his client is going to read his report, the psychologist strives all the more to be true to him, to capture his world as well as words allow, and to avoid overstatements, unintended implications, and loose descriptions [p. 74].

Then, the child and his parents are given the opportunity to clarify the points made, to add further material, and, if there is disagreement between the psychologist and the clients, to provide a dissenting view (in writing if warranted). Finally, the psychologist receives permission to disseminate the report to those whom the child and his parents agree to.

There is no doubt that adopting such an approach requires much rethinking and rebehaving on the part of school psychologists. . . . Admittedly, there may be some difficulty in implementing the approach fully. . . . A comment by Leo Goldman (1971), arguing against psychological secrecy and offering some suggestions for its reduction, may help put the matter in perspective:

> All of this may sound very unappealing to psychologists who would prefer to see themselves as the "good guys" who are there just to help people and make the world a better place. Unfortunately, that just isn't a viable arrangement when one is a member of the staff of a public school serving a community which contains diverse social, ethnic, and political elements. And it certainly is not possible in any pure sense in a setting such as the public schools, where the "clients" are not clients at all but mostly a captive, involuntary audience. We will just have to find a way to work out agreements in each school system . . . so that the professional helpers can do their thing, while the students and their families retain the power to decide *whether* they will be helped, what personal information they will divulge, and what the school may release to anyone. Although this will undoubtedly cramp our style to some extent, it will on the whole make for a healthier social institution than we now have [p. 11].

The suggestions made in this article for reorienting assessment will hopefully move us toward making the school a healthier social institution. At the very least we will treat the child and his parents as our equals, with the right to participate in the interpretations and decisions that will directly affect their lives. Certainly, the chances of damaging diagnoses and class placements will be lessened. And those diagnoses and placements that are made will have been a "co-constituted" decision, agreed on by those affected, increasing the probability of greater cooperation in making the changes that *all* have deemed appropriate.

References

Bersoff, D. N. "Current functioning" myth: An overlooked fallacy in psychological assessment. *Journal of Consulting and Clinical Psychology*, 1971, 37, 391–393. (a)

Bersoff, D. N., & Grieger, R. M. An interview model for the psychosituational assessment of children's behavior. *American Journal of Orthopsychiatry*, 1971, 41, 483–493.

Fischer, C. T. The testee as co-evaluator. *Journal of Counseling Psychology*, 1970, 17, 70–76.

Fischer, C. T. Paradigm changes which allow sharing of "results" with the client. In S. L. Brodsky (Chm.), Shared Results and Open Files with the Client: Professional Responsibility or Effective Involvement. Symposium presented at the annual meeting of the American Psychological Association, Washington, D.C., September 1971. (a)

Fischer, C. T. Toward the structure of privacy: Implications for psychological assessment. In A. Giorgi, W. F. Fischer, & R. vonEckartsberg (Eds.), *Duquesne studies in phenomenological psychology*. Pittsburgh: Duquesne University Press, 1971. (b)

Fischer, C. T. Contextual approach to assessment. *Journal of Community Mental Health*, in press. (a)

Fischer, C. T. A theme for the child-advocate: Sharable everyday life data of the child-in-the-world. *Journal of Clinical Child Psychology*, in press. (b)

Fiske, D. W. The subject reacts to tests. *American Psychologist*, 1967, 22, 287–296.

Fulkerson, S. C. Some implications of the new cognitive theory for projective tests. *Journal of Consulting Psychology*, 1965, 29, 191–197.

Goldman, L. Psychological secrecy and openness in the public schools. In S. L. Brodsky (Chm.), Shared Results and Open Files with the Client: Professional Responsibility or Effective Involvement. Symposium presented at the annual meeting of the American Psychological Association, Washington, D.C., September 1971.

Hamilton, J. Stimulus variables in clinical evaluation. *Professional Psychology*, 1970, 1, 151–153.

Jourard, S. M. Some reflections on a quiet revolution. In S. L. Brodsky (Chm.), Shared Results and Open Files with the Client: Professional Responsibility or

Effective Involvement. Symposium presented at the annual meeting of the American Psychological Association, Washington, D.C., September 1971.

Murstein, B. I. Assumptions, adaptation level, and projective techniques. In B. I. Murstein (Ed.), *Handbook of projective techniques*. New York: Basic Books, 1965.

Sattler, J. M., & Theye, F. Procedural, situational, and interpersonal variables in individual intelligence testing. *Psychological Bulletin*, 1967, 68, 347–361.

◆ ◆ ◆

Commentary: In almost all school systems, parental involvement in and consent for psychological or psychoeducational evaluations conducted on children suspected of being, or already labeled as, disabled are controlled by federal law and regulations. In 1975, Congress enacted the Education for All Handicapped Children's Act (Public Law 94-142), now amended as the Individuals with Disabilities in Education Act, and the administrative agency charged with enforcing the act promulgated implementing and detailed regulations. The following, found in Title 34 of the Code of Federal Regulations, (34 C.F.R. § 300.504–505) instructs school systems on the minimum obligations it must fulfill prior to testing:

> *(a) Notice. Written notice that meets the requirements of § 300.505 must be given to the parents of a child with a disability a reasonable time before the public agency—*
> *(1) Proposes to initiate or change the identification, evaluation, or educational placement of the child or the provision of FAPE[1] to the child; or*
> *(2) Refuses to initiate or change the identification, evaluation, or educational placement of the child or the provision of FAPE to the child.*
>
> *(b) Consent; procedures if a parent refuses consent. (1) Parental consent must be obtained before—*
> *(i) Conducting a preplacement evaluation; and*
> *(ii) Initial placement of a child with a disability in a program providing special education and related services.*

---

[1] *Ed. note:* FAPE stands for *free appropriate public education*.

(2) If State law requires parental consent before a child with a disability is evaluated or initially provided special education and related services, State procedures govern the public agency in overriding a parent's refusal to consent.

(3) If there is no State law requiring consent before a child with a disability is evaluated or initially provided special education and related services, the public agency may use the hearing procedures in §§ 300.506–300.508 to determine if the child may be evaluated or initially provided special education and related services without parental consent. If it does so and the hearing officer upholds the agency, the agency may evaluate or initially provide special education and related services to the child without the parent's consent, subject to the parent's rights under §§ 300.510–300.513.

(c) Additional State consent requirements. In addition to the parental consent requirements described in paragraph (b) of this section, a State may require parental consent for other services and activities under this part if it ensures that each public agency in the State establishes and implements effective procedures to ensure that a parent's refusal to consent does not result in a failure to provide the child with FAPE.

(d) Limitation. A public agency may not require parental consent as a condition of any benefit to the parent or the child except for the service or activity for which consent is required under paragraphs (b) or (c) of this section. . . .

§ 300.505 CONTENT OF NOTICE

(a) The notice under § 300.504 must include—

(1) A full explanation of all of the procedural safeguards available to the parents under § 300.500, §§ 300.502–300.515, and §§ 300.562–300.569;

(2) A description of the action proposed or refused by the agency, an explanation of why the agency proposes or refuses to take the action, and a description of any options the agency considered and the reasons why those options were rejected;

(3) A description of each evaluation procedure, test, record, or report the agency uses as a basis for the proposal or refusal; and

(4) A description of any other factors that are relevant to the agency's proposal or refusal.

(b) The notice must be—

(1) Written in language understandable to the general public; and

(2) Provided in the native language of the parent or other mode of communication used by the parent, unless it is clearly not feasible to do so.

(c) If the native language or other mode of communication of the parent is not a written language, the SEA or LEA shall take steps to ensure—

(1) That the notice is translated orally or by other means to the parent in his or her native language or other mode of communication;

(2) That the parent understands the content of the notice; and

(3) That there is written evidence that the requirements in paragraphs (c)(1) and (2) of this section have been met.

Although these regulations have salutary benefits in that they compel school systems to involve parents in material decisions, the children themselves do not have the right to notice or consent. Given the preceding articles, is this a serious omission or simply recognition that the law gives parents the right to act as children's primary decision makers?

For a more complete explanation of the parental consent and notice rules under Public Law 94-142 and its regulations, see Pryzwansky, W. B., & Bersoff, D. N. (1978). Parental consent for psychological evaluations: Legal, ethical, and practical considerations. Journal of School Psychology, 16, 274–281.

In addition to the Standards for Educational and Psychological Testing, cited earlier in this chapter, another document—one more directly related to practitioners—is General Guidelines for Providers of Psychological

Services, 1987, published in American Psychologist, 42, 712–723. The General Guidelines "are a set of aspirational statements" derived from the APA's 1981 Ethical Principles. Nevertheless, where the guidelines track the Ethical Principles, psychologists "have the same responsibility to uphold these specific General Guidelines as they would the corresponding Ethical Principles" (1987, p. 712).

Guideline 2.3.7 requires psychologists to "establish and maintain a system that protects the confidentiality of their users' [a term that includes recipients of psychological services] records" (p. 717; also see Standards 2.02(b), 5.04, and 5.10 of the 1992 Ethical Principles. In the commentary following Guideline 2.3.7, APA addresses the right of clients to information contained in their records:

> Users have the right to information in their agency records and to be informed as to any regulations that govern the release of such information. However, the records are the property of the psychologist or of the facility in which the psychologist works and are, therefore, under the control of the psychologist or of the facility. Users have the right to examine such psychological records. Preferably such examination should be in the presence of a psychologist who judges how best to explain the material in a meaningful and useful manner.
>
> In school settings, parents have the legal right to examine such psychological records, preferably in the presence of a psychologist. In the event that a family moves to another school system, the parents have the legal right to examine a copy of such records from the former school in the new school setting. In either circumstances, the rationale for allowing parents to examine such records is to assure that parents are not in a disadvantaged position if they choose to challenge a school's decision regarding the

child. Disclosure of such psychological information in the records from a former school is conducted under secure conditions: such records have been transmitted to the new school to a psychologist under whose supervision the records may be examined. Psychologists and the institutions in which they work have written policy regarding the storage and access of pupils' records. Parents are informed of the results of a psychological assessment of their child in a form most meaningful and useful to the parents.

> Raw psychological data (e.g., test protocols, therapy or interview notes, or questionnaire returns) in which a user is identified are ordinarily released only with the written consent of the user or of the user's legal representative, and are released only to a person recognized by the psychologist as competent to interpret the data. Any use made of psychological reports, records, or data for research or training purposes is consistent with this General Guideline. . . . (1987, pp. 717–718)

Does this guideline comport or conflict with the 1992 Ethical Principles?

The following, final section highlights two emerging and vital developments that have raised a number of ethical and legal issues: the use of computerized assessment systems and so-called integrity, or honesty, tests. With regard to the former, many essential articles have appeared in American Psychologist, Professional Psychology, and Computers in Human Behavior. In addition, papers presented at a symposium devoted to computerized testing, sponsored by the Buros Institute, in Nebraska, have appeared in Gutkin, T., & Wise, S. (Eds.). 1991. The computer and the decision-making process. Hillsdale, NJ: Erlbaum. The following materials are simply meant to introduce the reader to these important subjects.

Legal Issues in Computerized Psychological Testing

Donald N. Bersoff and Paul J. Hofer

. . .

PSYCHOLOGY'S RESPONSE TO CPT

. . .

There are several sources of ethical guidelines relevant to CPT. The APA first adopted interim standards of "Automated Test Scoring and Interpretation Practices" more than 20 years ago (APA, 1966). In addition, the 1974 Standards for Educational and Psychological Tests (APA, AERA, NCME, 1974), the revised 1985 Standards (APA, 1985), the 1977 *Standards for Providers of Psychological Services* (APA, 1977) and its recently adopted revision, the General Guidelines for Providers of Psychological Services (APA, 1987), as well as the 1981 *Specialty Guidelines for the Delivery of Services*, (APA, 1981) all contain references to computerized assessment. However, in these latter documents, many CPT issues are subsumed under general standards applicable to all types of testing or psychological practices and the specific implications for CPT may not be clear.

Several state associations and private groups have tackled the problem of CPT-specific standards. For example, the Colorado Psychological Association has adopted recommended "Guidelines for the Use of Computerized Testing Services" (Colorado Psychological Association, 1982) and the Kansas Psychological Association has apparently done so as well (Petterson, 1983). A group of respected psychometricians working on the implementation of an adaptive version of the Armed Services Vocational Aptitude Battery, produced some "Technical Guidelines for Assessing Computerized Adaptive Tests," (Green, Bock, Humphreys, Linn, & Reckase, 1984). A book (Schwartz, 1984) on the use of computers in clinical practice contains several chapters (e.g., Zachary & Pope, 1984) addressing ethical is-

sues. Many articles addressing the need for standards are appearing in the psychological literature (e.g., Skinner & Pakula, 1986; Matarazzo, 1986, in press; Burke & Normand, 1985; Hofer & Green, 1985). The present authors prepared a document (Hofer & Bersoff, 1983), "Standards for the Administration and Interpretation of Computerized Psychological Testing," for a testing service concerned about the void left by the absence of adequate guidelines.

Given all these sources, many observers have seen the need for organizing the issues unique to CPT under more specific, official, and national standards. The American Psychological Association's Board of Directors in January, 1984, instructed the Committee on Professional Standards and the Committee on Psychological Tests and Assessment to develop guidelines specific to CPT. These guidelines, having gone through several revisions and review by the APA governance, were adopted by the APA Council of Representatives in February, 1986. Importantly, at this point, the guidelines are considered advisory. After they have been tested in the real world, the APA may wish to revise them once again and make them binding standards. For now these guidelines are the clearest statement of the requirements of good practice, and professionals should familiarize themselves with them. Hofer (1985) and Hofer and Green (1985) provide an overview and discussion.

RIGHTS AND RESPONSIBILITIES OF PROFESSIONALS

Should there be any legal challenge to the administration, interpretation, and decisions related to computer-based tests, both the testing service and the test user are likely to be named as defendants. Both may be ultimately liable, either as joint wrongdoers or as individuals each responsible for their own negligence. In such cases, it might appear that clinicians could rely on a defense that they were ignorant of the underlying bases for the interpretations they accepted and passed along to their clients. But, such a defense would be an admission that the clinician violated the APA Ethical Principles and engaged in professional negligence. The *Ethical Principles of Psychologists*, Principle 8(e) (APA, 1981, p. 637) states: "Psychologists offering scoring and interpretation services are able to produce appropriate evidence for the validity of the programs and procedures used in arriving at interpretations."[1]

Conversely, testing services will probably not be able to place the entire blame on the user for injurious decisions resulting from negligent interpretations, and they could be held liable under a number of legal theories. Placing the responsibility for the validity of reports entirely on the user might erode the usefulness of CPT as reviewing the validity of each interpretative statement could be comparable with writing the entire report oneself, and most people use CPT to save time and effort. Actuarial interpretations and statistical predictions of behavior are best made using the power of the computer to summarize empirical relations. Interpretations that can be validated empirically should be. Predictive validation is often legally required when selecting applicants for jobs, and it should be encouraged for other important interpretations, such as treatment recommendations and prognoses. In cases where interpretations are based on empirical findings rather than clinical judgment, and where the clinician has no additional reason to believe the finding is invalid for that test taker, it may be better for practitioners to accept the computerized interpretation without alteration.

These considerations suggest that some division of labor and responsibility between developer and user must be found. The gist of the APA guidelines is: The validity and reliability of the computerized version of a test should be established by the developer, but CPT interpretations should be used only in conjunction with professional review. This rather general principle might be elaborated into a more specific assignment of responsibilities. The developer

seems in the best position to assure that the scales and research on which the report is based are not obsolete or otherwise inadequate. Actuarially based interpretations should use the best research and statistical equations. Developers can stay abreast of relevant research, incorporate new findings into the system, and direct practitioners to research that may assist them in properly using the report. Users can then concentrate on overseeing the context of the testing and evaluating the appropriateness of the norms and validation studies used by the system for interpreting any particular client's scores. They can concentrate on gathering clinical information not used by the CPT system but relevant to clinical decision making. By specializing and working together, developers and users can assure the full advantages of CPT are realized.

For users to meet their responsibilities to review the validity of a CPT report for each test taker, they must have information about the interpretation system. They need to know how interpretations are derived from original item responses. Some of this information is best suited for inclusion in each report, and some can be included in a manual outlining general features of the interpretation system. A major potential conflict in CPT is the tension between users' needs for sufficient information to review reports, and developers' proprietary interest in their algorithms, software, and other business assets.

This conflict is real, but a satisfactory compromise may be available. The APA guidelines call for disclosure of "how interpretations are derived" and information on "the nature of the relationship" between scores and interpretations. Users need not know all the decision rules and algorithms used by the testing service, but they must know enough to review any report they actually use. . . . In cases where interpretations are clinically based, users must have information needed to weigh the credibility of the expert. The names and credentials of these experts could be provided, along with their theoretical rationale. . . .

[*Ed. note:* I have omitted a long section on intellectual property issues—such as copyright, patents, and trade secrets. These problems, although beyond

---

[1] *Ed. note:* See Standard 2.08 of the APA's current (1992) Ethical Principles.

the scope of this text, are extremely important, and readers are referred to the full chapter for their discussion. The issue of copyright for norms and other data related to computerized testing has already been the subject of significant litigation.]

THE RIGHTS OF TEST TAKERS

. . .

A major concern about computer-generated reports is that they may not be as individualized as those generated in the conventional manner. Some information, such as demographic characteristics of the examinee, can be included in interpretation programs so that the computer will use more appropriate norms or base rates if they exist and qualify interpretations to take into account the particular test taker's characteristics. But no program can consider all the unique attributes of each individual and in most cases the same programmed decision rules will be applied to all test scores.

The revised *Standards for Educational and Psychological Testing* (APA et al., 1985), clearly indicates that test users are ultimately responsible for their test interpretations, no matter from what format the data are derived. Assessing the validity of interpretations requires that a human being observe the testing situation and decide if conditions are present that could invalidate test results. It is imperative that the final act of decision making be that of a qualified practitioner, consistent with state law, ethical principles, and professional standards, who takes responsibility for overseeing both the process of testing and judging the applicability of the interpretive report for individual examinees.

There must be an interposition of human judgment between the CPT report and decision making to ensure that decisions are made with full sensitivity to all the nuances of test administration and interpretation, and the unique constellation of attributes in each person is evaluated. Relying solely on test developers' computerized conception of the test taker's responses isolated from a clinician's trained observation of the test taker's behavior during the administration of the test, may tend to create bland, impersonal, and nonspecific assessments that fail to capture the test taker's cognitive, affec-

tive, and behavioral functioning across a variety of situations. . . .

References

American Psychological Association. (1966). Minutes of the annual meeting of the Council of Representatives. *American Psychologist, 21,* 1141.

American Psychological Association. (1977). *Standards for providers of psychological services.* Washington, DC: Author.

American Psychological Association. (1981). Specialty guidelines for the delivery of services. *American Psychologist, 36,* 640–681.

American Psychological Association. (1985). *Standards for educational and psychological tests.* Washington, DC: Author.

American Psychological Association. (1986). *Guidelines for computerized-based tests and interpretations.* Washington, DC: Author.

American Psychological Association. (1987). *General guidelines for providers of psychological services.* Washington, DC: Author.

American Psychological Association, American Educational Research Association, & National Council of Measurement in Education. (1974). *Standards for educational and psychological tests.* Washington, DC: Author.

Burke, M., & Normand, J. (1985). *Computerized psychological testing: An overview and critique.* Manuscript submitted for publication.

Colorado Psychological Association. (1982). *Guidelines for use of computerized testing services.* (Available from Colorado Psychological Association, 245 Columbine, Denver, CO 80206)

Green, B., Bock, R., Humphreys, L., Linn, R., & Reckase, M. (1984). Technical guidelines for assessing computerized adaptive tests. *Journal of Educational Measurement, 21,* 347–360.

Hofer, P. (1985). Developing standards for computerized psychological testing. *Computers in Human Behavior, 1,* 301–315.

Hofer, P., & Bersoff, D. (1983). *Standards for the administration and interpretation of computerized psychological testing.*

Hofer, P., & Green, B. (1985). The challenge of competence and creativity in computerized psychological testing. *Journal of Counseling and Clinical Psychology, 53,* 826–838.

Matarazzo, J. (1986). Computerized clinical psychological test interpretations: Unvalidated plus all mean and no sigma. *American Psychologist, 41,* 14–24.

Matarazzo, J. (in press). Clinical psychological test interpretation by computer: Hardware outpaces software. *Computers in Human Behavior.*

Petterson, J. (1983, November). Computer testing spurs writing of ethics codes. *Kansas City Times.*

Schwartz, M. (1984). (Ed.). *Using Computers in Clinical Practice.* New York: Haworth Press.

Skinner, H., & Pakula, A. (1986). Challenge of computers in psychological assessment. *Professional Psychology, 17,* 44–50.

Zachary, R., & Pope, K. (1984). Legal and ethical issues in the clinical use of computerized testing. In M. D. Schwartz (Ed.), *Using computers in clinical practice.* New York: Haworth Press.

◆ ◆ ◆

Commentary: Many psychologists are concerned that unqualified and untrained people in other professions will be sold computerized tests and scoring and interpretive services or may otherwise be given access to these. Is this a genuine concern or merely an argument to eliminate competition? For helpful readings on this problem and other legal and ethical issues, see, for example, these publications:

Eyde, L. D., & Kowal, D. M. (1987). Computerised test interpretation services: Ethical and professional concerns regarding U.S. producers and users. Applied Psychology: An International Review, 36, 401–417.

Hartman, D. E. (1986). On the use of clinical psychology software: Practical, legal, and ethical concerns. Professional Psychology: Research and Practice, 17, 462–465.

Zachary, R., & Pope, K. (1984). Legal and ethical issues in the clinical use of computerized testing. In M. D. Schwartz (Ed.), Using computers in clinical practice (pp. 151–164). New York: Haworth Press.

Computerized Clinical Psychological Test Interpretations: Unvalidated Plus All Mean and No Sigma

Joseph D. Matarazzo

PSYCHOLOGICAL ASSESSMENT, INVASION OF PRIVACY, AND PROFESSIONAL STANDARDS

I would like to set the stage for my comments by stating a truism that seems to have been forgotten recently in some quarters: The testing by one individual of another human's intellectual, personality, and related characteristics is an invasion of privacy to an extent no less intimate than that involved in an examination carried out on that same individual's person or resources by a physician, attorney, or agent of the Internal Revenue Service. Assessment of features of another person's intellect, interests, brain functioning, or personality, whether carried out by computer or by a clinician, is a professional act that, at its best, is executed with sensitive concern for the patient, client, his or her family, potential or present employer, the third-party payer who increasingly is paying for such a service, other professional colleagues, and the whole host of social institutions that potentially may be affected by the results of this individual, clinical assessment.

Alas, there is evidence that sensitivity to these concerns is not uniformly the norm today. In fact, there are alarming signals that the features of a responsible assessment that were first promulgated by Binet and Simon (Matarazzo, 1972) are today being overlooked by for-profit commercial companies and individual psychologist–entrepreneurs who are vigorously touting and over-selling the products of a new computer technology to some ill-prepared and professionally undereducated users who erroneously equate the products of this technology with a full and responsible psychological assessment.

. . . [M]y concern is not with the computer hardware being sold. Along with others in our profession, I believe this new technology, with its seemingly unlimited memory and capacity to store and integrate previously validated relationships, will significantly advance the art and science of assessment. My intention therefore is not to try to defend the work of today's human clinician nor to deny that computers will one day supplant some types of human clinical judgments. Rather, my concern is with the pages and pages of today's neatly typed, valid-sounding narrative interpretations that are the products, for the most part, of secretly developed disks of software that have not even been offered for scientific evaluation (as has clinical judgment), let alone met even the most rudimentary acceptable tests of science.

SOCIETY AND NOT THE INDIVIDUAL IS INCREASINGLY BEARING THE COSTS OF PSYCHOLOGICAL SERVICES

Referral of a patient or client for psychological assessment, in common with referral for other consultative procedures, was done until about a decade or two ago with careful weighing of the costs and benefits that might accrue to the individual who, to a large extent, was personally paying for such services. This weighing process seems to be less used today. The more recent large-scale increase in private and public third-party payment programs and the tremendous advances during the past five years in microcomputerized psychological testing hardware and software have made it possible and economically seductive for a psychologist, a physician, another health service provider or a hospital administrator to offer such testing to unprecedented numbers of pa-

Adapted from the *American Psychologist*, *41*, 14–24. Copyright 1986 by the American Psychological Association.

tients and clients. Whether provided in-house or purchased from a commercial firm, such psychological services are costly, and the inevitable result can only be a frightening escalation of fees being paid for psychological assessment by third-party payers. Given the nature of pooled risk in these private, state, and federal insurance industries, the annual costs perforce are passed on to all 230 million Americans and not only to the hundreds of thousands (or few millions) of actual consumers.

Therefore, given the ready-access computer's contribution to the potential massive increase in *alleged* need, we quite likely could see in the not-too-distant future repressive legislative and actuarial remedy aimed at the clinical psychological testing industry. Should such remedies begin to unfold, there will be little time for sorting out what is a legitimately needed clinical psychological service and what is one created solely by the availability of the technology in the offices of thousands of mental health service providers, many of whom have received no training in applied or theoretical psychometrics that would allow them better to evaluate the products of interpretative software.

RESPONSIBLE USE OF COMPUTERIZED CLINICAL INTERPRETATIONS REQUIRES MORE THAN A MANUAL

Today's automated and still "canned" clinical psychological interpretations, with almost no exceptions that I have been able to discern, do not offer the plausible interpretations by several well-respected and identified clinicians of the *same* test finding(s); nor, for that matter, do they offer several equally plausible interpretations by a single, publicly identified clinician. Thus, although computerized clinical psychological test interpretations present other problems, an issue that should seriously concern the experienced health service provider–user involves that critical missing element: namely, that the computer rarely delivers several different but equally plausible clinical interpretations. With almost no exceptions, today's software produces only a single, typically very lengthy, clinical narrative. Another danger of this clinical-appearing product is the aura of seeming validity that surrounds its objectively presented,

neatly typed page after page of narrative clinical statements.

PSYCHOLOGY BEGINS TO MEET THE CHALLENGE

. . . [T]he proliferation during the past decade of scores of for-profit companies producing hardware and software for yet-to-be-validated, computerized clinical psychological interpretations, without safeguards for the consumer or service provider, has presented the profession of psychology with a considerable threat to its integrity. Fortunately, however, developments within our profession since I first communicated my mounting alarm two years ago have begun to ease my anxiety. . . .

. . . [T]he 1985 Council of Representatives was provided a draft of a well-thought-out set of *Guidelines for Computer-Based Tests and Interpretations* that I hope will soon be ratified. These *Guidelines* were prepared jointly by the American Psychological Association's Committee on Professional Standards and its Committee on Psychological Tests and Assessment. Fortunately, these *Guidelines* include a series of detailed and well-reasoned principles by which to initiate and evaluate the needed further development and validation of the clinical and related products of computer software, as well as principles to guide the developer, publisher, and user of these new computer-generated tools.

There have been other equally important recent developments within our discipline. First, Hofer and Bersoff (1983) compiled and promulgated a series of ethical and professional standards for the administration and interpretation of computerized psychological testing tools. Second, a soon-to-be-published issue of the *Journal of Consulting and Clinical Psychology* will be devoted entirely to the problems and promises offered by the new software of clinical psychological interpretations. And third, a relative avalanche of symposia and paper sessions devoted to a concentrated, critical evaluation of this new computer-assisted, clinical psychological testing industry was presented at the 1984 Annual Meeting of the American Psychological Association in Toronto.

These and related developments will most likely help stimulate the effort in education, training, and research that must be undertaken by our discipline to meet the challenge sparked by the proffering of unvalidated software to unwary users and consumers by large numbers of for-profit companies and their consultants.

References

Hofer, P. J., & Bersoff, D. N. (1983). Standards for the administration and interpretation of computerized psychological testing.

Matarazzo, J. D. (1972). *Wechsler's measurement and appraisal of adult intelligence: Fifth and enlarged edition.* New York: Oxford University Press.

◆ ◆ ◆

Commentary: The Guidelines that Matarazzo referred to were ratified, as he hoped, by the APA's Council of Representatives, and they have been published. See American Psychological Association Committee on Professional Standards and Committee on Psychological Testing and Assessment. (1986). Guidelines for computer-based tests and interpretations. Washington, DC: American Psychological Association.[1]

The Guidelines are advisory in nature and, thus, are

not directly enforceable. Among other things, however, they recommend that "computer-generated interpretive reports should be used only in conjunction with professional judgment" (p. 12). It is the psychologist, not the testing company, "who takes responsibility for overseeing both the process of testing and judging the applicability of the interpretive report for individual test takers, consistent with legal, ethical, and professional requirements" (pp. 12–13). Thus, as these Guidelines suggest, psychologists "may need to amend the computer report to take into account their own observations and judgments and to ensure that the report is comprehensible, free of jargon, and true to the person evaluated" (p. 13).

Unfortunately, a portion of these Guidelines, not relevant here and thus not reprinted herein, cited several provisions from the 1981 APA ethics code that had been criticized by the Federal Trade Commission (see chap. 10). In accordance with a consent agreement between APA and the Federal Trade Commission, those portions of the Guidelines have been rescinded. To avoid further problems, the APA is revising all of the guidelines, and, at press time, had halted distribution of the current version. The major enforceable ethical principle concerning computerized testing is now found in Standard 2.08 of the 1992 Ethical Principles.

---

[1] These Guidelines have since been rescinded (see later discussion), and, at the time this book was in press, were not available from the APA.

Integrity Tests: Facts and Unresolved Issues

Wayne J. Camara and Dianne L. Schneider

Integrity tests, or honesty tests as they are often referred to, are paper-and-pencil instruments for personnel selection that are used to predict dishonesty or counterproductivity. These tests are composed of items that query job applicants about their attitudes toward theft and inquire about any past thefts. Over the past decade, integrity testing has greatly increased and has become a mainstream selection practice for a wide variety of jobs in which employees have access to cash or merchandise or perform security functions (Goldberg, Grenier, Guion, Sechrest, & Wing, 1991; Guastello & Rieke, 1991; O'Bannon, Goldinger, & Appleby, 1989).

In the past five years, integrity testing has received more scrutiny by the media, policymakers, and the public than has any other class of psychological tests. Much of this increased interest and use of integrity tests followed the passage of the Employee Polygraph Protection Act of 1988. Many of the technical flaws and misuses of polygraphs for employment screening (see Saxe, Dougherty, & Cross, 1985; U.S. Congress, 1983) have, in part, increased skepticism that any psychological instrument can accurately identify individuals who will be dishonest in a specific work environment (Saxe, 1991). Concerns about the reliance on integrity test scores in personnel selection decisions, the potential restriction of opportunities for job applicants, invasion of individuals' privacy, labeling, and basic psychometric issues of validity spurred investigations by Congress and the American Psychological Association (APA). The U.S. Congress Office of Technology Assessment (OTA) completed a two-year study of integrity testing that included several psychologists in advisory and consultant capacities (U.S. Congress, 1990). In addition, a task force of the APA established in conjunction with Division 5 (Division of Evaluation, Measurement, and Statistics) and Division 14 (The Society for Industrial and Organizational Psychology) completed a 20-month study of integrity tests (Goldberg et al., 1991), herein referred to as the APA report. . . .

The APA and OTA studies differed in foci, particularly their intended purposes, evidentiary bases, and conclusions regarding the implications of using integrity tests for employment screening. OTA's report was written to guide Congress in determining what, if any, legislative action on integrity tests was warranted. It focused on public policy issues, such as potential errors in selection decisions, the effect these tests have on labeling, and individuals' reduced employment opportunities—concerns that might generalize to all types of personnel selection processes. In contrast, APA's report was produced by psychologists for psychologists and test users. It targeted scientific and technical issues in integrity testing (e.g., defining the construct; identifying appropriate criteria; and examining the validity, reliability, and utility of the tests) and dealt with policy indirectly, by examining only those issues for which psychology can offer special expertise. . . .

PROFESSIONAL AND PUBLIC POLICY IMPLICATIONS

The continued use of integrity tests for employment screening raises professional and policy issues for psychology. As professionals, psychologists have a responsibility to reduce the misuse of integrity tests. Each of the following issues can best be discussed in light of several principles (2.02, 2.05, 2.06, and 2.08) concerning assessment in the *Ethical Principles of Psychologists and Code of Conduct* (APA, 1992).

Two of these principles address a psychologist's responsibility to prevent misuse of assessments and information from assessments by unqualified persons. Principle 2.02 (b) instructs psychologists to refrain from releasing test results or data to persons not qualified to use such information. This presents several dilemmas for the 56% of integrity test publishers who report using no formal screening practices for test users.

Demands for cutting scores by employers and the willingness of test publishers to produce them were cited as a major problem by both APA and OTA. Publishers often appear to have set cutting scores for some tests on purely arbitrary grounds, then created failing and passing categories (Goldberg et al., 1991) based on this scoring dichotomy. Scrivner (1991) pointed out that the integrity testing industry's own association specifies in its guidelines (Association of Personnel Test Publishers [APTP], 1990) that test users should know how a cutting score was derived. Yet, given the complexities of proper procedures to set cutting scores (see Rorer, Hoffman, & Hsieh, 1966), it is unrealistic to impose such responsibilities on the untrained persons who administer integrity tests (Cascio, Alexander, & Barrett, 1988). Similarly, APA's report recommended that standard error of measurement and score ranges be reported but noted that the typical test user may not be qualified to interpret anything more than dichotomous categories (e.g, hire vs. do not hire). When the competence level of test users is not known, test publishers will have difficulty inferring the appropriate amount and level of information that should be provided.

Principle 2.06 (APA, 1992) prohibits psychologists from promoting (e.g., through marketing or sales) the use of tests by unqualified persons. Integrity test publishers might note that test administration is often straightforward and that interpretation requires minimal understanding of categorical (e.g., low-, moderate-, or high-risk categories) or dichotomous data. One might argue that personnel responsible for the administration and use of integrity tests manage other facets of the employment screening process, such as interviews, reference checks, and possibly some cognitive ability tests. Yet, other principles and professional standards (e.g., APA, 1985) suggest that the use of tests and test data re-

quire a level of technical knowledge of statistics, measurement, and assessment that many integrity tests users lack. For example, when psychologists serve as test users, they should (a) be familiar with the reliability, validity, standardization, or outcome studies of the techniques (Principle 2.04 [a]); (b) recognize limits to the certainty of predictions made about individuals (Principle 2.04 [b]); (c) consider various test factors and individual characteristics that might limit the accuracy of interpretations, including automated interpretations (Principles 2.04 [c] and 2.05); (d) select scoring and interpretation services on the basis of evidence of the validity and other considerations (Principle 2.08 [b]); and (e) retain responsibility for the interpretation and use of assessments (including automated services; Principle 2.09). Although these principles are relevant for all test users, the *Ethical Principles* can be enforced only with APA members. Similarly, psychologists and all testing professionals responsible for the development, marketing, and sale of assessment products should consider these criteria when determining the qualifications of all test users.

Most integrity tests are classified as *proprietary* by their publishers. The APTP (1990) distinguishes between proprietary and nonproprietary tests [footnote omitted]. Nonproprietary tests are sold to users whom the publisher deems qualified to administer and interpret the test; publishers sell the test, scoring keys, and supporting materials to users possessing the necessary background (e.g., a doctoral degree) or experience (e.g., specialized training). In contrast, proprietary test users purchase a package deal from a publisher, who provides continuous client service. Publishers maintain technical responsibility for norming, scoring, validating, and interpreting tests for the user and providing ongoing psychological expertise to clients (APTP, 1990). Users are responsible for test administration, security of test scores, and final decisions based on the test scores. According to the APTP, "users of proprietary tests are not required to be credentialed by the publisher, although in general the more sophisticated users will make better use of such tests than users who do not have a comprehensive understanding of a test's psychometric properties" (p. 6). However, publishers with minimal or no screening procedures for test purchases and test services cannot evaluate the competence of users or risk of misuse for their services.

A working group of the Joint Committee on Testing Practices (Eyde, Moreland, Robertson, Primoff, & Most, 1988) made no distinctions between proprietary and nonproprietary tests in terms of potential test misuse or in qualifications for test use. Certainly, ensuring that test users are trained appropriately is a common problem in many forms of assessment: clinical, educational, and employment. The *Standards for Educational and Psychological Testing* (APA, 1985) state that "the ultimate responsibility for test use lies with the test user" (p. 41). However, risk of misuse can be reduced if those responsible for the sale of test materials and provision of services take some minimal steps, such as screening test users, requiring organizations that purchase products and services to limit access to only those persons considered competent by the publisher, and requiring test use training for organizations that employ persons who do not satisfy appropriate criteria for test use.

Publishers are justified in making distinctions about the level of competence required for using different types of test data. Few would argue that users who derive a diagnosis and treatment plan for a client using data from multiple scales on a personality test require substantially more expertise and training than users who receive data reported in dichotomous (e.g., hire vs. do not hire) categories on a preemployment assessment report. However, the responsibilities for proper test use (e.g., Eyde et al., 1993) and the importance of decisions based on assessment data may be no less important in employment settings than in clinical practice. Kay (1991) doubted that the unsophisticated test user will ever be competent enough to transform continuous test data into dichotomous selection decisions. He argued that many of the problems attributed to integrity tests result from end users who are largely unqualified to evaluate and interpret test scores. Kay urged publishers to adopt guidelines for the sale and use of integrity tests, similar to those currently used in qualifying users of other broadband-width personality inventories.

Psychologists are ethically bound (APA, 1992) to consider various test factors (e.g., situational vari-

ables, surveillance systems), individual characteristics, and limitations of tests when making recommendations and to ensure the integrity and security of tests and results. However, most users of integrity and employment tests are not psychologists (a situation similar to the administration and interpretation of most large-scale educational testing programs). Personnel managers, security specialists, and supervisors have no such ethical responsibilities and in addition probably lack familiarity with the *Ethical Principles of Psychologists and Code of Conduct* (APA, 1992) and the *Standards for Educational and Psychological Testing* (APA, 1985). Goldberg et al. (1991) acknowledged this problem and called for more concrete, comprehensive training for test users and for screening of potential users. These aspects of psychological testing are generally unregulated in employment settings. Test publishers currently represent the final check in ensuring that only qualified persons administer and interpret tests.

Currently, Massachusetts is the only state that bans integrity tests, although Rhode Island prohibits use of these tests as the sole basis for employment decisions. Both laws went into effect before the studies completed by OTA and APA. Since then, legislation aiming to ban or restrict the use of integrity and other forms of personality tests for preemployment screening has been introduced in at least five other states. However, not one piece of legislation has yet been signed into law. Inquiries about the attitudes and past conduct of applicants and employers have been a major concern of legislators seeking to restrict these tests; however, their misuse by unqualified users has also been cited as a rationale for such legislation (H. A. Fernandez, personal communication, June 18, 1991; Oregon Psychological Association, 1991). . . .

References

American Psychological Association. (1985). *Standards for Educational and Psychological Testing.* Washington, DC: Author.

American Psychological Association. (1992). Ethical principles of psychologists and code of conduct. *American Psychologist, 47,* 1597–1611.

Association of Personnel Test Publishers. (1990). *Model guidelines for pre-employment integrity testing programs.* Washington, DC: Author.

Cascio, W. F., Alexander, R. A., & Barrett, G. V. (1988). Setting cutoff scores: Legal, psychometric, and professional issues and guidelines. *Personnel Psychology, 41*, 1–24.

Employee Polygraph Protection Act of 1988, Sec. 200001 et sec., 29 U.S.C.

Eyde, L. D., Moreland, K. L., Robertson, G. J., Primoff, E. S., & Most, R. B. (1988). *Test user qualifications: A data-based approach to promoting good test use* (Report of the Test User Qualifications Working Group of the Joint Committee on Testing Practices). Washington, DC: American Psychological Association.

Eyde, L. D., Robertson, G. J., Krug, S. E., Moreland, K. L., Robertson, A. G., Shewan, C. M., Harrison, P. L., Porch, B. E., Hammer, A. L., & Primoff, E. S. (1993). *Responsible test use: Case studies for assessing human behavior* (Report of the Joint Committee on Testing Practices). Washington, DC: American Psychological Association.

Goldberg, L. R., Grenier, J. R., Guion, R. M., Sechrest, L. B., & Wing, H. (1991). *Questionnaires used in the prediction of trustworthiness in pre-employment selection decisions: An APA task force report.* Washington, DC: American Psychological Association.

Guastello, S. J., & Rieke, M. L. (1991). A review and critique of honesty test research. *Behavioral Sciences and the Law, 9*, 501–523.

Kay, G. C. (1991). Casting stones at integrity testing, not at integrity tests. *Forensic Reports, 4*, 163–169.

O'Bannon, R. M., Goldinger, L. A., & Appleby, G. S. (1989). *Honesty and integrity testing: A practical guide.* Atlanta: Applied Information Resources.

Oregon Psychological Association. (1991). [From insert distributed with newsletter]. *OPA Newsgram, 10*(8).

Rorer, L. G., Hoffman, P. J., & Hsieh, K. (1966). Utilities as base-rate multipliers in the determination of optimum cutting scores for the discrimination of groups of unequal size and variance. *Journal of Applied Psychology, 50*, 364–368.

Saxe, L. (1991). Lying: Thoughts of an applied social psychologist. *American Psychologist, 46*, 409–415.

Saxe, L., Dougherty, D., & Cross, T. (1985). The validity of polygraph testing: Scientific analysis and public controversy. *American Psychologist, 40*, 355–366.

Scrivner, E. (1991). Integrity testing: A new frontier for psychology. *Forensic Reports, 4*, 75–89.

U. S. Congress, Office of Technology Assessment. (1983). *Scientific validity of polygraph testing* (OTA-TM-H-15). Washington, DC: U.S. Government Printing Office.

U. S. Congress, Office of Technology Assessment. (1990). *The use of integrity tests for pre-employment screening* (OTA-SET-442). Washington, DC: U.S. Government Printing Office.

CHAPTER 7

THERAPY AND OTHER FORMS
OF INTERVENTION

Few human relationships so quickly attain the level of intimacy of a working therapeutic relationship. Although in most instances therapists are complete strangers at the beginning of treatment, clients are expected to reveal their innermost and private feelings, thoughts, and behavior to them, and with them, confront the clients' deepest, darkest, and most distasteful sides of themselves. At times, clients may be asked to do this not only in front of their therapists but also in the company of family members or even strangers who make up their therapeutic group.

To compound the problem, in most cases, people enter therapy only after considerable worry and rumination. They are experiencing such symptoms as debilitating feelings or nonproductive, even self-damaging behavior. Although they may want desperately to understand and ameliorate these indicators of distress, it is likely that they do not know much about the process of therapy.

Despite their anxiety, these potential clients are at least facing the prospect voluntarily. However, not all people come to treatment on their own initiative. Some patients—for example, those involuntarily committed to mental hospitals or forced by a court to seek treatment as a condition of probation or parole—may be compelled to see a psychologist. In either case, therapists are likely to encounter clients who, at their initial consultation, are confused, anxious, needy, and vulnerable—and sometimes, downright hostile and negative.

It is almost inevitable, then, that complex ethical issues will arise in settings where therapy and other forms of intervention take place. Preceding chapters have already explored some of these issues. In chapters 4 and 5, I provided materials in which crucial issues concerning confidentiality and multiple relationships, respectively, were debated. In chapter 10, I introduce some of the more ethically sensitive commercial aspects of providing psychological services. In this chapter, I concentrate on several additional issues that are not covered elsewhere in this book.

The previous APA code of ethics (1990) contained no divisible set of ethical principles related directly to therapy. In this regard, the 1992 Ethical Principles offered significant improvement. For example, Standard 4.02 of the 1992 code requires that "psychologists obtain appropriate informed consent to therapy or related procedures" (APA, 1992, p. 1605). As part of this process, psychologists are obliged to inform potential therapy participants "of significant information concerning the procedure" (p. 1605) in some documentable form. Although Standard 4.02 makes it clear that some manner of consent must be obtained from clients, it does not flesh out this requirement in any explicit way. Thus, many authors, reflecting on the 1990 and 1992 codes, have sought to advance their views on how the consent process should take place. Some have even questioned whether consent should be sought at all. Another matter of considerable debate is whether the therapist and the client should enter into a formal written informed-consent contract.

These controversies about the substance and procedure of informed consent to treatment are important in themselves, but they also raise larger, more overarching issues. What does the kind of consent process, if any, say about the nature of the relationship between the professional and the person seeking help? Which of the moral principles discussed in chapter 3 are promoted by consent? Does obtaining consent promote certain values, but endanger others? Can in fact obtaining consent damage—if not destroy—the value of certain forms of therapy?

Single client–therapist issues are complex enough; they become geometrically enlarged when therapists engage in couples, family, or group therapy. Confidentiality issues become paramount, of course, and the materials in this chapter on confidentiality amplify the ideas put forth in chapter 4. Added to this, however, is the complicating fact that family therapy often involves children. Should they have the right to consent to therapy? Do they have independent rights to privacy that should be respected? Should one assume that parents represent their children's interests? When, if ever, should therapists act as children's advocates?

It is essential that this chapter cover these traditional (though yet unresolved, and unsolved) problems. However, the world of psychology is not limited to spoken, face-to-face forms of treatment. For example, psychologists are increasingly involved in behavioral medicine, such as stress and pain management. Moreover, it is impossible to ignore the presently raging debate over the effort of many powerful and influential psychologists to obtain the right for licensed psychologists, given proper training, to prescribe antipsychotic and other psychotropic medications. In addition, some psychologists write self-help texts that become bestsellers, whereas others conduct therapy over the telephone (and probably by fax).

Not only do psychologists engage in different forms of treatment, but they are also confronted with a diversity of clients. Women in general, gays and lesbians, ethnic minorities, those from rural communities, and people with disabilities often confront the responsible psychotherapist (still predominantly men who are White and urban) with a plethora of ethical issues. Finally, ethical problems may even survive the death of the therapist. Consider, for example, what ethical obligations a psychologist has toward his or her patients in contemplation of his or her own death?

These are the issues covered in chapter 7. The challenges they represent clearly show that good therapy is more than technique, empathy, and sound theory.

References

American Psychological Association. (1990). Ethical principles of psychologists (amended June 2, 1989). *American Psychologist, 45,* 390–395.

American Psychological Association. (1992). Ethical principles of psychologists and code of conduct. *American Psychologist, 47,* 1597–1611.

Rights of Clients, Responsibilities of Therapists

Rachel T. Hare-Mustin, Jeanne Marecek, Alexandra G. Kaplan, and Nechama Liss-Levinson

Most psychotherapists formally uphold the ethical principles of their professions. These principles entail a commitment to promote the welfare of clients and to assure their rights. . . .

Although the content of the ethical codes concerns the rights and welfare of clients, their original intent was quite different. Historically, the ethical standards were developed to protect the professions, by permitting self-regulation, from regulation by outside agencies (Van Hoose & Kottler, 1977). The ethical codes allowed the psychotherapeutic professions to maintain their integrity by disavowing the unacceptable actions of individual members. Protecting the rights of clients was of secondary importance. Ethical codes are public affirmations of principles that may or may not guide actual practice (Hare-Mustin, 1974). It is unfortunate that statements of ethical standards represent more of a "salute to the flag" for therapists than a bill of rights for clients. . . .

ETHICAL PRINCIPLES IN THE THERAPY RELATIONSHIP

The *Ethical Standards* could be said to specify responsibilities of practitioners and the corresponding rights of their clients. In doing so, the *Ethical Standards* define reciprocal roles for therapist and client in the therapy relationship. Therapists' responsibilities and clients' rights converge on such issues as freedom of choice, disclosure of information about treatment, and protection of human dignity. By assuring clients' rights, therapists can accord their clients equality of status and responsibility for their participation in therapy and, ultimately, for their lives. In addition, assuring clients' rights places corresponding responsibilities on clients (Arbuckle,

1977). Clients are expected to choose wisely, to make use of information provided, and to assume control of their participation in therapy. By helping clients accept their rights and responsibilities, therapists are encouraging healthy functioning and, thus, mental health. Taken together, these responsibilities and rights that follow from the *Ethical Standards* constitute a model for the practice of therapy that can be contrasted with other models. . . .

This model can provide benefits to therapists and to the profession. Assuring clients' rights can make therapists more effective practitioners. Open communication about the methods and goals of therapy can encourage realistic expectations about treatment and outcome. The therapist who is sensitive to the client's rights may be able to minimize therapeutic impasses and unilateral terminations stemming from the client's unspoken dissatisfactions. Finally, assurance of clients' rights can protect the practitioner from criminal or malpractice actions (Roston & Sherrer, 1973). Unless the internal regulation of the profession is visibly effective in protecting clients, professional practice may be open to outside regulation.

Implications for Training

Few therapists are adequately prepared by their training to carry out the *Ethical Standards* in practice. . . . [T]raining should foster an image of clients as powerful, responsible adults and inculcate a sense of responsibility in therapists for clients' rights and dignity. As Kessler (1977) suggested, we must rethink and retool our training programs if our practice of therapy is to be consistent with our ethical principles. In the following sections we present four situations in therapy to illustrate how the model might be applied. We consider some specific issues that might arise in each situation and suggest possible ways of dealing with them. Our goal is to open a discussion among psychologists about some specific ways in which the *Ethical Standards* should be put into practice in the client–therapist relationship.

ASSURING THAT CLIENTS MAKE INFORMED CHOICES

. . .

First, clients need knowledge of procedures, goals, and side effects of therapy. Some of the issues involved in presenting a description of procedures and goals of therapy are discussed in the section below on Establishing a Contract. The issue of whether the client is to be informed of possible side effects of therapy generates more controversy. Information about possible indirect effects is essential if the client is to weigh the benefits and risks of entering treatment (Coyne, 1976; Graziano & Fink, 1973). An example of such an indirect effect is the possibility that progress in individual therapy will disrupt a marital relationship (Hurvitz, 1967). It is only recently that psychologists have turned their attention to the question of indirect effects of therapy (Strupp & Hadley, 1977). Thus, more research is needed to broaden our knowledge of indirect effects.

An issue that is now receiving much attention is confidentiality and privileged communication in therapy. The extent of confidentiality of communications and records is more limited than many assume. Third-party payers may require the therapist to furnish information that the client would not wish to disclose; such information may be available for later retrieval by others. The Tarasoff decision in California established that a therapist must warn a client's intended victim of possible danger (Whiteley & Whiteley, 1977). Confidentiality in group therapy may not be protected under the laws of privileged communication, although many therapists and clients assume that it is (Meyer & Smith, 1977). Some therapies by their nature offer fewer safeguards to confidentiality than others do. For example, clients "on the hot seat" in Gestalt therapy groups may be pressured to make revelations against their

wishes (Eberlein, 1977). In marital therapy, the therapist may provoke disclosures that further harm the marital relationship or that play into the hands of the more powerful partner (Rubin & Mitchell, 1976). Therapists may overlook the need to inform clients that their cases may sometimes be discussed with colleagues, supervisors, or at case conferences. Limitations on confidentiality must be conveyed to prospective clients; guarantees of complete secrecy are tantamount to "blatant misrepresentation of facts that should be known to all therapists" (Bersoff, 1975, p. 270).

Second, clients need information about the qualifications of the therapist to make informed choices about entering therapy. Clients may have uncertainties about the specialties and training of various professionals. As Winborn (1977) suggested, "honest labeling" is necessary if informed choices are to be made. Therapists disagree about the extent of information on skills, qualifications, and training to be presented to the client. However, therapists in training are not the only ones who should inform clients of their status and qualifications. Providing a description of skills and experience and responding to clients' queries safeguard both therapist and client from unrealistic expectations that the client might hold.

Third, clients need to know about alternatives to psychotherapy. It is unusual for therapists to share information on alternative resources with their clients, yet the *Standards for Providers* state that therapists have a responsibility to inform themselves about the network of human services in their communities and to use this knowledge in making referrals. Because clients' knowledge of the available resources is usually limited, therapists have the responsibility of providing this information. . . .

Issues About Informed Decisions
When should information be presented? . . .
Some therapists (e.g., Winborn, 1977) find that the optimal time for educating clients about therapy is the end of the first interview. However, this may not hold for clients who enter therapy in crisis. For clients who are deeply upset, the therapist may balance the need to offer immediate support and relief against the responsibility to explore whether the

client has come to the right place for help. Nonetheless, even if the examination of therapy and its alternatives is postponed for several sessions, it should not be foregone.

How should information about therapy and its alternatives be presented? The information may be presented orally, in writing, or on audio- or video-tape. Certain kinds of information can be presented by a receptionist or intake interviewer. Sometimes therapists may reduce or waive the fee for such an informational session.

The manner of presenting information to clients should be consistent with the ethical principle of informed choice. Biases and inaccurate information are violations of this principle. For example, therapists could be cautious to characterize alternative systems fairly. An ethical dilemma may occur when the therapist has very strong feelings about what course of action is best for a client. In such cases, the therapist may feel obligated to air these feelings to the client, particularly if the client is tending toward a different course of action. Recommending a course of action can be seen as promoting the client's welfare. However, when a course of action is insisted upon by the therapist, the client's right to free choice is diminished.

Are there disadvantages of assuring clients' rights to informed decisions? A premature or overly enthusiastic discussion of alternatives may convince the client that the therapist does not want him or her in therapy. Another disadvantage is that some potential clients may choose sources of help other than therapy. For therapists whose livelihoods depend on their clientele, this may be worrisome. However, concerns about losing clients must be viewed in perspective. Many potential clients terminate after the first interview anyway. An open discussion of therapy and its alternatives may lead some of these clients to continue in treatment.

Some psychoanalytic therapists may feel that detailed information about therapy and the therapist weakens the transference relationship (Wolberg, 1967). Other therapists feel that open disclosure promotes the client–therapist relationship.

ESTABLISHING A CONTRACT
. . .

Ethical principles assert that therapists should inform clients about the purpose and nature of therapy and that clients have freedom of choice about their participation. The process of providing information and obtaining agreement through the use of a contract defines the therapeutic relationship as a mutual endeavor to which the therapist contributes knowledge and skill in psychology and to which the client brings specialized personal knowledge and a commitment to work on his or her problems (Adams & Orgel, 1975; Schwitzgebel, 1976; Sulzer, 1962). Developing a contractual agreement is a negotiation between partners.

The purpose of a contract is to clarify the therapeutic relationship. The development of a contract, whether written or verbal, encourages the client and the therapist to specify the goals, expectations, and boundaries of therapy. Specifying both the problem (or diagnosis, if one is made) and the treatment makes the profession more accountable (Schulberg, 1976). In addition, the contract can prevent misunderstandings about the responsibilities, methods, and practical arrangements of therapy. In this regard, contracts can protect both the therapist and the client from disappointment or false expectations.

Most therapy contracts specify some or all of the following: the methods of therapy, its goals, the length and frequency of sessions, the duration of treatment, the cost and the method of payment, provisions for cancellation and renegotiation of the contract, the extent of each person's responsibility, and the degree of confidentiality. The issues covered by a contract vary according to the therapist's orientation and the inclination of the client. For example, behavior therapists tend to contract for specific behavioral goals to be accomplished according to a defined time schedule (Ayllon & Skuban, 1973; Stuart, 1975). Some therapists emphasize the nature of the relationship; other therapists provide precise specifications of the extent of confidentiality. A contract involving several clients, as in marital and family therapy or group therapy, raises special problems. Likewise, one must be especially sensitive to ethical issues when contracting with a child client, who may not be in a position to give meaningful agreement (Robinson, 1974). The more detailed a contract is, the more frequently it will require renegotiation as the client's circumstances change and the goals of therapy evolve. Periodic reassessment and revision are an integral part of the process of contracting.

The following example of a contract is adapted from a model proposed by the Health Research Group, a Ralph Nader group (Adams & Orgel, 1975):

> I, <u>Alice Bryant</u>, agree to join with Dr. J. Smith each <u>Tuesday</u> from <u>October 4, 1977</u> to <u>December 6, 1977</u>, at <u>3:00 p.m.</u>. During these <u>10</u> 45-minute sessions, we will direct our mutual efforts toward <u>3</u> goals:
>
> 1. Enabling me to have discussions with my spouse without losing my temper.
> 2. Explaining to my satisfaction why I avoid visiting my parents.
> 3. Overcoming my fears of meeting new people.
>
> I agree to pay <u>$35</u> per session for the use of her resources, training, and experience as a therapist. This amount is payable <u>at the time of the session</u>.
>
> If I am not satisfied with the progress made on these goals, I may <u>cancel any future appointments</u> provided I give Dr. Smith <u>3 days</u> warning of my intention to cancel. In that event, I (am/am not) required to pay for sessions not met. However, if I miss a session without <u>24</u> hrs. forewarning, I (am/am not) financially responsible for that missed session, exceptions to this arrangement being unforeseen and unavoidable accident or illness.
>
> At the end of <u>10</u> sessions, Dr. Smith and I agree to renegotiate this contract. We include the possibility that the stated goals will have changed during the <u>10-session</u> period. I understand that this agreement does not guarantee that I will have attained these goals; however,

it does constitute an offer on my part to pay Dr. Smith for access to her resources as a therapist and her acceptance to apply all those resources as a therapist in good faith.

> I further stipulate that this agreement become a part of the record which is accessible to both parties at will, but to no other person without my written consent. The therapist will respect my right to maintain the confidentiality of any information communicated by me to the therapist during the course of therapy.
>
> I (give/do not give) my permission to Dr. Smith to audiotape sessions for her review. However, she will not publish, communicate, or otherwise disclose, without my written consent, any such information, which, if disclosed, would injure me in any way.

_____
Client's signature

_____
Therapist's signature

_____
Date

Issues About Contracts
Should the contract specify all techniques?
. . .

Techniques that might be at odds with the client's values should be specified. The client should know whether the therapy will consist of talking, role playing, or body work, if aversive techniques will be used, if he or she is expected to take medication, if others, such as family members, will be involved, and if he or she will be expected to join a group. Therapists who follow up on clients should secure their permission in the contract, even if this might bias future responses. Some practices, such as sexual relations with clients, are unethical and remain so whether or not the client agrees to them. It has been argued that forms of treatment to which some therapists object, such as primal scream or "tickle" therapy, should be permitted if clients freely agree to them with full knowledge of the risks and benefits. The use of contracts cannot protect clients from making decisions that are not in their best interests. However, if there is gross inequity in the bargaining power of the contracting parties so that the client has no real choice or alternative, such a contract may be considered legally unconscionable (Schwitzgebel, 1975, 1976).

What if the therapist has personal or moral problems with the client's goal? . . . Special difficulties can arise in setting goals in therapies that involve more than one person, such as group, marital, or family therapy. Because encounter groups often attract persons ill suited for interpersonal confrontation (Hartley, Roback, & Abramowitz, 1976), the goals of applicants should be examined in screening interviews. Casualty status has been associated with clients who hold unrealistic expectations for groups (American Psychological Association, 1973; Lieberman, Yalom, & Miles, 1973). In family and marital therapy, various participants may have conflicting goals (Hines & Hare-Mustin, 1978). Therapists must be cautious about supporting goals for the maintenance of the family unit that override the rights of individuals.

Therapy with children also brings up special considerations. Some therapists who work with children advocate a contract because it encourages self-control and delay of gratification (Croghan & Frutiger, 1977). However, these seem to be goals of the parents and therapist, not goals of the child. The therapist may find it hard to support parental goals that deny the rights of the child client. Certain rights of children may not be waived by their parents (Sehdev, 1976; White House Conference on Children, 1970). It has been suggested that a child who does not have the capacity to give full unpressured agreement to goals and techniques should have an advocate other than the parent or therapist (Koocher, 1976). . . .

How should a therapist respond to a client who does not want a contract? For the therapist who feels strongly about the desirability of specifying the goals and arrangements for therapy, the contract may be such an integral part of the technique that he or she will not work without it. Some clients may reject a contract because they are suspicious that the contract is intended to benefit only the therapist. For those clients as well as others, a contract is such an unusual idea that considerable explanation may be required. However, the explanation must be presented in such a way that the client retains the right to refuse. . . .

References

Adams, S., & Orgel, M. *Through the mental health maze*. Washington, D.C.: Health Research Group, 1975.

American Psychological Association. Guildeines for psychologists conducting growth groups. *American Psychologist*, 1973, *28*, 933.

Arbuckle, D. S. Consumers make mistakes too: An invited response. *Personnel and Guidance Journal*, 1977, *56*, 226–228.

Ayllon, T., & Skuban, W. Accountability in psychotherapy: A test case. *Journal of Behavior Therapy and Experimental Psychiatry*, 1973, *4*, 19–30.

Bersoff, D. N. Professional ethics and legal responsibilities: On the horns of a dilemma. *Journal of School Psychology*, 1975, *13*, 359–376.

Coyne, J. C. The place of informed consent in ethical dilemmas. *Journal of Consulting and Clinical Psychology*, 1976, *44*, 1015–1016.

Croghan, L. M., & Frutiger, A. D. Contracting with children: A therapeutic tool. *Psychotherapy: Theory, Research and Practice*, 1977, *14*, 32–40.

Eberlein, L. Counselors beware! Clients have rights. *Personnel and Guidance Journal*, 1977, *56*, 219–223.

Graziano, A. M., & Fink, F. S. Second-order effects in mental health treatment. *Journal of Consulting and Clinical Psychology*, 1973, *40*, 356–364.

Hare-Mustin, R. T. Ethical considerations in the use of sexual contact in psychotherapy. *Psychotherapy: Theory, Research and Practice*, 1974, *11*, 308–310.

Hartley, D., Roback, H. B., & Abramowitz, S. I. Deterioration effects in encounter groups. *American Psychologist*, 1976, *31*, 247–255.

Hines, P., & Hare-Mustin, R. T. Ethical concerns in family therapy. *Professional Psychology*, 1978, *9*, 165–171.

Hurvitz, N. Marital problems following psychotherapy with one spouse. *Journal of Consulting Psychology*, 1967, *31*, 38–47.

Kessler, J. W. A problem of absorption. *APA Monitor*, March 1977, p. 2.

Koocher, G. P. Civil liberties and aversive conditioning for children. *American Psychologist*, 1976, *31*, 94–95.

Lieberman, M. A., Yalom, I. D., & Miles, M. B. *Encounter groups: First facts*. New York: Basic Books, 1973.

Meyer, R. G., & Smith, S. R. A crisis in group therapy. *American Psychologist*, 1977, *32*, 638–662.

Robinson, D. N. Harm, offense, and nuisance: Some first steps in the establishment of an ethics of treatment. *American Psychologist*, 1974, *29*, 233–238.

Roston, R., & Sherrer, C. Malpractice: What's new? *Professional Psychology*, 1973, *4*, 270–276.

Rubin, Z., & Mitchell, C. Couples research as couples counseling: Some unintended effects of studying close relationships. *American Psychologist*, 1976, *31*, 17–25.

Schulberg, H. C. Quality-of-care standards and professional norms. *American Journal of Psychiatry*, 1976, *133*, 1047–1051.

Schwitzgebel, R. K. A contractual model for the protection of the rights of institutionalized mental patients. *American Psychologist*, 1975, *30*, 815–820.

Schwitzgebel, R. K. Treatment contracts and ethical self-determination. *Clinical Psychologist*, 1976, *29*(3), 5–7.

Sehdev, H. S. Patients' rights or patients' neglect: The impact of the patients' rights movement on delivery systems. *American Journal of Orthopsychiatry*, 1976, *46*, 660–668.

Strupp, H. H., & Hadley, S. W. A tripartite model of mental health and therapeutic outcomes: With special reference to negative effects in psychotherapy. *American Psychologist*, 1977, *32*, 187–196.

Stuart, R. B. *Treatment contract*. Champaign, Ill.: Research Press, 1975.

Sullivan, F. W. Peer review and professional ethics. *American Journal of Psychiatry*, 1977, *134*, 186–188.

Sulzer, E. S. Reinforcement and the therapeutic contract. *Journal of Counseling Psychology*, 1962, *9*, 271–276.

Van Hoose, W. H., & Kottler, J. A. *Ethical and legal issues in counseling and psychotherapy*. San Francisco: Jossey-Bass, 1977.

White House Conference on Children. *Report to the President*. Washington, D.C.: U.S. Government Printing Office, 1970.

Whiteley, J., & Whiteley, R. California court expands privilege debate. *APA Monitor*, February 1977, pp. 5; 6; 18.

Winborn, B. B. Honest labeling and other procedures for the protection of consumers of counseling. *Personnel and Guidance Journal*, 1977, *56*, 206–209.

Wolberg, L. R. *The technique of psychotherapy* (2nd ed.). New York: Grune & Stratton, 1967.

Facilitating Informed Consent for Outpatient Psychotherapy: A Suggested Written Format

Mitchell M. Handelsman and Michael D. Galvin

Although the responsibility of psychologists to inform clients fully about psychotherapy is clear, an adequate procedure for doing so is not. We present a written format designed to facilitate the informed consent process. The format is a series of questions that clients have a right to ask and has several advantages over narrative forms: It preserves clients' rights to refuse information, it is less overwhelming, it fosters conversation between therapist and client, and it is readable.

Commentary: *Handelsman and Galvin have studied the effects of consent forms on patients and their therapy. Although these authors have been skeptical about whether such forms protect psychologists against legal liability, they have asserted that the forms "still have a role in facilitating the ethical goals of informed consent: increasing professionals' self-scrutiny, respecting the autonomy of clients, and allowing clients to enhance their welfare by becoming partners with the therapist in their mental health care" (1988, p. 223). In the Appendix to their article, Handelsman and Galvin provided the following form, written for a fourth-grade readability level, that therapists can give their clients to guide an informed decision about whether to enter therapy.*

When you come for therapy, you are buying a service. Therefore, you need information to make a good decision. Below are some questions you might want to ask. We've talked about some of them. You are entitled to ask me any of these questions, if you want to know. If you don't understand my answers, ask me again.

I. Therapy
   A. How does your kind of therapy work?
   B. What are the possible risks involved? (like divorce, depression)
   C. What percentage of clients improve? In what ways?
   D. What percentage of clients get worse?
   E. What percentage of clients improve or get worse without this therapy?
   F. About how long will it take?
   G. What should I do if I feel therapy isn't working?
   H. Will I have to take any tests? What kind?

II. Alternatives
   A. What other types of therapy or help are there? (like support groups)
   B. How often do they work?
   C. What are the risks of these other approaches?

III. Appointments
   A. How are appointments scheduled?
   B. How long are sessions? Do I have to pay more for longer ones?
   C. How can I reach you in an emergency?
   D. If you are not available, who is there I can talk to?
   E. What happens if the weather is bad, or I'm sick?

IV. Confidentiality
   A. What kind of records do you keep? Who has access to them? (insurance companies, supervisors)
   B. Under what conditions are you allowed to tell others about the things we discuss? (suicidal

Adapted from *Professional Psychology: Research and Practice, 19*, 223–225. Copyright 1988 by the American Psychological Association.

or homicidal threats, child abuse, court cases, insurance companies, supervisors)

  C. Do other members of my family, or of the group, have access to information?

V. Money

  A. What is your fee?

  B. How do I need to pay? At the session, monthly, etc.?

  C. Do I need to pay for missed sessions?

  D. Do I need to pay for telephone calls or letters?

  E. What are your policies about raising fees? (for example, How many times have you raised them in the past two years?)

  F. If I lose my source of income, can my fee be lowered?

  G. If I do not pay my fee, will you take me to small claims court? Do you use a collection agency or lawyer? Under what circumstances?

VI. General

  A. What is your training and experience? Are you licensed? Supervised? Board certified?

  B. Who do I talk to if I have a complaint about therapy which we can't work out? (e.g., Supervisor, State Board of Psychologist Examiners, APA ethics committee)

The contract [or brochure, or our conversation] dealt with most of these questions. I will be happy to ex-

plain them, and to answer other questions you have. This will help make your decision a good one. You can keep this information. Please read it carefully at home. We will also look this over from time to time.

◆ ◆ ◆

Commentary: In another study, Handelsman and his colleagues found that young adults evaluating a hypothetical male therapist rated him more highly if he used the consent form to evoke discussion in comparison with an identical male therapist who did not use the informed-consent procedure. See Sullivan, T., Martin, W. L., Jr., & Handelsman, M. (1993). Practical benefits of an informed-consent procedure: An empirical investigation. Professional Psychology: Research and Practice, 24, 160–163. They concluded that

these results provide evidence that an informed-consent procedure, when done well, can be used to provide ethical treatment to clients without risking damage at the beginning of the therapeutic relationship. Indeed, clients may be more favorably disposed to therapists who take the time and effort to provide information. For professional therapists, this consent procedure also seems to enhance impressions of trustworthiness and expertness. (p. 162)

The Responsible Psychotherapist

Thomas A. Widiger and Leonard G. Rorer

[*Ed. note:* These authors' arguments are grounded in the work of H. L. A. Hart (1968), a legal philosopher. Relying on this work, the authors defined four kinds of responsibility: (a) *role responsibility*, which refers to the fulfillment of duties, tasks, or obligations of one's position, office, or title; (b) *causal responsibility*, that is, causing or producing consequences, results, or outcomes; (c) *capacity responsibility*, which refers to the possession of qualities or abilities to govern one's actions; and (d) *liability responsibility*, being held accountable for acts and omissions. *See* Hart, H. L. A. (1968). *Punishment and responsibility: Essays in the philosophy of law.* Oxford, England: Clarendon Press.]

. . .

RECOMMENDED REQUISITES FOR AN ETHICAL PSYCHOTHERAPY

We will argue that the suggestions by those concerned with assuring an ethical psychotherapy (contracts, informed consent, and equal participation in decision making) are often incompatible with the role and causal responsibilities of the therapist and the capacity responsibilities of the therapist and the patient, and that they might have an effect opposite to that intended. The discussion focuses on the use of contracts and informed consent and subsumes the arguments concerned with equal participation in decisions.

Recommended Requisites Vis-à-Vis Role Responsibilities

Therapists are "bound by professional duty to be actively moral and virtuous in all their decisions" (Redlich & Mollica, 1976, p. 125) but "our greatest duty is to our patients or our client and the obligation is to render service" (Foster, 1975, p. 55). It is certainly within the role responsibility of the therapist to be ethical (APA, 1977, 1979), but at times being ethical may be antitherapeutic (Griffith & Griffith, 1978). What is ethical may not be effective, and what is effective may not be ethical (Begelman, 1971). "On the highest level of abstraction is the clash between the individual's right to freedom, autonomy, and personal choice, and the physician's professional duty to heal and cure" (Foster, 1978, p. 71) [footnote omitted].

Proponents of the ethical requisites seem not to have recognized the clash in responsibilities. For instance, Coyne and Widiger (1978) and Hare-Mustin et al. (1979) appear to believe that their recommendations not only would be applicable to all of the major forms of psychotherapy but also are themselves effective therapeutic techniques. "By helping clients accept their rights and responsibilities, therapists are encouraging healthy functioning" (Hare-Mustin et al., 1979, p. 4). Whether these or other therapeutic techniques have a beneficial effect is a matter of debate and is beyond the scope of this article.

The possibility of an inherent incompatibility between ethical and effective therapy derives in part from the fact that the ethical recommendations either do not follow from any theoretical model of psychotherapy or psychopathology or follow from some models but not from others. It follows from these considerations that some therapists may have difficulty in making certain practices congruent with their therapeutic techniques. For example, autonomy and freedom of choice are ethical positions consistent with a democratic ideal. While they are both a goal and a technique of existential psychotherapy consistent with its theoretical model of the person (Bugental, 1965), they are not easily derived from

Adapted from the *American Psychologist, 39,* 503–515. Copyright 1984 by the American Psychological Association.

the principles of psychoanalysis or behavior modification. We will consider specifically whether contracts and informed consent are consistent with the role responsibilities of the psychotherapist.

Contracts. Contracts are not inherently or absolutely incompatible with any form of psychotherapy. Indeed, all psychotherapy is conducted under some form of implicit or implied contract. The analyst and analysand, for instance, are implicitly under contract to follow certain guidelines of analytic treatment (e.g., not to give specific advice and to free associate, respectively). One could even have a contract that absolved all participants from any responsibilities, though it would probably not be legally acceptable.

A difficulty arises, however, when a contract suitable to one model of therapy is applied to another, incompatible model. The contracts recommended by Atthowe (1975), Hare-Mustin et al. (1979), Schwitzgebel (1975), and Stuart (1975), for instance, are congruent primarily with a behavioral perspective, and it is not coincidental that Atthowe, Schwitzgebel, and Stuart are behaviorally oriented. . . .

It is unclear how contracts specifying goals, length of therapy, and techniques of intervention would work with other models of treatment. Menninger (1958) and Szasz (1965) do use a "contractual model" within a psychoanalytic framework, but their contracts are much different from the specific and explicit contracts of Atthowe, Hare-Mustin, Schwitzgebel, and Stuart. Szasz (1965) leaves open and vague the frequency, duration, and focus of therapy precisely for the purpose of increasing the patient's control. Hare-Mustin et al. (1979) state that if the patient cannot be specific regarding a goal "this challenges the therapist to help translate vague complaints into specific problems" (p. 9). It is likely that an existential, analytic, or client-centered therapist would take issue with the therapeutic value of making such a translation. As Margolin (1982) indicates, in family therapy, "openly stated goals may differ from secret agendas and . . . goals that emerge during the course of therapy may differ from goals

stated at the outset" (p. 790). Parker (1976), in his comment on Schwitzgebel (1975), states that in "psychoanalytically oriented psychotherapy . . . such contracts of cure or even contracts outlining the specifics of the treatment process would be wholly inappropriate and, in fact, counterproductive. . . . There is enough built-in resistance to analytic psychotherapy . . . that we should avoid adding more coals to the fire" (p. 258). . . .

Though there are difficulties in making contracts consistent with various models of psychotherapy, there is no difficulty in making them consistent with a business or commercial model, from which they are more appropriately derived. The notion of a formal exchange of goods or services between autonomous participants with free choice is more evident in the purchase of services from professionals such as accountants, carpenters, and painters. A contractual model has been used within the physician–patient relationship, but it has been more of an implied than an explicit contract. As Schwitzgebel (1975), a proponent of the contractual model, indicates, this model has not been integrated very well into the physician–patient relationship. "The contractual model is not dependent upon medical conceptualizations of behavior or mental processes. The contractual model is more nearly based upon the notion of a social exchange of goods or services" (Schwitzgebel, 1975, p. 819). Many therapists, who prefer to act like therapists rather than business persons, have complained that patients' rights interfere with their ability to deliver effective treatment (Roth & Meisel, 1977; Stone, 1978; Wise, 1978) and that they are being forced to practice a "defensive psychotherapy" that is less effective and at times impotent (Gurevitz, 1977).

Informed consent. The APA's (1979) *Ethical Standards* state that "psychologists fully inform consumers as to the purpose and nature" (p. 5) of an intervention.[1] A consent is said to be informed if all risks and possible consequences of the procedure in question, and all alternative procedures, are presented to the patient and the patient has given evidence that the presentation was understood (Meisel,

---

[1] *Ed. note:* See Standards 1.07 and 4.02 of the APA's current (1992) Ethical Principles.

Roth, & Lidz, 1977). However, the instability, distress, confusion, or motivational defensive structure of the psychotherapy patient may make it difficult to disclose all of the relevant information (Morse, 1967). "If disclosure of certain information—especially the risks of treatment—is likely to upset the patient so seriously that he or she will be unable to make a rational decision, then the physician has the 'therapeutic privilege' to withhold such information" (Meisel et al., 1977, p. 286).

Not only do psychotherapists and patients lack the necessary capacities for implementation but informed consent is inherently incompatible with many therapeutic techniques. Both deception and covert manipulation are antithetical to informed consent but central to systems, strategic, and "social influence" models of psychotherapy (Gillis, 1979; Haley, 1978; Rabkin, 1977)...

There may in fact be a substantial amount of manipulation and social pressure in all forms of psychotherapy (Beutler, 1979; Frank, 1961; Strong, 1978). Margolin (1982) provides illustrations of the difficulty of being both an open and an effective family therapist. Lebensohn (1978), lamenting the deleterious effects of informed consent on analytic techniques, describes a procedure that forewarns the client of possible failure to get better; the possibility of getting worse; the potentially great dependency on, and emotional involvement with, the therapist; the possibility of a resulting divorce or suicide; and that anything said may be used for commitment. "Having properly executed the above form, you may now enter the private consulting room and feel free to tell the psychiatrist anything and everything that comes to mind" (Lebensohn, 1978, p. 36).

The conflict between ethical and effective treatment is illustrated in the paradoxical inconsistency of (a) Coyne's (1976a) and Coyne and Widiger's (1978) advocacy of open, equal, and honest participation by the client; and (b) Coyne's (1976b) model of depression and his support of manipulative, strategic techniques.

> [The patient] is assigned to monotonous, nongratifying, and repetitive tasks.... Although the patient is not ridiculed or belittled, his task perfor-

mance is continually criticized as not perfect. This continues ... until the patient "blows up," refuses to follow orders, or becomes verbally (seldom physically) aggressive.... [The staff is] instructed not to give in to the patient's pleadings to be left alone to suffer, not to try to cheer him up, and not to offer sympathy or encouragement. (Coyne, 1976b, p. 38)

This treatment certainly does not follow from an ethical model of mutual participation that grants "the patient the status of a responsible adult" (Coyne & Widiger, 1978, p. 701) with "extensive disclosure" and "an active and responsible role for the patient" (Coyne & Widiger, 1978, p. 707) [footnote omitted].

Recommended Requisites Vis-à-Vis Causal Responsibilities

A major difficulty in establishing legal liability has been the identification of the causal link between the injury and the acts of commission or omission by the therapist (Kennedy, 1975). There is little doubt that some change typically occurs during treatment, but the extent to which a therapist actually causes the results is an unresolved theoretical, empirical, and philosophical question.... Given conflicting attributions by different theoretical models combined with the inability to identify single causal effects empirically, it is clearly not possible to obtain agreement on causal responsibility and hence on liability (Rothblatt & Leroy, 1973)....

Recommended Requisites Vis-à-Vis Capacity Responsibilities

The APA (1979) *Ethical Standards* state that "psychologists fully inform consumers as to the purpose and nature [of an intervention] ... and they freely acknowledge that clients, students, or participants in research [and therapy] have freedom of choice with regard to participation" (p. 5). This is a commendable principle, but it may in actuality be beyond the capacities of the patient and the therapist. Therapists may not have the capacity to inform their patients fully, and patients, due to their inherent incapacities or their differential status with respect to the thera-

315

pist, may not have the capacity to offer a free choice. Each of these capacities is discussed in the following sections.

Patient capacity. The patient's capacity responsibility is a central issue when one considers contracts or informed consent within psychotherapy (Alexander & Szasz, 1973; Appelbaum & Roth, 1981; Roth, Miesel, & Lidz, 1977). Therapists opposing contracts and informed consent typically express the belief that patients, due to their mental illness or disorder, do not possess the necessary capacities to give an informed consent or to agree to a contract (Moore, 1978). Foster (1975) states that "quite competent patients by any standards" (p. 159) are not likely to understand the complex informed consent forms they sign upon admission to an inpatient unit, because they are too overwhelmed by the issues that brought them to the hospital, and are in a "distraught and distracted state of mind" (p. 159).

Appelbaum, Mirkin, and Bateman (1981) and Olin and Olin (1975) demonstrated in empirical studies that many voluntary mental hospital patients had little idea what they had consented to or what the consent involved. Appelbaum et al. (1981) state that their results "ought to give pause to those who are seeking to extend the ever growing formalization of the relationship, . . . especially those who speak of using a 'contract' " (p. 1175). . . .

. . . Informing the patient of treatment alternatives or risks may be of little value. "All the knowledge in the world will not help a depressed patient make a non-depressed choice. . . . How can the patient make a reasonable choice regarding behavior control when their choosing mechanism is so often the very object of the procedure?" (Neville, 1972, pp. 7–8).

> Mental disease is not an independent variable which is inversely related to the dependent variable of free choice, but is *by definition* inversely related to it. The relationship is tautological and not factual. Since responsibility is *by definition* a function of intention, it logically follows that responsibility is definitionally related to the diagnosis of mental illness. . . . That an act is the product of

mental illness logically *implies* lack of intention and, thus, lack of responsibility. (Leifer, 1964, p. 828)

The advocates of the ethical ameliorations, of course, adamantly reject the contention of patient incapacity. Coyne and Widiger (1978) would have it both ways. On the one hand they argue that there is no patient incapacity and that the appearance of it is created when therapists withhold information or describe therapy in intentionally vague terms. However, they simultaneously reject both informed consent and contracts on the basis of therapist and patient incapacities. "Patients often enter therapy in great distress. . . . While the explicitness and accountability of formal contracts may be desirable, many patients would find them threatening at the start of therapy and constraining as therapy progresses" (Coyne & Widiger, 1978, p. 706). Furthermore, while Coyne rejects the notion of an incompetent patient when he promotes his version of ethical responsibility (Coyne & Widiger, 1978), he clearly attributes incapacity when he promotes his theoretical model of depression (Coyne, 1976b), in which the depressed patient attempts, through interpersonal manipulations, to recruit new acquaintances into the pathological system of interaction. The system, once established, "tends to be largely beyond the control of its participants" (Coyne, 1976b, p. 35).

Alexander and Szasz (1973) and Finkel (1980) view the questioning of patient capacity as just another instance of paternalistic violation of liberty and freedom. An intervention is defined to be paternalistic when the therapist acts without the full consent, or against the resistance, of the patient. Dworkin (1972) indicates that paternalism is acceptable when "it preserves and enhances for the individual his ability to rationally consider and carry out his own decisions" (p. 83). This is precisely the goal of most psychotherapies. Dworkin (1972) also points out that those who would restrict the practice of therapists for the protection of the patient are as paternalistic as those who practice therapy, because both assume that patients cannot protect themselves.

The malleable nature of the attribution of capacity responsibility to mental patients is evident in other efforts to promote ethical rights. While patients are attributed the capacity to control their behavior and give consent when the use of contracts and informed consent is at issue, it is precisely the incapacity to control their behavior and give consent that is their defense in many malpractice suits. In the case of malpractice suits patients need not be psychotic to be assumed incapable of protecting, or deciding for, themselves. The judges in *Roy v. Hartogs* (1975) split on this very issue. A dissenting judge held that, because the patient was able to give consent, she was not entitled to claim that she was coerced into sexual relations by the overpowering influence of, or trust in, the therapist.

It appears that attributions of capacity in the patient, when motivated by a desire to protect ethical rights, can result in quite contradictory conclusions. Patients are capable if this entails their right to decision-making power but are incapable if they decided to engage in sexual activities. While Finkel (1980) may attribute complete capacity to the mental patient, thereby questioning involuntary treatment, Davison (1978) attributes incapacity to the mental patient (i.e., homosexuals), thereby questioning voluntary treatment. Both positions are based on an interest in protecting the ethical rights of patients.

Patient capacity and differential status. In discussions of informed consent, the question of capacity responsibility is often conflated with that of differential status or power. . . .

"If there is a gross inequity in the bargaining power of the parties to a contract so that the weaker party has no meaningful choice or no real alternatives the contract may be considered legally unconscionable" (Schwitzgebel, 1975, p. 818). What is ethically unconscionable may be even less stringent (Foster 1975). Schwitzgebel (1975) criticizes informed consent as a protection of a patient's rights precisely for its failure to deal adequately with the patient's disadvantageous, unfavorable position. He does not however, hold this to be a problem when a contract is used. It is unclear how the presence of a contract changes the status of patients and their unfavorable position (Parker, 1976). Coyne and Widiger (1978), while rejecting the notion of patient incapacity, argue that a patient's unfavorable position relative to a therapist belies a valid contractual rela-

tionship. The inconsistencies are clear. Patients have the capacity for participatory decision making but not for contracts (Coyne & Widiger, 1978); patients have the capacity to sign contracts but not to give an informed consent (Schwitzgebel, 1975); and patients have the capacity to give an informed consent (Redlich & Mollica, 1976) [footnote omitted].

Therapist capacity. Finally, we consider whether the ethical recommendations are compatible with the capacity responsibility of the therapist. Contracting for goals, length, means, or effects of therapy implies some capacity to govern or direct the process and outcome of therapy. It is unclear, however, how a therapist can assure a client that treatment will, or will not, affect certain beliefs, behaviors, or other persons. . . . It is unclear that the therapist has the capacity to present the necessary information for an informed consent, because the risks and consequences of the treatment and its alternatives are so vast, indeterminate, and complex that they belie adequate presentation. Therapists could tell their clients that they cannot provide an adequate informed consent or contract, or they could recite Lebensohn's (1978) list of possible catastrophic outcomes and add that the list is incomplete, but in the absence of probability values for these outcomes it is not clear that this would provide a basis for informed consent. . . .

CONCLUSIONS

. . .

Part of the role responsibility of a psychotherapist is to be ethical, but resolution of the therapeutic with the ethical involves inherent dilemmas. It is not simply a matter of including contracts and informed consent. Nor is it a matter of abandoning ethical principles. As Jung (1963) observed, "Nothing can spare us the torment of ethical decision" (p. 330).

Our analysis suggests that the torment is greater than has been acknowledged, because it is not possible to have a single set of ethical principles that is consistent with currently extant therapeutic orientations. Ethical principles consistent with some theoretical and philosophical positions will necessarily be inconsistent with others (unless they are vacuous).

Therefore, resolution of the ethical with the therapeutic will likely have to be relative to different therapeutic orientations. It may be that they will also have to be relative to different philosophical positions, but that again is a topic that is beyond the scope of this article. If some relativism is unavoidable, then a possible solution would be to require each therapist to formulate and to have on file with a designated ethics committee a set of ethical principles that would be made available to each prospective client. Each therapist's actions would be judged according to his or her set of ethical principles. Such a relativistic resolution obviously might not be acceptable to those who believe in absolute values and insist on universal standards, but some compromise appears to be necessary. It does not appear that the standards can be both universal and specific. The above proposal has the advantage that it would allow each therapist to formulate a consistent set of ethical guidelines and therapeutic principles.

We are not able to provide a solution for these dilemmas. Our hope is that this article will serve to stimulate thoughtful consideration and a tolerance for divergent positions.

References

Alexander, G. J., & Szasz, T. (1973). From contract to status via psychiatry. *Santa Clara Lawyer, 13*, 537–559.

American Psychological Association. (1977). *Standards for providers of psychological services.* Washington, DC: Author.

American Psychological Association. (1979). *Ethical standards of psychologist* (Rev. ed.). Washington, DC: Author.

Appelbaum, P. S., Mirkin, S. A., & Bateman, A. (1981). Empirical assessment of competency to consent to psychiatric hospitalization. *American Journal of Psychiatry, 138*, 1170–1176.

Appelbaum, P. S., & Roth, L. H. (1981). Clinical issues in the assessment of competency. *American Journal of Psychiatry, 138*, 1462–1467.

Atthowe, J. (1975). Legal and ethical accountability in everyday practice. *Behavioral Engineering, 3*, 25–38.

Begelman, D. A. (1971). The ethics of behavioral control and a new mythology. *Psychotherapy: Theory, Research and Practice, 8*, 165–169.

Beutler, L. (1979). Values, beliefs, religion, and the persuasive influence of psychotherapy. *Psychotherapy: Theory, Research and Practice, 16*, 432–440.

Bugental, J. (1965). *The search for authenticity.* New York: Holt, Rinehart & Winston.

Coyne, J. C. (1976a). Comments: The place of informed consent in ethical dilemmas. *Journal of Consulting and Clinical Psychology, 44*, 1015–1016.

Coyne, J. C. (1976b). Toward an interactional description of depression. *Psychiatry, 39*, 29–40.

Coyne, J. C., & Widiger, T. (1978). Toward a participatory model of psychotherapy. *Professional Psychology, 9*, 700–710.

Davison, G. C. (1978). Not can but ought: The treatment of homosexuality. *Journal of Consulting and Clinical Psychology, 46*, 170–172.

Dworkin, G. (1972). Paternalism. *The Monist, 52*, 64–84.

Finkel, N. J. (1980). *Therapy and ethics: The courtship of law and psychology.* New York: Grune & Stratton.

Foster, H. (1975). The conflict and reconciliation of the ethical interests of therapist and patient. *Journal of Psychiatry and Law, 2*, 39–61.

Foster, H. (1978). Informed consent of mental patients. In W. E. Barton & C. Sanborn (Eds.), *Law and the mental health professions.* New York: International Universities Press.

Frank, J. (1961). *Persuasion and healing.* Baltimore, MD: Johns Hopkins University Press.

Gillis, J. S. (1979). *Social influence in psychotherapy.* Jonesboro, TN: Pilgrimage Press.

Griffith, E. J., & Griffith, E. E. (1978). Duty to third parties, dangerousness, and the right to refuse treatment: Problematic concepts for psychiatrist and lawyer. *California Western Law Review, 14*, 241–274.

Gurevitz, H. (1977). *Tarasoff*: Protective privilege versus public peril. *American Journal of Psychiatry, 134*, 289–292.

Haley, J. (1978). *Problem-solving therapy.* San Francisco: Jossey-Bass.

Hare-Mustin, R. T., Marecek, J., Kaplan, A., & Liss-Levinson, N. (1979). Rights of clients, responsibilities of therapists. *American Psychologist, 34*, 3–16.

Jung, C. (1963). *Memories, dreams, reflections.* New York: Pantheon.

Kennedy, C. (1975). Injuries precipitated by psychotherapy: Liability without fault as a basis for recovery. *South Dakota Law Review, 20*, 401–417.

Lebensohn, Z. (1978). Defensive psychiatry or how to treat the mentally ill without being a lawyer. In W. Barton & C. Sanborn (Eds.), *Law and the mental health professionals.* New York: International Universities Press.

Leifer, R. (1964). The psychiatrist and tests of criminal responsibility. *American Psychologist, 19*, 825–830.

Margolin, G. (1982). Ethical and legal considerations in marital and family therapy. *American Psychologist, 37,* 788–801.

Meisel, A., Roth, L., & Lidz, C. (1977). Toward a model of the legal doctrine of informed consent. *American Journal of Psychiatry, 134,* 285–289.

Menninger, K. (1958). *Theory of psychoanalytic technique.* New York: Basic Books.

Moore, R. (1978). Ethics in the practice of psychiatry—Origins, functions, models and enforcement. *American Journal of Psychiatry, 135,* 157–163.

Morse, H. (1967). Psychiatric responsibility and tort liability. *Journal of Forensic Sciences, 12,* 305–358.

Neville, R. (1972, December 17). *Ethical and philosophical issues of behavior control.* Paper presented at the 139th annual meeting of the American Association for the Advancement of Science.

Olin, G., & Olin, H. (1975). Informed consent in voluntary mental hospital admissions. *American Journal of Psychiatry, 132,* 938–941.

Parker, K. (1976). Comment: On a contractual model of treatment. *American Psychologist, 31,* 257–258.

Rabkin, R. (1977). *Strategic psychotherapy.* New York: Basic.

Redlich, F., & Mollica, R. (1976). Overview: Ethical issues in contemporary psychiatry. *American Journal of Psychiatry, 133,* 125–136.

Roth, L., & Meisel, A. (1977). Dangerousness, confidentiality, and the duty to warn. *American Journal of Psychiatry, 134,* 508–511.

Roth, L., Meisel, A., & Lidz, C. (1977). Tests of competency to consent to treatment. *American Journal of Psychiatry, 134,* 279–284.

Rothblatt, H., & Leroy, D. (1973). Avoiding psychiatric malpractice. *California Western Law Review, 9,* 260–272.

Roy v. Hartogs, 381 N.Y.S. 2d 587 (New York, 1975).

Schwitzgebel, R. K. (1975). A contractual model for the protection of the rights of institutionalized mental patients. *American Psychologist, 30,* 815–820.

Stone, A. (1978). Psychiatry and law. In A. M. Nicholi, Jr. (Ed.), *The Harvard guide to modern psychiatry.* Cambridge, MA: Belknap Press.

Strong, S. (1978). Social psychological approach to psychotherapy research. In S. Garfield & A. Bergin (Eds.), *Handbook of psychotherapy and behavior change: An empirical analysis* (2nd ed.). New York: Wiley.

Stuart, R. B. (1975). *Guide to client-therapist treatment contract.* Champaign, IL: Research Press Co.

Szasz, T. (1965). *The ethics of psychoanalysis.* New York: Basic Books.

Wise, T. P. (1978). Where the public peril begins: A survey of psychotherapists to determine the effects of Tarasoff. *Stanford Law Review, 31,* 165–190.

◆ ◆ ◆

Commentary: *Graca (1985) disagreed that "treatment effectiveness should take precedence over ethical disclosure" (p. 1062):*

> *Leaving the ethical guidelines for obtaining informed consent to individual therapists to determine can only negatively affect the perception of our profession by consumers and members of the legal profession, who are already wary of our ethical fortitude. (pp. 1062–1063)*

What Graca suggested is that psychologists who take Widiger and Rorer's position inform their clients that because of their theoretical orientation, they will not discuss the specific techniques or objectives of therapy. See Graca, J. (1985). Whither informed consent to psychotherapy? American Psychologist, 40, 1062–1063. Would Graca's alternative comport with the informed consent provisions of the 1992 Ethical Principles?

Whether ethical or not, as Widiger and Rorer (1984) have argued, consent and contractual agreements may be incompatible with some forms of therapy. Perhaps the technique that raises the most ethical questions is paradoxical intention. Paradoxical strategies usually require the client to maintain or intensify a presenting symptom; for example, a therapist encourages an anxious client to act anxiously in an actual situation. For the strategy to work, it is at times necessary for the therapist to distort his or her rationale for using it. Thus, it is claimed, the use of paradoxical intention is unethical. Others respond that the ethical issues are no different in the use of this technique than in any other form of psychotherapy. What ethical principles are involved in the application of paradoxical strategies? For interesting and controversial discussions of this topic, see the following publications:

Betts, G. R., & Remer, R. (1993). The impact of paradoxical interventions on perceptions of the therapist and ratings of treatment acceptability. Professional Psychology: Research and Practice, 24, 164–170.

Brown, J. E., & Slee, P. T. (1986). Paradoxical strategies: The ethics of intervention. Professional Psychology: Research and Practice, 17, 487–491.

Hunsley, J. (1988). *Conceptions and misconceptions about the context of paradoxical therapy.* Professional Psychology: Research and Practice, 19, 553–559.

In a recent survey of 189 randomly selected doctoral-level APA members (63% men; 95% clinicians), only about 60% of the respondents informed all of their therapy clients about limits to confidentiality, and only 56% informed clients of the therapeutic procedures that might be used. Less than one third informed all of their clients about potential risks, alternatives to therapy, and potential length of treatment. When asked why they did not inform clients about confidentiality, almost 38% of respondents stated that the issue was not relevant, almost 10% felt it would have a negative impact on the client or the therapeutic relationship, and almost 8% said that their clients would not understand the information. See Somberg, D. R., Stone, G. L., & Claiborn, D. C. (1993). Informed consent: Therapists' beliefs and practices. Professional Psychology: Research and Practice, 24, 153–159.

Given the explicit provisions in the 1992 *Ethical Principles* about informed consent and the importance of self-determination as a fundamental moral principle, is there any justification for therapists to conclude that discussing the limits of confidentiality with clients is irrelevant? Are not the therapists in Somberg et al.'s survey being quite paternalistic? Regardless of diverging answers to these questions, there is consensus that the issue of informed consent with therapy clients remains complex, as Somberg et al. (1993) did acknowledge:

> The variability among therapists' self-reported practices and beliefs suggests that a singular focus on ethical standards may not be enough. Ethical standards need to be considered within the unique context of the therapist. This context includes the therapist's values, orientation, and work setting. For example, informing clients of the length of therapy would appear to be incongruent within the context of a psychodynamic orientation or an open-ended therapy setting. This example highlights the difficult task of applying ethical standards and principles to one's particular context. It seems essential that therapists continue to struggle with such ethical dilemmas presented by their unique therapeutic environment.

Some of the reasons given for not informing clients appear to reflect a concern for the welfare of the client. For example, therapists' concern for the negative impact on the client or therapeutic relationship suggests that informed consent is not only an ethical issue but has clinical implications as well. As potential negative effects appear to be of some relevancy for therapists, more research is needed regarding the negative impact of the consent procedures. It seems, however, that attention must also be given to the positive impact of obtaining informed consent. Because much of psychotherapy focuses on increasing a client's sense of control and autonomy, informed consent procedures have been suggested as a part of the treatment (Haas, 1991). From another perspective, viewing informed consent as a means of sharing power with the client can have clinical significance, especially for those clients who have been previously victimized. For such clients, issues of power and control can be of central concern, issues that also exist in each therapeutic relationship. Such therapeutic implications highlight the notion that informed consent is not simply an ethical issue but needs to be considered from a clinical perspective as well.

Reasons given for not informing clients also indicated that informed consent is not considered relevant or practical by some therapists. Hence, the value placed on informed consent becomes a central issue in regard to practice. The value given informed consent can be fostered through ethics education, graduate training, and professional discussion grounded in different and specific practice contexts.

The variability in practice issues and the significant differences among consent issues highlight the complexity of the informed consent process. While creating new standards for psychologists, consideration of the difficult challenge of implementation appears essential. (p. 159)

Reference

*Haas, L. J. (1991). Hide and seek or show and
tell? Emerging issues of informed consent.*
Ethics and Behavior, 1, 175–189.

For an intriguing study exploring the effects of informed-consent disclosure, including the risks of psychotherapy, on mothers' decisions to pursue psychological treatment for their elementary-school-aged children, see Gustafson, K. E., McNamara, J. R., & Jensen, D. A. (1994). Parents' informed consent decisions regarding psychotherapy for their children: Consideration of therapeutic risks and benefits. Professional Psychology: Research and Practice, 25, 16–22.

The Ethical Issue of Competence in Working With the Suicidal Patient

Bruce Bongar

Suicide has been found to be the most frequently encountered emergency situation for mental health professionals (Schein, 1976), with clinicians consistently ranking work with suicidal patients as the most stressful of all clinical endeavors (Deutsch, 1984). Also, patient suicides have an acute impact on the professional lives of many therapists (Chemtob, Bauer, Hamada, Pelowski, & Muraoka, 1989). A national survey found that psychologists responded to the loss of a patient to suicide in a manner akin to the death of a family member (Chemtob, Hamada, Bauer, Torigoe, & Kinney, 1988).

Furthermore, it is apparent from empirical findings that the average professional psychologist involved in direct patient care has greater than a 20% chance of losing a patient to suicide at some time during his or her professional career, with the odds being greater than 50% for psychiatrists (Chemtob, Hamada, Bauer, Torigoe, et al., 1988; Chemtob, Hamada, Bauer, Kinney, & Torigoe, 1988). Another study (Kleespies, Smith, & Becker, 1990) investigating the incidence, impact, and methods of coping with patient suicide during the training years of psychology graduate students found that one out of six students had experienced a patient's suicide at some time during their training. . . .

. . . The APA's ethical principles mandate that "Psychologists recognize the boundaries of their competence and the limitation of their techniques. They only provide services and only use the techniques for which they are qualified by training and experience" (APA, 1981, p. 634).[1] Harrar, VandeCreek, and Knapp (1990), in discussing the ethical and legal aspects of clinical supervision, pointed out that professional psychologists need to limit their practice to their demonstrated areas of professional competence, and that "direct liability could also occur if the supervisor assigned a task to a trainee whom the supervisor knew or should have known to be inadequately trained to execute it" (Harrar et al., 1990, p. 39).

. . . Because the APA COPS of the BPA has taken such an unambiguous position on the need for psychologists to manage the problem of suicide competently, and because "providers of psychological services have the same responsibility to uphold these specific General Guidelines as they would the corresponding Ethical Principles" (BPA, COPS, 1987b, p. 712), it is clear that formal graduate training in the study of suicide is a necessary part of our graduate curriculum for professional practice. . . .

CONFIDENTIALITY AND THE SUICIDAL PATIENT

. . .

In general, ethical considerations require that clinicians provide their clients with complete information about the limits to confidentiality. In addition, they should give careful thought regarding how they would handle various types of requests to release information or breach confidences before the specific situations occur. They should consider the lengths they would go to protect their clients' confidentiality (e.g., whether or not they would retain an attorney to fight a request or demand for information). They should decide whether they will fully discuss the implications of a privilege waiver with their clients upon receiving a subpoena. Finally,

[1] *Ed. note:* See Standard 1.04 of the APA's current (1992) Ethical Principles.

when an actual situation arises, a consultation with a senior colleague and/or attorney may help sort out the various options available and the clinical implications and management strategies associated with each strategy.

My essential advice is to develop a good understanding of the issues involved in breaching confidentiality with suicidal patients before the fact, that is, to have thought out carefully one's policy on breaching confidentiality before being required to implement it, and to seek consultation in any situation of uncertainty.

Simon (1988) pointed out that the competent patient's request for the maintenance of confidentiality must be honored unless the patient is a clear danger to himself or herself or to others. However, the legal duty to warn or inform third parties exists in some jurisdictions only if the danger of physical harm is threatened toward others (Simon, 1988).

Psychologists must understand laws and regulations related to breaching confidentiality when patients are a "danger to self" (VandeCreek & Knapp, 1989). Pope, Tabachnick, and Keith-Spiegel (1988) noted that:

> Apparently the argument made by the defense in many of the early "duty to protect" cases (e.g., *Tarasoff v. Regents of the University of California et al.*, 1976), that absolute confidentiality is necessary for psychotherapy, is not persuasive for many psychotherapists: Breaking confidentiality is seen by a large number of practitioners as uniformly good practice in cases of homicidal risk, suicidal risk, and child abuse. (p. 550)

Shneidman (1981) went even further and stated that confidentiality, when a patient has exhibited suicidal behavior, should not be an important issue between psychologists and their patients. He argued forcibly that the main goal of suicidal therapy is to defuse the potentially lethal situation. Thus, to hold to the principle of confidentiality is contradictory to a basic tenet of an ethical psychotherapeutic relationship.

The official policy of the APA states that psychologists have a primary obligation to respect the confidentiality of information obtained from persons in the course of their work and that they may reveal such information to others only with the consent of the person or her or his legal representative, except in those unusual circumstances when not doing so would result in clear danger to the person or to others (Keith-Speigel & Koocher, 1985). When appropriate, psychologists should inform their patients of the legal limits of confidentiality (see Bennett, Bryant, VandenBos, & Greenwood, 1990). . . .

Gutheil (1984) noted that, with patients for whom suicidal issues are predominant, it is important to assess their ability to participate in a therapeutic alliance with the clinician:

> The patient who is collaborative, who sees the issue as a joint problem for both patient and clinician, is in a completely different position from the patient who sees himself as being acted upon. . . . The distinction between the patient who can cooperate but does not and the patient who is too sick to cooperate may mean the difference between success and failure in the litigation area. (p. 3).

Therefore, at the most basic level, I believe that clinicians have a professional duty to take appropriate affirmative measures to prevent their patients from harming themselves. At times, this may well necessitate communicating with family members about the specifics of a patient's case, attempting to ameliorate toxic family interactions with the patient, or mobilizing support from the family and significant others (Bongar, 1991).

As with all other individual rights recognized by our society, the courts have held that the right to privacy must be balanced against the rights of other individuals and against the public interest (i.e., the legitimate regulatory functions of government) to determine which rights should prevail. As a result of this balancing process, the courts have carved out many exceptions to the general rule of therapeutic confidentiality. The critical point is that the psychologist should inform patients of the exceptions that exist to confidentiality before the patient enters treatment (Bongar, 1991).

Simon (1988) noted that common sense and good judgment can lead to a decision to breach patient confidentiality, specifically where "a patient will probably commit suicide and the act can be stopped only by the psychiatrist's intervention. . . . However, any limitations on the maintenance of confidentiality should be explained to patients from the beginning of any evaluation or treatment" (pp. 60–61).

Furthermore, regarding breaches of confidentiality, Stromberg et al. (1988) noted:

> Ethically, the therapist may be bound to disclose information concerning a patient in an emergency, when disclosure would obviously be best for the patient. Courts have increasingly defined "emergency" narrowly so that it does not cover all breaches of confidentiality which a particular therapist views as appropriate but only those made because the patient's health is seriously and imminently at stake. (p. 14)

Stromberg et al. continued that the scope of the disclosure should be limited to what is necessary for providing appropriate care and that, for example, disclosures made in good faith in seeking a civil commitment of the patient will be largely protected.

Bongar (1991) stated that if a breach of confidentiality is necessary to save the patient's life, the psychologist is bound to take this step. Bongar agreed with Shneidman (1981) that if such a breach of confidentiality is necessary to defuse the lethal situation, the psychologist must act to do so and "not ally herself/himself with death" (p. 348). (For an extended discussion of the complex ethical and legal dilemmas that often emerge when working with suicidal patients, e.g., the issues of rational suicide and euthanasia, the reader is directed to the work of Amchin, Wettstein, & Roth, 1990.) . . .

In summary, one of the critical tasks of the psychologist who is called on to treat the suicidal patient is to have evaluated a priori the strengths and limitations of his or her own training, education, and experience in the treatment of specific patient populations in certain clinical settings (e.g., an understanding of her or his own technical proficiencies, as well as her or his emotional tolerance levels for the intense demands required in treating suicidal patients). Specifically, psychologists must make the dif-

ficult and highly personal decision to conduct their own self-study of personal and professional competence to treat suicidal patients before the fact, not wait to assess this competence when suicidal thoughts or behaviors emerge in their patients. Pope (1986) noted that the APA's *Specialty Guidelines for the Delivery of Services by Clinical Psychologists* dictates that clinical psychologists limit their practice to demonstrated areas of professional competence, for example, "to ensure that you meet the legal, ethical and professional standards of competence in working with suicidal clients" (p. 19). Ultimately, the setting of such limits requires self-knowledge. . . .

References

Amchin, J., Wettstein, R. M., & Roth, L. H. (1990). Suicide, ethics and the law. In S. J. Blumenthal & D. J. Kupfer (Eds.), *Suicide over the life cycle: Risk factors, assessment, and treatment of suicidal patients* (pp. 637–664). Washington, DC: American Psychiatric Press.

Bennett, B. E., Bryant, B. K., VandenBos, G. R., & Greenwood, A. (1990). *Professional liability and risk management.* Washington, DC: American Psychological Association.

Board of Professional Affairs, Committee on Professional Standards. (1987b). General guidelines for providers of psychological services. *American Psychologist, 42,* 712–723.

Bongar, B. (1991). *The suicidal patient: Clinical and legal standards of care.* Washington, DC: American Psychological Association.

Chemtob, C. M., Bauer, G. B., Hamada, R. S., Pelowski, S. R., & Muraoka, M. Y. (1989). Patient suicide: Occupational hazard for psychologist and psychiatrists. *Professional Psychology: Research and Practice, 20*(5), 294–300.

Chemtob, C. M., Hamada, R. S., Bauer, G. B., Kinney, B., & Torigoe, R. Y. (1988). Patient suicide: Frequency and impact on psychiatrists. *American Journal of Psychiatry, 145,* 224–228.

Chemtob, C. M., Hamada, R. S., Bauer, G. B., Torigoe, R. Y., & Kinney, B. (1988). Patient suicide: Frequency and impact on psychologists. *Professional Psychology: Research and Practice, 19*(4), 421–425.

Deutsch, C. J. (1984). Self-report sources of stress among psychotherapists. *Professional Psychology: Research and Practice, 15,* 833–845.

Gutheil, T. G. (1984). Malpractice liability in suicide. *Legal Aspects of Psychiatric Practice, 1,* 1–4.

Harrar, W. R., VandeCreek, L., & Knapp, S. (1990). Ethical and legal aspects of clinical supervision. *Professional Psychology, 21*(1), 37–41.

Keith-Spiegel, P., & Koocher, G. P. (1985). *Ethics in Psychology*. New York: Random House.

Kleespies, P. M., Smith, M. R., & Becker, B. R. (1990). Psychology interns as patient suicide survivors: Incidence, impact, and recovery. *Professional Psychology: Research and Practice, 21*(4), 257–263.

Pope, K. (1986, January). Assessment and management of suicidal risks: Clinical and legal standards of care. *Independent Practitioner*, pp. 17–23.

Pope, K. S., Tabachnick, B. G., & Keith-Spiegel, P. (1988). Good and poor practices in psychotherapy: National survey of beliefs of psychotherapists. *Professional Psychology: Research and Practice, 19*(5), 547–552.

Schein, H. M. (1976). Obstacles in the education of psychiatric residents. *Omega, 7*, 75–82.

Shneidman, E. S. (1981). Psychotherapy with suicidal patients. *Suicide and Life-Threatening Behavior, 11*(4), 341–348.

Simon, R. I. (1988). *Concise guide to clinical psychiatry and the law*. Washington, DC: American Psychiatric Press.

Stromberg, C. D., Haggarty, D. J., Leibenluft, R. F., McMillan, M. H., Mishkin, B., Rubin, B. L., & Trilling, H. R. (1988). *The psychologist's legal handbook*. Washington, DC: The Council for the National Register of Health Service Providers in Psychology.

VandeCreek, L., & Knapp, S. (1989). *Tarasoff and beyond: Legal and clinical considerations in the treatment of life-endangering patients*. Sarasota, FL: Professional Resource Exchange, Inc.

◆ ◆ ◆

Commentary: For additional readings on legal, ethical, and competency issues in treating clients who threaten suicide, see, for example:

Bongar, B. (1991). The suicidal patient: Clinical and legal standards of care. Washington, DC: American Psychological Association.

Pope, K. S., & Vasquez, M. J. T. (1991). Ethics in psychotherapy and counseling (pp. 153–168). San Francisco: Jossey-Bass.

Bongar and the authors he cites appear to adopt a benef-icence–paternalism model in treating suicidal clients. Are there any moral principles or provisions in the 1992 Ethical Principles that would permit a therapist to abide by a client's wish to die?

Ethical and Legal Considerations in Marital and Family Therapy

Gayla Margolin

. . .

RESPONSIBILITY

The therapist's primary responsibilities are to protect the rights and to promote the welfare of his or her clients. The dilemma with multiple clients is that in some situations an intervention that serves one person's best interests may be countertherapeutic to another. Indeed, the very reason that families tend to seek therapy is because they have conflicting goals and interests. . . .

The family therapist must insure that improvement in the status of one family member does not occur at the expense of another family member. This objective is not entirely unique to family therapy. Since a person in individual therapy also makes changes that may cause unhappiness in those around him or her . . . , it is prudent for the individual therapist to encourage the client to explore potential ramifications of his or her actions. Yet what sets the family therapist apart from the individual therapist is the family therapist's clear commitment to promoting the welfare of each family member. Moreover, through direct involvement with all family members, the family therapist can directly assess how each person's behavior affects other family members. Thus, the family therapist has more responsibility for exercising judgment that takes those other individuals into account.

To work constructively in the face of conflicting family needs, some therapists identify the family system, rather than one or another individual, as "the patient." The family therapist then becomes an advocate of the family system and avoids becoming an agent of any one family member. Assuming that change by one person affects and is affected by other family members, the system advocate ensures that all problem definitions and plans for change are considered in the context of the entire family. The therapist, for example, may encourage the expression of strong feelings but structure a mode of expressing them that takes other family members into consideration (Grosser & Paul, 1964). If informed of the therapist's role as an advocate of the system, family members generally understand and accept this position, although at certain moments they still solicit the therapist as a personal ally. . . .

There are certain instances in which working as an advocate of the relationship system and changing patterns of interaction is not advised. Weiss and Birchler (1978) point out that a therapeutic alliance based on the ostensible goal of changing the relationship is countertherapeutic if one spouse seeks therapy as a way to exit from the relationship or to ease the burden of announcing a decision to separate. In this case, an emphasis on the relationship is likely to heighten the hope and emotional investment of the rejected individual, with further disappointment and sense of failure as the ultimate result for that person. Similarly, it is misleading to maintain a guise of working on the relationship when the actual objective is to change the behavior of one family member (e.g., to reduce a father's drinking or to increase a child's compliance). If the target individual in those cases is under the mistaken impression that there will be mutual change, she or he may end up feeling deceived by both the therapist and the other family members.

Finally, in addition to clinical considerations, there are legal prescriptions defining when the welfare of an individual takes precedence over relationship issues. The clearest obligation in this regard occurs in the instance of physical abuse among family members. Child abuse reporting laws require therapists to inform authorities if they suspect that a child has been abused, despite the possible consequences for the therapeutic alliance with other family members. Though the legal prescription for action is not quite as obvious for abuse between marital partners, the primary goal still is to reduce the danger of physical harm. If this objective cannot be realized within the context of conjoint therapy, it is the therapist's ethical responsibility to abdicate the role of relationship advocate and help the threatened person find protection (Margolin, 1979). More generally, it can be concluded that a family therapist's responsibility includes being an advocate of individual family members who cannot accurately represent their own rights and needs or recognize when these are infringed on by another family member. Toward this end, there are certain situations in which an intervention to help an individual extricate from the family takes precedence over the goals of the family as a system. . . .

CONFIDENTIALITY

. . .

How do standard practices of confidentiality translate from the traditional dyadic client–therapist relationship to a therapeutic relationship that includes several family members? There are two divergent positions in this regard. One preference is for the therapist to treat each family member's confidences as though that person were an individual client. That is, information obtained during a private session, during a telephone call, or from written material is not divulged to other family members. Some therapists, in fact, arrange for sessions with individual family members to actively encourage the sharing of "secrets" to better understand what is occurring in the family. The therapist then may work with the individual client in the hope of enabling that person to disclose the same information in the family session. Should that fail to occur, however, the therapist upholds the individual client's confidentiality and remains silent on that issue vis-à-vis other family members.

Other therapists adopt the policy of not keeping secrets from other family members. They explicitly discourage the sharing of any information that might lead to a special alliance with one individual and that excludes the remaining uninformed family members. Contrary to more traditional views of psychotherapy that hold the client–therapist confidence as a crucial factor in the overall effectiveness of therapy, this stance essentially blocks the occurrence of confidences between one family member and the therapist. Therapists who subscribe to this approach generally avoid receiving individual confidences by conducting joint, as opposed to individual, sessions. However, this one safeguard often proves insufficient against the sharing of individual confidences. Unless the client is directly informed of the therapist's policies, the client who seeks to divulge personal information will find a way to do so.

Between these two extreme positions are intermediary steps. Rather than treat all information shared in individual sessions as confidential, the therapist may indicate that (1) in general, confidentiality conditions do not apply, but (2) the client has the right to request that any specific information be kept confidential and the therapist will comply with any such requests. Likewise, it should be recognized that the therapist who does not promise to maintain confidences may, indeed, wish to exercise the option not to divulge certain information. For instance, faced with information that one spouse has had an affair, particularly one that has terminated long since, many therapists find it unnecessary and inadvisable to share such information. In conveying that she or he does not preserve the confidences of individual family members, the therapist should avoid implying that she or he will not conceal anything. Except for legal considerations mentioned previously, it is the therapist's discretion, not his or her responsibility, to divulge confidential information.

One instance that complicates issues of confidentiality is a change in the format of therapy, for example, individual therapy being replaced by marital therapy. How does the therapist handle the information that she or he has obtained during the course of individual therapy? One possibility is to obtain the individual client's permission to use such information, when necessary, in the conjoint sessions. If permission is not granted, however, that information must be kept confidential, a resolution far from desirable for the therapist who prefers not maintaining individual confidences in conjoint therapy. Even if the patient permits the information to be shared, this permission has been granted *after* the information was obtained. Does the client remember all that she or he has confided under the previously assumed condition of confidentiality? Would that person have responded differently in individual therapy if it were known from the outset that such information would be available to the spouse?

As in individual therapy, clients must be informed of the limits of their confidentiality. This is particularly important in family therapy, since the limits of confidentiality, vis-à-vis other family members, essentially are left to the therapist's discretion. Therapists who will not keep confidences must inform clients of this policy before any such information has been received. Otherwise, the client, particularly one who has had previous experience in individual therapy, is likely to presume that the therapist will maintain the confidentiality of his or her statements from other family members. The therapist who does keep individual confidences likewise should inform clients of this policy so that family members do not persist in trying to obtain information about one another through the therapist.

Although both sides of the decision about whether or not to maintain confidentiality are ethically defensible, they carry different clinical implications. In certain situations, maintaining one partner's confidences severely limits the therapist's options with another family member. Consider, for example, the situation in which marital therapy has been initiated by the wife on discovering that her husband had been having an affair. While willing to give the relationship one last try, she is adamant about terminating the marriage if the husband does not end his affair and then remain sexually faithful. Although the husband initially agrees to this condition, several months later he reveals to the therapist that he has resumed the extramarital relationship. Desperate to avoid the possibility of his wife's leaving him, the husband refuses to divulge this information in a conjoint session.

What is the therapist's course of action? If confi-

dentiality has been promised, the therapist may find himself or herself in a position of concealing information that is crucial to the wife's decision about remaining both in therapy and in the marriage. When the wife learns about the affair, she may believe that the therapist has neglected her welfare in favor of the husband and may even accuse the therapist of keeping her in therapy for personal gain. Even if the therapist were to terminate the case, an explanation is owed to the wife, which is likely to compromise the husband's confidentiality. Even though the therapist might believe that dealing openly with the husband's behavior would have long-range therapeutic benefit, this course of action is not possible without violating the husband's confidentiality.

The therapist who has not promised confidentiality has more options open and thus must carefully consider the therapeutic ramifications of his or her actions. Deciding not to divulge this information about the husband's affair might be justifiable if (1) the wife had made it clear that she did not want to know about the husband's indiscretions, (2) the affair would not interfere with the ongoing therapy, and (3) the affair had ended, so the therapist's action could not be construed as encouraging the husband's behavior. In view of the specifics of this case, however, in which the wife has clearly stated her preference not to be duped into believing her husband is sexually faithful, open discussion of the husband's affair and the wife's ultimatum is indicated. Such discussion is likely to precipitate a relationship crisis, the long-range effects of which cannot be predicted. One or both spouses may receive the information they need, finally, to pronounce the marriage over. Alternatively, the couple may make certain accommodations despite their divergent values regarding fidelity; for example, the husband could terminate his long-term liaison while not committing himself to sexual fidelity, and the wife could abandon her ultimatum regarding sexual faithfulness as long as there are no long-standing affairs.

The most difficult predicament for the therapist would be if she or he failed to convey a policy on confidentiality. In that case, it is possible that the husband and wife would be functioning under different assumptions, for example, the husband assuming confidentiality would be maintained and the wife assuming that there would be no individual secrets in marital therapy. Neither spouse knows the limits of confidentiality nor has made a conscious decision to accept those limits. As with the clinical options available to the other two therapists, any action taken by this therapist is potentially unsatisfactory to at least one spouse. However, this therapist faces the additional risk of misleading one or another partner about the conditions of the therapeutic relationship. . . .

This example . . . illustrates that the therapist's position in terms of confidentiality can have important ramifications for how marital therapy is conducted. By maintaining the confidentiality of individual partners, the therapist is likely to have information that otherwise might not be available. The therapist's options with that information are severely limited, however, and she or he may not find it possible to put the information to therapeutic advantage from a family-system perspective. On the other hand, obtaining permission to discuss conjointly information that either partner chooses to reveal individually poses risks to the spouses (i.e., that there is no safe environment for personal disclosures) and risks to the therapist (i.e., that she or he will not gain access to important information). When this stance is clearly understood, however, individual disclosures to the therapist may simply signal the desire for guidance on how to broach a particularly difficult topic with one's partner. . . .

Confidentiality issues also arise when a therapist has individual sessions with a child. Ethical standards of confidentiality apply to the child as a client just as they do for adult clients. In some states parents have the right to inspect the therapist's records, but they have no legal right to demand that the therapist reveal information to them. The therapist's foremost objective in child therapy is to protect the rights of the child, particularly since the child is less able to understand or guard his or her rights. Yet secondarily the therapist must show sensitivity to the concerns of interested parents, since their help and support is often quite influential in the overall effectiveness of child therapy. Before beginning child therapy sessions, it is important to set up an agreement with both the child and the parents about what, if any, information from the child's sessions will be discussed with the parents. The limits of con-

fidentiality should be determined; for example, can the child specifically request that the parents not be told certain information? The structure of this feedback also should be determined: for example, How often will the therapist meet with the parents? Will the child be present at those meetings? In setting up these conditions, the therapist may wish to indicate that other family members are not to pressure the child to reveal what has transpired in his or her individual sessions. . . .

PATIENT PRIVILEGE

Ethical issues related to confidentiality are closely intertwined with legal constraints dictated by state, and occasionally federal, laws regarding privileged communication. . . .

For the most part, privilege tends to be ill-defined for the situation in which two or more clients are seen simultaneously in therapy. Since privilege only covers communications that are uttered in confidence, the question arises of whether statements made in the presence of another family member indeed are confidential. The question also arises of whether privilege covers client-to-client communications. Since some states extend privilege to persons who aid in the delivery of personal services and are present during the uttering of confidential information (e.g., nurses, technicians), a liberal interpretation of privilege statutes might show that family members (or group members) are agents of the therapist (Bersoff & Jain, 1980). Lacking definitive legislation on these issues, however, family therapists cannot comfortably assume that existing privilege statutes protect the communications that occur during family therapy. In view of the inconsistencies of current laws, the therapist might wish to have a clear understanding with family members on these issues, for example, obtaining a written agreement that none of the members will call on the therapist to testify in litigation.

INFORMED CONSENT AND THE RIGHT TO REFUSE TREATMENT

The trend for clinicians to include some type of informed consent procedures as standard clinical practice reflects both an orientation toward clients as consumers and a recognition of increasing legal regulation of psychotherapeutic practices. The primary consideration in family therapy is that procedures for informed consent be conducted with all persons who participate in therapy, including those family members who join therapy at a later time. In addition to ethical reasons for taking the time to obtain informed consent from the entire family, this procedure communicates important therapeutic messages: No one family member is the "sick" or "crazy" person. No one person will be "treated" while others simply observe. No one will be excluded from knowledge about what is to transpire.

Recent reviews of informed consent (Everstine et al., 1980; Hare-Mustin et al., 1979) recommend that the following types of information be provided to clients before therapy is formally initiated: (a) an explanation of the procedures and their purpose, (b) the role of the person who is providing therapy and his or her professional qualifications, (c) discomforts or risks reasonably to be expected, (d) benefits reasonably to be expected, (e) alternatives to treatment that might be of similar benefit, (f) a statement that any questions about the procedures will be answered at any time, and (g) a statement that the person can withdraw his or her consent and discontinue participation in therapy or testing at any time.

Each of these guidelines also applies to marriage and family therapy. Guidelines c and d, for example, deserve special attention inasmuch as risks and benefits are different in family than in individual therapy. Since each family member has less control over the eventual outcome of family than of individual therapy, clients should be warned that marital and family therapy may lead to an outcome viewed as undesirable by one or another of the participants, for example, the decision to divorce or compromises in one's power over other family members.

Data on individual versus family therapy are central to Guideline e, particularly for the person torn between wanting to improve marital/family relationships and wanting the sanctuary of an individual therapeutic relationship. According to Gurman and Kniskern's (1978) comprehensive review, though marital therapy may be risky, individual therapy for marital problems is even riskier: Individual therapy for marital problems yields improvement in less than half of its consumers, whereas therapies that involve both partners yield improvement in approximately two thirds of the clients. . . .

It is typical of most families that some members are more eager to participate in therapy than others, raising the issue . . . of voluntary participation. Obviously, coercion of the reluctant individual by other family members or by the therapist is unethical; however, this does not mean that the therapist cannot strongly encourage a family member to attend at least one session to discover what therapy may offer. Nor does it suggest that the therapist ignore what may be underlying reasons contributing to the person's reluctance, such as feeling threatened. In sorting out whether or not a particular family member will participate in therapy, the therapist should identify the extent to which each person will be expected to participate, for example, whether some persons simply can attend the therapy sessions in the role of observer, learning enough about the therapeutic process so that they do nothing to impede its progress. The therapist also should explain to the reluctant member that if other family members still choose to participate, the family as a whole is likely to change regardless of that individual's lack of participation.

A potential source of coercion surrounding voluntary participation comes from the relatively common therapeutic policy of refusing to see families unless all family members are present. Do other family members go untreated just because one person is unwilling to participate? Does one person's decision to terminate mean that all family members must discontinue contact with the therapist? To avoid the conclusion that one family member denies the others access to therapeutic services, therapists with a strong preference for working with the entire family should inform the family that other therapists do not necessarily share this preference and should have available a list of competent referral sources.

Standards for informed consent are necessary, but the family therapist's conceptual model largely determines the degree of specificity in the information presented. . . . [M]ost therapists can give an overview of the objectives (e.g., better family adjustment) as well as the format of therapy (e.g., how often sessions will be held, approximately how long therapy will last). Full compliance with this guideline can be somewhat difficult, however, particularly for a strategic therapist who mobilizes the oppositional tendencies of family members through paradoxical interventions (Stanton, 1981; Watzlawick, Weakland, & Fisch, 1974). . . .

Moreover, most forms of marital and family therapy involve certain types of manipulation limiting "true" informed consent and free choice about therapy. For example, while not guaranteeing changes . . . , therapists often find it helpful to express optimism about the outcome of therapy in an effort to reduce the family's anxiety, to raise expectancies, and to increase the family's persistent efforts (Jacobson & Margolin, 1979). The therapist also might manipulate coalitions to fortify an intervention. Some therapists, for example, capitalize on parents' concern for their children, that is, "stressing the children's entitlements for a trustworthy climate for growth" (Boszormenyi-Nagy & Ulrich, 1981, p. 183) as therapeutic leverage to evoke collaboration in marital therapy. . . .

Thus, even though clients deserve an accurate portrayal of therapy in informed consent procedures, complete objectivity and openness may not be possible. At the same time that families need factual information to make an informed decision about therapy, they also need the therapist's support, encouragement, and optimism for taking this risky step. An overly enthusiastic discussion of alternatives to therapy or overly detailed explanation of the risks of therapy may convince the client that the therapist does not want him or her in therapy (Hare-Mustin et al., 1979).

Children's Right to Consent

Recently there has been an increasing ground swell of opinion that children should be allowed to exercise the right to consent to psychological treatment. Generally speaking it is the parent or legal guardian who takes responsibility for providing the child's consent to treatment (Morrison, Morrison, & Holdridge-Crane, 1979). Exceptions to this general policy are found in some state statutes that offer teenagers the right to obtain sexual counseling, abortions, or drug counseling. In view of the legal constraints for children, the psychological community

needs to address the issue of informed consent with children. The therapist needs to be sensitive to the fact that children constitute a consumer group who require extra protection, since even those parents who are well intentioned do not always know what is best for their children. It has been recommended that there be a child advocate to examine and protect what is in the best interest of the child client, particularly when a child is adamantly opposed to therapy (Morrison et al., 1979) or when the child does not have the capacity to give full unpressured consent (Koocher, 1976).

Perhaps children's rights to psychological treatment should become more similar to their rights to consent as research subjects. Regulations on the protection of human subjects from the biomedical and behavioral research of the Department of Health and Human Services propose that research should require the assent (not consent) of children over age seven in addition to permission from parents or guardians (Foltz, 1978). The rationale for obtaining informed consent from children who will be participating in therapy is at least as compelling as that for participating in research. Since the effectiveness of psychotherapy depends on a trusting relationship between the therapist and client, there is much to be gained by explaining what is to occur and having the child become involved in decisions that will contribute to the therapeutic endeavor (LoCicero, 1976). Describing procedures in simplified language that children can understand and questioning the children about what has been said reveals to both the therapist and parents the extent to which each child comprehends what will occur. Children who lack the experiential background or intellectual sophistication to weigh the risks and benefits of an informed decision should not be pressured to give written informed consent (Levy & Brackbill, 1979). Yet even partial understanding without formal consent, is preferable to proceeding with therapy in the absence of any explanation. . . .

THERAPIST VALUES

The impact of the therapist's values, inescapable in any therapeutic change process, can play a particularly weighty role in marital and family therapies. Issues discussed in family therapy elicit very important personal, familial, and societal values regarding preservation of the family system, extramarital relationships, and sex roles. Dealing therapeutically with these values is not easy, particularly when the therapist confronts a conflict in values among different family members and is inclined to reinforce the beliefs and attitudes of one family member over another.

Preservation of the Family

To what extent does a marital or family therapist express personal opinions about whether a couple should separate or divorce? The clearest professional standard on this issue is found in the Professional Code of the American Association for Marriage and Family Therapy (AAMFT), which states, "In all circumstances, the therapist will clearly advise a client that the decision to separate or divorce is the responsibility solely of the client" (AAMFT, 1979). Although appealing in principle, this stance is difficult, if not impossible, to exercise in practice. Certainly one function of marital therapy is to help distressed couples decide whether to stay together. Indeed, most couples who enter marital therapy have considered separation or divorce, and some seek therapy with the express purpose of making that decision. These couples "are primed to be influenced by the therapist and are quite sensitive to the cues which the therapist provides concerning his/her opinions about the relationship" (Jacobson & Margolin, 1979, p. 335).

Though few therapists would deny formulating impressions about whether a couple should remain together, there is substantial variability in how comfortable therapists feel in sharing those opinions. A debate on this issue by Yoell, Stewart, Wolpe, Goldstein, and Speierer (1971) conveys two extreme positions. Wolpe, for one, argues that "frequently the therapist needs to make the decision for the patient." He undertakes such a decision "if the patient is gravely unhappy in her marriage, if every step that could be taken seems to have been taken and has failed. If the prognosis for the relationship in terms of happiness is close to zero, then I accept the responsibility not only to advise the dissolution of the marriage but to help in every practical way to bring it about" (pp. 128–129). The opposite viewpoint is

expressed in Stewart's response, indicating "discomfiture about making decisions for a person. The thought constantly pops up—Is this going to be a meaningful decision for the individual if it is made by somebody else?" (p. 129).

Several other therapists endorse an explicit statement of one's opinion to the clients while claiming that the opinion is a personal one rather than a reflection of professional expertise (Gurman & Klein, 1981; Halleck, 1971). Perhaps by making this influence explicit, clients are better able to choose how much they want to be swayed by the therapist's opinions and to sort out their own reactions as distinct from those of the therapist. It is yet to be demonstrated, however, that differentiating a therapist's personal impression from his or her professional expertise is a meaningful distinction for the client. . . .

Extramarital Affairs

. . .

Does knowledge that one partner is currently engaging in an extramarital affair alter the course of therapy? Therapists who answer "no" to this question often focus on improving the primary relationship, which if successful may cause the other relationship to dwindle in importance. A small number of therapists even encourage one spouse to initiate or continue an affair for the well-being of that individual or perhaps even for the betterment of the relationship. . . .

There are, however, . . . potential drawbacks to advocating extramarital affairs for clients. First, even if the affair is beneficial to one person, the other is bound to suffer. Second, therapy that is directed toward the relationship is unlikely to work if one spouse is splitting his or her attention between two relationships. . . .

The other alternative is to actively discourage extramarital relationships or even to stipulate that extramarital affairs must be ended for therapy to commence (e.g., Ables & Brandsma, 1977; Jacobson & Margolin, 1979). This stance, typically described as strategic rather than moralistic, assumes that the affair would impede both partners' abilities to commit themselves fully to relationship improvement and would result in a halting and frustrating course of therapy. Though widely endorsed, this position represents a *professional value*, rather than an empirically derived conclusion. The therapeutic benefit of this stance is that it often prompts termination of an affair as a demonstration of that spouse's desire to work on the relationship. However, the drawback is that a spouse might carefully conceal information about an affair for fear of being excluded from therapy. . . .

Sex Roles

To what extent does the therapist accept the family's definition of sex role identities as opposed to attempting to influence and modify their attitudes in this regard? Recent attention to this question has led to the conclusion that marital and family therapy often tends to reinforce sex role stereotyping (Gurman & Klein, 1981; Hare-Mustin, 1978). Of the sexist attitudes found to characterize psychotherapy in general (APA Task Force on Sex Bias and Sex-Role Stereotyping, 1975), family therapists are particularly vulnerable to the following biases: (1) assuming that remaining in a marriage would result in better adjustment for a woman; (2) demonstrating less interest in or sensitivity to a woman's career than to a man's career; (3) perpetuating the belief that child rearing and thus the child's problems are solely the responsibility of the mother; (4) exhibiting a double standard for a wife's versus a husband's affair; and (5) deferring to the husband's needs over those of the wife.

How does the therapist respond when family members agree that they want to work toward goals that, in the therapist's viewpoint, represent sexist ideologies? By attempting to remain nonjudgmental about the client's objectives, the therapist may unwittingly reinforce these sexist attitudes. But by attempting to reorient them to an egalitarian viewpoint, the therapist might thwart the family from attaining their goals and alienate those individuals whose socialization is such that they are happy with traditional roles (Hare-Mustin, 1978). . . .

A more difficult dilemma arises when the woman challenges traditional sex roles while the husband seemingly is an intractable sexist. As soon as the therapist even privately identifies the husband's sexism as the problem, that therapist has violated guiding principles in marital therapy—balancing alliances with each partner and seeking to understand each

spouse's perspective on an issue. What needs to be sorted out is whether the conflict regarding roles reflects vastly divergent ideological positions or whether the ideological differences are accentuated by relationship issues; that is, the wife's demands threaten the husband, who becomes more rigid in his position, which causes the wife to make more demands, and so on. In this latter situation there are a number of ways to reverse the couple's intensifying polarity so that the therapist can avoid becoming embroiled in an ideological conflict. . . .

. . . Since inattention to gender role issues runs the risk of reinforcing sex role inequalities, it is recommended that family therapists examine therapeutic objectives in light of traditional versus nontraditional values. It also is recommended that therapists examine their own behavior for unwitting comments and questions that may imply that the husband and wife command differential roles and status. Subtle nonverbal behaviors, such as attending to the husband when discussing finances and to the wife when discussing child rearing, communicate the therapist's own expectations about sex role divisions. In contrast, eliciting each partner's perspective regarding both instrumental and expressive domains of the relationship models the absence of preconceptions about sex roles to the adults as well as to any children who may be present. Finally, it is recommended that the therapist be aware of his or her personal views about sex roles in order to avoid imposing these views on the family or judging the family from a predetermined perspective of how families should function. . . .

References

Ables, B. S., & Brandsma, J. M. *Therapy for couples*. San Francisco, Calif.: Jossey-Bass, 1977.

American Association for Marriage and Family Therapy. *Code of professional ethics and standards for public information and advertising*. Upland, Calif.: Author, 1979.

American Psychological Association Task Force. Report of the Task Force on Sex Bias and Sex-Role Stereotyping in Psychotherapeutic Practice. *American Psychologist*, 1975, *30*, 1169–1175.

Bersoff, D., & Jain, M. A practical guide to privileged communication for psychologists. In G. Cooke (Ed.), *The role of the forensic psychologist*. Springfield, Ill.: Charles C Thomas, 1980.

Boszormenyi-Nagy, I., & Ulrich, D. N. Contextual family therapy. In A. S. Gurman & D. P. Kniskern (Eds.), *Handbook of family therapy*. New York: Brunner/Mazel, 1981.

Everstine, L., et al. Privacy and confidentiality in psychotherapy. *American Psychologist*, 1980, *35*, 828–840.

Foltz, D. Proposed protection regs out on child research subjects. *APA Monitor*, September/October 1978, pp. 10; 37.

Grosser, G. H., & Paul, N. L. Ethical issues in family group therapy. *American Journal of Orthopsychiatry*, 1964, *34*, 875–884.

Gurman, A. S., & Klein, M. H. Women and behavioral marriage and family therapy: An unconscious male bias? In E. A. Blechman (Ed.), *Contemporary issues in behavior modification with women*. New York: Guilford, 1981.

Gurman, A. S., & Kniskern, D. P. Research on marital and family therapy: Progress, perspective, and prospect. In S. L. Garfield & A. E. Bergin (Eds.), *Handbook of psychotherapy and behavior change: An empirical analysis* (2nd ed.). New York: Wiley, 1978.

Halleck, S. L. *The politics of therapy*. San Francisco, Calif.: Jossey-Bass, 1971.

Hare-Mustin, R. T. A feminist approach to family therapy. *Family Process*, 1978, *17*, 181–194.

Hare-Mustin, R. T., Marecek, J., Kaplan, A. G., & Liss-Levinson, N. Rights of clients, responsibilities of therapists. *American Psychologist*, 1979, *34*, 3–16.

Jacobson, N. S., & Margolin, G. *Marital therapy: Strategies based on social learning and behavior exchange principles*. New York: Brunner/Mazel, 1979.

Koocher, G. P. Civil liberties and aversive conditioning for children. *American Psychologist*, 1976, *31*, 94–95.

Levy, C. M., & Brackbill, Y. Informed consent: Getting the message across to kids. *APA Monitor*, March 1979, pp. 3; 18.

LoCicero, A. The right to know: Telling children the results of clinical evaluations. In R. Koocher (Ed.), *Children's rights and the mental health profession*. New York: Wiley, 1976.

Margolin, G. Conjoint marital therapy to enhance anger management and reduce spouse abuse. *American Journal of Family Therapy*, 1979, *7*, 13–23.

Morrison, K. L., Morrison, J. K., & Holdridge-Crane, S. The child's right to give informed consent to psychiatric treatment. *Journal of Clinical Child Psychology*, 1979, *8*, 43–47.

Stanton, M. D. Strategic approaches to family therapy. In A. S. Gurman & D. P. Kniskern (Eds.), *Handbook of family therapy*. New York: Brunner/Mazel, 1981.

Watzlawick, P., Weakland, J., & Fisch, R. *Change: Principles of problem formation and problem resolution*. New York: Norton, 1974.

Weiss, R. L., & Birchler, G. R. Adults with marital dysfunction. In M. Hersen & A. S. Bellack (Eds.), *Behavior therapy in the psychiatric setting*. Baltimore: Williams & Wilkins, 1978.

Yoell, W., Stewart, D., Wolpe, J., Goldstein, A., & Speierer, G. Marriage, morals and therapeutic goals: A discussion. *Journal of Behavior therapy and Experimental Psychiatry*, 1971, *2*, 127–132.

Ethical Challenges of Group and Dyadic Psychotherapies: A Comparative Approach

Martin Lakin

. . .

. . . I focus on the ethical challenges generated by the group therapeutic context. . . . Ethical practice is not merely adherence to a professional code, but rather is based on understanding of how the modality itself—the group mode in this case—and the techniques that one uses are likely to affect a range of participants. . . .

ETHICAL DILEMMAS FOR LEADERS OF THERAPEUTIC GROUPS

. . .

The ethically significant point is that group interactions inevitably raise concerns about how much to intrude on another's privacy, how much to reveal to others, and how much to keep to oneself, what is to be kept secret from persons outside the group circle and what is to be shared, how much to trust and what constitutes trustworthiness, how much to encourage, to urge, and to push, and when to desist from pushing. It is essential that probing and confrontations do not exceed the capacities of participants. The provision of appropriate levels of support, the awareness of the vulnerabilities of members, and the avoidance of assaultive pressures are ethical as well as technical concerns. The ethical appropriateness of group interventions must be gauged by their relevance to group members in order to help them function more effectively and to cope with their life circumstances. . . .

ETHICAL GUIDELINES FOR GROUP LEADERS

Various professional associations have established special committees to review the ethical issues and to develop ethical guidelines for groups. Such codes are typically divided into two main components: (a) responsibility for providing information about the service to be offered, and (b) responsibility for providing ethical group services to participants. The following are examples drawn from one of these [footnote omitted].

1. The group leader should conduct a pregroup interview with each prospective member for purpose of screening and orientation in order to select group members whose goals are compatible with the established goals of the group and whose well-being will not be jeopardized by the group experience.
2. Group leaders should inform members that participation is voluntary and that they may exit from the group at any time.
3. Group leaders should fully inform group members of the goals of the group, qualifications of the leader, and procedures to be used.
4. Group leaders should stress personal risks involved in any group, especially the risks of potential life changes and help group members to explore their readiness to accept such risks.
5. Group leaders should protect members by defining clearly what confidentiality means, why it is important, and the difficulties involved in enforcement.

Responsibility for providing ethical group services is exemplified in the following guidelines:

1. Group leaders should refrain from imposing their own agendas, needs, and values on group members.

Adapted from *Professional Psychology: Research and Practice*, 17, 454–461. Copyright 1986 by the American Psychological Association.

2. Group leaders should make every effort to assist members in developing their personal goals.

3. Group leaders should protect members against physical threats, intimidations, coercion, and undue peer pressure.

4. Group leaders should promote independence of members from the group in the most efficient period of time.

5. Group leaders should not attempt any technique unless they are thoroughly trained in its use or are under supervision by an expert who is familiar with the technique.

SOME PROBLEMS IN FOLLOWING ETHICAL GUIDELINES

Informing the potential group member about group goals and procedures is easily prescribed, but can a leader share with members the techniques that will be used and the reasons for using them? Experienced group leaders know that members find it difficult to comprehend the rationale for intervention strategies, especially in screening interviews and in the beginning phases of a group. Despite leaders' wishes to provide them, their attempts to give detailed explanations are often irritating and exasperating rather than informative because beginning members are preoccupied with their emotional reactions. Moreover, one might argue that a participant should not, in fact, be prepared for a therapeutic experience because (a) the effects of the experience are context dependent: telling is so vastly different from experiencing; (b) much of the impact of the group experience will depend on its unpredictability: participants will be less able to rationalize or to defend against unanticipated reactions (whether critical or supportive) than those of which they have been forewarned; (c) the group interaction, to be effective, should appear to be spontaneous (i.e., experiences in which the participant plays an unprogrammed part); (d) the participant is not in the same position as the leader. The member is not familiar with research and practice literatures. Despite these considerations, it is ethically important for leaders to experiment with disclosing as much about their strategies as possible, just as they encourage members to try out new behaviors in facing multiple obstacles.

In every group, there are members who are better able to cope with confrontative responses than others; there are persons whose tolerance for candid interactions is quite low; there are individuals who require more latitude in the realm of emotional expression. There are unfortunately also those who readily become targets for group scapegoating. The need to take into account the vulnerabilities of members is an ethical as well as technical issue. Consequently, it is the leader's obligation to reduce or deflect group pressure when he or she thinks that such pressure jeopardizes the well being of a member. An emotional "procrustean bed" in which each member must have a certain kind of emotional "experience" is ethically indefensible. When one hears, for example, "Everybody has had a chance to express feelings except for Lucy—it's her turn!" or "Jim has been too quiet—he must want to get rid of his aggressive feelings!", it may indicate pressures by the group that are likely to result in a shift away from members' real problems to group insistence on a standardized "person who needs to be more expressive" ("assertive," "loving," "caring," etc.).

No leader can responsibly promise group confidentiality. Participants are made uneasy by a pretense of confidentiality when they know that it is not honored. How frank the group can be and the degree to which the group discussions are carried outside of the session is an important issue for any group.

Davis and Meara (1982) and Kottler (1982) appeared to be sensitive to this problem as it surfaces in group therapies. They recommended that group therapists not promise what cannot be delivered. Rather, there should be group discussion and involvement in setting forth the rules of confidentiality for group contexts. The leader can help the group to develop a more authentic standard for mutual trust by initiating discussions of the relation among disclosure, security, and confidentiality. Such discussions are important in providing a consensual basis for what is to be privileged: a base line by which violations may be judged and responded to. Ethical responsibility is not to be restricted to group leaders, but should become part of the therapy process itself. This is true for stranger groups, but holds even more strongly for within the organization (such as a university or a corporation). In such nonstranger groups, the issues of controlling one's fate are more immediate, and irresponsible talk could have dire consequences for participants. . . .

An increasingly frequent ethical problem arises when individual therapists group their individual patients, as many currently do. Problems of confidentiality are intensified when a therapist cannot separate what he or she hears in individual sessions from what transpires in a group. From the participant's point of view, the therapist may be interpreting from either or both contexts. The issue of authoritarian control becomes more salient when the therapist fills the function of group leader as well as that of individual therapist. Because therapy is an influence process, there is also a danger of fostering an attitude of unqualified faith as a consequence of being treated in individual and in group therapy by the same therapist.

Last, consider the ethical implications of exercises designed to promote or elicit specific feeling states. Use of such techniques invites the accusation that psychological helping groups promote a counterfeit image of human experience and feelings. This may be said of exercises for practicing expressing affection or for displaying anger because members are asked to accept such contrived experiences as emotional standards by which to judge their emotions and their expressions.

The techniques of psychotherapy and the ethics of psychotherapy have been viewed as distinct entities. But the lines between the "science" of therapy and the ethics of therapy are vague because therapies are also systems of beliefs and values about the nature of human experience (Karasu, 1980). Erickson (1976) said that the ethical position of psychotherapy can be found only if therapists take a stand between ideological extremes of aspiring for it to be an objective science and its representing an ideology of healthy conduct. If therapists are able to more clearly perceive and understand the kinds of ethical issues posed by context and process in psychotherapies, then they should be better able to act for the benefit of their patients. . . .

References

Davis, K. L., & Meara, N. M. (1982). So you think it is a secret. *Journal for Specialists in Group Work, 7*(3), 149–153.

Erikson, E. H. (1976). Psychoanalysis and ethics: Avowed or unavowed. *International Review of Psychoanalysis, 3,* 409–415.

Karasu, T. B. (1980). The ethics of psychotherapy. *The American Journal of Psychiatry, 137,* 1502–1512.

Kottler, J. A. (1982). Unethical behaviors we all do and pretend we do not. *Journal for Specialists in Group Work, 7*(3), 182–186.

◆ ◆ ◆

Commentary: Two recent and helpful articles summarize the literature on the ethical problems of providing services to families:

Patten, C., Barnett, T., & Houlihan, D. (1991). Ethics in marital and family therapy: A review of the literature. Professional Psychology: Research and Practice, 22, 171–175.

Hansen, J. C., Green, S., & Kutner, K. B. (1989). Ethical issues facing school psychologists working with families. Professional School Psychology, 4, 245–255.

Piercy and Sprenkle have described an interesting course designed to inform students of the wide variety of issues raised in conducting family therapy: Piercy, F. P., & Sprenkle, D. G. (1983). Ethical, legal, and professional issues in family therapy: A graduate level course. Journal of Marital and Family Therapy, 9, 393–401.

For an informative text on ethical issues related to children in general, see Koocher, G., & Keith-Spiegel, P. (1990). Children, ethics, and the law. Lincoln: University of Nebraska Press.

For readers still interested in conducting encounter groups, this article incorporating ethical issues may be helpful: American Psychological Association. (1973). Guidelines for psychologists conducting growth groups. American Psychologist, 28, 933.

One of the criticisms of the ethical codes written before 1992 was that they neglected marriage and family therapy issues. In addition to the more general provisions in the 1992 Ethical Principles, Standard 4.03 (Couple and Family Relationships) was included explicitly to address these issues. However, for critiques of the current code with regard to therapy for both individuals and groups, see these articles:

Lakin, M. (1994). Morality in group and family therapies: Multiperson therapies and the 1992 ethics code. Professional Psychology: Research and Practice, 25, 344–348.

Vasquez, M. J. T. (1994). Implications of the 1992 ethics code for the practice of individual psychotherapy. Professional Psychology: Research and Practice, 25, 321–328.

Ethical Issues in Rural Mental Health Practice

David S. Hargrove

Ethical behavior in mental health practice is forged from the interplay between practice and the environment in which it occurs. Specific courses of action in ethically and clinically complex situations often are suggested by both the particular clinical issues of a given case and the surrounding sociocultural context. . . .

Because the environmental context in which mental health workers practice gives shape to ethical concerns, the unique characteristics of the rural environment are important for a proper understanding of the ethical constraints on practice within its confines. The purpose of this article is to identify potentially troublesome ethical problems associated with work in rural areas and to suggest that their possible resolution may reside in the nature of the rural environment itself. . . .

CHARACTERISTICS OF RURAL AREAS

. . .

Longer distances between people and communities and fewer people in service areas characterize virtually every type of rural area in the United States. These characteristics force people in rural areas to live more independently and with greater interdependence with neighbors and relatives . . . To assure its economic and social integrity within the community, the family must be equally interdependent in how it functions, both within itself and in the surrounding community. Distances between people and the small population in a given area present particular psychological and economic factors that have an important impact on the lives of rural people.

Residing and working in smaller communities can increase the level of intensity of human relationships because there are fewer people with whom to relate and share experiences. Social and political relationships tend to be close, they frequently overlap, and monopolistic tendencies often characterize the economic environment. . . .

. . . This pattern of interlocking relationships may well constitute a significant component of the community's power structure. Knowledge of real relationships and those that may be represented in the literature reveals that they are, in fact, much more complex and can have deep historical, social, economic, political, and familial roots.

. . .

POTENTIAL ETHICAL ISSUES

. . .

The first, and perhaps most critical, ethical issue for rural mental health practitioners is the confidentiality of and within the professional relationship with a consumer of professional services. Both APA (1981) and NASW (1979) have stringent guidelines regarding the professional person's responsibility for maintaining the confidential nature of the relationship with the client.

APA's position is clearly set forth in its 1981 Principles:[1]

> Psychologists have a primary obligation
> to respect the confidentiality of informa-
> tion obtained from persons in the
> course of their work as psychologists.
> They reveal such information to others
> only with the consent of the person or
> the person's legal representative, except
> in those unusual circumstances in which

---

[1] *Ed. note:* See Standard 5.01 of the APA's current (1992) Ethical Principles.

not to do so would result in clear danger to the person or to others. Where appropriate, psychologists inform their clients of the legal limits of confidentiality. (APA, 1981, pp. 635–636)

Solomon et al. (1981) claimed that strict adherence to the ethical guidelines of APA do not provide sufficiently clear resolutions for some of the difficulties and conflicts faced by the psychologist who practices in a rural area. In addition, they identify at least one potential situation in which the ethical guidelines create a double-bind or no-win situation for rural psychologists and, possibly, for the agency for which he or she works. This situation is a result of APA's mandate of confidentiality of information on the one hand and the psychologist's responsibility to "be aware of the prevailing community standards" when community standards may be less restrictive than professional ethics on the other hand. . . .

The problem becomes paramount when there are adverse interprofessional and/or political consequences to behavior resulting from compliance with the ethical standards. Solomon et al. provide a realistic illustration of a referring physician who expects feedback regarding the referral regardless of whether the proper release documents are completed. When information about the referral is not forthcoming, the physician may well take offense and discontinue referrals to the mental health program. Because the physician is likely to be one of few medical providers in the community and certainly will have strong social and political influence, the consequences of alienating him or her could be great.

Another perspective of this dilemma is the reciprocal expectation of shared information among human service workers. Frequently in rural communities, in an effort to provide adequate continuity of care, many human service workers from a variety of agencies will be involved with the same case. It is not uncommon to have representatives from the welfare department, mental health, vocational rehabilitation, health department, Social Security Administration, and corrections involved with a family at the same time. Typically, one agency will refer to the others in the effort to provide access to comprehensive services. Many rural programs have cooperative staff

meetings that include personnel from other agencies to discuss mutual clients. The proper paperwork dealing with confidentiality may or may not be completed, and formal and informal communication about the case among the workers may or may not fall within the constraints of ethical practice. Frequently, it appears that clients assume that the necessary interagency and interprofessional communication will take place. I have known of more than a few clients who are amazed upon learning that they have not been discussed among human service professionals. Furthermore, they greet the explanation that it is for their own protection with amusement because of its seeming incompatibility with prevailing patterns of communication in the community.

The clear dilemma experienced by the human service professional in this situation is that if he or she communicates back to the referring physician that the client did, in fact, follow the referral or if the professional provides any information about the person, a violation in the privilege of confidence occurs. If the mental health staff person does not communicate back to the physician, the physician may be offended and refuse further referrals to the center and possibly may use his or her social and political prestige to the detriment on the local mental health program. This disruption would not only be injurious to the sociopolitical base of the center but would endanger both the quality and continuity of care for other clients in the community. If the mental health staff member shares in community service case conferences without permission from the client, there is a clear violation of ethical standards in that the client's confidence has been breached. If, on the other hand, the staff member refuses to participate, a valuable community resource is lost, and alienation of the mental health program from other community agencies results. Alienation between human service agencies in a small town is particularly harmful because of the already limited resources. Hollister (1982) pointed out the importance of developing smooth relationships between these agencies in small communities. These realistic situations certainly are not without ethical, legal, and potentially political consequences.

A second problematic ethical issue for rural professional persons concerns the limits of practice.

Principle 2 of the *Ethical Principles of Psychologists* states the following:

> Psychologists recognize the boundaries of their competence and the limitations of their techniques. They only provide services and only use techniques for which they are qualified by training and experience. In those areas in which recognized standards do not yet exist, psychologists take whatever precautions are necessary to protect the welfare of their clients. (APA, 1981, p. 634)[2]

The limit of professional competence is a serious and sensitive matter, and frequently a person's credibility rides on his or her interpretation of these limits. In a rural practice, the generalist model of practice prevails because of the lack of available resources and professionals (Hargrove, 1982b). As a consequence, the rural psychologist is likely to be called on to respond to a broad range of problems and people. If the mental health professional can assist in the identification of a client's clinical problem and refer that person to an appropriately trained specialist for further, more refined diagnosis and intervention, the client may be dealt with properly. Problems result, however, when there is no other local resource for diagnosis or treatment. In fact, there are situations in which the choice is either treatment from the person who is available or no treatment at all. . . .

The most appropriate response to this ethically murky situation is not at all clear. At issue is the definition of professional competence in a given area and the consequences of that definition. When is one deemed professionally competent and by whom? How narrow are the areas of professional competence in which one must be judged competent, and what impact does this have on the professional person who must function as a generalist, by either choice or job requirement?

The third ethical dilemma that is pertinent to the practice of mental health service delivery in rural environments is the multiple levels of relationships between persons who live and work in small communities. Mazer (1976) pointed out that in larger, more populous communities the clinician and the client will likely have one relationship at one level: the clinical or therapeutic relationship, in which one person is the helper and the other is receiving the help. In rural environments, however, it is likely that there will be many possible relationships between the person who is the clinician and the person who is the client. . . .

The rural mental health professional who resides in the community and takes an active part in community life doubtless will face the dilemma of dual relationships. The longer the person is in the role of the clinician in the community, the more likely dual relationships will occur. Because there are fewer people in the community, fewer trained individuals in any field who might be likely to assume some degrees of community leadership, there is greater possibility of having numerous multifaceted relationships with many people. Likewise, there is a greater possibility that one or more of these persons are either potential or actual clients. The choice of the clinician and the client in the event of a previously existing relationship is similar to that described in the discussion on limits of competence, in which a choice may be made that results in the lack of availability of help by a public agency. . . .

POTENTIAL RESOLUTION OF ETHICAL DILEMMAS

Resolutions of the ethical dilemmas that confront rural practitioners are as varied and creative as the situations and the persons in them. Frequently, mental health professionals find the solutions to problems in the nature of the environment itself and in a proper understanding of APA's Ethical Principles.

First, the rural practitioner needs to develop an appropriate view of the ethical standards themselves. The standards are guidelines for appropriate behavior fitting under the principle of the Preamble. They have built into their structure and content consider-

---

[2] *Ed. note:* See Standard 1.04 of the APA's current (1992) Ethical Principles.

able latitude enabling clinicians to make the best decisions possible under a given set of circumstances. The standards are not a substitute for clinical or ethical judgment on the part of the professional mental health worker. The attitude of the practitioner, including his or her intent, is critically important to arriving at proper courses of action in ethically unclear situations.

Second, the rural practitioner needs to look at the resources of the rural environment for solutions to problems that result from that environment. The rural context of practice may well hold the key to the solution of ethically difficult situations just as it may well create the problems in the first place. For example, in the case of the physician who refers a client to the mental health agency with the expectation that he or she will receive follow-up information, it is highly likely that the mental health clinician will have either a professional or personal (or both) relationship with the physician and will have ample opportunity to explain the situation in great detail. If the mental health worker does not have this sort of relationship with the physician, it is highly likely that a member of the board or another friend of the agency will have such a relationship. When a personal relationship with the physician is developed, a different setting enables issues of confidentiality and transfer of information to be discussed in a positive, collegial relationship. Given this relationship, matters are worked out in a personal way, which is the bread and butter of rural life.

With regard to the widely attended staff conferences, it is possible to design a release of information form that includes all the persons and/or agencies that attend. Presumably, the purpose of the meeting is the well-being of the client, and the client is aware of all the agencies' involvements and would have no objection to the sharing of information. If the client does object, there may be good reason. At this point, the clinician would have to question the propriety of a particular agency or staff person attending such conferences. If the client chooses not to allow discussion of his or her situation in an interagency case conference, the clinician has the responsibility to inform him or her of the possible consequences of this action so that the client's choice is an informed one.

The limits of clinical competence is a serious, double-edged issue that must be carefully and consistently addressed. It is particularly important in view of the psychotherapy research that affirms that people can, in fact, be harmed by the process of psychotherapy. First, the clinician must determine the nature of the problem for which assistance is being sought. Then, a decision must be made whether he or she is more competent to treat the disorder than are other available agencies or whether the client may benefit more from marginally competent intervention than none at all. If not, then this fact can be explained to the client, and the clinician can provide assistance in finding the closest available help. It is important that the client be involved in an informed decision, which is consistent with the ethical standards.

At this point, the entire agency can be of considerable help if it has a precedent of establishing reciprocal relationships with other mental health providers. Some agencies characteristically develop relationships with surrounding mental health agencies to provide whatever specialized services may be needed, thus expanding its own range of services. In this event, it is necessary for each clinician in either agency to be aware of the resources available in the others. . . .

It is important that rural mental health professionals and agencies recognize and respect the realities that underlie the ethical guidelines that govern professional behavior. Frequently, these realities also are factors that could lead to difficult agency problems unless approached in a careful, judicious manner. It is equally important that rural mental health administrators and clinicians anticipate the types of ethical problems that may arise and plan accordingly. . . .

References
American Psychological Association. (1981). Ethical principles of psychologists. *American Psychologist, 36,* 633–638.

Hargrove, D. S. (1982b). The rural psychologist as generalist: A challenge for professional identity. *Professional Psychology, 13,* 302–308.

Hollister, W. G. (1982). Principles guiding the development of an innovative low-cost, rural mental health program. In P. A. Keller & J. D. Murray (Eds.), *Handbook of rural community mental health* (pp. 86–99). New York: Human Sciences.

Mazer, M. (1976). *People and predicaments*. Cambridge, MA: Harvard University Press.

National Association of Social Workers. (1979). *Code of ethics of the National Association of Social Workers*. Washington, DC: Author.

Solomon, G., Hiesberger, J., & Winer, J. (1981). Confidentiality issues in rural community mental health. *Journal of Rural Community Psychology, 2*, 17–31.

Commentary: *One issue that Hargrove did not address was bartering for services, a problem that may confront those who serve rural or poor clients. In 1982, the APA ethics committee approved a policy that proclaimed bartering of services a violation of then Principle 6(a) (Dual Relationships). That policy was modified in the 1992 Ethical Principles. Standard 1.18 now generally discourages bartering, permitting it only if it is not clinically contraindicated and is not exploitative.*

Antiracism as an Ethical Imperative: An Example From Feminist Therapy

Laura S. Brown

Feminist therapy has from its inception been a field concerned with the ethics of practice. For feminist therapists, *ethics* is a term that has had broad connotations. Rather than framing ethics as simply being a set of rules or principles describing behaviors to be avoided, feminist therapists have attempted to construe ethical behavior in terms that integrated the process of thinking about ethics into all choices made by therapists about the underlying assumptions of our psychotherapy theory and the politics of our practice. Ethics holds a special place in feminist therapy; it is a unifying vision around which we have joined for the creation of our therapy theories. We have poured into the creation of feminist therapy ethics the best and clearest of our collective thought and the most focused of our work (Rave & Larsen, 1990). Feminist therapists may disagree on many aspects of how to practice, but we tend to converge around the idea that our work must reflect feminist ethical principles of empowerment, care, and the necessity of taking proactive rather than reactive stances (Lerman & Porter, 1990).

Over the two decades of its existence, feminist therapy has focused on a number of different ethical concerns. This article represents a divergence from the mainstream of that thought, which has been concerned primarily with the question of sexuality and sexual and social boundaries in psychotherapy, and instead attends to an issue that is painful and yet fertile with potential for enhancing our understanding of ethics in psychotherapy.

The issue is that of racism in feminist therapy. The questions to be raised here are several. How can we develop an ethic of antiracism within feminist therapy? How can we measure that ethical principle equal in weight to the other ethical concerns that have engaged feminist therapists until now? The issue is painful for many reasons. By raising it, White feminist therapists such as myself acknowledge what our sisters of color have been telling us from almost the beginning. Feminist therapy, as a discipline, and many White feminist therapists as individuals have in the main excluded the realities and living presence of women of color from our work, our theories, and our writing. We must attend to rather than deny or gloss over the discrepancy between our goals as feminists of nonoppressiveness and the realities of being participants in a process of institutionalized oppression. Until recently, antiracism has been neglected as an ethical consideration, in part because this self-confrontation is a difficult one that yields an image at odds with the self-concept of many feminist therapists. When it has been addressed, it has been framed by some White women as a political (as opposed to therapeutic) issue in such a way as to potentially minimize its core importance to matters of feminist therapy theory and practice. It has been seen by some White women as divisive, or inessential to the work and focus of feminist therapy, which may itself be a defensive rationalization for the neglect of the issue. Whatever the reasons, feminist therapy has been mostly a White women's movement in which the unconscious racism with which we were raised has been pervasive, our rhetoric of inclusiveness notwithstanding. . . .

It is important to note at this juncture that although the specifics to which I speak are derived from feminist therapy, the issues being raised here are more universal. That is, almost all current schools of psychotherapy are, by virtue of their participation in the dominant culture, inherently racist. The ethical questions raised here for feminist therapists are equally germane for any psychotherapist, and the importance of seeing antiracism as an ethical stance is no less valid outside the realm of feminist therapy practice. Placing my arguments within the context of feminist therapy, a socially and politically conscious school of thought, may help to illustrate the degree of difficulty White therapists of good will face when attempting to address our own racism. . . .

What I have begun to arrive at is a reframing of my understanding of racism as an ethical issue. I have conceptualized the presence of racism in therapy in the common language of feminist therapy ethics. That is, I suggest that we can more easily understand the need to be antiracist as an ethical imperative if we see racism through the lenses of failures of mutuality and lack of respect, violations of boundaries, and imbalances of power, terms that inhere to discussion of feminist therapy ethics in other realms such as sexuality or money.

Let us begin with the problem of failures of mutuality and lack of respect. Many women writers of color have criticized the second wave of the U.S. feminist movement (and by implication feminist therapy) for its overreliance on gender as a category of analysis for understanding women's oppression (Davis, 1983; Hooks, 1981; Lorde, 1980) . . . These women point out that the assumption of a generic woman makes invisible the experiences of women of color as people of color and that it eradicates the differences between living as a White woman versus living as a woman of color in a White racist society in which racism and sexism are intertwined.

In feminist therapy, White feminist therapists who constitute the bulk of the population have tended to share in this form of covert racism; we write and speak of "women's experiences" as if we are referring to all women when in fact our data bases are primarily or exclusively White (Brown, 1990; Kanuha, 1990). Thus, White feminist therapists have tended to annihilate women of color in our words and actions; we have made their lives invisible, their voices inaudible. We have communicated the meta-message that women of color are unimportant to feminist therapy theory and practice because we have not

moved to include them. Such behavior is destructive to mutuality and to the process of empathy and connection; it violates a feminist ethical standard of care (Noddings, 1984). This participation in the process of making women of color invisible does not allow the space to be in "right relationship" (Heyward, 1989, p. 10) where each person is known and attended to deeply by the other. Such participation in the process of institutionalized racism within the helping professions may be especially painful to women of color when it comes from feminist therapists because we have declared ourselves to be attentive to and concerned with oppression (Kanuha, 1990). We are, in effect, telling women of color that the only important oppression is gender based and that their experiences as targets of racism are of lesser or no importance. . . .

A second way to conceptualize racism as a problem of ethics is to construe it as a form of boundary violation. Typically, in feminist therapy (and other) ethical writings, we have thought of boundaries as sexual and physical; these terms have become so interchangeable that when someone is described as having "boundary problems" in her practice, the unspoken assumption is that she has sexually exploited a client. Yet personal boundaries are more than sexual. I propose that a woman's identity, her sense of self in her race and ethnicity, her pride or shame in her roots, and her awareness of her culture are all aspects of the boundary phenomenon and are at risk for violation. . . .

Finally, there is the question of power imbalance. Feminist therapists have a shared ethical commitment toward the development of egalitarian relationships. By this we have meant that we wish to practice in ways that reduce unnecessary asymmetries between the power of client and therapist, that empower the client to self-knowledge and self-value, and that lead to increasing mutuality in the therapist–client relationship while preserving those aspects of the frame of therapy (e.g., not having social or romantic relationships with clients) that are necessary for the well-being of the client.

This is clearly not to say that feminist therapists of color as a group are so weak and needy as to lack power or need special protections; they do not. Rather, it is to point to the ethical problem for

White feminist therapists that results when we fail to acknowledge the privilege given us by our skin color and the impact that our Whiteness has on colleagues who are women of color, in other words, the ethical conundrum of oppressive exclusivity that derives from a failure to be antiracist. . . .

References

Brown, L. S. (1990). The meaning of a multicultural perspective for theory-building in feminist therapy. In L. S. Brown & M. P. P. Root (Eds.), *Diversity and complexity in feminist therapy* (pp. 1–22). New York: Haworth.

Davis, A. Y. (1983). *Women, race and class.* New York: Vintage Books.

Heyward, C. (1989). *Touching our strength: The erotic as power and the love of God.* San Francisco: Harper & Row.

Hooks, B. (1981). *Ain't I a woman: Black women and feminism.* Boston: South End Press.

Kanuha, V. (1990). The need for an integrated analysis of oppression in feminist therapy ethics. In H. Lerman & N. Porter (Eds.), *Feminist ethics in psychotherapy* (pp. 24–36). New York: Springer.

Lerman, H., & Porter, N. (1990). The contribution of feminism to ethics in psychotherapy. In H. Lerman & N. Porter (Eds.), *Feminist ethics in psychotherapy* (pp. 5–13). New York: Springer.

Lorde, A. (1980, April). *Age, race, class, and sex: Women redefining difference.* Copeland Colloquium, Amherst College, Amherst, MA.

Noddings, N. (1984). *Caring: A feminine approach to ethics and moral education.* Berkeley: University of California Press.

Rave, E. J., & Larsen, C. C. (1990). Development of the code: The feminist process. In H. Lerman & N. Porter (Eds.), *Feminist ethics in psychotherapy* (pp. 14–23). New York: Springer.

◆ ◆ ◆

Commentary: APA has been reasonably forthcoming in producing documents designed to help therapists deal with such sensitive issues as sexism, racism, and the treatment of gays and lesbians. For example, in 1975, an APA task force on sexism in psychotherapy published this report: American Psychological Association. (1975). Report of the task force on sex bias and sex-role stereotyping in psychotherapeutic practice. American Psychologist, 30, 1169–1175. Like many other task force reports, this one has not been adopted by the Council of Representatives as APA policy. But it has raised many issues that are still of concern, such as the treatment of lesbians by therapists who are not fully trained or knowledgeable in this area and the problem of sexual attraction between therapist and patient.

The 1975 report recommended, among other things, that APA develop guidelines for nonsexist psychotherapeutic practice. APA appropriated funds for this endeavor, and in 1978, these guidelines were published in the American Psychologist, 33, 1122–1123.

Guidelines for Therapy With Women

Task Force on Sex Bias and Sex Role Stereotyping in Psychotherapeutic Practice

. . .

1. The conduct of therapy should be free of constrictions based on gender-defined roles, and the options explored between client and practitioner should be free of sex role stereotypes.

. . .

2. Psychologists should recognize the reality, variety, and implications of sex-discriminatory practices in society and should facilitate client examination of options in dealing with such practices.

. . .

3. The therapist should be knowledgeable about current empirical findings on sex roles, sexism, and individual differences resulting from the client's gender-defined identity.

. . .

4. The theoretical concepts employed by the therapist should be free of sex bias and sex role stereotypes.

. . .

5. The psychologist should demonstrate acceptance of women as equal to men by using language free of derogatory labels.

. . .

6. The psychologist should avoid establishing the source of personal problems within the client when they are more properly attributable to situational or cultural factors.

. . .

7. The psychologist and a fully informed client mutually should agree upon aspects of the therapy relationship such as treatment modality, time factors, and fee arrangements.

. . .

8. While the importance of the availability of accurate information to a client's family is recognized, the privilege of communication about diagnosis, prognosis, and progress ultimately resides with the client, not with the therapist.

. . .

9. If authoritarian processes are employed as a technique, the therapy should not have the effect of maintaining or reinforcing stereotypic dependency of women.

. . .

10. The client's assertive behaviors should be respected.

. . .

11. The psychologist whose female client is subjected to violence in the form of physical abuse or rape should recognize and acknowledge that the client is the victim of a crime.

. . .

12. The psychologist should recognize and encourage exploration of a woman client's sexuality and should recognize her right to define her own sexual preferences.

. . .

13. The psychologist should not have sexual relations with a woman client nor treat her as a sex object.

. . .

◆ ◆ ◆

Commentary: In 1984, APA's Division 17 (Counseling Psychology) produced a corollary set of precepts titled "Principles Concerning the Counseling and Psychotherapy of Women" that are worth studying (available from Division 17). For a recent book on this subject, see Lerman, H., & Porter, N. (Eds.) (1990). Feminist ethics in psychotherapy. New York: Springer.

In 1990, a report by the Task Force on Bias in Psychotherapy with Lesbians and Gay Men was approved by the APA Committee on Gay and Lesbian Concerns. In a survey conducted as part of this report, the task force found that the conduct of many therapists assessing and treating these client populations violated existing ethical principles that addressed competence and the welfare of the client. This important report, which has not been adopted as official APA-wide policy, is available from the APA's Committee on Gay and Lesbian Concerns.

Finally, the APA's Board of Ethnic Minority Affairs established a task force in 1988 to help psychologists better understand cultural and ethnic factors when providing psychological services to diverse populations. Guidelines from the board's report, which were subsequently adopted by the Council of Representatives as APA policy, are reprinted next.

Guidelines for Providers of Psychological Services to Ethnic, Linguistic, and Culturally Diverse Populations

American Psychological Association

. . .

GUIDELINES

Preamble: The Guidelines represent general principles that are intended to be aspirational in nature and are designed to provide suggestions to psychologists in working with ethnic, linguistic, and culturally diverse populations.

1. Psychologists educate their clients to the processes of psychological intervention, such as goals and expectations; the scope and, where appropriate, legal limits of confidentiality; and the psychologists' orientations.
   a. Whenever possible, psychologists provide information in writing along with oral explanations.
   b. Whenever possible, the written information is provided in the language understandable to the client.
2. Psychologists are cognizant of relevant research and practice issues as related to the population being served.
   a. Psychologists acknowledge that ethnicity and culture impact on behavior and take those factors into account when working with various ethnic/racial groups.
   b. Psychologists seek out educational and training experiences to enhance their understanding and thereby address the needs of these populations more appropriately and effectively. These experiences include cultural, social, psychological, political, economic, and historical material specific to the particular ethnic group being served.

c. Psychologists recognize the limits of their competencies and expertise. Psychologists who do not possess knowledge and training about an ethnic group seek consultation with, and/or make referrals to, appropriate experts as necessary.
   d. Psychologists consider the validity of a given instrument or procedure and interpret resulting data, keeping in mind the cultural and linguistic characteristics of the person being assessed. Psychologists are aware of the test's reference population and possible limitations of such instruments with other populations.
3. Psychologists recognize ethnicity and culture as significant parameters in understanding psychological processes.
   a. Psychologists, regardless of ethnic/racial background, are aware of how their own cultural background/experiences, attitudes, values, and biases influence psychological processes. They make efforts to correct any prejudices and biases.

Illustrative Statement: Psychologists might routinely ask themselves, "Is it appropriate for me to view this client or organization any differently than I would if they were from my own ethnic or cultural group?"
   b. Psychologists' practice incorporates an understanding of the client's ethnic and cultural background. This includes the client's familiarity and comfort with the majority culture as well as ways in which the client's culture may add to or improve various aspects of the majority culture and/or of society at large.

Illustrative Statement: The kinds of mainstream social activities in which families participate may offer information about the level and quality of acculturation to American society. It is important to distinguish acculturation from length of stay in the United States and not to assume that these issues are relevant only for new immigrants and refugees.

  c. Psychologists help clients increase their awareness of their own cultural values and norms, and they facilitate discovery of ways clients can apply this awareness to their own lives and to society at large.

Illustrative Statement: Psychologists may be able to help parents distinguish between generational conflict and culture gaps when problems arise between them and their children. In the process, psychologists could help both parents and children to appreciate their own distinguishing cultural values.

  d. Psychologists seek to help a client determine whether a "problem" stems from racism or bias in others so that the client does not inappropriately personalize problems.

Illustrative Statement: The concept of "healthy paranoia," whereby ethnic minorities may develop defensive behaviors in response to discrimination, illustrates this principle.

  e. Psychologists consider not only differential diagnostic issues but also the cultural beliefs and values of the client and his/her community in providing intervention.

Illustrative Statement: There is a disorder among the traditional Navajo called "Moth Madness." Symptoms include seizure-like behaviors. This disorder is believed by the Navajo to be the supernatural result of incestuous thoughts or behaviors. Both differential diagnosis and intervention should take into consideration the traditional values of Moth Madness.

4. Psychologists respect the roles of family members and community structures, hierarchies, values, and beliefs within the client's culture.

  a. Psychologists identify resources in the family and the larger community.

  b. Clarification of the role of the psychologist and the expectations of the client precede intervention. Psychologists seek to ensure that both the psychologist and client have a clear understanding of what services and roles are reasonable.

Illustrative Statement: It is not uncommon for an entire American Indian family to come into the clinic to provide support to the person in distress. Many of the healing practices found in American Indian communities are centered in the family and the whole community.

5. Psychologists respect clients' religious and/or spiritual beliefs and values, including attributions and taboos, since they affect world view, psychosocial functioning, and expressions of distress.

  a. Part of working in minority communities is to become familiar with indigenous beliefs and practices and to respect them.

Illustrative Statement: Traditional healers (e.g., shamans, curanderos, espiritistas) have an important place in minority communities.

  b. Effective psychological intervention may be aided by consultation with and/or inclusion of religious/spiritual leaders/practitioners relevant to the client's cultural and belief systems.

6. Psychologists interact in the language requested by the client and, if this is not feasible, make an appropriate referral.

  a. Problems may arise when the linguistic skills of the psychologist do not match the language of the client. In such a case, psychologists refer the client to a mental health professional who is competent to interact in the language of the client. If this is not possible, psychologists offer the client a translator with cultural knowledge and an appropriate professional background. When no translator is available, then a trained paraprofessional from the client's culture is used as a translator/culture broker.

  b. If translation is necessary, psychologists do not retain the services of translators/paraprofessionals who may have a dual role with the client, to avoid jeopardizing the validity of evaluation or the effectiveness of intervention.

  c. Psychologists interpret and relate test data in terms understandable and relevant to the needs of those assessed.

7. Psychologists consider the impact of adverse social, environmental, and political factors in assessing problems and designing interventions.

a. Types of intervention strategies to be used match the client's level of need (e.g., Maslow's hierarchy of needs).

Illustrative Statement: Low income may be associated with such stressors as malnutrition, substandard housing, and poor medical care; and rural residency may mean inaccessibility of services. Clients may resist treatment at government agencies because of previous experience (e.g., refugees' status may be associated with violent treatments by government officials and agencies).

b. Psychologists work within the cultural setting to improve the welfare of all persons concerned, if there is a conflict between cultural values and human rights.

8. Psychologists attend to, as well as work to eliminate, biases, prejudices, and discriminatory practices.

a. Psychologists acknowledge relevant discriminatory practices at the social and community level that may be affecting the psychological welfare of the population being served.

Illustrative Statement: Depression may be associated with frustrated attempts to climb the corporate ladder in an organization that is dominated by a top echelon of White men.

b. Psychologists are cognizant of sociopolitical contexts in conducting evaluations and providing interventions; they develop sensitivity to issues of oppression, sexism, elitism, and racism.

Illustrative Statement: An upsurge in the public expression of rancor or even violence between two ethnic or cultural groups may increase anxiety baselines in any member of those groups. This baseline of anxiety would interact with prevailing symptomatology. At the organizational level, the community conflict may interfere with open communication among staff.

9. Psychologists working with culturally diverse populations should document culturally and sociopolitically relevant factors in the records. These may include, but are not limited to

a. number of generations in the country
b. number of years in the country
c. fluency in English
d. extent of family support (or disintegration of family)

e. community resources
f. level of education
g. change in social status as a result of coming to this country (for immigrant or refugee)
h. intimate relationship with people of different backgrounds
i. level of stress related to acculturation.

Commentary: The APA's 1992 Ethical Principles of Psychologists and Code of Conduct is substantially more specific and sensitive to issues of assessment, intervention, and research with clients and participants of different genders, sexual preferences, and cultural, racial, and ethnic diversity than the 1981 ethics code that it replaced. Refer to the 1992 document, reprinted in chapter 1, and identify its applicable principles and enforceable provisions regarding these issues.

In the final section of this chapter, I address ethical issues related to more nontraditional forms of therapy. Conventional psychological interventions do not intrude into the client's body. Some psychophysical measurements, like electroencephalography, do involve the corpus of the client but do not "break the skin." Thus, they raise no special legal or ethical issues. But with the development of biofeedback, stress and pain management, and behavioral medicine—as well as psychologists' increasing participation in these fields—procedures that involve physical interventions, (particularly aversive conditioning) have come under increasing governmental and institutional scrutiny. To forestall inappropriate regulation, APA convened a task force to forge its position on physical interventions by psychologists and to make recommendations for their use. In 1981, the APA issued the document entitled Psychologists's Use of Physical Interventions: Task Force Report, *in which its task force members unanimously concluded that*

> *the use of physical interventions by psychologists is within the scope of psychological practice so long as the applications of such interventions are: (1) in the interest of more productive and comprehensive health care delivery; (2) within the scope of the practitioner's competence as determined by formal and appropriately supervised train-*

ing and experience in the application of the given intervention; and (3) primarily determined by a decision based on consumer welfare. (Unpublished manuscript, p. 14)

The task force then recommended, that psychologists, among others who use physical interventions, follow informed-consent procedures—providing clients with knowledge of the purposes, values, risks, and techniques of each particular intervention. It further advised that APA develop guidelines for the ethical use of physical procedures and substances.

This 1981 report was never adopted as APA policy by the Council of Representatives. But the task force envisioned "the development of appropriate training courses to qualify the psychologist to prescribe and utilize prescriptive medication . . . especially of the psychoactive types" (p. 16).

The 1981 report and a similar one published in 1985, were precursors to the current intensive effort toward securing for psychologists the privilege to prescribe certain psychotropic medications, although psychologists first raised the issue over a decade ago. See also, for example, Buscue, L. O., & Zlotowski, M. (1981). Psychologists' attitudes about prescribing medications. Psychological Reports, 48, 645–646.

The most comprehensive and recent report was issued in 1992 by the APA ad hoc Task Force on Psychopharmacology, although there is currently no consensus within organized psychology or its members favoring prescription privileges. See Massoth, N. A., McGrath, R. E., Bianchi, C., & Singer, J. (1990). Psychologists' attitudes toward prescription privileges. Professional Psychology: Research and Practice, 21, 147–149. However, the idea is gathering momentum and has stimulated the publication of a growing number of articles, both pro and con. Compare, for example, these first three articles with the last three:

Burns, S. M., DeLeon, P. H., Chemtob, C. M., Welch, B. L., & Samuels, R. M. (1988). Psychotropic medication: A new technique for psychology? Psychotherapy, 25, 508–515.

DeLeon, P. H., Fox, R. E., & Graham, S. R. (1991). Prescription privileges: Psychology's next frontier? American Psychologist, 46, 384–393.

Welsh, R. S. (1992). To medicate or not to medicate: Let us be honest about why we should. American Psychologist, 47, 1678.

Kingsbury, S. J. (1992). Some effects of prescribing privileges. American Psychologist, 47, 426–427.

Kovacs, A. L. (1988). Shall we take drugs? Just say no. Psychotherapy Bulletin, 23, 8–11.

May, W. T., & Belsky, J. (1992). Response to "Prescription privileges: Psychology's next frontier?" or the siren call: Should psychologists medicate? American Psychologist, 47, 427.

For an excellent review of relevant problems related to prescription privileges for psychologists who work with children, see DeMers, S. T. (1994). Legal and ethical issues in school psychologists' participation in psychopharmacological interventions with children. School Psychology Quarterly, 9, 41–52.

What provisions of the APA's Ethical Principles and Code of Conduct are implicated in the controversy over prescription privileges for psychologists?

The Development and Use of Nonprescription Behavior Therapies

Gerald M. Rosen

Psychologists are currently witnessing a proliferation of "nonprescription" behavior therapies that can be totally self-administered without professional consultation. Examples include self-help programs for weight reduction (Hagen, 1974; Stuart & Davis, 1972), toilet training (Azrin & Foxx, 1974), treatment of sexual dysfunctions (Kass & Stauss, in press), and progressive relaxation (Rosen, in press). Studies have demonstrated the effectiveness of self-administered systematic desensitization (Baker, Cohen, & Saunders, 1973; Clark, 1973; Kahn & Baker, 1968; Morris & Thomas, 1973; Phillips, Johnson, & Geyer, 1972; Rosen, Glasgow, & Barrera, 1976), and a self-instructional program for parents' management of retarded children has been empirically validated (Baker, Heifetz, & Brightman, 1972). . . . Other self-help programs for use on a nonprescription basis are likely to be developed in the near future.

When psychologists develop clinically effective behavior therapies that can be totally self-administered, a number of important issues are raised for our profession. . . .

DEVELOPING NONPRESCRIPTION BEHAVIOR THERAPIES

. . .

In light of recent developments, a set of standards to guide professionals and protect consumers of totally self-administered treatments appears desirable. One model for such standards is provided by the current regulatory system used for monitoring pharmaceutical products. Unlike earlier times when medical drugs went unregulated, federal legislation now ensures that products are subject to at least some empirical validation. Comparisons with untreated controls and double-blind placebos are common. Medical drugs are always accompanied by a set of warning or precautionary notes based on patients' reactions to controlled clinical trials. To ensure the enforcement of these guidelines, a governmental regulatory agency (the Food and Drug Administration) has been established.

Whether nonprescription behavior therapies should be monitored in a manner similar to medical drugs is subject to question. Most professionals are likely to react negatively to the development of an outside agency whose purpose it is to monitor their activities. In addition, issues related to freedom of the press make any control of published materials controversial.

An alternative to government regulations and restricted publishing might be found in a set of professionally defined standards that clarify those steps necessary to adequately validate a self-help program. . . . A set of standards would make it possible for clinically effective programs to receive formal approval from an APA standards committee or a professionally independent Nader-type consumer committee. . . . The official endorsement of adequately validated treatments would bring into play new contingencies that could significantly improve the quality of published materials. Informed consumers would be likely to purchase "approved" programs rather than unidentified publications to ensure the acquisition of safe and effective treatments. Professionals and publishers would then be rewarded for evaluating the clinical efficacy of their programs before marketing decisions were made.

The above suggestions broadly outline one

Adapted from the *American Psychologist, 48*, 139–141. Copyright 1976 by the American Psychological Association.

method for dealing with the development of nonprescription behavior therapies. It would be helpful if a committee within APA would begin a discussion on this and other approaches that could encourage the adequate development of self-help programs. Professional consideration of these issues is necessary if psychologists want to play a significant role in shaping future policies. The history of medical treatments suggests that governments inevitably move into a regulatory position when professionals fail to responsibly protect consumers.

CLINICAL IMPLICATIONS OF NONPRESCRIPTION THERAPIES

The development of self-help behavior therapies has tremendous implications for the health professions. What is perhaps most important is that these programs may enable therapists to more efficiently extend professional services to greater numbers of individuals. Effective programs that can be purchased in bookstores and totally self-administered may eliminate the need for many individuals to consult with professionals. Other people with focused behavioral complaints will be able to work largely on their own, with only minimal consultation from trained therapists. With these individuals, professionals could include weekly phone calls or infrequent office visits as supplements to available self-help programs. Therapists may also have patients who can work on specific problems at home while more general or central issues are focused on during regular therapy hours. A patient with chronic social anxiety and fear of driving might, for example, self-administer desensitization for the phobia while therapist time was spent modeling assertiveness and social skills. . . .

When considering the clinical implications of nonprescription treatments, a potentially controversial issue is raised. The issue is whether adequately developed self-administered programs should serve as a minimal standard against which clinical practices are assessed. Most professionals would probably agree that programs administered by private therapists should be at least as effective as empirically validated self-administered treatments. Otherwise, additional costs associated with a clinician's time and facilities would not be justi-

fied. What then are the responsibilities of a clinician once adequate self-help programs exist? Must therapists only employ techniques that are demonstrated to be more effective for particular behavior problems than readily available nonprescription programs? Or should therapists be free to employ whatever techniques are in accord with their personal preferences and theoretical orientations? If therapists can administer treatments without empirical restraints, should they be expected to inform their consumer clients of current evidence regarding alternative treatment formats? . . .

References

American Psychological Association. *Standards for educational and psychological tests and manuals.* Washington, D.C.: Author, 1966.

Azrin, N. H., & Foxx, R. M. *Toilet training in less than a day.* New York: Simon & Schuster, 1974.

Baker, B. L., Cohen, D. C., & Saunders, J. T. Self-directed desensitization for acrophobia. *Behaviour Research and Therapy*, 1973, *11*, 79–89.

Baker, B. L., Heifetz, L. J., & Brightman, A. J. *Parents as teachers.* Cambridge, Mass.: Behavioral Education Projects, 1972.

Clark, F. Self-administered desensitization. *Behaviour Research and Therapy*, 1973, *11*, 335–338.

Hagen, R. L. Group therapy versus bibliotherapy in weight reduction. *Behavior Therapy*, 1974, *5*, 222–234.

Kahn, M., & Baker, B. Desensitization with minimal therapist contact. *Journal of Abnormal Psychology*, 1968, *73*, 198–200.

Kass, D. J., & Stauss, F. *Sex therapy at home.* New York: Simon & Schuster, in press.

Morris, L. W., & Thomas, C. R. Treatment of phobias by a self-administered desensitization technique. *Journal of Behavior Therapy and Experimental Psychiatry*, 1973, *4*, 397–399.

Phillips, R. E., Johnson, G. D., & Geyer, A. Self-administered systematic desensitization. *Behaviour Research and Therapy*, 1972, *10*, 93–96.

Rosen, G. M. Self-administered progressive relaxation training. In J. P. Flanders, *Practical psychology.* New York: Harper & Row, in press.

Rosen, G. M., Glasgow, R. E., & Barrera, M., Jr. A controlled study to assess the clinical efficacy of totally self-administered systematic desensitization. *Journal of Consulting and Clinical Psychology*, 1976, *44*, 208–217.

Stuart, R. B., & Davis, B. *Slim chance in a fat world.* Champaign, Ill.: Research Press, 1972.

◆ ◆ ◆

Commentary: In 1978, APA created the Task Force on Self-Help Therapies. Its primary assignment was to evaluate the extent to which the then-current ethical principles could be applied to professional activity relative to self-help therapies and manuals. Analyzing principles related to responsibility, competence, and public statements, the task force concluded that many self-help books were violating the then-extant version of the APA ethics code, particularly because they failed both to fully inform purchasers of the limitations of the techniques that authors were espousing and to meet recognized standards for evaluating therapeutic procedures. However, because some self-help therapies do benefit the public, the task force urged the APA not to create an ethical bar to their promulgation and dissemination in books, in public lectures, or through the media. Were these recommendations adopted in the current Ethical Principles? What is the cumulative effect of current Standards 1.03, 2.01, 3.02, 3.03, and 3.04 on the use of self-help therapies and manuals?

The APA has always been ambivalent about psychologists giving personal advice through the media. On the one hand, permitting this was seen as potentially harmful to the public and demeaning to the profession if the advice was superficial and misleading. On the other hand, disallowing it precluded highly competent professionals from providing educational and, possibly, preventative information to the public. Until 1981 there was an ethical ban on media services. Standard 3.04 of the 1992 Ethical Principles, however, like its 1981 predecessor, does not prohibit giving advice through media presentations, as long as it is grounded in relevant scientific literature, it conforms to other provisions in the Ethical Principles, and there is no implication that a personal

"relationship" has been established. Does this mean that it is still unethical for a psychologist to provide a diagnosis or treatment through the media? What does the 1992 ethics code say, if anything, about asking current or former clients to appear on the radio or television with the psychologist? How would you view such a request?

What if the therapist conducts therapy with already established clients over the telephone or—more problematic perhaps—with a client that he or she has never (or only initially) personally seen? Telephone consultations provide immediacy and accessibility as well as financial savings that in-person therapy may not provide, particularly to clients who may need assurance and support during crises. What are some of the risks of providing such help? (Remember that an important element missing in telephone consultations is the information derived from face-to-face contact.)

Finally, although it is little discussed, the ethical therapist must contemplate taking appropriate steps to protect clients in case of his or her death or disability. In 1989, Jan Sonne, at the request of the APA ethics committee, produced a paper titled "Therapist Death or Disability: Ethical Responsibilities and Practical Considerations." Some of her recommendations found their way into the 1992 Ethical Principles. Standard 4.08, for example, now requires psychologists to plan for their clients' future care should services be interrupted by the clinician's "illness, death, [or] unavailability." Standard 5.09 requires psychologists to develop plans to protect records and data "in the event of the psychologist's death, incapacity, or withdrawal from the position or practice." For APA policy regarding records in general, see APA Committee on Professional Practice and Standards. (1993). Record keeping guidelines. American Psychologist, 48, 984–986.

CHAPTER 8

ACADEMIA: RESEARCH, TEACHING, AND SUPERVISION

The bricks and mortar of college buildings and the surrounding campus and the various forms of flora growing on them have long hid conduct of concern to ethicists and those in academia. Researchers, scholars, and supervisors have seemed to be beyond the scrutiny of ethics committees. Academicians, after all, were simply data gatherers, teachers, mentors, and thought-producing initiators of new theories. They were believed immune to the vagaries of professional practice that often landed their clinical colleagues in trouble, such as setting and collecting fees, mediating the needs of clients and the demands of insurance companies and other third-party payors, becoming sexually attracted to patients, or disclosing intimate information gathered in therapy.

But science and the public are becoming increasingly aware that donning a white lab coat or a tweed, elbow-patched jacket does not insulate one from unethical behavior. People now know, as one of the excerpts in this chapter briefly relates, that for over 60 years academic scientists working for the federal government engaged in risky research that proved harmful to participants, who were never fully informed about the nature, costs, and benefits of the studies. It has also been acknowledged that professors sometimes do appropriate students' ideas and works as their own; that teachers and supervisors more than rarely develop intimate, sometimes sexual, relations with students and trainees; and that some teachers are often unprepared to face their classes (or continue to lecture from the proverbial time-stained notes) and leave students languishing for months before returning examinations or seminar papers. These issues have become so salient that for the first time in nine revisions, the current (1992) set of APA Ethical Principles contains a specific section of standards (Section 6) that address teaching, training, supervision, research, and publishing.

Materials in this chapter introduce the reader to a broadening array of ethical issues within the university setting, although the bulk of the material is devoted to research. Research is an interesting enterprise from an ethical perspective because its purpose is not necessarily devoted to the betterment of those who participate in it. Psychological assessment, intervention, therapy, and other forms of treatment are, at the least, processes intended to benefit participants. Alternatively—although not true of all studies—research usually does not contribute to the welfare of participants at all. It is ironic, then, that subjects of research—animals as well as humans—may be the least well treated of all those with whom psychologists interact. The validity of this hypothesis may be supported by examining the controversy over *deception research*—studies in which the participant is either not fully informed or is misinformed about the purpose of the experiment so as not to contaminate the data. I have chosen to make such studies a focus of this chapter. This ethical dilemma is not only of central importance in research; rather, like other issues I highlight in this text, it evokes images of more universal conflicts that should be considered.

Issues concerning deception are at the surface of conflict between the interests of science and those of the participant in research. Such conflict has perhaps been best summarized by Shils (1959):

> The respect for privacy rests on the appreciation of human dignity, with its high evaluation of individual self-determination. . . . In this, respect for human dignity and individuality shares an historical comradeship with the freedom of scientific inquiry, which is equally precious to modern liberalism. The tension between these values, so essential to each other in so many profoundly important ways, is one of the antimonies of modern liberalism. The ethical problems with which we are dealing . . . arise from the confrontation of autonomy and privacy by a free intellectual curiosity, enriched by a modern awareness of the depth and complexity of the forces that work in us implemented by the devices of a passionate effort to transform this awareness into scientific knowledge. (pp. 120–121)

Similar note of this tension was made by psychologist Ross Stagner (*Problems Concerning Federal Support, 1967*) before a Senate subcommittee concerned with government research:

> Social scientists . . . have a genuine obligation to devise protections for the right of privacy, and to avoid mere psychic voyeurism. At the same time they have a compelling obligation to accumulate data—and meaningful generalizations— about the powerful impulses of loyalty, hostility, fear, and ambition which shape human history. . . .
>
> . . .
>
> There is an obvious conflict between the need of society to know and the right of the individual to dignity and privacy. (pp. 757–758)

The ambivalence between advancing science and protecting the integrity of the individual is also reflected in the APA's (1982) *Ethical Principles in the Conduct of Research With Human Participants*, which is now undergoing major revision. For example, Principle D states: "The investigator informs the participants of all aspects of the research that might reasonably be expected to influence willingness to participate" (APA, 1982, p. 32). But, with little pause, it cautions: "Failure to make full disclosure prior to obtaining informed consent requires additional safeguards to protect the welfare and dignity of the research participants" (APA, 1982, p. 32).

Beyond exploring this central conflict in social science research, the material in this chapter covers more mundane but crucial issues: exploitation of graduate students (both academically and socially), authorship issues (including publication credit), clinical supervision, and simply bad teaching. These topics have often been neglected in discussions of ethics. I hope that this compilation of materials reveals the seriousness of such issues and promotes even more extended attention to them.

References

American Psychological Association. (1982). *Ethical principles in the conduct of research with human participants.* Washington, DC: Author.

Problems Concerning Federal Support of Social Science Research: Hearings on S. 836 before the Subcommittee on Government Research of the Senate Committee on Government Operations, 90th Cong., 1st Sess. 757 (1967) (testimony of Ross Stagner).

Shils, E. A. (1959). Social inquiry and the autonomy of the individual. In D. Lerner (Ed.), *The human meaning of the social sciences* (pp. 114–148). New York: Meridian Books.

Science and Ethics in Conducting, Analyzing, and Reporting Psychological Research

Robert Rosenthal

. . .

CONDUCTING PSYCHOLOGICAL RESEARCH

Let us turn first to considerations of research design, procedures employed in a study, and the recruitment of human participants. In evaluating the ethical employment of our participants, we can distinguish issues of safety from more subtle issues of research ethics. Obviously, research that is unsafe for participants is ethically questionable. However, I propose that perfectly safe research in which no participant will be put at risk may also be ethically questionable because of the shortcomings of the design.

Issues of Design

Imagine that a research proposal that comes before an institutional review board proposes the hypothesis that private schools improve children's intellectual functioning more than public schools do. Children from randomly selected private and public schools are to be tested extensively, and the research hypothesis is to be tested by comparing scores earned by students from private versus public schools. The safety of the children to be tested is certainly not an issue, yet it can be argued that this research raises ethical issues because of the inadequacy of its design. The goal of the research is to learn about the causal impact on performance of private versus public schooling, but the design of the research does not permit reasonable causal inference because of the absence of randomization or even some reasonable attempt to consider plausible rival hypothesis (Cook & Campbell, 1979).

How does the poor quality of the design raise ethical objections to the proposed research? Because students', teachers', and administrators' time will be taken from potentially more beneficial educational experiences. Because the poor quality of the design is likely to lead to unwarranted and inaccurate conclusions that may be damaging to the society that directly or indirectly pays for the research. In addition, allocating time and money to this poor-quality science will serve to keep those finite resources of time and money from better quality science in a world that is undeniably zero-sum.

It should be noted that had the research question addressed been appropriate to the research design, the ethical issues would have been less acute. If the investigators had set out only to learn whether there were performance differences between students in private versus public schools, their design would have been perfectly appropriate to their question.

Issues of Recruitment

The American Psychological Association's (APA) Committee for the Protection of Human Participants in Research and its new incarnation, the Committee on Standards in Research, and such pioneer scholars of the topic as Herbert Kelman have thoughtfully considered a variety of ethical issues in the selection and recruitment of human participants (APA, 1982; Blanck, Bellack, Rosnow, Rotheram-Borus, & Schooler, 1992; Grisso et al., 1991; Kelman, 1968). Only a few comments need to be made here.

On the basis of several reviews of the literature, my friend and colleague Ralph Rosnow and I have proposed a number of procedures designed to reduce volunteer bias and therefore increase the generality of our research results (Rosenthal & Rosnow,

1975, 1991; Rosnow & Rosenthal, 1993). Employment of these procedures has led us to think of our human participants as another "granting agency"—which, we believe, they are, since they must decide whether to grant us their time, attention, and cooperation. Part of our treating them as such is to give them information about the long-term benefits of the research. In giving prospective participants this information, we have a special obligation to avoid hyperclaiming.

Hyperclaiming. Hyperclaiming is telling our prospective participants, our granting agencies, our colleagues, our administrators, and ourselves that our research is likely to achieve goals it is, in fact, unlikely to achieve. Presumably our granting agencies, our colleagues, and our administrators are able to evaluate our claims and hyperclaims fairly well. However, our prospective participants are not; therefore, we should tell them what our research can actually accomplish rather than that it will yield the cure for panic disorder, depression, schizophrenia, or cancer.

Causism. Closely related to hyperclaiming is the phenomenon of causism. Causism refers to the tendency to imply a causal relationship where none has been established (i.e., where the data do not support it).

Causism: characteristics and consequences. Characteristics of causism include (a) the absence of an appropriate evidential base; (b) the presence of language implying cause (e.g., "the effect of," "the impact of," "the consequence of," "as a result of") where the appropriate language would have been "was related to," "was predictable from," or "could be inferred from"; and (c) self-serving benefits to the causist. Causism is self-serving because it makes the causist's result appear more important or fundamental than it really is.

If a perpetrator of causism is unaware of the causism, its presence simply reflects poor scientific training. If the perpetrator is aware of the causism, it reflects blatantly unethical misrepresentation and deception.

Whereas well-trained colleagues can readily differentiate causist language from inferentially more

accurate language, potential research participants or policymakers ordinarily cannot. When a description of a proposed research study is couched in causal language, that description represents an unfair recruitment device that is at best inaccurate, when it is employed out of ignorance, and at worst dishonest, when it is employed as hype to increase the participation rates of potential participants. . . .

Bad Science Makes for Bad Ethics

Causism is only one example of bad science. Poor quality of research design, poor quality of data analysis, and poor quality of reporting of the research all lessen the ethical justification of any type of research project. I believe this judgment applies not only when deception, discomfort, or embarrassment of participants is involved, but for even the most benign research experience for participants. If because of the poor quality of the science no good can come of a research study, how are we to justify the use of participants' time, attention, and effort and the money, space, supplies, and other resources that have been expended on the research project? When we add to the "no good can come of it" argument the inescapable zero-sum nature of time, attention, effort, money, space, supplies, and other resources, it becomes difficult to justify poor-quality research on any ethical basis. For this reason, I believe that institutional review boards must consider the technical scientific competence of the investigators whose proposals they are asked to evaluate. Yes, that will increase the work required of board members and change boards' compositions somewhat to include a certain degree of methodological expertise. No, it will not always be easy to come to a decision about the scientific competence of an investigator and of a particular proposal, but then it is not always easy to come to a decision about the more directly ethical aspects of a proposal either.

Poor quality of research makes for poor quality of education as well. Especially when participation is quasi-coercive, the use of participants is usually justified in part by the fact that they will benefit educationally. But if participants are required to participate in poor-quality research, they are likely to acquire only misconceptions about the nature of science and of psychology. . . .

Costs and Utilities

Payoffs for doing research. When individual investigators or institutional review boards are confronted with a questionable research proposal, they ordinarily employ a cost-utility analysis in which the costs of doing a study, including possible negative effects on participants, time, money, supplies, effort, and other resources, are evaluated simultaneously against such utilities as benefits to participants, to other people at other times, to science, to the world, or at least to the investigator. The potential benefits of higher quality studies and studies addressing more important topics are greater than the potential benefits of lower quality studies and studies addressing less important topics. Any study with low utility and high cost should not be carried out. Studies in which costs equal utilities are very difficult to decide about.

Payoffs for failing to do research. However, Rosnow and I have become convinced that this cost-utility model is insufficient because it fails to consider the costs (and utilities) of *not* conducting a particular study (Rosenthal & Rosnow, 1984, 1991; Rosnow, 1990; Rosnow & Rosenthal, 1993).

The failure to conduct a study that could be conducted is as much an act to be evaluated on ethical grounds as is conducting a study. The oncology group that may have a good chance of finding a cancer preventive but feels the work is dull and a distraction from their real interest is making a decision that is to be evaluated on ethical grounds as surely as the decision of a researcher to investigate tumors with a procedure that carries a certain risk. The behavioral researcher whose study may have a good chance of reducing violence or racism or sexism, but who refuses to do the study simply because it involves deception, has not solved an ethical problem but only traded in one for another. The issues are, in principle, the same for the most basic as for the most applied research. In practice, however, it is more difficult to make even rough estimates of the probability of finding the cancer cure or the racism reducer for the more basic as compared with the more applied research.

This idea of lost opportunities has been applied with great eloquence by John Kaplan (1988), of Stanford University Law School. The context of his remarks was the use of animals in research and the efforts of "animal rights" activists to chip away "at our ability to afford animal research. . . . [I]t is impossible to know the costs of experiments not done or research not undertaken. Who speaks for the sick, for those in pain, and for the future?" (p. 839). . . .

DATA ANALYSIS AS AN ETHICAL ARENA

Data Dropping

Ethical issues in the analysis of data range from the very obvious to the very subtle. Probably the most obvious and most serious transgression is the analysis of data that never existed (i.e., that were fabricated). Perhaps more frequent is the dropping of data that contradict the data analyst's theory, prediction, or commitment.

Outlier rejection. There is a venerable tradition in data analysis of dealing with outliers, or extreme scores, a tradition going back over 200 years (Barnett & Lewis, 1978). Both technical and ethical issues are involved. The technical issues have to do with the best ways of dealing with outliers without reference to the implications for the tenability of the data analyst's theory. The ethical issues have to do with the relationship between the data analyst's theory and the choice of method for dealing with outliers. For example, there is some evidence to suggest that outliers are more likely to be rejected if they are bad for the data analyst's theory but treated less harshly if they are good for the data analyst's theory (Rosenthal, 1978; Rosenthal & Rubin, 1971). At the very least, when outliers are rejected, that fact should be reported. In addition, it would be useful to report in a footnote the results that would have been obtained had the outliers not been rejected.

Subject selection. A different type of data dropping is subject selection in which a subset of the data is not included in the analysis. In this case, too, there are technical issues and ethical issues. There may be good technical reasons for setting aside a subset of the data—for example, because the subset's sample size is especially small or because dropping the subset would make the data more comparable to some other research. However, there are also ethical issues, as when just those subsets are dropped that do not support the data analyst's theory. When a subset is dropped, we should be informed of that fact and what the results were for that subset. Similar considerations apply when the results for one or more variables are not reported.

Exploitation Is Beautiful

That data dropping has ethical implications is fairly obvious. An issue that has more subtle ethical implications is exploitation. Exploiting research participants, students, postdoctoral fellows, staff, and colleagues is of course reprehensible. But there is a kind of exploitation to be cherished: the exploitation of data.

Many of us have been taught that it is technically improper and perhaps even immoral to analyze and reanalyze our data in many ways (i.e., to snoop around in the data). We were taught to test the prediction with one particular preplanned test and take a result significant at the .05 level as our reward for a life well-lived. Should the results not be significant at the .05 level, we were taught, we should bite our lips bravely, take our medicine, and definitely not look further at our data. Such a further look might turn up results significant at the .05 level, results to which we were not entitled. All this makes for a lovely morality play, and it reminds us of Robert Frost's poem about losing forever the road not taken, but it makes for bad science and for bad ethics.

It makes for bad science because while snooping does affect p values, it is likely to turn up something new, interesting, and important (Tukey, 1977). It makes for bad ethics because data are expensive in terms of time, effort, money, and other resources and because the anti-snooping dogma is wasteful of time, effort, money, and other resources. If the research was worth doing, the data are worth a thorough analysis, being held up to the light in many different ways so that our research participants, our funding agencies, our science, and society will all get their time and their money's worth. . . .

Meta-Analysis as an Ethical Imperative

Meta-analysis is a set of concepts and procedures employed to summarize quantitatively any domain of research (Glass, McGaw, & Smith, 1981; Rosenthal, 1991). We know from both statistical and empirical research that, compared with traditional reviews of the literature, meta-analytic procedures are more accurate, comprehensive, systematic, and statistically powerful (Cooper & Rosenthal, 1980; Hedges & Olkin, 1985; Mosteller & Bush, 1954). Meta-analytic procedures use more of the information in the data, thereby yielding (a) more accurate estimates of the overall magnitude of the effect or relationship being investigated, (b) more accurate estimates of the overall level of significance of the entire research domain, and (c) more useful information about the variables moderating the magnitude of the effect or relationship being investigated.

Retroactive increase of utilities. Meta-analysis allows us to learn more from our data and therefore has a unique ability to increase retroactively the benefits of the studies being summarized. The costs of time, attention, and effort of the human participants employed in the individual studies entering into the meta-analysis are all more justified when their data enter into a meta-analysis. That is because the meta-analysis increases the utility of all the individual studies being summarized. Other costs of individual studies—costs of funding, supplies, space, investigator time and effort, and other resources—are similarly more justified because the utility of individual studies is so increased by the borrowed strength obtained when information from more studies is combined in a sophisticated way.

The failure to employ meta-analytic procedures when they could be used thus has ethical implications because the opportunity to increase the benefits of past individual studies has been forgone. In addition, when public funds or other resources are employed by scientists to prepare reviews of literatures, it is fair to ask whether those resources are being used wisely or ethically. Now that we know how to summarize literatures meta-analytically, it seems hardly justified to review a quantitative literature in the pre-meta-analytic, prequantitative manner. Money that funds a traditional review is not available to fund a meta-analytic review. . . .

REPORTING PSYCHOLOGICAL RESEARCH

Misrepresentation of Findings

Mother nature makes it hard enough to learn her secrets, without the additional difficulty of being misled by the report of findings that were not found or by inferences that are unfounded. Although all misrepresentations of findings are damaging to the progress of our science, some are more obviously unethical than others.

Intentional misrepresentation. The most blatant intentional misrepresentation is the reporting of data that never were (Broad & Wade, 1982). That behavior, if detected, ends (or ought to end) the scientific career of the perpetrator. A somewhat more subtle form of intentional misrepresentation occurs when investigators knowingly allocate to experimental or control conditions those participants whose responses are more likely to support the investigators' hypothesis. Another potential form of intentional misrepresentation occurs when investigators record the participants' responses without being blind to the participants' treatment condition, or when research assistants record the participants' responses knowing both the research hypothesis and the participants' treatment condition. Of course, if the research specifically notes the failure to run blind, there is no misrepresentation, but the design is unwise if it could have been avoided.

Unintentional misrepresentation. Various errors in the process of data collection can lead to unintentional misrepresentation. Recording errors, computational errors, and data analytic errors can all lead to inaccurate results that are inadvertent misrepresentations (Broad & Wade, 1982; Rosenthal, 1966). We would not normally even think of them as constituting ethical issues except for the fact that errors in the data decrease the utility of the research and thereby move the cost-utility ratio (which is used to justify the research on ethical grounds) in the unfavorable direction. . . .

Misrepresentation of Credit

I have been discussing misrepresentation of findings, or the issue of "what was really found?" In the present section, the focus is on the issue of "who really found it?"

Problems of authorship. Because so many papers in psychology, and the sciences generally, are multi-authored, it seems inevitable that there will be difficult problems of allocation of authorship credit. Who becomes a coauthor and who becomes a footnote? Among the coauthors, who is assigned first, last, or any other serial position in the listing? Such questions have been discussed in depth, and very general guidelines have been offered (APA, 1981, 1987; see also Costa & Gatz, 1992), but it seems that we could profit from further empirical studies in which authors, editors, referees, students, practitioners, and professors were asked to allocate authorship credit to people performing various functions in a scholarly enterprise.

Problems of priority. Problems of authorship are usually problems existing within research groups. Problems of priority are usually problems existing between research groups. A current example of a priority problem is the evaluation of the degree to which Robert C. Gallo and his colleagues were guilty of "intellectual appropriation" of a French research group's virus that was used to develop a blood test for HIV, the virus that is believed to cause AIDS (Palca, 1992). Priority problems also occur in psychology, where the question is likely to be not who first produced a virus but rather who first produced a particular idea.

Failing to Report or Publish

Sometimes the ethical question is not about the accuracy of what was reported or how credit should be allocated for what was reported, but rather about what was *not* reported and why it was not reported. The two major forms of failure to report, or censoring, are self-censoring and external censoring.

Self-censoring. Some self-censoring is admirable. When a study has been really badly done, it may be a service to the science and to society to simply start over. Some self-censoring is done for admirable motives but seems wasteful of information. For example, some researchers feel they should not cite their own (or other people's) unpublished data because the data have not gone through peer review. I would argue that such data should indeed be cited and employed in meta-analytic computations as long as the data were well collected.

There are also less admirable reasons for self-censoring. Failing to report data that contradict one's earlier research, or one's theory or one's values, is poor science and poor ethics. One can always find or invent reasons why a study that came out unfavorably should not be reported: The subjects were just starting the course; the subjects were about to have an exam; the subjects had just had an exam; the subjects were just finishing the course; and so on. A good general policy—good for science and for its integrity—is to report all results shedding light on the original hypothesis or providing data that might be of use to other investigators.

There is no denying that some results are more thrilling than others. If our new treatment procedure prevents or cures mental illness or physical illness, that fact may be worth more journal space or space in more prestigious journals than the result that our new treatment procedure does no good whatever. But that less thrilling finding should also be reported and made retrievable by other researchers who may need to know that finding.

External censoring. Both the progress and the slowing of progress in science depend on external censoring. It seems likely that sciences would be more chaotic than they are were it not for the censorship exercised by peers: by editors, by reviewers, and by program committees. All these gatekeepers help to keep the really bad science from clogging the pipelines of mainstream journals.

There are two major bases for external censorship. The first is evaluation of the methodology employed in a research study. I strongly favor such external censorship. If the study is truly terrible, it probably should not be reported.

The second major basis for external censorship is evaluation of the results. In my 35 years in psychology, I have often seen or heard it said of a study that "those results aren't possible" or "those results make no sense." Often when I have looked at such studies, I have agreed that the results are indeed implausible.

However, that is a poor basis on which to censor the results. Censoring or suppressing results we do not like or do not believe to have high prior probability is bad science and bad ethics (Rosenthal, 1975, 1994).

CONCLUSION

The purpose of this article has been to discuss some scientific and ethical issues in conducting, analyzing, and reporting psychological research. A central theme has been that the ethical quality of our research is not independent of the scientific quality of our research. Detailing some of the specifics of this general theme has, I hope, served two functions. First, I hope it has comforted the afflicted by showing how we can simultaneously improve the quality of our science and the quality of our ethics. Second, and finally, I hope it has afflicted the comfortable by reminding us that in the matter of improving our science and our ethics, there are miles to go before we sleep.

References

American Psychological Association. (1981). Ethical principles of psychologists. *American Psychologist, 36,* 633–638.

American Psychological Association. (1982). *Ethical principles in the conduct of research with human participants.* Washington, DC: Author.

American Psychological Association. (1987). *Casebook on ethical principles of psychologists.* Washington, DC: Author.

Barnett, V., & Lewis, T. (1978). *Outliers in statistical data.* New York: Wiley.

Blanck, P. D., Bellack, A. S., Rosnow, R. L., Rotheram-Borus, M. J., & Schooler, N. R. (1992). Scientific rewards and conflicts of ethical choices in human subjects research. *American Psychologist, 47,* 959–965.

Broad, W., & Wade, N. (1982). *Betrayers of the truth.* New York: Simon and Schuster.

Cook, T. D., & Campbell, D. T. (1979). *Quasi-experimentation: Design and analysis issues for field settings.* Chicago: Rand McNally.

Cooper, H. M., & Rosenthal, R. (1980). Statistical versus traditional procedures for summarizing research findings. *Psychological Bulletin, 87,* 442–449.

Costa, M. M., & Gatz, M. (1992). Determination of authorship credit in published dissertations. *Psychological Science, 3,* 354–357.

Glass, G. V., McGaw, B., & Smith, M. L. (1981). *Meta-analysis in social research*. Beverly Hills, CA: Sage.

Grisso, T., Baldwin, E., Blanck, P. D., Rotheram-Borus, M. J., Schooler, N. R., & Thompson, T. (1991). Standards in research: APA's mechanism for monitoring the challenges. *American Psychologist, 46,* 758–766.

Hedges, L. V., & Olkin, I. (1985). *Statistical methods for meta-analysis*. New York: Academic Press.

Kaplan, J. (1988). The use of animals in research. *Science, 242,* 839–840.

Kelman, H. C. (1968). *A time to speak: On human values and social research*. San Francisco: Jossey-Bass.

Mosteller, F., & Bush, R. R. (1954). Selected quantitative techniques. In G. Lindzey (Ed.), *Handbook of social psychology: Vol. 1. Theory and method* (pp. 289–334). Cambridge, MA: Addison-Wesley.

Palca, J. (1992). "Verdicts" are in on the Gallo probe. *Science, 256,* 735–738.

Rosenthal, R. (1966). *Experimenter effects in behavioral research*. New York: Appleton-Century-Crofts.

Rosenthal, R. (1975). On balanced presentation of controversy. *American Psychologist, 30,* 937–938.

Rosenthal, R. (1978). How often are our numbers wrong? *American Psychologist, 33,* 1005–1008.

Rosenthal, R. (1991). *Meta-analytic procedures for social research* (rev. ed.). Newbury Park, CA: Sage.

Rosenthal, R. (1994). On being one's own case study: Experimenter effects in behavioral research—30 years later. In W. R. Shadish & S. Fuller (Eds.), *The social psychology of science* (pp. 214–229). New York: Guilford Press.

Rosenthal, R., & Rosnow, R. L. (1975). *The volunteer subject*. New York: Wiley.

Rosenthal, R., & Rosnow, R. L. (1984). Applying Hamlet's question to the ethical conduct of research: A conceptual addendum. *American Psychologist, 39,* 561–563.

Rosenthal, R., & Rosnow, R. L. (1991). *Essentials of behavioral research: Methods and data analysis* (2nd ed.). New York: McGraw-Hill.

Rosenthal, R., & Rubin, D. B. (1971). Pygmalion reaffirmed. In J. D. Elashoff & R. E. Snow, *Pygmalion reconsidered* (pp. 139–155). Worthington, OH: C. A. Jones.

Rosnow, R. L. (1990). Teaching research ethics through role-play and discussion. *Teaching of Psychology, 17,* 179–181.

Rosnow, R. L., & Rosenthal, R. (1993). *Beginning behavioral research: A conceptual primer*. New York: Macmillan.

Tukey, J. W. (1977). *Exploratory data analysis*. Reading, MA: Addison-Wesley.

◆ ◆ ◆

Commentary: *Could Rosenthal's litany create the potential for finding almost any piece of research unethical? Would it be appropriate to make methodological flaws an ethical violation if they do not place research participants at risk or harm them? For discussions of these questions,* see

Parkinson, S. (1994). Scientific or ethical quality? Psychological Science, *5, 137–138.*

Pomerantz, J. R. (1994). On criteria for ethics in science: Commentary on Rosenthal. Psychological Science, *5, 135–136.*

Legal and Ethical Concerns in Research

Donald N. Bersoff

. . .

THE INFORMED CONSENT DOCTRINE

. . .

By the 1960s the contours of the legal duty of physicians to disclose significant aspects of proposed medical procedures to their patients had been fairly well established. Generally, it is now held that physicians violate their obligations to patients and subject themselves to liability for malpractice if they fail to reveal potential dangers and other important facts concerning suggested treatment or withhold information concerning available forms of treatment. . . . The underlying legal and philosophical premise of the informed consent doctrine is the notion of "thoroughgoing self-determination" (*Natanson v. Kline*, 1960, pp. 406; 1104). As a result, the patient is entitled to all the facts necessary to make an informed, intelligent choice before consenting to medical intervention.

Typically, the duty to disclose is not absolute. It is tempered by what may be called the materiality rule. . . . "Materiality may be said to be the significance a reasonable person, in what the physician knows or should know is his patient's position, would attach to the disclosed risk or risks in deciding whether to submit or not to submit to surgery or treatment" (*Wilkinson v. Vesey*, 1972, p. 689). . . . Some of the information falling within the materiality rule and thus necessitating disclosure are: (1) inherent and potential hazards of the proposed treatment; (2) alternatives to that treatment; (3) the likely result if the patient chooses to remain untreated. In brief, "To establish consent to a risk, it must be shown both that the patient was aware of the risk and that he assented to encounter it" (Waltz and Scheuneman, 1969, p. 643).

There was no reason for the informed consent doctrine to be limited to physician–patient relationships. In many ways the insensitivity of behavioral and medical researchers to the interests of those they studied matched that of the healers and by the mid-1950s it was clear that scientists were not to be immune from legal constraints. In 1954 a group of professors from law and the social sciences recorded and studied the deliberations of juries with "bugging devices." The researchers obtained the approval of the judges and the lawyers involved, but neither the jurors nor the litigants were aware that microphones had been concealed in the jury room. In 1963 three medical researchers injected "live cancer cells" into 22 chronically ill patients at a New York hospital with the approval of the institution's director of medicine but without the fully informed consent of those injected. (For a lengthy history and description of these cases see Katz, 1972.) In 1972 the American public was finally told that for 40 years, under the leadership, direction, and guidance of the United States Public Health Service there had been a continuing study of the effect of untreated syphilis in approximately 400 black males in Alabama. There was no evidence that consent for participation had ever been obtained.

Of overriding influence as far as behavior research is concerned, was Stanley Milgram's study of obedience (Milgram, 1963). Central to the startling results achieved was the deception, by the experimenter, of the subjects involved. To briefly recount the design, subjects were told that they would be taking part in a learning experiment. Each subject was assigned to a group of four people, three of whom, unknown to the subject, were Milgram's assistants. One of the assistants was the "learner" in the pseudoexperiment. The subject was to play the role of "teacher" whose function it was to instruct the learner by administering an electric shock when the learner made an error in the memory task. The naive subject was put at a control panel that regulated the shock from mild to extremely intense and painful. The teacher was told to deliver the painful stimulus whenever the learner erred. In reality, no electricity was hooked up to the panel and no learning took place. The subject was deceived concerning the purpose of the experiment. Learners deliberately made mistakes and pretended to feel pain so that the real investigators could determine to what levels subjects would raise the amount of electricity. When subjects hesitated they were urged to continue. Sixty-two percent of over 1000 subjects obeyed the experimenter's commands fully, raising the intensity level of the painful stimulus to the highest point possible. The experiment achieved notoriety not only because of the results obtained but because of the reactions of the deceived subjects. They expressed shame, revulsion, anxiety, and extreme tension during and after the experiment.

The ethics of conducting the research in the first place was soon debated in the psychological literature (Baumrind, 1964; Milgram, 1964) and eventually led to a reconsideration of the American Psychological Association (APA) Code of Ethics regarding research. That examination stimulated the drafting of a lengthy and separate reformulation of ethical principles concerning research with human beings (APA, 1973). In turn, these principles led to a vigorous discussion in print regarding the efficacy of the newly established Code (Baumrind, 1971; Berscheid, Baron, Dermer, and Libman, 1973; Gergan, 1973; Kelman, 1972; Kerlinger, 1972; Menges, 1973; Resnick and Schwartz, 1973; Waterman, 1974). Whatever the debatable points, the APA—the major organization representing behavioral scientists—had at least established minimal ethical guidelines for the design and implementation of research. Soon it would be the turn of the courts and the government to do the same. . . .

THE STATUTORY RESPONSE: THE FEDERAL GOVERNMENT SPEAKS

. . .

In mid 1974 the U.S. Department of Health, Education and Welfare (DHEW) published regulations regarding the protection of human subjects. These regulations govern the activities of those organizations who receive research funds or are accountable to DHEW. First published in the Federal Register (39 Federal Register 18917, May 30, 1974) and now codified as Federal regulations (45 CFR 46), the rules explicitly declare the Department's policy that "no activity involving human subjects to be supported by DHEW grants or contracts shall be undertaken unless a committee of the organization has reviewed and approved such activity and the organization has submitted to DHEW a certification of such review and approval . . ." (45 CFR 46.102(a)). These institutional review boards are to make four major determinations.

1. Whether the risks to the subject are outweighed by both the benefit to the individual and the importance of the knowledge to be gained so as to warrant a decision to allow the subject to accept these risks.
2. Whether the rights and welfare of these persons—called "subjects at risk"—will be adequately protected.
3. Whether legally effective informed consent can be obtained by appropriate and adequate methods.
4. Whether the design calls for periodic review of the research.

Two definitions made part of the regulations are pertinent here. One is the meaning of "subject at risk." The term includes

> [A]ny individual who may be exposed to the possibility of injury including physical, psychological, or social injury, as a consequence of participation as a subject in any research, development or related activity which departs from the application of those established and accepted methods necessary to meet his needs, or which increases the ordinary risks of daily life (45 CFR 46.103(b)).

The other definition is the Department's attempt to conceptualize informed consent. Broadly defined, it is conceived as the "knowing consent of an individual or his legally authorized representative so situated as to be able to exercise free power of choice without undue inducement or any element of force, fraud, deceit, duress, or other form of constraint or coercion" (45 CFR 46.103(c)). More specifically, the elements comprising consent include:

- Fair explanation of the procedures to be followed, and their purposes, including identification of any procedures that are experimental.
- Description of any attendant discomforts and risks reasonably to be expected.
- Description of any benefits reasonably to be expected.
- Disclosure of any appropriate alternative procedures that might be advantageous to the subject.
- An offer to answer any inquiries concerning the procedure.
- An instruction that the person is free to withdraw consent and to discontinue participating in the project or activity without prejudice to the subject.

Finally, the regulations prohibit the dissemination of personally identifiable information obtained through research without consent of the subjects or their legally authorized representative (45 CFR 46.119(b)).

Soon after DHEW published these regulations, Congress passed the National Research Act (Pub. L. 93-348, 88 Stat. 342), Title II of which is called "Protection of Human Subjects of Biomedical and Behavioral Research." Its primary purpose was to establish a National Commission whose major task is to identify basic ethical principles that underlie the conduct of human research. . . .

In developing ethical principles, the Commission is charged with considering ways in which it can be determined if human subjects are needed for planned research, constructing guidelines for the selection of human subjects, and arriving at a definition of informed consent. Another significant aspect of its work is to identify the requirements of informed consent for those persons whose capacity for giving consent is either absent or limited. In this category fall prisoners, institutionalized mental patients, and children. To accomplish this task the Commission is to consider the adequacy of information given to such persons about the research, the risks, discomforts, and anticipated benefits from the research, as well as the competence and freedom of

such people to make a choice for or against their involvement.

The concern for "limited capacity" populations was apparently stimulated by a recent decision that held that involuntarily detained mental patients could not give informed and adequate consent to experimental psychosurgery (*Kaimowitz v. Dep't of Mental Health* (1973)). . . . The invalidity of consent was predicated on the inherently coercive atmosphere of an institutional setting where release may depend on cooperation with those suggesting surgery as an alternative to indefinite confinement. The court assumed that the absence of meaningful choice on the part of one who has little bargaining power could vitiate any consent given by one in that position. [1977, *Federal Register*, 42, 26318–26326]

The Commission in its recommendations to the Secretary of DHEW has rejected the rationale of the *Kaimowitz* court. It agreed that institutionalization may lessen the ability of prisoners and mental patients to make uncoerced choices, but asserted that the diminished capacity to consent should not absolutely exclude involuntarily confined persons from the opportunity to benefit from new therapies if those interventions are their best or only hope for recovery from disabling disorders.

The Commission focused on the nature of the institution in which research might be conducted. Although prisons and hospitals may have potential for limiting the capacity of their residents to make "free" choices, the Commission believed it was possible to specify the necessary conditions under which research in closed institutions might continue to be supported by the federal government. With regard to prisons, for example, . . . it recommended that research concerning the possible causes, effects, and processes of incarceration and studies of prisons themselves could be supported provided that they presented no more than minimal risk or inconvenience to the subjects, that the research was performed by competent persons, and that the proposed study was approved by the Institutional Review Boards required by DHEW. With the same proviso, the Commission also agreed that research on innovative and accepted practices that had the intent and reasonable probability of improving the well-being of the individual prisoner might be conducted. Any other research—primarily that which would not have the goal of benefiting the individual prisoner—could only be conducted if the planned research filled an important social and scientific need, if the reasons for involving prisoners (in contrast to "free living" subjects) was compelling, and if there was a high degree of voluntariness on the part of prospective participants and openness on the part of the institution. Criteria of openness would include adequate living conditions, opportunity to effectively redress grievances, separation of research participation from parole considerations, and willingness of the prison to bear public scrutiny.

Thus, the Commission focused on standards of conduct for institutional authorities rather than on the capacity of the potential subject. As an alternative to forbidding all research in closed settings, it recommended research participation by inmates where there is evidence that a relatively free choice is probable. The consequence is at once to respect the autonomy of the individual as well as to stimulate positive change in living conditions in previously coercive institutions. The recommendations are, of course, not perfect. They may be considered paternalistic and protectionistic insofar as the prisoner is only allowed a choice when the institution meets the requirements of openness and voluntariness or when the research has substantial promise of benefit to the subject.

The situation regarding consent becomes even more complex when the potential subjects are children or those involuntarily committed to mental institutions. Unlike prisoners, these populations are not always presumed competent to make decisions. Substitute or proxy consent by a parent or legally appointed representative has been the traditional solution but there are those—including some members of the Commission, its staff, and its consultants—who feel that the use of third persons to consent for others is a basic denial of human dignity. It is this fundamental question of whether, or under what conditions, selected others may consent or refuse to consent to participation in research with which the National Commission for the Protection of Human Subjects is now grappling. . . .

This thicket of regulations, guidelines, codes, and statutes is no doubt confusing. . . . [T]he plethora of rules illustrates the progression from ethical standards, binding on only those researchers who belong to professional organizations but with little legal significance, to judicial decisions, binding on only the litigants involved, to statutes and regulations, binding on all those contemplated by the laws. Already, 90 percent of human medical research is sponsored by the federal government and for many who plan, conduct, or participate in research, ethical constraints are now legal mandates. . . .

References

American Psychological Association. *Ethical principles in the conduct of research with human participants.* Washington, D.C.: Author, 1973.

Baumrind, D. Principles of ethical conduct in the treatment of subjects. *American Psychologist*, 1971, 26, 887–896.

Baumrind, D. Some thoughts on ethics of research—after reading Milgram's "Behavioral Study of Obedience." *American Psychologist*, 1964, 19, 421–423.

Berscheid, E., Baron, R. D., Dermer, M., and Libman, S. Anticipating informed consent: An empirical approach. *American Psychologist*, 1973, 28, 913–925.

Gergan, K. J. The codification of research ethics: Views of a doubting Thomas. *American Psychologist*, 1973, 28, 907–912.

Katz, J. *Experimentation with human beings.* New York: Russell Sage Foundation, 1972.

Kelman, H. C. The rights of the subject in social research: An analysis in terms of relative power and legitimacy. *American Psychologist*, 1972, 27, 989–1016.

Kerlinger, F. Draft report of the APA Committee on Ethical Standards in Psychological Research: A critical reaction. *American Psychologist*, 1972, 27, 894–896.

Menges, R. J. Openness and honesty versus coercion and deception in psychological research. *American Psychologist*, 1973, 28, 1030–1034.

Milgram, S. Issues in the study of obedience: A reply to Baumrind. *American Psychologist*, 1964, 19, 848–852.

Milgram, S. Behavioral study of obedience. *Journal of Abnormal and Social Psychology*, 1963, 67, 371–378.

Natanson v. Kline, 186 Kan. 393, 350 P.2d 1093 (1960).

Resnick, J. H. and Schwartz, T. Ethical standards as an independent variable in psychological research. *American Psychologist*, 1973, 28, 134–139.

Waltz, J. R. and Scheuneman, T. W. Informed consent to therapy. *Northwestern Law Review*, 1969, 64, 628–650.

Waterman, S. The civil liberties of the participants in psychological research. *American Psychologist*, 1974, *29*, 470–471.

Wilkinson v. Vesey, 110 R.I. 606, 295 A.2d 676 (1972).

◆　◆　◆

Commentary: *The National Commission for the Protection of Human Subjects has long since completed its work, and the federal regulations described in the preceding excerpt have been refined and recodified. For example, some research is now exempt from scrutiny by Institutional Review Boards (IRBs), whereas other research may undergo expedited review. Recommendations that the commission had made concerning prisoners have been revised and promulgated as regulations by the Department of Health and Human Services (DHHS), as were regulations for research with children. Interestingly, commission recommendations concerning research with people who have been institutionalized as mentally disabled have never been adopted by DHHS. Relevant parts of the regulations for research conducted or funded by DHHS with human participants generally and with prisoners and children specifically are included in the following pages.*

Policy for Protection of Human Research Subjects

U.S. Department of Health and Human Services

SUBPART A—BASIC HHS POLICY FOR PROTECTION OF HUMAN RESEARCH SUBJECTS

AUTHORITY: 5 U.S.C. 301; 42 U.S.C. 289, 42 U.S.C. 300v–1(b).

SOURCE: 56 FR 28012, 28022, June 18, 1991, unless otherwise noted.

§ 46.101 To What Does This Policy Apply?

(a) Except as provided in paragraph (b) of this section, this policy applies to all research involving human subjects conducted, supported or otherwise subject to regulation by any federal department or agency which takes appropriate administrative action to make the policy applicable to such research. . . .

(b) Unless otherwise required by department or agency heads, research activities in which the only involvement of human subjects will be in one or more of the following categories are exempt from this policy:

(1) Research conducted in established or commonly accepted educational settings, involving normal educational practices, such as (i) research on regular and special education instructional strategies, or (ii) research on the effectiveness of or the comparison among instructional techniques, curricula, or classroom management methods.

(2) Research involving the use of educational tests (cognitive, diagnostic, aptitude, achievement), survey procedures, interview procedures or observation of public behavior, unless:

(i) Information obtained is recorded in such a manner that human subjects can be identified, directly or through identifiers linked to the subjects; and (ii) any disclosure of the human subjects' responses outside the research could reasonably place the subjects at risk of criminal or civil liability or be damaging to the subjects' financial standing, employability, or reputation.

(3) Research involving the use of educational tests (cognitive, diagnostic, aptitude, achievement), survey procedures, interview procedures, or observation of public behavior that is not exempt under paragraph (b)(2) of this section, if:

(i) The human subjects are elected or appointed public officials or candidates for public office; or (ii) federal statute(s) require(s) without exception that the confidentiality of the personally identifiable information will be maintained throughout the research and thereafter.

(4) Research, involving the collection or study of existing data, documents, records, pathological specimens, or diagnostic specimens, if these sources are publicly available or if the information is recorded by the investigator in such a manner that subjects cannot be identified, directly or through identifiers linked to the subjects.

(5) Research and demonstration projects which are conducted by or subject to the approval of department or agency heads, and which are designed to study, evaluate, or otherwise examine:

(i) Public benefit or service programs; (ii) procedures for obtaining benefits or services under those programs; (iii) possible changes in or alternatives to those programs or procedures; or (iv) possible changes in methods or levels of payment for benefits or services under those programs. . . .

§ 46.107 IRB Membership.

(a) Each IRB shall have at least five members, with varying backgrounds to promote complete and adequate review of research activities commonly conducted by the institution. The IRB shall be sufficiently qualified through the experience and expertise of its members, and the diversity of the members, including considera-

Adapted from 45 C.F.R. Part 46. Basic H.H.S. Policy for Protection of Human Research Subjects.

tion of race, gender, and cultural backgrounds and sensitivity to such issues as community attitudes, to promote respect for its advice and counsel in safeguarding the rights and welfare of human subjects. In addition to possessing the professional competence necessary to review specific research activities, the IRB shall be able to ascertain the acceptability of proposed research in terms of institutional commitments and regulations, applicable law, and standards of professional conduct and practice. The IRB shall therefore include persons knowledgeable in these areas. If an IRB regularly reviews research that involves a vulnerable category of subjects, such as children, prisoners, pregnant women, or handicapped or mentally disabled persons, consideration shall be given to the inclusion of one or more individuals who are knowledgeable about and experienced in working with these subjects.

(b) Every nondiscriminatory effort will be made to ensure that no IRB consists entirely of men or entirely of women, including the institution's consideration of qualified persons of both sexes, so long as no selection is made to the IRB on the basis of gender. No IRB may consist entirely of members of one profession.

(c) Each IRB shall include at least one member whose primary concerns are in scientific areas and at least one member whose primary concerns are in nonscientific areas.

(d) Each IRB shall include at least one member who is not otherwise affiliated with the institution and who is not part of the immediate family of a person who is affiliated with the institution.

(e) No IRB may have a member participate in the IRB's initial or continuing review of any project in which the member has a conflicting interest, except to provide information requested by the IRB.

(f) An IRB may, in its discretion, invite individuals with competence in special areas to assist in the review of issues which require expertise beyond or in addition to that available on the IRB. These individuals may not vote with the IRB. . . .

§ 46.110 Expedited Review Procedures for Certain Kinds of Research Involving No More Than Minimal Risk, and for Minor Changes in Approved Research.

(a) The Secretary, HHS, has established, and published as a Notice in the FEDERAL REGISTER, a list of categories of research that may be reviewed by the IRB through an expedited review procedure. The list will be amended, as appropriate after consultation with other departments and agencies, through periodic republication by the Secretary, HHS, in the FEDERAL REGISTER. A copy of the list is available from the Office for Protection from Research Risks, National Institutes of Health, HHS, Bethesda, Maryland 20892.

(b) An IRB may use the expedited review procedure to review either or both of the following:

(1) Some or all of the research appearing on the list and found by the reviewer(s) to involve no more than minimal risk,

(2) Minor changes in previously approved research during the period (of one year or less) for which approval is authorized.

Under an expedited review procedure, the review may be carried out by the IRB chairperson or by one or more experienced reviewers designated by the chairperson from among members of the IRB. In reviewing the research, the reviewers may exercise all of the authorities of the IRB except that the reviewers may not disapprove the research. A research activity may be disapproved only after review in accordance with the non-expedited procedure set forth in § 46.108(b). . . .

§ 46.111 Criteria for IRB Approval of Research.

(a) In order to approve research covered by this policy the IRB shall determine that all of the following requirements are satisfied:

(1) Risks to subjects are minimized: (i) By using procedures which are consistent with sound research design and which do not unnecessarily expose subjects to risk, and (ii) whenever appropriate, by using procedures already being performed on the subjects for diagnostic or treatment purposes.

(2) Risks to subjects are reasonable in relation to anticipated benefits, if any, to subjects, and the importance of the knowledge that may reasonably be expected to result. In evaluating risks and benefits, the IRB should consider only those risks and benefits that may result from the research (as distinguished from risks and benefits of therapies subjects would receive even if not participating in the research). The

IRB should not consider possible long-range effects of applying knowledge gained in the research (for example, the possible effects of the research on public policy) as among those research risks that fall within the purview of its responsibility.

(3) Selection of subjects is equitable. In making this assessment the IRB should take into account the purposes of the research and the setting in which the research will be conducted and should be particularly cognizant of the special problems of research involving vulnerable populations, such as children, prisoners, pregnant women, mentally disabled persons, or economically or educationally disadvantaged persons.

(4) Informed consent will be sought from each prospective subject or the subject's legally authorized representative, in accordance with, and to the extent required by § 46.116.

(5) Informed consent will be appropriately documented, in accordance with, and to the extent required by § 46.117.

(6) When appropriate, the research plan makes adequate provision for monitoring the data collected to ensure the safety of subjects.

(7) When appropriate, there are adequate provisions to protect the privacy of subjects and to maintain the confidentiality of data.

(b) When some or all of the subjects are likely to be vulnerable to coercion or undue influence, such as children, prisoners, pregnant women, mentally disabled persons, or economically or educationally disadvantaged persons, additional safeguards have been included in the study to protect the rights and welfare of these subjects. . . .

§ 46.116 General Requirements for Informed Consent.

Except as provided elsewhere in this policy, no investigator may involve a human being as a subject in research covered by this policy unless the investigator has obtained the legally effective informed consent of the subject or the subject's legally authorized representative. An investigator shall seek such consent only under circumstances that provide the prospective subject or the representative sufficient opportunity to consider whether or not to participate and that minimize the possibility of coercion or undue influence. The information that is given to the subject or the representative shall be in language understandable to the subject or the representative. No informed consent, whether oral or written, may include any exculpatory language through which the subject or the representative is made to waive or appear to waive any of the subject's legal rights, or releases or appears to release the investigator, the sponsor, the institution or its agents from liability for negligence.

(a) Basic elements of informed consent. Except as provided in paragraph (c) or (d) of this section, in seeking informed consent the following information shall be provided to each subject:

(1) A statement that the study involves research, an explanation of the purposes of the research and the expected duration of the subject's participation, a description of the procedures to be followed, and identification of any procedures which are experimental;

(2) A description of any reasonably foreseeable risks or discomforts to the subject;

(3) A description of any benefits to the subject or to others which may reasonably be expected from the research;

(4) A disclosure of appropriate alternative procedures or courses of treatment, if any, that might be advantageous to the subject;

(5) A statement describing the extent, if any, to which confidentiality of records identifying the subject will be maintained;

(6) For research involving more than minimal risk, an explanation as to whether any compensation and an explanation as to whether any medical treatment are available if injury occurs and, if so, what they consist of, or where further information may be obtained;

(7) An explanation of whom to contact for answers to pertinent questions about the research and research subjects' rights, and whom to contact in the

event of a research-related injury to the subject; and

(8) A statement that participation is voluntary, refusal to participate will involve no penalty or loss of benefits to which the subject is otherwise entitled, and the subject may discontinue participation at any time without penalty or loss of benefits to which the subject is otherwise entitled.

(b) Additional elements of informed consent. When appropriate, one or more of the following elements of information shall also be provided to each subject:

(1) A statement that the particular treatment or procedure may involve risks to the subject (or to the embryo or fetus, if the subject is or may become pregnant) which are currently unforeseeable;

(2) Anticipated circumstances under which the subject's participation may be terminated by the investigator without regard to the subject's consent;

(3) Any additional costs to the subject that may result from participation in the research;

(4) The consequences of a subject's decision to withdraw from the research and procedures for orderly termination of participation by the subject;

(5) A statement that significant new findings developed during the course of the research which may relate to the subject's willingness to continue participation will be provided to the subject; and

(6) The approximate number of subjects involved in the study.

(c) An IRB may approve a consent procedure which does not include, or which alters, some or all of the elements of informed consent set forth above, or waive the requirement to obtain informed consent provided the IRB finds and documents that:

(1) The research or demonstration project is to be conducted by or subject to the approval of state or local government officials and is designed to study, evalu-

ate, or otherwise examine: (i) Public benefit or service programs; (ii) procedures for obtaining benefits or services under those programs; (iii) possible changes in or alternatives to those programs or procedures; or (iv) possible changes in methods or levels of payment for benefits or services under those programs; and

(2) The research could not practicably be carried out without the waiver or alteration.

(d) An IRB may approve a consent procedure which does not include, or which alters, some or all of the elements of informed consent set forth in this section, or waive the requirements to obtain informed consent provided the IRB finds and documents that:

(1) The research involves no more than minimal risk to the subjects;

(2) The waiver or alteration will not adversely affect the rights and welfare of the subjects;

(3) The research could not practicably be carried out without the waiver or alteration; and

(4) Whenever appropriate, the subjects will be provided with additional pertinent information after participation.

(e) The informed consent requirements in this policy are not intended to preempt any applicable federal, state, or local laws which require additional information to be disclosed in order for informed consent to be legally effective.

(f) Nothing in this policy is intended to limit the authority of a physician to provide emergency medical care, to the extent the physician is permitted to do so under applicable federal, state, or local law. . . .

SUBPART C—ADDITIONAL PROTECTIONS PERTAINING TO BIOMEDICAL AND BEHAVIORAL RESEARCH INVOLVING PRISONERS AS SUBJECTS

SOURCE: 43 FR 53655, Nov. 16, 1978, unless otherwise noted.

. . .

§ 46.302 Purpose.

Inasmuch as prisoners may be under constraints because of their incarceration which could affect their ability to make a truly voluntary and uncoerced decision whether or not to participate as subjects in research, it is the purpose of this subpart to provide additional safeguards for the protection of prisoners involved in activities to which this subpart is applicable. . . .

§ 46.304 Composition of Institutional Review Boards Where Prisoners Are Involved.

In addition to satisfying the requirements in § 46.107 of this part, an Institutional Review Board, carrying out responsibilities under this part with respect to research covered by this subpart, shall also meet the following specific requirements:

(a) A majority of the Board (exclusive of prisoner members) shall have no association with the prison(s) involved, apart from their membership on the Board.

(b) At least one member of the Board shall be a prisoner, or a prisoner representative with appropriate background and experience to serve in that capacity, except that where a particular research project is reviewed by more than one Board only one Board need satisfy this requirement.

[43 FR 53655, Nov. 16, 1978, as amended at 46 FR 8386, Jan. 26, 1981]

§ 46.305 Additional Duties of the Institutional Review Boards Where Prisoners Are Involved.

(a) In addition to all other responsibilities prescribed for Institutional Review Boards under this part, the Board shall review research covered by this subpart and approve such research only if it finds that:

(1) The research under review represents one of the categories of research permissible under § 46.306(a)(2);

(2) Any possible advantages accruing to the prisoner through his or her participation in the research, when compared to the general living conditions, medical care, quality of food, amenities and opportunity for earnings in the prison, are not of such a magnitude that his or her ability to weigh the risks of the research against the value of such advantages in the limited choice environment of the prison is impaired;

(3) The risks involved in the research are commensurate with risks that would be accepted by nonprisoner volunteers;

(4) Procedures for the selection of subjects within the prison are fair to all prisoners and immune from arbitrary intervention by prison authorities or prisoners. Unless the principal investigator provides to the Board justification in writing for following some other procedures, control subjects must be selected randomly from the group of available prisoners who meet the characteristics needed for that particular research project.

(5) The information is presented in language which is understandable to the subject population; [and]

(6) Adequate assurance exists that parole boards will not take into account a prisoner's participation in the research in making decisions regarding parole, and each prisoner is clearly informed in advance that participation in the research will have no effect on his or her parole[.] . . .

§ 46.306 Permitted Research Involving Prisoners.

(a) Biomedical or behavioral research conducted or supported by DHHS may involve prisoners as subjects only if:

(1) The institution responsible for the conduct of the research has certified to the Secretary that the Institutional Review Board has approved the research under § 46.305 of this subpart; and

(2) In the judgment of the Secretary the proposed research involves solely the following:

(i) Study of the possible causes, effects, and processes of incarceration, and of criminal behavior, provided that the study presents no more than minimal risk and no more than inconvenience to the subjects;

(ii) Study of prisons as institutional structures or of prisoners as incarcerated persons, provided that the study presents no more than minimal risk and no more than inconvenience to the subjects;

(iii) Research on conditions particularly affecting prisoners as a class (for example, vaccine trials and other research on hepatitis which is much more prevalent in prisons than elsewhere; and research on social and psychological problems such as alcoholism, drug addiction and sexual assaults) provided that the study may proceed only after the Secretary has consulted with appropriate experts including experts in penology medicine and ethics, and published notice, in the FEDERAL REGISTER, of his intent to approve such research; or

(iv) Research on practices, both innovative and accepted, which have the intent and reasonable probability of improving the health or well-being of the subject. In cases in which those studies require the assignment of prisoners in a manner consistent with protocols approved by the IRB to control groups which may not benefit from the research, the study may proceed only after the Secretary has consulted with appropriate experts, including experts in penology medicine and ethics, and published notice, in the FEDERAL REGISTER, of his intent to approve such research.

(b) Except as provided in paragraph (a) of this section, biomedical or behavioral research conducted or supported by DHHS shall not involve prisoners as subjects.

SUBPART D—ADDITIONAL PROTECTIONS FOR CHILDREN INVOLVED AS SUBJECTS IN RESEARCH

SOURCE: 48 FR 9818, Mar. 8, 1983, unless otherwise noted.

. . .

§ 46.402 Definitions.

The definitions in § 46.102 of Subpart A shall be applicable to this subpart as well. In addition, as used in this subpart:

(a) *Children* are persons who have not attained the legal age for consent to treatments or procedures involved in the research, under the applicable law of the jurisdiction in which the research will be conducted.

(b) *Assent* means a child's affirmative agreement to participate in research. Mere failure to object should not, absent affirmative agreement, be construed as assent.

(c) *Permission* means the agreement of parent(s) or guardian to the participation of their child or ward in research.

(d) *Parent* means a child's biological or adoptive parent.

(e) *Guardian* means an individual who is authorized under applicable State or local law to consent on behalf of a child to general medical care.

§ 46.403 IRB Duties.

In addition to other responsibilities assigned to IRBs under this part, each IRB shall review research covered by this subpart and approve only research which satisfies the conditions of all applicable sections of this subpart.

§ 46.404 Research Not Involving Greater Than Minimal Risk.

HHS will conduct or fund research in which the IRB finds that no greater than minimal risk to children is presented, only if the IRB finds that adequate provisions are made for soliciting the assent of the children and the permission of their parents or guardians, as set forth in § 46.408.

§ 46.405 Research Involving Greater Than Minimal Risk but Presenting the Prospect of Direct Benefit to the Individual Subjects.

HHS will conduct or fund research in which the IRB finds that more than minimal risk to children is presented by an intervention or procedure that holds out the prospect of direct benefit for the individual subject, or by a monitoring procedure that is likely to contribute to the subject's well-being, only if the IRB finds that:

(a) The risk is justified by the anticipated benefit to the subjects;

(b) The relation of the anticipated benefit to the risk is at least as favorable to the subjects as that presented by available alternative approaches; and

(c) Adequate provisions are made for soliciting the assent of the children and permission of their parents or guardians, as set forth in § 46.408.

§ 46.406 Research Involving Greater Than Minimal Risk and No Prospect of Direct Benefit to Individual Subjects, but Likely to Yield Generalizable Knowledge About the Subject's Disorder or Condition.

HHS will conduct or fund research in which the IRB finds that more than minimal risk to children is presented by an intervention or procedure that does not hold out the prospect of direct benefit for the individual subject, or by a monitoring procedure which is not likely to contribute to the well-being of the subject, only if the IRB finds that:

(a) The risk represents a minor increase over minimal risk;

(b) The intervention or procedure presents experiences to subjects that are reasonably commensurate with those inherent in their actual or expected medical, dental, psychological, social, or educational situations;

(c) The intervention or procedure is likely to yield generalizable knowledge about the subjects' disorder or condition which is of vital importance for the understanding or amelioration of the subjects' disorder or condition; and

(d) Adequate provisions are made for soliciting assent of the children and permission of their parents or guardians, as set forth in § 46.408.

§ 46.407 Research Not Otherwise Approvable Which Presents an Opportunity to Understand, Prevent, or Alleviate a Serious Problem Affecting the Health or Welfare of Children.

HHS will conduct or fund research that the IRB does not believe meets the requirements of § 16.101, § 46.405, or § 46.406 only if:

(a) The IRB finds that the research presents a reasonable opportunity to further the understanding, prevention, or alleviation of a serious problem affecting the health or welfare of children; and

(b) The Secretary, after consultation with a panel of experts in pertinent disciplines (for example: science, medicine, education, ethics, law) and following opportunity for public review and comment, has determined either:

(1) That the research in fact satisfies the conditions of § 46.404, § 46.405, or § 46.406, as applicable, or

(2) The following:

(i) The research presents a reasonable opportunity to further the understanding, prevention, or alleviation of a serious problem affecting the health or welfare of children;

(ii) The research will be conducted in accordance with sound ethical principles;

(iii) Adequate provisions are made for soliciting the assent of children and the permission of their parents or guardians, as set forth in § 46.408.

§ 46.408 Requirements for Permission by Parents or Guardians and for Assent by Children.

(a) In addition to the determinations required under other applicable sections of this subpart, the IRB shall determine that adequate provisions are made for soliciting the assent of the children, when in the judgment of the IRB the children are capable of providing assent. In determining whether children are capable of assenting, the IRB shall take into account the ages, maturity, and psychological state of the children involved. This judgment may be made for all children to be involved in research under a particular protocol, or for each child, as the IRB deems appropriate. If the IRB determines that the capability of some or all of the children is so limited that they cannot reasonably be consulted or that the intervention or procedure involved in the research holds out a prospect of direct benefit that is important to the health or well-being of the children and is available only in the context of the research, the assent of the children is not a necessary condition for proceeding with the research. Even where the IRB determines that the subjects are capable of assenting, the IRB may still waive the assent requirement under circumstances in which consent may be waived in accord with § 46.116 of Subpart A.

(b) In addition to the determinations required under other applicable sections of this subpart, the IRB shall determine, in accordance with and to the extent that consent is required by § 46.116 of Subpart A, that adequate provisions are made for soliciting the permission of each child's parents or guardian. Where parental permission is to be obtained, the IRB may find that the permission of one parent is sufficient for research to be conducted under § 46.404 or § 46.405. Where research is covered by §§ 46.406 and 46.407 and permission is to be obtained from parents, both parents must give their permission unless one parent is deceased; unknown, incompetent, or not reasonably available, or when only one parent has legal responsibility for the care and custody of the child.

(c) In addition to the provisions for waiver contained in § 46.116 of Subpart A, if the IRB determines that a research protocol is designed for conditions or for a subject population for which parental or guardian permission is not a reasonable requirement to protect the subjects (for example, neglected or abused children), it may waive the consent requirements in Subpart A of this part and paragraph (b) of this section, provided an appropriate mechanism for protecting the children who will participate as subjects in the research is substituted, and provided further that the waiver is not inconsistent with Federal, state or local law. The choice of an appropriate mechanism would depend upon the nature and purpose of the activities described in the protocol, the risk and anticipated benefit to the research subjects, and their age, maturity, status, and condition.

(d) Permission by parents or guardians shall be documented in accordance with and to the extent required by § 46.117 of Subpart A.

(e) When the IRB determines that assent is required, it shall also determine whether and how assent must be documented.

§ 46.409 Wards.

(a) Children who are wards of the state or any other agency, institution, or entity can be included in research approved under § 46.406 or § 46.407 only if such research is:

(1) Related to their status as wards; or

(2) Conducted in schools, camps, hospitals, institutions, or similar settings in which the majority of children involved as subjects are not wards.

(b) If the research is approved under paragraph (a) of this section, the IRB shall require appointment of an advocate for each child who is a ward, in addition to any other individual acting on behalf of the child as guardian or in loco parentis. One individual may serve as advocate for more than one child. The advocate shall be an individual who has the background and experience to act in, and agrees to act in, the best interests of the child for the duration of the child's participation in the research and who is not associated in any way (except in the role as advocate or member of the IRB) with the research, the investigator(s), or the guardian organization. . . .

◆ ◆ ◆

Commentary: *As the regulations show, IRBs wield significant power in determining whether biomedical and behavioral research will be approved. Although only research conducted or funded by the federal government must receive IRB review, almost all proposed institutional research now undergoes such review. Some critics have alleged that IRB members are overly cautious and are guided more by personal and sociocultural values than by valid assessments of methodological rigor, risk to participants, and benefit to society. For example, in a provocative study, Ceci, Peters, and Plotkin (1985) found that, when asked to review hypothetical research proposals identical in their proposed treatment of human participants but differing in their sociopolitical sensitivity, IRBs were twice as likely to reject the socially sensitive proposals. Nonsensitive proposals that did not include ethical problems (such as deception or the absence of debriefing) were approved 95% of the time, but comparable, sensitive ones were approved only 40%–50% of the time. On the other hand, researchers asked to judge pairs of deliberately flawed experiments that were identical except for the importance of their subject matter were significantly more likely to overlook methodological problems and to recommend publication when they perceived the topic to be important. Thus, although regulations regarding the protection of human subjects specifically instruct IRBs not to consider the public policy effects of research, these studies show that, in fact, review boards do consider the sociopolitical consequences of the proposed research. See*

Ceci, S. J., Peters, D., & Plotkin, J. (1985). Human subjects review, personal values, and the regulation of social science research. American Psychologist, 40, 994–1002.

Wilson, T. D., DePaulo, B. M., Mook, D. G., & Klaaren, K. J. (1993). Scientists' evaluations of research: The biasing effects of the importance of the topic. Psychological Science, 4, 322–325.

Sieber and Stanley (1988) have provided a useful 4 × 10 matrix for identifying the ethical and professional dimensions of socially sensitive research. They saw four major aspects of scientific activity that engender ethical concerns: (a) formulation of the research question, (b) conduct of research and treatment of research participants, (c) institutional setting in which the research is conducted, and (d) interpretation and application of the findings. They then identified 10 ethical issues in socially sensitive research that may arise in these four areas: (a) the person's interest in controlling boundaries between the self and researcher (privacy), (b) confidentiality and control of data, (c) sound and valid methodology and design, (d) deception, (e) informed consent, (f) justice and equitable treatment (e.g., withholding experimental treatment from one group), (g) scientific freedom, (h) ownership of data, (i) humanistic versus scientific values, and (j) risk–benefit ratio. How would you apply this matrix to a pending decision about whether or not to conduct research on racial differences in intelligence or the patterns of the transmission of AIDS? See Sieber, J. E., & Stanley, B. (1988). Ethical and professional dimensions of socially sensitive research. American Psychologist, 43, 49–55.

As is the case with AIDS, research that may both benefit society by promoting human welfare and aid public health efforts to control disease may conflict with research participants' right to privacy. For example, as Melton and Gray (1988) have explained,

> disclosure of participants' status, even if simply as members of a risk group, may result in their being subjected to social stigma and legal sanctions (e.g., quarantine; punishment for engaging in prohibited risky behavior). Thus, participants may have a clear interest in avoiding participation and, if they choose to participate, preventing disclosures of data to third parties.
>
> At the same time, participants, particularly if they are patients themselves or members of risk groups, have a profound interest in promotion of research on the illness in question. They even have an interest in retention of identifiable data when it might be used for longitudinal research or sharing of data sets crucial to understanding the process of the disease. (p. 60)

Melton, G. B., & Gray, J. N. (1988). Ethical dilemmas in AIDS research: Individual privacy and public health. American Psychologist, 43, 60–64.

The disclosure of certain sensitive and confidential data gleaned from participants in government-funded mental health research may now be protected by obtaining a Confidentiality Certificate from the Department of Health and Human Services. See

42 C.F.R. Part 2a (Protection of Identity—Research Subjects).

Nelson, R. L., & Hetrick, T. E. (1983). The statutory protection of confidential research data: Synthesis and evaluation. In R. Boruch & J. Cecil (Eds.), Solutions to ethical and legal problems in social research (pp. 213–236). San Diego, CA: Academic Press.

Reatig, N. (1979). Confidentiality certificates: A measure of privacy protection. Institutional Review Board, 1(3), 1–4, 12.

For a recent, informative, and extended debate concerning the ethical conflict between protecting the confidentiality of research data generally and the tradition of open sharing in science, see the articles presented in the Adversary Forum of the June 1988 issue (Vol. 12) of Law and Human Behavior (pp. 159–206) and those in the Forum section of Ethics and Behavior (Vol. 3, pp. 311–317). The relevant standard in the APA's 1992 Ethical Principles is 6.25 (Sharing Data).

Standards 6.06–6.26 of the Ethical Principles are not the only guidelines that psychologists can consult concerning research. As the first two articles in this chapter cited, APA has produced the Ethical Principles in the Conduct of Research With Human Participants. These principles were first published in 1973 and were revised and republished in 1982. They are undergoing review, and a new edition should appear in late 1995.

When the 1973 edition of Research With Human Participants was being drafted, Gergen (1973) argued that "until we can provide scientific answers to questions about deception, coercion, informed consent, and so on, strong APA policies seem unwarranted" (p. 908). See Gergen, K. J. (1973). The codification of research ethics: Views of a doubting Thomas. American Psychologist, 28, 907–912. Since then, researchers have been attempting to answer these questions. And this research continues.

Informed Consent for Psychological Research: Do Subjects Comprehend Consent Forms and Understand Their Legal Rights?

Traci Mann

. . .

According to the American Psychological Association (1992), psychologists must "inform participants of the nature of the research; they [must] inform participants that they are free to participate or to decline to participate or to withdraw from the research; they [must] explain the foreseeable consequences of declining or withdrawing; they [must] inform participants of significant factors that may be expected to influence their willingness to participate" (p. 1608). Research subjects have to understand this information to make an informed decision about whether they wish to participate in an experiment. Research is needed on the critical question of whether subjects in psychology experiments understand the information on consent forms.

Even though it is unknown whether subjects comprehend consent forms, researchers continue to add more information to them. In an analysis of consent form readability, Baker and Taub (1983) found that the average length of consent forms for research in Veterans Administration hospitals doubled over the 7-year time span from 1975 to 1982. They concluded that consent forms increased in length in order to include more information about subjects' rights in accordance with federal guidelines. It is unclear, however, if these statements about rights, liability, and confidentiality are understood by research participants. Indeed, the quasi-legal language may cause research subjects to think they have signed a legal document designed to protect researchers.

This experiment compared psychology subjects' comprehension of two consent forms matched for readability level—a long, detailed form and a shorter, less detailed one. In addition, we looked specifically at the effectiveness of consent forms in conveying to subjects their legal rights by comparing subjects who had signed a consent form with subjects who had read an information sheet, but who had not signed a consent form. . . .

The data support three main conclusions. First, longer consent forms that attempt to describe a procedure fully may be comprehended less well than shorter forms that suppress some relevant details. Accordingly, federal regulations that require information to be added to already lengthy consent forms may end up reducing the amount of information subjects receive from consent forms. If a subject is to understand a consent form, the form should be as short and concise as possible.

Second, the 53 subjects who signed consent forms for an MRI scan did so without understanding important aspects of the experiment. Subjects answered only 60% of the specific questions correctly. These questions covered information crucial for deciding whether or not to participate in an experiment (e.g., risks, benefits, procedures). Because a consent is not considered valid unless the information on the consent form is understood (Beauchamp & Childress, 1989), subjects in this experiment did not give a valid consent.

In addition, subjects answered correctly only 50% of the general questions (which covered information they had presumably been exposed to in other experiments). Less than half of the subjects understood what the researchers would do for them if they got hurt, or could list even two of the four things their signature on the consent form meant. Only 39% of the subjects knew that the consent form included any information on what to do if one had complaints about an experiment, and only 1 of the 53 subjects was able to state the procedure for registering complaints about experiments. This last problem is particularly serious because institutional review boards (IRBs) use feedback from subjects to determine whether an experiment can be continued safely. If no subjects complain when they are upset or hurt in experiments, IRBs may be led to believe that there are no problems, even when problems exist.

The third conclusion supported by the data is that the very act of signing a consent form caused subjects to believe that they had lost the right to sue the researcher, even for negligence [footnote omitted]. Subjects who signed a consent form thought they had lost their right to sue the experimenter, whereas subjects who read the same information but did not sign a consent form generally did not think they had lost this right.

According to the U.S. Department of Health and Human Services (1983), "No informed consent, whether oral or written, may include any exculpatory language through which the subject is made to waive or appear to waive any of the subject's legal rights, or releases or appears to release the investigator, the sponsor, the institution, or its agents from liability for negligence" (5 CFR §46.115). The consent forms used in this study were not in violation of this code. They stated explicitly that subjects who signed the forms were not giving up any rights to sue. Despite this explicit statement on the consent forms, subjects thought they had given up their right to sue. To rectify this problem will require more than a statement about rights on a consent form.

This research suggests an argument for the use of oral consent procedures. Simply signing a consent form made subjects think they had lost the very rights the consent form was designed to protect. Perhaps subjects who consent orally but do not sign a legalistic form will not feel that they have lost their rights. Perhaps subjects simply need to be reminded

after signing a consent form that they have not given up any rights by signing it, but have merely consented to go ahead with the research. Future research will examine whether oral procedures and reminders are effective ways to overcome problems in informed consent.

References

American Psychological Association. (1992). Ethical principles of psychologists and code of conduct. *American Psychologist, 47,* 1597–1611.

Baker, M. T., & Taub, H. A. (1983). Readability of informed consent forms for research in a Veterans Administration medical center. *Journal of the American Medical Association, 250,* 2646–2648.

Beauchamp, T. L., & Childress, J. F. (1989). *Principles of biomedical ethics.* New York: Oxford University Press.

U.S. Department of Health and Human Services. (1983). Protection of human subjects. *Code of Federal Regulations, 45,* §46.115.

◆ ◆ ◆

Commentary: Mann asserted that consent is not valid unless the participant understands the information in the consent form. Is it the researcher's ethical obligation to ensure that participants comprehend what the form says, or is the obligation simply limited to a duty to disclose the information? What position does Standard 6.11 of the APA's (1992) Ethical Principles take?

One of the most controversial topics in research is the use of deception, which inevitably requires researchers to dilute, if not completely dispense with, the requirement for informed consent from participants. In many areas of psychology, disclosing to subjects the purposes and procedures of the study would significantly alter the data. Thus, researchers may disguise or misrepresent the nature of the experiment or, in some cases, may not even inform participants that they are the subjects of research. These practices have been both pilloried and justified, but "it is clear that over time deception has become normative practice for research in social psychology" (Adair, Dushenko, & Lindsay, 1985, p. 63). In fact, Adair et al. found that, for the studies they examined, researchers rarely reported on matters related to ethics, including informed consent and their attempts to debrief participants about the real purposes of the experiment after it was concluded. But they agreed with others that psychological research ... [should] be guided by neither methodological imperialism, in which the dignity and safety of the subject are disregarded in the interests of science, nor an ethical imperialism, in which research progress is thwarted at every turn by an obsession with individual rights. (p. 70)

See Adair, J. G., Dushenko, T. W., & Lindsay, R. C. L. (1985). *Ethical regulations and their impact on research practice*. American Psychologist, 40, 59–72.

Yet, Diana Baumrind (1985), perhaps the major critic of this position, has adamantly argued that "the use of intentional deception in the research setting is unethical, imprudent, and unwarranted scientifically" (p. 165) and that "effective debriefing does not nullify the wrong done participants ... and may not even repair their damaged self-image or ability to trust adult authorities" (p. 172). See Baumrind, D. (1985). *Research using intentional deception: Ethical issues revisited*. American Psychologist, 40, 165–174. An excellent recent article on this topic follows.

Participant Partners: College Students Weigh the Costs and Benefits of Deceptive Research

Celia B. Fisher and Denise Fyrberg

Since Milgram (1963) published his well-known obedience experiments, the use of deception in psychological research has gained popularity and drawn ethical debate. Surveys of the social psychology literature indicate that the proportion of studies using deceptive methodologies increased from 36.8% in 1963 to 47% in 1983 (Adair, Dushenko, & Lindsay, 1985; Gross & Fleming, 1982; Menges, 1973; Seeman, 1969). On the basis of these trends, some have argued that deception has become normative practice for research in social psychology (Adair et al., 1985). Debate regarding the ethical and moral issues surrounding deception has remained similarly unabated over the past three decades (Baumrind, 1964, 1985, 1990; Bok, 1978; Goldstein, 1981; Kelman, 1967; Milgram, 1964; Sieber, 1982, 1983a; M. B. Smith, 1976). Ethical arguments have focused on whether deceptive research practices are justified on the basis of their potential societal benefit or violate moral principles of beneficence and respect for individuals and the fiduciary obligations of psychologists to research participants.

According to the American Psychological Association's (APA's) *Ethical Principles of Psychologists and Code of Conduct* (hereinafter, *Ethical Principles*), investigators considering the use of deceptive methodologies have special ethical responsibility to determine (a) that the deceptive techniques are justified by the study's prospective scientific, educational, or applied value and whether equally effective alternative procedures are feasible; (b) whether significant aspects of the research, if known to the participants, would affect their willingness to participate; and (c) that participants are ensured sufficient explanation as soon as possible (APA, 1992, Standards 6.15a, 6.15b, 6.15c). The APA guidelines, therefore, while recognizing that deceptive research practices require special ethical concerns, leave the evaluation of a study's ethical acceptability to the judgment of the individual psychologist about how best to contribute to scientific knowledge and protect human welfare. When an ethical issue is unclear, researchers are encouraged "to resolve the issue through consultation with institutional review boards . . . peer consultations, or other proper mechanisms" (APA, 1992, Standard 6.06c).

In practice, the ethical advice that researchers receive is obtained informally from colleagues and formally through institutional review board (IRB) approval or disapproval of research proposals. Equally important but relatively untapped resources for ethical advice are members of the population who will serve as research participants (Bok, 1978; Gergen, 1973; Loo, 1982; Wilson & Donnerstein, 1976). Although there have been a fair number of empirical studies evaluating participant reactions to deception following debriefing (e.g., Milgram, 1964; Ross, Lepper, & Hubbard, 1975; S. S. Smith & Richardson, 1983), there is a paucity of data on how members of a participant population prospectively evaluate the ethical acceptability of deceptive research practices.

Moral arguments for the need to consider research participants as partners in ethical decision making include respect for persons, beneficence, and nonmaleficence. Veatch (1987), for example, has argued that it is morally unacceptable to consider individuals as "research material" rather than as "persons" who should be treated as human beings with dignity and respect.

Adapted from the *American Psychologist, 49,* 417–427. Copyright 1994 by the American Psychological Association. Table 1 has been omitted.

The principle of respect for personhood includes the recognition that prospective participants are themselves moral agents, with the right to apply a moral judgment to the purpose and procedures of research in which they are asked to participate. A second argument favoring prospective participant perspectives rests on the principle of beneficence (to do good) and assumes that society benefits from scientific research. This position warns of the danger of not using scientifically worthwhile procedures on the erroneous assumption that they would be harmful, when in fact prospective participants perceive them as innocuous (Farr & Seaver, 1975; Sullivan & Deiker, 1973). A third moral argument focuses on the principle of nonmaleficence (to do no harm). According to this position, the participant's point of view, rather than merely professional logic or scientific inference, may be essential to determine the degree of potential distress associated with a particular experimental condition (Farr & Seaver, 1975; Veatch, 1987; Wilson & Donnerstein, 1976). . . .

FACTORS IN THE CONSIDERATION OF THE COST–BENEFIT BALANCE

According to the APA *Ethical Principles*, psychologists design and conduct research "in accordance with recognized standards of scientific competence and ethical research" and "take reasonable steps to implement appropriate protections for the rights and welfare of human participants" (APA, 1992, Standards 6.06a, 6.06d). This dual consideration of scientific standards and human welfare is commonly referred to as the cost–benefit balance, where *cost* refers to the potential risks incurred by the research participant and *benefit* refers to the potential scientific and social value of research [footnote omitted].

Factors to be considered when weighing costs and benefits include the scientific value and validity of the research, the efficacy of alternative procedures, the possibility of experimentally induced harm, the ability to remove such harm through dehoaxing procedures, and the compatibility of deceptive practices with participants' moral values.

Scientific Value and Validity

The importance of scientific merit in deciding whether to conduct an experiment with human par-

ticipants was first formally articulated in the Nuremberg Code, which stated that an "experiment should be such as to yield fruitful results for the good of society" (Nuremberg Code, 1946, Principle 2). This statement places two aspects of scientific merit—scientific validity and scientific value—at the heart of the ethical decision to engage in human experimentation (B. Freedman, 1987). A study is scientifically valid provided it is designed to yield reliable information according to accepted principles of research practice. Accordingly, in evaluating the potential benefits of research using deceptive procedures, the psychologist must be confident that the design ensures a formal relationship between data and conclusions that can yield scientific facts relevant to the question under study (Rutstein, 1969). The validity of conclusions drawn from a study rests in part on confidence that participants believe the experimental situation to be realistic and take it seriously (Aronson & Carlsmith, 1968; J. Freedman, 1969). In this regard, participant perspectives may be more valuable than professional opinion in prospectively judging the "experimental realism" of a study.

A study may be well designed relative to its hypothesis but be of no value because the hypothesis itself is trivial (B. Freedman, 1987) or cannot be effectively translated into the body of scientific knowledge or into useful application (Sieber, 1990). Thus, the evaluation of the usefulness of both the experimental hypothesis and potential results of a study to science or society plays an integral role in cost–benefit decisions. Early on in the development of APA ethical guidelines, the Cook Committee (APA, Committee on Ethical Standards in Psychological Research, 1973) recognized the possibility that researchers, by definition of their training and professional investment, run the risk of overestimating the value of a study and suggested that opinions outside the psychological community be sought.

Methodological Alternatives

According to the APA *Ethical Principles*, once having made the decision that deceptive research methods are in accordance with standards of scientific competence, the psychologist must consider alternative procedures before concluding that the methodological requirements of a study make the use of concealment or deception necessary (APA, 1992, Standard 6.15). Implicit in this principle is the position that because acquisition of scientific knowledge about human behavior is itself valuable, methodologies, such as deception, cannot be ruled out if the knowledge cannot be achieved by other means (Kelman, 1967).

The search for alternative procedures to deception has been driven by both methodological and moral considerations. From a methodological perspective, deception is used on the premise that it is important to keep subjects naive about the purpose of a study so that they can respond to experimental manipulations spontaneously. According to this view, deception is an essential methodology because it enables researchers to obtain adequate stimulus control and random assignment of subjects and because it may be the only economical way to investigate a particular problem or obtain information that participants might otherwise be unwilling to provide (Sieber, 1982).

A number of researchers have argued that methodological deception, rather than providing stringent experimental control, leads to participant suspicion and subsequent nonsystematic, uncontrolled responding to experimental procedures (Orne, 1962). This suspicion can lead to role playing on the part of participants who seek to support what they believe to be the experimenter's hypothesis, to present themselves in the most favorable light, or to sabotage the experiment (Fillenbaum, 1966; Masling, 1966). Empirical studies document the influence of participant suspicion on response to deceptive procedures (Fillenbaum & Frey, 1970; Golding & Lichtenstein, 1970; Stricker, Messick, & Jackson, 1969; Toris & DePaulo, 1984). As a result, psychologists have examined whether role playing, naturalistic observation, or self-reports are methodologically equal or superior to the use of deception (Cooper, 1976; Forward, Canter & Kirsch, 1976; Geller, 1982; Weber & Cook, 1972; Willis & Willis, 1970). Empirical comparisons of alternative methodologies have been equivocal, leading some to argue that the prospects for these alternative procedures are poor (Aronson & Carlsmith, 1968; Miller, 1972) and others to conclude that across all methodologies "subjects tend to act in experimental situations as they

act in other public situations, by managing the impressions they convey to others" (Forward et al., 1976, p. 598). Accordingly, one factor influencing the cost–benefit balance of deceptive research is the value placed on deceptive procedures as the best way to contribute to scientific knowledge.

Those who seek to find alternatives to deceptive procedures on moral grounds focus on the fact that by failing to inform the participant of the true nature of the study, deception violates the moral value of respect for persons (Geller, 1982). In making this argument, scholars such as Baumrind (1979) distinguish between *nonintentional deception*, in which failure to fully inform cannot be avoided because of the complexity of the information, and *intentional deception*, which is the withholding of information in order to obtain participation that the subject might otherwise decline. On this basis, some have suggested that during the consent stage psychologists using deceptive procedures forewarn participants that deception might be used and that they may experience some form of the experimental manipulation (Geller, 1982; Sieber, 1982).

Forewarning, however, although addressing ethical concerns, raises methodological issues challenging the scientific validity of data collection. For example, forewarning prospective participants about certain elements of the study may create demand characteristics or participant hypothesizing similar to that ascribed to intentionally deceptive procedures and may threaten random sampling by discouraging participation (Resnick & Schwartz, 1973). In this regard, prospective data on the impact of forewarning on decisions to participate in research can provide important information about this methodological alternative.

Psychological Discomfort in Response to Planned Procedures

According to the APA *Ethical Principles*, psychologists take reasonable steps to avoid harming research participants, minimize harm where it is foreseeable and unavoidable, and never deceive research participants about significant aspects that would affect their willingness to participate, such as physical risks, discomfort, or unpleasant emotional experiences (APA, 1992, General Principle G; Standards 1.14, 6.15b).

When participant discomfort does arise in the course of an investigation, the psychologist must provide the participant sufficient explanation and desensitization as soon as possible following the experiment (APA, 1992, Standards 6.15c, 6.18a).

The psychological costs of participation in behavioral research using deceptive procedures can include invasion of privacy, stress and discomfort, loss of self-esteem, and negative reactions to being induced to commit reprehensible acts (Baumrind, 1985; Keith-Spiegel & Koocher, 1985). Because deceptive procedures by definition eliminate the possibility of fully informing the participant of potential harm, the weighing of "costs" posed by an experiment using deception rests on an evaluation of whether participants will experience harm as a consequence of the experimental manipulation and whether this harm can be alleviated during debriefing.

Participant reactions to experimental procedures may be underestimated or overestimated by psychologists (Gergen, 1973; Sullivan & Deiker, 1973). For example, Wilson and Donnerstein (1976) found cases in which the general public's reaction to naturalistic nonreactive research procedures was negative with respect to ethical acceptability and scientific justification as well as individual reactions to participation. On the other hand, Sullivan and Deiker found that undergraduates rated deceptive research practices as less unethical, more justified, and more attractive to volunteers than did psychologists. Along similar lines, Farr and Seaver (1975) were surprised to find that students would not be reluctant to fill out questionnaires about such seemingly personal issues as suicidal ideation and heterosexual–homosexual orientation and did not see such procedures as an invasion of privacy.

Participant Reactions to Dehoaxing

In weighing the welfare and rights of research participants against the scientific value of the deceptive research design, an investigator may determine that the research entails a risk of producing psychological discomfort. Further evaluation of the experimental risk depends on expectations regarding participant reactions to debriefing. Among the elements necessary for successful dehoaxing are these: (a) The participant must believe the investigator when informed

of the deception, (b) debriefing should not in and of itself lead to psychological discomfort, and (c) the experimenter must be aware of any negative reactions so that he or she may successfully desensitize the participant (APA, 1973; Mills, 1976; Sieber, 1983b).

Research on the efficacy of debriefing procedures has produced equivocal results. Some studies indicate that a majority of participants experience no harm from participation in deceptive research following dehoaxing (Holmes, 1976a, 1976b; Holmes & Bennett, 1974; Milgram, 1964; S. S. Smith & Richardson, 1983). Other studies find self-reports of harm and increased suspiciousness (Fillenbaum, 1966; Keisner, 1971; Ring, Wallston, & Corey, 1970; S. S. Smith & Richardson, 1983). Several scholars have questioned the adequacy of self-report data following the experience of being deceived, suggesting that cognitive dissonance, distrust of the investigator, masochistic obedience, deferential compliance, and embarrassment, among other mechanisms, may reduce honest responding on the part of the participant (Baumrind, 1985; Rubin, 1985; C. P. Smith, 1981). In the absence of information from prospective participants, investigators considering the use of deceptive procedures must rely on their own a priori judgments concerning the potential cost or benefits that debriefing will provide.

Metaethical Positions

Moral discussions involving deception include consequential philosophies, most notably *act-utilitarianism* and *rule-utilitarianism*, and nonconsequential positions, most notably the deontological perspective. Scholars taking an act-utilitarian position argue that the immediate consequences of conducting the study, rather than universal moral principles, should govern ethical decision making in deceptive research. For example, Baron (1981) proposed that because deceptive research practices are necessary to accomplish beneficial scientific ends, they are ethical when accompanied by the scrutiny of an IRB, limited consent procedures, and thorough debriefing. The weighing of costs and benefits recommended in the APA ethical guidelines can be interpreted as an example of this metaethical position because according to Standard 6.15, deceptive research procedures are ethically acceptable if they have the potential to produce significant scientific benefits and do not cause discomfort that would affect a participant's willingness to participate.

In contrast, the rule-utilitarian applies a consequential argument resulting in the nonrelativistic position that deception in research is never acceptable (Baumrind, 1985). From this metaethical position, truth telling and promise keeping are necessary to promote an ordered and coherent environment in which individuals are held fully accountable for the consequences of their actions (Baumrind, 1990). Accordingly, a violation of trust is particularly immoral in a fiduciary relationship, such as that of a psychologist to a research participant, which is based on the perceived trustworthiness of the fiduciary (Baumrind, 1985; Cupples & Gochnauer, 1985; Holder, 1982).

The deontological argument rests on the nonconsequential Kantian position that we must not treat an individual as a means to an end. From this moral perspective, psychologists should never conduct studies that either violate an individual's autonomy, and thus personhood, or cause harm to an individual (Goldstein, 1981). Consistent with such an approach, Kelman (1972) argued that the experimenter–subject relationship must be considered a real relationship "in which we have responsibility toward the subject as another human being whose dignity we must preserve" (p. 5).

Most of the discussion surrounding the morality of deception has focused on the ethical ideologies of the investigator. Of equal importance, but less scholarly attention, is the compatibility of deceptive research practices with the moral values of the research participant. . . . [*Ed. note*: The authors describe a study designed to gather information on how prospective participants evaluate deception research. Forty-five male and 45 female undergraduates were randomly assigned to read and answer questions about one of three studies selected from the *Journal of Personality and Social Psychology* exemplifying deceptive procedures. The following is a summary of major results:

1. Most students judged the deception studies to be scientifically valuable and valid and the use of deception important even when alternative methodologies were available.

2. A majority believed that individuals would be less willing to participate if they were forewarned that the study might include deception, supporting those who argue that forewarning narrows the subject population, thereby reducing the generalizability of results.

3. The vast majority of students thought that participants would believe the researcher when they were told of the deception; but about 50% thought that they would also be embarrassed by debriefing revelations, and most of these thought they would not reveal these feelings to the researcher.

4. In the main, students thought that the societal benefits of the studies were greater than the cost to participants. Most took an "act-utilitarian" position, stating that the decision to conduct deception research should rest on a consideration of the social, scientific, or personal benefits of the study; the minimization or alleviation of harm; or full debriefing after the experiment. Only 6 of the 90 participants viewed deception as wrong under any conditions.]

The moral ideologies reflected in the responses of the majority of students are consistent with the APA *Ethical Principles* (1992) emphasis on cost–benefit analyses of deceptive research designs. Most of the students believed that deceptive research was justifiable if the study had the potential to produce scientific or societal benefits or if harm was minimal or alleviated during debriefing. Many of the students operating within a nonconsequential framework saw avoidance of harm rather than deception as the major moral imperative for the conduct of psychological research. Thus, the moral positions reflected in the responses of the students we surveyed did not indicate that they found deception per se to be inconsistent with their own moral principles.

THE CHALLENGE OF INVESTIGATOR–PARTICIPANT PARTNERSHIPS

. . .

Majority Rule

When using prospective participant surveys in ethical evaluations of deceptive research, investigators and ethics review committees need to consider the emphasis given to majority versus minority opinions (Wilson & Donnerstein, 1976). In the preceding section we used group means and percentages to guide ethical decisions regarding the design and implementation of deceptive research. On the basis of prospective participant opinion, we concluded that the majority of introductory psychology students recruited from subject pools for the three studies summarized would find them ethically acceptable if systematic procedures for reducing the potentially coercive and distressful aspects of dehoaxing were included in the design. However, individual psychologists and IRB members must struggle, as we did, with the question of whether a particular deceptive procedure can be justified if a substantial, or even small, minority of prospective participants believe the costs of participation outweigh potential social benefits. For example, from 40% to 87% of our respondents thought participants would be embarrassed or annoyed to learn that they had been deceived, and as many as 27% of the students . . . thought the costs to participants outweighed societal benefits of the deceptive methodology. As Wilson and Donnerstein pointed out, even one extremely upset research participant can weigh heavily on a researcher's conscience and create a potentially devastating professional and legal problem.

One way to empirically approach this problem is to utilize prospective participant surveys to establish baseline responses to research designs that do not use deception or experimentally induced participant discomfort and then to use these baselines as a way of judging meaningful substantive differences in majority–minority ratios in responding to specific deceptive designs. A second empirical approach is to use the prospective participant survey procedure to ascertain individual characteristics predictive of those who might be negatively impacted by the study. The results of such a survey should not, however, be used to screen out prospective participants because this would inequitably exclude them from our base of scientific understanding (see Rawls, 1971, on the moral value of justice). Rather, knowledge of individual differences in response to descriptions of deceptive procedures can be applied to the design of individually tailored informed consent and debriefing procedures (Fisher & Rosendahl, 1990).

Description Versus Prescription

Early in this century Sidgwick (1902) made the argument that ethics should be concerned with what ought to be rather than with what actually is. Any consideration of participant or professional opinion surveys runs the risk of accepting descriptions of ethical decision making as prescriptions for ethical decisions (Steininger, Newell, & Garcia, 1984). We do not propose that empirical information on the reactions of prospective participants to research designs be a deciding criterion for ethics approval or disapproval of deceptive research. Empirical information can assist but not substitute for ethical decisions by individual psychologists and their IRBs on the basis of the moral values of beneficence, respect, and justice. Using prospective participant opinions in ethical decision making will help realize these moral principles by contributing to the design and approval of research that protects the participant's welfare and treats participants with the respect due all persons as moral agents in their own right.

References

Adair, J. G., Dushenko, T. W., & Lindsay, R. C. L. (1985). Ethical regulations and their impact on research practice. *American Psychologist, 40*, 59–72.

American Psychological Association. (1992). Ethical principles of psychologists and code of conduct. *American Psychologist, 47*, 1597–1611.

American Psychological Association, Committee on Ethical Standards in Psychological Research. (1973). *Ethical principles in the conduct of research with human participants*. Washington, DC: Author.

Aronson, E., & Carlsmith, J. M. (1968). Experimentation in social psychology. In G. Lindzey & E. Aronson (Eds.), *The handbook of social psychology* (Vol. 2, pp. 1–79). Reading, MA: Addison-Wesley.

Baron, R. A. (1981). The "Costs of deception" revisited: An openly optimistic rejoinder. *IRB: A Review of Human Subjects Research, 3*, 8–10.

Baumrind, D. (1964). Some thoughts on ethics of research: After reading Milgram's "Behavioral study of obedience." *American Psychologist, 26*, 887–896.

Baumrind, D. (1979). IRBs and social science research: The costs of deception. *IRB: A Review of Human Subjects Research, 1*, 1–4.

Baumrind, D. (1985). Research using intentional deception: Ethical issues revisited. *American Psychologist, 40*, 165–174.

Baumrind, D. (1990). Doing good well. In C. B. Fisher & W. W. Tryon (Eds.), *Ethics in applied developmental psychology: Emerging issues in an emerging field* (pp. 17–28). Norwood, NJ: Ablex.

Bok, S. (1978). *Lying: Moral choice in public and private life.* New York: Pantheon.

Cooper, J. (1976). Deception and role playing: On telling the good guys from the bad guys. *American Psychologist, 31,* 605–610.

Cupples, B., & Gochnauer, M. (1985). The investigator's duty not to deceive. *IRB: A Review of Human Subjects Research, 7,* 1–6.

Farr, J. L., & Seaver, W. B. (1975). Stress and discomfort in psychological research: Subject perceptions of experimental procedures. *American Psychologist, 30,* 770–773.

Fillenbaum, S. (1966). Prior deception and subsequent experimental performance: The "faithful" subject. *Journal of Personality and Social Psychology, 4,* 532–537.

Fillenbaum, S., & Frey, R. (1970). More on the "faithful" subject. *Journal of Personality and Social Psychology, 38,* 43–51.

Fisher, C. B., & Rosendahl, S. A. (1990). Psychological risks and remedies of research participation. In C. B. Fisher & W. W. Tryon (Eds.), *Ethics in applied developmental psychology: Emerging issues in an emerging field* (pp. 43–60). Norwood, NJ: Ablex.

Forward, J., Canter, R., & Kirsch, N. (1976). Role-enactment and deception methodologies: Alternative paradigms. *American Psychologist, 31,* 595–604.

Freedman, B. (1987). Scientific value and validity as ethical requirements for research: A proposed explication. *IRB: A Review of Human Subjects Research, 9,* 7–10.

Freedman, J. (1969). Role playing: Psychology by consensus. *Journal of Personality and Social Psychology, 13,* 107–114.

Geller, D. M. (1982). Alternatives to deception: Why, what, and how? In J. E. Sieber (Ed.), *The ethics of social research: Surveys and experiments* (pp. 40–55). New York: Springer-Verlag.

Gergen, K. J. (1973). The codification of research ethics: Views of a doubting Thomas. *American Psychologist, 8,* 907–912.

Golding, S. L., & Lichtenstein, E. (1970). Confession of awareness and prior knowledge of deception as a function of interview set and approval motivation. *Journal of Personality and Social Psychology, 14,* 213–223.

Goldstein, R. (1981). On deceptive rejoinders about deceptive research: A reply to Baron. *IRB: A Review of Human Subjects Research, 3,* 5–6.

Gross, A. E., & Fleming, I. (1982). Twenty years of deception in social psychology. *Personality and Social Psychology Bulletin, 8,* 402–408.

Holder, A. R. (1982). Do researchers and subjects have a fiduciary relationship? *IRB: A Review of Human Subjects Research, 4,* 6–7.

Holmes, D. S. (1976a). Debriefing after psychological experiments: 1. Effectiveness of postdeception dehoaxing. *American Psychologist, 31,* 858–867.

Holmes, D. S. (1976b). Debriefing after psychological experiments: 2. Effectiveness of postdeception desensitizing. *American Psychologist, 31,* 868–875.

Holmes, D. S., & Bennett, D. H. (1974). Experiments to answer questions raised by the use of deception in psychological research: 1. Role playing as an alternative to deception; 2. Effectiveness of debriefing after a deception; 3. Effect of informed consent on deception. *Journal of Personality and Social Psychology, 29,* 348–367.

Keisner, R. (1971). *Debriefing and responsiveness to overt experimenter expectancy cues.* Unpublished manuscript, Long Island University, NY.

Keith-Spiegel, P., & Koocher, G. P. (1985). *Ethics in psychology.* New York: Random House.

Kelman, H. C. (1967). Human use of human subjects: The problem of deception in social psychological experiments. *Psychological Bulletin, 27,* 1–11.

Kelman, H. C. (1972). The rights of the subject in social research: An analysis in terms of relative power and legitimacy. *American Psychologist, 27,* 1–11.

Loo, C. M. (1982). Vulnerable populations: Case studies in crowding research. In J. E. Sieber (Ed.), *The ethics of social research: Surveys and experiments* (pp. 105–129). New York: Springer-Verlag.

Masling, J. (1966). Role-related behavior of the subject and psychologist and its effects upon psychological data. *Nebraska Symposium on Motivation, 14,* 67–103.

Menges, R. J. (1973). Openness and honesty versus coercion and deception in psychological research. *American Psychologist, 28,* 1030–1034.

Milgram, S. (1963). Behavioral study of obedience. *Journal of Abnormal and Social Psychology, 7,* 371–378.

Milgram, S. (1964). Issues in the study of obedience: A reply to Baumrind. *American Psychologist, 19,* 848–852.

Miller, A. G. (1972). Role-playing, an alternative to deception: A review of the evidence. *American Psychologist, 27,* 623–636.

Mills, J. (1976). A procedure for explaining experiments involving deception. *Personality and Social Psychology Bulletin, 2,* 3–13.

Nuremberg Code. (1946). *Journal of the American Medical Association, 132,* 1090.

Orne, M. T. (1962). On the social psychology of the psychological experiment: With particular reference to demand characteristics and their implications. *American Psychologist, 17,* 776–783.

Rawls, J. (1971). *A theory of justice.* Cambridge, MA: Harvard University Press.

Resnick, J. H. & Schwartz, T. (1973). Ethical standards as an independent variable in psychological research. *American Psychologist, 28,* 134–139.

Ring, K., Wallston, K., & Corey, M. (1970). Mode of debriefing as a factor affecting subjective reaction to a Milgram-type obedience experiment: An ethical inquiry. *Journal of Representative Research in Social Psychology, 1,* 67–88.

Ross, L., Lepper, M. R., & Hubbard, M. (1975). Perseverance in self-perception and social perception: Biased attributional processes in the debriefing paradigm. *Journal of Personality and Social Psychology, 32,* 880–892.

Rubin, Z. (1985). Deceiving ourselves about deception: Comment on Smith and Richardson's "Amelioration of deception and harm in psychological research." *Journal of Personality and Social Psychology, 48,* 252–253.

Rutstein, D. D. (1969). The ethical design of human experiments. In P. Freund (Ed.), *Experimentation with human subjects* (pp. 383–401). New York: Braziller Daedulus Library.

Seeman, J. (1969). Deception in psychological research. *American Psychologist, 24,* 1025–1028.

Sidgwick, H. (1902). *Philosophy: Its scope and relations.* New York: Macmillan.

Sieber, J. E. (1982). Kinds of deception and the wrongs they may involve. *IRB: A Review of Human Subjects Research, 4,* 1–5.

Sieber, J. E. (1983a). Evaluating the potential for harm or wrong. *IRB: A Review of Human Subjects Research, 5,* 1–6.

Sieber, J. E. (1983b). The nature and limits of debriefing. *IRB: A Review of Human Subjects Research, 5,* 1–4.

Sieber, J. E. (1990). How to be ethical in applied developmental psychology: Examples from research on adolescent drinking behavior. In C. B. Fisher & W. W. Tryon (Eds.), *Ethics in applied developmental psychology: Emerging issues in an emerging field* (pp. 61–78). Norwood, NJ: Ablex.

Smith, C. P. (1981). How (un)acceptable is research involving deception? *IRB: A Review of Human Subjects Research, 3,* 1–4.

Smith, M. B. (1976). Some perspectives on ethical/political issues in social science research. *Personality and Social Psychology Bulletin, 2,* 445–453.

Smith, S. S., & Richardson, D. (1983). Amelioration of deception and harm in psychological research. *Journal of Personality and Social Psychology, 44,* 1075–1082.

Steininger, M., Newell, J. D., & Garcia, L. T. (1984). *Ethical Issues in Psychology.* Homewood, IL: Dorsey Press.

Stricker, L. J., Messick, S., & Jackson, D. N. (1969). Evaluating deception in psychological research. *Psychological Bulletin, 71,* 343–351.

Sullivan, D. S., & Deiker, T. E. (1973). Subject–experimenter perceptions of ethical issues in human research. *American Psychologist, 28,* 587–591.

Toris, C., & DePaulo, B. M. (1984). Effects of actual deception and suspiciousness of deception on interpersonal perceptions. *Journal of Personality and Social Psychology, 47,* 1063–1073.

Veatch, R. M. (1987). *The patient as partner.* Bloomington: Indiana University Press.

Weber, S. J., & Cook, T. D. (1972). Subject effects in laboratory research: An examination of subject roles, demand characteristics, and valid inference. *Psychological Bulletin, 77,* 273–295.

Willis, R., & Willis, Y. (1970). Role playing versus deception: An experimental comparison. *Journal of Personality and Social Psychology, 16,* 472–477.

Wilson, D. W. & Donnerstein, W. (1976). Legal and ethical aspects of nonreactive social psychological research: An excursion into the public mind. *American Psychologist, 31,* 765–773.

◆ ◆ ◆

Commentary: If research participants will, indeed, be embarrassed to find during debriefing that they were deceived, then can any deception research pass muster under Standard 6.15(b) of the APA's 1992 Ethical Principles, which forbids psychologists from ever deceiving "research participants about significant aspects that would affect their willingness to participate, such as physical risks, discomfort, or unpleasant emotional experiences?"

In light of the preceding material, it would be helpful to review the 1992 Ethical Principles that address consent and deception in psychological research (see Standards 6.11, 6.12, and 6.15). Which side of the "scientist versus humanist" ledger do these provisions fall on? Do they address Baumrind's concerns? If you were contemplating doing research that involved deception, would these standards be an adequate guide to help you avoid ethical pitfalls?

Designing and conducting psychotherapy research presents special ethical problems, particularly because scientific rigor may conflict with clinical care. A prime example is the controlled clinical trial in which some groups may receive placebo treatment or no treatment at all. The brief excerpt below provides an introduction to the ethical dilemmas that arise when conducting clinical trials.

Informed Consent and Deception in Psychotherapy Research: An Ethical Analysis

Richard T. Lindsey

. . .

One of the most problematic of ethical dilemmas . . . is the use of "placebos" in counseling and clinical research. Placebos, by definition, are inert and not expected or designed to do anything really helpful for the subject. By contrast, when people enter treatment and develop a contact with a therapist/agency, it is with the understanding they will receive an active treatment designed to help them. If clients are given a placebo in place of the active treatment they seek, that contract is violated. In addition, if and when clients discover that they have received a placebo rather than the active treatment they sought, they may feel angered and betrayed by a profession committed to their betterment. As a result, their autonomous choice is violated by using inaccurate and insufficient information. The principle of nonmaleficence is also violated because the possibility of deterioration in the absence of psychotherapy cannot be eliminated. Finally, the principle of beneficence is violated, for they may be no better after "treatment" than before. These ethical violations would be all the more severe in cases where effective alternative forms of treatment were available (O'Leary & Borkovec, 1978). These arguments could hold for no treatment control groups as well.

It is important to point out that there do seem to be alternative designs available that could be used in place of placebos and no treatment control groups. For example, O'Leary and Borkovec (1978) argue that since placebo conditions are difficult to create, researchers ought to compare a treatment of interest with an alternative treatment which also appears to be effective for a problem.

As long as two treatments are equated for duration of contact time and other nonspecific variables, and as long as independent assessments . . . indicate equivalent generation of expectancy for improvement through the treatment trial, such a design provides control for some of the usual factors addressed by placebo conditions. (p. 826)

Also, by replacing control groups with comparison groups, as O'Leary and Borkovec have argued ought to be done for placebo groups, we avoid the ethical problem of leaving some clients without treatment who stand in need of it.

The one exception to this procedure would be in situations where resources are scarce, such that the relatively large number of clients needing treatment exceed the available psychotherapists. In such a situation, to randomly assign some to no treatment control groups would be ethically acceptable (Stricker, 1982).

By using comparison groups, the assignment of clients to the various treatment groups becomes important. It would seem that randomization is the wisest choice, with each client being informed that s/he will be randomly assigned to one of a number of treatments, each of which is viewed as potentially capable of being helpful (Stricker, 1982; O'Leary & Borkovec, 1978). The clients could then make an informed choice (O'Leary & Borkovec, 1978) as to whether they would be willing to be randomly assigned or not. At the conclusion of the study, if one particular method proved to be the more effective treatment, then it could be offered to members of

From the *Counseling Psychologist*, 12, 79–86. Copyright 1986 by Sage. Adapted with permission of the publisher.

the other treatment groups if they still needed assistance (Stricker, 1982). . . .

References

O'Leary, K. D. & Borkovec, T. D. (1978). Conceptual, methodological, and ethical problems of placebo groups in psychotherapy research. *American Psychologist, 33,* 821–830.

Stricker, G. (1982). Ethical issues in psychotherapy research. In M. Rosenbaum (Ed.), *Ethics and values in psychotherapy: A guidebook.* New York: Free Press, pp. 403–424.

◆ ◆ ◆

Commentary: For a more extensive exploration of ethical problems in conducting not only controlled clinical trials but also collaborative research among several institutional sites, see Imber, S. D., Glanz, L. M., Elkin, E., Sotsky, S. M., Boyer, J. L., & Leber, W. R. (1986). Ethical issues in psychotherapy research. American Psychologist, 41, 137–146. They described a multisite collaborative investigation in which a clinical trials design was used to evaluate the effectiveness and safety of two forms of brief psychotherapy for depression (cognitive–behavioral therapy and interpersonal therapy) in comparison with the administration of imipramine (psychopharmacological medication) and a placebo-controlled condition. What ethical problems are raised by such a protocol? What are the potential conflicts among the demands of science, the traditional reliance on professional judgment, and the ultimate responsibility for patient welfare? In what ways are these problems exacerbated by the fact that, in the Imber et al. example, the patients were depressed? Read the entire article for a helpful discussion of these rarely analyzed questions.

In 1979, Mirvis and Seashore complained that the APA's then-current (1977) ethics documents

> *evolved largely from clinical and counseling practice, from research with unorganized subjects, and from a preoccupation with collegial relationships; they do not adequately address the issues that arise in the context of organizational settings. (p. 778)*

See Mirvis, P. H., & Seashore, S. E. (1979). Being ethical in organizational research. American Psychologist, 34, 766–780. Has the situation improved? What provi-

sions, other than Standard 8.03 in the 1992 Ethical Principles, guide the researcher who must deal "with a social system composed of people who have positions in a hierarchy and who, in their collective identity as an organization, also have relationships with supporters, consumers, government, unions, and other public institutions" (Mirvis & Seashore, 1979, p. 766)? For readers who will face this issue, Mirvis and Seashore have provided a helpful discussion of strategies for addressing ethical dilemmas in organizational research.

McConnell and Kerbs (1993) have offered this reminder:

> *Successful research with human subjects depends on the cooperation of potential subjects and the organizations which they are affiliated with as clients, staff, or administrators. Maintaining viable subject pools requires that researchers be viewed positively by both subjects and nonresearch professionals who are involved in the research process. This is accomplished by adherence to human-subject requirements, including providing appropriate feedback in a timely way. (p. 269).*

See McConnell, W. A., & Kerbs, J. J. (1993). Providing feedback in research with human subjects. Professional Psychology: Research and Practice, 24, 266–270. Yet, they and others have complained that subjects (both those included in the experiment and those screened out by preexperimental procedures), institutions in which the research is conducted, and funding agencies often do not receive information about the results of research. Only a few have viewed this as an ethical issue. In addition to McConnell and Kerbs (1993), see

Gurman, E. B. (1994). Debriefing for all concerned: Ethical treatment of human subjects. Psychological Science, 5, 139.

Sieber, J. E., & Saks, M. J. (1989). A census of subject pool characteristics and policies. American Psychologist, 44, 1053–1061.

Interested readers have certainly become aware that experimentation with human participants is not the only kind of research that has engendered controversy. As Galvin and Herzog (1992) have noted, "The use of animals as subjects in behavioral and biomedical research has become a major issue with social, political, philo-

sophical, and psychological ramifications" (p. 263). See Galvin, S. L., & Herzog, H. A. (1992). The ethical judgment of animal research. Ethics and Behavior, 2, 263–286. *Because of these ramifications as well as pressure from animal activists, like human research, animal* research conducted at universities is scrutinized by review boards called Institutional Animal Care and Use Committees. *In addition to the provisions in the 1992 Ethical Principles, the APA has developed its own policies concerning animal research (reprinted next).*

Guidelines for Ethical Conduct in the Care and Use of Animals

American Psychological Association

. . .

The following guidelines were developed by the American Psychological Association (APA) for use by psychologists working with nonhuman animals.[1] They are based on and are in conformity with Section 6.20 of the *Ethical Principles of Psychologists and Code of Conduct of* APA. In the ordinary course of events, the acquisition, care, housing, use, and disposition of animals should be in compliance with applicable federal, state, local, and institutional laws and regulations and with international conventions to which the United States is a party. APA members working outside the United States are to follow all applicable laws and regulations of the country in which they conduct research.

I. JUSTIFICATION OF THE RESEARCH

A. Research should be undertaken with a clear scientific purpose. There should be a reasonable expectation that the research will a) increase knowledge of the processes underlying the evolution, development, maintenance, alteration, control, or biological significance of behavior; b) increase understanding of the species under study; or c) provide results that benefit the health or welfare of humans or other animals.

B. The scientific purpose of the research should be of sufficient potential significance to justify the use of animals. Psychologists should act on the assumption that procedures that would produce pain in humans will also do so in other animals.

C. The species chosen for study should be best suited to answer the question(s) posed. The psychologist should always consider the possibility of using other species, nonanimal alternatives, or procedures that minimize the number of animals in research, and should be familiar with the appropriate literature.

D. Research on animals may not be conducted until the protocol has been reviewed by the institutional animal care and use committee (IACUC) to ensure that the procedures are appropriate and humane.

E. The psychologist should monitor the research and the animals' welfare throughout the course of an investigation to ensure continued justification for the research.

II. PERSONNEL

A. Psychologists should ensure that personnel involved in their research with animals be familiar with these guidelines.

B. Animal use procedures must conform with federal regulations regarding personnel, supervision, record keeping, and veterinary care. [footnote omitted]

C. Behavior is both the focus of study of many experiments as well as a primary source of information about an animal's health and well-being. It is therefore necessary that psychologists and their assistants be informed about the behavioral characteristics of their animal subjects, so as to be aware of normal, species-specific behaviors and unusual behaviors that could forewarn of health problems.

D. Psychologists should ensure that all individuals who use animals under their supervision receive explicit instruction in experimental methods and in the care, maintenance, and handling of the species being studied. Responsibilities and activities of all individuals dealing with animals should be consistent with their respective competencies, training, and experience in either the laboratory or the field setting.

III. CARE AND HOUSING OF ANIMALS

The concept of "psychological well-being" of animals is of current concern and debate and is included in Federal Regulations (United States Department of Agriculture [USDA], 1991). As a scientific and professional organization, APA recognizes the complexities of defining psychological well-being. Procedures appropriate for a particular species may well be inappropriate for others. Hence, APA does not presently stipulate specific guidelines regarding the maintenance of psychological well-being of research animals. Psychologists familiar with the species should be best qualified professionally to judge measures such as enrichment to maintain or improve psychological well-being of those species.

A. The facilities housing animals should meet or exceed current regulations and guidelines (USDA, 1990, 1991) and are required to be inspected twice a year (USDA, 1989).

B. All procedures carried out on animals are to be reviewed by a local IACUC to ensure that the procedures are appropriate and humane. The committee should have representation from within the institution and from the local community. In the event that it is not possible to constitute an appropriate local IACUC, psychologists are encouraged to seek advice from a corresponding committee of a cooperative institution.

C. Responsibilities for the conditions under which animals are kept, both within and outside of the context of active experimentation or teaching, rests with the psychologist under the supervision of the IACUC (where required by federal regulations) and with individuals appointed by the institution to oversee animal care. Animals are to be provided with humane care and healthful conditions during their stay in the facility. In addition to the federal requirements to provide for the psychological well-being of nonhuman primates used in research, psychologists are encouraged to consider enriching the environments of their laboratory animals and should keep abreast of literature on well-being and enrichment for the species with which they work.

IV. ACQUISITION OF ANIMALS

A. Animals not bred in the psychologist's facility are to be acquired lawfully. The USDA and local ordinances should be consulted for information regarding regulations and approved suppliers.

B. Psychologists should make every effort to ensure that those responsible for transporting the animals to the facility provide adequate food, water, ventilation, space, and impose no unnecessary stress on the animals.

C. Animals taken from the wild should be trapped in a humane manner and in accordance with applicable federal, state, and local regulations.

D. Endangered species or taxa should be used only with full attention to required permits and ethical concerns. Information and permit applications can be obtained from the Fish and Wildlife Service, Office of Management Authority, U.S. Dept. of the Interior, 4401 N. Fairfax Dr., Rm. 432, Arlington, VA 22043, 703-358-2104. Similar caution should be used in work with threatened species or taxa.

V. EXPERIMENTAL PROCEDURES

Humane consideration for the well-being of the animal should be incorporated into the design and conduct of all procedures involving animals, while keeping in mind the primary goal of experimental procedures—the acquisition of sound, replicable data. The conduct of all procedures is governed by Guideline I.

A. Behavioral studies that involve no aversive stimulation or overt sign of distress to the animal are acceptable. This includes observational and other noninvasive forms of data collection.

B. When alternative behavioral procedures are available, those that minimize discomfort to the animal should be used. When using aversive conditions, psychologists should adjust the parameters of stimulation to levels that appear minimal, though compatible with the aims of the research. Psychologists are encouraged to test painful stimuli on themselves, whenever reasonable. Whenever consistent with the goals of the research, consideration should be given to providing the animals with control of the potentially aversive stimulation.

C. Procedures in which the animal is anesthetized

and insensitive to pain throughout the procedure and is euthanized before regaining consciousness are generally acceptable.

D. Procedures involving more than momentary or slight aversive stimulation, which are not relieved by medication or other acceptable methods, should be undertaken only when the objectives of the research cannot be achieved by other methods.

E. Experimental procedures that require prolonged aversive conditions or produce tissue damage or metabolic disturbances require greater justification and surveillance. This includes prolonged exposure to extreme environmental conditions, experimentally induced prey killing, or infliction of physical trauma or tissue damage. An animal observed to be in a state of severe distress or chronic pain that cannot be alleviated and is not essential to the purposes of the research should be euthanized immediately.

F. Procedures that use restraint must conform to federal regulations and guidelines.

G. Procedures involving the use of paralytic agents without reduction in pain sensation require particular prudence and humane concern. Use of muscle relaxants or paralytics alone during surgery, without general anesthesia, is unacceptable and shall not be used.

H. Surgical procedures, because of their invasive nature, require close supervision and attention to humane considerations by the psychologist. Aseptic (methods that minimize risks of infection) techniques must be used on laboratory animals whenever possible.

1. All surgical procedures and anesthetization should be conducted under the direct supervision of a person who is competent in the use of the procedures.
2. If the surgical procedure is likely to cause greater discomfort than that attending anesthetization, and unless there is specific justification for acting otherwise, animals should be maintained under anesthesia until the procedure is ended.
3. Sound postoperative monitoring and care, which may include the use of analgesics and antibiotics, should be provided to minimize discomfort and to prevent infection and other untoward consequences of the procedure.

4. Animals can not be subjected to successive surgical procedures unless these are required by the nature of the research, the nature of the surgery, or for the well-being of the animal. Multiple surgeries on the same animal must receive special approval from the IACUC.

I. When the use of an animal is no longer required by an experimental protocol or procedure, in order to minimize the number of animals used in research, alternatives to euthanasia should be considered. Such uses should be compatible with the goals of research and the welfare of the animal. Care should be taken that such an action does not expose the animal to multiple surgeries.

J. The return of wild-caught animals to the field can carry substantial risks, both to the formerly captive animals and to the ecosystem. Animals reared in the laboratory should not be released because, in most cases, they cannot survive or they may survive by disrupting the natural ecology.

K. When euthanasia appears to be the appropriate alternative, either as a requirement of the research or because it constitutes the most humane form of disposition of an animal at the conclusion of the research:

1. Euthanasia shall be accomplished in a humane manner, appropriate for the species, and in such a way as to ensure immediate death, and in accordance with procedures outlined in the latest version of the "American Veterinary Medical Association (AVMA) Panel on Euthanasia." [footnote omitted]
2. Disposal of euthanized animals should be accomplished in a manner that is in accord with all relevant legislation, consistent with health, environmental, and aesthetic concerns, and approved by the IACUC. No animal shall be discarded until its death is verified.

VI. FIELD RESEARCH

Field research, because of its potential to damage sensitive ecosystems and ethologies, should be subject to IACUC approval. Field research, if strictly observational, may not require IACUC approval (USDA, 1989, pg. 36126).

A. Psychologists conducting field research should disturb their populations as little as possible—consistent with the goals of the research. Every effort should be made to minimize potential harmful effects of the study on the population and on other plant and animal species in the area.

B. Research conducted in populated areas should be done with respect for the property and privacy of the inhabitants of the area.

C. Particular justification is required for the study of endangered species. Such research on endangered species should not be conducted unless IACUC approval has been obtained and all requisite permits are obtained (see above, III D).

VII. EDUCATIONAL USE OF ANIMALS

APA has adopted separate guidelines for the educational use of animals in precollege education, including the use of animals in science fairs and demonstrations. For a copy of APA's "Ethical Guidelines for the Teaching of Psychology in the Secondary Schools," write to: High School Teacher Affiliate Program, Education Directorate, APA, 750 First St., NE, Washington, DC 20002 4242.

A. Psychologists are encouraged to include instruction and discussion of the ethics and values of animal research in all courses that involve or discuss the use of animals.

B. Animals may be used for educational purposes only after review by a committee appropriate to the institution.

C. Some procedures that can be justified for research purposes may not be justified for educational purposes. Consideration should always be given to the possibility of using nonanimal alternatives.

D. Classroom demonstrations involving live animals can be valuable as instructional aids in addition to videotapes, films, or other alternatives. Careful consideration should be given to the question of whether this type of demonstration is warranted by the anticipated instructional gains.

References

U.S. Department of Agriculture. (1989, August 21). Animal welfare; Final rules. *Federal Register.*

U.S. Department of Agriculture. (1990, July 16). Animal welfare; Guinea pigs, hamsters, and rabbits. *Federal Register.*

U.S. Department of Agriculture. (1991, February 15). Animal welfare; Standards; Final rule. *Federal Register.*

◆ ◆ ◆

Commentary: The federal regulations referenced in the APA's Animal Guidelines concerning the well-being of primates and dogs were printed in the Federal Register, *56, 6425–6505 (February 15, 1991), and they also appeared in the* Code of Federal Regulations. *(Animal Welfare Standards, 9 C.F.R. Part 3). However, in 1993, a federal court ordered the United States Department of Agriculture (USDA) to rewrite these regulations. In overturning the 1991 regulations, the court said that they did not provide the minimum standards that Congress had intended under the Animal Welfare Act. However, the court of appeals later reversed this decision, allowing the USDA regulations to stand. These developments have made it difficult for researchers constructing animal facilities to conform their conduct to the law and ethical demands.*

Obviously, there have been strong reactions to many of the restrictions on animal research advocated by those who identify themselves as protectors of animal rights. For some critiques of the animal rights movement, see, for example

King, F. A. (1991). Animal research: Our obligation to educate. In M. A. Novak & A. J. Petto (Eds.), Through the looking glass: Issues of psychological well-being in captive nonhuman primates (pp. 212–230). Washington, DC: American Psychological Association.

Lansdell, H. (1993). The three Rs: A restrictive and refutable rigmarole. Ethics and Behavior, 3, 177–185.

The most notorious case in the annals of animal activism concerned psychologist Edward Taub and his laboratory monkeys, whose nerves he cut in an experiment at the Institute for Behavioral Research in Maryland. For an extensive and reasonably balanced discussion of that case, see Fraser, C. (1993, April 19). The raid at Silver Spring. The New Yorker, 66–74, 76–84. Partly in response to violent disruptions by those opposed to biomedical and behavioral research using animal subjects, Congress in 1992 passed the Animal Enterprise Protection Act, amending the U.S. Criminal Code (18 U.S.C. § 43). It provides, in relevant part:

SEC. 2. ANIMAL ENTERPRISE TERRORISM.

(a) In General.—Title 18, United States Code, is amended by inserting after section 42 the following: . . .

"§ 43. Animal Enterprise Terrorism

"(a) Offense.—Whoever—

"(1) travels in interstate or foreign commerce, or uses or causes to be used the mail or any facility in interstate or foreign commerce, for the purpose of causing physical disruption to the functioning of an animal enterprise; and

"(2) intentionally causes physical disruption to the functioning of an animal enterprise by intentionally stealing, damaging, or causing the loss of, any property (including animals or records) used by the animal enterprise, and thereby causes economic damage exceeding $10,000 to that enterprise, or conspires to do so;

shall be fined under this title or imprisoned not more than one year, or both.

"(b) Aggravated Offense.—

"(1) Serious Bodily Injury.—Whoever in the course of a violation of subsection (a) causes serious bodily injury to another individual shall be fined under this title or imprisoned not more than 10 years, or both.

"(2) Death.—Whoever in the course of a violation of subsection (a) causes the death of an individual shall be fined under this title and imprisoned for life or for any term of years.

"(c) Restitution.—An order of restitution under section 3663 of this title with respect to a violation of this section may also include restitution—

"(1) for the reasonable cost of repeating any experimentation that was interrupted or invalidated as a result of the offense; and

"(2) the loss of food production or farm income reasonably attributable to the offense.

Empirical Studies of Ethical Issues in Research: A Research Agenda

Barbara Stanley, Joan E. Sieber, and Gary B. Melton

. . .

WHY CONDUCT EMPIRICAL STUDIES OF RESEARCH ETHICS?

Although the definition of the ethical conduct of research is a normative enterprise, the application of normative ethical principles is often dependent on empirical assumptions. For example, the capacity of potential research participants to make informed decisions may be a crucial assumption underlying determination of ethical obligations for participant consent or consultation of a proxy decision maker. Understanding of the ability of both normal and special populations to comprehend and weigh facts critical to an informed decision whether to participate may clarify both whether special restrictions should be placed on potential participants' power of autonomous consent and how relevant information may be disclosed in a way that participants might best process it. Similarly, social psychological research on persuasion and experimenter effects may provide information about ways of preserving participants' perceived freedom to withdraw from a study or to decline to participate at all. . . .

Psychological science is also important in another way to research ethics. As a practical matter, applied ethics is dependent on an understanding of possibilities. The ethical calculus about the acceptability of a particular research design is often affected by the methodological rigor of the proposed study (i.e., Does the proposed design have sufficient validity to ensure that participants' investment of their time and, in a sense, themselves will result in a significant contribution to knowledge?) and the nature of alternatives (e.g., Are other designs available that are less

intrusive but just as likely to result in social benefit?). Thus, an appreciation of psychological science itself complements an understanding of the ethical issues often raised by psychological research with human participants. Creativity in methodology often can enhance the likelihood of significant increases in knowledge about the human condition without undue risk to, intrusion on, or wrong of participants.

However, such psychological questions in research ethics have seldom been addressed. Although the APA ethical principles relating to research were based on a survey of ethical issues confronted by psychological researchers using a critical incidents technique, no empirical investigation of the assumptions underlying the ethical principles was undertaken. Policies and standards typically have been formulated without empirical data to guide their development. . . .

COMMUNICATION BETWEEN THE RESEARCHER AND PARTICIPANTS

. . .

Disclosure and Comprehension of Consent Information

In most instances, individuals must be asked to volunteer for a research project (as opposed to being drafted) and must be informed of the nature, purpose, risks, and benefits of the proposed study. It is presumed that, once so informed, individuals understand and use the consent information in their decision to participate or refuse participation. However, researchers actually know very little about this process. A large number of studies have examined how much of the information given to research par-

Adapted from the *American Psychologist*, 7, 735–741. Copyright 1987 by the American Psychological Association.

ticipants (or individuals receiving nonexperimental treatments) is understood and retained over a period of time. However, many of these studies suffer from serious methodological flaws (Meisel & Roth, 1981). . . . Despite these flaws, these studies show a general trend: Comprehension of consent information is relatively poor.

These studies also indicate that more questions are left unanswered than answered. For example, what techniques can be used to increase comprehension of consent information? Some studies have explored the use of videotape aids (Barbour & Blumenkrantz, 1978), discussion groups (Faden, 1977), or objective testing (Silberstein, 1974) to ensure comprehension of consent information. However, no large-scale, well-controlled multimethod study with varied populations has been conducted. In addition, no study has addressed the question, Do the characteristics of the individual conveying the consent information have an impact on the level of comprehension? . . .

Another question that needs to be addressed concerns the format of consent information. What format and level of complexity lead to the fullest comprehension of consent information? Not surprisingly, the level of comprehension diminishes as the complexity and length of the consent material increase (Epstein & Lasagna, 1969). However, although there is an extensive body of literature on learning and educational psychology, it has not been brought to bear on the development of understandable consent information.

Reactions to Informed Consent Procedures

In addition to studies of the amount of consent information that individuals understand, some studies have been conducted on how patients feel about being informed (Alfidi, 1971; Denney, Williamson, & Penn, 1975; Golden & Johnston, 1970; Lankton, Batchelder, & Ominslay, 1977). Besides its obvious relevance to decision making about treatment, this area of investigation has special significance for therapeutic research, in which participants' consideration of risks and benefits of an experimental treatment and its alternatives may make grave prognoses appear especially stark. . . .

Reaction to consent information is typically assessed by asking individuals whether the information disclosed in the consent session made them upset or anxious. Although there are anecdotal reports that the disclosure made patients anxious or fearful, empirical studies generally find no differences between the anxiety levels, either self-reported or reported by observers, of informed individuals receiving standard treatment and those of uninformed individuals receiving such treatment (Denney et al., 1975; Houts & Leaman, 1980; Lankton et al., 1977). Two studies without uninformed controls (Alfidi, 1971; Houts & Leaman, 1980) found that although consent information disturbed about 40% of the patients, only 1% decided to refuse the recommended procedure and virtually all individuals regarded the information as useful. It is interesting to note that one study (Denney et al., 1975) found that postoperative anxiety levels were lower in informed patients than in uninformed patients, thus suggesting that knowledge of expected results makes the actual results more emotionally tolerable and less frightening. In fact, this notion serves as the basis for presurgical counseling, which prepares patients through support and information. . . .

Decision Making

. . .

A few studies have attempted to relate comprehension of consent information to decision making (Epstein & Lasagna, 1969; Stuart, 1978). The findings indicate that higher levels of comprehension are associated with higher rates of agreement to the proposed procedure by the patient.

As an outgrowth of studies that show that risk disclosure often has only a minimal influence on decision making with regard to medical procedures, some studies have begun to identify other factors that influence decisions. In a study of participation in psychology experiments (Geller & Faden, 1979), the relative influence of standard consent information and personal testimony of one individual was examined. Although recall of consent information was affected by testimony that contraindicated it, the decision to participate was not affected. In another study, subjects reported that disclosed information was not the primary determinant in decisions regarding contraception. Personal feelings were reported to have a greater influence on the decision (Faden & Beauchamp, 1980).

As an extension of this work, it would be worthwhile to use and adapt some of the techniques developed by investigators who research decision making and information processing (Janis & Mann, 1977; Jungerman, 1980). For example, one might try to adapt the technique of "policy capturing" to research on informed consent. In addition to asking participants what influenced them, researchers could place them in a variety of hypothetical situations and ask them to make a decision about participation. In this way, participants' ability to report influences would not be depended upon as heavily. This approach, with its pitfalls, could be supplemented with individual self-reports to obtain a fuller picture of the decision-making process. In addition, research that combines available knowledge of the psychology of the volunteer with the cognitive aspects of risk perception and decision making would provide a much clearer picture of research participants than is now available.

Furthermore, researchers have little knowledge of the effect of the institutional setting on decision making with respect to research participation. Do certain settings in which individuals are not permitted to leave (e.g., prisons, schools, psychiatric hospitals) have a coercive influence and therefore increase the likelihood of research participation irrespective of the individual's real wishes? If so, are there ways in which the research setting itself can be altered to increase perceived choice?

COMPETENCY OF RESEARCH PARTICIPANTS

Competency to give an informed consent recently has been the subject of empirical studies. A major difficulty with conducting research on competency lies in the lack of a uniform standard of competency (Meisel, Roth, & Lidz, 1977; Roth, Meisel, & Lidz, 1977). Three populations are most often identified as having questionable competency: (a) mentally disabled persons, (b) cognitively impaired elderly persons, and (c) children.

Mentally Disabled Persons

The empirical evidence that is available with respect to severely disordered persons presents a somewhat mixed picture. One conclusion that can be safely drawn with respect to psychiatric patients is that they do no better than medical patients in the consent process. The evidence that they are less able to give consent is somewhat equivocal and to a certain extent depends on the definition of competency that is used. With respect to comprehension of consent information, a few studies have assessed psychiatric patients' ability to understand consent information (Appelbaum, Mirkin, & Bateman, 1981; Grossman & Summers, 1980; Roth et al., 1982; Soskis & Jaffe, 1979). In general, psychiatric patients do not have a very high level of understanding of consent information. However, when studies of medical patients are compared with studies of psychiatric patients, their understanding seems nearly equal (Grossman & Summers, 1980; Soskis & Jaffe, 1979). For example, one study found that schizophrenic patients understood only about 50% of the material on a consent form that was read to them (Grossman & Summers, 1980). However, in a direct comparison of psychiatric and medical patients, schizophrenic patients were found to be more aware of the risks and side effects of their medication than were medical patients (Soskis, 1978). On the other hand, medical patients were better informed about the name and dosage of their medication, as well as their diagnosis. Psychiatric patients' poor knowledge of their diagnosis may have been partly the result of a general reluctance by hospital staff to tell patients that they have schizophrenia.

Related to the comprehension level of psychiatric patients are studies that have examined their literacy skills. Although acutely hospitalized psychiatric patients' comprehension of consent information seems to be equal to that of medical patients, research indicates that reading comprehension scores of chronic patients are only at the fifth-grade level (Berg & Hammit, 1980; Coles, Roth, & Pollack, 1978). Thus, hospital documents should be simplified for psychiatric patients (Berg & Hammit, 1980), as some have suggested they be for medical patients. . . .

Overall, the empirical research on informed consent shows that psychiatric patients do have some impairment in their abilities. However, the research also shows that in some respects they do not differ from medical patients. As a result, further studies that use comparison groups, particularly medical patients, are necessary to draw conclusions about the competency of mentally disordered persons as a group to consent to research.

Cognitively Impaired Elderly Persons

Studies of the elderly have shown some impairment in their ability to comprehend consent information (Stanley, Guido, Stanley, & Shortell, 1984). Impaired recall of consent information has been noted in elderly persons who have poor verbal skills (Taub, 1980). However, it appears that the overall quality of decision making is not affected by age, although comprehension and recall may be (Stanley et al., 1984). In other words, elderly people typically reach decisions regarding agreement to proposed procedures that are similar to those of younger people.

Children

As with the other groups, the competence of minors to consent to research probably is often underestimated. A large body of research has developed about children's competence in making personal decisions, including consent to treatment (see generally Melton, 1984; Melton, Koocher, & Saks, 1983). Generally, such studies show that even elementary school children commonly are able to express a preference and, indeed, to make the same decision that average adults make (Weithorn & Campbell, 1982). By age 14, for most decisions, minors are as competent as adults to understand and weigh the risks and benefits of the available alternatives.

Few studies have examined minors' competence to consent to research. However, the studies that are available are consistent with the general findings about minors' decision making (Keith-Spiegel, 1983; Keith-Spiegel & Maas, 1981; Lewis, Lewis, & Ifekwunigue, 1978). . . .

ADDRESSING ETHICAL ISSUES IN RESEARCH

The social sciences in some ways have lagged behind other disciplines, including medicine and law, in addressing ethical issues in science (Kaufmann, 1983) and particularly in research. Although psychology was a forerunner in developing a set of ethical principles governing research, it has been slow to address the nuances of the range of ethical issues in research, as indicated, for example, by the relatively few articles on informed consent in the social sciences

(Kaufmann, 1983). Social science methods can be readily applied to the study of a broad range of ethical issues in research. Use of these techniques may ultimately help to develop a more informed public policy and standards with respect to research. . . .

References

Alfidi, R. J. (1971). Informed consent: A study of patient reaction. *Journal of the American Medical Association, 216,* 1325–1329.

Appelbaum, P. S., Mirkin, S., & Bateman, A. (1981). Competency to consent to psychiatric hospitalization: An empirical assessment. *American Journal of Psychiatry, 138,* 1170–1176.

Barbour, G. L., & Blumenkrantz, M. J. (1978). Videotape aids informed consent decisions. *Journal of the American Medical Association, 240,* 2741–2742.

Berg, A., & Hammit, K. B. (1980). Assessing the psychiatric patient's ability to meet the literacy demands of hospitalization. *Hospital and Community Psychiatry, 31,* 266–268.

Coles, G., Roth, L., & Pollack, L. (1978). Literacy skills of long-term hospitalized mental patients. *Hospital and Community Psychiatry, 29,* 512–516.

Denney, M., Williamson, D., & Penn, R. (1975). Informed consent: Emotional responses of patients. *Postgraduate Medicine, 60,* 205–209.

Epstein, L., & Lasagna, L. (1969). Obtaining informed consent: Form or substance? *Archives of Internal Medicine, 123,* 682–685.

Faden, R. (1977). Disclosure and informed consent: Does it matter how we tell it? *Health Education Monographs, 5,* 198–214.

Faden, R., & Beauchamp, T. (1980). Decision-making and informed consent: A study of the impact of disclosed information. *Social Indicators Research, 7,* 13–36.

Geller, D., & Faden, R. (1979, September). *Decision-making in informed consent: Base rate and individuating information.* Paper presented at the meeting of the American Psychological Association, New York.

Golden, J., & Johnston, G. (1970). Problems of distortion in doctor–patient communication. *Psychiatry Medicine, 1,* 127–148.

Grossman, L., & Summers, F. (1980). A study of the capacity of schizophrenic patients to give informed consent. *Hospital and Community Psychiatry, 31,* 205–207.

Houts, P., & Leaman, D. (1980, September). *Patient response to information about possible complications of medical procedures.* Paper presented at the meeting of the American Psychological Association, Montreal, Canada.

Janis, L., & Mann, L. (1977). *Decision-making: A psychological analysis of conflict choice and commitment.* New York: Free Press.

Jungerman, H. (1980). Speculations about decision–theoretic aids for personal decision making. *Acta Psychologica, 45,* 7–34.

Kaufmann, C. L. (1983). Informed consent and patient decision making: Two decades of research. *Social Science and Medicine, 17,* 1657–1664.

Keith-Spiegel, P. (1983). Children and consent to participate in research. In G. B. Melton, G. P. Koocher, & M. J. Saks (Eds.), *Children's competence to consent* (pp. 179–211). New York: Plenum Press.

Keith-Spiegel, P., & Maas, T. (1981, August). *Consent to research: Are there developmental differences?* Paper presented at the meeting of the American Psychological Association, Los Angeles, CA.

Lankton, J., Batchelder, B., & Ominslay, A. (1977). Emotional responses to detailed risk disclosure for anesthesia. *Anesthesiology, 46,* 294–296.

Lewis, C. E., Lewis, M. A., & Ifekwunigue, M. (1978). Informed consent by children and participation in an influenza vaccine trial. *American Journal of Public Health, 68,* 1079–1082.

Meisel, A., & Roth, L. (1981). What we do and do not know about informed consent. *Journal of the American Medical Association, 246,* 2473–2477.

Meisel, A., Roth, L., & Lidz, C. (1977). Towards a model of the legal doctrine of informed consent. *American Journal of Psychiatry, 134,* 285–289.

Melton, G. B. (1984). Developmental psychology and the law: The state of the art. *Journal of Family Law, 22,* 445–482.

Melton, G. B., Koocher, G. P., & Saks, M. J. (Eds.). (1983). *Children's competence to consent.* New York: Plenum.

Roth, L. H., Lidz, C. W., Meisel, A., Soloff, P. H., Kaufmen, K., Spiker, D. G., & Foster, F. G. (1982). Competency to decide about treatment or research: An overview of some empirical data. *International Journal of Law and Psychiatry, 5,* 29–50.

Roth, L. H., Meisel, A., & Lidz, C. W. (1977). Tests of competency to consent to treatment. *American Journal of Psychiatry, 134,* 279–284.

Silberstein, E. (1974). Extension of two part consent form. *New England Journal of Medicine, 291,* 155–156.

Soskis, D. A. (1978). Schizophrenic and medical inpatients as informed drug consumers. *Archives of General Psychiatry, 35,* 645–647.

Soskis, D. A., & Jaffe, R. L. (1979). Communicating with patients about antipsychotic drugs. *Comprehensive Psychiatry, 20,* 126–131.

Stanley, B., Guido, J., Stanley, M., & Shortell, D. (1984). The elderly patient and informed consent. *Journal of the American Medical Association, 252,* 1302–1306.

Stuart, R. B. (1978). Protection of the right to informed consent to participate in research. *Behavior Therapy, 9,* 73–82.

Taub, H. A. (1980). Informed consent, memory and age. *The Gerontologist, 20,* 686–690.

Weithorn, L. A., & Campbell, S. B. (1982). The competency of children and adolescents to make informed treatment decisions. *Child Development, 53,* 1589–1598.

◆ ◆ ◆

Commentary: Although it has been phased out, the APA Committee on Standards in Research issued periodic reports that are still worth reading. See, for example,

Rosnow, R. L., Rotheram-Borus, M. J., Ceci, S. J., Blanck, P. D., & Koocher, G. P. (1993). The institutional review board as a mirror of scientific and ethical standards. American Psychologist, 48, *821–826.*

Blanck, P. D., Bellak, A. S., Rosnow, R. L., Rotheram-Borus, M. J., & Schooler, N. R. (1992). Scientific rewards and conflicts of ethical choices in human subjects research. American Psychologist, 47, *959–965.*

Grisso, T., Baldwin, E., Blanck, P. D., Rotheram-Borus, M. J., Schooler, N., & Thompson, T. (1991). Standards in research: APA's mechanism for monitoring the challenges. American Psychologist, 46, *758–766.*

There are also many well-regarded texts that address the issues introduced in this chapter in a more detailed and comprehensive way. The following are just a few examples:

Boruch, R. F., & Cecil, J. S. (1983). Solutions to ethical and legal problems in social research: Quantitative studies in social relations. San Diego, CA: Academic Press.

Kimmel, A. J. (1988). Ethics and values in applied social research. Newbury Park, CA: Sage.

Levine, R. J. (1988). Ethics and regulation of clinical research (2nd ed.). New Haven, CT: Yale University Press.

Miller, D. J., & Hersen, M. (1992). Research fraud in the behavioral and biomedical sciences. New York: Wiley.

Sieber, J. E. (1992). Planning ethically responsible research: A guide for students and internal review boards. Newbury Park, CA: Sage.

For a thoughtful critique of the provisions affecting research in the APA's 1992 Ethical Principles, see Sieber, J. E. (1994). Will the new code help researchers to be more ethical? Professional Psychology: Research and Practice, 25, *369–375.*

Ethical Issues in the Supervision of Student Research: A Study of Critical Incidents

Rodney K. Goodyear, Clyde A. Crego, and Michael W. Johnston

[*Ed. note*: In this study, 57 well-published and experienced professional psychologists were asked to describe, in free-response form, up to three instances of ethical problems related to student–faculty research collaboration. Respondents reported 114 critical incidents. The results are summarized by category in Table 1. Under the heading "Applicable APA Ethical Principles," provide the appropriate standards in the 1992 Ethical Principles. Then continue with the authors' consideration of each of the categories.]

Kitchener (1984) suggested five broad principles as being especially important bases for ethical behavior: doing no harm, benefiting others, respecting other's autonomy, being fair, and acting faithfully in relationships. These "higher level norms" are broader and more basic than APA's Ethical Principles. For that reason, they are used as criteria for considering the ethically problematic aspects of each of the following categories.

Incompetent supervision. Psychologists recognize that, because of the risk of harm to clients, it is unethical to practice outside their areas of competence when they provide client services. This same principle should extend to the research supervisor, though this application of it has received scant discussion in the literature. Although the critical incidents addressed only the supervisor's methodological competence, another area of competence that is important in research supervision is that of subject matter.

Subject matter competence seems to arise most often as an issue in the supervision of dissertation or thesis research. The ethical tension is between that of respecting the student's autonomy, on the one hand,

and that of being able to benefit the student and act faithfully, on the other. In fact, it seems possible to array the ways in which faculty have responded to this matter along a continuum. At one end of the continuum are faculty who would allow each student whom they supervise to follow his or her own interests, regardless of faculty knowledge of that area. Often these seem to be faculty who believe that conducting "independent" research means that the student is to have complete freedom in topic choice. On the other end of the continuum are faculty who define specific areas of expertise for themselves and refuse to supervise any student research that does not fall into one of these areas.

Neither of these extreme solutions is wholly satisfactory. The second approach, however, probably offers the better balance of the competing ethical principles as long as students have the freedom within a program to pair with the faculty member whose interests are closest to their own: Students who feel coerced into research on a topic of little interest to them lose perceived autonomy and may suffer harm (e.g., in their attitudes toward research, in the quality of their work).

The second issue of competence concerns the research supervisor's mastery of research methodology and statistics. Competence, of course, exists on a continuum, and few people are as competent as they could be. However, in the words of one respondent, "Ultimately the authors of articles must assume sole responsibility for all aspects of their scholarly product and their interpretations. It is insufficient to simply say 'Because the statistician said so.'" There does seem to be a point at which the supervisor's lack of

Adapted from *Professional Psychology: Research and Practice, 23*, 203–210. Copyright 1992 by the American Psychological Association. Part of Table 1 has been omitted.

TABLE 1

Ethical Problems in Faculty Supervision of Student Research

Category	Examples of Critical Incidents	Applicable APA Ethical Principles
Incompetent supervision	(a) Faculty member knows so little about statistics that he refers his students to consultants or other faculty for even the most basic information; (b) Data analysis for a thesis conducted by a statistician without the student's or advisor's knowledge of the statistics being used.	
Inadequate supervision	(a) The faculty advisor to a senior honors thesis was only peripherally involved in the student's research, did not read her thesis draft, and was unavailable prior to the day of her defense meeting. The resulting paper was awful and the student was humiliated. (b) A faculty member participated little in a thesis project and provided minimal supervision. Just before the defense, the faculty member berated the student for the topic as well as the obtained results. (c) Dissertation chair sets inadequate standards for student performance, fails to have the student follow-through on suggestions made by the dissertation committee, and argues that "no one is going to read it anyway."	
Supervision abandonment	(a) "I have seen students dropped in the middle of research projects either because the faculty weren't interested, had moved away, or some other reason." (b) "Three years ago, I was, as an intern, part of a research team that conducted a large treatment outcome study. None of the several papers we outlined have yet been done—and despite my repeated offers to assist in writing/analyzing/editing, I am told my help is not needed." (c) Faculty member gets research teams together, makes them do a great deal of work, says she will write it up, then doesn't.	
Intrusion of supervisor values	(a) Faculty member refused to chair her advisee's dissertation because she was an atheist and the student wanted to study a religious issue; (b) Faculty member insisted her student employ a radical feminist perspective in his dissertation study of campus date rape even though the student did not find the perspective useful.	
Abusive supervision	(a) A student's advisor verbally and emotionally abused her, leading to her hatred of research, self-doubt, and thought of leaving the program. (b) To gain access to needed data, a student was required to join a research team, do work she was not interested in—and to be ridiculed as incompetent in front of the group (her contribution, which ultimately resulted in a publication with the faculty member, was minimized and ridiculed). (c) Professor took student off as coauthor after she confronted his sexual harassment behavior.	
Exploitive supervision	(a) Professor requires graduate assistants to assist in the teaching of his courses. They are afraid to confront him for fear of reprisals. (b) Professor consistently exploited a student's time and regularly insisted that she work on a research project during a time she was scheduled to be in class with another professor.	

(table continues)

	TABLE 1 *(cont.)*	
Category	**Examples of Critical Incidents**	**Applicable APA Ethical Principles**
Dual relationships	(a) Dissertation advisor and student were involved romantically, but the relationship went sour, they broke up, and he gave her a hard time on her dissertation research and written document. (b) A professor provided research assistantships and authorships to a student who was in a sexual relationship with him.	
Encouragement to fraud	(a) Faculty member urged students to skew a report of data analyses that failed to support his preferred theory. (b) Student was an RA for a faculty member, doing house-to-house survey: Faculty member told the student to make up data if no one was home.	
Authorship issues		
1. Plagiarism	(a) A GA essentially ghost wrote several chapters of a faculty member's book, but received no credit. (b) A professor published the ideas of one of his students without crediting her. (c) Student wrote a critique of a book; it then was published with the professor who assigned the task as the sole author.	
2. Failure to give (expected) credit	(a) Student and faculty member collaborate on a project; unbeknownst to the student, the faculty member submitted it for convention presentation. (b) A PI wrote up the results of a study and submitted it for publication without inviting the RA (who had been substantially involved) to coauthor. (c) The senior author dropped the 3rd author from authorship on page proofs without notifying 2nd or 3rd authors—who found out after publication.	
3. Giving unwarranted credit	(a) I have observed faculty giving students authorship for activities that likely do not fall under the rubric of authorship. (b) A student conducted a thesis, relying primarily on faculty other than his advisor for guidance and support—then in a nice gesture, gave his advisor second authorship of a resulting article (though uncomfortable, the advisor consented). (c) Faculty member and student are sole collaborators on an article. But galleys arrive, faculty member adds spouse third author.	

expertise impairs his or her ability to benefit the supervisee or to act faithfully in that relationship; conceivably, it also could cause actual harm to the supervisee.

It might be that a hallmark of research supervisors who could be considered to practice outside their methodological competence is their unwillingness to master new models and procedures along with the students they are supervising (by, for example, joining the student for meetings with the statistical consultant for tutoring in unfamiliar procedures). Fortunately, by tradition there is a committee to whom thesis and dissertation students answer. This

can moderate many, though not all, effects of incompetent supervision.

Inadequate supervision. It is possible, of course, for a research supervisor to be competent but still leave students to fend for themselves, with neither the support nor the skills they will need for truly successful completion of their research project. There is no way of knowing what percentage of research supervisors provide consistently inadequate supervision. But it is likely that even the most conscientious of us occasionally is guilty of a less serious version of this type of behavior: providing students with tardy responses to or inadequate critiques of their work (see, e.g., Magoon & Holland, 1984). Of Kitchener's (1984) ethical principles, the one that seems to apply most to inadequate research supervision is that of acting faithfully, although the principles of being fair, benefiting others, and doing no harm apply as well.

Supervision abandonment. Occasionally, a supervisor will fail to fulfill an implicit or explicit contract with the student to see a research project through to completion. The supervisor has not acted faithfully or provided benefit to these supervisees. In fact, she or he actually may cause them some degree of harm (e.g., in graduation delays, in time invested that could have been used more profitably elsewhere).

There seem to be two qualitatively different manifestations of this ethical problem category. In one version, the students participate in a research project, often as members of a research group. They may have done a great deal of work, but the supervising faculty member fails to follow through with his or her promised efforts, and the project is not completed. Because of the power differential or because the faculty member has physical possession of the data, research supervisees are unable to reap the expected (and deserved) rewards of their efforts.

A second type of abandonment occurs when the faculty member leaves the student midway through his or her thesis or dissertation. Although faculty occasionally will do this when they take a sabbatical, this seems to occur more often when faculty move to another university. The degree to which this is a breach of ethical principles (especially those of faithfulness and doing no harm) is moderated by such factors as the stage of the student's research and the extent to which he or she has been given prior information about the likelihood of the supervisor leaving.

It is important to recognize, too, that because research supervision typically occurs in an institutional context, institutional policies and norms have a great deal to do with how research supervision is handled if a faculty member leaves that setting. Some universities, for example, will provide the travel costs and even some stipend to a departing faculty member in order to see a dissertation through to completion. But if the situation will not permit the departing faculty member to continue as the student's primary research supervisor, he or she should be active in helping to arrange the student's transition to another faculty supervisor (just as a psychologist would arrange a client's referral under parallel circumstances).

Intrusion of the supervisor's values. Certainly most people have beliefs about what is important to study and the perspective or perspectives from which that should be done. Research supervision can be no less value free than psychotherapy. There is, though, a fine line between merely sharing those values and actively imposing them on students, a behavior that violates the principles of autonomy and fairness. It is possible to provide reasonable protection to students from this problem by ensuring that the students (a) are clear about strongly held values of faculty members, and (b) have freedom within their training program not to work with faculty members whose guiding values would prove problematic to them.

Abusive and exploitive supervision. Although abusive and exploitive supervision share some similar characteristics, the raters judged that they were sufficiently different to merit separate clustering. The difference seemed to be one of the supervisor's intent: Whereas with exploitive supervision the research supervisor subjects the supervisee to inconvenience for some selfish end, in abusive supervision the supervisor's motive seems to be punishment of the supervisee for some real or imagined "shortcoming." In either case, the offending supervisor is likely to have violated the principles of fairness and of doing no harm.

Dual relationships. Dual relationships apparently constitute a problem in research supervision just as in other areas of psychological practice. Goodyear and Sinnett (1984) have noted that people who choose the same occupation tend to share common values and beliefs, and that such similarities can provide the basis for the mutual attraction that sometimes occurs between faculty and students. Moreover, in contrast to therapist–client relationships, faculty and students interact in multiple contexts and therefore experience fewer boundary constraints on their behaviors. In fact, as Tabachnick et al. (1991) have observed, "sometimes, what with so many social and other types of activities available to both students and faculty on and off campus, boundary blurring seems practically built into the academic system" (p. 514).

The salient issue, though, is one of protecting the student from exploitation, for the power differential is such that the student is at greater risk in these relationships than the faculty member—no matter how well intentioned the involved parties might be. Certainly the critical incidents summarized in Table 1 concerning romantic attachments and research supervision illustrate that concerns about these risks are grounded in reality. The principles of faithfulness and of doing no harm are at issue in these cases.

Encouragement to fraud. Encouraging students to engage in such fraudulent research activity as faking data or results seems especially reprehensible. To the extent that these efforts are "successful," science is tainted and students are exposed to unfortunate role models who have failed to behave faithfully. As important, though, is the fact that students are placed at risk of harm by such behaviors. One respondent recounted the substantial lengths to which a psychologist, now herself a faculty member, had to go to clear her reputation following an incident of data falsification by her faculty collaborator on a project in which she was involved as a student.

Authorship issues. Finally, there is the important and often-troublesome matter of authorship credit: Who should be an author and in what order? This matter often emerges as a basis of disputes between or among well-intentioned people who have honest disagreements about authorship. A number of the reported incidents were of this type. It was difficult, however, to identify ethical principles that would justify these situations as being ethically problematic.

It was possible, though, to identify three subcategories of authorship problem that were ethically problematic. The first two of these subcategories involve supervisee exploitation, with consequent harm to the supervisee and a breach of faithfulness on the part of the supervisor. These subcategories differ,

though, in that with the first category, plagiarism, the person from whom the ideas of work was taken may either be unaware of the infraction or actually have colluded in it. Although in the second category, failure to give credit, one or more persons who expected author credit did not receive it.

Some of the more contentious problems arise in determining what authorship, if any, a faculty member can take on an article developed from a dissertation. This, in turn, seems grounded in assumptions about what a dissertation is or should be: If it literally is independent research in which the student has formulated the problem, developed the design, gathered data, and conducted analyses with relative independence, the authorship certainly is the student's. Some faculty apparently believe this is how all dissertations are to be developed. One respondent asked, for example, "Is it ever appropriate for an advisor to coauthor an article based on a student's dissertation?"

In practice, few dissertations would meet such a rigorous standard of independence. This is so because students approach their dissertations with differing levels of preparation and therefore faculty often must assume substantial roles in the conceptualization and execution of the projects. Moreover, students often participate in larger research projects, from which they obtain real benefits.

One element in the debate about what level of authorship, if any, a faculty member should have on dissertation-based articles likely derives from psychology's failure to adopt uniform guidelines for the research preparation of students. Compare this situation, for example, with the practitioner training that students receive in professional psychology programs. For this training, students participate in a series of practica and internship experiences; APA accreditation guidelines provide some general consistency across training programs for these experiences. No such uniformity exists, however, in the research training of students, even in those programs that espouse a scientist–practitioner model. . . . Thus, whereas a dissertation is for some students akin to an internship in research, for many others it is more akin to a first practicum. That is, whereas some students have multiple experiences in conducting research prior to undertaking a dissertation, for too many it is their first research project. In the latter case, it is difficult for the faculty supervisor to avoid making major contributions to the project, thereby earning eventual authorship.

Another cause of authorship uncertainties seems to come from the common use of the implicit metaphor of authorship as a type of currency to purchase resources. Researchers often offer junior authorship as compensation for any of a variety of possible contributions that might be made to a research project, from conducting literature searches to providing access to existing databases. But this metaphor can become a source of problems for the many students who engage in supervised research as graduate assistants and are receiving real currency as compensation. The results of several critical incidents have suggested that the question in many such cases is whether receiving a paycheck adequately compensates for research participation. Perhaps the alternative question is, Does receiving both a paycheck and a junior authorship constitute "double-dipping." (Faculty, of course, receive both salary and authorship for their contributions with no such questions being raised.) In the absense of clear norms for these matters, the best way of handling such issues probably is to have the ground rules for research participation clear to all parties at the outset of a project.

In contrast to the possible "theft" involved in the first two of these authorship subcategories, the third subcategory involves unwarranted gifts of credit. A real difficulty in this case is that the psychologist may operate with the best of motives. He or she may, for example, wish to help promote the career of a mentee. In this way, the supervisor actually is adhering to the principle of benefiting another. A possible difficulty, though, is that if others are involved as coauthors on the basis of having made real contributions to the project, their benefits are "diluted" with the inclusion of the noncontributor (i.e., generally, the greater the number of authors, the less the perceived contribution of each). This raises both the principle of fairness and that of doing no harm. . . .

References

Goodyear, R. K., & Sinnett, E. R. (1984). Current and emerging ethical issues for counseling psychologists. *The Counseling Psychologist, 12,* 87–93.

Kitchener, K. S. (1984). Intuition, critical evaluation, and ethical principles: The foundation for ethical decisions in counseling psychology. *The Counseling Psychologist, 12,* 43–45.

Magoon, T. M., & Holland, J. L. (1984). Research training and supervision. In S. D. Brown & R. W. Lent (Eds.), *Handbook of counseling psychology* (pp. 682–715). New York: Wiley.

Tabachnick, B. G., Keith-Spiegel, P., & Pope, K. S. (1991). Ethics of teaching: Beliefs and behaviors of psychologists as educators. *American Psychologist, 46,* 506–515.

◆　◆　◆

Commentary: For a more extended discussion of the assignment of publication credit in student–faculty collaborations, see Costa, M. M., & Gatz, M. (1992). Determination of authorship credit in published dissertations. Psychological Science, 3, *354–357. Using vignettes distributed to all students and faculty at seven geographically diverse doctoral-level psychology departments, Costa and Gatz found that students were given more credit by faculty on published dissertations than on nondegree research but that second authorship credit by the faculty member for dissertations was almost automatic. Contrary to expectations, students were more generous to advisors than advisors were to themselves, with senior faculty giving greater credit to graduate students than did junior faculty. Another helpful resource is Fine, M. A., & Kurdek, L. A. (1993). Reflections on determining authorship credit and authorship order on faculty–student collaborations.* American Psychologist, 48, *1141–1147. This article was particularly educational because it contained four realistically based but hypothetical cases involving authorship credit, suggested ethical principles to guide decision making, proposed some decision rules, and then applied these principles and rules to the four cases. Readers may not agree with the outcomes, but these cases will surely provoke useful discussion.*

Although guidelines for authorship credit appear in the fourth edition of the Publication Manual of the American Psychological Association *(1994), an enforceable provision concerning assignment of publication credit is now found in Section 6.23 of the 1992 Ethical Principles. Other relevant standards are 6.21 (Reporting of Results), 6.22 (Plagiarism), 6.24 (Duplicate Publication of Data), and 6.25 (Sharing Data). For a rare discussion of ethical issues related to the peer review of manuscripts submitted for publication, see Rogers, R. (1992). Investigating psychology's taboo: The ethics of editing.* Ethics and Behavior, 2, 253–261.

The conduct, reporting, and publishing of research are not the only arenas within the academic environment that engender ethical concerns. Yet, with the exception of the problem of multiple relationships between faculty and students (see chap. 5), few writers have paid attention to a host of ethical dilemmas that may arise in the univer-sity. There is beginning to be some literature on the ethics of supervision. See, for example,

Russell, R. K., & Petrie, T. (1994). Issues in training effective su-pervisors. Applied and Preventive Psychology, 3, 27–42.

Vasquez, M. T. (1992). Psychologist as clinical supervisor: Promoting ethical practice. Professional Psychology: Research and Practice, 23, 196–202.

Other issues have yet to be addressed in any compre-hensive way. The following excerpt, the last in this chapter, represents a step toward filling this void.

Ethics in Academia: Students' Views of Professors' Actions

Patricia C. Keith-Spiegel, Barbara G. Tabachnick, and Melanie Allen

The bulk of the burgeoning literature debating the ethical standards to which psychologists should be held applies to psychologists engaged in clinical work or research (Hogan & Kimmel, 1992; Tabachnick, Keith-Spiegel, & Pope, 1991). When ethical issues are presented as they apply to academic settings, they largely fall into four circumscribed areas: sexual harassment, rights of "subject-pool" participants, teaching values to students, and scientific misconduct. The general ethical obligations of teaching psychologists—especially those involving responsibilities toward students—have been largely neglected, confined to a spate of articles and book chapters (e.g., Blevins-Knabe, 1992; Goodstein, 1981; Hogan & Kimmel, 1992; Keith-Spiegel & Koocher, 1985; Matthews, 1991). When college students appear in empirical ethics literature, the focus has been on the problems that students themselves cause for professors and the academic institution (e.g., academic dishonesty or psychological impairment).

Given the large number of psychologists who teach on at least a part-time basis, this gap in our literature is curious when one considers how convenient it is to obtain students' opinions. Perhaps teaching psychologists, as members of a larger academic establishment, are presumed to be monitored effectively by policies and standards set in place by the institutions that employ them. And perhaps academic psychologists have been intimidated by a genre of literature seeking to expose professors as self-centered; lazy; politicized and biased; and barely tolerant of, or outrightly repelled by, undergraduate students (e.g., Anderson, 1992; D'Souza, 1991; Sykes, 1989). Such denouncements may leave academics wary about engaging in scholarly activity that could appear to further undermine the public image of the professorate. Furthermore, professors who are mandated to obtain teaching evaluations from students may not relish the prospect of additionally subjecting themselves to students' judgments about their general conduct. However, a better understanding of how students view their professors as "ethical beings" could help guide our roles as models and exemplars as well as educators. Knowledge of students' views of the conduct of professors may also uncover areas of misunderstanding between the two groups.

METHOD

Sample

An urban, West Coast (Los Angeles) sample of 200 undergraduate students and a Midwest (rural Indiana) sample of 282 undergraduate students attending large, comprehensive universities completed a questionnaire requesting ratings of professors' behaviors. . . .

Questionnaire

Fifty-nine items in the questionnaire were adapted from the form used in a study of psychology department faculty (Tabachnick et al., 1991). An additional 48 items were culled from incidents contributed by students responding to a request to supply what they saw to be ethical problems that they had experienced with their professors. Students were asked to rate the 107 faculty behaviors in terms of how ethical they considered the behavior to be. General definitions of unethical behavior (exploitation, causing harm, poor judgment, disrespect, etc.) were offered to assist student respondents with their decision making. Students rated each behavior on the following 5-point scale: *It would not be an unethical act/nothing wrong with this* (1), *it would be poor manners or "tacky" but not unethical* (2), *it would be unethical under rare circumstances* (3), *it would be unethical under many circumstances* (4), *it would be unethical under virtually all circumstances* (5), and *don't know* (DK). . . .

RESULTS

. . .

Table 2 shows the percentages of respondents' ratings of ethicality for each of the 107 behaviors.

. . .

Comparisons Between Students and Professors

Fifty-one of the items (the first 51 items in Table 2) either were identical on this survey to those used in the companion article (Tabachnick et al., 1991) or had only minor changes in wording to accommodate student respondents. Responses were highly correlated, $r(49) = -.81$, $p < .001$. (The negative correlation was produced by opposite coding of the response scales.)

These items could not be compared statistically because of differences in response scales. However, six items showed differences of at least one scale unit (after teacher ratings were reflected to make directions comparable) between students and professors.

Disagreement was strongest for "teaching full-time and holding down another job for at least 20 hours a week." Students were more accepting of moonlighting on the part of faculty. Their mean rating was well within the range of ethical judgments. The average faculty rating indicated a judgment between "ethical under rare circumstances" and "don't know/not sure."

Ratings for "requiring students to use electric shock on rats" were also discrepant. Students found the practice to be "unethical under rare circumstances" whereas teachers judged it between "unquestionably not ethical" and "ethical under rare circumstances." Students were also more accepting of "teaching in a nonobjective or incomplete manner," according ratings between "unethical under rare circumstances" and "unethical under many circum-

stances." Teachers accorded the behavior a rating between "unquestionably not ethical" and "ethical under rare circumstances."

Students considered "accepting an invitation to a student's party" to be "poor manners or 'tacky' but not unethical" on the average, whereas teachers produced an average rating of "don't know/not sure."

"Using university funds or resources to write a 'popular' psychology book for personal profit" was the only item considered less ethical by students than teachers by at least one category. Students considered creating a popular book with school funds to be unethical under many circumstances. Faculty responses were more equivocal, indicating a response of "don't know/not sure."

DISCUSSION

Rather than adversaries, it appears that professors have allies in their students when it comes to expectations of appropriate ethical behavior. When comparisons were possible with the earlier survey of teaching psychologists, students were generally less condemnatory than teaching psychologists were toward themselves.

We would not have been surprised to discover some differences between freshmen and upper division students, but none was discovered. Students apparently enter college with already-set notions of appropriate and inappropriate behavior expected of their teachers, and these do not alter as they mature. We would not have been surprised with differences between ratings made by students living in a huge, diverse, metropolitan city and students in a small, rural, Midwest town: However, there were almost no differences.

We found intriguing patterns in the students' views of the most egregious acts that professors might commit. Defining *egregious* as any action receiving 80% or more ratings of unethical under many or most circumstances, 16 meet the criteria. Practices that could be described as "unfair" because they hinder or bias open competition among students or violate a presumed class contract account for the majority of the acts that students judge to be the most unethical. These are "ignoring strong evidence of cheating," "using a grading procedure that does not adequately measure what students have learned," "allowing how

---

TABLE 2

Percentage of Students Responding in Each Category (*N* = 482)

Item	Rating[a]					
	1	2	3	4	5	DK
1. Using university funds or resources to write a "popular" psychology book for personal profit (e.g., *How to Be Your Own Best Friend*).	5.4	11.2	9.5	28.8	43.6	1.5
2. Ignoring strong evidence of student's cheating.	1.0	3.5	4.8	31.7	58.7	0.2
3. Giving easy courses to ensure popularity with students.	3.9	13.3	14.9	39.0	28.6	0.2
4. Giving academic credit instead of salary for student assistants to perform work for the professor because there are no funds available to hire students.	47.3	17.0	17.2	11.4	4.1	2.9
5. Teaching full-time and holding down another job for at least 20 hours a week.	62.4	16.0	13.3	6.0	1.2	1.0
6. Dating a student.	10.8	25.7	11.8	34.0	17.4	0.2
7. Asking small favors (such as a ride home) from students.	30.9	36.7	18.7	9.8	3.9	0.0
8. Hugging a student.	31.7	22.8	23.4	17.2	4.8	0.0
9. Requiring students to use electric shock on rats.	5.8	6.4	23.4	32.4	29.7	2.3
10. Accepting a student's expensive gift.	16.6	22.0	21.6	24.3	15.4	0.2
11. Teaching classes when too distressed to be effective.	8.3	23.4	30.3	26.1	8.1	3.7
12. Becoming sexually involved with a student.	6.2	14.7	8.3	28.4	42.1	0.2
13. Lending money to a student.	27.2	16.8	25.5	21.2	8.7	0.6
14. Accepting a student's invitation to a party.	30.0	19.1	19.7	17.2	4.6	0.6
15. Selling goods (such as a car or books) to a student.	48.5	20.5	18.0	8.1	3.3	1.5
16. Being sexually attracted to a student.	36.7	27.4	12.9	14.7	7.7	0.6
17. Teaching material that they haven't really mastered or know very much about themselves.	8.1	12.7	16.0	33.6	29.0	0.6
18. Teaching that homosexuality is a mental sickness.	8.9	7.5	9.5	21.8	50.0	2.3
19. Accepting a student's inexpensive gift (i.e., worth less than $5).	57.3	16.0	15.8	6.6	3.9	0.4
20. Teaching a class without being adequately prepared that day.	4.1	38.8	21.4	25.1	10.2	0.4
21. Making deliberate or repeated sexual comments, gestures, or physical contact toward a student that are unwanted by the student.	0.6	2.1	0.8	5.8	90.7	0.0
22. Teaching while under the influence of alcohol.	0.6	1.5	2.3	5.8	89.8	0.0
23. Choosing a particular textbook for a class primarily because the publisher would pay them a "bonus" to do it.	2.1	9.3	11.2	29.3	47.7	0.4
24. Helping a student file a complaint against another professor.	33.2	19.9	25.1	14.3	6.0	1.5
25. Teaching that certain races are intellectually inferior.	0.8	1.7	3.3	10.0	83.8	0.4
26. Encouraging students to volunteer to participate in their research projects as "subjects."	50.6	12.9	20.1	11.2	3.5	1.7
27. Having students be research participants as part of a course requirement (with no alternative way of satisfying the class requirement).	14.3	12.9	21.4	27.8	22.2	1.5
28. Using a grading procedure that does not adequately measure what students have learned.	0.6	4.1	14.1	35.3	44.8	1.0
29. Teaching content in a nonobjective or incomplete manner.	0.8	6.2	15.8	42.3	32.4	2.5
30. Teaching while under the influence of alcohol, cocaine, or some other illegal drug.	0.4	1.0	1.0	3.9	93.6	0.0
31. Refusing to write a letter of recommendation for a particular student because he or she doesn't like that student.	10.2	12.0	14.7	24.3	38.0	0.8
32. Choosing a textbook because the publisher would give the department some free films and software to do it.	11.8	16.4	21.2	33.2	16.2	1.2
33. Allowing how much a student is liked to influence what grade the student gets.	0.6	1.7	7.1	25.5	64.7	0.4
34. Using profanity in class during lectures.	18.0	36.7	17.2	19.3	7.9	0.8
35. Allowing students to drop a class for reasons not officially approved of by the university.	14.7	13.1	36.1	28.0	7.7	0.4
36. Engaging in sexual relationships with other faculty members in the same department.	55.4	25.3	9.1	5.6	3.9	0.6

(table continues)

TABLE 2 (cont.)

Item	Rating[a]					
	1	2	3	4	5	DK
37. Inadequately supervising teaching assistants.	3.7	14.9	28.4	36.7	13.9	2.3
38. Using university funds or resources to create a scholarly textbook.	33.8	10.0	21.2	18.5	13.7	2.9
39. Telling a student "I'm sexually attracted to you."	1.5	18.7	7.9	24.1	47.7	0.2
40. Intentionally leaving out something very important that would help the student when writing a letter of recommendation.	0.0	6.4	7.7	27.8	57.9	0.2
41. Including false or misleading information that hurt the student's chances when writing a letter of recommendation for a student.	0.4	1.7	3.1	14.3	80.3	0.2
42. Grading on a strict curve regardless of class performance level.	8.1	11.4	23.0	35.3	21.4	0.8
43. Using films and videos to fill class time without regard for their educational value to students.	2.5	7.5	19.1	45.0	25.7	0.2
44. Teaching ethics and values to students.	55.8	10.0	16.4	11.4	4.8	1.7
45. Failing to periodically update class lecture notes.	3.3	17.0	26.6	36.3	15.8	1.0
46. Assigning unpaid students to carry out work for the professors that has little educational value for the students.	2.3	8.9	17.4	38.0	32.0	1.5
47. Privately tutoring students in the department for a fee.	20.5	15.4	16.4	23.0	22.4	2.3
48. Taking advantage of a student's offer such as getting wholesale prices at a parent's store.	17.6	25.1	17.8	19.1	19.3	1.0
49. Criticizing all theoretical approaches except those the professor personally prefers.	1.5	9.1	15.8	32.6	39.6	1.5
50. Using cocaine or other illegal drugs in their personal (nonteaching) life.	12.0	17.4	12.2	20.3	37.1	0.8
51. Insulting or ridiculing a student in the student's presence.	1.0	6.0	5.6	23.7	63.5	0.2
52. Encouraging competition among students.	36.1	14.5	24.7	17.2	6.8	0.6
53. Ignoring unethical behavior committed by their colleagues.	1.9	8.9	19.7	39.6	28.6	1.2
54. Becoming sexually involved with a student after the class is over and the grades have been assigned.	39.2	24.1	13.5	12.7	9.5	1.0
55. Picking their favorite students to do projects with them.	11.6	17.4	23.2	29.5	18.3	0.0
56. Being absent from class often due to illness.	49.0	22.8	16.2	8.1	3.3	0.6
57. Being absent from class often to travel to professional workshops and conventions.	20.3	28.6	19.7	21.6	9.5	0.2
58. Giving only multiple choice exams as the basis for the course grade.	56.6	16.8	18.0	5.2	2.3	1.0
59. Giving only essay exams and assigning written projects (i.e., no multiple choice exams).	42.5	14.3	19.5	14.9	7.3	1.5
60. Assigning three thick textbooks for a three-unit course.	15.1	21.2	19.1	26.3	16.6	1.7
61. Giving "pop" (unannounced) quizzes.	45.9	19.9	17.8	10.2	5.8	0.4
62. Spending 25–30 hours during the week doing writing and research in their offices or laboratories.	65.4	8.7	13.3	7.1	3.1	2.5
63. Agreeing to write a recommendation letter for a student, but not getting it in until 2 weeks past the deadline.	1.0	15.0	7.3	25.1	50.8	0.0
64. Lecturing only from material taken directly from the textbook.	39.2	25.3	18.0	13.9	3.3	0.2
65. Flirting with students.	4.1	24.3	11.2	29.7	30.3	0.4
66. Humiliating a student for falling asleep in class.	7.1	23.0	25.1	25.3	19.5	0.0
67. Giving an F on a term paper because it was a week late.	30.5	15.1	24.5	17.4	11.4	1.0
68. Not allowing any student to enter the room the instant the "hour" starts.	4.8	17.8	12.0	31.3	33.6	0.4
69. Giving every student an A regardless of the quality of their work.	2.7	2.9	5.8	19.5	68.7	0.4
70. Refusing to let students take makeup exams.	6.4	6.8	24.5	33.8	28.2	0.2
71. Giving only one or two As in each class.	8.5	7.5	17.4	31.7	33.6	1.2
72. Gives 15 hours worth of homework a week for a three-unit class.	10.0	13.5	17.8	33.4	24.3	1.0
73. Giving a very difficult exam during the third week of school in an attempt to encourage some students to drop the course.	1.0	5.4	10.2	35.7	47.7	0.0
74. Setting up a course so that students are encouraged to share aspects of their very personal life in class.	21.2	14.9	26.1	24.7	12.2	0.8
75. Refusing to write a letter of recommendation for a student because he or she doesn't know the student well enough.	48.8	16.4	20.7	9.8	4.4	0.0
76. Assigning reading that is difficult to get to (e.g., articles in journals that cannot be taken home from the library).	5.8	21.4	22.8	35.9	13.9	0.2

(table continues)

TABLE 2 (cont.)

Item	Rating[a]					
	1	2	3	4	5	DK
77. Requiring students to read materials (text, articles, etc.) that the professor acknowledges are "not very good."	8.3	16.4	22.0	36.1	16.0	1.2
78. Taking a "royalty" percentage payment on a collection of previously published readings that the professor puts together himself or herself, and requires students to purchase at the bookstore or a copy store.	10.4	12.7	18.7	28.4	26.8	3.1
79. Not getting exams graded and handed back until 4 weeks after the exam was given.	0.8	19.3	10.4	35.7	33.2	0.6
80. Changing the criteria for successful completion of a class in the middle of the semester (e.g., adding an extra term paper or saying that something was going to count more and changing to it counting less).	1.0	6.0	15.6	31.7	45.2	0.4
81. Announcing exam grades of each student, by name, in front of the class.	0.4	8.1	7.1	23.4	61.0	0.0
82. Running a film that might offend or emotionally upset some students without prior warning.	1.0	9.3	9.3	39.0	41.3	0.0
83. Including material on the test that was not covered in the lectures or assigned reading.	0.4	2.7	5.4	18.7	72.8	0.0
84. Changing the expected format of a test on the day of the test.	1.2	6.4	6.6	28.4	57.3	0.0
85. Accepting current students as psychotherapy clients in a professor's private practice.	11.8	12.2	19.9	25.3	25.9	4.8
86. Ridiculing or discounting the opinion of another professor in a student's presence.	1.9	15.6	16.8	31.3	33.2	1.2
87. Requiring students to disclose highly personal information in a group discussion class (i.e., the student who remains silent or "closed up" is graded down for that).	0.8	2.9	7.5	26.3	61.6	0.8
88. Advising a student not to take a certain professor's class.	7.9	13.7	25.5	30.3	22.4	0.2
89. Giving a student advice in areas in which the professor is not really qualified to offer guidance.	5.8	12.4	25.9	38.6	16.8	0.4
90. Talking to students (in private) about a student's personal problems.	46.3	14.5	19.5	14.1	5.2	0.4
91. Talking to students (in private) about their own personal problems.	18.7	23.0	14.9	24.7	17.6	1.0
92. Telling a student that he or she has problems and should go to the counseling center.	38.2	18.3	24.3	13.3	5.4	0.6
93. Telling a student during a class discussion, "That was a stupid comment."	0.8	7.7	7.7	23.7	60.2	0.0
94. Requiring students to watch a film on how to do surgical brain implant techniques on monkeys.	13.1	15.4	21.0	23.9	24.1	2.7
95. Never learning any of the students' names in a class of 30 students.	6.4	37.8	11.4	22.6	21.6	0.2
96. Teaching in jeans and a sweatshirt.	64.3	23.9	5.6	3.9	2.1	0.2
97. Inability to control class (e.g., too-talkative students who dominate class time are not curtailed).	1.7	16.8	18.0	35.3	27.6	0.6
98. Always letting class out 15 minutes early.	43.6	21.0	21.6	10.6	3.3	0.0
99. Requiring students to visit a "locked ward" (most disturbed) patients in a mental hospital.	10.0	11.2	21.2	29.3	26.8	1.7
100. Being more friendly to some students than to others.	9.5	26.1	19.5	27.2	17.4	0.2
101. Telling "off-color" stories or jokes in class.	12.2	22.2	11.8	20.5	32.0	1.2
102. Writing comments on tests or assignments that are illegible.	8.1	42.7	14.1	17.4	17.0	0.6
103. Handing back term projects with a grade, but no other marks on it or indication as to why the grade was assigned.	6.4	23.0	16.4	33.2	20.1	0.8
104. Allowing only students who have English as their second language to use a dictionary during lecture.[b]	12.7	8.9	20.3	26.6	27.6	1.5
105. Offering students no opportunities for "extra credit."	27.6	18.5	23.4	17.4	12.4	0.6
106. Taking points off for assignments handed in late.	68.3	10.6	15.1	5.0	0.8	0.2
107. Grading handwritten papers lower than papers that are typed or done on a computer.	18.5	22.6	24.3	19.5	14.3	0.8

[a]Students rated each behavior on the following 5-point scale: *would not be an unethical act/nothing wrong with this* (1), *would be poor manners or "tacky" but not unethical* (2), *it would be unethical under rare circumstances* (3), *it would be unethical under many circumstances* (4), *it would be unethical under virtually all circumstances* (5), and *don't know* (DK). [b]Row does not sum to 100% because of missing data.

much a student is liked to influence grading," "including false or misleading harmful information in a student's letter of recommendation," "giving every student an *A* regardless of the quality of their work," "giving a very difficult exam during the third week of school in an attempt to encourage some students to drop the course," "changing the criteria for successful completion of the class in the middle of the semester," and "including material on an exam that was not covered in the lectures or assigned reading." Students appear to be very sensitive to ridicule, embarrassment, or other emotionally upsetting experiences. Five of the eight survey behaviors reflecting these themes were ranked among the most unethical: "insulting or ridiculing a student in the student's presence," "running a film that might offend or emotionally upset some students without prior warning," "requiring students to disclose highly personal information in a group discussion class," "telling a student during a class discussion, 'That was a stupid comment,'" and sexual harassment. Three items involved the infliction of direct emotionally upsetting experiences on students: "flirting with students," "telling a student 'I'm sexually attracted to you,'" and "humiliating a student for falling asleep in class." Rounding out the list of acts judged as the most unethical are, "teaching while under the influence of alcohol, cocaine, or some other illegal drug" and "teaching that certain races are intellectually inferior."

Some issues that are often informally debated among professors are not generally perceived as ethical problems for students. Defining less troublesome items as those receiving more than 60% of the ratings in the "would not be an unethical act/nothing wrong with this" or "would be poor manners or 'tacky,' but not unethical" category, such items include the following: "giving only multiple choice exams as the basis for the course grade," "lecturing only from material taken directly from the textbook," "giving academic credit instead of salaries to student assistants," "always letting class out 15 minutes early," "engaging in sexual relationships with other faculty members in the same department," and moonlighting.

Although these baseline data provide a portrait in very broad strokes, they provide some insights into how students view the ethical obligations of teaching psychologists. Students, being the consumers of the services of teaching psychologists, deserve to be heard and better understood.

References

Anderson, M. (1992). *Impostors in the temple.* New York: Simon & Schuster.

Blevins-Knabe, B. (1992). The ethics of dual relationship in higher education. *Ethics & Behavior, 2,* 151–163.

D'Souza, D. (1991). *Illiberal education: The politics of race and sex on campus.* New York: Free Press.

Goodstein, L. D. (1981). Ethics are for academics too! *Professional Psychology, 12,* 191–193.

Hogan, P. M., & Kimmel, A. J. (1992). Ethical teaching of psychology: One department's attempts at self-regulation. *Teaching of Psychology, 19,* 205–210.

Keith-Spiegel, P., & Koocher, G. P. (1985). *Ethics in psychology: Standards and cases.* New York: McGraw-Hill.

Matthews, J. (1991). The teaching of ethics and the ethics of teaching. *Teaching of Psychology, 18,* 80–85.

Sykes, C. J. (1989). *ProfScan: Professors and the demise of higher education.* Washington, DC: Regnery Gateway, Inc.

Tabachnick, B. G., Keith-Spiegel, P., & Pope, K. S. (1991). Ethics of teaching: Beliefs and behaviors of psychologists as educators. *American Psychologist, 46,* 506–515.

◆　◆　◆

Commentary: The APA's 1992 Ethical Principles address some heretofore neglected issues in academia, including the design and description of educational programs and the accurate and objective evaluation of students and supervisees (see Standards 6.01 to 6.05). But is the new code too intrusive? For example, should an inaccurate description of a doctoral program become an ethical issue? The code also prohibits faculty members from "personally demeaning" students. What if a teacher writes this on a student's paper or states it in class?: "This is the worst review of the literature I have ever seen. Don't you know where the library is?" Should this lead to an ethics complaint? Although there is probably a consensus that making fools of individuals in the classroom is not good practice, does making it an ethical issue create an atmosphere in which professors' freedom to speak is unduly chilled? For a discussion of the 1992 Ethical Principles relative to academia, see Keith-Spiegel, P. (1994). Teaching psychologists and the new APA ethics code: Do we fit in? Professional Psychology: Research and Practice, 25, 362–368.

CHAPTER 9

FORENSIC SETTINGS

The American legal system is complex. One of the complicating factors is that there are two parallel sets of courts: one national network of federal courts and 51 sets of separate state courts (including the District of Columbia). Furthermore, within each there is a criminal justice system and a civil justice system. State courts also have a hybrid criminal–civil system that deals with matters affecting juveniles. Forensic psychologists are called on to provide these systems and divisions within them with useful expert information that, it is hoped, will lead to more informed decisions by judges and juries about human behavior.

A "forensic psychologist refers to any psychologist, experimental or clinical, who specializes in producing or communicating psychological research or assessment information intended for application to legal issues" (Grisso, 1987, p. 831; see also Committee on Ethical Guidelines for Forensic Psychologists, 1991). In the criminal system, a forensic psychologist's traditional role may include evaluating criminal defendants (a) to determine whether they are competent to stand trial, (b) to determine what their mental state was at the time of the crime, or (c) to help the judge or the jury determine the proper sentence, including, in capital cases, whether the defendant should suffer the death penalty. In the civil system, a forensic psychologist may testify about the mental capacity and propensity for violence of someone that the state wishes to involuntary hospitalize (civilly commit) and then offer recommendations for appropriate inpatient treatment. In the juvenile system, the forensic psychologist may offer an opinion, after an assessment, about whether a minor should be tried in juvenile court or waived for trial to an adult court (e.g., when the minor has allegedly been involved in a serious crime, particularly a violent one). Finally, a more academically oriented psychologist may consult with a party in litigation about legal tactics, jury selection, or the influence of pretrial publicity on jury objectivity.

Many of these, as well as other, functions are performed by psychologists who identify themselves as *forensic specialists*. They may belong to Division 41 (American Psychology–Law Society) of the American Psychological Association, or they may have been awarded a diploma by the American Board of Forensic Psychology—signifying that they meet certain educational, experiential, and evaluative criteria identifying them as having forensic expertise. They usually are employed by state-run institutions, but they are also found in community mental health centers and in independent practice (Grisso, 1987). These psychologists, primarily clinicians, spend a great deal of time in the courtroom and are frequent visitors to the witness stand.

It would be a mistake, however, to believe that only those psychologists who identify themselves as *forensic mental health professionals* will find themselves involved with the law. Every psychologist—whether clinician, scientist, or academician—is a potential expert witness, and each must be prepared to interact with the legal system. For example, clinicians who see children or families may be called to testify in divorce, child custody, or abuse litigation. A therapist whose client is in a serious automobile accident and claims to have been traumatized by it may be called to testify by the plaintiff–client or by the defendant about the client's mental or emotional condition before the accident. A neuropsychologist may be asked to give an opinion about the capacity of an elderly client to make a will or the extent of brain injury suffered by a worker in an industrial accident. An industrial psychologist who has developed a preemployment screening test claimed to discriminate against, for example, people with disabilities, may be compelled to explain how the instrument was constructed and validated. An academician conducting studies on adolescent gang violence or on other socially sensitive issues may be ordered by a judge to reveal otherwise confidential data concerning some or all of the participants in those studies. Likewise, a researcher who specializes in perception may be called by the defense in a criminal matter to inform a jury about the vagaries of eyewitness identification. Finally, psychologists, whatever their training, may wish to inform legislative or regulatory bodies about pending enactments or to lobby for a certain measure.

The psychologist's part in each of these scenarios is guided by ethical considerations. Although lawyers are obligated to champion their clients' causes through zealous and unbridled representation, different ethical imperatives may guide the behavior of psychologists who enter the hallowed halls of the law. This chapter examines the ethical dimensions of three major questions that face forensic psychologists: (a) Should an expert witness be an advocate or an objective teacher? (b) When performing psychological services at the behest of the court, who is the psychologist's ultimate client? and (c) Are there forensic functions that an ethical psychologist should refuse to perform?

References

Committee on Ethical Guidelines for Forensic Psychologists. (1991). Specialty guidelines for forensic psychologists. *Law and Human Behavior, 15*, 655–665.

Grisso, T. (1987). The economic and scientific future of forensic psychological assessment. *American Psychologist, 42*, 831–839.

On Being Ethical in Legal Places

Patricia Anderten, Valerie Staulcup, and Thomas Grisso

. . .

. . . Entrance into the courtroom thrusts the psychologist into a dynamic relationship with the legal system, its adversarial process, and its participants. Participation in this relationship can produce conflict and, perhaps, insensitivity about ethical principles that guide our profession. Our basic concern is that the ethical standards of the psychologist potentially can be jeopardized in the courtroom setting because of the psychologist's failure to recognize that the basic tenets of the legal system and the science of psychology are often at odds. At the heart of this matter is the difference between the role of the attorney and the role of the psychologist in what may be called the search for truth.

The two systems differ markedly. The first difference is in the prescribed roles of the participants. The logic of jurisprudence is based on the assumption that truth may best be discovered when two persons who support differing conclusions confront each other with passionate, bipartisan debate regarding the merits of their conclusions. . . . In contrast, the rules of science are predicated on the assumption that truth may be discovered by a single person dispassionately employing the scientific method to make all relevant observations and to test all possible conclusions.

The second way the two systems differ is in their tolerance of indecision. Of necessity, the law requires that a decision about "truth" be made on the basis of the evidence available at a given point in time regardless of the degree of ambiguity of that evidence. On the other hand, the philosophical underpinnings of science do not require a conclusion to problems investigated by the methods of science. There is, in theory, an indefinite tolerance of ambiguous findings—a situation that is endured as a necessity for avoiding conclusions based on inadequate data.

The description of these two distinct approaches to the acquisition of knowledge is admittedly abstract and may seem far removed from the everyday practices of lawyers and psychologists. But these approaches are offered here as the most general systematic differences underlying the ethical conflicts that the psychologist faces as an expert witness. . . .

Adapted from *Professional Psychology, 11,* 764–773. Copyright 1980 by the American Psychological Association.

Use and Then Prove, or Prove and Then Use? Some Thoughts on the Ethics of Mental Health Professionals' Courtroom Involvement

David Faust

. . .

The psychology–law interface obviously involves two systems or institutions in which, however, psychology and law are not equal partners. Rather, in the legal arena, psychology is subsumed under law. It is not the judge who enters the clinician's office and lies down on the couch but the psychologist who enters his or her honor's home field. The legal system dominates in determining not only whether participation occurs but, when allowing it, the rules and procedures under which it takes place.

The court's authority, however, is incomplete. Most important, the potential psychologist–expert usually is not compelled to participate but rather does so voluntarily. For example, although the judge may allow testimony on the likelihood of future violent behavior, a psychologist asked to assist in the determination can refuse the request. The choice to not participate when one could paves the way for the expression of personal or professional (i.e., inter-

nal) standards and eases or alleviates the pressure to defer to the court's external standards. Usually, one can make the choice of nonparticipation without violating the rules of the dominant authority structure or without creating legal jeopardy. In contrast, if the law required professionals to serve as expert witnesses whether they wanted to or not, and one's own standards dictated noninvolvement, this would create an immediate legal conflict and put one at risk for official sanction. Of course, one can still live by personal standards under such circumstances, but it is more difficult to do so, and the balance of pluses and minuses may shift dramatically.

Obviously, the court's standards, which are external to the psychologist, and the psychologist's internal or professional standards may clash. At opposing ends of the spectrum are psychologists who always follow external standards and those who always follow internal standards, and in between are various possible combinations. . . .

From *Ethics and Behavior*, 3, 359–380. Copyright 1993 by Erlbaum. Adapted with permission of the publisher.

Reclaiming the Integrity of Science in Expert Witnessing

Bruce D. Sales and Daniel W. Shuman

. . .

Perhaps because of its importance to litigation and its frequent use, it is commonplace to hear complaints about the behavior of expert witnesses. Critics complain that many experts who testify abandon their scientific integrity and that the legal system stimulates this result. . . .

Given the importance of expert testimony and the pool of competent attorneys and scientists, what explains the perceived problems with expert witnessing? An important reason lies in the inherent conflicts between the goals of attorneys and the goals of scientists/experts (Champagne, Shuman, & Whitaker, 1991 . . .). Because the legal system is an adversarial system and science is not, the goals of the attorneys and the goals of the scientist/experts differ. Attorneys need partisan experts to persuade the trier of fact (judge or jury), which weighs in favor of the selection of the most articulate, understandable, presentable, and persuasive expert rather than the best scientist. Even when there are good scientists who fit the bill, attorneys have a strong incentive to choose the person whose presentation and interpretation of the data is most sympathetic to the attorney's cause. As Champagne et al. (1991) noted in their empirical study of the use of experts, "lawyers seemingly want articulate, partisan experts with integrity" (p. 387).

Science, on the other hand, demands that scientists focus only on scientific knowledge without the influence—whether subtle or explicit—of the attorney's goals. Of equal concern is that the attorneys respond to current cases, which causes them to pressure experts to reach firm conclusions on the witness stand, even if the science on the issue and the scientific enterprise is tentative and iterative in nature or if the scientific information is available. . . .

Although the law has attempted to address some of these problems (e.g., through the rules of evidence and the cases interpreting them), its solutions have neither quieted the legal debate nor provided helpful guidance to the dilemmas scientists experience as expert witnesses. . . . Thus, to the extent that scientists have placed their hopes for a resolution of this dilemma on the legal system, they have been disappointed. Perhaps the law should not be expected to be overly concerned about the needs of science given that it is not the law's focus; the law focuses on the resolution of disputes between parties.

Prior discussions of these problems by scientists are not terribly helpful. In the main, when those writings have focused on what scientists can do to address these problems, they have reflected the values of the individual author, rather than on a rule or principled analysis. The intervention of a rule or principled analysis could provide a systematic approach to generating insights and guidelines for solutions. To the extent that ethics governs all scientific and professional behavior—which it does—it is only appropriate that it become the first metric against which to judge the expert witnessing of scientists and professionals.

Although the problems of expert witnessing transcend the presentation of a particular type of scientific expert, focusing on the use of psychologists and other mental health professionals as expert witnesses provides important insights on this issue. The usefulness of their information is debated within and without the legal system, and they have not been spared criticism in the debate over the lost integrity of scientists as expert witnesses. In addition, because psychologists have a well-developed system of ethics that bears on their activities (see, e.g., Section 8.01 of the "Ethical Principles of Psychologists and Code of Conduct," American Psychological Association [APA], 1992, referred to hereafter as ethics code), an ethical analysis of expert testimony by psychologists is informative. . . .

References

American Psychological Association. (1992). *Ethical principles of psychologists and code of conduct.* Washington, DC: Author.

Champagne, A., Shuman, D. W., & Whitaker, E. (1991). The use of expert witnesses in American courts. *Judicature, 31,* 375–392.

Mental Health Professionals and the Courts: The Ethics of Expertise

Stephen L. Golding

. . .

. . . [I]n the ideal, mental health expertise enters the courtroom in the following steps:

1. An area of expertise, which is beyond the ordinary knowledge and understanding of the trier of fact, is accepted as one which will assist the trier of fact in understanding evidence or determining a fact at issue.
2. An expert in that area is qualified by the trial judge after hearing evidence that the individual is an expert, by virtue of "knowledge, skill, experience, training, or education."
3. The evidence upon which the expert will rely must be judged to be "trustworthy" or "reliable" (i.e., of a type "reasonably relied upon") by experts in the area of expertise. Furthermore, the nature of the evidence and the opinion must be judged to be more probative than it is prejudicial, confusing, misleading, or redundant with other evidence.

SUMMARY CRITIQUE OF MENTAL HEALTH EXPERTISE

It comes as no surprise, of course, that the ideal and the real are frequently at variance with one another. Controversy has surrounded the role of mental health expertise in the courtroom for several centuries. . . . While an exhaustive catalogue of the controversial issues would be quite long, a set of central issues will first be outlined and then discussed under the major section headings which follow.

Moral Advocacy Versus Expertise

While some nihilists argue that mental health expertise simply does not exist or should be banned completely from the courtroom, the more cogent argument has been that such expertise as does exist is quite limited, and that the *real* role of the forensic expert in the courtroom has been that of moral advocate. . . . That is, the problem with forensic expertise is identified with a hidden moral agenda in which the moral controversies underlying the ascription of responsibility and blame-worthiness are played out through the roles of the experts.

The Qualification of Experts

In principle, a trial judge accepts an individual as a qualified expert only after a thorough hearing as to the person's training, knowledge, and experience with respect to a circumscribed area of expertise. In practice, judges rarely exercise this discretionary authority. The resulting problem is the level of expertise available to courts varies widely with many generically trained mental health professionals giving "expert opinions" on complex forensic mental health questions. The court is thereby misled into believing that it is hearing opinions based upon the most current scholarship, research, and experience in the area.

Prejudicial Versus Probative Aspects of Expertise

While judges have the discretionary authority to limit expert evidence, even when relevant, on the basis of the balance between its prejudicial versus probative effects, they are rarely asked to evaluate this issue. As a consequence, it has become common practice for both defense and prosecution to (mis)use their experts to introduce evidence that

From the *International Journal of Law and Psychiatry*, 13, 281–307. Copyright 1990 by Pergamon Press. Adapted with permission of the publisher.

would otherwise be inadmissible, obfuscatory, or prejudicial. A related claim is that the "aura of science" which surrounds expert testimony leads to undue weight being given to the expert's opinions and inferences. Furthermore, since these opinions themselves are frequently seen as "invading the province of the trier of fact," experts are seen as inappropriately influencing the legal system.

Expertise Is Distorted in an Adversarial System

The fundamental structure of evidence production in an adversarial system is seen as incompatible with the basic tenets of expert knowledge systems which are grounded in the scientific methods of evidence appraisal. . . .

Expertise Is for Hire

This claim is expressed most stridently as experts are "whores for hire." The more reasoned critiques question whether the combination of economic forces and a strongly structured adversarial system produces the most useful and probative expert testimony. Thus, the combination of "doctor shopping," inadequate qualification of experts, vaguely defined boundaries of expertise, and adversarial as opposed to court-appointed experts may deprive the court of the most probative expertise available. . . .

◆ ◆ ◆

Commentary: One hundred years ago, an author writing on expert testimony quoted this from an unidentified trial lawyer's closing statement: "Gentlemen of the jury," the attorney began, "there are three kinds of liars—the common liar, the damned liar, and the scientific expert"

(p. 169). See Foster, W. L. (1897). Expert testimony— Prevalent complaints and proposed remedies. Harvard Law Review, 11, 169–186.

There is some evidence that lawyers do frequently coach experts; that experts are generally receptive to this process; and as a result, that these "hired guns" vary their testimony to suit the needs of the side by which they have been retained. See, for example,

Champagne, A., Shuman, D. W., & Whitaker, E. (1991). The use of expert witnesses in American courts. Judicature, 31, 375–392

Homant, R. J., & Kennedy, D. B. (1987). Subjective factors in clinicians' judgments of insanity: A comparison of a hypothetical and an actual case. Professional Psychology: Research and Practice, 18, 439–446

Otto, R. K. (1989). Bias and expert testimony of mental health professionals in adversarial proceedings: A preliminary investigation. Behavioral Sciences and the Law, 7, 267–273.

For a general review of biases to which forensic clinicians are subject, see Bersoff, D. N. (1992). Judicial deference to nonlegal decision-makers: Imposing simplistic solutions on problems of cognitive complexity in mental disability law. Southern Methodist Law Review, 46, 327–370.

If there is one category of cases that most frequently evokes the accusation of "hired gun," it is in the assessment of children during custody disputes between two divorcing parents. It is here that the confluence of incompetence, multiple relationships, role conflicts, and biased advocacy is most rampant. Unless these disputes are settled amicably, there are always going to be parents who feel aggrieved by the decision. Rightly or wrongly, such disgruntled parents are increasingly filing ethics complaints against assessors. In an attempt to diminish the number of these complaints and to educate its members, the APA developed the following document, which is now APA policy.

Guidelines for Child Custody Evaluations in Divorce Proceedings

American Psychological Association

INTRODUCTION

Decisions regarding child custody and other parenting arrangements occur within several different legal contexts, including parental divorce, guardianship, neglect or abuse proceedings, and termination of parental rights. The following guidelines were developed for psychologists conducting child custody evaluations, specifically within the context of parental divorce. These guidelines build upon the American Psychological Association's *Ethical Principles of Psychologists and Code of Conduct* (APA, 1992) and are aspirational in intent. *As guidelines, they are not intended to be either mandatory or exhaustive. The goal of the guidelines is to promote proficiency in using psychological expertise in conducting child custody evaluations.*

Parental divorce requires a restructuring of parental rights and responsibilities in relation to children. If the parents can agree to a restructuring arrangement, which they do in the overwhelming proportion (90%) of divorce custody cases (Melton, Petrila, Poythress, & Slobogin, 1987), there is no dispute for the court to decide. However, if the parents are unable to reach such an agreement, the court must help to determine the relative allocation of decision making authority and physical contact each parent will have with the child. The courts typically apply a "best interest of the child" standard in determining this restructuring of rights and responsibilities.

Psychologists provide an important service to children and the courts by providing competent, objective, impartial information in assessing the best interests of the child; by demonstrating a clear sense of direction and purpose in conducting a child custody evaluation; by performing their roles ethically; and by clarifying to all involved the nature and scope of the evaluation. The Ethics Committee of the American Psychological Association has noted that psychologists' involvement in custody disputes has at times raised questions in regard to the misuse of psychologists' influence, sometimes resulting in complaints against psychologists being brought to the attention of the APA Ethics Committee (APA Ethics Committee, 1985; Hall & Hare-Mustin, 1983; Keith-Spiegel & Koocher, 1985; Mills, 1984) and raising questions in the legal and forensic literature (Grisso, 1986; Melton et al., 1987; Mnookin, 1975; Ochroch, 1982; Okpaku, 1976; Weithorn, 1987).

Particular competencies and knowledge are required for child custody evaluations to provide adequate and appropriate psychological services to the court. Child custody evaluation in the context of parental divorce can be an extremely demanding task. For competing parents the stakes are high as they participate in a process fraught with tension and anxiety. The stress on the psychologist/evaluator can become great. Tension surrounding child custody evaluation can become further heightened when there are accusations of child abuse, neglect, and/or family violence.

Psychology is in a position to make significant contributions to child custody decisions. Psychological data and expertise, gained through a child custody evaluation, can provide an additional source of information and an additional perspective not otherwise readily available to the court on what appears to be in a child's best interest, and thus can increase the fairness of the determination the court must make.

Adapted from *American Psychologist*, 49, 677–680. Copyright 1994 by the American Psychological Association.

These guidelines were drafted by the Committee on Professional Practice and Standards, a committee of the Board of Professional Affairs, with input from the Committee of Children, Youth, and Families. They were adopted by the Council of Representatives of the American Psychological Association in February 1994.

GUIDELINES FOR CHILD CUSTODY EVALUATIONS IN DIVORCE PROCEEDINGS

I. Orienting Guidelines: Purpose of a Child Custody Evaluation

1. The primary purpose of the evaluation is to assess the best psychological interests of the child. The primary consideration in a child custody evaluation is to assess the individual and family factors that affect the best psychological interests of the child. More specific questions may be raised by the court.

2. The child's interests and well-being are paramount. In a child custody evaluation, the child's interests and well-being are paramount. Parents competing for custody, as well as others, may have legitimate concerns, but the child's best interests must prevail.

3. The focus of the evaluation is on parenting capacity, the psychological and developmental needs of the child, and the resulting fit. In considering psychological factors affecting the best interests of the child, the psychologist focuses on the parenting capacity of the prospective custodians in conjunction with the psychological and developmental needs of each involved child. This involves (a) an assessment of the adults' capacities for parenting, including whatever knowledge, attributes, skills, and abilities, or lack thereof, are present; (b) an assessment of the psychological functioning and developmental needs of each child and of the wishes of each child where appropriate; and (c) an assessment of the functional ability of each parent to meet these needs, including an evaluation of the interaction between each adult and child.

The values of the parents relevant to parenting, ability to plan for the child's future needs, capacity to provide a stable and loving home, and any potential for inappropriate behavior or misconduct that might negatively influence the child also are considered. Psychopathology may be relevant to such an assessment, insofar as it has impact on the child or the ability to parent, but it is not the primary focus.

II. General Guidelines: Preparing for a Child Custody Evaluation

4. The role of the psychologist is that of a professional expert who strives to maintain an objective, impartial stance. The role of the psychologist is as a professional expert. The psychologist does not act as a judge, who makes the ultimate decision applying the law to all relevant evidence. Neither does the psychologist act as an advocating attorney, who strives to present his or her client's best possible case. The psychologist, in a balanced, impartial manner, informs and advises the court and the prospective custodians of the child of the relevant psychological factors pertaining to the custody issue. The psychologist should be impartial regardless of whether he or she is retained by the court or by a party to the proceedings. If either the psychologist or the client cannot accept this neutral role, the psychologist should consider withdrawing from the case. If not permitted to withdraw, in such circumstances, the psychologist acknowledges past roles and other factors that could affect impartiality.

5. The psychologist gains specialized competence.
A. A psychologist contemplating performing child custody evaluations is aware that special competencies and knowledge are required for the undertaking of such evaluations. Competence in performing psychological assessments of children, adults, and families is necessary but not sufficient. Education, training, experience, and/or supervision in the areas of child and family development, child and family psychopathology, and the impact of divorce on children help to prepare the psychologist to participate competently in child custody evaluations. The psychologist also strives to become familiar with applicable legal standards and procedures, including laws governing divorce and custody adjudications in his or her state or jurisdiction.

B. The psychologist uses current knowledge of scientific and professional developments, consistent with accepted clinical and scientific standards, in selecting data collection methods and procedures. The *Standards for Educational and Psychological Testing* (APA, 1985) are adhered to in the use of psychological tests and other assessment tools.

C. In the course of conducting child custody evaluations, allegations of child abuse, neglect, family violence, or other issues may occur that are not necessarily within the scope of a particular evaluator's expertise. If this is so, the psychologist seeks additional consultation, supervision, and/or specialized knowledge, training, or experience in child abuse, neglect, and family violence to address these complex issues. The psychologist is familiar with the laws of his or her state addressing child abuse, neglect, and family violence and acts accordingly.

6. The psychologist is aware of personal and societal biases and engages in nondiscriminatory practice. The psychologist engaging in child custody evaluations is aware of how biases regarding age, gender, race, ethnicity, national origin, religion, sexual orientation, disability, language, culture, and socioeconomic status may interfere with an objective evaluation and recommendations. The psychologist recognizes and strives to overcome any such biases or withdraws from the evaluation.

7. The psychologist avoids multiple relationships. Psychologists generally avoid conducting a child custody evaluation in a case in which the psychologist served in a therapeutic role for the child or his or her immediate family or has had other involvement that may compromise the psychologist's objectivity. This should not, however, preclude the psychologist from testifying in the case as a fact witness concerning treatment of the child. In addition, during the course of a child custody evaluation, a psychologist does not accept any of the involved participants in the evaluation as a therapy client. Therapeutic contact with the child or involved participants following a child custody evaluation is undertaken with caution.

A psychologist asked to testify regarding a therapy client who is involved in a child custody case is aware of the limitations and possible biases inherent in such a role and the possible impact on the ongoing therapeutic relationship. Although the court may require the psychologist to testify as a fact witness regarding factual information he or she became aware of in a professional relationship with a client, that psychologist should generally decline the role of an expert witness who gives a professional opinion regarding custody and visitation issues (see Ethical Standard 7.03) unless so ordered by the court.

III. Procedural Guidelines: Conducting a Child Custody Evaluation

8. The scope of the evaluation is determined by the evaluator, based on the nature of the referral question. The scope of the custody-related evaluation is determined by the nature of the question or issue raised by the referring person or the court, or is inherent in the situation. Although comprehensive child custody evaluations generally require an evaluation of all parents or guardians and children, as well as observations of interactions between them, the scope of the assessment in a particular case may be limited to evaluating the parental capacity of one parent without attempting to compare the parents or to make recommendations. Likewise, the scope may be limited to evaluating the child. Or a psychologist may be asked to critique the assumptions and methodology of the assessment of another mental health professional. A psychologist also might serve as an expert witness in the area of child development, providing expertise to the court without relating it specifically to the parties involved in a case.

9. The psychologist obtains informed consent from all adult participants and, as appropriate, informs child participants. In undertaking child custody evaluations, the psychologist ensures that each adult participant is aware of (a) the purpose, nature, and method of the evaluation; (b) who has requested the psychologist's services; and (c) who will be paying the fees. The psychologist informs adult participants about the nature of the assessment instruments and techniques and informs those participants about the possible disposition of the data collected. The psychologist provides this information, as appropriate, to children, to the extent that they are able to understand.

10. The psychologist informs participants about the limits of confidentiality and the disclosure of information. A psychologist conducting a child custody evaluation ensures that the participants, including children to the extent feasible, are aware of the limits of confidentiality characterizing the professional relationship with the psychologist. The psychologist informs participants that in consenting to the evaluation, they are consenting to disclosure of the evaluation's findings in the context of the forth-coming litigation and in any other proceedings deemed necessary by the courts. A psychologist obtains a waiver of confidentiality from all adult participants or from their authorized legal representatives.

11. The psychologist uses multiple methods of data gathering. The psychologist strives to use the most appropriate methods available for addressing the questions raised in a specific child custody evaluation and generally uses multiple methods of data gathering, including, but not limited to, clinical interviews, observation, and/or psychological assessments. Important facts and opinions are documented from at least two sources whenever their reliability is questionable. The psychologist, for example, may review potentially relevant reports (e.g., from schools, health care providers, child care providers, agencies, and institutions). Psychologists may also interview extended family, friends, and other individuals on occasions when the information is likely to be useful. If information is gathered from third parties that is significant and may be used as a basis for conclusions, psychologists corroborate it by at least one other source wherever possible and appropriate and document this in the report.

12. The psychologist neither overinterprets nor inappropriately interprets clinical or assessment data. The psychologist refrains from drawing conclusions not adequately supported by the data. The psychologist interprets any data from interviews or tests, as well as any questions of data reliability and validity, cautiously and conservatively, seeking convergent validity. The psychologist strives to acknowledge to the court any limitations in methods or data used.

13. The psychologist does not give any opinion regarding the psychological functioning of any individual who has not been personally evaluated. This guideline, however, does not preclude the psychologist from reporting what an evaluated individual (such as the parent or child) has stated or from addressing theoretical issues of hypothetical questions, so long as the limited basis of the information is noted.

14. Recommendations, if any, are based on what is in the best psychological interests of the child. Although the profession has not reached consensus about whether psychologists ought to make recommendations about the final custody determination to the courts, psychologists are obligated to be aware of the arguments on both sides of this issue and to be able to explain the logic of their position concerning their own practice.

If the psychologist does choose to make custody recommendations, these recommendations should be derived from sound psychological data and must be based on the best interests of the child in the particular case. Recommendations are based on articulated assumptions, data, interpretations, and inferences based upon established professional and scientific standards. Psychologists guard against relying on their own biases or unsupported beliefs in rendering opinions in particular cases.

15. The psychologist clarifies financial arrangements. Financial arrangements are clarified and agreed upon prior to commencing a child custody evaluation. When billing for a child custody evaluation, the psychologist does not misrepresent his or her services for reimbursement purposes.

16. The psychologist maintains written records. All records obtained in the process of conducting a child custody evaluation are properly maintained and filed in accord with the APA *Record Keeping Guidelines* (APA, 1993) and relevant statutory guidelines.

All raw data and interview information are recorded with an eye toward their possible review by other psychologists or the court, where legally permitted. Upon request, appropriate reports are made available to the court.

References

American Psychological Association. (1985). *Standards for educational and psychological testing*. Washington, DC: Author.

American Psychological Association. (1992). Ethical principles of psychologists and code of conduct. *American Psychologist, 47,* 1597–1611.

American Psychological Association. (1993). *Record keeping guidelines*. Washington, DC: Author.

American Psychological Association, Ethics Committee. (1985). *Annual report of the American Psychological Association Ethics Committee*. Washington, DC: Author.

Grisso, T. (1986). *Evaluating competencies: Forensic assessments and instruments*. New York: Plenum.

Hall, J. E., & Hare-Mustin, R. T. (1983). Sanctions and the diversity of ethical complaints against psychologists. *American Psychologist, 38*, 714–729.

Keith-Spiegel, P., & Koocher, G. P. (1985). *Ethics in psychology*. New York: Random House.

Melton, G. B., Petrila, J., Poythress, N. G., & Slobogin, C. (1987). *Psychological evaluations for the courts: A handbook for mental health professionals and lawyers*. New York: Guilford Press.

Mills, D. H. (1984). Ethics education and adjudication within psychology. *American Psychologist, 39*, 669–675.

Mnookin, R. H. (1975). Child-custody adjudication: Judicial functions in the face of indeterminacy. *Law and Contemporary Problems, 39*, 226–293.

Ochroch, R. (1982, August). *Ethical pitfalls in child custody evaluations*. Paper presented at the 90th Annual Convention of the American Psychological Association, Washington, DC.

Okpaku, S. (1976). Psychology: Impediment or aid in child custody cases? *Rutgers Law Review, 29*, 1117–1153.

Weithorn, L. A. (Ed.). (1987). *Psychology and child custody determinations: Knowledge, roles, and expertise*. Lincoln: University of Nebraska Press.

◆ ◆ ◆

Commentary: Although the issue of biased advocacy most often surfaces in the context of testimony by professional psychologists—as in child custody cases and other litigation (e.g., the presence of insanity in a criminal defendant, the emotional damage of victims of sexual or physical abuse, the extent of disability in a child needing special education, or the validity of employment tests)—it has become perhaps an even more significant issue for researchers. The controversy has been most heated in cases involving eyewitness identification of a criminal defendant.

The Experimental Psychologist in Court:
The Ethics of Expert Testimony

Michael McCloskey, Howard Egeth, and Judith McKenna

. . .

The psychologist who is asked to serve as an expert witness faces several difficult ethical questions, first in deciding whether to testify and then, if this decision is in the affirmative, in considering what duties and responsibilities inhere in the expert witness role. These issues were the topic of a conference held at Johns Hopkins University in the summer of 1983. Approximately thirty psychologists, legal professionals, and ethnicists explored the ethics of expert testimony by experimental psychologists, with the aim of defining the critical questions and articulating the considerations relevant to answering these questions. . . .

THE ETHICAL QUESTIONS

Advocate or Educator?

The experimental psychologist who testifies as an expert witness is virtually always hired by the attorneys for one side in a case. Because attorneys' ethics require them to be zealous advocates for their clients, they often want the psychologist to discuss in expert testimony only those points for which the available psychological research supports their client's position. Psychologists who offer different testimony depending on who has hired them act at least to some extent as advocates; psychologists whose testimony does not differ according to employer act as impartial educators of the jury.

In some unusual circumstances the roles of advocate and impartial educator may coincide (i.e., on all relevant points the available research may clearly support the contentions of the side hiring the expert). Usually, however, the roles are in conflict

(Fersch, 1980). Consider the psychologist who is hired by the defense in a criminal case to testify about research on eyewitness performance. In the role of advocate for the defense, the psychologist would emphasize in expert testimony only those perceptual and memorial factors that suggest that the identification(s) in the case at hand may have been inaccurate (e.g., brief exposure, stress experienced by the eyewitness). In contrast, the psychologist adopting the role of impartial educator would also discuss factors suggesting that the eyewitness identification of the defendant may have been accurate (e.g., good lighting, short retention interval). Current practice in this sort of expert testimony is probably closer to advocacy than to impartial education (e.g., Loftus, 1979, 1980, . . . ; Loftus & Monahan, 1980).

Most conference participants agreed that the most desirable role for the expert is that of impartial educator, and some held that this is the only ethically defensible position. It is clear that the law defines the role of the expert as that of an impartial educator called to assist the trier of fact. A scientist is called upon to assist the jury to understand the evidence or determine a fact in issue (see, e.g., Federal Rules of Evidence, Rule 702, 1975, p. 80). Therefore, it was argued, the psychologist has the ethical responsibility to present a complete and unbiased picture of the psychological research relevant to the case at hand.

Many conference participants disagreed, however, contending that the educator role is difficult if not impossible to maintain, both because of pressures toward advocacy from the attorneys who hire the expert, and because of a strong tendency to identify with the side for which one is working. Hence, they suggested, the psychologist should accept the reali-

From *Law and Human Behavior, 10,* 1–13. Copyright 1986 by Plenum Publishing. Adapted with permission of the publisher.

ties of working within an adversary system, and seek to be a responsible advocate, presenting one side of an issue without distorting or misrepresenting the available psychological research.

The discussions at the conference also made clear that additional ethical problems arise once a stance has been taken on the basic advocate/educator issue. The psychologist who decides that some degree of advocacy is ethically acceptable must consider how to draw the line between using research to argue one side of an issue fairly, and distorting and misrepresenting the available research.

The psychologist who decides that the role of impartial educator is the only ethically acceptable one also faces difficult problems. An attorney may fail to accept or even to understand the psychologist's desire to be even-handed in expert testimony. Thus, the psychologist who wishes to act as an impartial educator may be faced with a choice between accommodating the attorney's desire for a one-sided presentation, or not being called to testify. . . .

Effects of Expert Testimony

Expert psychological testimony is offered to assist jurors in understanding or evaluating other evidence in a case. However, whenever an experimental psychologist gives expert testimony, there is the possibility that the testimony will affect the jury in some unanticipated and undesirable way. Jurors may misinterpret, overgeneralize, or misapply the information presented by the psychologist, and so may come to unwarranted conclusions. Further concerns expressed in rules of evidence and appellate decisions regarding expert testimony include the possibility that expert testimony may confuse the issues in a case, or that the expert's opinions may be accorded undue weight by the jury.

The risk of deleterious effects is especially evident in light of the fact that the expert witness does not offer to the jury an exhaustive and uninterpreted recitation of research results. Rather, the expert typically states conclusions based upon the available research, often without discussing the studies that form the basis for this conclusion. For example, an expert on eyewitness psychology might state that cross-race identifications (e.g., black witness, white defendant) are less reliable than within-race identifi-

cations. Expert testimony in this form carries the risk that jurors may accept the expert's statements as scientific fact, when in fact these statements are often better characterized as tentative conclusions drawn on the basis of limited and perhaps inconsistent evidence. . . .

At present little is known about the effects of expert psychological testimony concerning cognitive or social processes. A few preliminary studies on effects of expert testimony about eyewitness performance have been conducted (Hosch, Beck, & McIntyre, 1980; Loftus, 1980; . . . Wells, Lindsay, & Tousignant, 1980), but the results are far from definitive. The effects of other sorts of expert testimony by experimental psychologists have not been investigated. Given the paucity of data, what consideration should the experimental psychologist give to the potential effects of expert testimony when deciding whether and how to testify?

Some of the conference participants suggested that in the absence of definitive data, psychologists should rely upon their professional judgments about the likely effects of their expert testimony. One problem with this position is that in the absence of data concerning effects of expert testimony, the psychologist must rely primarily upon intuition in assessing potential effects. Psychologists' intuitions, it may be argued, have no special claim to validity (Morse, 1978; Nisbett & Wilson, 1977), and so do not provide an adequate basis for a sound professional judgment about effects of expert testimony. . . .

Bases for Statements

What constitutes an adequate basis for a statement by an expert witness? How should the line be drawn between statements that are adequately supported by psychological research, and statements that are based to an inappropriately great extent upon speculation and intuition?

The issue of bases for statements made in expert testimony generated more discussion—and more disagreement—than any other issue considered at the conference. The discussions made clear that the issue subsumes two distinct questions: (1) how well supported should a statement be?; and (2) how much support do the available data provide for the sorts of statements experimental psychologists commonly make in expert testimony?

On the first issue two quite distinct positions were apparent in the discussions. Proponents of the "best available evidence" position held that it is appropriate for a psychologist to state in expert testimony conclusions based on the best available evidence, even if these conclusions must be very tentative. In support of this position it was argued that the judicial system cannot withhold decisions on cases until psychologists have a complete understanding of cognition and social psychology; decisions must be made on the basis of information currently available. Thus, if as the result of psychological research some information relevant to an issue under adjudication is available, psychologists have the right, and perhaps even the ethical obligation, to provide the judicial system with this information.

In contrast, proponents of the "well-established knowledge" position asserted that while absolute certainty about the validity of a statement is not necessary, a conclusion should be scientifically well established before it is offered in expert testimony. In support of this position it was argued that matters at the frontiers of a science—matters that are poorly understood or vigorously debated within the discipline—are not appropriate subjects for expert testimony. In the first place, it may be argued that for issues on which the available research yields no clear conclusions, the expert's judgment has no greater claim to validity than that of the layperson. In addition, if a conclusion is stated in an appropriately tentative fashion (e.g., witness confidence may sometimes be a good indicator and sometimes a poor

indicator of witness accuracy, but the circumstances in which it is a good or poor indicator are not understood) it may be of little use to the jury, but if the conclusion is asserted without indication of its tentative nature the jury may inappropriately accept it as scientific fact. . . .

References

Federal Rules of Evidence for United States Courts and Magistrates. (1975). St. Paul, Minnesota: West Publishing Company.

Fersch, E. A., Jr. (1980). Ethical issues for psychologists in court settings. In J. Monahan (Ed.), *Who is the client? The ethics of psychological intervention in the criminal justice system.* Washington, DC: American Psychological Association.

Hosch, H. M., Beck, E. L., & McIntyre, P. (1980). Influence of expert testimony regarding eyewitness accuracy on jury decisions. *Law and Human Behavior, 4,* 287–296.

Loftus, E. F. (1979). *Eyewitness testimony.* Cambridge, Massachusetts: Harvard University Press.

Loftus, E. F. (1980). Impact of expert psychological testimony on the unreliability of eyewitness identification. *Journal of Applied Psychology, 65,* 9–15.

Loftus, E. F., & Monahan, J. (1980). Trial by data: Psychological research as legal evidence. *American Psychologist, 35,* 270–283.

Morse, S. J. (1978). Law and mental health professionals: The limits of expertise. *Professional Psychology, 9,* 389–399.

Nisbett, R. E., & Wilson, T. D. (1977). Telling more than we can know: Verbal reports on mental processes. *Psychological Review, 84,* 231–259.

Wells, G. L., Lindsay, R. C. L., & Tousignant, J. P. (1980). Effects of expert psychological advice on human performance in judging the validity of eyewitness testimony. *Law and Human Behavior, 4,* 275–285.

Experimental Psychologist as Advocate or Impartial Educator

Elizabeth F. Loftus

. . .

The view that psychologists may serve as advocates, presenting only the beneficial side of the case, begins with the argument that the trial is an adversary process in which each side has the right to make the best possible case. As participants in this process, experts may limit their testimony to points that support the arguments of one side, leaving the opposing attorneys the task of presenting evidence and arguments favoring their position. The opposition can resort to vigorous cross-examination to bring out weaknesses in the testimony offered by the other side. One staunch advocate of this position is Marvin Wolfgang, sociologist and criminologist, whose court-related experience has been largely in the area of discrimination (Wolfgang, 1974). Proponents of his position suggest that unsupportive evidence may be fine if published in a scientific article, but it "has no function in the adversary game" (p. 246). In court, there is selectivity unlike that which exists in science.

Rivlin (1973) went so far as to suggest that we acknowledge the development of a "forensic social science" rather than pretend to be balanced, objective, free of personal biases, and acting as if we are offering all sides of the case so that people can judge for themselves. If left to Rivlin's design, a psychologist would simply prepare a position paper for or against a particular proposition. The position would be clearly stated, and the evidence that supports one side of the argument would be brought together. The job of critiquing the case that has been presented and of detailing the counterevidence would be left to a scholar working for the opposition. One advantage of a forensic social science is that it would reduce the hypocrisy of pseudo-objectivity and hidden biases that now pervade the so-called scientifically balanced approach. If used properly, Rivlin argues, forensic social science can sharpen public issues and make social scientific research more relevant to real policy questions than it has ever been in the past. This is probably an extreme version of the advocacy side of the issue. Yet even while advocating the forensic social science approach, Rivlin is careful to point out that there must be some rules. We still must guard against misrepresentation of facts or findings of studies cited. Moreover, she claims, the evidence has to be available for examination by the advocates on the other side, and by the judge and jury.

Will this approach be good for science? Pollack (1973) thinks so: ". . . the adversary process is best suited to explore, expose, and challenge the 'scientific facts' . . ." (p. 177). For Pollack, the system of obtaining justice through challenging "legal truth" provides the opportunity for questioning the absoluteness, fixity, and degree of error in "scientific truth," and for evaluating the significance of scientific data when it is presented as evidence.

Now consider an opposing point of view. All witnesses take an oath before they take the stand, and that oath is to tell "the truth, the whole truth, and nothing but the truth." By selectively leaving out studies that are crucial to some particular question, the psychologists may be failing to perform according to the oath. The "whole truth" is not being told. For this reason, some social scientists have suggested that the expert may have an obligation to bring up research evidence that runs counter to the thrust of his or her testimony. . . .

POSSIBLE GUIDES TO ETHICAL DECISIONS

Laws of Evidence

The law itself does not require "full disclosure." More specifically, the Federal Rules of Evidence (1975) do not require an expert to disclose facts or data that underlie the opinion or inference being offered. Rule 705 says:

> The expert may testify in terms of opinions or inference and give his reasons therefore without prior disclosure of underlying facts or data, unless the court requires otherwise. The expert may in any event be required to disclose the underlying facts or data on cross-examination (p. 84).

In other words, counsel can disclose the underlying facts (including supportive and contradictory facts) when presenting its case, but is not necessarily obligated to do so. The revealing of underlying facts could, however, be forced on cross-examination. Some have argued that it is unfair to require the cross-examiner to bring out the weaknesses in the expert testimony, but the legal commentary on Rule 705 disagrees. Those who cross-examine are assumed to have advance knowledge, typically through traditional procedures of discovery, necessary for effective challenging of expert testimony. This safeguard is reinforced by the discretionary power of the judge to require preliminary disclosure of the identity of the experts and their findings. Even if this information is not discovered in advance of trial, the opposing attorney is always free to ask the right questions, such as "Do you know of any studies that show the opposite result?"

How should a psychologist decide what role to play? In addition to deciding whether to mention studies that run counter to the general point being made, the psychologist has other choices to make. For example, there is considerable latitude regarding what topics to discuss in expert testimony. In a case involving a long exposure and a short interval between the crime and subsequent identification, the impartial educator might discuss both the factors of exposure duration and retention interval, while the advocate or the defense might discuss only one. It is

worth noting that current practice in expert testimony on eyewitness reliability is probably closer to advocacy than to impartial education (Loftus, 1979; Loftus & Monahan, 1980). However, this is not the only approach one could take. It would certainly be useful if psychologists had some reasonable basis upon which to choose the approach to take.

Ethics of Psychological Practice

It is natural to ask what role the legal principles (that do not require full disclosure) should play in a psychologist's decision. If the legal principles permit less than full disclosure, is this sufficient justification for the expert to adopt the advocate's role; or must ethical principles independent of the legal criteria be taken into account?

A reasonable position is that the ethics of one's own field should govern the choice. In considering the ethics of psychology as a means of resolution, we must turn to the set of ethical standards for the profession of psychology. . . . (Ethical Principles of Psychologists, 1981). These Standards are continually updated and revised, but we can look to the most recent version (1981) for advice. The preamble suggests some difficulties we might face in court settings:

> Psychologists respect the dignity and worth of the individual and strive for the preservation and protection of fundamental human rights. They are committed to increasing knowledge of human behavior and of people's understanding of themselves and others and to the utilization of such knowledge for the promotion of human welfare. While pursuing these objectives, they make every effort to protect the welfare of those who seek their services and of any research participants that may be the object of study. They use their skills only for purposes consistent with these values and do not knowingly permit their misuse by others (Ethical Principles of Psychologists, 1981, p. 633).

As Fersch (1980) has noted, these standards do not go far toward resolving the troubling ethical issues that psychologists might face when they find themselves in court. And it is easy to see why. Foremost among the difficulties is the question of who the client is. If psychologists are to protect "fundamental human rights," whose rights are we to protect—the rights of the defendant in a criminal case to present the strongest case possible, or the rights of citizens to see the guilty convicted of crimes they have committed? If we are committed to the "promotion of human welfare," whose welfare? If psychologists must "make every effort to protect the welfare of those who seek their services", does this imply a duty to the defendant who has hired the psychologist to help in the advocacy role? Fersch (1980) has stated rather explicitly that when a defendant has hired a psychologist to point out the unreliability of eyewitness identification (or to help pick a jury or offer some other service), the psychologist "has but one client—the defendant—and owes responsibility solely to him or her" (1980, p. 54). But, taking into account the ethical principles, how far should the psychologist go in satisfying this responsibility? Adding fuel to these troubled waters is another one of the ethical principles, which states:

> Psychologists present the science of psychology and offer their services, products, and publications fairly and accurately, avoiding misrepresentation through sensationalism, exaggeration, or superficiality. Psychologists are guided by the primary obligation to aid the public in developing informed judgments, opinions, and choices (p. 635).

What does the psychologist do, then, if the needs of the client (such as the defendant) run somewhat counter to the needs of the public? In short, the Ethical Principles, while usually useful concerning the matter of responsibility to clients seen in a clinical setting, provide little help to the expert in court.

If the Ethical Principles do not provide the necessary guidance, we must tackle the problem in another way. Does the expert have an obligation to present both sides of the case? As a start, it seems fruitful to ask this question: Does the case have two "reasonable" sides? If there is contrary evidence to the major thrust of the expert's testimony, it can be of two sorts:

1. Contradictory evidence that calls into question the general rule being proffered, and
2. An exception that still maintains the general rule.

The second case is the easier one, for the expert could decide that a minor exception need not be discussed since it will only confuse the jury and prolong the testimony needlessly. The first case, by contrast, is the more difficult one for it presumes that the case has two reasonable sides. The psychologist could still choose the advocacy or the education path. Whatever the choice, trouble may lurk ahead. In any given case, or when it comes to any given issue within a case, neither the advocacy nor the education path is likely to be straight and easy.

Problems With the Advocacy Option

Suppose the psychologist decides that it is ethically responsible to be an advocate. Several problems will still arise. Say, for example, the expert is testifying that cross-racial identifications are more difficult for witnesses, and suppose that 99% of all investigations support this conclusion. Here, the expert may have little problem. He or she could easily decide that any discussion of the other 1% of the studies would simply confuse the jury and prolong the testimony unduly. On the other hand, suppose that 51% of the investigations support the expert's conclusions. Or even a mere 25%. The expert must decide whether selective presentation of this research would seriously distort and misrepresent the available psychological research. In good conscience, the expert could decide that the supportive studies are solid and reliable while the unsupportive ones are shoddily conducted and must be discarded from consideration. But when this happens, it is conceivable that the expert will become immersed in a battle involving opposing experts that could be rather unpleasant.

Indeed, the advocacy position may have one discomforting side effect. It could lead to a battle of the experts similar to that which exists in the psychiatric area. (See Ziskin, 1975; Tunstall et al., 1982; Heim, 1982 for a discussion of how unpleasant this can be.) Several experimental psychologists have already suggested that such a battle in the area of eyewitness reliability is practically a foregone conclusion (Egeth & McCloskey, 1984).

Problems With the Education Option

Suppose the psychologist decides that it is ethically responsible to be an impartial educator. Several problems will arise in this case too. After all, the psychologist is working within an adversary system, the essence of which is that one side of the case is presented, and subsequently challenged by the other. As Schofield (1956) noted almost 30 years ago, there is something in the very nature of this system, and in a court trial in particular, that "arouses the adrenals" (p. 2). During cross-examination, attorneys will try to portray witnesses as "ignorant, irresponsible, or biased" (Brodsky, 1977). Based upon his own participation and observations of trials, Schofield came to believe that only a superhuman person could avoid becoming identified with one of the sides, and avoid the sense of wanting his or her side to win. Thus motivated, the person may become guilty of distorting testimony and potentially frustrate the process of justice.

Whether knowingly or not, psychologists may find that "the whole truth" is not revealed, or worse, a distorted truth is given, because of the procedures required by law. For example, when testifying on the reliability of eyewitness accounts, an expert cannot necessarily control the specific questions posed to elicit information and opinions. If questions that might reveal weaknesses in the testimony are never asked, the information may never reach the jury. Thus, even when a psychologist wants to present more information, or a less distorted picture of the psychological research, it may in practice be impossible to do so.

Even more likely is the probability that the "impartial educator" will never get the chance to participate in the case. One distinguished trial lawyer who spoke to a conference for lawyers on the subject of "relations with the expert witness" warned his colleagues about the so-called impartial educator:

> Many people are convinced that the expert who really persuades a jury is the independent, objective, nonarticulate type ... I disagree. I would go into a lawsuit with an objective, uncommitted, independent expert about as willingly as

I would occupy a foxhole with a couple of non-combatant soldiers (Meier, 1982).

. . .

References

Brodsky, S. L. (1977). The mental health professional on the witness stand: A survival guide. In B. D. Sales (Ed.), *Psychology in the legal process*. New York: Spectrum.

Egeth, H., & McCloskey, M. (1984). Expert testimony about eyewitness behavior: Is it safe and effective? In G. Wells and E. Loftus (Eds.), *Eyewitness testimony: Psychological perspectives*. London: Cambridge University Press.

Ethical Principles of Psychologists. *American Psychologist*, 1981, *36*, 633–638.

Federal Rules of Evidence for United States Courts and Magistrates. (1975). St. Paul, Minnesota: West.

Fersch, E. A., Jr. (1980). Ethical issues for psychologists in court settings. In J. Monahan (Ed.), *Who is the client? The ethics of psychological intervention in the criminal justice system*. Washington D.C.: American Psychological Association.

Heim, A. (1982). Professional issues arising from psychological evidence presented in court: A reply. *Bulletin of the British Psychological Society*, *35*, 332–333.

Loftus, E. F. (1979). *Eyewitness testimony*. Cambridge, Massachusetts: Harvard University Press.

Loftus, E. F., & Monahan, J. (1980). Trial by data: Psychological research as legal evidence. *American Psychologist*, *35*, 270–283.

Meier, P. (1982). Damned liars and expert witnesses. Presidential Address. American Statistical Association, Annual Meeting.

Pollack, S. (1973). Observations on the adversary system and the role of the forensic scientist: "Scientific truth" v. "Legal truth." *Journal of Forensic Sciences*, *18*, 173–177.

Rivlin, A. (1973). Forensic social science. *Harvard Educational Review*, *43*, 61–75.

Schofield, W. (1956). Psychology, law and the expert witness. *American Psychologist*, *11*, 1–7.

Tunstall, O., Gudjonsson, G., Eysenck, H., & Haward, L. (1982). Professional issues arising from psychological evidence presented in court. *Bulletin of the British Psychological Society*, *35*, 329–331.

Wolfgang, M. E. (1974). The social scientist in court. *Journal of Criminal Law and Criminology*, *65*, 239–247.

Ziskin, J. (1975). *Coping with psychiatric and psychological testimony*. (2nd edition). Beverly Hills, California: Law and Psychology Press.

◆ ◆ ◆

Commentary: In a recent review, Elliott criticized Loftus's position. Specifically, he remarked that the notion that

> as between the expert as educator–
> scientist and the expert as advocate we
> can settle claims to merit by waiting to see
> which survives seems to me to be both
> misplaced Darwinism and bad advice.

> Lawyers and other policy actors will almost always choose advocates over impartial scientists, which only means that the adversary system is not a fit environment for science. Why let the world of policy be the touchstone of the value of science?
> (pp. 433–434)

See Elliott, R. (1993). Expert testimony about eyewitness identification. Law and Human Behavior, 17, 423–448.

Cognitive Psychologists as Expert Witnesses:
A Problem in Professional Ethics

Alan H. Goldman

. . .

If role differentiation were accepted by the psychologist, then he would accept the role defined for him in the natural working of the trial process. Officially, the justice system defines his role as that of an impartial expert. In practice, since he will be retained by one attorney (normally the defense attorney), the pressure toward an adversarial role will be great (Anderton et al., 1980; Haney, 1980). If the psychologist simply accepts these pressures as part of the proper working of the system, then he will be content to serve as an advocate, to present only that testimony elicited by the defense attorney as helpful to his client's cause. He would cooperate fully at pretrial conferences in educating the lawyer as to just those aspects of the total evidence that might suggest inaccuracy on the part of the witnesses in the case. If the psychologist takes the defendant to be his client as well in this context, this view will lend additional support to the legal concept of the advocate role, especially if he believes that his first duty is always to his client in his own professional role. His desire to cooperate with the attorney who seeks his services, rewards him for providing them, and can recommend his services to others may further motivate his acceptance of an adversarial role. Finally, his advocacy of a particular position may be intensified by defensiveness in the face of aggressive cross-examination. Thus there will be extramoral pressures on the psychologist to accept the advocate role in the trial context. The question is whether there is moral justification as well for doing so. The answer is negative.

I have argued against the acceptance of role differentiation in this context. In any case the proper role for the psychologist here is not that of client advocate, but that of educator of the jury. Neither the defense lawyer nor the defendant is the psychologist's patient. Doing his best in treating a patient is therefore not analogous to doing his best to win acquittal for a defendant in a trial (even if he were a clinician). The psychologist can fulfill his function of serving as an expert only by informing the jury in as impartial and objective manner as possible of the current state of knowledge regarding eyewitness accuracy and the variables affecting it. The requirement of adopting the role of impartial educator follows directly from our justification for testifying. Given that the moral aim of such testimony is to inform the decision-making process in the jury so as to make it more rational, the proper manner of testifying is that which best achieves this aim. . . .

Acceptance of this function for the expert is compatible with the advocate role only under the assumption that truth or knowledge will emerge in the end from the clash of opposing witnesses or of examination and cross-examination. But we have questioned that assumption. It is even more obvious than in the case of lawyers that the psychologist can assume neither the existence of an equally knowledgable expert for the other side nor sufficient expertise or will on the part of the prosecutor to elicit an objective view of the subject matter.

Having decided that the psychologist ought to be impartial in his testimony, the problem becomes how he can achieve this aim within the adversarial setting. Since the defense lawyer will not be anxious to elicit both sides of the research results in the area, the psychologist ought to serve notice at the beginning that impartiality will be the price of his testimony. While a defense attorney will not solicit the

From *Law and Human Behavior, 10,* 29–45. Copyright 1986 by Plenum Publishing. Adapted with permission of the publisher.

testimony of an expert unless he takes it to benefit his client's cause, he can be put on notice prior to the trial that a strictly adversarial role for the psychologist is not considered proper. The lawyer might at that point seek a different expert, but the fact that this second expert might be less scrupulous is no excuse for complicity in an improper role.

Having made his position clear, the psychologist should, if permitted to testify, attempt to bring out the tentative nature of the experimental results (when they have not been thoroughly corroborated), difficulties in generalization, and contrary experimental results when they exist. Of course he should also confine his testimony to reporting experimental studies that he considers sound, resisting controversial inferences or applications to the present case, that is, testimony beyond his area of expertise. The defense lawyer who hires him will of course emphasize those variables that call into question an adverse witness's reliability. It may be unreasonable to expect the psychologist to introduce on his own testimony on counterindicative variables, that is those which indicate favorable circumstances for identification. Some balancing here may have to be left to the competence of the prosecutor in cross-examination. Given the limitations of the context, the psychologist might not succeed in the impartial and complete presentation of the relevant data that he seeks. But, as noted, the considerations that justify his testifying at all demand as well a presentation that will enable the jury to weigh the other evidence in a more reasonable and informed manner. If the adversary system does not in general destroy the ability of the jury to arrive at a reasonable conclusion, it should not destroy the contribution of the psychologist's expert testimony toward that aim, provided that he rejects the role of advocate and follows his direct professional and personal conscience.

References

Anderton, P., Staulcup, V., & Crisso, T. (1980). On being ethical in legal places. *Professional Psychology, 11,* 764–773.

Haney, C. (1980). Psychology and legal change: On the limits of a factual jurisprudence. *Law and Human Behavior, 4,* 147–199.

◆　◆　◆

Commentary: Perhaps the most succinct summary of the consensus position comes from Adams, K. M., & Putnam, S. H. (1994). Coping with professional skeptics: Reply to Faust. Psychological Assessment, 6, *5–7:*

> *Psychologists called to court are best advised to act as psychologists first and best, allowing the legal arena to evolve as it must and will. Psychologists and lawyers are professionals with different goals, cultures, and rules and who operate in epistemologically diverse ways. (p. 6)*

This issue is not simply a matter of academic debate, however. As the next excerpt reveals, the courts have begun to be concerned about misguided advocacy.

Psychologists and the Judicial System: Broader Perspectives

Donald N. Bersoff

. . .

. . . In June 1980, Judge John Grady of the federal district court in northern Illinois, issued his opinion in *PASE v. Hannon* (1980). The plaintiffs had challenged the use of individual intelligence scales to place black children in classes for the educably mentally retarded. A disproportionate number of black children had been misclassified as retarded, they claimed, because the tests upon which the determinations were based were racially and culturally biased. During the three week trial on this controversial issue, Judge Grady heard the testimony of several prominent psychologists, including a past president of the American Psychological Association, a former member of its Board of Directors, and other acknowledged experts who would comprise a veritable Who's Who of American Measurement, if such a compendium existed. Some of the experts agreed with the plaintiffs that, indeed, there were data to support the assertion that the tests unduly favored those from the white middle-class culture; others concurred with the defendant school system that there was no evidence that the tests disfavored blacks because of inherent bias in their construction.

Actually, the gathering of the experts in *PASE* was something of a reunion. Many of these same witnesses had appeared earlier in San Francisco in a much more heralded case, *Larry P. v. Riles* (1972; 1979). There Judge Robert Peckham found in favor of the minority plaintiffs on both statutory and constitutional grounds. He concluded the tests were culturally biased and permanently enjoined the defendant state of California "from utilizing, permitting the use of, or approving the use of any standardized tests . . . for the identification of black EMR children or their placement into EMR classes, without first securing prior approval by this court" (p. 989).

The plaintiffs in *PASE* apparently expected a replay of the trial in *Larry P.* However, rather than ruling that the tests in question were culturally biased, Judge Grady held that individual intelligence tests "do not discriminate against black children in the Chicago public schools" (p. 883). Judge Grady's reference to *Larry P.* occupied a bit less than one page of his 52-page opinion and he virtually rejected its tenability out of hand. "The witnesses and the arguments," Judge Grady said, "which persuaded Judge Peckham have not persuaded me" (p. 882).

One of the most intriguing aspects of Judge Grady's decision was his almost utter rejection of the testimony of expert psychologists who testified on behalf of both parties. The reason for this rejection is, at the same time, illuminating, instructive, and very troublesome:

> None of the witnesses in this case has so impressed me with his or her credibility or expertise that I would feel secure in basing a decision on his or her opinion. In some instances, I am satisfied that the opinions expressed are more the result of doctrinaire commitment to a preconceived idea than they are the result of scientific inquiry. I need something more than the conclusions of the witnesses in order to arrive at my own conclusions (p. 836).

This perception of the behavior of the expert witnesses who testified before Judge Grady raises some formidable and disturbing, if not painful, ethical issues. If he is correct in that perception, each of the psychologists who offered opinions out of a "doctrinaire commitment to a preconceived idea" rather than as a "result of scientific inquiry" may be guilty of violating several important provisions of the Ethical Principles of Psychologists (APA, 1981), of which the following may serve as examples:

1. The Code's Preamble, while recognizing that psychologists must be free to inquire and communicate, reminds them that this freedom also demands "objectivity in the application of skills . . ." (p. 633).
2. Principle 1(a) requires psychologists to "provide a thorough discussion of the limitations of their data, especially where their work touches on social policy . . ." (p. 633).
3. Psychologists, under Principle 2, are ordered to "recognize the boundaries of their competence and the limitations of their techniques . . ." (p. 634).
4. Under Principle 4, psychologists providing psychological information in a public forum must "base their statements on scientifically acceptable psychological findings and techniques with full recognition of the limits and uncertainties of such evidence" (pp. 634–635).
5. Principle 4(g) more specifically mandates that psychologists who offer statements on the science of psychology do so "fairly and accurately, avoiding misrepresentation through sensationalism, exaggeration, or superficiality." This provision further compels psychologists to remain aware that their primary obligation is "to aid the public in developing informed judgments, opinions, and choices" (p. 635).

These are genuinely serious concerns. If the ethical integrity and scientific objectivity of experimental psychologists begin to be questioned, the significant and potentially useful information they produce may be permanently neglected by the judicial system. This will be detrimental not only to the just resolution of legal disputes between parties that involve empirical issues, but to the advancement of social policy in general. It is imperative, therefore, that social scientists remain true to the primary role they serve in society. . . .

Several years ago Cronbach (1975) warned psychologists involved in assessment issues not to act as advocates. His admonition, of course, is applicable to a wide range of social policy and scientific issues adjudicated by the legal system. While social scientists perform a valuable service when they testify as expert witnesses for one side or the other, belief in the rightness of a particular cause does not justify abandonment of evenhandedness, dispassion, and neutrality. Monahan and Loftus (1982) have served a useful purpose in denoting the variety of ways in which psychologists can enrich the legal system and in cautioning that the disinterested and simple arraying of facts may "foster an asceptic aloofness from the human problems with which the law attempts to deal" (p. 466). But, while unbridled advocacy may be a moral imperative for attorneys, it may be directly antagonistic to the ethical principles that control the behavior of psychologists. Social scientists must continually be conscious of the fact that their data, interpretations, and opinions will be tested in the crucible of courtroom cross-examination whose very purpose it is to destroy credibility and evoke evidence of bias. Although the distillation of that process may yield testimony of great consequence and weight to the court, it can be highly anxiety provoking for psychologists who act as injudicious advocates, pleading for a position rather than as cautious scientists presenting data in an evenhanded manner. I am not suggesting that it is inappropriate to testify on behalf of a particular party in a legal dispute, but, in doing so, psychologists should exhibit the prudence of a circumspect, rational, scrupulous scientist.

Through their publications, collaboration with attorneys and judges, participation in the drafting of *amicus* briefs, testimony before legislative committees, and administrative agencies, as well as serving as expert witnesses, there are many ways social scientists can influence public policy effectively. . . . Within the bounds of scientific and professional ethics, these are important, if not crucial roles. But, if experimental psychologists are to be respected by the courts and treated as more than mere numerologists attempting to convince the judiciary of doctrinaire positions, they must offer more situation-specific, ecologically valid, objective data that serve science, not a particular adversary. In that way, perhaps, courts may finally arrive at, not only judicially sound but, empirically justified decisions that will withstand both appellate and scientific scrutiny.

References

American Psychological Association (1981). Ethical principles of psychologists. *American Psychologist, 36,* 633–638.

Cronbach, L. (1975). Five decades of public controversy over mental testing. *American Psychologist, 30,* 1–14.

Larry P. v. Riles, 343 F.Supp. 1306 (N.D. Cal. 1972) (order granting preliminary injunction) *aff'd* 502 F.2d 963 (9th Cir. 1974); 495 F.Supp. 926 (N.D. Cal. 1979) *appeal docketed* No. 80–4027 (9th Cir., Jan. 17, 1980).

Monahan, J., & Loftus, E. (1982). The psychology of law. *Annual Review of Psychology, 33,* 441–475.

PASE v. Hannon, 506 F.Supp. 831 (N.D. Ill. 1980).

Commentary: As a middle-ground position, consider Hastie's (1986) recommendations:

> I would like to suggest a concrete image in place of Loftus's teacher–advocate dichotomy. I think that the psychologist should assume the role of a watchdog. When he or she honestly believes, based on scientific findings, that, for example, eyewitness testimony is unreliable, then he or she should take the witness stand to testify against the eyewitness. If any other expert improperly applies scientific findings to impugn eyewitness testimony, then the psychologist should testify against the expert. My watchdog image is meant to exclude two other roles. The psychologist should not be a timid lapdog who never believes there is sufficient reason to leave the comfort of the laboratory to challenge an unreliable eyewitness or misleading expert in the courtroom. Nor should

> the psychologist be a rabid attack dog who assaults every eyewitness who appears in the courtroom. (p. 80)

Hastie, R. (1986). Notes on the psychologist expert witness. Law and Human Behavior, 10, 79–82.

In any event, despite attempts to seek help from the then-current version of the APA code of ethics to resolve the advocacy–educator issue, by the 1980s there began to be a call for specific guidance to be provided for psychologists who enter the legal arena:

> As a profession psychology must decide for itself the standards and level of quality that should apply to its forensic assessments. The most important reason for doing this is consumer and public welfare. Moreover, every industry knows that a high level of internally imposed standards and quality control is important to ensure a high-quality product and to avoid personal and corporate liability.
>
> Both APA's Division 41 and the ABFP can play a role in the development of such standards. The standards should reflect the values not only of psychological practitioners, but also of researchers in psychology and law and scientific psychology in general. The standards should reflect these values because psychologists who perform forensic assessments represent psychology—not merely forensic clinical psychology—when they enter the courtroom. Furthermore, as noted earlier, experimental psychologists themselves are entering the courtroom in increasing numbers. They are facing the same questions regarding the limits of their testimony. (p. 837)

See Grisso, T. (1987). The economic and scientific future of forensic psychological assessment. American Psychologist, 42, 831–839.

Four years later, the call was answered.

Specialty Guidelines for Forensic Psychologists

Committee on Ethical Guidelines for Forensic Psychologists

The *Specialty Guidelines for Forensic Psychologists*, while informed by the *Ethical Principles of Psychologists* (APA, 1990) and meant to be consistent with them, are designed to provide more specific guidance to forensic psychologists in monitoring their professional conduct when acting in assistance to courts, parties to legal proceedings, correctional and forensic mental health facilities, and legislative agencies. The primary goal of the *Guidelines* is to improve the quality of forensic psychological services offered to individual clients and the legal system and thereby to enhance forensic psychology as a discipline and profession. The *Specialty Guidelines for Forensic Psychologists* represent a joint statement of the American Psychology–Law Society and Division 41 of the American Psychological Association and are endorsed by the American Academy of Forensic Psychology. The *Guidelines* do not represent an official statement of the American Psychological Association.

The *Guidelines* provide an aspirational model of desirable professional practice by psychologists, within any subdiscipline of psychology (e.g., clinical, developmental, social, experimental), when they are engaged regularly as experts and represent themselves as such, in an activity primarily intended to provide professional psychological expertise to the judicial system. This would include, for example, clinical forensic examiners; psychologists employed by correctional or forensic mental health systems; researchers who offer direct testimony about the relevance of scientific data to a psycholegal issue; trial behavior consultants; psychologists engaged in preparation of *amicus* briefs; or psychologists, appearing as forensic experts, who consult with, or testify before, judicial, legislative, or administrative agencies acting in an adjudicative capacity. Individuals who provide only occasional service to the legal system and who do so without representing themselves as *forensic experts* may find these *Guidelines* helpful, particularly in conjunction with consultation with colleagues who are forensic experts.

While the *Guidelines* are concerned with a model of desirable professional practice, to the extent that they may be construed as being applicable to the advertisement of services or the solicitation of clients, they are intended to prevent false or deceptive advertisement or solicitation and should be construed in a manner consistent with that intent.

I. PURPOSE AND SCOPE

A. Purpose

1. While the professional standards for the ethical practice of psychology, as a general discipline, are addressed in the American Psychological Association's *Ethical Principles of Psychologists*, these ethical principles do not relate, in sufficient detail, to current aspirations of desirable professional conduct for forensic psychologists. By design, none of the *Guidelines* contradicts any of the *Ethical Principles of Psychologists*; rather, they amplify those *Principles* in the context of the practice of forensic psychology, as herein defined.

From *Law and Human Behavior*, 15, 655–665. Copyright 1991 by Plenum Publishing. Reprinted with permission of the publisher. Footnotes 1 and 2 have been omitted.

The *Specialty Guidelines for Forensic Psychologists* were adopted by majority vote of the members of Division 41 [American Psychological Association] and the American Psychology–Law Society. They have also been endorsed by majority vote by the American Academy of Forensic Psychology. The Executive Committee of Division 41 and the American Psychology–Law Society formally approved these *Guidelines* on March 9, 1991.

2. The *Guidelines* have been designed to be national in scope and are intended to conform with state and Federal law. In situations where the forensic psychologist believes that the requirements of law are in conflict with the *Guidelines*, attempts to resolve the conflict should be made in accordance with the procedures set forth in these *Guidelines* [IV(G)] and in the *Ethical Principles of Psychologists*.

B. Scope

1. The *Guidelines* specify the nature of desirable professional practice by forensic psychologists, within any subdiscipline of psychology (e.g., clinical, developmental, social, experimental), when engaged regularly as forensic psychologists.

   a. "Psychologist" means any individual whose professional activities are defined by the American Psychological Association or by regulation of title by state registration or licensure, as the practice of psychology.

   b. "Forensic psychology" means all forms of professional psychological conduct when acting, with definable foreknowledge, as a psychological expert on explicitly psycholegal issues, in direct assistance to courts, parties to legal proceedings, correctional and forensic mental health facilities, and administrative, judicial, and legislative agencies acting in an adjudicative capacity.

   c. "Forensic psychologist" means psychologists who regularly engage in the practice of forensic psychology as defined in I(B)(1)(b).

2. The *Guidelines* do not apply to a psychologist who is asked to provide professional psychological services when the psychologist was not informed at the time of delivery of the services that they were to be used as forensic psychological services as defined above.

The *Guidelines* may be helpful, however, in preparing the psychologist for the experience of communicating psychological data in a forensic context.

3. Psychologists who are not forensic psychologists as defined in I(B)(1)(c), but occasionally provide limited forensic psychological services, may find the *Guidelines* useful in the preparation and presentation of their professional services.

C. Related Standards

1. Forensic psychologists also conduct their professional activities in accord with the *Ethical Principles of Psychologists* and the various other statements of the American Psychological Association that may apply to particular subdisciplines or areas of practice that are relevant to their professional activities.

2. The standards of practice and ethical guidelines of other relevant "expert professional organizations" contain useful guidance and should be consulted even though the present *Guidelines* take precedence for forensic psychologists.

II. RESPONSIBILITY

A. Forensic psychologists have an obligation to provide services in a manner consistent with the highest standards of their profession. They are responsible for their own conduct and the conduct of those individuals under their direct supervision.

B. Forensic psychologists make a reasonable effort to ensure that their services and the products of their services are used in a forthright and responsible manner.

III. COMPETENCE

A. Forensic psychologists provide services only in areas of psychology in which they have specialized knowledge, skill, experience, and education.

B. Forensic psychologists have an obligation to present to the court, regarding the specific matters to which they will testify, the boundaries of their competence, the factual bases (knowledge, skill, experience, training, and education) for their qualifications as an expert, and the relevance of those factual bases to their qualification as an expert on the specific matters at issue.

C. Forensic psychologists are responsible for a fundamental and reasonable level of knowledge and understanding of the legal and professional standards that govern their participation as experts in legal proceedings.

D. Forensic psychologists have an obligation to understand the civil rights of parties in legal proceedings in which they participate, and manage their professional conduct in a manner that does not diminish or threaten those rights.

E. Forensic psychologists recognize that their own personal values, moral beliefs, or personal and professional relationships with parties to a legal proceeding may interfere with their ability to practice competently. Under such circumstances, forensic psychologists are obligated to decline participation or to limit their assistance in a manner consistent with professional obligations.

IV. RELATIONSHIPS

A. During initial consultation with the legal representative of the party seeking services, forensic psychologists have an obligation to inform the party of factors that might reasonably affect the decision to contract with the forensic psychologist. These factors include, but are not limited to

1. the fee structure for anticipated professional services;

2. prior and current personal or professional activities, obligations, and relationships that might produce a conflict of interests;

3. their areas of competence and the limits of their competence; and

4. the known scientific bases and limitations of the methods and procedures that they employ and their qualifications to employ such methods and procedures.

B. Forensic psychologists do not provide professional services to parties to a legal proceeding on the basis of "contingent fees," when those services involve the offering of expert testimony to a court or administrative body, or when they call upon the psychologist to make affirmations or representations intended to be relied upon by third parties.

C. Forensic psychologists who derive a substantial portion of their income from fee-for-service arrangements should offer some portion of their professional services on a *pro bono* or reduced fee basis where the public interest or the welfare of clients may be inhibited by insufficient financial resources.

D. Forensic psychologists recognize potential conflicts of interest in dual relationships with parties to a legal proceeding, and they seek to minimize their effects.

1. Forensic psychologists avoid providing professional services to parties in a legal proceeding with whom they have personal or professional relationships that are inconsistent with the anticipated relationship.

2. When it is necessary to provide both evaluation and treatment services to a party in a legal proceeding (as may be the case in small forensic hospital settings or small communities), the forensic psychologist takes reasonable steps to minimize the potential negative effects of these circumstances on the rights of the party, confidentiality, and the process of treatment and evaluation.

E. Forensic psychologists have an obligation to ensure that prospective clients are informed of their legal rights with respect to the anticipated forensic service, of the purpose of any evaluation, of the nature of procedures to be employed, of the intended uses of any product of their services, and of the party who has employed the forensic psychologist.

1. Unless court ordered, forensic psychologists obtain the informed consent of the client or party, or their legal representative, before proceeding with such evaluations and procedures. If the client appears unwilling to proceed after receiving a thorough notification of the purposes, methods, and intended uses of the forensic evaluation, the evaluation should be postponed and the psychologist should take steps to place the client in contact with his/her attorney for the purpose of legal advice on the issue of participation.

2. In situations where the client or party may not have the capacity to provide informed consent to services or the evaluation is pursuant to court order, the forensic psychologist provides reasonable notice to the client's legal representative of the nature of the anticipated forensic service before proceeding. If the client's legal representative objects to the evaluation, the forensic psychologist notifies the court issuing the order and responds as directed.

3. After a psychologist has advised the subject of a clinical forensic evaluation of the intended uses of the evaluation and its work product, the psychologist may not use the evaluation work product for other purposes without explicit waiver to do so by the client or the client's legal representative.

F. When forensic psychologists engage in research or scholarly activities that are compensated financially by a client or party to a legal proceeding, or when the psychologist provides those services on a *pro bono* basis, the psychologist clarifies any anticipated further use of such research or scholarly product, discloses the psychologist's role in the resulting research or scholarly products, and obtains whatever consent or agreement is required by law or professional standards.

G. When conflicts arise between the forensic psychologist's professional standards and the requirements of legal standards, a particular court, or a directive by an officer of the court or legal authorities, the forensic psychologist has an obligation to make those legal authorities aware of the source of the conflict and to take reasonable steps to resolve it. Such steps may include, but are not limited to, obtaining the consultation of fellow forensic professionals, obtaining the advice of independent counsel, and conferring directly with the legal representatives involved.

V. CONFIDENTIALITY AND PRIVILEGE

A. Forensic psychologists have an obligation to be aware of the legal standards that may affect or limit the confidentiality or privilege that may attach to their services or their products, and they conduct their professional activities in a manner that respects those known rights and privileges.

1. Forensic psychologists establish and maintain a system of record keeping and professional communication that safeguards a client's privilege.

2. Forensic psychologists maintain active control over records and information. They only release information pursuant to statutory requirements, court order, or the consent of the client.

B. Forensic psychologists inform their clients of the limitations to the confidentiality of their services and their products (see also Guideline IV E) by providing them with an understandable statement of their rights, privileges, and the limitations of confidentiality.

C. In situations where the right of the client or party to confidentiality is limited, the forensic psychologist makes every effort to maintain confidentiality with regard to any information that does not bear directly upon the legal purpose of the evaluation.

D. Forensic psychologists provide clients or their authorized legal representatives with access to the information in their records and a meaningful explanation of that information, consistent with existing Federal and state statutes, the *Ethical Principles of Psychologists, the Standards for Educational and Psychological Testing*, and institutional rules and regulations.

VI. METHODS AND PROCEDURES

A. Because of their special status as persons qualified as experts to the court, forensic psychologists have an obligation to maintain current knowledge of scientific, professional and legal developments within their area of claimed competence. They are obligated also to use that knowledge, consistent with accepted clinical and scientific standards, in selecting data collection methods and procedures for an evaluation, treatment, consultation or scholarly/empirical investigation.

B. Forensic psychologists have an obligation to document and be prepared to make available, subject to court order or the rules of evidence, all data that form the basis for their evidence or services. The standard to be applied to such documentation or recording *anticipates* that the detail and quality of such documentation will be subject to reasonable judicial scrutiny; this standard is higher than the normative standard for general clinical practice. When forensic psychologists conduct an examination or engage in the treatment of a party to a legal proceeding, with foreknowledge that their professional services will be used in an adjudicative forum, they incur a special responsibility to provide the best documentation possible under the circumstances.

   1. Documentation of the data upon which one's evidence is based is subject to the normal rules of discovery, disclosure, confidentiality, and privilege that operate in the jurisdiction in which the data were obtained. Forensic psychologists have an obligation to be aware of those rules and to regulate their conduct in accordance with them.

   2. The duties and obligations of forensic psychologists with respect to documentation of data that form the basis for their evidence apply from the moment they know or have a reasonable basis for knowing that their data and evidence derived from it are likely to enter into legally relevant decisions.

C. In providing forensic psychological services, forensic psychologists take special care to avoid undue influence upon their methods, procedures, and products, such as might emanate from the party to a legal proceeding by financial compensation or other gains. As an expert conducting an evaluation, treatment, consultation, or scholarly/empirical investigation, the forensic psychologist maintains professional integrity by examining the issue at hand from all reasonable perspectives, actively seeking information that will differentially test plausible rival hypotheses.

D. Forensic psychologists do not provide professional forensic services to a defendant or to any party in, or in contemplation of, a legal proceeding prior to that individual's representation by counsel, except for persons judicially determined, where appropriate, to be handling their representation *pro se*. When the forensic services are pursuant to court order and the client is not represented by counsel, the forensic psychologist makes reasonable efforts to inform the court prior to providing the services.

   1. A forensic psychologist may provide emergency mental health services to a pretrial defendant prior to court order or the appointment of counsel where there are reasonable grounds to believe that such emergency services are needed for the protection and improvement of the defendant's mental health and where failure to provide such mental health services would constitute a

substantial risk of imminent harm to the defendant or to others. In providing such services the forensic psychologist nevertheless seeks to inform the defendant's counsel in a manner consistent with the requirements of the emergency situation.

2. Forensic psychologists who provide such emergency mental health services should attempt to avoid providing further professional forensic services to that defendant unless that relationship is reasonably unavoidable [see IV(D)(2)].

E. When forensic psychologists seek data from third parties, prior records, or other sources, they do so only with the prior approval of the relevant legal party or as a consequence of an order of a court to conduct the forensic evaluation.

F. Forensic psychologists are aware that hearsay exceptions and other rules governing expert testimony place a special ethical burden upon them. When hearsay or otherwise inadmissible evidence forms the basis of their opinion, evidence, or professional product, they seek to minimize sole reliance upon such evidence. Where circumstances reasonably permit, forensic psychologists seek to obtain independent and personal verification of data relied upon as part of their professional services to the court or to a party to a legal proceeding.

1. While many forms of data used by forensic psychologists are hearsay, forensic psychologists attempt to corroborate critical data that form the basis for their professional product. When using hearsay data that have not been corroborated, but are nevertheless utilized, forensic psychologists have an affirmative responsibility to acknowledge the uncorroborated status of those data and the reasons for relying upon such data.

2. With respect to evidence of any type, forensic psychologists avoid offering information from their investigations or evaluations that does not bear directly upon the legal purpose of their professional services and that is not critical as support for their product, evidence or testimony, except where such disclosure is required by law.

3. When a forensic psychologist relies upon data or information gathered by others, the origins of those data are clarified in any professional product. In addition, the forensic psychologist bears a special responsibility to ensure that such data, if relied upon, were gathered in a manner standard for the profession.

G. Unless otherwise stipulated by the parties, forensic psychologists are aware that no statements made by a defendant, in the course of any (forensic) examination, no testimony by the expert based upon such statements, nor any other fruits of the statements can be admitted into evidence against the defendant in any criminal proceeding, except on an issue respecting mental condition on which the defendant has introduced testimony. Forensic psychologists have an affirmative duty to ensure that their written products and oral testimony conform to this Federal Rule of Procedure (12.2[c]), or its state equivalent.

1. Because forensic psychologists are often not in a position to know what evidence, documentation, or element of a written product may be or may lend to a "fruit of the statement," they exercise extreme caution in preparing reports or offering testimony prior to the defendant's assertion of a mental state claim or the defendant's introduction of testimony regarding a mental condition. Consistent with the reporting requirements of state or federal law, forensic psychologists avoid including statements from the defendant relating to the time period of the alleged offense.

2. Once a defendant has proceeded to the trial stage, and all pretrial mental health

issues such as competency have been resolved, forensic psychologists may include in their reports or testimony any statements made by the defendant that are directly relevant to supporting their expert evidence, providing that the defendant has "introduced" mental state evidence or testimony within the meaning of Federal Rule of Procedure 12.2(c), or its state equivalent.

H. Forensic psychologists avoid giving written or oral evidence about the psychological characteristics of particular individuals when they have not had an opportunity to conduct an examination of the individual adequate to the scope of the statements, opinions, or conclusions to be issued. Forensic psychologists make every reasonable effort to conduct such examinations. When it is not possible or feasible to do so, they make clear the impact of such limitations on the reliability and validity of their professional products, evidence, or testimony.

VII. PUBLIC AND PROFESSIONAL COMMUNICATIONS

A. Forensic psychologists make reasonable efforts to ensure that the products of their services, as well as their own public statements and professional testimony, are communicated in ways that will promote understanding and avoid deception, given the particular characteristics, roles, and abilities of various recipients of the communications.

  1. Forensic psychologists take reasonable steps to correct misuse or misrepresentation of their professional products, evidence, and testimony.

  2. Forensic psychologists provide information about professional work to clients in a manner consistent with professional and legal standards for the disclosure of test results, interpretations of data, and the factual bases for conclusions. A full explanation of the results of tests and the bases for conclusions should be given in language that the client can understand.

   a. When disclosing information about a client to third parties who are not qualified to interpret test results and data, the forensic psychologist complies with Principle 16 of the *Standards for Educational and Psychological Testing*. When required to disclose results to a nonpsychologist, every attempt is made to ensure that test security is maintained and access to information is restricted to individuals with a legitimate and professional interest in the data. Other qualified mental health professionals who make a request for information pursuant to a lawful order are, by definition, "individuals with a legitimate and professional interest."

   b. In providing records and raw data, the forensic psychologist takes reasonable steps to ensure that the receiving party is informed that raw scores must be interpreted by a qualified professional in order to provide reliable and valid information.

B. Forensic psychologists realize that their public role as "expert to the court" or as "expert representing the profession" confers upon them a special responsibility for fairness and accuracy in their public statements. When evaluating or commenting upon the professional work product or qualifications of another expert or party to a legal proceeding, forensic psychologists represent their professional disagreements with reference to a fair and accurate evaluation of the data, theories, standards, and opinions of the other expert or party.

C. Ordinarily, forensic psychologists avoid making detailed public (out-of-court) statements about particular legal proceedings in which they have been involved. When there is a strong justification to do so, such public statements are designed to assure accurate representation of their role or their evidence, not to advocate the positions of parties in the legal proceeding. Forensic psychologists address particular legal proceedings in publications or communications only to the extent that the information relied upon is part of a public record, or consent for that use has been properly obtained from the party holding any privilege.

D. When testifying, forensic psychologists have an obligation to all parties to a legal proceeding to present their findings, conclusions, evidence, or other professional products in a fair manner. This principle does not preclude forceful representation of the data and reasoning upon which a conclusion or professional product is based. It does, however, preclude an attempt, whether active or passive, to engage in partisan distortion or misrepresentation. Forensic psychologists do not, by either commission or omission, participate in a misrepresentation of their evidence, nor do

they participate in partisan attempts to avoid, deny, or subvert the presentation of evidence contrary to their own position.

E. Forensic psychologists, by virtue of their competence and rules of discovery, actively disclose all sources of information obtained in the course of their professional services; they actively disclose which information from which source was used in formulating a particular written product or oral testimony.

F. Forensic psychologists are aware that their essential role as expert to the court is to assist the trier of fact to understand the evidence or to determine a fact in issue. In offering expert evidence, they are aware that their own professional observations, inferences, and conclusions must be distinguished from legal facts, opinions, and conclusions. Forensic psychologists are prepared to explain the relationship between their expert testimony and the legal issues and facts of an instant case.

The Relation Between Ethical Codes and Moral Principles

Donald N. Bersoff and Peter M. Koeppl

[*Ed. note:* This article, from which the following is an excerpt, appeared in a special issue of *Ethics and Behavior* devoted to forensic expert testimony. The article defines the prima facie duties of nonmaleficence, beneficence, fidelity, justice, and autonomy (see chap. 3) and examines how these same duties have been addressed in the 1992 APA Ethical Principles and the Specialty Guidelines for Forensic Psychologists].

There are two sets of standards that directly address the activities of psychologists who do forensic work and serve as expert witnesses. The first is Part 7 of the APA (1992) code, denominated Forensic Activities. The second is the "Specialty Guidelines for Forensic Psychologists" (CEGFP, 1991). [footnote omitted] The Forensic Activities section of the code and the specialty guidelines do not embody as explicitly the moral principles we have found in other provisions of the code. But Provision 7.01 reminds forensic psychologists that they "must comply with all other provisions of the Ethics Code" (APA, 1992, p. 1610) and the guidelines' purpose is to "amplify" the provisions of the APA ethics code "in the context of the practice of forensic psychology" (CEGFP, 1991, p. 656). Thus, to the extent that the philosophical duties we described are represented in the other enforceable provisions of the code, they may be said to be incorporated by reference in Part 7 and in the specialty guidelines.

Although less explicit, some allusion to prima facie duties are found in Part 7 of the code (APA, 1992), particularly fidelity, justice, and to some extent autonomy. If one defines *fidelity* not only as faithfulness to one's client but as allegiance to scientific roots of one's profession (Diener &

Crandall, 1978; Kitchener, 1984), then the code's Forensic Activities provisions are particularly salutary. Provision 7.04, for example, requires that "psychologists testify truthfully, honestly, and candidly . . . (APA, 1992, p. 1610). Similarly, when necessarily compelled to testify with incomplete data, "psychologists clarify the impact of their limited information on the reliability and validity of their reports and testimony, and they appropriately limit the nature and extent of their conclusions or recommendations" (Provision 7.02, p. 1610). This emphasis on acting as a cautious, objective scientists, not as advocates for an empirically unsupported and predetermined position, also, of course, implements the obligation to act justly and equitably.

The requirements in the code (APA, 1992) that "psychologists avoid . . . potentially conflicting roles in forensic matters" (Provision 7.03, p. 1610) and "take into account ways in which . . . prior relationship[s] might affect their professional objectivity" (Provision 7.05, p. 1610) translate the duty of fidelity more traditionally. In addition, these mandates and the corollary responsibilities (i.e., to clarify role expectations and the conflicts that prior relationships with one or more of the parties to a legal proceedings might produce and clarify the limits of confidentiality found in Provisions 7.03 and 7.05) foster the principles of autonomy and justice.

In like manner, the specialty guidelines (CEGFP, 1991) contain translations of the moral obligations found in the prima facie duties. For example, the responsibility to perform forensic tasks in ways that "do . . . not diminish or threaten" the civil rights of the parties (CEGFP, 1991, p. 658) and to decline to participate in activities in which one's competence as a forensic clinician would be impaired as a result of one's "personal values [or] moral beliefs" (p. 658) implement principles of nonmaleficence, justice, and fidelity. Similarly, the duty to refrain from testifying to any incriminating statements made by a criminal defendant during a forensic examination not only comports with constitutional requirements but exemplifies the principle of nonmaleficence as well (see Guideline VI[G], pp. 662–663). The guidelines ubiquitous references to fairness and accuracy in evaluations, testimony, and other public statements and the corollary obligations to avoid bias, partisanship, and misrepresentation are the most salutary translations of the duties of justice and fidelity.

The prima facie duty of autonomy is also well represented in the guidelines (CEGFP, 1991). Forensic psychologists are obligated to "inform the party of factors that might reasonably affect the decision to contract" with them (p. 658). They also have the responsibility to

> ensure that prospective clients are informed of their legal rights with respect to the anticipated forensic service, of the purposes of any evaluation, of the nature of procedures to be employed, of the intended uses of any product of their services, and of the party who has employed [them]. (p. 659)

Similarly, forensic psychologists are to "inform their clients of the limitations to the confidentiality of their services and their products . . . by providing them with an understandable statement of their rights, privileges, and the limitations of confidentiality" (p. 660). On the other hand, the suggested prohibition in the guidelines that potential experts refrain from providing forensic services to parties unrepresented by legal counsel (Guideline VI[C], p. 661), although beneficial in its intent, diminishes a party's right to self-determination. A duty to disclose the risks of such undertakings might have satisfied the dual obligations of autonomy and beneficence.

Finally, as a result of their role, expert witnesses will always be confronted with questions of loyalty and concerns about acting as double agents (Monahan, 1980), particularly if they perform court-compelled examinations. Although, the code encourages psychologists to "clarify role expectations and the extent of confidentiality in advance to the extent feasible" (APA, 1992, p. 1610) and the specialty guidelines require forensic experts to "recognize potential conflicts of interest in dual relationships" (CEGFP, 1991, p. 659), they will always be faced with moral dilemmas. For instance, to whom do forensic psychologists owe ultimate loyalty, and to what extent do they abide by the duty of nonmaleficence when it is the products of their endeavors that may lead to the conviction and punishment of a defendant? Because many examinees seen by forensic psychologists are referred by a third party such as a court these referrals raise questions regarding the voluntariness of the client's participation. To which set of moral or professional principles do psychologists hold allegiance in these cases? The moral principle of autonomy assures clients that their choices will be respected. If clients do not agree to undergo a forensic evaluation, do psychologists have the prima facie duty to respect this desire? Or do they owe an overriding duty of fidelity to the referring agency? If the forensic evaluation is mandated by the court, this obligation may not be rescinded, even when the client is opposed to the procedure. As a result, a forensic psychologist may indeed be acting in accordance with the specialty guidelines but yet still be in conflict with the grander moral principles.

References

American Psychological Association. (1992). Ethical principles of psychologists and code of conduct. *American Psychologist, 47,* 1597–1611.

Committee on Ethical Guidelines for Forensic Psychologists. (1991). Specialty guidelines for forensic psychologists. *Law and Human Behavior, 15,* 655–665.

Diener, E., & Crandall, R. (1978). *Ethics in social and behavioral research.* Chicago: University of Chicago.

Kitchener, K. S. (1984). Intuition, critical evaluation and ethical principles: The foundation for ethical decisions in counseling psychology. *The Counseling Psychologist, 12,* 43–55.

Monahan, J. (Ed.). (1980). *Who is the client? The ethics of psychological intervention in the criminal justice system.* Washington, DC: American Psychological Association.

◆ ◆ ◆

Commentary: Pfeifer and Brigham (1993) surveyed 37 academic forensic psychologists to identify ethical issues that they had encountered while consulting in pretrial phases of litigation or as experts during trials. Every one of the respondents reported that they had never "resolved their current ethical dilemmas by referring either to the APA's ethical principles or the [Committee on Ethical Guidelines for Forensic Psychologists's] specialty guidelines" (p. 341–342). See Pfeifer, J. E., & Brigham, J. C. (1993). Ethical concerns of nonclinical forensic witnesses and consultants. Ethics and Behavior, 3, 329–343. Many of the respondents suggested that ethical conflicts should be resolved through personal choice, beliefs, and values. What do these findings say about the utility of these two documents for scientists who serve as experts?

Institutional Constraints on the Ethics of Expert Testimony

Bruce D. Sales and Leonore Simon

. . .

A dramatic improvement in the quality of expert testimony could occur if experts reflected on their ethical obligations prior to becoming experts witnesses.

For example, Principle A of the *Ethical Principles of Psychologists and Code of Conduct* (APA, 1992) admonishes psychologists to recognize the boundaries of their competencies and the limitations of their expertise. If an expert witness has not kept up with the literature and testifies using out-of-date information, he or she would be violating the responsibility to be competent. And what of clinical psychologists who testify on a topic without training in the area? The issue of competence becomes salient once again.

Principle B of the ethical principles (APA, 1992) suggests that psychologists should promote integrity in psychology. Is the integrity benefitted or harmed by psychologists who assume the hired gun role or advocate their personal values, rather than presenting scientific knowledge? Advocacy that is one sided and intentionally presented to aid the client rather than present accurate scientific information runs afoul of this principle.

Manipulating testimony to achieve a personal goal might also run afoul of Principle F of the ethical principles (APA, 1992). It admonishes psychologists to apply their knowledge to contribute to and improve the society in which they live and work. For example, some testimony on the battered woman syndrome that passes for expertise involves expert witnesses who misuse their profession by failing to raise the existence of professional criticism about the accuracy of the diagnostic classification (e.g., Vidmar & Schuller, 1989). Such expert testimony would thus constitute a violation of the social responsibility ethic.

Similar examples can be found in the ethical standards that set down enforceable rules for conduct. For example, Ethical Standard 1.04 (APA, 1992) mandates that psychologists perform only within their area of competence, whereas Ethical Standard 1.05 requires psychologists to keep abreast of current scientific information to maintain their competence.

Clearly, ethical principles and standards are important to proscribe certain behaviors. But perhaps most important, if studied and applied regularly and consistently in the normal course of activities, ethical principles and standards provide the impetus for potential expert witnesses to evaluate (a) their decision to participate, (b) the way in which they will prepare for participation, and (c) the way in which they will participate. This self-reflection can improve the quality of expert witnessing.

The use of ethical principles and standards is not without its limits however. By their very nature, ethics documents do not specifically address all issues and conundrums that experts will face in the courtroom. Indeed, ethical principles are typically broadly drawn so that they can be applied to a wide variety of behaviors. For example, Ethical Standard 1.16 (APA, 1992) prohibits psychologists from participating in activities in which their skills or knowledge are misused by others unless corrective mechanisms are available. Does this standard place a duty on psychologists to take reasonable steps to ensure that their testimony is not distorted even by the side that hired them? A potential solution is for the ethi-

From *Ethics and Behavior*, 3, 231–249. Copyright 1993 by Erlbaum. Adapted with permission of the publisher.

cal principles to be supplemented by practice standards, such as the "Specialty Guidelines for Forensic Psychologists" (Committee on Ethical Guidelines for Forensic Psychologists, 1991). But whether this document or other practice standards comprehensively address the issues of concern will have to await further analysis. . . . In addition, if not adopted by the entire organization, such standards will have limited applicability. For example, the specialty guidelines was adopted by the American Psychology–Law Society/a Division of the APA. As such, it is applicable to the approximately 1,500 members of this division but not the remaining members of the APA.

There are other limitations as well. Standards of practice, including ethical principles and standards, do not guarantee excellence. They only institutionalize the minimum level of acceptable performance—competence. Competence in some court cases may not be sufficient when people's lives and/or property are at stake, particularly if we take our social responsibility ethic seriously. How then would ethical principles specify the expertise needed for different types of cases? A uniform standard may be too low in some cases and too high in others. The ethical principles should focus on the necessity of having requisite skills and engaging in a process of competent preparation to meet the demands of a task. But future research will need to explore the mechanics of implementing such an approach.

Finally, even if someone's behavior violated the ethical principles and standards, sanctioning the scientist would be a problem. Although the scientific organization that promulgated the ethical principles could enforce them, it could only do so against members. If scientists chose to drop out of the organization, the organization cannot force its rules on them. Even if violators maintained membership, sanctioning the majority of them is unlikely. It takes significant resources to identify and investigate potential violations, hold hearings to give potential violators an opportunity to present their side of the facts, and implement corrective interventions.

Another solution would be to enforce ethical principles and standards through malpractice actions; the principles could be used to designate the acceptable level of practice to which the scientist–consultant would have to adhere. However,

expert witness immunity might prevent potential malpractice claims (e.g., *Bruce v. Byrne-Stevens & Associates Engineers, Inc.,* 1989). Even if permissible, the difficulty of this approach is that there would not be a party who would be likely to sue the scientist and have legal standing to do so. The scientist's employer—the lawyer and the client—would not sue if the scientist's testimony included what they hoped to hear; if the scientist was not going to support the lawyer and client's cause, he or she would not have been retained after the initial interview or would not appear in court. The other side would be unlikely to sue because malpractice actions require that the wrong-doer owe the complaining party a duty to adhere to a certain standard. Because the scientist was hired by the opposing side, the duty would be owed to that side. Some creative lawyering might get the courts to make certain that experts understand that they have a duty to both parties to perform competently on the argument that not to do so would hamper the factfinding process in trials or perhaps perpetrate a fraud on the court. We know of no cases that have considered this issue, however, and would not be optimistic that it would be a winning argument.

The truly injured party is an amorphous one—science, most likely as embodied in one of its scientific organizations. Yet, the scientific organization would not have standing to sue. And even if one did, it is unlikely that an organization would use this approach in any but the most flagrant cases because to do so might open up to question and public scrutiny the competence of the professional behaviors of all members. . . .

References

American Psychological Association. (1992). Ethical principles of psychologists and code of conduct. *American Psychologist, 47,* 1597–1611.

Bruce v. Byrne-Stevens & Associates Engineers, Inc., 776 P.2d 666 (Wash. 1989).

Committee on Ethical Guidelines for Forensic Psychologists. (1991). Specialty guidelines for forensic psychologists. *Law and Human Behavior, 15,* 655–665.

Vidmar, N. J., & Schuller, R. A. (1989). Juries and expert evidence: Social framework testimony. *Law and Contemporary Problems, 52,* 133–176.

◆ ◆ ◆

Commentary: Sales and Simon conjectured that the immunity from lawsuits (but not from perjury) that expert witnesses enjoy regarding their in-court testimony makes it unlikely that incompetent experts will be sanctioned by the legal system. However, a California appeals court recently upheld the APA's right to censure one of its members for presenting false testimony in a child custody hearing. The court held that, although court-appointed psychologists are protected from liability (such as malpractice) arising from communications made during judicial proceedings or when acting for courts in resolving custody disputes, that did not preclude professional associations from disciplining their members for violating their ethics. See Budwin v. American Psychological Association, 24 Cal. App. 4th 875, 29 Cal. Rptr. 2d 453 (Cal. App. 3d Dist. 1994).

In an article published contemporaneously with Sales and Simon's, Perrin and Sales (1994) concluded that the 1992 APA Ethical Principles "provides an initial, but modest attempt to address ethical issues related to forensic practice" (p. 380); but they also found many of the forensic provisions to be so vague as to "provide virtually no specific guidance" (p. 379). See Perrin, G. I., & Sales, B. D. (1994). Forensic standards in the American Psychological Association ethics code. Professional Psychology: Research and Practice, 25, 376–382.

In this same article, Perrin and Sales (1994) stated that

> *providers of forensic services must be aware of, and sensitive to, the potential conflicts between the psychological roles of examiner, therapist, and consultant; between the legal roles of expert witness and fact witness; and between the roles of advocate for the client and advocate for the professional opinion.*
>
> . . .
>
> *The identification of who is the client has important ramifications in the determination of what service is to be provided, who is to have access to the information, what information is to be confidential, what product is to be generated by the psychologist, to whom the psychologist is to report, and who is to pay the fee for the service. (pp. 377–378)*

Standard 7.03 (Clarification of Role) provides some guidance on these issues, but they are much more complex than the Standard contemplates. Some of their complexities are addressed in the next set of materials.

Expert Opinion

American Psychology–Law Society

THE QUESTION

You are a psychologist in private practice and have been working in therapy with a client whose complaints include anxiety and depression attributed to a variety of problems, including dissatisfaction at work, problems in her marriage, and unresolved anger toward family members for events that occurred long ago. During the fourth month of therapy you receive a call from an attorney who reports that she is representing the client in a lawsuit against her employer, alleging that the client has been the victim of sexual harassment and a hostile work environment, resulting in emotional disability. The lawyer advises that, as a mental health professional intimately knowledgeable about her client's mental condition, she intends to call you as an expert witness in the upcoming trial in civil court. She inquires about your hourly fee for forensic evaluation and expert testimony, and then asks you to conduct whatever additional evaluations are needed to prepare for court. She also indicates that she will ask you to testify about the client's diagnosis, treatment and adjustment. The attorney advises that she has already informed your client of this possibility; a faxed release that you receive later in the afternoon confirms that your client is agreeable to this. What should you do?

THE RESPONSE

The response is from Stephen Golding, Ph.D., Professor, Department of Psychology, University of Utah. Dr. Golding is past-president of AP-LS and was involved in development of the Specialty Guidelines for Forensic Psychologists.

I am basing my response on both the Specialty Guidelines for Forensic Psychologists (SGFP) and the most recent Ethical Principles for Psychologists and Code of Conduct (EPPCC). Obviously, the opinion given here represents my own view and should not be construed as an official interpretation of the SGFP or EPPCC.

This situation bears most directly on the problem of dual-role relationships, although other facets of the ethics codes and guidelines are also involved. The EPPCC sections 7.02 [Forensic assessments], 7.03 [Clarification of role] and 7.05 [Prior relationships] are directly applicable to this vignette, as are the (roughly) corresponding sections of the Specialty Guidelines–IV-D [Dual roles], VI [Methods and procedures].

First for the easy part. No particular problems with respect to confidentiality exist in that the client has explicitly waived her privilege [EPPCC 5.05, Disclosures]. However, the therapist should discuss this matter with the client and not rely solely upon the client's lawyer to have adequately informed her of what sorts of information would be disclosed at trial. That is, the informed consent obtained at the start of therapy would not ordinarily have included this sort of information, and the therapist should ensure that the client fully understands the nature of the personal disclosures that would be entailed by her testifying [SGFP sections IV-E, and V, as well as corresponding sections of EPPCC].

Now for the hard part. In my view, the therapist cannot agree to become an "expert" witness in this case. While she may have detailed professional information about the client's "diagnosis, treatment and adjustment," this information was obtained in the context of a therapeutic relationship, not in the context of an independent and neutral evaluation of the client's response to the alleged sexual harassment. Thus, according to the EPPCC [7.05], the therapist may testify as a "fact witness," conveying her profes-

Adapted from the *American Psychology–Law Society News*, 14(2), 5. Copyright 1994 by Division 41 of the American Psychological Association.

sional information as to diagnosis, treatment progress and the like, but she should not agree to offer "expert" testimony on the underlying psycholegal issue, namely, the causative connection between the alleged harassment and any "emotional harm." Clearly, the therapist is in a professional position to offer the former sort of testimony, but should make clear [SGFP III-B, Boundaries of Competence; EPPCC 7.02, Forensic assessments] that she did not undertake, in the course of diagnosing and treating this client, the kind of psycholegal assessment that would be required to address the causation-harm issues. The sort of expert testimony requested would, in my view, require an analysis of the client's level of emotional adjustment prior to the alleged sexual harassment as well as an analysis of her emotional state during and consequent to that harassment. In performing such an analysis competently and independently, a forensic examiner would ordinarily rely upon data from prior records as well as interviews of a number of third parties, and would not base her findings solely upon the self-report of the client. This is a very different data base than that to which the therapist would typically have access. In addition, the therapist's pre-existing relationship with the client would constitute a dual-role which would make it difficult, if not impossible, for her to assume the "neutral" role (and to gather that "additional information") having already formed a therapeutic relationship with the client.

Hence, I see this vignette as primarily involving problems of dual roles, which in turn raise issues about the adequacy of the assessment. In my view, the therapist can testify as a "fact" witness, but not as an "expert." If she has performed an adequate assessment of her client prior to and during their therapeutic relationship, she can greatly assist her client, but she does not have either the objectivity or the data that would be required for her to agree to change from the role of therapist to that of expert.

◆ ◆ ◆

Commentary: *It would be a useful exercise to draft a rebuttal to Golding's analysis. What provisions in the APA Ethical Principles or the forensic guidelines, if any, would support acting in the role of expert in this case? To what extent is a client's request for his or her psychologist to testify as an expert significant?*

Role Conflicts in Coercive Assessments: Evaluation and Recommendations

Jose M. Arcaya

Although the ways in which a therapist's emotional reactions to a client's personality and problems distort the psychotherapy situation—technically called *countertransference*—are well known . . . , their counterpart in the administration and formulation of psychological assessments is much less discussed. . . . This distortion manifests itself when evaluators, instead of basing their conclusions primarily on the empirical data obtained during the interview, unknowingly permit their own ideology, values, and feelings to intrude into and unduly influence their assessment recommendations and decisions. . . .

Although such countertransferencelike tendencies are liable to appear in any assessment situation, they are most prominently observed in the mandatory context of the criminal justice system. In contrast with the voluntary, "free-world" setting, in which the client independently agrees to be evaluated and in which matters related to such social concerns as retribution, deterrence, and incapacitation are not at issue, the coercive environment requires that the evaluator make recommendations directly affecting the client's personal rights, freedom, and property. This responsibility places significant emotional pressures on these psychologists because their findings can have direct and important long-term consequences on a client's life.

As well, because forensic psychologists who work for the criminal justice system must often evaluate individuals who are likely to have engaged in criminal behaviors (e.g., robbery, assault, rape) that strongly arouse their passions and outrage, their personal reactions to this kind of client are often more intense than are reactions to clients encountered in the volunteer setting. Because they are individuals who have problems that have negative consequences only for themselves and for whom such feelings as empathy, concern, and benevolent neutrality are thus naturally engendered, voluntary clients do not normally evoke in the evaluator conflicting feelings as strong. Criminal justice clients, on the other hand, because they almost always have harmed other people, tend to stir the evaluator's own prejudices and unexamined convictions regarding punishment, justice, and fairness.

Therefore, given that the latter can elicit strong and elemental reactions (e.g., anger at a convicted offender's callousness; sympathy with inmates because of their dismal childhood circumstances; impatience about the administrative policies of a correctional facility), it becomes important to clarify the professional role of psychologists working in the criminal justice system lest such emotional issues unduly distort their formal evaluations. . . .

These are different ways in which psychologists engaged in mandatory psychological evaluations can unconsciously resolve the role conflicts inherent in working for the criminal justice system. More specifically, they are compromises used by many examining psychologists to reduce the anxiety arising from their own contradictory or unacceptable feelings about the client–offender, the agency for whom they are employed, and the community that they serve. . . .

BACKGROUND CONSIDERATIONS

Psychologists normally are trained to administer evaluations in situations in which the clients freely pre-

Adapted from *Professional Psychology: Research and Practice, 18*, 422–428. Copyright 1987 by the American Psychological Association.

sent themselves for testing or examination. These settings—for example, mental health clinics, hospitals, and private practice offices—generally operate according to administrative philosophies that are consistent with the psychologist's own ethical standards to respect the client's privacy and confidentiality. . . .

However, when traditionally trained psychologists—who are thus taught to be protective of the client's privacy, freedom, and integrity—are hired by the various agencies of the criminal justice system (e.g., courts, police departments, prisons, community treatment centers) to conduct assessments, they are required to establish a different kind of professional understanding with their client–offenders. These agencies require that psychologists diversify their professional allegiances. They expect the psychologists to be concerned not only about their clients' welfares, but also about the practical exigencies facing these forensic employers (e.g., maintaining institutional order, upholding court-ordered legal standards, fulfilling governmental mandates) and the general safety of the community.

In the criminal justice system, psychologists are necessarily expected to share their assessment results with many more individuals (e.g., lawyers, administrators, probation-parole officers) than in the free-world situation. Because by definition all criminal justice cases are adversarial, the readership of such forensic reports must be inevitably composed of parties opposed to one another, representing the concerns of the client–offender, the criminal justice system, and the community. Therefore, forensic psychologists automatically find themselves in the midst of controversy whenever they submit their results as neutral professionals, having displeased somebody along the way (e.g., displeasing a prosecutor by advocating lenient treatment, the client by recommending the denial of parole).

These two differences—role diversity and role conflict—are the bases for the role confusion of psychologists working in the criminal justice system. As noted by the American Psychological Association's (APA) Task Force Report on the Role of the Psychologist in the Criminal Justice System (American Psychological Association, 1980), "What

psychology appears to lack at the present time is an effective way to differentiate obligations owed to organizational as opposed to individual clients" (p. 2). It indicates, for example, that of 203 criminal justice psychologists surveyed by the Task Force, 75% reported that one of the major ethical issues that they faced concerned confidentiality: how much and what kind of information should be revealed to their criminal justice employers. . . .

THE COERCIVE SETTING

The coercive setting differs markedly from the voluntary situation mainly because client–offenders do not hire their psychologists. They are forced to undergo the evaluation under penalty of law or deprivation of certain rights and privileges. These client–offenders, therefore, are in no position to dictate their terms to their examiners. They must submit to their psychologists' tests and inquiries whether they like it or not, knowing that if they refuse, such intransigency might result in possible negative consequences (e.g., denial of parole, more stringent sentencing, loss of institutional perquisites).

Because client–offenders have been pressured to go to their psychologists, they avoid having to take responsibility for this participation and for solving the problems that are the focus of the evaluation. Instead, they tend to approach their psychologists warily and resistively. The psychologists, therefore, have the task of penetrating these facades of self-sufficiency and denial before being able to reliably assess their client–offenders' true strengths and vulnerabilities.

In portraying themselves in as positive a light as possible, client–offenders tend to exclude from view anything that would block them from attaining their goals (e.g., outright freedom, less severe sentencing, day passes from a locked facility to the community). This guardedness arises, of course, because the evaluation results are not confidential but are used to decide important matters about the client–offenders' lives. Indeed, in many forensic settings the psychologists are required to warn their client–offenders that whatever they divulge may be used against them in court (see Principle 5, *Ethical Standards of Psychologists*; American Psychological Association, 1981).[1]

---

[1] *Ed. note:* See Standard 1.07 of the APA's current (1992) Ethical Principles.

Because an assessment report is a legal document that is subject to perusal by a variety of individuals in the criminal justice system, the psychologist in the forensic agency has little control over how the findings will be used and understood. Many judges, lawyers, administrators, counselors, and probation officers associated with a particular client–offender's case have the right to read its contents. This fact makes it difficult for psychologists to tailor their comments to particular individuals or suit the needs of specific referral sources. It also makes it difficult to establish rapport with their client–offenders. However, because forensic psychologists are paid to conduct their evaluations by their agency employers, there exists less incentive to build a working alliance with the typical criminal justice client than with the voluntary subject. Such forensic evaluations are conducted primarily for the benefit of various criminal justice personnel, insofar as they, not the examinees, are the main critics of the psychologists' work.

Despite this reality, forensic psychologists are typically still concerned about their client–offenders' plights. However, they worry about the social institutions with which client–offenders might eventually become involved (such as employers in the case of employment screening), the safety of the community (in the case of probation or parole evaluations), and the well-being of other involved third parties (such as the offspring of mothers charged with child neglect). Thus divided in their concern—to their client–offenders (e.g., "How will my decision affect the long-term interest of this person?"), the community (e.g., "Will this individual pose a threat to other people?"), and the criminal agency for which they are employed (e.g., "Is this agency properly equipped to handle this kind of individual?"—thoughtful forensic psychologists find themselves forced to consider many more variables in making their determinations than are their free-world counterparts.

Obviously, different kinds of cases tend to demand different kinds of priorities among these competing interests. In some instances, the priority of community safety comes first (e.g., when the client–offender has the potential for violence); in others, needs of client–offenders become more central (e.g., when they seem to be good prospects for education or rehabilitation and are not dangerous to others); and in still others, the requirements concerning the institution or agency entrusted to care for client–offenders assumes maximum importance (e.g., avoiding recommending a facility that is overcrowded and understaffed). However, sometimes forensic psychologists can adopt one way of approaching all criminal justice clients. When such a way is predictable and habitual, it can stem from unconscious motives and is analogous to the kinds of countertransference encountered in psychotherapy. . . .

THE HELPER BIAS

. . . This stance leads the psychologist to side with the client–offender in practically every instance. According to this person-centered, humanitarian perspective, the needs of the client–offender are more important than the agency's needs or the concerns of the community. The helper bias is based on a kind of antibureaucratic and antiorganizational philosophy, and its followers tend to be oblivious to dimensions of the evaluation other than the offenders' viewpoints. . . .

THE PROSECUTORIAL BIAS

The prosecutorial bias is relatively rare in comparison with the helper bias; the psychologist adopting the prosecutorial bias considers client–offenders with suspicion and tends to make negative value judgments about their conduct. This position is identified closely with the feelings of the community, and the client–offender is considered more from a moral than from a humanitarian perspective. This bias is prosecutorial because the psychologist is assumed to be an extension of the judicial system. The psychologist is more likely to consider the offender's behavior in a condemning rather than a clinical fashion. Reflecting a "law and order" attitude, psychologists operating from this bias are minimally empathetic with their client–offenders' plights.

Because the prosecutorial evaluators tend to adopt a negative view about the future of the client–offender, their recommendations are likely to be conservative and guarded. These evaluators predictably tend to favor the interests of the community over the welfare of their client–offenders. . . .

THE UNCOMMITTED BIAS

This bias reflects the classic bureaucratic mentality. It is more responsive to the implicit demands of the institution for which the evaluator works than to the needs of the client–offender or of the community. These psychologists avoid taking risks because they dislike conflict and controversy. Psychologists personifying this attitude tend to write their evaluations in terms of the preferences of the agency administrators reading their reports, rather than in terms of their true convictions. For example, uncommitted psychologists, knowing that their criminal justice agency administrators like to read reports making hopeful rather than pessimistic predictions about their wards, would be prone to make their evaluations conform to that conclusion. . . .

ADVERSARIAL MODEL

The adversarial model is proposed to help avoid the biases inherent in the previous stances. . . .

Following the same rationale as the legal system itself, the adversarial evaluator assumes that final judgments and recommendations about forensic clients are best decided after all opposing viewpoints have been considered. In effect, the adversarial model extends this rationale into the assessment process itself; the report is to be organized and communicated as though it were a courtroom debate between hypothetical psychologists representing opposed vested interests (i.e., the defendant, the prosecutor). Only after these viewpoints are fully discussed could psychologists present their final recommendations.

This model requires psychologists to act as "devil's advocates" who, instead of trying to fit disparate findings about their client–offenders into a consistent narrative (possibly because they want to convey a sense of scientific certainty to the reader), disclose these contradictions honestly. Because evaluators are charged with multiple role responsibilities anyway (to the client–offender, the institution, and the community), there is no reason why all of their judgments, findings, and opinions should to be in total agreement. Indeed, as a result of exposure to diverse and opposed information, the readers of reports written from this perspective would be in a better position to evaluate the merits of the evaluator's final recommendations.

Rather straightforward in its format, this model requires forensic psychologists to subdivide their reports into as many sections as there are legal perspectives on their client–offenders. They would then consider their clients from each one of these viewpoints. Most often the typical client–offender would be evaluated from only two perspectives: one favoring the client–offender's interests (the defendant's viewpoint) and one opposing them (the prosecutor's viewpoint). However, in more complex cases, involving other parties with different claims (such as the children in child custody or neglect evaluations), the psychologist would add other viewpoints as well (e.g., how the children might be affected were they to be separated from client–offender) to the report. Each division would contain any information believed to be pertinent to the particular perspective under consideration. After presenting all of the relevant information appropriate to these subsections, psychologists would then make their final recommendations and conclusions.

The standard forensic assessment format, on the other hand, makes it easy for psychologists to present their data impersonally, thereby obscuring their biases. It helps them to avoid dealing with the legal context in which the assessment takes place, in which there is no single truth . . . and in which radically different views of reality are in contention. Modeled to fit a setting in which role conflict or professional ambiguity is absent, the standard forensic assessment format does not dignify the multiperspectival nature of legal proceedings. The adversarial model, in contrast, forces psychologists to be more reflective and to think through their rationales before reaching their conclusions. . . .

References

American Psychological Association (1980). *Who is the client? The psychological intervention in the criminal justice system.* Washington, DC: Author.

American Psychological Association (1981). Ethical principles of psychologists. *American Psychologist, 36,* 633–638.

Role Conflict in Forensic Clinical Psychology: Reply to Arcaya

Dewey G. Cornell

. . .

The various roles of clinical psychologists in the criminal justice system cannot be characterized in the same way. Psychologists who conduct pretrial evaluations of criminal defendants typically deal with very different legal and clinical issues than do psychologists employed in prison settings. Psychologists who are regular employees of a court- or state-administered clinic experience a different relationship with defendants than do psychologists in independent practice who may be hired by the defendant. Also, psychologists whose contact with a defendant is limited to a forensic evaluation have different goals, ethical obligations, and clinical responsibilities than do psychologists involved in a treatment relationship. Arcaya's concerns about the psychologist–client relationship need more careful explication for each different role. The issue of role conflict at a minimum must be examined separately with regard to defendant versus convict status, the interaction of employer and client, and whether the professional relationship is for assessment or treatment purposes.

For purposes of this discussion, attention will be focused on psychologists who conduct pretrial evaluations of criminal defendants. Typically, these evaluations concern one or both of two legal issues: competency to stand trial or criminal responsibility (legal insanity). An evaluation of competency to stand trial concerns the defendant's present mental state: whether the defendant suffers from a mental condition that impairs his or her ability to defend himself or herself at the trial. Criminal responsibility concerns the defendant's mental state at the time of the alleged offense: whether the defendant suffered from a mental condition that would exculpate him or her from criminal charges. Specific legal criteria and guidelines for these evaluations vary from state to state.

However, the psychologist–defendant/client relationship differs in important ways for these two legal issues. For example, in Michigan . . . a defendant has no choice about submitting to an evaluation of competency to stand trial. Although this evaluation is usually conducted on an outpatient basis, the defendant could be committed for inpatient evaluation. If adjudicated incompetent to stand trial, the defendant could be committed involuntarily for a period as long as 15 months.

The circumstances are quite different for evaluations of criminal responsibility. Here the defendant is the one initiating the claim of insanity, and the defendant retains complete authority to refuse or cancel an evaluation. Contrary to Arcaya's global characterization of forensic evaluations, there are important differences according to the legal issue involved, and the defendant does retain voluntary status in some circumstances. Last, the defendant who disagrees with a psychologist's clinical opinion in a pretrial evaluation retains the right to request an independent evaluation by another professional.

As this example indicates, it is misleading for Arcaya to contrast evaluations conducted for the criminal justice system with all other evaluations by describing the former as "coercive" and the latter as "free-world" evaluations. Moreover, many evaluations outside of the criminal justice system are far from fully voluntary. Probably the most "coercive" evalua-

Adapted from *Professional Psychology: Research and Practice, 18,* 429–432. Copyright 1987 by the American Psychological Association.

tion in mental health today occurs when an individual is evaluated for involuntary commitment, a civil court matter. A close second would be evaluations of adolescent minors whose parents are seeking to have them admitted for inpatient treatment. Psychologists also face less-than-willing subjects when they conduct child custody evaluations or when they are hired by the defense to examine the complainant in personal injury cases. These examples are not to minimize the difficulties of conducting evaluations with criminal defendants; however, many of the ethical problems, role conflicts, and potential biases that Arcaya described are not specific to criminal forensic work. Perhaps a broader recognition of these problems would facilitate identifying possible solutions.

ROLE CONFLICT AND BIAS IN FORENSIC EVALUATIONS

. . .

The psychoanalytic terminology that Arcaya used in his conceptualization of role conflict seems inappropriate and unnecessary to his argument. . . .

What is valuable about Arcaya's argument is the contention that psychologists are vulnerable to bias in their attitudes toward defendants. There is no need to couch this view in psychoanalytic terminology (or any other specific theoretical framework), even though a well-thought-out psychoanalytic approach may generate useful hypotheses for study. It is more important to examine first whether psychologists *are* biased and whether the criminal justice system does place undue pressure on them. The role of unconscious childhood conflicts in determining whether a psychologist is biased or succumbs to institutional pressure is a question that should be considered later.

Arcaya's position can be reformulated as a call for research in an important area of clinical practice. The argument that he presented is really a set of hypotheses that demand to be examined in empirical study. Some of the more salient research questions can be articulated as follows:

1. Do psychologists experience role conflict, or other forms of stress, on conducting evaluations for the criminal justice system? . . .

2. Are clinical opinions influenced by pressures or expectations of the criminal justice system? . . .

3. What emotional factors influence clinical opinions in forensic evaluations? . . .

PROPOSALS FOR CHANGE

Arcaya's (partial) solution to the problem of psychologist bias was to modify the format for psychological reports. He proposed that psychologists write their reports in a manner more consistent with the legal system's adversarial model. Evidence supporting each side of the case would be presented and weighed before the psychologist expressed a final opinion.

There are several problems with this approach. First, if Arcaya was correct in stating that psychologists are biased because of unconscious personality conflicts and countertransference reactions to the defendant, it is highly unlikely that any change in report format would be effective. . . .

If bias is primarily a result of institutional pressures and professional role conflict, again it seems that merely changing report format would be too weak an intervention. The legal system, rather than the individual, would be the appropriate target for intervention. . . .

Last, many of Arcaya's concerns about bias and role conflict can be addressed from the standpoint of the Ethical Principles of the American Psychological Association (APA, 1981; see also Keith-Spiegel & Koocher, 1985). Psychologists are *already* obligated to assume an objective and evenhanded approach in their report of psychological findings. For example, Principle 1, Section a, of the Ethical Principles states, in part, "In publishing reports of their work, they [psychologists] never suppress disconfirming data, and they acknowledge the existence of alternative hypotheses and explanations of their findings" (APA, 1981, p. 633). In addition, psychologists are ethically obligated to point out and attempt to resolve professional conflicts with institutional policies or expectations (APA, 1981, Principles 3 and 6).[1]

ALTERNATIVES

Psychologists should not attempt to cope with the adversarial pressures of the legal system by mimick-

[1] *Ed. note:* See Standards 3.03, 6.21, 7.06, and 8.03 of the APA's current (1992) Ethical Principles.

ing an adversarial approach in their report writing. Instead, psychologists need to resist being co-opted by the system and to reassert their professional identity as scientist-practitioners. Forensic psychologists need to make clear, as often as is necessary, that their role is objective and neutral, and that although they may reach clinical opinions favorable to either defense or prosecution, they are never advocates of one side or the other in legal proceedings. . . .

References

American Psychological Association (1981). Ethical principles of psychologists (revised). *American Psychologist*, 36, 633–638.

Keith-Spiegel, P., & Koocher, G. (1985). *Ethics in psychology: Professional standards and cases*. Hillsdale, NJ: Erlbaum.

◆ ◆ ◆

Commentary: *Despite their differences, Arcaya and Cornell did agree that forensic clinicians experience significant role conflicts, particularly when they conduct court-compelled evaluations in criminal prosecutions. These role conflicts not only create the potential for ethical violations but may impair the defendant's rights under the U.S. Constitution as well. The Fifth Amendment states in relevant part: "no person shall be compelled in any criminal case to be a witness against himself." Also, the Sixth Amendment provides that "in all criminal prosecutions, the accused shall enjoy the right . . . to have the assistance of counsel for his defense." Consider how these constitutional protections might be endangered under the following scenario:*

> *When Smith was indicted for murder, the state announced that it would seek the death penalty. The trial judge ordered Dr. Grigson, a psychiatrist, to evaluate whether Smith was competent to stand trial. After a 90-minute interview, Dr. Grigson determined that Smith was competent. Smith was then tried and convicted of murder. Subsequently, a separate sentencing proceeding was held before a jury to decide whether Smith should be executed. One of the issues the jury had to determine in the positive, if it were to give Smith a death sentence, was the probability that Smith would commit violent criminal acts again. At the sentencing hearing, Dr. Grigson was called by the state to testify about Smith's proclivity toward future violence. Basing his testimony on the pretrial competency evaluation, Dr. Grigson stated that Smith would be a danger to society. The jury then sentenced Smith to death. Smith charged this procedure violated his rights under the Fifth and Sixth Amendments. The Supreme Court agreed to review his claims, with the following result.*

Estelle v. Smith

. . .

. . . [W]e turn first to whether the admission of Dr. Grigson's testimony at the penalty phase violated respondent's Fifth Amendment privilege against compelled self-incrimination because respondent was not advised before the pretrial psychiatric examination that he had a right to remain silent and that any statement he made could be used against him at a sentencing proceeding. . . .

The fact that respondent's statements were uttered in the context of a psychiatric examination does not automatically remove them from the reach of the Fifth Amendment. . . . The state trial judge, *sua sponte*, ordered a psychiatric evaluation of respondent for the limited, neutral purpose of determining his competency to stand trial, but the results of that inquiry were used by the State for a much broader objective that was plainly adverse to respondent. Consequently, the interview with Dr. Grigson cannot be characterized as a routine competency examination restricted to ensuring that respondent understood the charges against him and was capable of assisting in his defense. Indeed, if the application of Dr. Grigson's findings had been confined to serving that function, no Fifth Amendment issue would have arisen.

Nor was the interview analogous to a sanity examination occasioned by a defendant's plea of not guilty by reason of insanity at the time of his offense. When a defendant asserts the insanity defense and introduces supporting psychiatric testimony, his silence may deprive the State of the only effective means it has of controverting his proof on an issue that he interjected into the case. Accordingly, several Courts of Appeals have held that, under such circumstances, a defendant can be required to submit to a sanity examination conducted by the prosecution's psychiatrist. . . .

Respondent, however, introduced no psychiatric evidence, nor had he indicated that he might do so. Instead, the State offered information obtained from the court-ordered competency examination as affirmative evidence to persuade the jury to return a sentence of death. Respondent's future dangerousness was a critical issue at the sentencing hearing, and one on which the State had the burden of proof beyond a reasonable doubt. . . . To meet its burden, the State used respondent's own statements, unwittingly made without an awareness that he was assisting the State's efforts to obtain the death penalty. In these distinct circumstances, the Fifth Amendment privilege was implicated.

. . . *Miranda v. Arizona* . . . held that "the prosecution may not use statements, whether exculpatory or inculpatory, stemming from custodial interrogation of the defendant unless it demonstrates the use of procedural safeguards effective to secure the privilege against self-incrimination." . . . Thus, absent other fully effective procedures, a person in custody must receive certain warnings before any official interrogation, including that he has a "right to remain silent" and that "anything said can and will be used against the individual in court." . . .

The considerations calling for the accused to be warned prior to custodial interrogation apply with no less force to the pretrial psychiatric examination at issue here. Respondent was in custody at the Dallas County Jail when the examination was ordered and when it was conducted. That respondent was questioned by a psychiatrist designated by the trial court to conduct a neutral competency examination, rather than by a police officer, government informant, or prosecuting attorney, is immaterial. When Dr. Grigson went beyond simply reporting to the court on the issue of competence and testified for the prosecution at the penalty phase on the crucial issue of respondent's future dangerousness, his role changed and became essentially like that of an agent of the State recounting unwarned statements made in a postarrest custodial setting. During the psychiatric evaluation, respondent assuredly was

Adapted from *Estelle v. Smith*, 451 U.S. 459 (1981).

"faced with a phase of the adversary system" and was "not in the presence of [a] perso[n] acting solely in his interest." . . . Yet he was given no indication that the compulsory examination would be used to gather evidence necessary to decide whether, if convicted, he should be sentenced to death. He was not informed that, accordingly, he had a constitutional right not to answer the questions put to him. . . .

A criminal defendant, who neither initiates a psychiatric evaluation nor attempts to introduce any psychiatric evidence, may not be compelled to respond to a psychiatrist if his statements can be used against him at a capital sentencing proceeding. Because respondent did not voluntarily consent to the pretrial psychiatric examination after being informed of his right to remain silent and the possible use of his statements, the State could not rely on what he said to Dr. Grigson to establish his future dangerousness. If, upon being adequately warned, respondent had indicated that he would not answer Dr. Grigson's questions, the validly ordered competency examination nevertheless could have proceeded upon the condition that the results would be applied solely for that purpose. In such circumstances, the proper conduct and use of competency and sanity examinations are not frustrated, but the State must make its case on future dangerousness in some other way.

"Volunteered statements . . . are not barred by the Fifth Amendment," but under *Miranda v. Arizona* we must conclude that, when faced while in custody with a court-ordered psychiatric inquiry, respondent's statements to Dr. Grigson were not "given freely and voluntarily without any compelling influences" and, as such, could be used as the State did at the penalty phase only if respondent had been apprised of his rights and had knowingly decided to waive them. . . . These safeguards of the Fifth Amendment privilege were not afforded respondent and, thus, his death sentence cannot stand [footnote omitted].

When respondent was examined by Dr. Grigson, he already had been indicted and an attorney had been appointed to represent him. The Court of Appeals concluded that he had a Sixth Amendment right to the assistance of counsel before submitting to the pretrial psychiatric interview. . . . We agree. . . .

Here, respondent's Sixth Amendment right to counsel clearly had attached when Dr. Grigson ex-

amined him at the Dallas County Jail [footnote omitted], and their interview proved to be a "critical stage" of the aggregate proceedings against respondent. . . . Defense counsel, however, were not notified in advance that the psychiatric examination would encompass the issue of their client's future dangerousness [footnote omitted], and respondent was denied the assistance of his attorneys in making the significant decision of whether to submit to the examination and to what end the psychiatrist's findings could be employed. . . .

Therefore, in addition to Fifth Amendment considerations, the death penalty was improperly imposed on respondent because the psychiatric examination on which Dr. Grigson testified at the penalty phase proceeded in violation of respondent's Sixth Amendment right to the assistance of counsel [footnote omitted]. . . .

◆ ◆ ◆

Commentary: If a psychologist were to act as Grigson did, what provisions of the APA's 1992 Ethical Principles would the clinician violate? What sections of the Specialty Guidelines would be implicated?

Is it not the psychologist's duty to disclose at the initiation of therapy such important information as limits to confidentiality (i.e., in a manner equivalent to the police officer's Miranda warnings)? As chapter 4 illustrated, the legal system compels psychologists at times to act as agents of the state, such as when they are required to report child abuse or to protect a private third party from a patient's violent threats. In instances like these, should not psychologists, regardless of the setting in which they work, inform their clients of those situations in which they feel obligated to serve society and in which, like Grigson, they determine that the duty of fidelity has shifted from their clients to the state?

Role conflicts are an inevitable fact of life for academicians and practitioners, but they occur more often—as Estelle v. Smith proves—when the client is an involuntary participant in assessment or treatment. In many such cases, the forensic clinician is asked to predict whether the involuntary client might engage in an act of violence. Such predictions are not restricted to death penalty cases but are also requested in more commonplace instances, with regard to civil commitment, bail and parole hearings, detention of juveniles, and child abuse.

Is it Unethical to Offer Predictions of Future Violence?

Thomas Grisso and Paul S. Appelbaum

For many years, scholars have been warning mental health professionals that the results of our research on predictors of future violence set serious limits for experts who testify about future dangerous behavior (e.g., Cocozza & Steadman, 1976; Ennis & Litwack, 1974; Monahan, 1981). Megargee's (1981) conclusion is representative: "The identification of the potentially violent individual with sufficient accuracy to warrant preventative detention . . . is an impossible quest" (p. 181).

Recognition of these predictive limits often has given rise to recommendations that clinicians should not render opinions about "dangerousness" or future violence in legal forums. For example, the American Psychiatric Association (1974) long ago suggested that "clinicians should avoid 'conclusory' judgments" (p. 33) about such matters in expert testimony. This recommendation seems to have been reached most often with regard to testimony in criminal cases (Brody, 1990), although Stone's (1975) review of the empirical evidence led him to recommend that violence prediction should be placed outside the clinician's role in civil commitment as well.

More recently, some analysts of the state of the art in violence prediction have stated outright that which earlier writers may only have implied: It is unethical to do what our research says we cannot do reliably. Melton, Petrila, Poythress, and Slobogin (1987), after concluding that "there is no specialized clinical knowledge that permits categorical, or even relative, conclusions about dangerousness" (p. 204), observed that "in view of this research, clinicians may decide that they cannot ethically offer prediction testimony" (p. 205). Ethicist Philippa Foot (1990) stated the point more forcefully in the context of capital sentencing, admonishing clinicians to refuse to offer predictive testimony that they know is unreliable: "Such a refusal," she observed, "seems right in the center of the area of professional ethics" (p. 213).

Ewing's (1983, . . . , 1991) statements of this position have been the most sweeping: "[There] is good reason to conclude that psychologists and psychiatrists act unethically when they render predictions of dangerousness that provide a legal basis for restricting another person's interest in life and liberty" (Ewing, 1991, p. 162). The foundation for this assertion is that "such predictions cannot be said to be founded on a scientific basis . . . The psychiatrist or psychologist who makes a prediction of dangerousness violates his or her ethical obligation to register judgments that rest on a scientific basis" (Ewing, 1983, pp. 417–418).

Ewing's conclusions were reached after his review of research on clinical judgment, expert testimony, and legal considerations in delinquency and criminal cases involving questions of detention and sentencing. But the broad reference to violence predictions affecting restrictions of liberty suggests, as have others (e.g., Stone, 1975), that predictions in matters concerning juvenile and adult offenders are not the only ones that are being condemned. Emergency and involuntary admissions to mental hospitals, as well as decisions about discharge, also involve violence predictions and potential restrictions of liberty. So do the decisions of psychotherapists who fulfill legal obligations to protect children or other persons when they become aware of potential violence by their clients. Therefore, it would appear that a broad-based conclusion that predictions of future violence are unethical indicts most mental health professionals in general clinical or forensic work of unethical behavior at least some time in their careers, and a substantial proportion of them on a daily basis.

From *Law and Human Behavior*, 16, 621–633. Copyright 1992 by Plenum Publishing. Adapted with permission of the publisher.

We believe that a more differentiated analysis of predictive testimony about future violence, which we offer in this article, does not support an assertion that experts' judgments about violent behavior are necessarily or always unethical, even in legal cases involving potential loss of liberty [footnote omitted]. We submit that there may be several ethically significant dimensions along which predictions of future violence can be differentiated, which are not taken into account by a blanket condemnation of predictive testimony. These dimensions include, but may not be limited to, (a) the nature of the predictive testimony, (b) the foundation for the predictive testimony, and (c) the legal consequences of the prediction [footnote omitted].

THE NATURE OF THE PREDICTIVE TESTIMONY

Let us presume that when critics have spoken against "predictions of dangerousness," they have been referring to "predictions of future violent behavior." Expert testimony about future violence can take several forms, all of which might be considered predictions as the term is used broadly in the behavioral and social sciences. We can cite no authority for the forms of testimony that such predictions take, but the following are examples from our experience:

a. *Dichotomous:* Statement that a particular behavior (or type of behavior) will or will not occur in the future. ("In my opinion, he will engage in serious violent behavior in the future.")

b. *Dichotomous with Qualified Confidence:* Dichotomous statement, with additional testimony concerning expert's confidence in his or her opinion. ("In my opinion, he will engage in a serious violent behavior in the future, and I believe that it is more likely than not [or 'reasonably certain' or 'very certain'] that my judgment would prove accurate.")

c. *Risk, Individual-Based:* Statement of the degree of likelihood that this individual will engage in a particular behavior (or type of behavior) in the future. ("In my opinion, there is a 40% probability that he will engage in serious violent behavior in the future.")

d. *Risk, Class-Based:* Statement of likelihood or probability, but offered in reference to a class of persons of which the individual is alleged to be a member. ("In my opinion, about 25% of people with this individual's characteristics engage in violent behavior after release from a mental hospital.") May be combined with individual-based. (". . . but I believe that he presents somewhat greater/less risk than that group" [e.g., based on future environmental circumstances].)

All of these forms of testimony may be construed as predictions [footnote omitted]. They attempt to inform the listener about the clinician's professional opinion concerning behaviors that may occur in the future. Statements of risk are no less predictions than statements in dichotomous form; they simply provide additional information concerning the likelihood that others will be right or wrong in drawing their own dichotomous conclusion.

Broad arguments for a ban on predictions of violent behavior appear not to have been limited to dichotomous statements of prediction, but would prohibit all types of predictive testimony involving questions of future violence and restriction of liberty. The scope of the applicable definition of *prediction* may be significant in evaluating arguments such as Ewing's (1991). If one intends to condemn all forms of predictive testimony as unethical, and if the basis for this conclusion is inadequate scientific support for predictions, then the conclusion is wrong if there is reasonable scientific support for any of the above forms of predictive testimony. It would seem that there is.

Let us consider first the evidence as it relates to dichotomous predictive testimony, our types *a* and *b*. Research demonstrating the lack of scientific support for the validity of predictions of future violence is derived primarily from publications in the 1970s, which have been reviewed extensively (e.g., Monahan, 1981; Webster & Menzies, 1987). Collectively, those studies demonstrated that even for groups with characteristics that often are associated with violent behavior, no more than 20%–40% of individuals, at best, were identified later (e.g., on parole) as engaging in violent acts resulting in recidivism. Reviews of the literature concluded that clinicians have no ability, or no special ability, to predict whether or not a person will engage in a violent act in the future and that they would be right in at best about one in three cases in which they made such predictions (e.g., Cocozza & Steadman, 1976, 1978; . . . Ennis & Litwack, 1974) [footnote omitted].

In a thoughtful, critical review of this literature, Litwack and Schlesinger (1987) have argued that "none of these statements has been established by the relevant research findings and, in all probability, they are simply wrong" (p. 206). Their primary argument was that the design of the studies simply did not allow such sweeping conclusions. Given that some studies demonstrated a high number of false-positive predictions in certain circumstances with certain populations, it still did not follow that there were no circumstances in which clinicians might make more accurate predictions or might have something more to offer than lay persons. . . .

In one sense, Litwack and Schlesinger's observations appear to challenge the conclusion that all dichotomous predictions are unethical. Research on the invalidity of such predictions has focused only on certain populations and circumstances; one might argue, therefore, that the impropriety of dichotomous predictions in those types of cases need not extend to other types of cases for which validity has not yet been challenged. This reasoning is less persuasive, however, if it is also unethical (as some critics have claimed: Dix, 1980) to make dichotomous predictions when we *do not know* their validity for the type of case at hand because of the *absence* of relevant research. Dichotomous predictions of future violence, therefore, remain vulnerable to arguments that they violate ethical propriety.

Turning now to predictive testimony of types *c* and *d*, some of the same studies of the 1970s that challenged the validity of dichotomous predictions provided the earliest scientific support for offering predictive testimony in the form of probabilistic or comparative risk statements. For example, the State of Michigan's (1978) Parole Risk Study identified a small class of parolees with a 40% rate of violent recidivism. Accurate classification of a parole candidate in that group, therefore, would allow scientifically supported predictive testimony that the risk of vio-

lent recidivism was much greater for this person than for most parolees (for whom the baserate was shown to be about 10%).

Much more sophisticated research during the 1980s significantly augmented the scientific support for identification of groups with relatively high baserates of future violence (e.g., Binder & McNiel, 1988; Klassen & O'Connor, 1988, 1990; Link, Cullen, & Andrews, 1990; Swanson, Holzer, Ganju, & Jono, 1990). For example, studies identified hospitalized groups, based on a combination of background and demographic characteristics, for which the risk of subsequent violent behavior in the community was over 50% (Klassen & O'Connor, 1988), as well as groups identified merely by a reliable diagnosis (alcohol or drug abuse/dependence) for which prior-year baserates of violence in the community were 25%–35%, or 12–17 times greater than for persons with no DSM-III diagnosis (Swanson et al., 1990).

These newer studies, of course, do not provide scientific evidence with which to claim validity for predictive testimony in dichotomous form (predictive testimony of types a and b in our characterization above). They merely provide research support, in some cases, for predictive testimony that offers courts a sense of the relative risk of violence associated with individuals in question (predictive testimony of types c and d). Yet this is enough to contradict the generalized assertion that *all* predictive testimony regarding future violence is unethical for lack of a scientific basis. . . .

THE FOUNDATION OF THE PREDICTIVE TESTIMONY

As the preceding discussion makes clear, the scientific basis for predictions of future violence is derived from studies identifying particular characteristics of research subjects who subsequently engaged in violent behavior. This suggests three important limitations on the appropriateness even of predictive risk statements, consistent with a general standard of competence in clinicians' performance of evaluations (Section I: American Psychiatric Association, 1989; Principle 1: American Psychological Association, 1981).

First, the person about whom the estimate of risk is being made must be similar to the research subjects in the studies from which the predictive model is derived. Second, the estimate of risk must be based on types of data comparable to those available in the studies that are being relied upon. Third, the expert's evaluation process and methods by which data are gathered must be sufficiently reliable to assure accurate identification of the relevant characteristics of the individual in question.

Many of the arguments against the use of predictions by mental health professionals have focused on a single type of situation in which none of these limiting conditions has been respected: the prediction of a defendant's future violent behavior at the sentencing phase of a capital trial (Ewing, 1983). In that situation, mental health professionals have testified routinely about the likelihood of future violence when there were no data about comparable groups of subjects (Dix, 1980), or when such data began to be available (Marquart, Ekland-Olsen, & Sorenson, 1989; Marquart & Sorenson, 1989), often in disregard of them. Moreover, such testimony often has been based on evaluation procedures or methods that manifest little regard for a reliable description of the defendant's characteristics. Such is the case when predictions are offered on the basis of information provided in a hypothetical question posed by the prosecutor, typically without the expert having had an opportunity to examine the defendant or to become acquainted with documentary evidence relevant to the defendant's history (Appelbaum, 1984).

The ethics of predictions of future violence in such a context indeed are questionable. But it is not clear that one can generalize from these troublesome practices to all other predictive testimony. For example, predictive testimony may be ethically appropriate when a mental health professional who has examined a potential patient offers testimony at a commitment hearing about an increased risk of future violence, based on (a) data suggesting that certain diagnostic groups, or persons manifesting certain symptoms, are at increased risk for violent behavior, and (b) data indicating that the prospective patient reliably can be associated with those groups. The closer the match between the characteristics of

the subject of the prediction and the data available about those characteristics in the studies on which the predictive statement is based, the less problematic such testimony will be.

In summary, predictive testimony sometimes has met the foundational criteria described here and sometimes has not. But the frequent failure of experts to have satisfied these conditions in a particular situation (sentencing in capital trials) does not warrant the conclusion that *all* violence predictions are unethical.

THE LEGAL CONSEQUENCES OF THE PREDICTION

. . .

We sometimes have the necessary research support and assessment data to state a probability of violence in a given case. That probability usually will be less than 0.5. As noted in our first discussion, this probability may be sufficient to lead the factfinder to conclude that the identified level of risk satisfies a sociolegal definition of dangerousness for purposes of restricting liberties. When decision makers are satisfied that a level of risk below 0.5 warrants the restriction of liberty, however, across cases the majority of persons about whom the decision is being made will be the "victims" of a high false-positive rate.

Society may believe that it is justified in "mistakenly" restricting the liberties of a majority in order to achieve the proper objectives in relation to the minority who are "correctly" restricted. Yet that which society can justify for itself may not always satisfy the ethical obligations of clinicians, as interpreted individually or by their professional organizations. For example, psychologists are urged by their profession's ethical standards to be alert to, and to refuse to engage in or condone, unjustifiable decisions by others as a consequence of their own actions, and to make known their concern about conflicts of these types that they encounter in their work (American Psychological Association, 1981: Principle 1(f), 2(b) and (d)). Psychiatrists are urged to respect the rights of patients and to seek changes in laws when they are contrary to the best interests of patients (American Psychiatric Association, 1989: Section 3 and 4). Therefore independent of that which is accepted by society or the law, professionals have an obligation to consider the potential effects of their testimony about risk statements with high false-positive rates and to question whether the law's use of their testimony violates their professional ethical standards.

When we participate in legal proceedings in which our predictive testimony results in decisions with high false-positive rates and their consequences, do we practice unethically? There are at least three ways that one might address the question.

First, one can argue that *any* restriction of liberty based on predictive testimony about risk involving large false-positive rates constitutes a misuse of psychological or psychiatric information by the legal system. This position would be based on either of two views: (1) that it is wrong for society to restrict liberties on the basis of less than 0.5 probability of future violence, and that to do so demeans the rights of the individual, is "unjustifiable," and does not "promote human welfare" (e.g., American Psychological Association, 1981: Preamble, and Principle 3(b)); or (2) that even with an expert's attempts to inform the court about the limits of testimony based on probabilities with high false-positive rates, there is an unacceptable potential for misunderstanding or misuse of the information in the legal forum. Experts who testify about risk probabilities with high false-positive rates, therefore, would be perceived as participating unethically in the process.

A second approach would leave questions of justification to the courts and society to determine, not the mental health professional. Statutes and procedures of law define the conditions under which society "justly" restricts the liberties of its citizens. The expert who provides reliable risk probability information (and clearly explains its limitations) to courts within that legal framework engages in ethical practice, according to this view, even if the legal outcome deprives the individual of liberty "mistakenly." The duties of the forensic expert are different in this regard from those of the clinician in a doctor–patient relationship, wherein the obligation to maximize the welfare of the patient is paramount. Therefore, the consequences of a court's restrictions of liberty present no ethical burden for the expert beyond that of

presenting reliable testimony and clearly explaining its limitations.

A third position is intermediate in relation to the other two. It would not leave questions of justification only to the courts. On the other hand, it would observe that not all types of liberty restrictions are of equal consequence, especially given variability across circumstances (e.g., civil commitment vs. capital sentencing) in potential, counterbalancing benefits to the person whose liberty is restricted. This position might also recognize variability in the quality of legal justice across jurisdictions (e.g., known patterns of racial bias in sentencing in certain jurisdictions). This perspective would see predictive testimony about risk probabilities with high false-positive rates as neither ethical nor unethical *per se*. Instead, it would encourage professional debate regarding the circumstances (e.g., degree and type of liberty restrictions associated with the legal questions, types of benefits that may accrue) in which the various magnitudes of false-positive error resulting from risk probability testimony would be ethically acceptable or unacceptable in relation to the balance of consequences for the individual and society.

Our purpose here is not to evaluate, endorse, or refine any of these approaches. We merely observe that they reach different answers to the questions of ethical propriety in predictive testimony about risk probabilities. The second approach would not consider such predictive testimony unethical, and the third might consider it unethical for certain types of legal proceedings, but not for all.

The first approach would, indeed, see all such testimony as unethical. If it is to be used as a basis for arguing that risk-related predictive testimony should be banned because it contributes to unjust legal decisions, then its proponents should make explicit the assumptions and unanswered questions underlying the position so that it can be debated on its merits. For example, on what basis are our professional associations to determine that society's justifications for restrictions of liberty (based partly on our testimony) are wrong? What is the foundation for the argument that our testimony, if carefully presented, will be misunderstood or misused by legal fact-finders? Do the gains in "human welfare" associated with a prohibition on risk-related testimony outweigh the potential negative effects on "human welfare?"[1] . . .

References

American Psychiatric Association. (1974). *Clinical aspects of the violent individual*. Washington, DC: American Psychiatric Association.

American Psychiatric Association. (1989). *Principles of medical ethics with annotations especially applicable to psychiatry*. Washington, DC: American Psychiatric Association.

American Psychological Association. (1981). *Ethical principles of psychologists*. Washington, DC: American Psychological Association.

Appelbaum, P. (1984). Hypotheticals, psychiatric testimony, and the death sentence. *Bulletin of the American Academy of Psychiatry and the Law, 12*, 169–177.

Binder, R., & McNiel, D. (1988). Effects of diagnosis and context on dangerousness. *American Journal of Psychiatry, 145*, 728–732.

Brody, B. (1990). Prediction of dangerousness in different contexts. In R. Rosner & R. Weinstock (Eds.), *Ethical practice in psychiatry and the law* (pp. 185–196). New York: Plenum.

Brooks, A. (1974). *Law, psychiatry and the mental health system*. Boston: Little, Brown.

Cocozza, J., & Steadman, H. (1976). The failure of psychiatric predictions of dangerousness: Clear and convincing evidence. *Rutgers Law Review, 29*, 1084–1101.

Cocozza, J., & Steadman, H. (1978). Prediction in psychiatry: An example of misplaced confidence in experts. *Social Problems, 25*, 265–276.

Dix, G. (1980). Clinical evaluation of the "dangerousness" of "normal" criminal defendants. *Virginia Law Review, 66*, 523–581.

Ennis, B., & Litwack, T. (1974). Psychiatry and the presumption of expertise: Flipping coins in the courtroom. *California Law Review, 62*, 693–752.

Ewing, C. (1983). "Dr. Death" and the case for an ethical ban on psychiatric and psychological predictions of dangerousness in capital sentencing proceedings. *American Journal of Law and Medicine, 8*, 407–428.

Ewing, C. (1991). Preventive detention and execution: The constitutionality of punishing future crimes. *Law and Human Behavior, 15*, 139–163.

Foot, P. (1990). Ethics and the death penalty: Participation of forensic psychiatrists in capital trials. In R. Rosner and R. Weinstock (Eds.), *Ethical practice in psychiatry and the law* (pp. 207–217). New York: Plenum.

Klassen, D., & O'Connor, W. (1988). A prospective study of predictors of violence in adult male mental health admissions. *Law and Human Behavior, 12*, 143–158.

Klassen, D., & O'Connor, W. (1990). Assessing the risk of violence in released mental patients: A cross-validational study. *Psychological Assessment, 1*, 75–81.

Link, B., Cullen, F., & Andrews, H. (1990, August). *Violent and illegal behavior of current and former mental patients compared to community controls*. Paper presented at the meeting of the Society for the Study of Social Problems.

Litwack, T., & Schlesinger, L. (1987). Assessing and predicting violence: Research, law, and application. In I. Weiner & A. Hess, (Eds.), *Handbook of forensic psychology* (pp. 205–257). New York: Wiley.

Marquart, J., Ekland-Olsen, S., & Sorenson, J. (1989). Gazing into the crystal ball: Can jurors accurately predict dangerousness in capital cases? *Law and Society Review, 23*, 449–468.

Marquart, J., & Sorensen, J. (1989). A national study of the *Furman*-committed inmates: Assessing the threat to society from capital offenders. *Loyola of Los Angeles Law Review, 23*, 5–28.

Megargee, E. (1981). Methodological problems in the prediction of violence. In J. Hays, T. Roberts, & K. Solway (Eds.), *Violence and the violent individual* (pp. 179–191). New York: Spectrum.

Melton, G., Petrila, J., Poythress, N., & Slobogin, C. (1987). *Psychological evaluations for the courts*. New York: Guilford.

Monahan, J. (1981). *The clinical prediction of violent behavior*. Rockville, MD: National Institute of Mental Health.

State of Michigan, Department of Corrections (June 29, 1978). *The parole risk study*. Unpublished manuscript.

[1] Two examples of potential negative consequences of the first position may be offered. *First*, a blanket prohibition of risk probability testimony involving high false-positive rates would disallow not only predictions of violence, but also predictions of nonviolence. According to past research, our predictions that individuals will *not* engage in future violence are quite likely to be accurate (low false-negatives). Therefore, testimony about nonviolence is immune to consequentialist arguments that focus on unjust restrictions of liberty as a result of the effects of testimony on legal dispositions. Prohibiting risk-related predictive testimony could deprive individuals of testimony that might reduce the likelihood of liberty restrictions due to alleged violence potential. *Second*, additional questions are raised by the apparent limitation of the argument (that testimony on future violence is unethical) to situations in which "liberty" is at stake (e.g., Ewing, 1991). If cases involving restrictions on liberty are construed narrowly as only referring to decisions about detention or release, we arrive at the paradoxical argument that the same testimony about a child abuser's future violence that could not be offered at a parole hearing could be tendered at a custody proceeding. On the other hand, if liberty is construed broadly, such that, for example, denial of access to one's child consequent to a custody determination infringes liberty, then testimony on future violence would never be permissible. We question whether proponents of the view that predictions of future violence are unethical truly desire to exclude testimony from child custody hearings (presuming the testimony meets scientific standards that a parent has a 40% likelihood of harming his or her child).

Stone, A., (1975). *Mental health and law: A system in transition*. Rockville, MD: National Institute of Mental Health.

Swanson, J., Holzer, C., Ganju, V., & Jono, R. (1990). Violence and psychiatric disorder in the community: Evidence from the Epidemiologic Catchment Area Surveys. *Hospital and Community Psychiatry, 41,* 761–770.

Webster, C., & Menzies, R. (1987). The clinical prediction of dangerousness. In D. Weisstub (Ed.), *Law and mental health: International perspectives*, Vol. 3 (pp. 158–208). New York: Pergamon.

◆ ◆ ◆

Commentary: *For perhaps the most recent review of the literature on this topic, see Litwack, T. R. (1994). Assessments of dangerousness: Legal, research, and clinical developments. Administration and Policy in Mental Health, 21, 361–378.*

Contrast the views in the Grisso and Appelbaum article presented above with the following, from Goldman (1986):

> The psychologist ought to weigh directly the probable moral consequences of his testimony and use his full powers of moral reasoning in deciding whether and how to testify as an expert. It is not sufficient from a moral point of view that he tell the truth and do what the court asks of him. He must also desist from contributing directly to outcomes to which he is morally opposed on good grounds.
>
> There are many areas in which psychologists might be called as experts. A preliminary example that can be cited here relates to the predictability of violent behavior. Suppose that methods for prediction improve until a high degree of reliability is achieved and that courts increasingly use such predictions as bases for imposing the death penalty (the example is from Loftus & Monahan, 1980). In my view a psychologist who is morally opposed to capital punishment cannot rightly agree to provide testimony that will lead to its imposition on grounds that he is only telling the truth and providing "ethically neutral" scientific

> knowledge that the judge has the authority to seek and use. Rather than usurping the role of the judge, the psychologist who refuses to testify in such a case is taking a stand as an individual against what he perceives to be unjustifiable homicide. Since individual psychologists cannot themselves determine the law on the matter, such input into the system does not represent the usurpation of lawmaking authority. Just as citizens in general need not support on moral grounds or contribute to the enforcement of laws they consider seriously unjust, so here the psychologist need not aid the imposition of a morally abominable sentence. (p. 37)

Goldman, A. H. (1986). Cognitive psychologists as expert witnesses: A problem in professional ethics. *Law and Human Behavior, 10, 29–45.*

Goldman raised the final question to be considered in this chapter: Are there some functions that an ethical psychologist should refuse to perform? This question has been broached most poignantly in the debate over implementation of the death penalty. Specifically, in Ford v. Wainwright *(477 U.S. 399, 1986), the U.S. Supreme Court held that the execution of a psychotic and incompetent death row inmate would violate the Eighth Amendment ban on cruel and unusual punishment. Do mental health professionals act unethically if they participate in treating seriously mentally ill criminals so that they may become competent enough to be executed? The American Medical Association has advised physicians that they should not take part in legally authorized executions. And, the Louisiana Supreme Court has held that it is unconstitutional for the state to forcibly medicate condemned inmates with antipsychotic drugs so that they can become competent enough to be executed.*

Psychologists are not yet entitled to prescribe psychotropic medication, but they are qualified to either assess whether a death row inmate is competent to be executed or design and implement psychotherapeutic and behavioral interventions to achieve competency. Should psychologists participate in such endeavors? Readers whose immediate reaction is no should consider this: What about prisoners who choose to be executed rather than live in a psychotic state during a lifetime in prison?

For a variety of perspectives on these issues, see these publications:

Bonnie, R. (1990). Dilemmas in administering the death penalty: Conscientious abstention, professional ethics, and the needs of the legal system. Law and Human Behavior, 14, 67–90.

Brodsky, S. L. (1990). Professional ethics and professional morality in the assessment of competence for execution: A response to Bonnie. Law and Human Behavior, 14, 91–97.

Salguero, R. G. (1986). Medical ethics and competency to be executed. Yale Law Journal, 96, 167–186.

White, W. S. (1987). Defendants who elect execution. University of Pittsburgh Law Review, 48, 853–877.

What guidance, if any, do the APA Ethical Principles and the Specialty Guidelines give the forensic practitioner about these issues? What are the relevant provisions in these documents? What moral principles, described in chapter 3 (e.g., justice and nonmaleficence), should prevail?

On Being Ethical in Legal Places

Patricia Anderten, Valerie Staulcup, and Thomas Grisso

. . .

SAFEGUARDING ETHICAL STANDARDS

Given that the courtroom presents ethical difficulties and professional conflicts for psychologists, one need not conclude that psychologists should avoid either the courtroom or consultation to attorneys and their clients. A weighing of the potential benefits and liabilities of placing psychological information at the disposal of courts would probably find the potential benefits weighing heavier in the balance. The focus, then, should be on how we can offer our services within the legal system in the most effective and professional manner. An examination of the dynamics of the situations we have discussed suggests several general recommendations for psychologists who would wish to reduce the chances of ethical malfeasance in their participation in legal cases.

First, knowledge of the legal process and of the problems inherent in psychological testimony is essential to maintaining competent and ethical practice as an expert witness. Acquiring this knowledge is presently a matter of individual initiative. Few graduate courses on professional and ethical issues deal more than cursorily with the complexities of psychologist–attorney relationships or the expert witness role. However, workshops in these areas are increasing in number, and earlier we cited a growing literature that should be read by any psychologist who anticipates professional involvement in legal cases.

Second, especially if one is inclined to actively seek involvement in legal cases, it is important to examine seriously one's needs and motives in relation to this intent. . . . [E]xcessive influence by altruistic motives and self-serving motives alike can easily cloud one's judgment. Clinical psychologists will re-

call similar admonitions by their supervisors in the early stages of psychotherapy training. For most psychologists, the role of expert witness is as foreign and complex as was the psychotherapist's role in their earlier training and, therefore, requires no less by way of awareness of personal motivations if competent and ethical practice is to prevail.

Third, psychologists who have passed beyond that period of professional development in which they obtained case consultation from another psychologist may wish to reinstate that practice. Peer review of assessment data can provide a hedge against bias during one's initial explorations into legal casework when the threat to autonomous objectivity may be greatest because of one's initial insecurity in a new professional situation.

Finally, we urge psychologists to be assertive concerning the establishment of a truly collaborative relationship with the attorney and the client (be this an individual or a court). . . . Careful joint preparation will reduce the number of "surprises" encountered by psychologists in the courtroom and allow the psychologists to avoid various ethical pitfalls. It is also through active involvement with the attorney that the psychologist can best educate the attorney regarding ethical problems as they arise and can attend closely to events that may unduly jeopardize the psychological well-being of the client.

As more psychologists take the witness stand, the courtroom may become a major source of information with which the public forms its impressions of psychology as a science and a profession. There is a commensurate responsibility for psychologists to adequately prepare themselves to meet the special ethical demands of the expert witness role, not only because they represent the profession in the public's eye but also for the welfare of the clients who are served.

Adapted from *Professional Psychology, 11*, 764–773. Copyright 1980 by the American Psychological Association.

Commentary: As Anderten et al. (1980) stressed, it is essential that forensic psychologists maintain current information about the problems that will confront them in the legal process. Perhaps the most hotly debated topic at the present time concerns the disclosure of psychological test data, particularly raw scores. The issue arises most often when the attorney for one of the parties— usually the party opposing the one for which the examining psychologist will testify—subpoenas (i.e., compels the production of) all of the psychologist's records, including the test items as printed on the test protocol, clients' responses to the items, the correct answers printed in the manual (if there is one), and test norms. The issue is controversial for several reasons. First, publishers assert that disclosure will violate their copyright and destroy the validity of their tests. Second, clients complain that disclosure will violate their right to confidentiality and to consent to disclosure. And, finally, psychologists believe that disclosure will place raw data into the hands of unqualified persons and destroy test security. The APA is attempting to provide guidance to its members on this difficult issue. The APA Committee on Psychological Tests and Assessment is drafting a statement on the disclosure of test data, and the APA ad hoc Committee on Legal Issues is preparing strategies for coping with subpoenas or compelled testimony for test data. Neither document is in final form, however, and neither has been adopted as APA policy.

Disclosure is not only an ethical issue but also a legal one; thus, it is resolvable in part by knowledge of relevant state laws (if they exist) in the jurisdiction in which one practices or testifies. Until there is an APA policy on this knotty topic, what provisions in the Ethical Principles or the forensic guidelines are relevant? If the client does consent to disclosure, is there any reason that the psychologist should not honor that consent, regardless of the interests that test publishers assert? As should be evident by now, there is no escaping the need for psychological professionals to sort out competing ethical obligations.

As the final substantive words in this chapter, I can find no more eloquent or elegant summary than this, by Butcher and Pope (1993):

> The psychologist who conducts forensic assessments holds a sometimes overwhelming power over the lives of others. The results of a forensic assessment may influence— perhaps even determine—whether a person receives custody of his or her child, is forced to pay damages to another litigant, returns home from the courtroom, or spends years in prison. In some cases, the assessment results may literally determine whether a person accused of a capital crime lives or dies. Whatever other implications this power has, it mandates that we never take it for granted or treat it carelessly. The explicit ethical and professional standards reviewed . . . are the profession's attempt to ensure that this power is used competently, carefully, appropriately, and responsibly. Our responsibility as forensic practitioners includes not only upholding these standards in our own work of conducting assessments but also constantly rethinking the nature of these standards, their presence in our education and training, the degree to which the profession ensures accountability or, alternatively, passively tolerates and tacitly accepts or encourages violations, and the care with which we spell out responsibilities that fit the current and constantly evolving demands of forensic assessment. (p. 285)

See Butcher, J. N., & Pope, K. S. (1993). Seven issues in conducting forensic assessments: Ethical responsibilities in light of new standards and new tests. *Ethics and Behavior, 3,* 267–288.

The literature in forensic psychology is burgeoning. Although this chapter was devoted to examining ethical issues, other recent material is available for readers interested in more intensive knowledge about forensic mental health testimony, including the sharp controversies in the field:

Ackerman, M. J. (1995). Clinician's guide to child custody evaluations. *New York: Wiley.*

Ackerman, M. J., & Kane, E. (1993). Psychological experts in divorce, personal injury, and other civil actions (2nd ed., Vols. 1–2). *New York: Wiley.*

Brodsky, S. L. (1991). Testifying in court: Guidelines and maxims for the expert witness. *Washington, DC: American Psychological Association.*

Brodzinsky, D. M. (1993). On the use and misuse of psychological testing in child custody evaluations. Professional Psychology: Research and Practice, 24, 213–219.

Heilbrun, K. (1992). The role of psychological testing in forensic assessment. Law and Human Behavior, 16, 257–272.

Lykken, D. T. (1993). Predicting violence in the violent society. Applied and Preventive Psychology, 2, 13–20.

Ogloff, J. R. P., Roberts, C. F., & Roesch, R. (1993). The insanity defense: Legal standards and clinical assessment. Applied and Preventive Psychology, 2, 163–178.

Roesch, R., Ogloff, J. R. P., & Golding, S. L. (1993). Competency to stand trial: Legal and clinical issues. Applied and Preventive Psychology, 2, 43–51.

Shapiro, D. L. (1991). Forensic psychological assessment. Boston: Allyn & Bacon.

Skinner, L. J., & Berry, K. K. (1993). Anatomically detailed dolls and the evaluation of child sexual abuse allegations. Law and Human Behavior, 17, 399–421.

Wolfner, G., Faust, D., & Dawes, R. M. (1993). The use of anatomically detailed dolls in sexual abuse evaluations: The state of the science. Applied and Preventive Psychology, 2, 1–11.

Ziskin, J., & Faust, D. (1988). Coping with psychiatric and psychological testimony (4th ed., Vols. 1–3). Beverly Hills, CA: Law and Psychology Press.

CHAPTER 10

THE BUSINESS OF PSYCHOLOGY

During the time that I wrote this chapter, there was a joke being bandied about by disgruntled mental health professionals. Relating it to the reader in an attempt at humor may be a dubious reward for wending one's way through the world of ethics reflected in this book, but it will also serve a useful purpose in making the point of this chapter.

> Three physicians happened to die on the same day and arrived at the proverbial Pearly Gates, waiting to be interviewed by St. Peter to determine whether they would be allowed to enter the Kingdom of Heaven.
>
> "And who are you?" asked St. Peter of the first candidate.
>
> "I'm Jonas Salk," he replied meekly.
>
> "Oh, the discoverer of the vaccine that saved so many children from the perils of polio. Come right in."
>
> Turning to the second healer, St. Peter asked the same question. "I'm Benjamin Spock. I wrote a book on children's health and development," the second physician responded authoritatively.
>
> "Ah, yes, and a wise counselor to millions of otherwise anxious and worried parents. We welcome you to Heaven for the remainder of eternity." He then turned to the third supplicant, saying "And who might you be?"
>
> "Well, I'm Gordon Smiley."
>
> "Don't think I recognize the name. What have you done?"
>
> "I," Smiley said proudly, "invented the concept of managed health care."[1]
>
> "Really?" St. Peter said, "Okay. You're approved for 3 days."

The logistics of doing professional psychology no longer simply involves renting an office; buying an oriental rug, an aquarium, and comfortable couches and chairs; and exercising independent professional discretion. Psychology is becoming, and will very likely be for the foreseeable future, a business. Psychologists are no longer therapists or doctors; they are health service providers (or, worse yet, vendors). Those who receive treatment are no longer patients or clients; they are consumers of psychological services. Patients no longer remit fees; bills are submitted for reimbursement to third-party payors. For good or ill, and regardless of this kind of "new speak," these are the realities that psychologists face.

---

[1] For those still innocent, managed health care involves, among other things, attempts by health care systems and third-party payors (like insurance companies) to control costs. They do this in a variety of ways, including requiring permission before certain procedures, such as surgery or psychotherapy, are undertaken and determining length of treatment, such as limiting a hospital stay to 1 day or therapy to 8–10 sessions.

477

The changing world of professional psychology confronts the concerned clinician with an array of ethical issues. The modern psychologist must traverse the metaphorical minefield in which are hidden such explosive and competing values as controlling the quickly rising costs of health care, exercising proper professional autonomy, and serving what are perceived to be the needs and best interests of the patient. Even more generally, the health care revolution raises the question of what effects the commercialization of psychology will have on such fundamental moral principles as beneficence, autonomy, fidelity, and justice.

Another part of the new environment for psychologists is the specter of malpractice. Although psychologists rarely are successfully sued for professional negligence, the threat still looms. Performing incompetent child custody evaluations, invading the boundaries of professional relationships through sexual relationships with clients, damaging patients by improperly administering psychotropic medication (increasingly possible as prescription privileges for psychologists become more likely), and committing other vagaries of practice all may lead to malpractice claims. In an attempt to prevent such claims from succeeding and to alert readers to the concurrent ethical problems that may arise from malpractice suits, this chapter presents material on such important issues as proper record keeping and keeping one's financial "house" in order.

Finally, because the federal government views the provision of psychological services as a commercial, competitive enterprise, it has sought to regulate both the profession and its professionals. In particular, the Federal Trade Commission (FTC) has scrutinized ethical principles of such associations as APA to see if they restrict competition inappropriately. As a result, there are now fewer controls on setting fees, advertising, and soliciting clients. These changes may increase competition within and between professions (e.g., psychology and psychiatry), but they may also lead to dubiously ethical conduct. I hope that the material in this chapter helps discern the differences among sleazy behavior, bad form, illegal actions, and unethical conduct.

The Commerce of Professional Psychology and the New Ethics Code

Gerald P. Koocher

No one will dispute the notion that the practice of professional psychology demands both clinical competence and up-to-date scientific knowledge. Increasingly, however, successful practice demands a sophisticated understanding of commercial issues not routinely addressed in graduate training. The increasing prevalence of managed mental health care, the range of payment mechanisms, and economic hard times contribute to compounding the complexity of the business aspects of running a mental health practice, whether it is done on a solo basis or as part of a large agency. This article focuses on the impact of the new American Psychological Association (APA) ethics code (APA, 1992) with respect to the commercial aspects of the professional practice of psychology. . . .

RECORDS

New specifics on record maintenance (Standard 5.04), preservation (Standard 5.09), ownership (Standard 5.10), and withholding records for nonpayment (Standard 5.11) are provided in the new code. It is now clear, for example, that protection of the confidentiality of records demands consideration of all media (e.g., magnetic, electronic, and optical computer storage, as well as paper and ink records). The new code reiterates the obligation of clinicians to plan in advance for the protection of confidential records in the event of their death or incapacity. Similarly, psychologists must ensure the continuing availability of records and data that may be needed to serve the best interests of their clients (Standard 5.10). The new code also clearly addresses the issue of withholding records solely because of nonpayment

(Standard 5.11). Although the code provides a loophole (i.e., "except as otherwise provided by law"; APA, 1992, p. 1607), it is clear that records that are needed to serve the client's imminent welfare cannot be held hostage to unpaid bills. At the same time, however, there is no clear requirement that the psychologist prepare reports or summaries that require additional professional work to produce when a bill for prior services remains unpaid. The new code addresses only preexisting records under this provision. . . .

New *Record Keeping Guidelines* (APA, 1993), adopted at the APA Council meeting immediately following the one at which the new code was approved, are not technically a part of the new code. They do, however, provide an important set of instructions regarding the minimum acceptable standards for psychologists' records. It will always be necessary to monitor special statutes or regulations governing medical and psychological records in one's own legal jurisdiction, as state and local laws may exceed the APA (1993) specifications or have special features demanding particular care. . . .

Although not specifically cited in the new code, the so-called electronic superhighway of communications calls for special cautions. The dissemination of records (discussed in Standard 1.24) by electronic mail and facsimile requires special caution. For example, confidential records should not be transmitted to E-mail accounts or fax destinations that are not secure or appropriately monitored. Similarly, it is important to recognize that conversations on cellular or cordless telephones are not quite as private as those on standard wired phones. . . .

Adapted from *Professional Psychology: Research and Practice*, 25, 355–361. Copyright 1994 by the American Psychological Association.

Some psychotherapists have occasionally asserted with misguided pride that they keep no records other than those needed to issue bills (e.g., dates of appointments, charges, and payments). One such psychologist attempted to argue to a state licensing board investigating concerns about her record keeping practices that case records would be of little use to anyone else because, in her opinion, the only truly important aspect of the treatment was the transference, and that could not be picked up using written notes. The standards explicit in both the new code and the *Record Keeping Guidelines* ensure that her practice of not keeping more detailed notes would be deemed negligent (Standards 1.23 and 1.24). . . .

FEES AND FINANCIAL ARRANGEMENTS

As described earlier, with respect to both the therapeutic contract and advertising issues, the key point in the ethics of financial arrangements, aside from basic honesty and fairness as discussed in Standard 1.25(b), is disclosure. As stated in Standard 1.25(a), the client should know from the initiation of the professional relationship what to expect in terms of fees and payments. In addition, the psychologists are warned in Standard 1.25(c) that they must be mindful that their practices (even solo practices) are businesses and, as a result, are regulated by many state and local laws. For example, a psychologist might think it is a good idea to charge interest or late payment penalties on client bills; however, such practices may well run afoul of state debtor and creditor laws without special legally approved credit agreements. . . .

Discussing fees up front and taking into account the client's ability to pay, restrictions imposed by third-party payers, and similar issues are very important matters. The psychologist's goal should be to thoughtfully avoid the risk of abandoning the client for financial reasons, to obey applicable laws on financial matters, to be nonexploitative, to make no misrepresentation, to anticipate limitations, to discuss collection practices, and to make accurate reports to payers (Standard 1.26). Although not mentioned in the code, it would be wise for psychologists' special fee requirements (e.g., billing for missed appointments or appointments that were

cancelled late) to secure clients' agreement on this point at the start of the relationship. . . .

Providing bribes or kickbacks in exchange for referrals has never been acceptable. However, from the FTC's perspective, some ethics panels or licensing boards interpreted such prohibitions as forbidding participation in health maintenance organizations, preferred provider organizations, or certain referral services. The FTC regards referral services as procompetitive, and barring them per se was regarded as a significant problem. Unfortunately, what constitutes a bribe, as opposed to a legitimate fee reduction or membership payment, is open to a wide range of opinion. The key to discriminating between an appropriate and an inappropriate payment will depend on the rationale and justification for the charges or fee reductions and the openness of information on these arrangements to the consumers of the services.

In the new code it is clear that payments for referrals and dividing of fees must be based on services rather than the referral per se (Standard 1.27). It is also very important that any referral be justified principally on the basis of the client's best interests, rather than on some financial arrangement between the referral source and the service provider (Standard 1.20). Both their payers and recipients of referral fees should be prepared to document the actual costs of services provided (e.g., office space rental, secretarial costs, or utilities) and the qualifications of the recipient of the referral to meet the particular needs of the client. . . .

Fraud or lying about services actually provided is illegal under most circumstances and has always been unethical. In Standard 1.26, the new code, however, specifically addresses the issue of accuracy in reporting to payers and funding sources. This would include giving accurate accounts of fees charged and copayments made. Similarly, it is clearly unethical to misrepresent the identity of the actual service provider (e.g., failing to disclose that a service was provided by an assistant) or the actual diagnosis (e.g., exaggerating symptoms to ensure insurance coverage). . . .

The most common business issue that leads to ethical disputes between colleagues involves departures from a practice. This may mean leaving an institution for private practice, leaving a partnership or group practice to strike out on one's own, or simply moving on. Often such career transitions are either not entirely voluntary or not uniformly welcomed by those departing and those staying behind. At such times clients can too often be lost in the shuffle or used as pawns with each side claiming to righteously respect the needs of the client with its own proposed solution.

The new code addresses this issue in Standard 4.08 by focusing appropriately on the client's needs with respect to interrupted services. Psychologists are cautioned to carefully consider how they will resolve their clinical responsibilities on departure at the time they propose to enter an employment or contractual relationship. In this way, the client's best interests can be focused on hypothetically (i.e., before they are actually the new hire's clients), and the sensitive issue of parting can be addressed during a period of maximal goodwill between employer and employee.

The paramount issue to be considered is client welfare. The client's needs must never be held hostage to a practitioner's business or personal interests. A reasonable plan should be in place to define procedures for notifying clients, providing freedom of choice, and ensuring their best interests whenever a disruption in services or continuity of care occurs. . . .

References

American Psychological Association. (1992). Ethical principles of psychologists and code of conduct. *American Psychologist, 47*, 1597–1611.

American Psychological Association. (1993). *Record keeping guidelines*. Washington, DC: Author.

◆　◆　◆

Commentary: In their survey, Fulero and Wilbert (1988) found wide variability in psychologists' record-keeping policies and practices. They strongly recommended the promulgation of "a specific set of guidelines propounded under the auspices of the APA" that, they speculated, "could help to reduce the variability in record-keeping practices found in [their] study" (p. 660). Fulero, S. M., & Wilbert, J. R. (1988). Record-keeping practices of clinical and counseling psychologists: A survey of practitioners. Professional Psychology: Research and Practice, 19, 658–660. In 1993, the APA responded to this and similar suggestions with its Record-Keeping Guidelines (1993; see the next article). Review these guidelines, and consider to what extent they provide concrete guidance to practitioners.

Record Keeping Guidelines

Committee on Professional Practice and Standards, Board of Professional Affairs

INTRODUCTION[1]

The guidelines that follow are based on the General Guidelines, adopted by the American Psychological Association (APA) in July 1987 (APA, 1987). The guidelines receive their inspirational guidance from specific APA *Ethical Principles of Psychologists and Code of Conduct* (APA, 1992).

These guidelines are aspirational and professional judgment must be used in specific applications. They are intended for use by providers of health care services.[2,3] The language of these guidelines must be interpreted in light of their aspirational intent, advancements in psychology and the technology of record keeping, and the professional judgment of the individual psychologist. It is important to highlight that professional judgment is not preempted by these guidelines; rather, the intent is to enhance it.

UNDERLYING PRINCIPLES AND PURPOSE

Psychologists maintain records for a variety of reasons, the most important of which is the benefit of the client. Records allow a psychologist to document and review the delivery of psychological services. The nature and extent of the record will vary depending upon the type and purpose of psychological services. Records can provide a history and current status in the event that a user seeks psychological services from another psychologist or mental health professional.

Conscientious record keeping may also benefit psychologists themselves, by guiding them to plan and implement an appropriate course of psychological services, to review work as a whole, and to self-monitor more precisely.

Maintenance of appropriate records may also be relevant for a variety of other institutional, financial, and legal purposes. State and federal laws in many cases require maintenance of appropriate records of certain kinds of psychological services. Adequate records may be a requirement for receipt of third party payment for psychological services.

In addition, well documented records may help protect psychologists from professional liability, if they become the subject of legal or ethical proceedings. In these circumstances, the principal issue will be the professional action of the psychologist, as reflected in part by the records.

Adapted from the *American Psychologist, 48*, 984–986. Copyright 1993 by the American Psychological Association.

[1] In 1988 the Board of Professional Affairs (BPA) directed the Committee on Professional Practice and Standards (COPPS) to determine whether record keeping guidelines would be appropriate. COPPS was informed that these guidelines would supplement the provisions contained in the *General Guidelines for Providers of Psychological Services*, which had been amended two years earlier. The Council of Representatives approved the General Guidelines records provisions after extended debate on the minimum recordation concerning the nature and contents of psychological services. The General Guidelines reflect a compromise position that psychologists hold widely varying views on the wisdom of recording the content of the psychotherapeutic relationship. In light of the Council debate on the content of psychological records and the absence of an integrated document, BPA instructed COPPS to assess the need for such guidelines, and, if necessary, the likely content.

COPPS undertook a series of interviews with psychologists experienced in this area. The consensus of the respondents indicated that practicing psychologists could benefit from guidance in this area. In addition, an APA legal intern undertook a 50-state review of laws governing psychologists with respect to record keeping provisions. The survey demonstrated that while some states have relatively clear provisions governing certain types of records, many questions are often left unclear. In addition, there is a great deal of variability among the states, so that consistent treatment of records as people move from state to state, or as records are sought from other states, may not be easy to achieve.

Based on COPPS' survey and legal research, BPA in 1989 directed COPPS to prepare an initial set of record keeping guidelines. This document resulted. [These guidelines were adopted as APA policy by the Council of Representatives in February 1993.]

[2] These guidelines apply to Industrial/Organizational psychologists providing health care services but generally not to those providing non-health care I/O services. For instance, in I/O psychology, written records may constitute the primary work product, such as a test instrument or a job analysis, while psychologists providing health care services may principally use records to document non-written services and to maintain continuity.

[3] Rather than keeping their own record system, psychologists practicing in institutional settings comply with the institution's policies on record keeping, so long as they are consistent with legal and ethical standards.

At times, there may be conflicts between the federal, state or local laws governing record keeping, the requirements of institutional rules, and these guidelines. In these circumstances, psychologists bear in mind their obligations to conform to applicable law. When laws or institutional rules appear to conflict with the principles of these guidelines, psychologists use their education, skills and training to identify the relevant issues, and to attempt to resolve it in a way that, to the maximum extent feasible, conforms both to law and to professional practice, as required by ethical principles.

Psychologists are justifiably concerned that, at times, record keeping information will be required to be disclosed against the wishes of the psychologist or client, and may be released to persons unqualified to interpret such records. These guidelines assume that no record is free from disclosure all of the time, regardless of the wishes of the client or the psychologist.

1. Content of Records

a. Records include any information (including information stored in a computer) that may be used to document the nature, delivery, progress, or results of psychological services. Records can be reviewed and duplicated.

b. Records of psychological services minimally include (a) identifying data, (b) dates of services, (c) types of services, (d) fees, (e) any assessment, plan for intervention, consultation, summary reports, and/or testing reports and supporting data as may be appropriate, and (f) any release of information obtained.

c. As may be required by their jurisdiction and circumstances, psychologists maintain to a reasonable degree accurate, current, and pertinent records of psychological services. The detail is sufficient to permit planning for continuity in the event that another psychologist takes over delivery of services, including, in the event of death, disability, and retirement. In addition, psychologists maintain records in sufficient detail for regulatory and administrative review of psychological service delivery.

d. Records kept beyond the minimum requirements are a matter of professional judgment for the psychologist. The psychologist takes into account the nature of the psychological services, the source of the information recorded, the intended use of the records, and his or her professional obligation.

e. Psychologists make reasonable efforts to protect against the misuse of records. They take into account the anticipated use by the intended or anticipated recipients when preparing records. Psychologists adequately identify impressions and tentative conclusions as such.

2. Construction and Control of Records

a. Psychologists maintain a system that protects the confidentiality of records. They must take reasonable steps to establish and maintain the confidentiality of information arising from their own delivery of psychological services, or the services provided by others working under their supervision.

b. Psychologists have ultimate responsibility for the content of their records and the records of those under their supervision. Where appropriate, this requires that the psychologist oversee the design and implementation of record keeping procedures, and monitor their observance.

c. Psychologists maintain control over their clients' records, taking into account the policies of the institutions in which they practice. In situations where psychologists have control over their clients' records and where circumstances change such that it is no longer feasible to maintain control over such records, psychologists seek to make appropriate arrangements for transfer.

d. Records are organized in a manner that facilitates their use by the psychologist and other authorized persons. Psychologists strive to assure that record entries are legible. Records are to be completed in a timely manner.

e. Records may be maintained in a variety of media, so long as their utility, confidentiality and durability are assured.

3. Retention of Records

a. The psychologist is aware of relevant federal, state and local laws and regulations governing record retention. Such laws and regulations supersede the requirements of these guidelines. In the absence of such laws and regulations, complete records are maintained for a minimum of 3 years after the last contact with the client. Records, or a summary, are then maintained for an additional 12 years before disposal.[4] If the client is a minor, the record period is extended until 3 years after the age of majority.

b. All records, active and inactive, are maintained safely, with properly limited access, and from which timely retrieval is possible.

4. Outdated Records

a. Psychologists are attentive to situations in which record information has become outdated, and may therefore be invalid, particularly in circumstances where disclosure might cause adverse effects. Psychologists ensure that when disclosing such information that its outdated nature and limited utility are noted using professional judgment and complying with applicable law.

b. When records are to be disposed of, this is done in an appropriate manner that ensures nondisclosure (or preserves confidentiality) (see Section 3a).

5. Disclosure of Record Keeping Procedures

a. When appropriate, psychologists may inform their clients of the nature and extent of their record keeping procedures. This information includes a statement on the limitations of the confidentiality of the records.

b. Psychologists may charge a reasonable fee for review and reproduction of records. Psychologists do not withhold records that are needed for valid health care purposes solely because the client has not paid for prior services.

References

American Psychological Association. (1987). General guidelines for providers of psychological services. *American Psychologist, 42,* 712–723.

American Psychological Association. (1992). Ethical principles of psychologists and code of conduct. *American Psychologist, 47,* 1597–1611.

---

[4] These time limits follow the APA's specialty guidelines. If the specialty guidelines should be revised, a simple 7 year requirement for the retention of the complete record is preferred, which would be a more stringent requirement than any existing state statute.

Thorough Record Keeping: A Good Defense in a Litigious Era

Ellen L. Soisson, Leon VandeCreek, and Samuel Knapp

. . .

DOCUMENTATION OF SIGNIFICANT DECISIONS AND EVENTS

The record should provide an explanation of significant treatments as well as patient–therapist decisions. Klein, Macbeth, and Onek (1984) recommended that for each significant decision, the record should include (a) what the choice is expected to accomplish, (b) why the clinician believes it will be effective, (c) any risks that might be involved and why they are justified, (d) what alternative treatments were considered, (e) why they were rejected, and (f) what steps were taken to improve the effectiveness of the chosen treatments.

Forensically significant events such as involuntary commitments and possible malpractice suits should be anticipated, and the record should be written from the perspective of future readers (Gutheil & Appelbaum, 1982). For example, in the case of a suicidal client, psychotherapists should document an assessment of the risk, the options considered for the prevention of suicide, and possible treatments of the client (including advantages and disadvantages).

Psychotherapists should record the details of emergencies with special care because they result in a disproportionate number of malpractice suits (Gutheil & Appelbaum, 1982). Consultation and its documentation in such cases can be invaluable. In emergencies and in standard practice, it may also help to document the cooperation or resistance of significant others to an individual's treatment so that the responsibility can be placed where it ought to be if malpractice is claimed (Cohen, 1979). In addition, when a clinician is about to take a calculated risk or make a nonroutine intervention, it is appropriate to "think out loud for the record." According to Gutheil (1980), thinking for the record "stacks the deck heavily in favor of a finding of error in judgment rather than negligence" (p. 482).

DECIDING WHAT NOT TO DOCUMENT

Some members of the medical profession have argued that "no amount of documentation is too much and no detail is too small" ("Physician team," 1985, p. 2). However, the principle of extreme inclusiveness does not necessarily hold true for psychological records. The developing right of clients to gain access to their records and the widespread release of records to third-party payers and others emphasize that records should focus on facts and not hunches or value judgments (Cohen, 1979). As a result, records should exclude emotional statements and other personal opinions. Information about illegal behavior, sexual practices, or other sensitive information that may embarrass or harm the client or others is rarely appropriate for the record.

CLIENT ACCESS TO RECORDS

Psychiatric and psychological records are considered to be the property of the health care provider. The consumer controls its dissemination, although the right of patients to have direct access to their records varies from state to state (Hirsh, 1978). The trend, however, is toward increasing patient access to records. Patients may request that information be altered or corrected, and agency policies frequently afford a process for appeal if the correction request is

Adapted from *Professional Psychology: Research and Practice*, 18, 498–502. Copyright 1987 by the American Psychological Association.

denied. The right of client access to the records further increases the professional's accountability, heightening the pressure to write records as clearly and accurately as possible. Access may be denied in cases in which disclosure could be harmful to the patient, but psychologists generally should assume that one's clients will eventually review their records.

Despite the fears of professionals, researchers examining the impact of allowing patients access to their records have found favorable patient responses. Research with psychiatric inpatients (Roth, Wolford, & Meisel, 1980; Stein, Furedy, Simonton, & Neuffer, 1979) who were granted access to their records indicated that many records contained errors. Nonetheless, both patients and staff believed that client access improved treatment.

In states without access statutes, patients may often obtain access to their records by authorizing their release to another professional or to an attorney by initiating a lawsuit against the psychologist (*Palmer v. Durso*, 1977).

That records pose a threat to clients was dramatically reaffirmed by the court in *Wolfe v. Beal* (1978), in which an ex-client successfully brought suit to expunge and destroy the records of her hospitalization on the grounds that the record resulted from an illegal commitment. The court agreed that the continued existence of the record, even though held in confidence by the facility, posed a continual threat to her reputation.

DUAL RECORDS

Some psychologists keep a separate record of material of a sensitive or speculative nature that does not become a part of the client's formal record but remains in the clinician's possession (Brown, 1982). State law is not always clear in regard to the status of such records. In Illinois, however, the term *personal notes* is a part of the Mental Health and Developmental Disabilities Confidentiality Act of 1979. Such notes are not considered to be part of the patient's record, and they are immune from subpoena [Mental and Developmental Disabilities Confidentiality Act, 1979, ¶802, §2(4)].

The concept of maintaining dual records is controversial. Pollack (1977) warned that a double set of records could lead to an embarrassing legal confrontation if they came to light. However, an ethics code for health professionals proposed by the American Orthopsychiatric Association (Schuchman, Nye, Rafferty, & Freedman, 1982) suggested that a dual record system is appropriate. In general, the distinction between the patient's record and personal notes is considered defensible and potentially analogous to the work product privilege that protects lawyers' records (Klein et al., 1984). The Illinois statute has been upheld twice in court tests (Shutz, 1982).

We are aware of no court tests of dual records in states without explicit protection. However, in a related matter, a court (*White v. United States*, 1986) recently found that a "therapist–administrator split" for treatment and record keeping of a hospital patient was an acceptable practice. This arrangement entailed keeping individual psychotherapy independent of other forms of hospital treatment in order to ensure a trusting relationship. The best solution would be for states to clarify in the statutes the status of personal notes and dual records.

RECORD RETENTION

. . .

In the event of the death or incapacitation of the psychotherapist in independent practice, special provisions must be made for the retention or transferral of the records and for continuity of services. Ideally, the psychotherapist should have a written set of instructions incorporated into a will or into the records of the practice that specify the disposition of the records. The Specialty Guidelines (American Psychological Association, 1980) suggest that if no provisions have been made for records, it is appropriate for another psychologist, acting under the auspices of a local professional standards review committee, to review the records with patients and to recommend a course of action. To facilitate such a process psychotherapists should keep their records current and in good order. It would not be wise for the records to contain inflammatory material that might lead a reviewing patient to initiate a lawsuit against the deceased psychotherapist's estate. . . .

References

American Psychological Association. (1980). Specialty guidelines for delivery of services by clinical psychologists. *American Psychologist, 36*, 652–663.

Brown, S. (1982). Record content. In H. Schuchman, L. Foster, S. Nye, E. Brown, J. Gutman, R. Lanman, & S. Pettee (Eds.), *Confidentiality of health records* (pp. 45–64). New York: Gardner.

Cohen, R. J. (1979). *Malpractice: A guide for mental health professionals.* New York: The Free Press.

Gutheil, T. G. (1980). Paranoia and progress notes: A guide to forensically informed psychiatric record keeping. *Hospital and Community Psychiatry, 13*, 479–482.

Gutheil, T. G., & Appelbaum, P. S. (1982). *The clinical handbook of psychiatry and the law.* New York: McGraw-Hill.

Hirsh, H. L. (1978). Will your medical records get you into trouble? *Legal Aspects of Medical Practice, 6*, 46–51.

Klein, J. I., Macbeth, J. E., & Onek, J. N. (1984). *Legal issues in the private practice of psychiatry.* Washington, DC: American Psychiatric Press.

Mental Health and Developmental Disabilities Confidentiality Act, (1979, January). *Ill. Stat. Ann.*, CA 91$\frac{1}{2}$, ¶801 et. seq.

Palmer v. Durso, 90 Misc. 2d 110, 393 N.Y.S. 2d 898 (1977).

Physician team studies OB claims. (1985, June). *Malpractice Digest, 12*, 2.

Pollack, S. (1977). Psychiatric–legal problems of office practice. *Current Psychiatric Therapies, 1977*, 31–46.

Roth, L. H., Wolford, J., & Meisel, A. (1980). Patient access to records: Tonic or toxin. *American Journal of Psychiatry, 137*, 592–596.

Schuchman, H., Nye, S., Rafferty, F. T., & Freedman, L. (1982). Appendix II: Ethics codes for health professionals. In H. Schuchman, L. Foster, S. Nye, E. Brown, J. Gutman, R. Lanman, & S. Pettee (Eds.), *Confidentiality of health records* (pp. 199–224). New York: Gardner.

Shutz, B. M. (1982). *Legal liability in psychotherapy.* San Francisco: Jossey-Bass.

Stein, E. J., Furedy, R. L., Simonton, M. J., & Neuffer, C. H. (1979). Patient access to medical records on a psychiatric inpatient unit. *American Journal of Psychiatry, 136*, 327–329.

White v. United States, 780 F.2d 97 (D.C. Cir. 1986).

Wolfe v. Beal, 384 A.2d 1187 (Pa. 1978).

Commentary: In recent years, the FTC has scrutinized the business practices of health care entities. It has charged that these entities have placed restrictions on professionals that both reduce competition among practitioners and reduce the free flow of truthful information to consumers. Among the entities scrutinized are state boards that license health care professionals and professional associations that regulate the ethical conduct of their members. As the APA ethics committee noted in the following excerpt from its annual report, the APA has not been immune to FTC scrutiny:

> In July 1986, the Federal Trade Commission (FTC) began an investigation charging that APA's Ethical Principles of Psychologists *were in violation of the federal antitrust laws. In particular, the Federal Trade Commission expressed concern about Principles 4.b.iii, 4.b.v, 4.b.vi, 4.b.vii, 4.b.viii, and portions of Principles 6.d and 7.b. The APA voluntarily placed a moratorium on the adjudication of complaints of unethical conduct under the challenged principles and informed the APA membership of this action. Thereafter, a long series of letter exchanges took place between APA and the FTC, and in June 1989, the APA Board of Directors, on advise[sic] of legal counsel, declared an emergency and voted to rescind the challenged ethical principles. In October 1989, on the advise[sic] of legal counsel, the Board of Directors authorized APA to sign the renegotiated complaint, consent agreement, and order.*
>
> In the opinion of expert legal counsel, the portions of APA's Ethical Principles of Psychologists *in question were clearly in violation of the antitrust laws. Similar principles to those rescinded by the APA Board of Directors contained in the American Medical Association's ethical code were declared in violation of the antitrust laws by the federal district and appellate courts.*
> (p. 874)

See APA Ethics Committee. (1990). *Report of Ethics Committee, 1988*. American Psychologist, 45, 874. For a more complete history, see also Koocher, G. P. (1994). *APA and the FTC: New adventures in consumer protection*. American Psychologist, 49, 322–328 (some of which is reprinted on the following pages).

As a result of negotiations with the FTC, the following sections from the 1981 ethics code were deleted in 1989:

> 4(b)(iii) [Public statements by psychologists do not contain] a testimonial from a patient regarding the quality of a psychologists' services or products. . . ; (v) a statement implying unusual, unique, or one-of-a-kind abilities; (vi) a statement intended or likely to appeal to a client's fears, anxieties or emotions concerning the possible results of failure to obtain the offered services; (vii) a statement concerning the comparative desirability of offered services; (viii) a statement of direct solicitation of individual clients.
>
> 6(d) [Psychologists] neither give nor receive any remuneration for referring clients for professional services.
>
> 7(b) If a person is receiving similar services from another professional, psychologists do not offer their own services directly to such a person.

In what ways could these deleted standards be said to restrict competition and the free flow of information to the clients of psychologists? In what ways do the deletion of these standards disserve client welfare and interfere with the goals of effective assessment, therapy, and research?

APA and the FTC: New Adventures in Consumer Protection

Gerald P. Koocher

. . .

THE NATURE OF RESTRICTIONS ON ADVERTISEMENTS

If the general goals of the FTC were to make useful information available to the general public, it is understandable that clinging to vestiges of sameness in public statements for the sake of a sense of professionalism would not survive. However, some limits on advertising may well serve legitimate public interests. This is especially true in professions such as psychology, in which the consumers are often particularly vulnerable to undue influence because of their intellectual or emotional status. . . .

Is Commercial Speech Free Speech Too?

Do restraints imposed by professional association restrictions on advertising violate commercial free speech? Although it is not the same as political free speech, in the constitutional sense, the concept is still highly relevant and has often been an issue in efforts to limit advertising by lawyers. Commercial speech is protected under the First and Fourteenth Amendments, just as political speech is protected (*Virginia State Board of Pharmacy*, 1975); however, the courts have ruled that it is still reasonable to demand substantiation in the face of alleged false or deceptive advertising. The FTC's thrust has been to expand access to truthful information in the marketplace, although there are some exceptions that are discussed later as "in-your-face" solicitations. A good example of the commercial free speech argument involved an enterprising Kentucky lawyer named Shapero.

In *Shapero v. Kentucky Bar Association* (1988), the Supreme Court dealt with the case of a young lawyer who wanted to solicit business by sending truthful, nondeceptive letters to potential clients known to be confronting certain legal problems. The letter in question was to go to "potential clients who have had a foreclosure suit filed against them" and advised "you may be about to lose your home" and that "federal law may allow you to . . . ORDER your creditor to STOP." Potential clients were invited to "call my office for FREE information. . . . it may surprise you what I may be able to do for you" (p. 1919).

Mr. Shapero had the foresight to ask the Kentucky state bar whether his proposed letter to people facing foreclosure was acceptable. Although the state bar commissioners ruled that the letter was not misleading, they said no to Shapero, citing a then-existing Kentucky Supreme Court rule prohibiting the direct solicitation of individuals (i.e., as opposed to members of the general public) as a directed result of some specific event. Shapero appealed to the U.S. Supreme Court and won. The key point in the decision was that the content of his notice was not false or deceptive and held genuine potential interest for the intended recipients—which they could then choose to act on or ignore.

"In-Your-Face" Solicitation

What if the nature of the commercial exercise of free speech involves a more intense approach than Attorney Shapero's letter or takes advantage of a client in a vulnerable position? The bottom line seems to be that so-called in-your-face solicitation of clients, especially vulnerable ones, will not be tolerated.

Adapted from the *American Psychologist, 49,* 322–328. Copyright 1994 by the American Psychological Association.

Consider the case of an enterprising attorney named Ohralik from Montville, Ohio (*Ohralik v. Ohio State Bar Association*, 1978). On February 13, 1974, Ohralik was picking up his mail at the Montville post office when he learned in casual conversation with the postmaster's brother that 18-year-old Carol McClintock had been injured in an automobile accident a week and a half earlier. Ohralik decided to pay a call on Carol's parents, from whom he learned that she and her passenger, Wanda Lou Holbert, were riding together in the McClintock family car when they were struck by an uninsured motorist. Both girls required hospitalization. Because Carol was 18 years old and no longer a minor, Ohralik immediately set out for the hospital, where he found Carol lying in traction. He attempted to sign her up as a client in the hospital room, but she demurred so that she could seek parental advice. He then went off to find Wanda Lou, but she had just been released by the hospital. On his way back to the McClintock home, Ohralik stopped to take photos of the accident scene and concealed a tape recorder under his raincoat. He reviewed the family insurance policy and discovered that both Carol and Wanda Lou could recover up to $12,500 each under an uninsured motorist clause. Ohralik made a variety of different misrepresentations to the girls, who were initially swayed by his arguments but soon sought to discharge him from representing them in this matter. He sued them for breach of contract, using excerpts from the surreptitiously made tape recordings in an effort to prove that an oral contract existed. Both girls complained to the county bar association, which passed the action on to the state bar. Ohralik was found to have violated the Ohio Code of Professional Responsibility, despite his claim of First and Fourteenth Amendment protections.

In particular, the Ohio Supreme Court found that this direct solicitation of business was inconsistent with the profession's ideal of the attorney–client relationship. Ohralik had claimed that this solicitation was no different from the *Bates* (1977) case, but the U.S. Supreme Court (*Ohralik v. Ohio State Bar Association*, 1978) ruled that Ohralik's conduct posed "dangers that the state has a right to prevent" (p. 449), noting that the "appellant not only foisted

himself upon these clients; he acted in gross disregard for their privacy" (p. 469).

Testimonials

The use of testimonials by "satisfied users" has a kind of inherent face validity that appeals to the FTC. Unfortunately, like many forms of face validity, the true predictive potential of a testimonial endorsement is far more complex so far as psychological services are concerned. If psychotherapy research has taught us anything, it is that any given psychotherapist is not equally efficacious with all potential clients.

One ironic inconsistency in the latest version of the *EP* is obvious when one contrasts the two-year interval during which sexual intimacies with former psychotherapy clients are absolutely proscribed (Section 4.07) with the instant availability of the client as a testimonial provider upon the moment of terminating therapy. Psychotherapists know very well that their influence in the life of their clients does not end at the close of the last treatment session. The FTC did allow APA to bar the use of testimonials from "current psychotherapy patients" or from "persons who because of their particular circumstances are vulnerable to undue influence." Apparently, the FTC does not regard the lingering influence of the transference relationship and its potential consequences as an automatic barrier to testimonial advertising (e.g., potentially unfair and deceptive endorsements provided in the glow of a positive transference).

Although most private practitioners know that satisfied clients and the people who referred those clients are their best sources of future referrals, there are few data to suggest that the public will rely on commercially advertised testimonials in selecting medical care providers. The one exception may be plastic and cosmetic surgery, in which the concept of "face" validity takes on a unique meaning to the viewer.

Appeals to Fear

Many psychologists wondered why the FTC would object to APA's ban of advertising that appealed to potential clients' fears. After all, some of our clients are emotionally insecure and may be even more vulnerable to inappropriate duress than were Carol

McClintock and Wanda Lou Holbert. From the FTC's perspective, global bans on advertising that "appeals to fear if services are not obtained" were simply unacceptable in general. Lots of effective advertising appeals to emotions and fears at some level (e.g., fear of tooth decay if you don't brush, fear of accidental injury or death if you ride in a car without benefit of seat belts and air bags, or fear of AIDS as a result of not practicing "safe sex"). In fact, social psychology has taught us that an "appeal to fear" coupled with a designated course of action is highly effective in evoking attitude change.

How might an ethics committee have become involved in such complaints? In one instance, actual complaints were filed when consumers objected to advertising by psychologists running programs to help people quit smoking. The advertisements powerfully cited potential death from lung cancer and other pulmonary diseases. A more troubling example is the coupling of an appeal to fear with so-called in-your-face solicitation, as was the case in the Ohralik decision, described earlier. Imagine the situation in which a psychologist arrives unsolicited at the home of a child who witnessed a playground shooting and urges the parents to subscribe to a course of therapy to prevent inevitable posttraumatic stress syndrome in their as-yet asymptomatic child.

It is interesting that FTC Commissioner Azcuenaga disagreed with her colleagues on this point. She supported APA's wish to continue a ban on scare advertising, noting that the justification for banning such advertising by psychologists was plausible and that the FTC ought not to substitute its judgment on the matter without having a sound basis for doing so. She cited the FTC's lack of expertise concerning psychotherapy and noted that "nothing, even hypothetically, suggests that the [APA's] justification is either implausible or invalid" (Azcuenaga, 1990, p. 2). She was outvoted.

Fee Splitting

Providing bribes or kickbacks in exchange for referrals was never an acceptable practice, but from the FTC's perspective some ethics panels or licensing boards were interpreting prohibitions on this point as forbidding psychologists' participation in health maintenance organizations, preferred provider orga-

nizations, or referral services during the 1980s. The FTC regards referral services as procompetitive, and barring them per se was regarded as a significant problem. Unfortunately, what constitutes a bribe, as opposed to a legitimate fee reduction or membership payment, is open to a wide range of opinion. The FTC consent order does permit APA to issue "reasonable" principles requiring disclosures to consumers regarding fees paid to referral services or similar entities. The key to discriminating between reasonable and inappropriate payment will have to depend on the rationale for the charges or fee reductions and the openness of information on these arrangements to the consumers of the services.

1992 APA ETHICS CODE

The FTC did not intend that psychologists should necessarily adopt the market tactics of used car dealers and carnival barkers but rather focused on bans against all advertising. Potential harm that could result from hucksterism and abuses of advertising was deemed a valid focus of specific tailored restrictions by professional associations. Claims to "professional dignity" and the imagined need for "uniformity" would no longer constitute a valid basis for limiting advertising by professionals.

For the reader interested in reviewing the relevant sections of the current version of the *EP* (APA, 1992) most directly covered by the FTC order are the following:

> *Standard 1.27 Referrals and Fees*, which prohibits improper payments between professionals based on referrals;
> *Standard 3.01*, which defines what is considered a "Public Statement";
> *Standard 3.02*, which requires reasonable efforts to correct misstatements made about or on behalf of the psychologist by others and prohibits compensation of media personnel to get publicity;
> *Standard 3.03*, which deals with avoiding "False or Deceptive Statements" regarding psychologists' credentials and the scientific bases for claims of efficacy;
> *Standard 3.05*, which bars psychologists from soliciting testimonials from

current therapy clients or other persons who are vulnerable to "undue influence" by virtue of their particular circumstances;

Standard 3.06, which bars the uninvited, in-person solicitation for psychotherapy of persons vulnerable to undue influence (except for collateral contact with significant others of existing patients); and

Standard 4.04, which adds back specific requirements to be followed when considering whether to offer services to a client already receiving them elsewhere.

Indirectly, *Standard 1.20*, Sections a and c, which deal with consultation and referral practices (focus on clients' best interests and obeying the law); *Standard 1.25*, Sections a, b, c, and d, which deal with specifying financial, billing, compensation, and fee arrangements, and nonexploitation in that regard, are also relevant. Also Section 4.01, which addresses structuring the therapeutic relationship, so far as fee information is concerned, applies.

Did the FTC–APA interaction lead to an improved ethics code? I believe that some improvements resulted by directing the APA and other professional associations concerned with advertising to focus on substance, rather than on style. On the other hand, I also believe that the FTC failed to fully accept the principle that the relationships between mental health professionals and their clients are qualitatively different from those that exist in many other professions. The result will be a greater reluctance on the part of ethics enforcement groups in psychology to tackle complaints in this arena. What does all of this mean for the psychologist who wants to consider advertising in light of the current code? How about the state licensing board that wants to impose restrictions greater or more specific than those adopted by APA?

The following guidelines summarize the key factors to focus on.

1. Advertising by psychologists is clearly acceptable and cannot be banned, although the content of advertisements should ideally focus on facts of meaningful interest to the potential consumer.

2. One must take great care when listing affiliations, degrees, and other data so as to assure that the public is not misled, confused, or otherwise deceived. Both intentional deception and inadvertent errors that are not corrected can be prosecuted.

3. Once completely prohibited, soliciting testimonials or quotes from "satisfied users" is now permissible, so long as they are not solicited from current psychotherapy clients or others subject to "undue influence." The effectiveness of such advertising for psychologists is unknown.

4. The uninvited, direct, in-your-face solicitation of individuals as clients is also prohibited to the extent that it subjects the potential client to "undue influence," as opposed to mass solicitation through media advertising. However, this does not include barriers to inviting the significant others of current clients for collateral treatment.

5. Psychologists who serve organizational or industrial clients are entitled to broader latitude than those who serve individuals (e.g., current organizational clients could be solicited for endorsements), lay groups, and families; however, they too must observe factual validity-based criteria and avoid deception in their advertising claims.

6. Fees may be mentioned in advertisements but must also be reasonably honored for the reasonable life of the announcement.

7. Referral services may ethically charge a fee to clients, therapists, or both, although this should not be secret from the client, and the fee should not be the primary basis for making the specific referral. When portions of fees are paid to others parties, such fees should be in payment for services actually rendered (e.g., referral service, consultation, supervision, office space rental).

8. Although there is no longer any prohibition to offering treatment to a client who is receiving services from another professional, specific discussion with the client of the potential risks and conflicts is now required. It would also be wise to seek authorization from the client to contact the other professional and to consult with that person.

9. Psychologists must consider their style of presentation-of-self and public statements carefully in any public context, whether or not advertising per se is involved.

10. States may impose more stringent restrictions on professional advertising than do professional associations, so long as a legitimate state's interest is documented and so long as that state's interest does not violate a customer's access to useful information.

References

American Psychological Association. (1992). Ethical principles of psychologists and code of conduct. *American Psychologist, 47*, 1597–1611.

Azcuenaga, M. L. (1990). *Separate statement of Commissioner Mary L. Azcuenaga concurring in part and dissenting in part in American Psychological Association File 861–0082.* Washington, DC: Federal Trade Commission.

Bates et al. v. State Bar of Arizona, 433 U.S. 350 (1977).

Ohralik v. Ohio State Bar Association, 436 U.S. 447 (1978).

Shapero v. Kentucky Bar Association, 486 U.S. 466 (1988).

Virginia State Board of Pharmacy et al. v. Virginia Citizens Consumer Council, Inc., et al., 425 U.S. 747 (1975).

◆ ◆ ◆

*Commentary: Koocher correctly stated that the 1992 Ethical Principles bar uninvited in-person solicitation of actual or potential psychotherapy clients who are vulnerable to undue influence (see Standard 3.06). The FTC approved Standard 3.06 on the basis of the Supreme Court's decision in Ohralik v. State Bar Association, 436 U.S. 447 (1978), concerning in-person solicitation by lawyers of clients suffering personal injuries (such as in auto accidents, like the case summarized by Koocher in the preceding excerpt). However, in 1993, the Supreme Court struck down a Florida rule precluding certified public accountants from engaging in direct in-person solicitation. The Court noted that it had not banned all such attempts to garner business and that distinctions among professions were significant in assessing whether such bans were reasonable and constitutional. In Edenfield v. Fane, 113 S. Ct. 1792 (1993), the Court ruled that solicitation by certified public accountants was different than solicitation by lawyers because lawyers are trained in the art of persuasion whereas accountants' training emphasizes independence and objectivity, not advocacy. Who are psychologists more like—lawyers or accountants? Should not the proper analysis involve ex-*amining the nature of the client, not the nature of the profession? From that perspective, is the APA's Standard 3.06 appropriate?*

Consider the following advertisement:

> *Premature ejaculation, impotence and vaginisumus, cured by World's Who's Who psychotherapist. Ninety-five percent success, revolutionary short term program, compassionate, scientific, sincere. All anxieties treated between 11:00 a.m. and 1 p.m. Area code . . . .*

This ad, quoted by Frisch and Rebert (1991, p. 176), in their article, appeared in the Village Voice in 1989. The authors argued that such self-advertising is not in the best interest of psychology. Instead, they advocated "that psychology should, in fact, expand its efforts to advertise the profession as a whole, bringing the public information about the use of psychological services and where to find those services" (p. 179). Such collective public education programs, they believed, offer a more positive image of the profession. See Frisch, G. R., & Rebert, D. (1991). Effects of advertising on psychology. Canadian Psychology, 32, 176–180. In any event, is the ad that they quoted in violation of the APA Ethical Principles?

With regard to another controversial matter, Koocher correctly stated that Standard 1.27 of the 1992 Ethical Principles does not bar referral fees as long as the fees are based on services provided and are not simply "kickbacks" for the referral itself. But the line between a kickback and a proper referral fee may be difficult to draw. Furthermore, under the statutes regulating Medicare (nationwide health insurance for the elderly) and Medicaid (state medical assistance programs for the poor), "whoever knowingly and willfully solicits or receives any remuneration" or "whoever knowingly and willfully offers to pay any remuneration (including any kickback, bribe, or rebate) directly or indirectly, overtly or covertly, in cash or in kind in return for referring an individual to a person for the furnishing of [Medicare or Medicaid] service" is guilty of a felony, punishable by a fine of up to $25,000 and imprisonment of up to 5 years. See Social Security Spending Reduction Act of 1984, 42 U.S.C. § 1320a-7b(b). Thus, although some referral-fee practices may be ethical, they may be illegal within federal health systems. Furthermore, some state ethics codes, incorporated into their licensure laws, may be more restrictive than the

APA code of ethics. Thus, the prudent practitioner will obtain sound legal advice before offering or receiving referral fees. For an informative and cautionary article concerning fraud in federal programs generally, see Geis, G., Pontell, H. N., Keenan, C., Rosoff, S. M., O'Brien, M. J., & Jesilow, P. D. (1985). Peculating psychologists: Fraud and abuse against Medicaid. Professional Psychology: Research and Practice, 16, 823–832.

Finally, in reviewing the 1981 APA code of ethics, Faustman (1982) raised another difficult money-related concern:

> The ethical standards seem somewhat vague on the act of referring [delinquent accounts] to an external collection service. Under the intent of the standards, the use of a collection agency may be ethical if the therapist, prior to the initiation of therapy, obtains the expressed consent (e.g., written and/or verbal consent) of the client to release information should the client not pay the fee. (p. 209)

See Faustman, W. O. (1982). Legal and ethical issues in debt collection strategies of professional psychologists. Professional Psychology, 13, 208–214.

Standard 1.25f of the 1992 Ethical Principles is much clearer on this issue. Psychologists planning to use collection agencies may do so, provided that they "first [inform] the person that such measures will be taken and [provide] that person an opportunity to make prompt payment." However, a collection agency's "aggressive attempts to obtain payment . . . may result in the client's bringing suit against the therapist" (Faustman, 1982, p. 210). For a helpful guide to all these knotty matters, see Yenney, S. L., & American Psychological Association Practice Directorate. (1994). Business strategies for a caring profession. Washington, DC: American Psychological Association.

When 1994 began, debate about health care reform was raging. To provide for the estimated 35 million Americans with no health coverage in an era of ever-escalating health care costs, President Clinton sought to secure the twin goals of universal access and cost containment. Central to this universal system is the concept of "managed competition." Managed competition would divide the health care system into networks of providers and networks of health purchasers. The providers would be called Accountable Health Partnerships and would consist of hospitals, physicians, and other health care providers, presumably including psychologists. The purchasers would be called Health Insurance Purchasing Cooperatives and would consist of nonprofit cooperatives of employers, self-employed persons, and those who would otherwise have no group medical coverage. Various committees of Congress proposed different plans, but all systems envisioned strict control of costs. By 1995, as this book went to press, health care reform for the forseeable future was no longer viable.

The complexities of health care reform are far beyond the scope of this text. The relevant question here is whether government regulation of the provision of mental health services, under the rubric of managed care, will create a significant number of ethical dilemmas for psychologists and others who provide those services. Whatever the eventual legislation, it is clear, as Kiesler and Morton (1988) have presciently observed, that "health policy is in a state of upheaval in the United States, brought about by the so-called 'health care revolution.' The rapid evolution of health policy has potentially dramatic implications for psychologists, as scientists, professionals, and advocates" (p. 993). Kiesler, C. A., & Morton, T. L. (1988). Psychology and public policy in the "health care revolution." American Psychologist, 43, 993–1003. As the three, more recent articles that follow show, what was true then is decidedly more true now.

Legal Liability and Managed Care

Paul S. Appelbaum

. . .

OVERVIEW OF MANAGED CARE

Managed care as a generic term subsumes a wide variety of practices designed to regulate the utilization of health care (Dorwart, 1990; Tischler, 1990; Zimet, 1989). The key element shared by all managed care approaches, however, is the prospective or concurrent review of care provided to individual patients, with the power to deny payment for care thought to be unnecessary or not cost effective. Although managed care programs often maintain that their efforts will lead to an improvement in the quality of care—for example, through the elimination of unnecessary procedures or treatments—it is clear that the goal of reducing health care costs lies at the heart of managed care systems (Institute of Medicine, 1989).

Management of care now takes place as part of every type of payment system for health care. In traditional indemnity programs, under which patients select their own providers who are reimbursed on a fee-for-service basis, preadmission or pretreatment authorization with continuing periodic review is often required. Preferred provider organizations (PPOs), in which patients are limited to predetermined panels of providers (or at least have economic incentives to select a provider from the panels), may also require prospective or concurrent review, and in addition may recruit practitioners on the basis of their predisposition to use lower-cost treatments (e.g., short-term psychotherapies) and their willingness to cooperate with cost-control measures (Dorwart, 1990; Tischler, 1990).

In health maintenance organizations (HMOs), in which care is delivered by a preset group of providers for a fixed annual fee, designated gatekeepers (e.g., primary care physicians) may serve the prescreening role, and selection of treatment modalities may be governed by uniform protocols that restrict provider discretion. Providers' compensation may be affected by their abilities to control costs, either directly, through bonuses or penalties, or indirectly, through payments linked to the overall profit of the organization (Bennett, 1988). New organizational forms for financing and delivering health care are evolving rapidly, often combining elements of two or more of the indemnity, HMO, or PPO models. Almost all, however, have some managed care component (Task Force on Managed Health Care, 1991). Even public health insurance programs, such as Medicare and Medicaid are rapidly embracing managed care models (Hadley & Langwell, 1991).

Oversight of clinical care in managed systems may be performed by health insurers themselves, using in-house reviewers. In the past decade, however, there has been explosive growth of independent companies providing managed care services to insurers (Goleman, 1991; Tischler, 1990). Whether these companies, which usually have financial incentives to hold down utilization, inappropriately deny coverage to the detriment of patients is the subject of fierce controversy (Borenstein, 1990; Gabbard, Takahashi, Davidson, Bauman-Bork, & Ensroth, 1991; Moran, 1991). . . .

LIABILITY IMPLICATIONS FOR CLINICIANS

Managed Care: The Clinician's Dilemma

Since the growth of employer-provided health insurance after World War II, health professionals generally have been free to order for their patients any ac-

Adapted from the *American Psychologist, 48*, 251–257. Copyright 1993 by the American Psychological Association.

cepted diagnostic procedure or treatment, knowing that third-party payers would cover the costs. Thus, clinicians had both the obligation to determine what care their patients reasonably required and the power to provide or otherwise obtain that care (Morreim, 1991).

Although this situation obtained for health care generally, it was not always strictly true for mental health treatment, because many policies limited the amount of coverage by dollars, hospital days, or outpatient visits, or imposed copayment requirements. Nonetheless, benefits were adequate for many patients, and when they were not, there was often the possibility of shifting more severely ill patients into public-sector mental health systems, in which insurance coverage was typically not an issue. At a minimum, treatment was always available up to the limits imposed by the insurance policy.

In a managed care system, however, clinicians are not always able to provide or obtain care that they believe is necessary for patients, even when that care would appear to be covered by patients' insurance. If a reviewer for the entity managing the insurer's mental health benefits concludes that the recommended care is not "medically necessary" (the standard ordinarily applied), coverage may be denied, despite the patient's not having exhausted available benefits (Hall & Anderson, 1992). Although mental health professionals have always had to deal with the problem of limited benefits, denial of coverage is now a potential problem for every insured patient, and may occur early in the course of treatment.

To demonstrate the issues that can arise for clinicians in such circumstances, consider the following hypothetical (but, as will be seen, not unimaginable) case. A depressed, suicidal patient is hospitalized, then followed in psychotherapy for two months by an outpatient clinician. The clinician believes long-term treatment is indicated to help the patient remain stable, even though the acute symptoms of depression have resolved. Adequate coverage remains under the patient's insurance plan, but the patient has no personal resources to pay for further care. An employee of the managed care entity overseeing the treatment, on the basis of a record review and a telephone discussion with the clinician, determines that further treatment is not medically necessary. Because

of recent cutbacks in state funding, no public sector resources are available for patients of this sort.

What should a clinician do in a case like this? Should one continue treatment of the patient without compensation? If one is expected to extend free care to this patient, how much of one's caseload must be nonpaying before it is permissible to decline to offer such services? Or should one simply terminate the patient's care, despite one's belief that further treatment is needed to prevent relapse? If so, who will bear responsibility if the patient again becomes suicidal and injures himself or herself severely?

Such questions are usually answered by reference to the *standards of care* of the mental health professions, which evolve from the collective experience of clinicians, shaped by the recommendations of educators and experts in the field. Failure to conform to a recognized standard of care can be the basis for a finding of malpractice. Thus, clinicians concerned about reducing risks of liability naturally will want to know what their colleagues and the courts have accepted as reasonable standards of practice in situations like these.

The task of identifying appropriate standards in this case, however, is complicated by the limited opportunities clinicians and the courts have had to deal with these questions. Standards addressing previously unprecedented situations often crystallize at an agonizingly slow pace, with both the professional literature and appellate court decisions taking a decade or more to catch up to changes in practice. Moreover, standards of care are not static, but are modified continuously as new treatment techniques are developed and innovations are introduced in the delivery of care. Early data suggest that the introduction of managed care itself has led to modifications in professional standards, included marked shifts from inpatient to outpatient treatment (Thompson, Burns, Goldman, & Smith, 1992) and reductions in the number of outpatient sessions per episode of treatment (Norquist & Wells, 1991). As the approaches to mental health treatment reflected in these data become widely practiced, it is likely that the professions and the courts will recognize them as constituting legitimate alternative standards of care (Hall, 1989; Hirshfeld, 1990a).

Therefore, although it is possible to begin to address the questions posed above, it would be well to keep in mind, at this point, definitive answers are not possible. Managed care in its present form is a relatively new phenomenon on the mental health scene. There is little relevant case law and almost no relevant statutes. The legal literature in this area is skimpy and highly speculative, but one can begin to discern the developing outlines of the answers to these questions. In particular, there are three duties that might be relevant to a clinician caught in the circumstances of the case described above.

Duty to Appeal Adverse Decisions

At a minimum, a clinician whose patient has been denied payment for care that he or she believes is indicated may have an obligation to contest, on the patient's behalf, the decision of the managed care entity. All such systems have some appellate procedures, and the new generation of state statutes regulating managed care practices often sets certain parameters for their availability and speed of response (American Medical Association, 1990). . . .

Even if one accepts a general obligation to advocate for patients' needs, however, several questions remain. How far must appeals be pursued? Managed care companies and insurers usually have several levels of review. Must every case be taken through the entire process? Because managed care entities are often accused of creating time-consuming procedural obstacles to discourage appeals, does the extent of a caregiver's obligation to spend uncompensated time on this process depend on the amount of time required?

Must appeals be taken in every case? Is this obligation limited to urgent or emergent situations, or does it include cases in which treatment merely would be beneficial to the patient? Perhaps most important, does the likelihood of success affect the duty? If previous appeals have always, or almost always, been rejected . . . , is a clinician obligated to try again every time? In Virginia, for example, Blue Cross/Blue Shield has a 4.6% rate of approving appeals (Task Force on Managed Health Care, 1991). Is that sufficiently high to justify a requirement that appeals always be pursued?

The answers to these questions are unclear, but there does seem to be an evolving belief that clinicians are obligated to undertake at least some efforts to obtain approval for needed treatment. Moreover, lawyers advising managed care entities on how to avoid liability for their actions (discussed more fully below) recommend that they never discontinue coverage when caregivers feel adamantly that further care is needed. Instead, they suggest the reviewers authorize care for an interim period while additional review (perhaps by a neutral third party) takes place (Hinden & Elden, 1990). If this advice is followed, appeals are likely to have greater potency, at least over the short term, making imposition of a duty to appeal more meaningful.

What constitutes a reasonable approach from a clinician's point of view? At least an initial appeal of adverse decisions should be undertaken when a clinician believes that the treatment in question is necessary for a patient's well-being. Further levels of appeal probably should be pursued only after consultation with the patient, taking into consideration the likelihood of success, whether the patient still desires to proceed with treatment, and the availability of alternative means of paying for care. Clinicians, to this point, generally have assumed the burden of these procedures without directly seeking compensation for their time, although that may change in the future, particularly with patients who can afford to defray the cost of exceptional periods of time spent contesting adverse decisions. Many mental health professionals, in response to the greater bureaucratic demands of working with managed care systems, including appellate procedures, have shortened the standard length of treatment sessions (e.g., treatment "hours" have dropped from 50 to 45 minutes in many places) while maintaining fees at a constant level.

Duty to Disclose

Morreim (1991) has suggested that the entry of managed care into the clinical setting creates an additional obligation on caregivers to discuss with patients the economic implications of their treatment. This duty could be based on clinicians' fiduciary duties, contractual obligations, or the underlying duty to disclose information relevant to obtaining patients' informed consent.

What might such a duty include? At the initiation of therapy, clinicians might want to discuss with patients the potential effects of managed care on the course of treatment, including the possibility that payment for therapy might be terminated before either the patient or the clinician believes that the goals of treatment have been achieved. Patients who are about to embark on therapy involving painful self-disclosure and the activation of disturbing affects might well find such information important to their decision to proceed. Disclosure of the nature and extent of information that may have to be released to managed care reviewers may also be useful to patients.

When further coverage is denied, clinicians will probably need to enter into a full discussion of patients' options. Denial of coverage does not in itself mean that treatment must end. Patients may elect to pay for care out of pocket, or to proceed with therapy during the appeals process, risking in the interim being held responsible for charges accrued. Referral to alternative sources of care that are free or less expensive may also be an option.

The duty to disclose this information to patients seems neither onerous nor unreasonable. Nonetheless, it is not a duty that the courts have yet had an opportunity to rule on, and thus its legal status remains unclear.

Duty to Continue Treatment

When coverage for further treatment has been denied by a managed care entity, a clinician always retains the option of continuing to care for a patient without payment or at a reduced rate. This is obviously not an attractive option from the clinician's perspective, but there may be circumstances in which it is required, and others in which its status is unclear.

Most authorities would probably agree that when clinicians believe an emergency exists—such as in the case example above, if the patient had been acutely suicidal—there is an obligation to continue with treatment until the emergent state resolves or until an alternative provider of care can be found (Appelbaum & Gutheil, 1991). The same is true when insurance coverage is exhausted completely ("Court Finds," 1992). In principle, these situations should arise infrequently, because coverage should not be refused in such cases.

The nature of clinicians' obligations in nonemergent situations, such as in the case example, is less evident. Some court cases dating from before the managed care era indicate that, once accepting a patient for treatment, clinicians and hospitals must provide all necessary care (Marsh, 1985). Such language can be found in more recent cases as well. One opinion, rejecting the attempt of a group of psychiatrists to abrogate a managed care agreement because of alleged negative effects on patient care, noted, "Whether or not the proposed treatment is approved, the physician retains the right and indeed the ethical and legal obligation to provide appropriate treatment to the patient" (*Varol v. Blue Cross and Blue Shield of Michigan*, 1989, p. 833).

As a matter of public policy, however, this approach makes no sense, and it is clearly not sustainable over the long run. Clinicians and hospitals cannot simply be required to provide unlimited amounts of uncompensated care. What then of the duty not to abandon patients whose care one has undertaken? It should be evident that this duty is not absolute, particularly in nonemergent situations. As has always been the case when insurance benefits expired and patients could not or would not assume responsibility for the costs of care, clinicians' obligations are limited to referral (if free or low-cost care is available) or appropriate termination. Depending on the length of time that therapy has gone on, termination may require from one to several sessions to wrap up and consolidate the gains of treatment. Inpatients, of course, will need enough time to make discharge plans. No more can be reasonably required, although it is noteworthy that this is another issue that the courts have yet to address.

The new economic realities embodied in managed care in all likelihood have created a new set of obligations for clinicians, including advocacy of their patients' interests and disclosure of the economic consequences of their treatment decisions. Unlimited responsibilities for the provision of uncompensated care, however, are not likely to be part of clinicians' duties. . . .

References

American Medical Association. (1990). Utilization review. *State Health Legislation Report*, 18(2), 30–35.

Appelbaum, P. S., & Gutheil, T. G. (1991). *Clinical Handbook of Psychiatry and the Law* (2nd ed.) Baltimore: Williams & Wilkins.

Bennett, M. J. (1988). The greening of the HMO: Implications for prepaid psychiatry. *American Journal of Psychiatry, 145*, 1544–1549.

Borenstein, D. B. (1990). Managed care: A means of rationing psychiatric treatment. *Hospital and Community Psychiatry, 41*, 1095–1098.

Court finds Charter negligent in discharge of suicidal teen: Hospital will appeal. (1992, March 20). *Psychiatric News*, pp. 1.

Dorwart, R. A. (1990). Managed mental health care: Myths and realities in the 1990s. *Hospital and Community Psychiatry, 41*, 1087–1091.

Gabbard, G. O., Takahashi, T., Davidson, J., Bauman-Bork, M., & Ensroth, E. (1991). A psychodynamic perspective on the clinical impact of insurance review. *American Journal of Psychiatry, 148*, 318–323.

Goleman, D. (1991, October 24). Battle of insurers vs. therapists: Cost control pitted against proper care. *New York Times*, pp. D1, D9.

Hadley, J. P., & Langwell, K. (1991). Managed care in the United States: Promises, evidence to date and future directions. *Health Policy, 19*, 91–118.

Hall, M. A. (1989). The malpractice standard under health care cost containment. *Law, Medicine, and Health Care, 17*, 347–355.

Hall, M. A., & Anderson, G. F. (1992). Health insurers' assessment of medical necessity. *University of Pennsylvania Law Review, 140*, 1637–1712.

Hinden, R. A., & Elden, D. L. (1990). Liability issues for managed care entities. *Seton Hall Legislative Journal, 14*, 1–63.

Hirshfeld, E. B. (1990a). Economic considerations in treatment decisions and the standard of care in medical malpractice litigation. *JAMA: The Journal of the American Medical Association, 264*, 2004–2012.

Institute of Medicine (1989). *Controlling costs and changing patient care? The role of utilization management.* Washington, DC: National Academy Press.

Marsh, F. H. (1985). Health care cost containment and the duty to treat. *Journal of Legal Medicine, 6*, 157–190.

Moran, M. (1991, May 17). Report criticizes managed care firm. *Psychiatric News*, pp. 1, 20.

Morreim, E. H. (1991). Economic disclosure and economic advocacy: New duties in the medical standard of care. *Journal of Legal Medicine, 12*, 275–329.

Norquist, G. S., & Wells, K. B. (1991). How do HMOs reduce outpatient mental health care costs? *American Journal of Psychiatry, 148*, 96–101.

Task Force on Managed Health Care, Board of Health Professions. (1991). *Report to the Commission on Health Care for All Virginians.* Richmond: Virginia Department of Health Professions.

Thompson, J. W., Burns, B. J., Goldman, H. H., & Smith, J. (1992). Initial level of care and clinical status in a managed mental health program. *Hospital and Community Psychiatry, 43*, 599–603.

Tischler, G. L. (1990). Utilization management of mental health services by private third parties. *American Journal of Psychiatry, 147*, 967–973.

Varol v. Blue Cross and Blue Shield of Michigan, 708 F.Supp. 826 (E.D. Mich. 1989).

Zimet, C. N. (1989). The mental health care revolution: Will psychology survive? *American Psychologist, 44*, 703–708.

Parameters of Managed Mental Health Care: Legal, Ethical, and Professional Guidelines

Russ Newman and Patricia M. Bricklin

Although some form of capitated health care has been in existence for many years, such as that sponsored by Kaiser Permanente, recently there has been a virtual explosion in alternatives to the traditional fee-for-service model of health care. *Managed care*, as it has become known, grew out of substantial changes in the economic realities of the health care marketplace in an attempt to contain the rising costs of health services.

Some people have argued that within the fee-for-service delivery system, health care was provided without regard to cost, and often without regard to necessity. This resulted in continued high costs of care during a period when the general economy was experiencing deflation. New cost-control and cost-reduction methods integrated into the service delivery system to prevent continued health care inflation have ultimately shaped the direction and spurred the growth of managed care. Enrollment in health maintenance organizations (HMOs), for example, grew 11.9% from December 1986 to September 1987, and included 28.8 million members. It is estimated that by 1993, 50 million people will be enrolled in HMOs nationwide (Martinsons, 1988). This dramatic growth has been stimulated, in part, by legislation that removed some legal and financial obstacles to the creation of new managed care entities.

Reaction to this change in the health care industry, particularly in the mental health care arena, has been mixed. A survey of psychologists and other mental health care professionals who subscribed to *Behavior Today* revealed that 86% of respondents believed that the quality of mental health care suffers when provided through managed care structures ("BT Survey Results," July 20, 1987). The most frequent reason cited for the concern about quality in managed care was the limits or *caps* placed on the number of sessions a patient could receive—a complaint expressed by 79% of those surveyed. Other major complaints expressed included increased paperwork (67% of the respondents), the gatekeeping system (55%), decreased flexibility in the treatment approaches allowed (47%), and the long wait for reimbursements (46%); ("BT Survey Results," July 27, 1987). Approximately two thirds of respondents specifically objected to physicians and nurses with insufficient training and qualifications in mental health acting as gatekeepers.

Some advantages of managed health care were cited: increased client flow, less marketing needed by providers, added stability in an otherwise changing marketplace, and increased income–cash flow ("BT Survey Results," July 27, 1987). In general the survey indicated that managed care was an economic benefit to providers at the expense of quality mental health care.

Perhaps the greatest focus of concern stimulated by managed care has been the potential adverse impact of financial incentives on the quality of care provided. Prepaid health care, the *sine qua non* of managed care, establishes a financial incentive to control costs. If the actual cost of treatment exceeds the prepaid amount, the managed care entity loses money. Therefore, it is in the best financial interest of the entity to provide no more treatment than the prepaid amount will support. Some fear this will lead to a treatment attitude focused on protecting some minimum level of care, in contrast to a fee-for-

Adapted from *Professional Psychology: Research and Practice*, 22, 26–35. Copyright 1991 by the American Psychological Association.

service treatment attitude of enhancing or maximizing the health of patients (Brook & Lohr, 1985). Furthermore, managed care entities often give their participating providers financial incentives, such as bonuses, to hold down the actual cost of care rendered or arranged. Many are concerned that the incentives given to participating providers may be so strong that they pose a potential threat to the quality of care by encouraging inappropriate reduction in services (General Accounting Office [GAO], 1988). In fact, a recent study of depression found that patients receiving care financed by prepayment were significantly less likely to have their depression detected or treated than were similar patients receiving fee-for-service care (Wells et al., 1989). However, numerous mechanisms are potentially available within managed care systems to provide parameters to counterbalance the potential adverse impact of cost-containment mechanisms and financial incentives. Strong management controls, such as quality assurance and utilization review, provider credentialing, medical records review, and enrollee satisfaction and grievance procedures, are necessary mechanisms to help identify and prevent provider behavior that adversely affects quality (GAO, 1988). Within an individual profession such as psychology, professional standards, ethical principles, and the risk of malpractice suits may also prevent behavior that adversely affects quality. . . .

ETHICAL AND PROFESSIONAL PRACTICE GUIDELINES

Given the relatively limited statutory controls on the use of cost-containment mechanisms within managed care entities and the potential for provider liability, it is incumbent upon individual providers to balance quality with cost containment. In fact, the effects of incentive arrangements on good providers are believed to be distinguishable from the effects on bad providers (ICF, 1987). More specifically, the result of incentives for good providers is likely to be cost-effective quality care, whereas the result for bad providers is likely to be inexpensive but poor care. This is perhaps not unlike the result of financial con-

cerns in a traditional fee-for-service model of health care. In other words, it may be speculated that some providers may take advantage of lucrative insurance funds by extending care beyond what is medically or psychologically necessary.

It is difficult, if not impossible, to screen out those providers who will sacrifice quality for financial rewards, but appropriate ethical parameters for provider behavior can minimize such abuses. Some guidance for psychologists working in managed care settings can be found in the *Ethical Principles of Psychologists* (APA, 1990), although none of these principles expressly refers to psychological services in managed care settings.

Principle 1(f), pertaining to responsibility, mandates that psychologists as practitioners "are alert to personal, social, and organizational, financial, or political situations and pressures that might lead to misuse of their influence" (p. 633).[1] Every psychologist must be cognizant of the organizational structure of managed care entities focused on cost containment and the related financial pressures. More to the point, psychologists are ethically bound to take care that these pressures not result in treatment that is to the detriment of patients.

In addition, Principle 6 (welfare of the consumer) provides that "when conflicts of interest arise between clients and psychologists' employing institution, psychologists clarify the nature and direction of their loyalties and responsibilities and keep all parties informed of their commitments" (p. 636).[2] This principle may be construed to resolve any conflict arising between a managed care entity (or provider's financial interest) and quality of care concerns in favor of the latter. At the very least, the principle argues for disclosure to the client that a financial incentive exists to keep the amount or type of service limited.

Although not proscriptive in the same way as the *Ethical Principles*, the *General Guidelines for Providers of Psychological Services* (*Guidlines*; APA, 1987) may delineate parameters of behavior within managed care settings. In fact, the *Guidelines* are intended to apply to psychological services "at any time and *in*

---

[1] See Standard 1.15 of the APA's current (1992) Ethical Principles.

[2] See Standard 8.03 of the APA's current (1992) Ethical Principles.

any setting [italics added]" for the purpose of promoting the "best interests and the welfare of users of such service" (p. 1). Furthermore, the Preamble recognizes that principles of conduct "evolves over the history of every profession . . . [which] guide the relationships of the members of the profession to their users, to each other, and to the community of which both professional and users are members" (p. 1). Yet few of the actual guidelines appear relevant to the unique concerns of managed care's cost-containment emphasis.

Only Guideline 3 (accountability) has some relevance to the dilemma created for psychologists by the competing concerns of cost containment and quality of care. In particular, Guideline 3.1, indicates that "the promotion of human welfare is the primary principle guiding the professional activities of all members of the psychological service unit" (p. 7). A plausible interpretation of this guideline is, in effect, that cost containment stops where quality of care begins to be compromised. The illustrative statement intended to clarify this guideline expressly prohibits the withholding of services to a potential user. Unfortunately, the influences listed as potential causes of withholding of services—national or ethnic origin, religion, gender, affectional orientation, or age—indicate that the *Guidelines* did not envision the possibility of services being withheld because of financial incentives or cost-containment concerns.

Guideline 2.3.4 is of similar indirect relevance to the unique situation created by managed care structures, particularly the situation of disclosure of a provider's financial incentives to consumers. That guideline states "Professional psychologists clarify early on to users and sanctioners the exact fee structure or financial arrangements and payment schedule when providing services for a fee," (APA, 1987, p. 6). Unfortunately, the illustrative statement speaks only to traditional fee-for-service reimbursement procedures.

Additionally, Guideline 3.4 makes professional psychologists accountable for all aspects of the service they provide, including financial concerns. The illustrative statement indicates that this accountability includes the provision of accurate and full information to the user regarding the qualifications of providers, the nature and extent of services offered, and, where appropriate, financial costs and potential risks.

Although the ideal incorporated by this guideline

is laudable and relevant to managed care, the feasibility of implementation may be questionable. If a psychologist is held accountable for all aspects of his or her services provided within a managed care structure, the result may be individual accountability for aspects over which the psychologist has no control. For example, should a psychologist–provider employed by a managed care entity be held accountable for corporate policies that emphasize the financial bottom line or implement financial incentives to the point that quality of care suffers? Or should the psychologist–provider be held accountable for the corporation's advertising that does not thoroughly describe the financial incentives inherent in managed care to reduce the amount or type of treatment it provides? Taken to its logical extreme, this guideline might make it impossible for psychologists to work within some managed care settings. Whether one agrees with this result or not, it is unlikely that such an outcome was envisioned by the drafters of the *Guidelines*.

APA POLICY ON MANAGED CARE

Although some legislative, ethical, professional, and common law parameters for providing treatment within managed care settings do exist, they are considered by many in organized psychology to be either slow in developing or insufficient to deal with the unique characteristics of the newly emerging health care system. As a result, the American Psychological Association's Council of Representatives promulgated a policy statement in 1988 designed to articulate organized psychology's concerns about the potential effects of managed care on psychological services. Furthermore, the policy was intended to offer some recommendations to providers and consumers, in an attempt to minimize the potential for managed care's adverse effects on services (APA, Council of Representatives, 1989). Since that time, APA boards and committees have taken various steps to implement the spirit of the council policy statement, which remains as APA policy to the present.

Background and Policy Development

In the early 1980s, as a result of activities at the federal level and the emergence of new alternative health care delivery models, many psychologists in practice approached the APA through individual letters expressing interest and concern about these new service delivery systems. In response APA, through its Board of Professional Affairs (BPA) began to explore managed care in the context of future markets for psychological practice. At that time, there was both a growing excitement about the possibility of managed care as a creative solution to service delivery problems and a concern about the possible legal and ethical issues presented by such an alternative model.

Between 1982 and 1984, BPA sponsored a major APA convention program to review the issues, and as a result established a Subcommittee on Future Markets. While developing a manual for providers interested in preferred provider organizations (PPOs), HMOs, and other managed care models, the Subcommittee on Future Markets considered issues of helping psychologists cope with the other emerging cost-containment measures, the need for peer review in the system, and especially the need to educate providers on both the negative and positive aspects of involvement in alternative delivery systems. Despite these efforts to educate the APA membership about the changing health care marketplace, by 1985 it was clear that changes and events in this arena were occurring more rapidly than had been anticipated. These changes had serious ramifications for the delivery of psychological services as evidenced by the growing concern expressed by state associations, divisions of APA, and individuals (APA, Committee for the Advancement of Professional Psychology, 1988). Additionally, other APA governance groups associated with public interest expressed particular concern over access-to-care and quality-of-care needs of special populations within these systems.

In response, the BPA approved the development of a manual to educate the APA membership about the opportunities and challenges facing psychologists interested in joining HMOs and PPOs. The manual, *Marketing Psychological Services: A Practitioner's Guide* (APA, 1986) was completed in late 1985 and published in 1986.

During the same time period, the APA Committee on Women, the Committee on Gay and Lesbian Concerns, and the Board of Social and Ethical Responsibility reviewed managed care issues with respect to care and quality-of-care needs of special populations within managed care systems. As a result of their deliberation, they expressed the following concerns:

1. As the primary aim of new service delivery systems is cost containment, comprehensiveness of service or provision for services for special populations or special needs may not be specified.
2. There are serious problems with preferred provider organizations and other newly emerging healthcare delivery systems which, because of lack of built-in regulatory mechanisms, do not ensure consumer access to a diversity of providers. This is an issue of particular importance for gay and lesbian clients, ethnic minority populations, and women.
3. The new models of healthcare delivery are not bound by regulations that would require psychologists, especially those who specialize in working with specific populations (i.e., women, ethnic minorities, lesbians and gays, older persons), to be included. As a result, there is a strong probability that women and other special populations, will have to accept less-than-optimal services or pay for psychotherapy outside their health plans (APA, The Committee on Gay Concerns, 1984, p. 6; APA, Board of Social and Ethical Responsibility, 1985, p. 5; APA, Committee on Women, 1985, p. 11).
4. Regarding HMOs, there are four areas of particular concern: training of personnel to deal with minority populations; quality assurance with ethnic minority populations; truth in packaging issues; and the need for legislation that affects ethnic minorities (APA Board of Ethnic and Minority Affairs, 1986, Minute #19).

The particular concern for public interest groups, especially those that work with minority populations, is that the majority of managed care systems designate care providers. In a managed care model the patient generally has the choice only of providers who are part of the system. These providers may or may not be sensitive to minority issues. In a really free enterprise system, the client is free to choose a provider who is sensitive to his or her specific minority concerns. It is critically important that clients who enter into managed care systems be aware that they may be limited in the choice of service provider. This is a real truth in packaging issue.

The issues of psychologists' participation in alternative managed health care delivery systems continued to be of concern to various APA groups, including public interest and practice oriented constituencies. With the creation of the Office of Professional Practice within APA, its Interim Advisory Committee became a coordinating mechanism for consideration of managed care.

The Interim Advisory Committee (later Committee for the Advancement of Professional Practice) expressed concern over additional issues in managed care in 1988 (APA, Interim Advisory Committee, 1988). The concern that cost containment would be the major driving force in treatment decisions at the expense of the consumer was a major issue. It affirmed that it is especially important that decisions regarding quantity and quality of care be based on consumers' needs as well as on the economic interest of the health care delivery system. A proposed policy statement developed by the Interim Advisory Committee was circulated to all interested APA governance groups, including the BPA, and appropriate public interest groups, including the Committee on Women and the Committee on Gay and Lesbian Concerns (APA, Committee for the Advancement of Professional Psychology, 1988). This culminated in a document unanimously agreed upon by all of the participating groups, which was presented to the Council of Representatives in August 1988 and became APA policy at that time.

Policy Statement by the Council of Representatives

WHEREAS, many mental health problems are reflective of profound problems of living, substantial intrapsychic disorganization or severe physical and psychological disruption; and

WHEREAS, some psychological services are specifically focused on the alleviation of the personal distress attendant thereto; and

WHEREAS, managed care or other healthcare delivery systems should not unduly discriminate against those consumers who need intensive care, against those who need specialty care, and should not systematically endorse short-term or biomedical intervention as the treatment of choice for all patients at the expense of individual needs; and

WHEREAS, managed care delivery programs, by their very nature, frequently impose artificial and/or economic barriers to consumer access to health care services and, as such, are as subject to mismanagement as are traditional funding and delivery systems; and

WHEREAS, many managed healthcare programs may unfairly exclude those with the greatest need from adequate care and/or otherwise put both consumer and participating professional at substantial economic/psychological risk; and

WHEREAS, it is important that mental health care delivery programs provide appropriate and equally high quality services to all persons in diverse client and undeserved populations; and

WHEREAS, providers and patients should be informed of the limitations and restrictions to types and access of psychological services prior to subscribing to a plan (i.e., truth in advertising or explicit statements regarding any financial disincentives to treat and refer patients in need of psychological services),

THEREFORE, BE IT RESOLVED that the American Psychological Association urges consumers, subscribers and psychologists to review carefully the mechanisms, procedures, practices and policies of managed care programs before deciding to participate. Although such programs may offer the potential to expand access to appropriate mental health care, they may also restrict the availability of necessary psychological services.

It is further recommended that providers may wish to require as a condition of their participation that such managed healthcare delivery systems adequately and concretely demonstrate provisions to serve the consumer's interest with sufficient quantity and highest quality of health care based on the available scientific evidence of efficacy.

It is further recommended that consumers, subscribers and psychologists, as a condition of their participation, require that these programs practice truth in advertising regarding the range and duration of psychological services available through the plan and that these programs provide patients access to diversity of psychological health care competencies based on the available scientific evidence of efficacy.

It is also recommended that providers require that such systems operate in accordance with prevailing standards of care and prevailing scientific knowledge, applicable ethical principles, and that the systems have sufficient economic resources to cover the delivery system's liability.

Finally, individual members, state psychological association and divisions are strongly urged to monitor and inform themselves of the legal and regulatory requirements imposed on managed health care systems and to advocate that such requirements meet the principles enumerated herein. (APA, Council of Representatives, 1989 p. 1024)

This alternative health care delivery policy continues to be APA policy into the 1990s. Since its passage, APA has initiated a number of activities to implement this policy statement. Specifically, APA through its boards and committees has initiated the following implementation steps:

1. Communication of the APA Council of Representatives policy and its advisory statements to state associations.
2. The development of a manual on alternative health care delivery systems to be distributed to psychologists in professional practice.
3. Active lobbying on the part of the Practice Directorate of the American Psychological Association for HMO and PPO legislation to protect consumers and members.

The APA is not the only professional mental health provider group expressing concerns about the potential effects of managed care on mental health services. The American Psychiatric Association Board of Trustees recently created the Ad Hoc Committee on Managed Care Issues and voted to earmark up to $50,000 to investigate legal issues and concerns about managed care (American Psychiatric Association, 1990). The board also voted to support the concept of developing acceptable practice parameters for psychiatric care. . . .

References

American Psychiatric Association. (1990, January 5). Trustees attack managed care threat. *Psychiatric News*, p. 1.

American Psychological Association. (1986). *Marketing psychological services: A practitioners guide.* Washington, DC: Author.

American Psychological Association. (1987). *General guidelines for providers of psychological services.* Washington, DC: American Psychological Association; Committee on Professional Standards.

American Psychological Association, Board of Ethnic and Minority Affairs. (1986, May 1–3). *Minutes.* Washington, DC: American Psychological Association, Public Interest Directorate.

American Psychological Association, Board of Social and Ethical Responsibilities. (1984, November 2–4). *Minutes.* Washington, DC: American Psychological Association, Public Interest Directorate.

American Psychological Association, Committee for the Advancement of Professional Practice. (1988, March 18–20). *Exhibit 1, Summary Board of Professional Affairs actions related to alternative healthcare delivery systems.* Washington, DC: American Psychological Association, Practice Directorate.

American Psychological Association, Committee on Gay Concerns. (1984, September 28–29). *Minutes.* Washington DC: American Psychological Association, Public Interest Directorate.

American Psychological Association, Committee on Women in Psychology. (1985, March 28–30). *Minutes.* Washington, DC: American Psychological Association, Public Interest Directorate.

American Psychological Association, Council of Representatives. (1989). Proceedings of the American Psychological Association, Incorporated, for the year 1988. *American Psychologist, 44,* 996–1028.

American Psychological Association, Interim Advisory Committee. (1988, January 8–10). *Managed care systems.* Washington, DC: American Psychological Association, Practice Directorate.

American Psychological Association. (1990). Ethical principles of psychologists (amended June 2, 1989). *American Psychologist, 45,* 390–395.

Brook, R., & Lohr, K. N. (1985, May). Efficacy, effectiveness, variations, and quality: Boundary-crossing research. *Medical Case,* 720–722.

BT survey results: The changing mental healthcare delivery system. (1987, July 20). *Behavior Today,* 1–2.

BT survey results: Advantages and disadvantages of HMOs. (1987, July 27). *Behavior Today,* 1–2.

General Accounting Office. (1988). *Medicare physician incentive payment by prepaid health plans could lower quality of care* (GAO/HRD-89-29). Washington, DC: U.S. Government Printing Office.

ICF. (1987). *Physician incentive arrangements used by HMOs and PPOs* (Report submitted to the Office of the Assistant Secretary for Planning and Evaluation, DHHS). Washington, DC: U.S. Government Printing Office.

Wells, K. B., Hays, R. D., Burnam, A., Rogers, W., Greenfield, S., & Ware, J. E. (1989, December). Detection of depressive disorder for patients receiving prepaid or fee-for-service care. *Journal of the American Medical Association,* 3298–3302.

Managed Outpatient Mental Health Plans: Clinical, Ethical, and Practical Guidelines for Participation

Leonard J. Haas and Nicholas A. Cummings

THE RISE OF MANAGED OR LIMITED MENTAL HEALTH BENEFITS

The continued emphasis on cost containment in health care, and in mental health care in particular, has stirred strong feelings (both pro and con) among psychologists in recent years. With regard to outpatient psychological treatment, it is increasingly the case that "psychotherapy" is coming to be synonymous with brief or time-limited psychotherapy. For individual providers who examine "managed" mental health outpatient care options carefully, three questions arise forcefully: (a) Does managed mental health care present some unique set of problems for providers or patients?; (b) How can psychologists make sensible decisions about participation in the "new" mental health care plans?; and (c) For psychologists who are providers in managed care environments, are there ethical or clinical considerations in deciding who should or should not be provided treatment? . . .

THE NEW ERA

Increasingly in mental health service delivery, fee-for-service arrangements are a relic of the past (Cummings, 1986). The "revolution in health care" has almost guaranteed that some form of managed care will be the service used in this country by all but the extremely affluent (Zimet, 1989) or the extremely poor. Although managed care can take several forms [footnote omitted] its common ingredient is restriction on freedom (Morriem, 1988) or intrusion into the formerly private contractual world of

provider and consumer. From the provider's perspective, managed mental health care plans constrain the ability of the provider to establish whatever treatment plans he or she believes will be effective for the presenting problem. From the perspective of the patient, managed care imposes some restrictions on the patient's freedom to obtain third-party reimbursement for whatever he or she thinks should be treated. And from the perspective of the offeror of insurance plans, managed mental health care offers the hope that health care costs can be contained (and the continued existence of the insurance plan promoted). . . .

THE RESPONSE OF PSYCHOLOGIST PROVIDERS

Strong emotions are generated on both sides of the issue when psychologists consider the rise in managed mental health care plans. Interestingly, the focus is almost entirely on the issue of limitations to outpatient treatment, or the institution of some sort of benefit cap that might tend to shorten the length of psychotherapy. Thus, the debate seems primarily to center on time-limited [footnote omitted] or brief psychotherapy versus long-term treatment. Reaction in the professional literature ranges from suggestions that psychologists have made a mistake in opting to be considered health care providers, to suggestions that those who fail to embrace the new systems are "dinosaurs." Even the old "symptom substitution" argument, not much in evidence since the heyday of the psychodynamic–behavioral wars, is periodically

Adapted from *Professional Psychology: Research and Practice*, 22, 45–51. Copyright 1991 by the American Psychological Association.

heard (e.g., time-limited treatment cannot really treat the underlying problem, but will inevitably lead to a recurrence of symptoms).

THE CHANGING FACE OF PSYCHOTHERAPY ECONOMICS

These questions have to some extent stemmed from perceived threats to livelihood (Cummings, 1988), but there is undeniably some ethical and clinical substance at their core. Psychologists are primarily in the business of offering outpatient mental health services, and almost all consumers of such services except for the very poor and the very wealthy depend in part on some third party to help them to afford such services. Increasingly, those third parties are imposing limits on outpatient psychotherapy to attempt to contain costs. Initially, these efforts took the form of "benefit design," or alterations in the amount of money patients must pay as they receive longer treatment (e.g., first 5 visits at no copayment, next 10 visits at 20% copayment, and the next 20 visits at 50% copayment). More recently, these efforts have taken the form of "management" of treatment, which inserts the third-party payor into a more active role in the treatment planning or monitoring. And, among some plans (notably, but not exclusively, certain health maintenance organizations [HMOs]), there is the feature of treatment limitation, which caps the number of sessions, not simply the number of dollars, that will be reimbursed. Although we will argue against the notion of treatment limitation by third parties, we are enthusiastic about the practitioner's use of brief methods. The ideal environment in which to contain costs would be one in which providers well trained in the rapid treatment of disorder were free to use their professional discretion in the service of their patients' welfare.

MANAGED MENTAL HEALTH CARE: UNIQUE THREAT?

Although managed-care programs in general health care were developed as a means to limit the constantly increasing cost of health care in the United States, cost containment has proved to be an elusive goal (Doleuc & Dougherty, 1985; Frank & McGuire, 1986). Rather, health care costs have escalated at a dizzying rate, and with them, mental health care costs as well. This article focuses primarily on outpatient mental health care plans; ironically, however, the vast proportion of mental health care costs are incurred through use of inpatient services (Lowman, 1987; Manning, Wells, Duan, Newhouse, & Ware, 1984). Although this is a "perverse incentive" (Lowman, 1987) in that such a policy encourages the use of higher cost alternatives, the use by managed mental health care programs of limitations on outpatient benefits has continued as a cost-containment strategy. One or more of the following limitations is usually used in attempts to contain costs: increasing the patient's share of treatment costs (raising copayments); limiting dollars available per insured per year (total-cost cap); limiting treatment to conditions falling into certain diagnostic categories (prospective payment schemes); limiting treatment by number of episodes, or in inpatient settings, length of stay (treatment-episode limits); limiting treatment to specific approved techniques; and limiting treatment through requiring prior approval by "gatekeepers" (pre-authorization).

Although the new realities of managed mental health care do affect the traditional relationship between provider and patient (as we will discuss here later), they also fail to end the risk to the survival of the plan itself, as industry spokespeople note (e.g., Jones, in VandenBos, 1983). Insurers are in constant competition for the contracts of large employers. To the extent that insurers cannot contain costs, they will suffer the consequences of loss of business to lower cost competitors or to large employers' willingness to self-insure, often with much-reduced benefit options. Hence, it is good policy for the manager of an insurance program or mental health care program to attempt to constrain costs as vigorously as possible, while of course maintaining the quality of service.

There are various means to limit the access of prospective insurance policyholders or patients to a plan or to a service. These means may be examined from clinical, fiscal, and ethical perspectives, because these are the usual types of concerns expressed about such policy decisions. That is, the clinician is most concerned about the clinical aspects of delivering quality care. The plan administrator has the clearest concern for the financial realities, because they directly affect whether the plan may survive. And both "stakeholders" (Haas & Malouf, 1989) should be concerned about the ethical dimension of their policy, in part to make it consistent with psychologists' ethical principles and in part to make it morally sound on more general grounds. A description of the options and relevant ethical concerns follows:

1. A plan may simply impose limitations on treatment. These limitations are for the present purposes being called *time limits*, although they are most clearly so primarily in HMOs. In other plans, time limits are translated into dollar limits. Thus, a plan could offer (as many do) a $2000 yearly maximum for outpatient mental health coverage, occurring in a maximum of 50 sessions. In many HMOs, the limit is 20 sessions annually, with annual and lifetime cost caps. From a clinical perspective, this policy may be risky: Patients may be denied needed care that extends beyond their benefits. From a fiscal perspective, this policy is sensible: There is a known cap on the amount of financial risk the program takes (although there is the fiscal risk that patients may, justly or unjustly, accuse the program of depriving them of needed care). From an ethical perspective, the policy is problematic: It shifts the risk to the therapist, because therapists are ethically bound to care for their patients and not abandon them. Thus, to provide care to patients whose benefits have been exceeded puts the therapist in the position of needing to make a referral of the patient if continued treatment is appropriate. Alternatively, therapists could provide *pro bono* service, although doing this frequently might eventually lower the therapist's income to an unacceptable level.

2. A plan may institute no time limits but may carefully select its policyholders so that they are unlikely to exceed some (actuarially derived) time limits or expenditure limits. This is called *skimming* (McGuire, 1989), or selecting to insure those individuals who are least likely to make a claim. Although no managed-care program would admit to selecting patients in this manner, careful marketing (Nelson, Clark, Goldman, & Schore, 1989) may accomplish the same end. For example, plans may only be open to retired persons, teachers, or military

dependents. However, despite the fears of critics (e.g., Nelson et al., 1989) in practice it is almost impossible to select low-utilization policyholders. One strategy that may work involves adverse selection: Lowering premiums and benefits carefully will attract those who perceive themselves to have low need for the service and to have low risk for the noncovered condition and thus expect not to need the benefits and wish to save the money. However, even if the plan administrator is judicious, this may be a relatively risky strategy in terms of financial exposure. Clinically, if it can actually be implemented, this is a relatively low-risk strategy, because it tends to amount to offering treatment to those who do not need it. Ethically, the primary problem involves informed consent; as long as the program gives policyholders clear information on the limits of coverage and they are free to choose other plans, there is no coercion into inappropriate service. However, there is the more abstract ethical concern that by selecting only low-utilization patients, the plan unfairly burdens other health insurers with higher utilization patients.

3. A plan may opt for the policy of limiting access to treatment, and limiting access to the policy itself through selection criteria or marketing strategies. There is little data on this option; however, it is likely to be fiscally the safest; a clearly known financial risk is involved. It is, on the other hand, clinically risky: Unless very clear diagnostic criteria are specified, the situation is similar to Paragraph 2, just discussed; it poses the danger that a patient who needs treatment will be denied it. Such a plan is potentially ethically problematic in the same way as other treatment limits are, because it changes the therapist's role to one of resource rationer and restricts his or her ability to act in the best interests of the patient.

4. A program may impose no limitations on outpatient treatment and may offer reimbursement (minus the copayment) to any policyholder. Although this is not a widespread policy (Cummings, 1988), it has proven viable when carefully implemented. Presumably, most plans avoid this arrangement out of fear that it expands their risks uncontrollably. This policy option is clinically safe (patients who need more extensive treatment will get it); it is eco-

nomically risky (the plan has no way of limiting the amount of expenses it is exposed to); and it is ethically sound (the competent and ethical provider decides in conjunction with the patient what treatment is indicated).

Overall, then, "managed" or "designed" benefits packages are not so unique; all of the issues of limiting access to treatment are present (perhaps in a less stark form) in any third-party-reimbursed scheme. All involve, in one way or another, intrusions into the traditional relationship between provider and patient. These issues will be considered next.

CONSIDERATIONS BEFORE JOINING A MANAGED-CARE SYSTEM

First and foremost, the prospective provider in a managed-care plan must know exactly what the plan involves and what constraints it will impose. Beyond this, several features of mental health care plans should raise questions.

1. *Who takes the risks?* In the usual arrangement, the insurer takes the risks: The plan and its benefits assume a probability of particular treatment needs, and if the patient should need more treatment, the plan reimburses for it. In managed-care plans, some of this risk is shifted to the patient: If costs go above a certain level, the patient pays. In other plans, notably HMOs, some of the risk is shifted onto providers: If costs go above the limits, or if referrals to specialists become necessary, the provider's reimbursement drops. One side effect of the shifting of risk to providers is that this tempts them to hoard resources (Morriem, 1988), in the sense that they may be reluctant to refer or extend treatment if it costs them too much.

2. *How much does the plan intrude into the patient–provider relationship?* The professional who agrees to participate in a mental health care plan incurs obligations both to the plan provider and to the patient. In the traditional doctor–patient relationship, there is substantial contractual freedom. The prototypical consumer experiences a need for a service, chooses a provider from among some alternatives, and has some degree of participation in the treatment planning process (e.g., selection of procedures if alternatives are available, agreement to follow the doctor's orders if called on to do so, and informing

provider if treatment appears to be working). For the prototypical provider, the relationship involves loyalty to the patient; that is, the provider has the freedom to accept or decline to treat the patient, to select appropriate treatment or treatments from among those in which he or she is competent, and then to honor his or her duty to treat the patient until the presenting problem is resolved, a referral is made, or the patient discontinues treatment. In theoretical terms, the principles of beneficence, autonomy, and justice are relevant (Beauchamp & Childress, 1988). In more conventional language, the relationship is marked by freedom and responsibility; freedom to treat as the provider sees fit, and responsibility, primarily to the patient, to resolve the presenting problem. Although some commentators have argued that this arrangement provides incentives to offer more care than necessary, others (e.g., Nelson et al., 1989) argue that it also highlights the primary loyalty of provider to consumer. The risk to the clinician participating in managed-care arrangements becomes that of balancing loyalty to the patient with responsibilities as an agent of the mental health program. If the program takes on undue risks from a particular case (e.g., the patient's care becomes too costly), the program may suffer damage, as may the therapist and other potential patients of the program.

3. *What provisions exist for exceptions to the rules?* A provider who is willing to incur the financial risk (or who works in a noncapitated arrangement) may want to continue providing treatment to a particular patient who has exceeded benefits. The provider may be tempted to change the diagnosis or the description of treatment so that the patient can be reimbursed. These maneuvers are possible in any third-party paid arrangement, of course. However, they illustrate that tightening limits on benefits may simply challenge the creativity of clinicians loyal to their patients and that the risks of altering that loyalty extend beyond simply the escalation of costs.

4. *Are there referral resources if patient needs should exceed plan benefits?* Psychologists, like other mental health professionals, have a duty to treat the patient until the presenting problem is resolved, a referral is made, or the patient discontinues treatment. To do otherwise is to abandon the patient, and this is unethical (American Psychological Association, 1990). Thus,

a key question before joining a plan that limits benefits may well become, How do practitioners avoid abandoning their patients without going bankrupt?

5. *Does the plan provide assistance or training in helping the provider to achieve treatment goals?* An alternative to the dilemma just mentioned involves the clinician in becoming more knowledgeable about short-term treatment options. A variety of brief therapy approaches exists (Budman, 1978; Sperry, 1989). If prospective providers have not been trained in these approaches, plans should either not select them or should make provisions to train them appropriately.

6. *Does the plan minimize economic incentives to hospitalize patients?* The "perverse incentives" noted above operate in many plans. Providers should carefully investigate their existence and perhaps lobby for alternative incentive systems.

7. *Are there ways in which the plan is open to provider input?* Given the proliferation of benefit options and plan arrangements, it is essential that some feedback mechanisms be built into these plans. Otherwise, the provider becomes simply an employee rather than a professional treating patients.

8. *Do plans clearly inform their policyholders of the limits of benefits?* Just as providers have loyalties to both other parties in the system, they should avoid being trapped in the middle, having to explain benefit limits to naive patients after the benefit limits have been reached.

Of course, the ideal policy for a managed mental health care program is one that does not create dual loyalties among therapists and that provides benefits both to specific patients in need of services and to potential patients who may require program resources in the future. This is a difficult policy option to implement because pressing immediate needs are those most likely to claim our loyalties even though alleviating present needs may increase the suffering of patients who will have needs in the future. . . .

ADDITIONAL ETHICAL ISSUES

Consideration of additional ethical issues in managed mental health care plans brings several to the forefront. First . . . the issue of competence is crucial. Consistent with the ethical obligation to offer services within the domain of their competence, psychologists must be capable of delivering service in a time-limited context if they are to be involved in managed-care plans.

Second is the issue of informed consent. The prospective patient must be given clear information about the benefits to which he or she is entitled and clear information about the limits of treatment as the clinician envisions them.

A third issue of ethical importance concerns divided loyalties. Third-party payment arrangements always elicit such issues, but never so clearly as in managed mental health care plans. The principal of fidelity (Beauchamp & Childress, 1988) demands that the provider or professional be loyal to those with whom he or she has a contractual relationship. Thus, if a therapist agrees to work in a managed health-care program, he or she should believe in the service philosophy it endorses. If the therapist agrees to work with a particular patient, he or she should be loyal to that patient's interests (this is part of what is meant by a fiduciary relationship). The Ethical Principles of Psychologists (APA, 1990) focuses on fidelity in Principle 6, in terms of the psychologist's obligation to obtain informed consent from consumers, and on avoiding relationships in which there is a conflict of interest that may impair his or her objectivity. On this last point, the Ethical Principles of Psychologists (APA, 1990) is also clear. When demands of an organization conflict with the ethics code, psychologists attempt to bring the conflict to the attention of relevant parties and resolve it. In this case, the conflict would likely be between the demands of the plan that reimbursement for treatment cease or change versus the needs of the patient and the psychologist's ethical responsibility to act for the benefit of the client ("welfare of the consumer"). Psychologists may have a corollary obligation to ensure that plans with which they are associated have mechanisms to receive their input and recommendations for change. . . .

References

American Psychological Association. (1990). Ethical principles of psychologists (amended June 2, 1989). *American Psychologist, 45,* 390–395.

Beauchamp, T., & Childress, W. (1988). *Principles of biomedical ethics* (3rd ed.). Baltimore, MD: Johns Hopkins University Press.

Budman, S. H. (1978). *Forms of brief therapy*. New York: Guilford Press.

Cummings, N. A. (1986). The dismantling of our health system: Strategies for the survival of psychological practice. *American Psychologist, 41*, 426–431.

Cummings, N. A. (1988). Emergence of the mental health complex: Adaptive and maladaptive responses. *Professional Psychology: Research and Practice, 19*, 308–315.

Doleuc, D. A., & Dougherty, L. J. (1985). The counterrevolution in financing health care. *Hastings Center Report, 15*, 19–29.

Frank, R., & Dougherty, L. J. (1986). A review of studies of the impact of insurance on the demand and utilization of specialty mental health services. *Health Services Research, 21*, 241–266.

Haas, L. J., & Malouf, J. L. (1989). *Keeping up the good work: A practitioner's guide to mental health ethics*. Sarasota, FL: Professional Resource Exchange.

Lowman, R. L. (1987, August). *Economic incentives in the delivery of alternative mental health services*. Paper presented at the 95th Annual Convention of the American Psychological Association, New York, NY.

Manning, W. G., Wells, K. B., Duan, N., Newhouse, J. P., & Ware, J. E. (1984). Cost sharing and the use of ambulatory mental health services. *American Psychologist, 39*, 1077–1084.

McGuire, T. G. (1989). Outpatient benefits for mental health services in medicare: Alignment with the private sector? *American Psychologist, 44*, 818–824.

Morreim, E. H. (1988). Cost containment: Challenging fidelity and justice. *Hastings Center Report, 18*, 20–25.

Nelson, L. J., Clark, H. W., Goldman, R. L., & Schore, J. E. (1989). Taking the train to a world of strangers: Health care marketing and ethics. *Hastings Center Report, 19*, 36–43.

Sperry, L. (1989). Contemporary approaches to brief psychotherapy: A comparative analysis. *Individual psychology: The Journal of Adlerian Therapy, Research and Practice, 45*, 3–25.

VandenBos, G. R. (1983). Health financing, service utilization, and national policy: A conversation with Stan Jones. *American Psychologist, 38*, 948–955.

Zimet, C. N. (1989). The mental health care revolution: Will psychology survive? *American Psychologist, 44*, 703–708.

◆ ◆ ◆

Commentary: *The articles by Newman and Bricklin (1991) and by Haas and Cummings (1991) excerpted above were written before the 1992 Ethical Principles and Code of Conduct was adopted. Haas and Cummings, in fact, cited some provisions of the former code that were relevant to providing ethical mental health services in an era of managed care. Nevertheless, in their conclusions and recommendations, Newman and Bricklin suggested that the APA's "existing Ethical Principles . . . be amended to reflect the potential impact of cost-containment strategies on psychological services" (p. 34). Does the 1992 revision reflect their suggestion? Identify those current provisions that underscore the importance of maintaining quality care in the face of attempts to contain mental health costs.*

Index

About the Author

DONALD N. BERSOFF currently directs the JD–PhD Program in Law and Psychology jointly sponsored by Villanova Law School and the Medical College of Pennsylvania—Hahnemann Graduate School. He is a tenured full professor at both institutions. He received his PhD from New York University in 1965 and his JD in 1976 from Yale Law School, where he was an editor of the *Yale Law Journal*.

After obtaining his doctorate and before attending law school, Bersoff served as a clinical psychologist in the U.S. Air Force (1965–1968), spending 2 of those years in Southeast Asia. Then, after 5 years in academia training future psychologists (during which he had a part-time private practice), he attended law school. In 1976 he joined the faculties of both the University of Maryland School of Law and the Johns Hopkins University Department of Psychology, where he developed the nation's second Law and Psychology Program.

In 1979, Bersoff became the first general counsel of the American Psychological Association (APA). Two years later, he helped found the Washington, DC, law firm of Ennis, Friedman, Bersoff & Ewing, which merged with Jenner & Block in 1988. In his capacity as APA legal counsel (1979–1989) he prepared over 25 briefs in the U.S. Supreme Court and an equal number in lower federal and state courts. Many of these briefs sought to inform the court of social science evidence relevant to the issue before it. During this time, he also served as legal consultant to the APA Ethics Committee. In that role, he participated in all of the 30 meetings that the committee held for the decade, particularly when cases before the committee posed legal issues.

Bersoff is the author of over 100 book chapters, articles, and papers on ethics and the interaction of law, psychology, and the social sciences. He is a Fellow of the APA and a Diplomate in School Psychology. He has been elected to two terms as a member of the APA Council of Representatives—the APA's legislative body. During each of these terms (1977 and 1992), he has participated in passing a revised ethics code. He is currently serving a 3-year term on the APA Board of Directors (1994–1997), which functions in one capacity to independently review the work of the Ethics Committee in cases that have resulted in recommendations to assess the most serious of sanctions.

Bersoff has served as President of the American Psychology–Law Society, on the American Bar Association's Commission on the Mentally Disabled, and as Chair of the Section on Mental Disability Law of the Association of American Law Schools. He is a member of the Pennsylvania, District of Columbia, and Maryland Bars as well as of the Bar of the U.S. Supreme Court.